CDX Learning System

FUNDAMENTALS OF

Medium/Heavy Duty Diesel Engines

SECOND EDITION

TASKSHEET MANUAL

We Support
ASE | Education Foundation

CDX Learning Systems

JONES & BARTLETT
LEARNING

World Headquarters
Jones & Bartlett Learning
5 Wall Street
Burlington, MA 01803
978-443-5000
info@jblearning.com
www.jblearning.com

Jones & Bartlett Learning books and products are available through most bookstores and online booksellers. To contact Jones & Bartlett Learning directly, call 800-832-0034, fax 978-443-8000, or visit our website, www.jblearning.com.

Substantial discounts on bulk quantities of Jones & Bartlett Learning publications are available to corporations, professional associations, and other qualified organizations. For details and specific discount information, contact the special sales department at Jones & Bartlett Learning via the above contact information or send an email to specialsales@jblearning.com.

ISBN: 978-1-284-19650-4

Production Credits
General Manager: Kimberly Brophy
VP, Product Development: Christine Emerton
Product Owner: Chris Benson
Product Development Manager: Amanda Brandt
Manager, Project Management: Kristen Rogers
Project Specialist: Brooke Haley
Project Specialist: Jamie Reynolds
Director of Marketing Operations: Brian Rooney
VP, Manufacturing and Inventory Control: Therese Connell
Composition: S4Carlisle Publishing Services
Project Management: S4Carlisle Publishing Services
Cover Design: Scott Moden
Senior Media Development Editor: Troy Liston
Rights Specialist: Maria Leon Maimone
Cover Image (Title Page): Courtesy of Gus Wright
Printing and Binding: Sheridan Books, Inc.

6048

Printed in the United States of America
24 23 22 21 20   10 9 8 7 6 5 4 3 2 1

Contents

Section 1: Foundations and Safety

Section 2: Diesel Engine Fundamentals, Construction, and Operation

Section 3: Diesel Fuel and Fuel Systems

Section 4: Air Induction and Exhaust Systems

Section 5: Engine Electrical

Acknowledgments

Contributors

Joseph Berhausen

Mia Bevacqua

Mark DeHart

Michael Glaeser

Scott Heard

John Lee

Trace Phillis

Jonathan Williams

Section 1: Foundations and Safety

General Safety

Learning Objective/Task	CDX Tasksheet Number	ASE Foundation Reference Number
• Identify general shop safety rules and procedures.	MHTS001	SPS01
• Identify marked safety areas.	MHTS006	SPS06
• Identify the location and the types of fire extinguishers and other fire safety equipment; demonstrate knowledge of the procedures for using fire extinguishers and other fire safety equipment.	MHTS007	SPS07
• Identify the location and use of eye wash stations.	MHTS008	SPS08
• Identify the location of the posted evacuation routes.	MHTS009	SPS09
• Locate and demonstrate knowledge of safety data sheets (SDS).	MHTS015	SPS15

Materials Required
- Program's shop policy and other safety information
- Safety Data Sheets (SDS) book
- Fire extinguisher(s) from the shop
- SDS for the products listed

Safety Considerations
- Comply with personal and environmental safety practices associated with clothing; eye protection; hand tools; power equipment; proper ventilation; and the handling, storage, and disposal of chemicals/materials in accordance with local, state, and federal safety and environmental regulations.

- Shop rules and procedures are critical to your safety. Please give these your utmost attention.
- Marked safety areas play an important role in maintaining a safe work environment. Always understand and heed marked safety areas.
- Fire blankets are an important component of fire safety in the shop. Always know their location, purpose, and use.
- Fire extinguishers come in a variety of types and sizes. It pays to understand the differences before they are needed.
- Eye wash stations are an important component of shop safety. Always know their location, purpose, and use.
- Pre-planned evacuation routes are an important component of shop safety. Always know the location of all evacuation routes for your shop.
- Being able to locate information in an SDS is critical to your safety and health. Make sure you are familiar with their location and use.

CDX Tasksheet Number: MHTS001

Student/Intern Information

Name _____ Date _____ Class _____

Vehicle, Customer, and Service Information

Vehicle used for this activity:

Year _____ Make _____ Model _____

Odometer _____ VIN _____

Materials Required

- Program's shop policy and other safety information
- Safety Data Sheets (SDS) book
- Fire extinguisher(s) from the shop
- SDS for the products listed

Task-Specific Safety Considerations

- Shop rules and procedures are critical to your safety. Please give these your utmost attention.
- Marked safety areas play an important role in maintaining a safe work environment. Always understand and heed marked safety areas.
- Pre-planned evacuation routes are an important component of shop safety. Always know the location of all evacuation routes for your shop.

▶ **TASK** Identify general shop safety rules and procedures. _____ **MHT** SPS01

Time off_____

Time on_____

Student Instructions: Read through the entire procedure prior to starting. Prepare your workspace and any tools or parts that may be needed to complete the task. When directed by your supervisor/instructor, begin the procedure to complete the task and check the box as each step is finished. Track your time on this procedure for later comparison to the standard completion time (i.e., "flat rate" or customer pay time).

Total time_____

Procedure:	Step Completed
1. List the location(s) of the following items:	
a. Program's general shop rules and policies.	☐

b. Safety data sheet (SDS) book.	☐
c. Procedure for operation of a fire extinguisher.	☐
d. Procedure for operation of a vehicle hoist.	☐
2. List the shop's policy for the wearing of safety glasses while in the shop:	☐
3. List the shop's policy for driving vehicles:	☐
4. List the shop's policy for clothing in the shop:	☐
5. List the shop's policy for jewelry in the shop:	☐
6. Pass the shop's safety test and record your score here:	☐

Non-Task–Specific Evaluations:	Step Completed
1. Tools and equipment were used as directed and returned in good working order.	☐
2. Complied with all general and task-specific safety standards, including proper use of any personal protective equipment.	☐
3. Completed the task in an appropriate time frame (recommendation: 1.5 or 2 times flat rate).	☐
4. Left the workspace clean and orderly.	☐
5. Cared for customer property and returned it undamaged.	☐

Student signature _____ Date _____

Comments:

Have your supervisor/instructor verify satisfactory completion of this procedure, any observations found, and any necessary action(s) recommended.

Evaluation Instructions: The scoring box below is intended to act as a guide for both student and supervisor/instructor. Each criterion listed will help students to understand what is expected of them and help supervisors/instructors articulate the level of success at a particular task. The scoring is set up to allow a second attempt at each task (see the Test and Retest columns). Scoring is also designed to award students points only for task criteria that were completed correctly. Points are lost for failure to complete the employability requirements (see Non-Task-Specific Evaluation criteria). When all criteria are evaluated, tally the points for a total at the bottom of each column.

Tasksheet Scoring

Evaluation Items	Test		Retest	
	Pass	**Fail**	**Pass**	**Fail**
Task-Specific Evaluation	**(1 pt)**	**(0 pts)**	**(1 pt)**	**(0 pts)**
Student listed the shop safety rules.				
Student listed procedures used in the lab.				
Student identified the location of the SDS book.				
Student reviewed fire extinguisher operation and physically located extinguishers in the shop.				
Non-Task-Specific Evaluation	**(0 pts)**	**(−1 pt)**	**(0 pts)**	**(−1 pt)**
Student successfully completed at least three of the non-task-specific steps.				
Student successfully completed all five of the non-task-specific steps.				
Total Score: <total # of points/4 = %>				

Supervisor/Instructor:

Supervisor/instructor signature _____ Date _____

Comments:

Retest supervisor/instructor signature _____ Date _____

Comments:

CDX Tasksheet Number: MHTS006

Student/Intern Information

Name _____ Date _____ Class _____

Vehicle, Customer, and Service Information

Vehicle used for this activity:

Year _____ Make _____ Model _____

Odometer _____ VIN _____

Materials Required

- Program's shop policy and other safety information
- Safety Data Sheets (SDS) book
- Fire extinguisher(s) from the shop
- SDS for the products listed

Task-Specific Safety Considerations

- Marked safety areas play an important role in maintaining a safe work environment. Always understand and heed marked safety areas.

▶ TASK Identify marked safety areas. **MHT SPS06**

Time off_____

Time on_____

Student Instructions: Read through the entire procedure prior to starting. Prepare your workspace and any tools or parts that may be needed to complete the task. When directed by your supervisor/instructor, begin the procedure to complete the task and check the box as each step is finished. Track your time on this procedure for later comparison to the standard completion time (i.e., "flat rate" or customer pay time).

Total time_____

Procedure:	Step Completed
1. Identify different safety signs in the shop. List some of the words and symbols used on those signs.	
a. Word/symbol	☐
b. Word/symbol	☐
c. Word/symbol	☐
d. Word/symbol	☐

2. Identify all of the marked safety areas of the shop.	☐

Non-Task–Specific Evaluations:	Step Completed
1. Tools and equipment were used as directed and returned in good working order.	☐
2. Complied with all general and task-specific safety standards, including proper use of any personal protective equipment.	☐
3. Completed the task in an appropriate time frame (recommendation: 1.5 or 2 times flat rate).	☐
4. Left the workspace clean and orderly.	☐
5. Cared for customer property and returned it undamaged.	☐

Student signature _____ Date _____

Comments:

Have your supervisor/instructor verify satisfactory completion of this procedure, any observations found, and any necessary action(s) recommended.

Evaluation Instructions: The scoring box below is intended to act as a guide for both student and supervisor/instructor. Each criterion listed will help students to understand what is expected of them and help supervisors/instructors articulate the level of success at a particular task. The scoring is set up to allow a second attempt at each task (see the Test and Retest columns). Scoring is also designed to award students points only for task criteria that were completed correctly. Points are lost for failure to complete the employability requirements (see Non-Task-Specific Evaluation criteria). When all criteria are evaluated, tally the points for a total at the bottom of each column.

Tasksheet Scoring

	Test		Retest	
Evaluation Items	**Pass**	**Fail**	**Pass**	**Fail**
Task-Specific Evaluation	**(1 pt)**	**(0 pts)**	**(1 pt)**	**(0 pts)**
Student explained the purpose of marked safety areas in the lab/shop.				
Student described the areas and equipment that are generally marked in the lab/shop.				
Student identified safety signs used in the shop.				
Student identified areas of the shop marked as safety areas.				
Non-Task-Specific Evaluation	**(0 pts)**	**(−1 pt)**	**(0 pts)**	**(−1 pt)**
Student successfully completed at least three of the non-task-specific steps.				
Student successfully completed all five of the non-task-specific steps.				
Total Score: <total # of points/4 = %>				

Supervisor/Instructor:

Supervisor/instructor signature _____ Date _____

Comments:

```




```

Retest supervisor/instructor signature _____ Date _____

Comments:

```




```

CDX Tasksheet Number: MHTS007

Student/Intern Information

Name _____ Date _____ Class _____

Vehicle, Customer, and Service Information

Vehicle used for this activity:

Year _____ Make _____ Model _____

Odometer _____ VIN _____

Materials Required

- Program's shop policy and other safety information
- Safety Data Sheets (SDS) book
- Fire extinguisher(s) from the shop
- SDS for the products listed

Task-Specific Safety Considerations

- Fire blankets are an important component of fire safety in the shop. Always know their location, purpose, and use.
- Fire extinguishers come in a variety of types and sizes. It pays to understand the differences before they are needed.

▶ **TASK** Identify the location and the types of fire extinguishers and other fire safety equipment; demonstrate knowledge of the procedures for using fire extinguishers and other fire safety equipment. **MHT SPS07**

Time off_____

Time on_____

Total time_____

Student Instructions: Read through the entire procedure prior to starting. Prepare your workspace and any tools or parts that may be needed to complete the task. When directed by your supervisor/instructor, begin the procedure to complete the task and check the box as each step is finished. Track your time on this procedure for later comparison to the standard completion time (i.e., "flat rate" or customer pay time).

Procedure:	Step Completed
1. Research the types, location, and use of fire extinguishers.	

a. List the different types of fire extinguishers (dry chemical, CO_2, etc.) available:
  i. Type:　　　　　　　　for use on what class of fire:
  ii. Type:　　　　　　　for use on what class of fire:
  iii. Type:　　　　　　　for use on what class of fire:
  iv. Type:　　　　　　　for use on what class of fire:
In the above list, put a star next to the type(s) of fire extinguishers in this shop.
	☐

2. List the steps for proper use of a fire extinguisher:	☐
3. Research the location, purpose, and use of fire blankets in your shop:	
a. Describe the purpose of a fire blanket (under what circumstances should a fire blanket be used?).	☐
b. Describe how a fire blanket puts out a fire.	☐
4. Label the location of all fire extinguishers on the diagram of the shop at the end of this section.	☐
5. Label the location of the fire blanket(s) on the diagram of the shop at the end of this section.	☐

Non-Task–Specific Evaluations:	Step Completed
1. Tools and equipment were used as directed and returned in good working order.	☐
2. Complied with all general and task-specific safety standards, including proper use of any personal protective equipment.	☐
3. Completed the task in an appropriate time frame (recommendation: 1.5 or 2 times flat rate).	☐
4. Left the workspace clean and orderly.	☐
5. Cared for customer property and returned it undamaged.	☐

Student signature _____ Date _____

Comments:

Have your supervisor/instructor verify satisfactory completion of this procedure, any observations found,

and any necessary action(s) recommended.

Evaluation Instructions: The scoring box below is intended to act as a guide for both student and supervisor/instructor. Each criterion listed will help students to understand what is expected of them and help supervisors/instructors articulate the level of success at a particular task. The scoring is set up to allow a second attempt at each task (see the Test and Retest columns). Scoring is also designed to award students points only for task criteria that were completed correctly. Points are lost for failure to complete the employability requirements (see Non-Task-Specific Evaluation criteria). When all criteria are evaluated, tally the points for a total at the bottom of each column.

Tasksheet Scoring

	Test		Retest	
Evaluation Items	**Pass**	**Fail**	**Pass**	**Fail**
Task-Specific Evaluation	**(1 pt)**	**(0 pts)**	**(1 pt)**	**(0 pts)**
Student determined the location and level of charge for fire extinguishers located in the lab/shop.				
Student located the fire blanket in the lab/shop and demonstrated knowledge of how to use this item.				
Student selected the correct type of fire extinguisher for a given type of fire.				
Student described how to properly operate a fire extinguisher.				
Non-Task-Specific Evaluation	**(0 pts)**	**(−1 pt)**	**(0 pts)**	**(−1 pt)**
Student successfully completed at least three of the non-task-specific steps.				
Student successfully completed all five of the non-task-specific steps.				
Total Score: <total # of points/4 = %>				

Supervisor/Instructor:

Supervisor/instructor signature _____ Date _____

Comments:

_____

_____

Retest supervisor/instructor signature _____ Date _____

Comments:

_____

_____

CDX Tasksheet Number: MHTS008

Student/Intern Information

Name _____ Date _____ Class _____

Vehicle, Customer, and Service Information

Vehicle used for this activity:

Year _____ Make _____ Model _____

Odometer _____ VIN _____

Materials Required

- Program's shop policy and other safety information
- Safety Data Sheets (SDS) book
- Fire extinguisher(s) from the shop
- SDS for the products listed

Task-Specific Safety Considerations

- Eye wash stations are an important component of shop safety. Always know their location, purpose, and use.

▶ **TASK** Identify the location and use of eye wash stations.

MHT SPS08

Time off_____

Time on_____

Student Instructions: Read through the entire procedure prior to starting. Prepare your workspace and any tools or parts that may be needed to complete the task. When directed by your supervisor/instructor, begin the procedure to complete the task and check the box as each step is finished. Track your time on this procedure for later comparison to the standard completion time (i.e., "flat rate" or customer pay time).

Total time_____

Procedure:	Step Completed
1. Research the location, purpose, and use of eye wash stations in your shop:	
a. Describe the purpose of an eye wash station.	☐
b. Describe the proper use of an eye wash station (including time).	☐

	Step Completed
c. What type of eye injury would use of an eye wash station NOT be appropriate for?	☐
2. Label the location of the eye wash station(s) on the diagram of the shop at the end of this section.	☐

Non-Task–Specific Evaluations:	Step Completed
1. Tools and equipment were used as directed and returned in good working order.	☐
2. Complied with all general and task-specific safety standards, including proper use of any personal protective equipment.	☐
3. Completed the task in an appropriate time frame (recommendation: 1.5 or 2 times flat rate).	☐
4. Left the workspace clean and orderly.	☐
5. Cared for customer property and returned it undamaged.	☐

Student signature _____ Date _____

Comments:

Have your supervisor/instructor verify satisfactory completion of this procedure, any observations found, and any necessary action(s) recommended.

Evaluation Instructions: The scoring box below is intended to act as a guide for both student and supervisor/instructor. Each criterion listed will help students to understand what is expected of them and help supervisors/instructors articulate the level of success at a particular task. The scoring is set up to allow a second attempt at each task (see the Test and Retest columns). Scoring is also designed to award students points only for task criteria that were completed correctly. Points are lost for failure to complete the employability requirements (see Non-Task-Specific Evaluation criteria). When all criteria are evaluated, tally the points for a total at the bottom of each column.

Tasksheet Scoring

	Test		Retest	
Evaluation Items	**Pass**	**Fail**	**Pass**	**Fail**
Task-Specific Evaluation	**(1 pt)**	**(0 pts)**	**(1 pt)**	**(0 pts)**
Student described the location of the eye wash station.				
Student explained how to operate the eye wash station.				
Student explained how long to use an eye wash station.				
Student explained which eye injuries should not use an eye wash station.				
Non-Task-Specific Evaluation	**(0 pts)**	**(−1 pt)**	**(0 pts)**	**(−1 pt)**
Student successfully completed at least three of the non-task-specific steps.				
Student successfully completed all five of the non-task-specific steps.				
Total Score: <total # of points/4 = %>				

Supervisor/Instructor:

Supervisor/instructor signature _____ Date _____

Comments:

Retest supervisor/instructor signature _____ Date _____

Comments:

CDX Tasksheet Number: MHTS009

Student/Intern Information

Name _____ Date _____ Class _____

Vehicle, Customer, and Service Information

Vehicle used for this activity:

Year _____ Make _____ Model _____

Odometer _____ VIN _____

Materials Required
- Program's shop policy and other safety information
- Safety Data Sheets (SDS) book
- Fire extinguisher(s) from the shop
- SDS for the products listed

Task-Specific Safety Considerations
- Pre-planned evacuation routes are an important component of shop safety. Always know the location of all evacuation routes for your shop.

▶ **TASK** Identify the location of the posted evacuation routes.   **MHT** *SPS09*

Time off_____

Time on_____

Student Instructions: Read through the entire procedure prior to starting. Prepare your workspace and any tools or parts that may be needed to complete the task. When directed by your supervisor/instructor, begin the procedure to complete the task and check the box as each step is finished. Track your time on this procedure for later comparison to the standard completion time (i.e., "flat rate" or customer pay time).

Total time_____

Procedure:	Step Completed
1. Research the location and purpose of evacuation routes:	
a. Describe the purpose of evacuation routes.	☐
2. Label the evacuation route(s) on the diagram of the shop at the end of this section. Also label the location of the posted evacuation route diagram(s).	☐

Non-Task–Specific Evaluations:	Step Completed
1. Tools and equipment were used as directed and returned in good working order.	☐
2. Complied with all general and task-specific safety standards, including proper use of any personal protective equipment.	☐
3. Completed the task in an appropriate time frame (recommendation: 1.5 or 2 times flat rate).	☐
4. Left the workspace clean and orderly.	☐
5. Cared for customer property and returned it undamaged.	☐

Student signature _____ Date _____

Comments:

Have your supervisor/instructor verify satisfactory completion of this procedure, any observations found, and any necessary action(s) recommended.

Evaluation Instructions: The scoring box below is intended to act as a guide for both student and supervisor/instructor. Each criterion listed will help students to understand what is expected of them and help supervisors/instructors articulate the level of success at a particular task. The scoring is set up to allow a second attempt at each task (see the Test and Retest columns). Scoring is also designed to award students points only for task criteria that were completed correctly. Points are lost for failure to complete the employability requirements (see Non-Task-Specific Evaluation criteria). When all criteria are evaluated, tally the points for a total at the bottom of each column.

Tasksheet Scoring

	Test		Retest	
Evaluation Items	**Pass**	**Fail**	**Pass**	**Fail**
Task-Specific Evaluation	**(1 pt)**	**(0 pts)**	**(1 pt)**	**(0 pts)**
Student described the location of the posted evacuation routes.				
Student described the route of evacuation.				
Student identified gathering points during an evacuation.				
Student explained the purpose of an established evacuation route.				
Non-Task-Specific Evaluation	**(0 pts)**	**(−1 pt)**	**(0 pts)**	**(−1 pt)**
Student successfully completed at least three of the non-task-specific steps.				
Student successfully completed all five of the non-task-specific steps.				
Total Score: <total # of points/4 = %>				

Supervisor/Instructor:

Supervisor/instructor signature _____ Date _____

Comments:

Retest supervisor/instructor signature _____ Date _____

Comments:

CDX Tasksheet Number: MHTSO15

Student/Intern Information

Name _____ Date _____ Class _____

Vehicle, Customer, and Service Information

Vehicle used for this activity:

Year _____ Make _____ Model _____

Odometer _____ VIN _____

Materials Required
- Program's shop policy and other safety information
- Safety Data Sheets (SDS) book
- Fire extinguisher(s) from the shop
- SDS for the products listed

Task-Specific Safety Considerations
- Being able to locate information in an SDS is critical to your safety and health. Make sure you are familiar with their location and use.

▶ **TASK** Locate and demonstrate knowledge of safety data sheets (SDS). **MHT SPS15**

Time off_____

Time on_____

Student Instructions: Read through the entire procedure prior to starting. Prepare your workspace and any tools or parts that may be needed to complete the task. When directed by your instructor, begin the procedure to complete the task and check the box as each step is finished. Track your time on this procedure for later comparison to the standard completion time (i.e., "flat rate" or customer pay time).

Total time_____

Procedure:	Step Completed
1. List the safety precautions when handling motor oil:	☐
2. List the flash point of gasoline/petroleum: _____ °F/°C	☐

	Step Completed
3. List the firefighting equipment needed to put out a gasoline/petroleum fire:	☐
4. List the first aid treatment for battery acid in the eyes:	☐
5. List the first aid treatment for ingestion of antifreeze (ethylene glycol):	☐
6. Label the location of the SDS books on the diagram of the shop at the end of this section.	☐

Non-Task–Specific Evaluations:	Step Completed
1. Tools and equipment were used as directed and returned in good working order.	☐
2. Complied with all general and task-specific safety standards, including proper use of any personal protective equipment.	☐
3. Completed the task in an appropriate time frame (recommendation: 1.5 or 2 times flat rate).	☐
4. Left the workspace clean and orderly.	☐
5. Cared for customer property and returned it undamaged.	☐

Student signature _____ Date _____

Comments:

Have your supervisor/instructor verify satisfactory completion of this procedure, any observations found, and any necessary action(s) recommended.

Evaluation Instructions: The scoring box below is intended to act as a guide for both student and supervisor/instructor. Each criterion listed will help students to understand what is expected of them and help supervisors/instructors articulate the level of success at a particular task. The scoring is set up to allow a second attempt at each task (see the Test and Retest columns). Scoring is also designed to award students points only for task criteria that were completed correctly. Points are lost for failure to complete the employability requirements (see Non-Task-Specific Evaluation criteria). When all criteria are evaluated, tally the points for a total at the bottom of each column.

Tasksheet Scoring

Evaluation Items	Test Pass	Test Fail	Retest Pass	Retest Fail
Task-Specific Evaluation	**(1 pt)**	**(0 pts)**	**(1 pt)**	**(0 pts)**
Student described the location of the MSDS in your lab/classroom.				
Student listed types of potential hazards documented in an MSDS.				
Student described the procedures/safety measures documented in an MSDS.				
Student explained how to decipher the sections of the NFPA fire diamond detailed for a given product.				
Non-Task-Specific Evaluation	**(0 pts)**	**(−1 pt)**	**(0 pts)**	**(−1 pt)**
Student successfully completed at least three of the non-task-specific steps.				
Student successfully completed all five of the non-task-specific steps.				
Total Score: <total # of points/4 = %>				

Supervisor/Instructor:

Supervisor/instructor signature _____ Date _____

Comments:

```



```

Retest supervisor/instructor signature _____ Date _____

Comments:

```



```

Personal Safety

Learning Objective/Task	CDX Tasksheet Number	ASE Foundation Reference Number
• Comply with the required use of safety glasses, ear protection, gloves, and shoes during lab/shop activities.	MHTS010	SPS10
• Identify and wear appropriate clothing for lab/shop activities.	MHTS011	SPS11
• Secure hair and jewelry for lab/shop activities.	MHTS012	SPS12

Materials Required

- Regular safety glasses
- Gloves
- Shoes

Safety Considerations

- Comply with personal and environmental safety practices associated with clothing; eye protection; hand tools; power equipment; proper ventilation; and the handling, storage, and disposal of chemicals/materials in accordance with local, state, and federal safety and environmental regulations.
- Shop rules and procedures are critical to your safety. Please give these your utmost attention.

CDX Tasksheet Number: MHTS010

Student/Intern Information

Name _____ Date _____ Class _____

Vehicle, Customer, and Service Information

Vehicle used for this activity:

Year _____ Make _____ Model _____

Odometer _____ VIN _____

Materials Required
- Regular safety glasses
- Gloves
- Shoes

Task-Specific Safety Considerations
- Comply with personal and environmental safety practices associated with clothing; eye protection; hand tools; power equipment; proper ventilation; and the handling, storage, and disposal of chemicals/materials in accordance with local, state, and federal safety and environmental regulations.
- Shop rules and procedures are critical to your safety. Please give these your utmost attention.

▶ **TASK** Comply with the required use of safety glasses, ear protection, gloves, and shoes during lab/shop activities.

MHT SPS10

Time off_____

Time on_____

Total time_____

Student Instructions: Read through the entire procedure prior to starting. Prepare your workspace and any tools or parts that may be needed to complete the task. When directed by your supervisor/instructor, begin the procedure to complete the task and check the box as each step is finished. Track your time on this procedure for later comparison to the standard completion time (i.e., "flat rate" or customer pay time).

Procedure:	Step Completed
1. Describe the safety glasses policy for your shop (be specific):	☐

2. Describe the policy related to ear protection in the shop (be specific):	☐
3. Describe the policy related to gloves for your shop (be specific):	☐
4. Describe the policy related to work shoes for your shop (be specific):	☐
5. These tasks require observation of the student over a prolonged period. Ask your supervisor/instructor to give you a date for your evaluation:	
a. Write that date here.	☐
6. Continue with your projects, complying with the safe use of safety glasses, gloves, shoes, clothing, and hair containment during all lab/shop activities.	☐

Non-Task-Specific Evaluations:	Step Completed
1. Tools and equipment were used as directed and returned in good working order.	☐
2. Complied with all general and task-specific safety standards, including proper use of any personal protective equipment.	☐
3. Completed the task in an appropriate time frame (recommendation: 1.5 or 2 times flat rate).	☐
4. Left the workspace clean and orderly.	☐
5. Cared for customer property and returned it undamaged.	☐

Student signature _____ Date _____

Comments:

Have your supervisor/instructor verify satisfactory completion of this procedure, any observations found, and any necessary action(s) recommended.

Evaluation Instructions: The scoring box below is intended to act as a guide for both student and supervisor/instructor. Each criterion listed will help students to understand what is expected of them and help supervisors/instructors articulate the level of success at a particular task. The scoring is set up to allow a second attempt at each task (see the Test and Retest columns). Scoring is also designed to award students points only for task criteria that were completed correctly. Points are lost for failure to complete the employability requirements (see Non-Task-Specific Evaluation criteria). When all criteria are evaluated, tally the points for a total at the bottom of each column.

Tasksheet Scoring

Evaluation Items	Test		Retest	
	Pass	Fail	Pass	Fail
Task-Specific Evaluation	**(1 pt)**	**(0 pts)**	**(1 pt)**	**(0 pts)**
Student listed the personal protective equipment required when working in the lab.				
Student used the necessary personal protective equipment (eyewear) at appropriate times.				
Student wore appropriate shoes and personal clothing as required for shop safety at appropriate times.				
Student identified and wore the proper type of gloves at appropriate times.				
Non-Task-Specific Evaluation	**(0 pts)**	**(−1 pt)**	**(0 pts)**	**(−1 pt)**
Student successfully completed at least three of the non-task-specific steps.				
Student successfully completed all five of the non-task-specific steps.				
Total Score: <total # of points/4 = %>				

Supervisor/Instructor:

Supervisor/instructor signature _____ Date _____

Comments:

Retest supervisor/instructor signature _____ Date _____

Comments:

CDX Tasksheet Number: MHTSO11

Student/Intern Information

Name _____ Date _____ Class _____

Vehicle, Customer, and Service Information

Vehicle used for this activity:

Year _____ Make _____ Model _____

Odometer _____ VIN _____

Materials Required
- Regular safety glasses
- Gloves
- Shoes

Task-Specific Safety Considerations
- Comply with personal and environmental safety practices associated with clothing; eye protection; hand tools; power equipment; proper ventilation; and the handling, storage, and disposal of chemicals/materials in accordance with local, state, and federal safety and environmental regulations.

▶ TASK Identify and wear appropriate clothing for lab/shop activities. **MHT SPS11**

Time off_____

Time on_____

Total time_____

Student Instructions: Read through the entire procedure prior to starting. Prepare your workspace and any tools or parts that may be needed to complete the task. When directed by your supervisor/instructor, begin the procedure to complete the task and check the box as each step is finished. Track your time on this procedure for later comparison to the standard completion time (i.e., "flat rate" or customer pay time).

Procedure:	Step Completed
1. Describe the clothing requirements for your shop (be specific):	☐

2. These tasks require observation of the student over a prolonged period. Ask your supervisor/instructor to give you a date for your evaluation:	
a. Write that date here.	☐
3. Continue with your projects, complying with the safe use of safety glasses, gloves, shoes, clothing, and hair containment during all lab/shop activities.	☐

Non-Task-Specific Evaluations:	Step Completed
1. Tools and equipment were used as directed and returned in good working order.	☐
2. Complied with all general and task-specific safety standards, including proper use of any personal protective equipment.	☐
3. Completed the task in an appropriate time frame (recommendation: 1.5 or 2 times flat rate).	☐
4. Left the workspace clean and orderly.	☐
5. Cared for customer property and returned it undamaged.	☐

Student signature _____ Date _____

Comments:

_____

Have your supervisor/instructor verify satisfactory completion of this procedure, any observations found, and any necessary action(s) recommended.

Evaluation Instructions: The scoring box below is intended to act as a guide for both student and supervisor/instructor. Each criterion listed will help students to understand what is expected of them and help supervisors/instructors articulate the level of success at a particular task. The scoring is set up to allow a second attempt at each task (see the Test and Retest columns). Scoring is also designed to award students points only for task criteria that were completed correctly. Points are lost for failure to complete the employability requirements (see Non-Task-Specific Evaluation criteria). When all criteria are evaluated, tally the points for a total at the bottom of each column.

Tasksheet Scoring

	Test		Retest	
Evaluation Items	**Pass**	**Fail**	**Pass**	**Fail**
Task-Specific Evaluation	**(1 pt)**	**(0 pts)**	**(1 pt)**	**(0 pts)**
Student explained what clothing material type should be worn when working in the lab.				
Student explained what type of shoe should be worn in the lab.				
Student explained what types of protective equipment should be worn when working around flames and loud noises.				
Student wore appropriate clothing and PPE at all times.				
Non-Task-Specific Evaluation	**(0 pts)**	**(−1 pt)**	**(0 pts)**	**(−1 pt)**
Student successfully completed at least three of the non-task-specific steps.				
Student successfully completed all five of the non-task-specific steps.				
Total Score: <total # of points/4 = %>				

Supervisor/Instructor:

Supervisor/instructor signature _____ Date _____

Comments:

_____

Retest supervisor/instructor signature _____ Date _____

Comments:

_____

CDX Tasksheet Number: MHTS012

Student/Intern Information

Name _____ Date _____ Class _____

Vehicle, Customer, and Service Information

Vehicle used for this activity:

Year _____ Make _____ Model _____

Odometer _____ VIN _____

Materials Required
- Regular safety glasses
- Gloves
- Shoes

Task-Specific Safety Considerations
- Comply with personal and environmental safety practices associated with clothing; eye protection; hand tools; power equipment; proper ventilation; and the handling, storage, and disposal of chemicals/materials in accordance with local, state, and federal safety and environmental regulations.

▶ **TASK** Secure hair and jewelry for lab/shop activities.

MHT SPS12

Time off_____

Time on_____

Total time_____

Student Instructions: Read through the entire procedure prior to starting. Prepare your workspace and any tools or parts that may be needed to complete the task. When directed by your supervisor/instructor, begin the procedure to complete the task and check the box as each step is finished. Track your time on this procedure for later comparison to the standard completion time (i.e., "flat rate" or customer pay time).

Procedure:	Step Completed
1. List your shop's policy concerning securing hair in the shop (be specific):	☐
2. List your shop's policy concerning jewelry in the shop (be specific):	☐

3. These tasks require observation of the student over a prolonged period. Ask your supervisor/instructor to give you a date for your evaluation:	
a. Write that date here.	☐
4. Continue with your projects, complying with the safe use of safety glasses, gloves, shoes, clothing, and hair containment during all lab/shop activities.	☐

Non-Task-Specific Evaluations:	Step Completed
1. Tools and equipment were used as directed and returned in good working order.	☐
2. Complied with all general and task-specific safety standards, including proper use of any personal protective equipment.	☐
3. Completed the task in an appropriate time frame (recommendation: 1.5 or 2 times flat rate).	☐
4. Left the workspace clean and orderly.	☐
5. Cared for customer property and returned it undamaged.	☐

Student signature _____ Date _____

Comments:

Have your supervisor/instructor verify satisfactory completion of this procedure, any observations found, and any necessary action(s) recommended.

Evaluation Instructions: The scoring box below is intended to act as a guide for both student and supervisor/instructor. Each criterion listed will help students to understand what is expected of them and help supervisors/instructors articulate the level of success at a particular task. The scoring is set up to allow a second attempt at each task (see the Test and Retest columns). Scoring is also designed to award students points only for task criteria that were completed correctly. Points are lost for failure to complete the employability requirements (see Non-Task-Specific Evaluation criteria). When all criteria are evaluated, tally the points for a total at the bottom of each column.

Tasksheet Scoring

	Test		Retest	
Evaluation Items	**Pass**	**Fail**	**Pass**	**Fail**
Task-Specific Evaluation	**(1 pt)**	**(0 pts)**	**(1 pt)**	**(0 pts)**
Student explained how long hair, jewelry, and loose clothing can be dangerous during lab activities.				
Student complied with rules regarding hair and jewelry when working in the lab.				
Student identified shop policy on long hair.				
Student identified shop policy on personal jewelry.				
Non-Task-Specific Evaluation	**(0 pts)**	**(−1 pt)**	**(0 pts)**	**(−1 pt)**
Student successfully completed at least three of the non-task-specific steps.				
Student successfully completed all five of the non-task-specific steps.				
Total Score: <total # of points/4 = %>				

Supervisor/Instructor:

Supervisor/instructor signature _____ Date _____

Comments:

Retest supervisor/instructor signature _____ Date _____

Comments:

Tool Safety

Learning Objective/Task	CDX Tasksheet Number	ASE Foundation Reference Number
• Identify tools and their usage in automotive applications.	MHTS016	TE01
• Identify standard and metric designation.	MHTS017	TE02
• Utilize safe procedures for handling of tools and equipment.	MHTS002	SPS02
• Demonstrate safe handling and use of appropriate tools.	MHTS018	TE03
• Demonstrate proper cleaning, storage, and maintenance of tools and equipment.	MHTS019	TE04
• Demonstrate proper use of precision measuring tools (e.g., micrometer, dial-indicator, dial-caliper).	MHTS020	TE05

Materials Required
- Standard toolkit and other tools as required
- Precision measuring tools: micrometer, dial-indicator, dial-caliper, etc.
- Various standard and metric fasteners.

Safety Considerations
- Comply with personal and environmental safety practices associated with clothing; eye protection; hand tools; power equipment; proper ventilation; and the handling, storage, and disposal of chemicals/materials in accordance with local, state, and federal safety and environmental regulations.
- Tools allow us to increase our productivity and effectiveness. However, they must be used according to the manufacturer's procedures. Failure to follow those procedures can result in serious injury or death.

CDX Tasksheet Number: MHTS016

Student/Intern Information

Name _____ Date _____ Class _____

Vehicle, Customer, and Service Information

Vehicle used for this activity:

Year _____ Make _____ Model _____

Odometer _____ VIN _____

Materials Required
- Standard toolkit and other tools as required
- Precision measuring tools: micrometer, dial-indicator, dial-caliper, etc.

Task-Specific Safety Considerations
- Tools allow us to increase our productivity and effectiveness. However, they must be used according to the manufacturer's procedures. Failure to follow those procedures can result in serious injury or death.

▶ **TASK** Identify tools and their usage in automotive applications. **MHT TE01**

Time off_____

Time on_____

Student Instructions: Read through the entire procedure prior to starting. Prepare your workspace and any tools or parts that may be needed to complete the task. When directed by your supervisor/instructor, begin the procedure to complete the task and check the box as each step is finished. Track your time on this procedure for later comparison to the standard completion time (i.e., "flat rate" or customer pay time).

Total time_____

Procedure:	Step Completed
1. Using the following list, describe the specific function/purpose of each of the following tools and any disadvantages/problems with using the tool:	
a. Open-end wrench.	☐
b. Box-end wrench.	☐

c. Socket.	☐
d. Ratchet.	☐
e. Torque wrench.	☐
f. Slotted screwdriver.	☐
g. Phillips screwdriver.	☐
h. Tap.	☐
i. Die.	☐
j. Feeler blade.	☐
k. Line wrench/flare-nut wrench.	☐
l. Allen wrench.	☐

m. Torx screwdriver or socket.	☐
n. Hacksaw.	☐
o. Oil filter wrench.	☐
p. Compression gauge.	☐
q. DVOM/DMM.	☐
r. Test light.	☐
s. Diagonal side cutters.	☐
t. Locking pliers.	☐
u. Needle-nose pliers.	☐
v. Brake spoon.	☐

w. Micrometer.	☐
x. Dial indicator.	☐
y. Antifreeze hydrometer.	☐
z. Snap-ring pliers.	☐

Non-Task-Specific Evaluations:	Step Completed
1. Tools and equipment were used as directed and returned in good working order.	☐
2. Complied with all general and task-specific safety standards, including proper use of any personal protective equipment.	☐
3. Completed the task in an appropriate time frame (recommendation: 1.5 or 2 times flat rate).	☐
4. Left the workspace clean and orderly.	☐
5. Cared for customer property and returned it undamaged.	☐

Student signature _____ Date _____

Comments:

Have your supervisor/instructor verify satisfactory completion of this procedure, any observations found,

and any necessary action(s) recommended.

Evaluation Instructions: The scoring box below is intended to act as a guide for both student and supervisor/instructor. Each criterion listed will help students to understand what is expected of them and help supervisors/instructors articulate the level of success at a particular task. The scoring is set up to allow a second attempt at each task (see the Test and Retest columns). Scoring is also designed to award students points only for task criteria that were completed correctly. Points are lost for failure to complete the employability requirements (see Non-Task-Specific Evaluation criteria). When all criteria are evaluated, tally the points for a total at the bottom of each column.

Tasksheet Scoring

	Test		Retest	
Evaluation Items	**Pass**	**Fail**	**Pass**	**Fail**
Task-Specific Evaluation	**(1 pt)**	**(0 pts)**	**(1 pt)**	**(0 pts)**
Student identified various types of hand tools and describe their appropriate usage.				
Student identified various types of torque wrenches and describe their appropriate usage.				
Student identified various types of cutting tools and describe their appropriate usage.				
Student identified various types of measuring tools and described their usage.				
Non-Task-Specific Evaluation	**(0 pts)**	**(−1 pt)**	**(0 pts)**	**(−1 pt)**
Student successfully completed at least three of the non-task-specific steps.				
Student successfully completed all five of the non-task-specific steps.				
Total Score: <total # of points/4 = %>				

Supervisor/Instructor:

Supervisor/instructor signature _____ Date _____

Comments:

[   ]

Retest supervisor/instructor signature _____ Date _____

Comments:

[   ]

CDX Tasksheet Number: MHTS017

Student/Intern Information

Name _____ Date _____ Class _____

Vehicle, Customer, and Service Information

Vehicle used for this activity:

Year _____ Make _____ Model _____

Odometer _____ VIN _____

Materials Required

- Standard toolkit and other tools as required
- Precision measuring tools: micrometer, dial-indicator, dial-caliper, etc.
- Various standard and metric fasteners.

Task-Specific Safety Considerations

- There are no task-specific safety considerations for this task.

▶ **TASK** Identify standard and metric designation.

MHT TE02

Time off_____

Time on_____

Total time_____

Student Instructions: Read through the entire procedure prior to starting. Prepare your workspace and any tools or parts that may be needed to complete the task. When directed by your supervisor/instructor, begin the procedure to complete the task and check the box as each step is finished. Track your time on this procedure for later comparison to the standard completion time (i.e., "flat rate" or customer pay time).

Procedure:	Step Completed
1. Examine a fastener. How can you determine whether it is metric or standard?	☐
2. Obtain a set of wrenches in both standard and metric designations. Compare the size similarities and differences between them and note that information below. Then arrange the wrenches in size from small to large for both designations.	☐

© 2021 Jones & Bartlett Learning, LLC, an Ascend Learning Company

	Step Completed
3. Examine different fasteners.	
a. How are standard fasteners graded for strength?	☐
b. How are metric fasteners designated for strength?	☐
4. Using a measuring device such as a caliper, measure the size of the fastener to determine what size wrench/socket will be needed to remove and install it. Note the fastener type and size here.	☐

Non-Task-Specific Evaluations:	Step Completed
1. Tools and equipment were used as directed and returned in good working order.	☐
2. Complied with all general and task-specific safety standards, including proper use of any personal protective equipment.	☐
3. Completed the task in an appropriate time frame (recommendation: 1.5 or 2 times flat rate).	☐
4. Left the workspace clean and orderly.	☐
5. Cared for customer property and returned it undamaged.	☐

Student signature _____ Date _____

Comments:

Have your supervisor/instructor verify satisfactory completion of this procedure, any observations found, and any necessary action(s) recommended.

Evaluation Instructions: The scoring box below is intended to act as a guide for both student and supervisor/instructor. Each criterion listed will help students to understand what is expected of them and help supervisors/instructors articulate the level of success at a particular task. The scoring is set up to allow a second attempt at each task (see the Test and Retest columns). Scoring is also designed to award students points only for task criteria that were completed correctly. Points are lost for failure to complete the employability requirements (see Non-Task-Specific Evaluation criteria). When all criteria are evaluated, tally the points for a total at the bottom of each column.

Tasksheet Scoring

	Test		Retest	
Evaluation Items	**Pass**	**Fail**	**Pass**	**Fail**
Task-Specific Evaluation	**(1 pt)**	**(0 pts)**	**(1 pt)**	**(0 pts)**
Student selected the correct standard/metric designation for a given fastener.				
Student arranged standard and metric hand tools in order from small to large.				
Student described how SAE standard and metric fasteners are graded for strength.				
Student described the difference between SAE standard and metric measure.				
Non-Task-Specific Evaluation	**(0 pts)**	**(−1 pt)**	**(0 pts)**	**(−1 pt)**
Student successfully completed at least three of the non-task-specific steps.				
Student successfully completed all five of the non-task-specific steps.				
Total Score: <total # of points/4 = %>				

Supervisor/Instructor:

Supervisor/instructor signature _____ Date _____

Comments:

Retest supervisor/instructor signature _____ Date _____

Comments:

CDX Tasksheet Number: MHTS002

Student/Intern Information

Name _____ Date _____ Class _____

Vehicle, Customer, and Service Information

Vehicle used for this activity:

Year _____ Make _____ Model _____

Odometer _____ VIN _____

Materials Required
- Standard toolkit and other tools as required
- Precision measuring tools: micrometer, dial-indicator, dial-caliper, etc.

Task-Specific Safety Considerations
- Comply with personal and environmental safety practices associated with clothing; eye protection; hand tools; power equipment; proper ventilation; and the handling, storage, and disposal of chemicals/materials in accordance with local, state, and federal safety and environmental regulations.
- Tools allow us to increase our productivity and effectiveness. However, they must be used according to the manufacturer's procedures. Failure to follow those procedures can result in serious injury or death.

▶ **TASK** Utilize safe procedures for handling of tools and equipment.   **MHT SPS02**

Time off_____

Time on_____

Total time_____

Student Instructions: Read through the entire procedure prior to starting. Prepare your workspace and any tools or parts that may be needed to complete the task. When directed by your supervisor/instructor, begin the procedure to complete the task and check the box as each step is finished. Track your time on this procedure for later comparison to the standard completion time (i.e., "flat rate" or customer pay time).

Procedure:	Step Completed
1. These tasks will require observation of the student over a prolonged period after the initial check. Ask your supervisor/instructor to give you a date for your evaluation:	
a. Write that date here.	☐

2. Continue with your other projects, utilizing safe handling of tools and equipment, including proper cleaning, maintenance, and storage of the tools and equipment, until the date of your evaluation.	☐

Non-Task-Specific Evaluations:	Step Completed
1. Tools and equipment were used as directed and returned in good working order.	☐
2. Complied with all general and task-specific safety standards, including proper use of any personal protective equipment.	☐
3. Completed the task in an appropriate time frame (recommendation: 1.5 or 2 times flat rate).	☐
4. Left the workspace clean and orderly.	☐
5. Cared for customer property and returned it undamaged.	☐

Student signature _____ Date _____

Comments:

_____

Have your supervisor/instructor verify satisfactory completion of this procedure, any observations found, and any necessary action(s) recommended.

Evaluation Instructions: The scoring box below is intended to act as a guide for both student and supervisor/instructor. Each criterion listed will help students to understand what is expected of them and help supervisors/instructors articulate the level of success at a particular task. The scoring is set up to allow a second attempt at each task (see the Test and Retest columns). Scoring is also designed to award students points only for task criteria that were completed correctly. Points are lost for failure to complete the employability requirements (see Non-Task-Specific Evaluation criteria). When all criteria are evaluated, tally the points for a total at the bottom of each column.

Tasksheet Scoring

	Test		Retest	
Evaluation Items	**Pass**	**Fail**	**Pass**	**Fail**
Task-Specific Evaluation	**(1 pt)**	**(0 pts)**	**(1 pt)**	**(0 pts)**
Student identified various hand tools used in vehicle repair.				
Student identified various power tools used in vehicle repair.				
Student identified large equipment used in a vehicle repair facility.				
Student listed safety precautions for using related tools and equipment.				
Non-Task-Specific Evaluation	**(0 pts)**	**(−1 pt)**	**(0 pts)**	**(−1 pt)**
Student successfully completed at least three of the non-task-specific steps.				
Student successfully completed all five of the non-task-specific steps.				
Total Score: <total # of points/4 = %>				

CDX Tasksheet Number: MHTS018

Student/Intern Information

Name _____ Date _____ Class _____

Vehicle, Customer, and Service Information

Vehicle used for this activity:

Year _____ Make _____ Model _____

Odometer _____ VIN _____

Materials Required

- Standard toolkit and other tools as required
- Precision measuring tools: micrometer, dial-indicator, dial-caliper, etc.

Task-Specific Safety Considerations

- Comply with personal and environmental safety practices associated with clothing; eye protection; hand tools; power equipment; proper ventilation; and the handling, storage, and disposal of chemicals/materials in accordance with local, state, and federal safety and environmental regulations.
- Tools allow us to increase our productivity and effectiveness. However, they must be used according to the manufacturer's procedures. Failure to follow those procedures can result in serious injury or death.

▶ **TASK** Demonstrate safe handling and use of appropriate tools. | **MHT** **TE03**

Time off_____

Time on_____

Total time_____

Student Instructions: Read through the entire procedure prior to starting. Prepare your workspace and any tools or parts that may be needed to complete the task. When directed by your supervisor/instructor, begin the procedure to complete the task and check the box as each step is finished. Track your time on this procedure for later comparison to the standard completion time (i.e., "flat rate" or customer pay time).

Procedure:	Step Completed
1. These tasks will require observation of the student over a prolonged period after the initial check. Ask your supervisor/instructor to give you a date for your evaluation:	
a. Write that date here.	☐

	Step Completed
2. Continue with your other projects, demonstrating safe handling and proper cleaning, maintenance, and storage of the tools until the date of your evaluation.	☐

Non-Task-Specific Evaluations:	Step Completed
1. Tools and equipment were used as directed and returned in good working order.	☐
2. Complied with all general and task-specific safety standards, including proper use of any personal protective equipment.	☐
3. Completed the task in an appropriate time frame (recommendation: 1.5 or 2 times flat rate).	☐
4. Left the workspace clean and orderly.	☐
5. Cared for customer property and returned it undamaged.	☐

Student signature _____ Date _____

Comments:

> [blank comment box]

Have your supervisor/instructor verify satisfactory completion of this procedure, any observations found, and any necessary action(s) recommended.

Evaluation Instructions: The scoring box below is intended to act as a guide for both student and supervisor/instructor. Each criterion listed will help students to understand what is expected of them and help supervisors/instructors articulate the level of success at a particular task. The scoring is set up to allow a second attempt at each task (see the Test and Retest columns). Scoring is also designed to award students points only for task criteria that were completed correctly. Points are lost for failure to complete the employability requirements (see Non-Task-Specific Evaluation criteria). When all criteria are evaluated, tally the points for a total at the bottom of each column.

Tasksheet Scoring

	Test		Retest	
Evaluation Items	**Pass**	**Fail**	**Pass**	**Fail**
Task-Specific Evaluation	**(1 pt)**	**(0 pts)**	**(1 pt)**	**(0 pts)**
Student used the correct tool for the type of fastener being serviced (e.g., used 6-point fasteners when needed instead of 12-point).				
Student used the correct style of tool for the fastener being serviced (e.g., used an impact socket on an impact gun).				
Student used hand tools in the proper manner (e.g., screwdriver NOT used as a chisel or punch).				
Student used the correct driver for the correct socket (e.g., removed transmission pan bolts with a speed brace or wheel lug nuts with a lug wrench).				
Non-Task-Specific Evaluation	**(0 pts)**	**(−1 pt)**	**(0 pts)**	**(−1 pt)**
Student successfully completed at least three of the non-task-specific steps.				
Student successfully completed all five of the non-task-specific steps.				
Total Score: <total # of points/4 = %>				

Supervisor/Instructor:

Supervisor/instructor signature _____ Date _____

Comments:

Retest supervisor/instructor signature _____ Date _____

Comments:

CDX Tasksheet Number: MHTS019

Student/Intern Information

Name _____ Date _____ Class _____

Vehicle, Customer, and Service Information

Vehicle used for this activity:

Year _____ Make _____ Model _____

Odometer _____ VIN _____

Materials Required

- Standard toolkit and other tools as required
- Precision measuring tools: micrometer, dial-indicator, dial-caliper, etc.

Task-Specific Safety Considerations

- Comply with personal and environmental safety practices associated with clothing; eye protection; hand tools; power equipment; proper ventilation; and the handling, storage, and disposal of chemicals/materials in accordance with local, state, and federal safety and environmental regulations.
- Tools allow us to increase our productivity and effectiveness. However, they must be used according to the manufacturer's procedures. Failure to follow those procedures can result in serious injury or death.

▶ **TASK** Demonstrate proper cleaning, storage, and maintenance of tools and equipment.

MHT TE04

Time off_____

Time on_____

Total time_____

Student Instructions: Read through the entire procedure prior to starting. Prepare your workspace and any tools or parts that may be needed to complete the task. When directed by your supervisor/instructor, begin the procedure to complete the task and check the box as each step is finished. Track your time on this procedure for later comparison to the standard completion time (i.e., "flat rate" or customer pay time).

Procedure:	Step Completed
1. These tasks will require observation of the student over a prolonged period after the initial check. Ask your supervisor/instructor to give you a date for your evaluation:	
a. Write that date here.	☐

	Step Completed
2. Continue with your other projects, demonstrating safe handling and proper cleaning, maintenance, and storage of the tools until the date of your evaluation.	☐

Non-Task-Specific Evaluations:	Step Completed
1. Tools and equipment were used as directed and returned in good working order.	☐
2. Complied with all general and task-specific safety standards, including proper use of any personal protective equipment.	☐
3. Completed the task in an appropriate time frame (recommendation: 1.5 or 2 times flat rate).	☐
4. Left the workspace clean and orderly.	☐
5. Cared for customer property and returned it undamaged.	☐

Student signature _____ Date _____

Comments:

Have your supervisor/instructor verify satisfactory completion of this procedure, any observations found, and any necessary action(s) recommended.

Evaluation Instructions: The scoring box below is intended to act as a guide for both student and supervisor/instructor. Each criterion listed will help students to understand what is expected of them and help supervisors/instructors articulate the level of success at a particular task. The scoring is set up to allow a second attempt at each task (see the Test and Retest columns). Scoring is also designed to award students points only for task criteria that were completed correctly. Points are lost for failure to complete the employability requirements (see Non-Task-Specific Evaluation criteria). When all criteria are evaluated, tally the points for a total at the bottom of each column.

Tasksheet Scoring

	Test		Retest	
Evaluation Items	**Pass**	**Fail**	**Pass**	**Fail**
Task-Specific Evaluation	**(1 pt)**	**(0 pts)**	**(1 pt)**	**(0 pts)**
Student described how hand tools should be maintained.				
Student described how pneumatic tools should be maintained.				
Student described how large equipment such as a vehicle hoist should be maintained.				
Student demonstrated proper care of all tools and equipment.				
Non-Task-Specific Evaluation	**(0 pts)**	**(−1 pt)**	**(0 pts)**	**(−1 pt)**
Student successfully completed at least three of the non-task-specific steps.				
Student successfully completed all five of the non-task-specific steps.				
Total Score: <total # of points/4 = %>				

Supervisor/Instructor:

Supervisor/instructor signature _____ Date _____

Comments:

[   ]

Retest supervisor/instructor signature _____ Date _____

Comments:

[   ]

CDX Tasksheet Number: MHTS020

Student/Intern Information

Name _____ Date _____ Class _____

Vehicle, Customer, and Service Information

Vehicle used for this activity:

Year _____ Make _____ Model _____

Odometer _____ VIN _____

Materials Required
- Standard toolkit and other tools as required
- Precision measuring tools: micrometer, dial-indicator, dial-caliper, etc.

Task-Specific Safety Considerations
- Comply with personal and environmental safety practices associated with clothing; eye protection; hand tools; power equipment; proper ventilation; and the handling, storage, and disposal of chemicals/materials in accordance with local, state, and federal safety and environmental regulations.
- Tools allow us to increase our productivity and effectiveness. However, they must be used according to the manufacturer's procedures. Failure to follow those procedures can result in serious injury or death.

▶ **TASK** Demonstrate proper use of precision measuring tools (e.g., micrometer, dial-indicator, dial-caliper).

MHT TE05

Time off_____

Time on_____

Total time_____

Student Instructions: Read through the entire procedure prior to starting. Prepare your workspace and any tools or parts that may be needed to complete the task. When directed by your supervisor/instructor, begin the procedure to complete the task and check the box as each step is finished. Track your time on this procedure for later comparison to the standard completion time (i.e., "flat rate" or customer pay time).

Procedure:	Step Completed
1. These tasks will require observation of the student over a prolonged period after the initial check. Ask your supervisor/instructor to give you a date for your evaluation:	
a. Write that date here.	☐

2. Continue with your other projects, demonstrating safe handling and proper cleaning, maintenance, and storage of the tools until the date of your evaluation.	☐

Non-Task-Specific Evaluations:	Step Completed
1. Tools and equipment were used as directed and returned in good working order.	☐
2. Complied with all general and task-specific safety standards, including proper use of any personal protective equipment.	☐
3. Completed the task in an appropriate time frame (recommendation: 1.5 or 2 times flat rate).	☐
4. Left the workspace clean and orderly.	☐
5. Cared for customer property and returned it undamaged.	☐

Student signature _____ Date _____

Comments:

Have your supervisor/instructor verify satisfactory completion of this procedure, any observations found, and any necessary action(s) recommended.

Evaluation Instructions: The scoring box below is intended to act as a guide for both student and supervisor/instructor. Each criterion listed will help students to understand what is expected of them and help supervisors/instructors articulate the level of success at a particular task. The scoring is set up to allow a second attempt at each task (see the Test and Retest columns). Scoring is also designed to award students points only for task criteria that were completed correctly. Points are lost for failure to complete the employability requirements (see Non-Task-Specific Evaluation criteria). When all criteria are evaluated, tally the points for a total at the bottom of each column.

Tasksheet Scoring

Evaluation Items	Test		Retest	
	Pass	Fail	Pass	Fail
Task-Specific Evaluation	**(1 pt)**	**(0 pts)**	**(1 pt)**	**(0 pts)**
Student listed different types of precision measuring tools and described their usage.				
Student measured a given item accurately within 0.0005" using a micrometer.				
Student measured a given item accurately within 0.0005" using a dial-indicator.				
Student measured a given item accurately within 0.0005" using a dial-caliper.				
Non-Task-Specific Evaluation	**(0 pts)**	**(−1 pt)**	**(0 pts)**	**(−1 pt)**
Student successfully completed at least three of the non-task-specific steps.				
Student successfully completed all five of the non-task-specific steps.				
Total Score: <total # of points/4 = %>				

Supervisor/Instructor:

Supervisor/instructor signature _____ Date _____

Comments:

Retest supervisor/instructor signature _____ Date _____

Comments:

Vehicle Protection and Jack and Lift Safety

Learning Objective/Task	CDX Tasksheet Number	ASE Foundation Reference Number
• Identify purpose and demonstrate proper use of fender covers, mats.	MHTS022	VS02
• Utilize proper ventilation procedures for working within the lab/shop area.	MHTS005	SPS05
• Identify and use proper placement of floor jacks and jack stands.	MHTS003	SPS03
• Identify and use proper procedures for safe lift operation.	MHTS004	SPS04
• Ensure vehicle is prepared to return to customer per school/company policy (floor mats, steering wheel cover, etc.).	MHTS026	VC01

Materials Required

- Vehicle
- Fender, seat, steering wheel, and carpet covers
- Floor jack
- Jack stand(s)
- Wheel chocks
- Vehicle hoist
- Shop rag
- Possible cleaning supplies

Safety Considerations

- Comply with personal and environmental safety practices associated with clothing; eye protection; hand tools; power equipment; proper ventilation; and the handling, storage, and disposal of chemicals/materials in accordance with local, state, and federal safety and environmental regulations.
- Floor jacks and jack stands must have a capacity rating higher than the load lifted.
- Floor jacks and jack stands must be used on a hard, level surface. Do not attempt to lift or support a vehicle under any other conditions.
- Jacks are designed to lift a vehicle, not to support it. Always use jack stands once the vehicle has been lifted.
- Have the jack stands ready, and at hand, prior to lifting the vehicle.
- Vehicle hoists are important tools that increase productivity and make the job easier. But they also can cause severe injury or death if used improperly. Make sure you follow the hoist's and vehicle manufacturers' operation procedures. Also, make sure you have your supervisor's/instructor's permission to use a vehicle hoist.
- It is critical that the vehicle be returned to the customer in proper working order. Double-check your work before releasing the vehicle to the customer.

CDX Tasksheet Number: MHTS022

Student/Intern Information

Name _____ Date _____ Class _____

Vehicle, Customer, and Service Information

Vehicle used for this activity:

Year _____ Make _____ Model _____

Odometer _____ VIN _____

Materials Required

- Vehicle
- Fender, seat, steering wheel, and carpet covers
- Floor jack
- Jack stand(s)
- Wheel chocks
- Vehicle hoist
- Shop rag
- Possible cleaning supplies

Task-Specific Safety Considerations

- It is critical that the vehicle be returned to the customer in proper working order. Double-check your work before releasing the vehicle to the customer.

▶ **TASK** Identify purpose and demonstrate proper use of fender covers, mats.

MHT VS02

Time off_____

Time on_____

Total time_____

Student Instructions: Read through the entire procedure prior to starting. Prepare your workspace and any tools or parts that may be needed to complete the task. When directed by your supervisor/instructor, begin the procedure to complete the task and check the box as each step is finished. Track your time on this procedure for later comparison to the standard completion time (i.e., "flat rate" or customer pay time).

Procedure:	Step Completed
1. Identify the purpose of the following items:	
a. Fender cover.	☐

	Step Completed
b. Seat cover.	☐
c. Steering wheel cover.	☐
d. Carpet cover/floor mat.	☐
2. Properly prepare a vehicle for service or repair, using the above covers.	☐

Non-Task-Specific Evaluations:	Step Completed
1. Tools and equipment were used as directed and returned in good working order.	☐
2. Complied with all general and task-specific safety standards, including proper use of any personal protective equipment.	☐
3. Completed the task in an appropriate time frame (recommendation: 1.5 or 2 times flat rate).	☐
4. Left the workspace clean and orderly.	☐
5. Cared for customer property and returned it undamaged.	☐

Student signature _____ Date _____

Comments:

Have your supervisor/instructor verify satisfactory completion of this procedure, any observations found, and any necessary action(s) recommended.

Evaluation Instructions: The scoring box below is intended to act as a guide for both student and supervisor/instructor. Each criterion listed will help students to understand what is expected of them and help supervisors/instructors articulate the level of success at a particular task. The scoring is set up to allow a second attempt at each task (see the Test and Retest columns). Scoring is also designed to award students points only for task criteria that were completed correctly. Points are lost for failure to complete the employability requirements (see Non-Task-Specific Evaluation criteria). When all criteria are evaluated, tally the points for a total at the bottom of each column.

Tasksheet Scoring

	Test		Retest	
Evaluation Items	**Pass**	**Fail**	**Pass**	**Fail**
Task-Specific Evaluation	**(1 pt)**	**(0 pts)**	**(1 pt)**	**(0 pts)**
Student listed the ways to protect a vehicle's interior from dirt or grease during service.				
Student listed the ways to protect a vehicle's exterior from damage during service.				
Student explained why it is important to protect a vehicle while service is being performed.				
Student demonstrated proper measures of vehicle care during service.				
Non-Task-Specific Evaluation	**(0 pts)**	**(−1 pt)**	**(0 pts)**	**(−1 pt)**
Student successfully completed at least three of the non-task-specific steps.				
Student successfully completed all five of the non-task-specific steps.				
Total Score: <total # of points/4 = %>				

Supervisor/Instructor:

Supervisor/instructor signature _____ Date _____

Comments:

Retest supervisor/instructor signature _____ Date _____

Comments:

CDX Tasksheet Number: MHTS005

Student/Intern Information

Name _____ Date _____ Class _____

Vehicle, Customer, and Service Information

Vehicle used for this activity:

Year _____ Make _____ Model _____

Odometer _____ VIN _____

Materials Required

- Vehicle
- Fender, seat, steering wheel, and carpet covers
- Floor jack
- Jack stand(s)
- Wheel chocks
- Vehicle hoist
- Shop rag
- Possible cleaning supplies

Task-Specific Safety Considerations

- Comply with personal and environmental safety practices associated with clothing; eye protection; hand tools; power equipment; proper ventilation; and the handling, storage, and disposal of chemicals/materials in accordance with local, state, and federal safety and environmental regulations.

▶ **TASK** Utilize proper ventilation procedures for working within the lab/ shop area.

MHT SPS05

Time off_____

Time on_____

Total time_____

Student Instructions: Read through the entire procedure prior to starting. Prepare your workspace and any tools or parts that may be needed to complete the task. When directed by your supervisor/instructor, begin the procedure to complete the task and check the box as each step is finished. Track your time on this procedure for later comparison to the standard completion time (i.e., "flat rate" or customer pay time).

Procedure:	Step Completed
1. List the OSHA personal exposure limit for carbon monoxide over an 8-hour work period: _____ ppm	☐
2. Properly position a vehicle in a work stall.	☐
3. Properly connect the exhaust extraction system to the vehicle exhaust.	☐
4. Turn on, or verify that the extraction system is on.	☐
5. With your supervisor's/instructor's permission, start the vehicle and verify the extraction equipment is secure and operating properly.	☐
6. Have your supervisor/instructor verify your previously given answer and your proper exhaust extraction usage. Supervisor's/instructor's initials:	☐
7. Turn off the vehicle, return the exhaust hoses to their proper storage places, and shut off the extraction system if it isn't being used anymore.	☐

Non-Task-Specific Evaluations:	Step Completed
1. Tools and equipment were used as directed and returned in good working order.	☐
2. Complied with all general and task-specific safety standards, including proper use of any personal protective equipment.	☐
3. Completed the task in an appropriate time frame (recommendation: 1.5 or 2 times flat rate).	☐
4. Left the workspace clean and orderly.	☐
5. Cared for customer property and returned it undamaged.	☐

Student signature _____ Date _____

Comments:

Have your supervisor/instructor verify satisfactory completion of this procedure, any observations found, and any necessary action(s) recommended.

Evaluation Instructions: The scoring box below is intended to act as a guide for both student and supervisor/instructor. Each criterion listed will help students to understand what is expected of them and help supervisors/instructors articulate the level of success at a particular task. The scoring is set up to allow a second attempt at each task (see the Test and Retest columns). Scoring is also designed to award students points only for task criteria that were completed correctly. Points are lost for failure to complete the employability requirements (see Non-Task-Specific Evaluation criteria). When all criteria are evaluated, tally the points for a total at the bottom of each column.

Tasksheet Scoring

Evaluation Items	Test		Retest	
	Pass	**Fail**	**Pass**	**Fail**
Task-Specific Evaluation	**(1 pt)**	**(0 pts)**	**(1 pt)**	**(0 pts)**
Student described the purpose of proper ventilation.				
Student identified the location of ventilation system components (controls/hoses/fans).				
Student verified that the ventilation system is in good working condition.				
Student used the ventilation system correctly at appropriate times.				
Non-Task-Specific Evaluation	**(0 pts)**	**(−1 pt)**	**(0 pts)**	**(−1 pt)**
Student successfully completed at least three of the non-task-specific steps.				
Student successfully completed all five of the non-task-specific steps.				
Total Score: <total # of points/4 = %>				

Supervisor/Instructor:

Supervisor/instructor signature _____ Date _____

Comments:

_____

Retest supervisor/instructor signature _____ Date _____

Comments:

_____

CDX Tasksheet Number: MHTS003

Student/Intern Information

Name _____ Date _____ Class _____

Vehicle, Customer, and Service Information

Vehicle used for this activity:

Year _____ Make _____ Model _____

Odometer _____ VIN _____

Materials Required
- Vehicle
- Fender, seat, steering wheel, and carpet covers
- Floor jack
- Jack stand(s)
- Wheel chocks
- Vehicle hoist
- Shop rag
- Possible cleaning supplies

Task-Specific Safety Considerations
- Comply with personal and environmental safety practices associated with clothing; eye protection; hand tools; power equipment; proper ventilation; and the handling, storage, and disposal of chemicals/ materials in accordance with local, state, and federal safety and environmental regulations.
- Floor jacks and jack stands must have a capacity rating higher than the load lifted.
- Floor jacks and jack stands must be used on a hard, level surface. Do not attempt to lift or support a vehicle under any other conditions.
- Jacks are designed to lift a vehicle, not to support it. Always use jack stands once the vehicle has been lifted.
- Have the jack stands ready, and at hand, prior to lifting the vehicle.

▶ **TASK** Identify and use proper placement of floor jacks and jack stands. **MHT SPS03**

Time off_____

Time on_____

Student Instructions: Read through the entire procedure prior to starting. Prepare your workspace and any tools or parts that may be needed to complete the task. When directed by your supervisor/instructor, begin the procedure to complete the task and check the box as each step is finished. Track your time on this procedure for later comparison to the standard completion time (i.e., "flat rate" or customer pay time).

Total time_____

Procedure:	Step Completed
1. Research the jacking and lifting procedures for this vehicle in the appropriate service manual.	
a. Draw a diagram of the vehicle's lift points.	☐
2. Check to make sure the vehicle is on a hard, level surface. If not, move it to a safe location.	☐
3. Install wheel chocks. Prepare the floor jack and stands for use.	☐
4. Lift and support one end of the vehicle on jack stands according to the manufacturer's procedure.	
a. Have your supervisor/instructor initial to verify proper jack stand placement.	☐
5. Lift the vehicle and remove the jack stands. Return the jack and stands to their proper storage places.	☐
6. Return the vehicle to its beginning condition and return any tools you used to their proper locations.	☐

Non-Task-Specific Evaluations:	Step Completed
1. Tools and equipment were used as directed and returned in good working order.	☐
2. Complied with all general and task-specific safety standards, including proper use of any personal protective equipment.	☐
3. Completed the task in an appropriate time frame (recommendation: 1.5 or 2 times flat rate).	☐
4. Left the workspace clean and orderly.	☐
5. Cared for customer property and returned it undamaged.	☐

Student signature _____ Date _____

Comments:

Have your supervisor/instructor verify satisfactory completion of this procedure, any observations found,

and any necessary action(s) recommended.

Evaluation Instructions: The scoring box below is intended to act as a guide for both student and supervisor/instructor. Each criterion listed will help students to understand what is expected of them and help supervisors/instructors articulate the level of success at a particular task. The scoring is set up to allow a second attempt at each task (see the Test and Retest columns). Scoring is also designed to award students points only for task criteria that were completed correctly. Points are lost for failure to complete the employability requirements (see Non-Task-Specific Evaluation criteria). When all criteria are evaluated, tally the points for a total at the bottom of each column.

Tasksheet Scoring

Evaluation Items	Test		Retest	
	Pass	**Fail**	**Pass**	**Fail**
Task-Specific Evaluation	**(1 pt)**	**(0 pts)**	**(1 pt)**	**(0 pts)**
Student utilized service information to identify correct lifting points and jacking instructions.				
Student listed safety precautions for raising and lowering a vehicle using a floor jack and jack stands.				
Student used a floor jack correctly when raising and lowering a vehicle.				
Student used jack stands to support the vehicle.				
Non-Task-Specific Evaluation	**(0 pts)**	**(−1 pt)**	**(0 pts)**	**(−1 pt)**
Student successfully completed at least three of the non-task-specific steps.				
Student successfully completed all five of the non-task-specific steps.				
Total Score: <total # of points/4 = %>				

Supervisor/Instructor:

Supervisor/instructor signature _____ Date _____

Comments:

Retest supervisor/instructor signature _____ Date _____

Comments:

CDX Tasksheet Number: MHTS004

Student/Intern Information

Name _____ Date _____ Class _____

Vehicle, Customer, and Service Information

Vehicle used for this activity:

Year _____ Make _____ Model _____

Odometer _____ VIN _____

Materials Required

- Vehicle
- Fender, seat, steering wheel, and carpet covers
- Floor jack
- Jack stand(s)
- Wheel chocks
- Vehicle hoist
- Shop rag
- Possible cleaning supplies

Task-Specific Safety Considerations

- Comply with personal and environmental safety practices associated with clothing; eye protection; hand tools; power equipment; proper ventilation; and the handling, storage, and disposal of chemicals/materials in accordance with local, state, and federal safety and environmental regulations.
- Floor jacks and jack stands must have a capacity rating higher than the load lifted.
- Floor jacks and jack stands must be used on a hard, level surface. Do not attempt to lift or support a vehicle under any other conditions.
- Jacks are designed to lift a vehicle, not to support it. Always use jack stands once the vehicle has been lifted.
- Have the jack stands ready, and at hand, prior to lifting the vehicle.
- Vehicle hoists are important tools that increase productivity and make the job easier. But they also can cause severe injury or death if used improperly. Make sure you follow the hoist's and vehicle manufacturers' operation procedures. Also, make sure you have your supervisor's/instructor's permission to use a vehicle hoist.

Time off_____

Time on_____

Total time_____

▶ **TASK** Identify and use proper procedures for safe lift operation.

MHT
SPS04

Student Instructions: Read through the entire procedure prior to starting. Prepare your workspace and any tools or parts that may be needed to complete the task. When directed by your supervisor/instructor, begin the procedure to complete the task and check the box as each step is finished. Track your time on this procedure for later comparison to the standard completion time (i.e., "flat rate" or customer pay time).

Procedure:	Step Completed
1. Position the vehicle in proper relation to the lift, taking into consideration the center of gravity of the vehicle. **(Note:** Check the vehicle for unusual loading, such as heavy loads in the trunk or truck bed. If you find this situation, notify your instructor immediately.)	☐
2. Position the lift arms in the proper location as specified by the manufacturer.	☐
3. Raise the lift until one of the arms lightly contacts the lift point. Check the position of the lift arms to make sure they are in contact with (or just about to contact) the proper points. **(Note:** Make sure the lift arms are not touching or pinching anything they shouldn't be in contact with, including the rocker panel, running boards, and fuel or brake lines.)	☐
4. If the arms are in the proper position, raise the vehicle a few inches off the ground. Using a strong part of the vehicle, moderately shake the vehicle to make sure it is stable. **(Note:** If the vehicle shifts position at all or is out of balance, lower the vehicle and reset the lift arms or reposition the vehicle.)	☐
5. If the vehicle is stable, lift the vehicle to the height indicated by your instructor and engage the locks or lower the lift onto the locks. Supervisor/instructor initials:	☐

© 2021 Jones & Bartlett Learning, LLC, an Ascend Learning Company

84 Vehicle Protection and Jack and Lift Safety

	Step Completed
6. Verify that there are no obstacles under the vehicle, and that all doors are closed. Lower the vehicle and move the lift arms out of the way of the vehicle.	☐
7. Return the vehicle to its beginning condition and return any tools you used to their proper locations.	☐

Non-Task-Specific Evaluations:	Step Completed
1. Tools and equipment were used as directed and returned in good working order.	☐
2. Complied with all general and task-specific safety standards, including proper use of any personal protective equipment.	☐
3. Completed the task in an appropriate time frame (recommendation: 1.5 or 2 times flat rate).	☐
4. Left the workspace clean and orderly.	☐
5. Cared for customer property and returned it undamaged.	☐

Student signature _____ Date _____

Comments:

Have your supervisor/instructor verify satisfactory completion of this procedure, any observations found, and any necessary action(s) recommended.

Evaluation Instructions: The scoring box below is intended to act as a guide for both student and supervisor/instructor. Each criterion listed will help students to understand what is expected of them and help supervisors/instructors articulate the level of success at a particular task. The scoring is set up to allow a second attempt at each task (see the Test and Retest columns). Scoring is also designed to award students points only for task criteria that were completed correctly. Points are lost for failure to complete the employability requirements (see Non-Task-Specific Evaluation criteria). When all criteria are evaluated, tally the points for a total at the bottom of each column.

Tasksheet Scoring

Evaluation Items	Test		Retest	
	Pass	**Fail**	**Pass**	**Fail**
Task-Specific Evaluation	**(1 pt)**	**(0 pts)**	**(1 pt)**	**(0 pts)**
Student listed safety precautions for operating a vehicle lift.				
Student described how to operate the lift/lower control mechanisms.				
Student used the proper procedure to position the lift arms and raise the vehicle, including checking the vehicle stability before raising it completely.				
Student checked for obstructions and signaled when lowering the vehicle according to shop procedure.				
Non-Task-Specific Evaluation	**(0 pts)**	**(−1 pt)**	**(0 pts)**	**(−1 pt)**
Student successfully completed at least three of the non-task-specific steps.				
Student successfully completed all five of the non-task-specific steps.				
Total Score: <total # of points/4 = %>				

Supervisor/Instructor:

Supervisor/instructor signature _____ Date _____

Comments:

Retest supervisor/instructor signature _____ Date _____

Comments:

CDX Tasksheet Number: MHTS026

Student/Intern Information

Name _____ Date _____ Class _____

Vehicle, Customer, and Service Information

Vehicle used for this activity:

Year _____ Make _____ Model _____

Odometer _____ VIN _____

Materials Required
- Vehicle
- Fender, seat, steering wheel, and carpet covers
- Floor jack
- Jack stand(s)
- Wheel chocks
- Vehicle hoist
- Shop rag
- Possible cleaning supplies

Task-Specific Safety Considerations
- It is critical that the vehicle be returned to the customer in proper working order. Double-check your work before releasing the vehicle to the customer.

▶ **TASK** Ensure vehicle is prepared to return to customer per school/company policy (floor mats, steering wheel cover, etc.). **MHT VC01**

Time off_____

Time on_____

Student Instructions: Read through the entire procedure prior to starting. Prepare your workspace and any tools or parts that may be needed to complete the task. When directed by your supervisor/instructor, begin the procedure to complete the task and check the box as each step is finished. Track your time on this procedure for later comparison to the standard completion time (i.e., "flat rate" or customer pay time).

Total time_____

Procedure:	Step Completed
(**Note:** A properly protected vehicle and good work habits will make this task much easier.)	
1. Double check that all work has been completed. Nothing can be missing, loose, or leaking.	☐
2. If your supervisor/instructor deems it necessary, test-drive the vehicle to be sure of proper repair and operation of the vehicle.	

a. Have your supervisor/instructor initial here.	☐
3. Double-check that all tools are put away and stored properly.	☐
4. Remove all fender covers, seat covers, floor covers, and steering wheel covers. Return them to their storage place or dispose of them properly, depending on the type of cover.	☐
5. Check the exterior of the vehicle for greasy fingerprints or grime. Clean with an appropriate cleaner. Follow your shop's policies on this procedure.	☐
6. Check the following interior locations for dirt or greasy spots. Clean with an appropriate cleaner. Follow your shop's policies on this procedure.	
a. Carpet and floor mats.	☐
b. Seats.	☐
c. Steering wheel and parking brake handle.	☐
d. Door panel and handles.	☐

7. If the vehicle is ready to return to the customer, the vehicle may need to be moved out of the shop. Get your supervisor's/instructor's permission to move the vehicle to the customer pick-up area.	
a. Have your supervisor/instructor initial here.	☐
8. Return to your work stall and clean up the floor, benches, and related area.	☐

Non-Task-Specific Evaluations:	Step Completed
1. Tools and equipment were used as directed and returned in good working order.	☐
2. Complied with all general and task-specific safety standards, including proper use of any personal protective equipment.	☐
3. Completed the task in an appropriate time frame (recommendation: 1.5 or 2 times flat rate).	☐
4. Left the workspace clean and orderly.	☐
5. Cared for customer property and returned it undamaged.	☐

Student signature _____ Date _____

Comments:

Have your supervisor/instructor verify satisfactory completion of this procedure, any observations found,

and any necessary action(s) recommended.

Evaluation Instructions: The scoring box below is intended to act as a guide for both student and supervisor/instructor. Each criterion listed will help students to understand what is expected of them and help supervisors/instructors articulate the level of success at a particular task. The scoring is set up to allow a second attempt at each task (see the Test and Retest columns). Scoring is also designed to award students points only for task criteria that were completed correctly. Points are lost for failure to complete the employability requirements (see Non-Task-Specific Evaluation criteria). When all criteria are evaluated, tally the points for a total at the bottom of each column.

Tasksheet Scoring

Evaluation Items	Test		Retest	
	Pass	**Fail**	**Pass**	**Fail**
Task-Specific Evaluation	**(1 pt)**	**(0 pts)**	**(1 pt)**	**(0 pts)**
Student listed the procedures for preparing a vehicle to be returned to a customer as per school/company policy.				
Student washed and wiped the vehicle to remove residual dirt or grease.				
Student removed protective interior mats/covers.				
Student reset all lights, warnings, and reminders related to the vehicle service.				
Non-Task-Specific Evaluation	**(0 pts)**	**(−1 pt)**	**(0 pts)**	**(−1 pt)**
Student successfully completed at least three of the non-task-specific steps.				
Student successfully completed all five of the non-task-specific steps.				
Total Score: <total # of points/4 = %>				

Supervisor/Instructor:

Supervisor/instructor signature _____ Date _____

Comments:

Retest supervisor/instructor signature _____ Date _____

Comments:

Vehicle, Customer, and Service Information

Learning Objective/Task	CDX Tasksheet Number	ASE Foundation Reference Number
• Identify information needed and the service requested on a repair order.	MHTS021	VS01
• Demonstrate use of the three Cs (concern, cause, and correction).	MHTS023	VS03
• Review vehicle service history.	MHTS024	VS04
• Complete work order to include customer information, vehicle identifying information, customer concern, related service history, cause, and correction.	MHTS025	VS05

Materials Required

- Vehicle
- Service information
- Completed repair order assigned by your supervisor/instructor
- Several repair orders for the same vehicle from repairs/services performed over an extended period of time
- Scheduled maintenance chart for this vehicle
- Blank repair order

Safety Considerations

- Shop rules and procedures are critical to your safety. Please give these your utmost attention.

CDX Tasksheet Number: MHTSO21

Student/Intern Information

Name _____ Date _____ Class _____

Vehicle, Customer, and Service Information

Vehicle used for this activity:

Year _____ Make _____ Model _____

Odometer _____ VIN _____

Materials Required

- Vehicle
- Service information
- Completed repair order assigned by your supervisor/instructor
- Several repair orders for the same vehicle from repairs/services performed over an extended period of time
- Scheduled maintenance chart for this vehicle
- Blank repair order

Task-Specific Safety Considerations

- Shop rules and procedures are critical to your safety. Please give these your utmost attention.

▶ **TASK** Identify information needed and the service requested on a repair order.

MHT VSO1

Time off_____

Time on_____

Total time_____

Student Instructions: Read through the entire procedure prior to starting. Prepare your workspace and any tools or parts that may be needed to complete the task. When directed by your supervisor/instructor, begin the procedure to complete the task and check the box as each step is finished. Track your time on this procedure for later comparison to the standard completion time (i.e., "flat rate" or customer pay time).

Procedure:	Step Completed
1. Familiarize yourself with the assigned repair order. Locate and list the following information.	
a. Date.	☐

b. Customer.	☐
c. Address.	☐
d. Daytime phone number.	☐
e. Year.	☐
f. Make.	☐
g. Model.	☐
h. Color.	☐
i. License and state.	☐
j. Odometer reading.	☐

	Step Completed
k. VIN.	☐
l. Customer concern(s)/service requested:	☐
2. Did the customer sign the repair order authorizing the repairs? Yes: _____ No: _____	☐
3. Return the sample repair order to its proper storage place.	☐

Non-Task-Specific Evaluations:	Step Completed
1. Tools and equipment were used as directed and returned in good working order.	☐
2. Complied with all general and task-specific safety standards, including proper use of any personal protective equipment.	☐
3. Completed the task in an appropriate time frame (recommendation: 1.5 or 2 times flat rate).	☐
4. Left the workspace clean and orderly.	☐
5. Cared for customer property and returned it undamaged.	☐

Student signature _____ Date _____

Comments:

Have your supervisor/instructor verify satisfactory completion of this procedure, any observations found,

and any necessary action(s) recommended.

Evaluation Instructions: The scoring box below is intended to act as a guide for both student and supervisor/instructor. Each criterion listed will help students to understand what is expected of them and help supervisors/instructors articulate the level of success at a particular task. The scoring is set up to allow a second attempt at each task (see the Test and Retest columns). Scoring is also designed to award students points only for task criteria that were completed correctly. Points are lost for failure to complete the employability requirements (see Non-Task-Specific Evaluation criteria). When all criteria are evaluated, tally the points for a total at the bottom of each column.

Tasksheet Scoring

Evaluation Items	Test		Retest	
	Pass	**Fail**	**Pass**	**Fail**
Task-Specific Evaluation	**(1 pt)**	**(0 pts)**	**(1 pt)**	**(0 pts)**
Student listed the customer contact information needed to complete a repair order.				
Student listed the vehicle information needed to complete a repair order.				
Student described how to document the service requested for a customer's vehicle.				
Student explained how to communicate with a customer to gain the most insight on their concern.				
Non-Task-Specific Evaluation	**(0 pts)**	**(−1 pt)**	**(0 pts)**	**(−1 pt)**
Student successfully completed at least three of the non-task-specific steps.				
Student successfully completed all five of the non-task-specific steps.				
Total Score: <total # of points/4 = %>				

Supervisor/Instructor:

Supervisor/instructor signature _____ Date _____

Comments:

Retest supervisor/instructor signature _____ Date _____

Comments:

CDX Tasksheet Number: MHTS023

Student/Intern Information

Name _____ Date _____ Class _____

Vehicle, Customer, and Service Information

Vehicle used for this activity:

Year _____ Make _____ Model _____

Odometer _____ VIN _____

Materials Required

- Vehicle
- Service information
- Completed repair order assigned by your supervisor/instructor
- Several repair orders for the same vehicle from repairs/services performed over an extended period of time
- Scheduled maintenance chart for this vehicle
- Blank repair order

Task-Specific Safety Considerations

- Shop rules and procedures are critical to your safety. Please give these your utmost attention.

▶ **TASK** Demonstrate use of the three Cs (concern, cause, and correction).

MHT VS03

Time off_____

Time on_____

Total time_____

Student Instructions: Read through the entire procedure prior to starting. Prepare your workspace and any tools or parts that may be needed to complete the task. When directed by your supervisor/instructor, begin the procedure to complete the task and check the box as each step is finished. Track your time on this procedure for later comparison to the standard completion time (i.e., "flat rate" or customer pay time).

Procedure:	Step Completed
1. Using the following scenario, write up the three Cs as listed on most repair orders. Assume that the customer authorized the recommended repairs. A customer complains that his vehicle is leaving what looks like oil spots on the landlord's driveway after he ran over something in the road a few days ago. You check the engine oil and find that it is about 1/2 a quart low, but looks pretty clean, like it was changed recently. The engine oil life monitor indicates 92% oil life remaining. You safely raise and secure the vehicle on the hoist. While visually inspecting the underside of the vehicle, you notice oil dripping off the engine oil drain plug. Checking the torque of the drain plug shows that the drain plug isn't loose. Closer inspection reveals a shiny spot on the aluminum oil pan near the drain plug. There is a small crack in the oil pan that is seeping oil and is dripping slowly off the drain plug.	
a. Concern/complaint.	☐
b. Cause.	☐
c. Correction.	☐

Non-Task-Specific Evaluations:	Step Completed
1. Tools and equipment were used as directed and returned in good working order.	☐
2. Complied with all general and task-specific safety standards, including proper use of any personal protective equipment.	☐
3. Completed the task in an appropriate time frame (recommendation: 1.5 or 2 times flat rate).	☐
4. Left the workspace clean and orderly.	☐
5. Cared for customer property and returned it undamaged.	☐

Student signature _____ Date _____

Comments:

Have your supervisor/instructor verify satisfactory completion of this procedure, any observations found, and any necessary action(s) recommended.

Evaluation Instructions: The scoring box below is intended to act as a guide for both student and supervisor/instructor. Each criterion listed will help students to understand what is expected of them and help supervisors/instructors articulate the level of success at a particular task. The scoring is set up to allow a second attempt at each task (see the Test and Retest columns). Scoring is also designed to award students points only for task criteria that were completed correctly. Points are lost for failure to complete the employability requirements (see Non-Task-Specific Evaluation criteria). When all criteria are evaluated, tally the points for a total at the bottom of each column.

Tasksheet Scoring

Evaluation Items	Test		Retest	
	Pass	**Fail**	**Pass**	**Fail**
Task-Specific Evaluation	**(1 pt)**	**(0 pts)**	**(1 pt)**	**(0 pts)**
Student used appropriate questions to provide a detailed report of the customer's concern when writing a repair order.				
Student focused on an appropriate customer concern when diagnosing a vehicle.				
Student provided a detailed description of the cause of a given customer concern, complete with results from various tests/procedures performed.				
Student provided a detailed description of measures taken to repair a vehicle.				
Non-Task-Specific Evaluation	**(0 pts)**	**(−1 pt)**	**(0 pts)**	**(−1 pt)**
Student successfully completed at least three of the non-task-specific steps.				
Student successfully completed all five of the non-task-specific steps.				
Total Score: <total # of points/4 = %>				

CDX Tasksheet Number: MHTS024

Student/Intern Information

Name _____ Date _____ Class _____

Vehicle, Customer, and Service Information

Vehicle used for this activity:

Year _____ Make _____ Model _____

Odometer _____ VIN _____

Materials Required

- Vehicle
- Service information
- Completed repair order assigned by your supervisor/instructor
- Several repair orders for the same vehicle from repairs/services performed over an extended period of time
- Scheduled maintenance chart for this vehicle
- Blank repair order

Task-Specific Safety Considerations

- Shop rules and procedures are critical to your safety. Please give these your utmost attention.

▶ **TASK** Review vehicle service history.

MHT VS04

Time off_____

Time on_____

Total time_____

Student Instructions: Read through the entire procedure prior to starting. Prepare your workspace and any tools or parts that may be needed to complete the task. When directed by your supervisor/instructor, begin the procedure to complete the task and check the box as each step is finished. Track your time on this procedure for later comparison to the standard completion time (i.e., "flat rate" or customer pay time).

Procedure:	Step Completed
1. Familiarize yourself with the repair history as listed on the repair orders and answer the following questions.	
a. What was the first date this vehicle was serviced?	☐

	Step Completed
b. What was the last date this vehicle was serviced?	☐
c. What was the most major repair performed?	☐
d. Was this vehicle ever returned for the same problem more than once? Yes: _____ No: _____	☐
i. If so, for what and how many times?	☐
e. Compare this list to the scheduled maintenance chart and list any missed maintenance tasks between the first service and the last service.	☐

Non-Task-Specific Evaluations:	Step Completed
1. Tools and equipment were used as directed and returned in good working order.	☐
2. Complied with all general and task-specific safety standards, including proper use of any personal protective equipment.	☐
3. Completed the task in an appropriate time frame (recommendation: 1.5 or 2 times flat rate).	☐
4. Left the workspace clean and orderly.	☐
5. Cared for customer property and returned it undamaged.	☐

Student signature _____ Date _____

Comments:

Have your supervisor/instructor verify satisfactory completion of this procedure, any observations found, and any necessary action(s) recommended.

Evaluation Instructions: The scoring box below is intended to act as a guide for both student and supervisor/instructor. Each criterion listed will help students to understand what is expected of them and help supervisors/instructors articulate the level of success at a particular task. The scoring is set up to allow a second attempt at each task (see the Test and Retest columns). Scoring is also designed to award students points only for task criteria that were completed correctly. Points are lost for failure to complete the employability requirements (see Non-Task-Specific Evaluation criteria). When all criteria are evaluated, tally the points for a total at the bottom of each column.

Tasksheet Scoring

	Test		Retest	
Evaluation Items	**Pass**	**Fail**	**Pass**	**Fail**
Task-Specific Evaluation	**(1 pt)**	**(0 pts)**	**(1 pt)**	**(0 pts)**
Student used service information to access vehicle service history.				
Student identified previous repairs that may be related to current customer concern.				
Student explained why you would use vehicle service history as a service advisor.				
Student explained why you would use vehicle service history as a technician.				
Non-Task-Specific Evaluation	**(0 pts)**	**(−1 pt)**	**(0 pts)**	**(−1 pt)**
Student successfully completed at least three of the non-task-specific steps.				
Student successfully completed all five of the non-task-specific steps.				
Total Score: <total # of points/4 = %>				

Supervisor/Instructor:

Supervisor/instructor signature _____ Date _____

Comments:

Retest supervisor/instructor signature _____ Date _____

Comments:

CDX Tasksheet Number: MHTS025

Student/Intern Information

Name _____ Date _____ Class _____

Vehicle, Customer, and Service Information

Vehicle used for this activity:

Year _____ Make _____ Model _____

Odometer _____ VIN _____

Materials Required

- Vehicle
- Service information
- Completed repair order assigned by your supervisor/instructor
- Several repair orders for the same vehicle from repairs/services performed over an extended period of time
- Scheduled maintenance chart for this vehicle
- Blank repair order

Task-Specific Safety Considerations

- Shop rules and procedures are critical to your safety. Please give these your utmost attention.

▶ **TASK** Complete work order to include customer information, vehicle identifying information, customer concern, related service history, cause, and correction.

MHT VS05

Time off_____

Time on_____

Total time_____

Student Instructions: Read through the entire procedure prior to starting. Prepare your workspace and any tools or parts that may be needed to complete the task. When directed by your supervisor/instructor, begin the procedure to complete the task and check the box as each step is finished. Track your time on this procedure for later comparison to the standard completion time (i.e., "flat rate" or customer pay time).

Procedure:	Step Completed
1. Use your company's repair order to complete this task. Fred Smith brings in a 2008 Hyundai Santa Fe AWD, with a 3.3 L engine, automatic transmission, 72,426 miles on the odometer, silver paint, VIN 5NMSH73E28H192794. It needs some work before going on a 3000-mile trip. He would like an estimate of repairs needed and has agreed to let your technician inspect the vehicle while you write up the repair order. He gives you the following information: • Home address: 1234 NE Main Street, Anytown, CA 13579 • Cell phone: (111) 222-1234 • Work phone: (111) 333-4567 • Vehicle license number: CDX-111	☐
2. The customer listed the following concerns/complaints: • Small oil leak from under the engine. • Small coolant leak from under the engine. • Squealing noise coming from the front brakes.	☐
3. The technician found the following conditions: • Both valve covers have leaking gaskets. • The water pump is leaking from the shaft and the bearing is worn. • The front brake pads are worn down to the wear indicators, the rotors are a bit under specifications, and the calipers are starting to seep brake fluid past the caliper piston seal and need to be replaced.	☐
4. Complete the repair order as if all tasks were completed, including parts, their cost, and labor.	☐

Non-Task-Specific Evaluations:	Step Completed
1. Tools and equipment were used as directed and returned in good working order.	☐
2. Complied with all general and task-specific safety standards, including proper use of any personal protective equipment.	☐
3. Completed the task in an appropriate time frame (recommendation: 1.5 or 2 times flat rate).	☐
4. Left the workspace clean and orderly.	☐
5. Cared for customer property and returned it undamaged.	☐

Student signature _____ Date _____

Comments:

Have your supervisor/instructor verify satisfactory completion of this procedure, any observations found, and

any necessary action(s) recommended.

© 2021 Jones & Bartlett Learning, LLC, an Ascend Learning Company

Vehicle, Customer, and Service Information   107

Evaluation Instructions: The scoring box below is intended to act as a guide for both student and supervisor/instructor. Each criterion listed will help students to understand what is expected of them and help supervisors/instructors articulate the level of success at a particular task. The scoring is set up to allow a second attempt at each task (see the Test and Retest columns). Scoring is also designed to award students points only for task criteria that were completed correctly. Points are lost for failure to complete the employability requirements (see Non-Task-Specific Evaluation criteria). When all criteria are evaluated, tally the points for a total at the bottom of each column.

Tasksheet Scoring

Evaluation Items	Test		Retest	
	Pass	**Fail**	**Pass**	**Fail**
Task-Specific Evaluation	**(1 pt)**	**(0 pts)**	**(1 pt)**	**(0 pts)**
Student included customer contact information on repair order.				
Student included vehicle information on repair order.				
Student accessed service history and identified any related repairs.				
Student provided detailed descriptions for the customer concern, root cause of the concern, and the action taken to repair the vehicle.				
Non-Task-Specific Evaluation	**(0 pts)**	**(−1 pt)**	**(0 pts)**	**(−1 pt)**
Student successfully completed at least three of the non-task-specific steps.				
Student successfully completed all five of the non-task-specific steps.				
Total Score: <total # of points/4 = %>				

Supervisor/Instructor:

Supervisor/instructor signature _____ Date _____

Comments:

```



```

Retest supervisor/instructor signature _____ Date _____

Comments:

```



```

SRS and ABS Safety

Learning Objective/Task	CDX Tasksheet Number	ASE Foundation Reference Number
• Demonstrate awareness of the safety aspects of supplemental restraint systems (SRS), electronic brake control systems, and hybrid vehicle high voltage circuits.	MHTS013	SPS13
• Demonstrate awareness of the safety aspects of high voltage circuits (such as high-intensity discharge [HID] lamps, ignition systems, injection systems, etc.).	MHTS014	SPS14

Materials Required

- Vehicle with SRS and anti-lock brake system (ABS)
- Special tools or equipment, if specified

Safety Considerations

- Comply with personal and environmental safety practices associated with clothing; eye protection; hand tools; power equipment; proper ventilation; and the handling, storage, and disposal of chemicals/materials in accordance with local, state, and federal safety and environmental regulations.
- Deployment of the SRS could cause serious injury or death. Follow all the manufacturer's procedures before working on this system.
- The ABS may hold brake fluid under extremely high pressure. Follow the manufacturer's procedures to relieve this pressure before working on this system.
- Hybrid and electric vehicles have batteries with VERY high voltage, which can kill you if handled improperly. Always get permission from your supervisor/instructor before working on or near the system. Also, ALWAYS follow the manufacturer's procedure when servicing a hybrid or electric vehicle.

CDX Tasksheet Number: MHTS013

Student/Intern Information

Name _____ Date _____ Class _____

Vehicle, Customer, and Service Information

Vehicle used for this activity:

Year _____ Make _____ Model _____

Odometer _____ VIN _____

Materials Required

- Vehicle with SRS and anti-lock brake system (ABS)
- Special tools or equipment, if specified

Task-Specific Safety Considerations

- Comply with personal and environmental safety practices associated with clothing; eye protection; hand tools; power equipment; proper ventilation; and the handling, storage, and disposal of chemicals/materials in accordance with local, state, and federal safety and environmental regulations.
- Deployment of the SRS could cause serious injury or death. Follow all the manufacturer's procedures before working on this system.
- The ABS may hold brake fluid under extremely high pressure. Follow the manufacturer's procedures to relieve this pressure before working on this system.
- Hybrid and electric vehicles have batteries with VERY high voltage, which can kill you if handled improperly. Always get permission from your supervisor/instructor before working on, or near, the system. Also, ALWAYS follow the manufacturer's procedure when servicing a hybrid or electric vehicle.

▶ **TASK** Demonstrate awareness of the safety aspects of supplemental restraint systems (SRS), electronic brake control systems, and hybrid vehicle high voltage circuits.

MHT
SPS13

Time off_____

Time on_____

Total time_____

Student Instructions: Read through the entire procedure prior to starting. Prepare your workspace and any tools or parts that may be needed to complete the task. When directed by your supervisor/instructor, begin the procedure to complete the task and check the box as each step is finished. Track your time on this procedure for later comparison to the standard completion time (i.e., "flat rate" or customer pay time).

Procedure:	Step Completed
1. Research the following procedures for a hybrid vehicle in the appropriate service information.	
a. List the precautions when working around or on the SRS on this vehicle.	☐
b. List the steps to disable the SRS on this vehicle.	☐
c. List the steps to enable the SRS on this vehicle.	☐
d. List the precautions when working on or around the electronic brake control system on this vehicle.	☐
e. Identify the high-voltage circuit wiring on this vehicle. What color is the wire conduit?	☐
f. List or print out the high-voltage disable procedure for this vehicle.	☐

Non-Task-Specific Evaluations:	Step Completed
1. Tools and equipment were used as directed and returned in good working order.	☐
2. Complied with all general and task-specific safety standards, including proper use of any personal protective equipment.	☐
3. Completed the task in an appropriate time frame (recommendation: 1.5 or 2 times flat rate).	☐
4. Left the workspace clean and orderly.	☐
5. Cared for customer property and returned it undamaged.	☐

Student signature _____ Date _____

Comments:

Have your supervisor/instructor verify satisfactory completion of this procedure, any observations found,

and any necessary action(s) recommended.

Evaluation Instructions: The scoring box below is intended to act as a guide for both student and supervisor/instructor. Each criterion listed will help students to understand what is expected of them and help supervisors/instructors articulate the level of success at a particular task. The scoring is set up to allow a second attempt at each task (see the Test and Retest columns). Scoring is also designed to award students points only for task criteria that were completed correctly. Points are lost for failure to complete the employability requirements (see Non-Task-Specific Evaluation criteria). When all criteria are evaluated, tally the points for a total at the bottom of each column.

Tasksheet Scoring

Evaluation Items	Test		Retest	
	Pass	Fail	Pass	Fail
Task-Specific Evaluation	**(1 pt)**	**(0 pts)**	**(1 pt)**	**(0 pts)**
Student listed general precautions for servicing and handling of SRS components.				
Student listed general precautions for servicing electronic brake control systems.				
Student listed general precautions for servicing hybrid vehicle high-voltage systems.				
Student demonstrated use of necessary precautions when working on these systems.				
Non-Task-Specific Evaluation	**(0 pts)**	**(−1 pt)**	**(0 pts)**	**(−1 pt)**
Student successfully completed at least three of the non-task-specific steps.				
Student successfully completed all five of the non-task-specific steps.				
Total Score: <total # of points/4 = %>				

Supervisor/Instructor:

Supervisor/instructor signature _____ Date _____

Comments:

Retest supervisor/instructor signature _____ Date _____

Comments:

CDX Tasksheet Number: MHTSO14

Student/Intern Information

Name _____ Date _____ Class _____

Vehicle, Customer, and Service Information

Vehicle used for this activity:

Year _____ Make _____ Model _____

Odometer _____ VIN _____

Materials Required
- Vehicle with SRS and anti-lock brake system (ABS)
- Special tools or equipment, if specified

Task-Specific Safety Considerations
- Comply with personal and environmental safety practices associated with clothing; eye protection; hand tools; power equipment; proper ventilation; and the handling, storage, and disposal of chemicals/materials in accordance with local, state, and federal safety and environmental regulations.
- Hybrid and electric vehicles have batteries with VERY high voltage, which can kill you if handled improperly. Always get permission from your supervisor/instructor before working on, or near, the system. Also, ALWAYS follow the manufacturer's procedure when servicing a hybrid or electric vehicle.

▶ **TASK** Demonstrate awareness of the safety aspects of high voltage circuits [such as high-intensity discharge (HID) lamps, ignition systems, injection systems, etc.]

MHT SPS14

Time off_____

Time on_____

Total time_____

Student Instructions: Read through the entire procedure prior to starting. Prepare your workspace and any tools or parts that may be needed to complete the task. When directed by your supervisor/instructor, begin the procedure to complete the task and check the box as each step is finished. Track your time on this procedure for later comparison to the standard completion time (i.e., "flat rate" or customer pay time).

Procedure:	Step Completed
1. Using appropriate service information, identify system voltage and safety precautions associated with high-intensity discharge headlights, ignition systems, and injection systems.	
a. HID lamp voltage: _____ volts	☐

b. List the safety precautions required when working on HID systems.	☐
c. Maximum secondary ignition system voltage: _____ volts	☐
d. List the safety precautions required when working around ignition systems.	☐
e. Injection system voltage (on a vehicle with a high-voltage injection system): _____ volts	☐
f. List the safety precautions required when working around high-voltage injection systems.	☐

Non-Task-Specific Evaluations:	Step Completed
1. Tools and equipment were used as directed and returned in good working order.	☐
2. Complied with all general and task-specific safety standards, including proper use of any personal protective equipment.	☐
3. Completed the task in an appropriate time frame (recommendation: 1.5 or 2 times flat rate).	☐
4. Left the workspace clean and orderly.	☐
5. Cared for customer property and returned it undamaged.	☐

Student signature _____ Date _____

Comments:

Have your supervisor/instructor verify satisfactory completion of this procedure, any observations found, and any necessary action(s) recommended.

Evaluation Instructions: The scoring box below is intended to act as a guide for both student and supervisor/instructor. Each criterion listed will help students to understand what is expected of them and help supervisors/instructors articulate the level of success at a particular task. The scoring is set up to allow a second attempt at each task (see the Test and Retest columns). Scoring is also designed to award students points only for task criteria that were completed correctly. Points are lost for failure to complete the employability requirements (see Non-Task-Specific Evaluation criteria). When all criteria are evaluated, tally the points for a total at the bottom of each column.

Tasksheet Scoring

Evaluation Items	Test		Retest	
	Pass	Fail	Pass	Fail
Task-Specific Evaluation	**(1 pt)**	**(0 pts)**	**(1 pt)**	**(0 pts)**
Student listed general precautions for servicing and handling HID lamps.				
Student listed general precautions for servicing ignition systems.				
Student listed general precautions for servicing fuel injection systems.				
Student demonstrated use of necessary precautions when working on these systems.				
Non-Task-Specific Evaluation	**(0 pts)**	**(−1 pt)**	**(0 pts)**	**(−1 pt)**
Student successfully completed at least three of the non-task-specific steps.				
Student successfully completed all five of the non-task-specific steps.				
Total Score: <total # of points/4 = %>				

Supervisor/Instructor:

Supervisor/instructor signature _____ Date _____

Comments:

```



```

Retest supervisor/instructor signature _____ Date _____

Comments:

```



```

Section 2: Diesel Engine Fundamentals, Construction, and Operation

I.A Diesel Engines: General

Learning Objective/Task	CDX Tasksheet Number	ASE Foundation MTST Reference Number; Priority Level
• Research vehicle service information, including fluid type, vehicle service history, service precautions, and technical service bulletins.	MHT1A001	I.A.1; P-1
• Inspect level and condition of fuel, oil, diesel exhaust fluid (DEF), and coolant.	MHT1A002	I.A.2; P-1
• Inspect engine assembly for fuel, oil, coolant, air, and other leaks; determine needed action.	MHT1A003	I.A.3; P-1
• Diagnose engine operation (starting and running), including: noise, vibration, smoke, etc.; determine needed action.	MHT1A004	I.A.4; P-2
• Use appropriate electronic service tool(s) and procedures to diagnose problems; check, record, and clear diagnostic codes; check and record trip/operational data; reset maintenance monitor (if applicable); interpret digital multimeter (DMM) readings.	MHT1A005	I.A.5; P-1
• Identify system components, configurations, and types of the following: cylinder head(s), valve train, engine block, engine lubrication, engine cooling, air induction, exhaust, fuel, and engine braking.	MHT1A006	I.A.6; P-1
• Diagnose engine no-crank, cranks but fails to start, hard starting, and starts but does not continue to run problems; determine needed action.	MHT1A007	I.A.7; P-2
• Diagnose engine surging, rough operation, misfiring, low power, slow deceleration, slow acceleration, and/or shutdown problems; determine needed action.	MHT1A008	I.A.8; P-2

Materials Required

- Vehicle with possible engine concern
- Engine manufacturer's workshop materials
- Manufacturer-specific tools depending on the concern/procedure(s)
- Vehicle/component lifting equipment, if applicable

Safety Considerations

- Activities may require test-driving the vehicle on the school grounds or on a hoist, both of which carry severe risks. Attempt this task only with full permission from your supervisor/instructor, and follow all the guidelines exactly.
- Lifting equipment and machines such as vehicle jacks and stands, vehicle hoists, and engine hoists are important tools that increase productivity and make the job easier. However, they can also cause severe injury or death if used improperly. Make sure you follow the manufacturer's operation procedures. Also make sure you have your supervisor's/instructor's permission to use any particular type of lifting equipment.
- Comply with personal and environmental safety practices associated with clothing; eye protection; hand tools; power equipment; proper ventilation; and the handling, storage, and disposal of chemicals/materials in accordance with federal, state, and local regulations.
- Always wear the correct protective eyewear and clothing and use the appropriate safety equipment, as well as fender covers, seat protectors, and floor mat protectors.
- Make sure you understand and observe all legislative and personal safety procedures when carrying out practical assignments. If you are unsure of what these are, ask your supervisor/instructor.

CDX Tasksheet Number: MHT1A001

Student/Intern Information

Name _____ Date _____ Class _____

Vehicle, Customer, and Service Information

Vehicle used for this activity:

Year _____ Make _____ Model _____

Odometer _____ VIN _____

Materials Required
- Vehicle with possible engine concern
- Engine manufacturer's workshop materials
- Manufacturer-specific tools depending on the concern/procedure(s)
- Vehicle/component lifting equipment, if applicable

Task-Specific Safety Considerations
- Activities may require test-driving the vehicle on the school grounds or on a hoist, both of which carry severe risks. Attempt this task only with full permission from your supervisor/instructor, and follow all the guidelines exactly.
- Lifting equipment and machines such as vehicle jacks and stands, vehicle hoists, and engine hoists are important tools that increase productivity and make the job easier. However, they can also cause severe injury or death if used improperly. Make sure you follow the manufacturer's operation procedures. Also make sure you have your supervisor's/instructor's permission to use any particular type of lifting equipment.
- Comply with personal and environmental safety practices associated with clothing; eye protection; hand tools; power equipment; proper ventilation; and the handling, storage, and disposal of chemicals/materials in accordance with federal, state, and local regulations.
- Always wear the correct protective eyewear and clothing and use the appropriate safety equipment, as well as wheel chocks, fender covers, seat protectors, and floor mat protectors.
- Make sure you understand and observe all legislative and personal safety procedures when carrying out practical assignments. If you are unsure of what these are, ask your supervisor/instructor.

▶ **TASK** Research vehicle service information, including fluid type, vehicle service history, service precautions, and technical service bulletins.

MTST
I.A.1; P1

Time off_____

Time on_____

Total time_____

Student Instructions: Read through the entire procedure prior to starting. Prepare your workspace and any tools or parts that may be needed to complete the task. When directed by your supervisor/instructor, begin the procedure to complete the task and check the box as each step is finished.

Note: This tasksheet may require the student to check the condition of miscellaneous vehicle fluids, some of which may be flammable and could damage the environment or cause health problems if not handled properly. Observe all safety precautions and follow local regulations for the proper disposal of fluids.

Procedure:	Step Completed
1. Reference the manufacturer's vehicle data plate, and record the vehicle identification number (VIN):	☐
2. Reference the manufacturer's engine data plate, and record the engine serial number and model:	☐
3. Reference the manufacturer's transmission data plate, and record the transmission serial number and model:	☐
4. Reference the manufacturer's rear end(s) data plate, and record the rear end(s) serial number(s) and model:	☐
5. Reference the manufacturer's workshop materials, and record the recommended oil change intervals for the engine, transmission, and rear ends and oil type and quantity. Include information for any miscellaneous manufacturer's specific fluid(s).	
a. Engine oil change interval: _____ miles/km	☐
b. Engine oil type:	☐
c. Engine oil quantity: _____ qts/gallons	☐
d. Transmission oil change interval: _____ miles/km	☐
e. Transmission oil type:	☐

f. Transmission oil quantity: _____ qts/gallons	☐
g. Rear end oil change interval: _____ miles/km	☐
h. Rear end oil type:	☐
i. Rear end oil quantity: _____ qts/gallons	
j. Misc. oil change interval: _____ miles/km	☐
k. Misc. oil type:	☐
l. Misc. oil quantity: _____ qts/gallons	
6. Reference the manufacturer's workshop materials, and record any special service precautions or conditions:	☐
7. Reference the manufacturer's online information, and record any recent technical service bulletins (TSBs):	☐
8. Discuss the findings with your supervisor/instructor.	☐

Non-Task-Specific Evaluations:	Step Completed
1. Tools and equipment were used as directed and returned in good working order.	☐
2. Complied with all general and task-specific safety standards, including proper use of any personal protection equipment.	☐
3. Completed the task in an appropriate time frame (recommendation: 1.5 or 2 times flat rate).	☐
4. Left the workspace clean and orderly.	☐
5. Cared for customer property and returned it undamaged.	☐

Student signature _____ Date _____

Comments:

Have your supervisor/instructor verify satisfactory completion of this procedure, any observations made, and any necessary action(s) recommended.

Evaluation Instructions: The scoring box below is intended to act as a guide for both student and supervisor/instructor. Each criterion listed will help students to understand what is expected of them and help supervisors/instructors articulate the level of success at a particular task. The scoring is set up to allow a second attempt at each task (see the Test and Retest columns). Scoring is also designed to award students points only for task criteria that were completed correctly. Points are lost for failure to complete the employability requirements (see Non-Task-Specific Evaluation criteria). When all criteria are evaluated, tally the points for a total at the bottom of each column.

Tasksheet Scoring

Evaluation Items	Test		Retest	
	Pass	Fail	Pass	Fail
Task-Specific Evaluation	**(1 pt)**	**(0 pts)**	**(1 pt)**	**(0 pts)**
Student properly recorded the VIN number.				
Student properly recorded the drivetrain component serial and model numbers.				
Student properly researched and recorded recommended oil change intervals for the engine, transmission, and rear ends and oil type and quantity.				
Student properly researched and recorded TSBs.				
Non-Task-Specific Evaluation	**(0 pts)**	**(−1 pt)**	**(0 pts)**	**(−1 pt)**
Student successfully completed at least three of the non-task-specific steps.				
Student successfully completed all five of the non-task-specific steps.				
Total Score: <total # of points/4 = %>				

Supervisor/Instructor:

Supervisor/instructor signature _____ Date _____

Comments:

Retest supervisor/instructor signature _____ Date _____

Comments:

CDX Tasksheet Number: MHT1A002

Student/Intern Information

Name _____ Date _____ Class _____

Vehicle, Customer, and Service Information

Vehicle used for this activity:

Year _____ Make _____ Model _____

Odometer _____ VIN _____

Materials Required

- Vehicle with possible engine concern
- Engine manufacturer's workshop materials
- Manufacturer-specific tools depending on the concern/procedure(s)
- Vehicle/component lifting equipment, if applicable

Task-Specific Safety Considerations

- Activities may require test-driving the vehicle on the school grounds or on a hoist, both of which carry severe risks. Attempt this task only with full permission from your supervisor/instructor, and follow all the guidelines exactly.
- Lifting equipment and machines such as vehicle jacks and stands, vehicle hoists, and engine hoists are important tools that increase productivity and make the job easier. However, they can also cause severe injury or death if used improperly. Make sure you follow the manufacturer's operation procedures. Also make sure you have your supervisor's/instructor's permission to use any particular type of lifting equipment.
- Comply with personal and environmental safety practices associated with clothing; eye protection; hand tools; power equipment; proper ventilation; and the handling, storage, and disposal of chemicals/materials in accordance with federal, state, and local regulations.
- Always wear the correct protective eyewear and clothing and use the appropriate safety equipment, as well as wheel chocks, fender covers, seat protectors, and floor mat protectors.
- Make sure you understand and observe all legislative and personal safety procedures when carrying out practical assignments. If you are unsure of what these are, ask your supervisor/instructor.

▶ **TASK** Inspect level and condition of fuel, oil, diesel exhaust fluid (DEF), and coolant.

MTST
I.A.2; P1

Time off_____

Time on_____

Student Instructions: Read through the entire procedure prior to starting. Prepare your workspace and any tools or parts that may be needed to complete the task. When directed by your supervisor/instructor, begin the procedure to complete the task and check the box as each step is finished.

Total time_____

Note: This tasksheet will require the student to check the condition of miscellaneous vehicle fluids, some of which may be flammable and could damage the environment or cause health problems if not handled properly. Observe all safety precautions and follow local regulations for the proper disposal of fluids.

Procedure:	Step Completed
1. Reference the appropriate manufacturer's workshop materials.	

a. Identify the engine oil type and quantity.
  i. Recommended type of engine oil: _____
  ii. Recommended engine oil quantity: _____
	☐

b. Identify the engine coolant type and quantity.
  i. Recommended type of coolant:
 	
  ii. Recommended engine coolant quantity: _____ qts
	☐

2. Check the engine oil level as outlined in the manufacturer's workshop materials.	
a. Within manufacturer's specifications: Yes: ☐ No: ☐	☐
If No, describe the recommended corrective action(s):	
3. Using proper equipment and procedure, retrieve an oil sample from the engine. Record the procedure for obtaining the oil sample:	☐
4. Are any of the above tests outside of the manufacturer's specifications? Yes: ☐ No: ☐	☐
If Yes, describe the recommended corrective action(s):	
5. Using a clean glass container, drain off a sample of the diesel fuel from the fuel tank(s).	
a. Inspect the sample for any contaminations (e.g., water). (**Note:** In case of poor running conditions or catastrophic failure, it may be necessary to send the sample out to an independent lab to check the fuel.)	☐
b. Is the sample within the manufacturer's specifications? Yes: ☐ No: ☐	☐
If No, describe the recommended corrective action(s):	

6. Using a clean glass container, drain off a sample of the engine coolant from the radiator.	
a. Check the freeze point of coolant and record: _____ degrees below zero	☐
b. Test the pH level of coolant and record: _____	☐
c. Test the supplemental coolant additive (SCA) level and record: _____	☐
d. Are any of the above tests outside of the manufacturer's specifications? Yes: ☐ No: ☐	☐
If Yes, describe the recommended corrective action(s).	
7. Using a clean glass container, drain off a sample of DEF.	
a. Inspect DEF for visible contaminates and record:	☐
b. Using a DEF refractometer, check the DEF concentration and record: _____	☐
c. Using DEF test strips, check for diesel/oil contamination and record: _____	☐
d. Are any of the above tests outside of the manufacturer's specifications? Yes: ☐ No: ☐	☐
If Yes, describe the recommended corrective action(s).	
8. Return the vehicle to its beginning condition, and return any tools you used to their proper locations.	☐
9. Discuss your findings with your supervisor/instructor.	☐

Non-Task-Specific Evaluations:	Step Completed
1. Tools and equipment were used as directed and returned in good working order.	☐
2. Complied with all general and task-specific safety standards, including proper use of any personal protection equipment.	☐
3. Completed the task in an appropriate time frame (recommendation: 1.5 or 2 times the flat rate).	☐
4. Left the workspace clean and orderly.	☐
5. Cared for customer property and returned it undamaged.	☐

Student signature _____ Date _____

Comments:

Have your supervisor/instructor verify satisfactory completion of this procedure, any observations made, and any necessary action(s) recommended.

Evaluation Instructions: The scoring box below is intended to act as a guide for both student and supervisor/instructor. Each criterion listed will help students to understand what is expected of them and help supervisors/instructors articulate the level of success at a particular task. The scoring is set up to allow a second attempt at each task (see the Test and Retest columns). Scoring is also designed to award students points only for task criteria that were completed correctly. Points are lost for failure to complete the employability requirements (see Non-Task-Specific Evaluation criteria). When all criteria are evaluated, tally the points for a total at the bottom of each column.

Tasksheet Scoring

Evaluation Items	Test		Retest	
	Pass	Fail	Pass	Fail
Task-Specific Evaluation	**(1 pt)**	**(0 pts)**	**(1 pt)**	**(0 pts)**
Student used the appropriate service information to determine engine oil and coolant levels/types.				
Student properly sampled engine oil, diesel fuel, test engine coolant, and DEF.				
Student properly tested engine oil, diesel fuel, test engine coolant, and DEF.				
Student reinstalled all removed components undamaged and in working order.				
Non-Task-Specific Evaluation	**(0 pts)**	**(−1 pt)**	**(0 pts)**	**(−1 pt)**
Student successfully completed at least three of the non-task-specific steps.				
Student successfully completed all five of the non-task-specific steps.				
Total Score: <total # of points/4 = %>				

Supervisor/Instructor:

Supervisor/instructor signature _____ Date _____

Comments:

Retest supervisor/instructor signature _____ Date _____

Comments:

CDX Tasksheet Number: MHT1A003

Student/Intern Information

Name _____ Date _____ Class _____

Vehicle, Customer, and Service Information

Vehicle used for this activity:

Year _____ Make _____ Model _____

Odometer _____ VIN _____

Materials Required

- Vehicle with possible engine concern
- Engine manufacturer's workshop materials
- Manufacturer-specific tools depending on the concern/procedure(s)
- Vehicle/component lifting equipment, if applicable

Task-Specific Safety Considerations

- Activities may require test-driving the vehicle on the school grounds or on a hoist, both of which carry severe risks. Attempt this task only with full permission from your supervisor/instructor, and follow all the guidelines exactly.
- Lifting equipment and machines such as vehicle jacks and stands, vehicle hoists, and engine hoists are important tools that increase productivity and make the job easier. However, they can also cause severe injury or death if used improperly. Make sure you follow the manufacturer's operation procedures. Also make sure you have your supervisor's/instructor's permission to use any particular type of lifting equipment.
- Comply with personal and environmental safety practices associated with clothing; eye protection; hand tools; power equipment; proper ventilation; and the handling, storage, and disposal of chemicals/materials in accordance with federal, state, and local regulations.
- Always wear the correct protective eyewear and clothing and use the appropriate safety equipment, as well as wheel chocks, fender covers, seat protectors, and floor mat protectors.
- Make sure you understand and observe all legislative and personal safety procedures when carrying out practical assignments. If you are unsure of what these are, ask your supervisor/instructor.

▶ **TASK** Inspect engine assembly for fuel, oil, coolant, air, and other leaks; determine needed action.

MTST
I.A.3; P1

Time off_____

Time on_____

Total time_____

Student Instructions: Read through the entire procedure prior to starting. Prepare your workspace and any tools or parts that may be needed to complete the task. When directed by your supervisor/instructor, begin the procedure to complete the task and check the box as each step is finished.

Note: This tasksheet will require the student to check the condition of miscellaneous vehicle fluids, some of which may be flammable and could damage the environment or cause health problems if not handled properly. Observe all safety precautions and follow local regulations for the proper disposal of fluids.

Procedure:	Step Completed
1. Reference the manufacturer's workshop materials for the correct procedure for checking and identifying the main causes of engine fuel leaks.	
a. List all possible causes of engine fuel leaks:	☐
2. Reference the manufacturer's workshop materials for the correct procedure for checking and identifying the main causes of engine oil leaks.	
a. List all possible causes of engine oil leaks:	☐
3. Reference the manufacturer's workshop materials for the correct procedure for checking and identifying the main causes of engine coolant leaks.	
a. List all possible causes of coolant leaks:	☐
4. Reference the manufacturer's workshop materials for the correct procedure for checking and identifying the main causes of DEF leaks.	
a. List all possible causes of DEF leaks:	☐
5. Reference the manufacturer's workshop materials for the correct procedure for checking and identifying the main causes of compressed air system leaks.	
a. List all possible causes of compressed air system leaks:	☐
6. Reference the manufacturer's workshop materials for the correct procedure for checking and identifying the main causes of intake air system leaks.	
a. List all possible causes of intake air system leaks:	☐

7. Reference the manufacturer's workshop materials for the correct procedure for checking and identifying the main causes of exhaust system leaks.	
a. List all possible causes of exhaust system leaks:	☐
8. Return the vehicle to its beginning condition and return any tools you used to their proper locations.	☐
9. Discuss your findings with your supervisor/instructor.	☐

Non-Task-Specific Evaluations:	Step Completed
1. Tools and equipment were used as directed and returned in good working order.	☐
2. Complied with all general and task-specific safety standards, including proper use of any personal protection equipment.	☐
3. Completed the task in an appropriate time frame (recommendation: 1.5 or 2 times the flat rate).	☐
4. Left the workspace clean and orderly.	☐
5. Cared for customer property and returned it undamaged.	☐

Student signature _____ Date _____

Comments:

Have your supervisor/instructor verify satisfactory completion of this procedure, any observations made, and any necessary action(s) recommended.

Evaluation Instructions: The scoring box below is intended to act as a guide for both student and supervisor/instructor. Each criterion listed will help students to understand what is expected of them and help supervisors/instructors articulate the level of success at a particular task. The scoring is set up to allow a second attempt at each task (see the Test and Retest columns). Scoring is also designed to award students points only for task criteria that were completed correctly. Points are lost for failure to complete the employability requirements (see Non-Task-Specific Evaluation criteria). When all criteria are evaluated, tally the points for a total at the bottom of each column.

Tasksheet Scoring

Evaluation Items	Test		Retest	
	Pass	**Fail**	**Pass**	**Fail**
Task-Specific Evaluation	**(1 pt)**	**(0 pts)**	**(1 pt)**	**(0 pts)**
Student inspected engine assembly for leaks.				
Student referenced the appropriate service information to research different leaks.				
Student correctly listed all possible causes of diesel fuel, engine oil, coolant, DEF, compressed air system, intake air system, and exhaust system leaks.				
Student reinstalled all removed components undamaged and in working order.				
Non-Task-Specific Evaluation	**(0 pts)**	**(−1 pt)**	**(0 pts)**	**(−1 pt)**
Student successfully completed at least three of the non-task-specific steps.				
Student successfully completed all five of the non-task-specific steps.				
Total Score: <total # of points/4 = %>				

Supervisor/Instructor:

Supervisor/instructor signature _____ Date _____

Comments:

Retest supervisor/instructor signature _____ Date _____

Comments:

CDX Tasksheet Number: MHT1A004

Student/Intern Information

Name _____ Date _____ Class _____

Vehicle, Customer, and Service Information

Vehicle used for this activity:

Year _____ Make _____ Model _____

Odometer _____ VIN _____

Materials Required
- Vehicle with possible engine concern
- Engine manufacturer's workshop materials
- Manufacturer-specific tools depending on the concern/procedure(s)
- Vehicle/component lifting equipment, if applicable

Task-Specific Safety Considerations
- Activities may require test-driving the vehicle on the school grounds or on a hoist, both of which carry severe risks. Attempt this task only with full permission from your supervisor/instructor, and follow all the guidelines exactly.
- Lifting equipment and machines such as vehicle jacks and stands, vehicle hoists, and engine hoists are important tools that increase productivity and make the job easier. However, they can also cause severe injury or death if used improperly. Make sure you follow the manufacturer's operation procedures. Also make sure you have your supervisor's/instructor's permission to use any particular type of lifting equipment.
- Comply with personal and environmental safety practices associated with clothing; eye protection; hand tools; power equipment; proper ventilation; and the handling, storage, and disposal of chemicals/materials in accordance with federal, state, and local regulations.
- Always wear the correct protective eyewear and clothing and use the appropriate safety equipment, as well as wheel chocks, fender covers, seat protectors, and floor mat protectors.
- Make sure you understand and observe all legislative and personal safety procedures when carrying out practical assignments. If you are unsure of what these are, ask your supervisor/instructor.

▶ **TASK** Diagnose engine operation (starting and running), including: noise, vibration, smoke, etc.; determine needed action.

MTST
I.A.4; P2

Time off_____

Time on_____

Student Instructions: Read through the entire procedure prior to starting. Prepare your workspace and any tools or parts that may be needed to complete the task. When directed by your supervisor/instructor, begin the procedure to complete the task and check the box as each step is finished.

Total time_____

Note: This tasksheet will require the student to check the condition of miscellaneous vehicle fluids, some of which may be flammable and could damage the environment or cause health problems if not handled properly. Observe all safety precautions and follow local regulations for the proper disposal of fluids.

Procedure:	Step Completed
1. Start the engine and bring it to operating temperature.	
a. List any hard-starting problems (e.g., extended cranking):	☐
2. Observe and record exhaust color.	
a. Exhaust color upon initial startup:	☐
b. Exhaust color after engine is at operating temperature at idle:	☐
c. Exhaust color after engine is at operating temperature at governed RPM (high idle):	☐
3. Record the quantity of smoke coming from the exhaust (e.g., short burst, then cleared; longer burst, then cleared; large amount after startup, at idle, and at governed RPM):	☐
a. List possible causes for excessive exhaust (e.g., white, blue, black in color):	☐
b. Determine what action will be required for an engine's possible excessive exhaust problems:	☐
4. With the engine running at operating temperature, record the following.	
a. Record the idle RPM: _____ RPM	☐

b. Record the governed RPM (high idle): _____ RPM	☐
5. Record any mechanical, whistling, knocking, or grinding noises at idle and governed RPM:	
a. List possible causes for mechanical, whistling, knocking, or grinding noises: (**Note:** Shut down the engine immediately and notify your instructor if you hear any of the above noises.)	☐
b. Determine what action will be required for an engine's knocking, whistling, or grinding problems:	☐
6. Record excessive vibrations at idle and governed RPM with the clutch disengaged (pushed in) and engaged (released); if it is an automatic transmission, engage air-conditioning (A/C):	
a. List possible causes for excessive vibrations:	☐
b. Determine what action(s) will be required to resolve an engine's excessive vibrations:	☐
7. Return the vehicle to its beginning condition, and return any tools you used to their proper locations.	☐
8. Discuss your findings with your supervisor/instructor.	☐

Non-Task-Specific Evaluations:	Step Completed
1. Tools and equipment were used as directed and returned in good working order.	☐
2. Complied with all general and task-specific safety standards, including proper use of any personal protection equipment.	☐
3. Completed the task in an appropriate time frame (recommendation: 1.5 or 2 times the flat rate).	☐
4. Left the workspace clean and orderly.	☐
5. Cared for customer property and returned it undamaged.	☐

Student signature _____ Date _____

Comments:

Have your supervisor/instructor verify satisfactory completion of this procedure, any observations made,

and any necessary action(s) recommended.

Evaluation Instructions: The scoring box below is intended to act as a guide for both student and supervisor/instructor. Each criterion listed will help students to understand what is expected of them and help supervisors/instructors articulate the level of success at a particular task. The scoring is set up to allow a second attempt at each task (see the Test and Retest columns). Scoring is also designed to award students points only for task criteria that were completed correctly. Points are lost for failure to complete the employability requirements (see Non-Task-Specific Evaluation criteria). When all criteria are evaluated, tally the points for a total at the bottom of each column.

Tasksheet Scoring

Evaluation Items	Test		Retest	
	Pass	**Fail**	**Pass**	**Fail**
Task-Specific Evaluation	**(1 pt)**	**(0 pts)**	**(1 pt)**	**(0 pts)**
Student started the engine and brought it to operating temperature.				
Student listed hard-starting problems.				
Student observed and recorded exhaust color, exhaust quantity, unusual noises, and unusual vibrations at idle and at governed RPM.				
Student reinstalled all removed components undamaged and in working order.				
Non-Task-Specific Evaluation	**(0 pts)**	**(−1 pt)**	**(0 pts)**	**(−1 pt)**
Student successfully completed at least three of the non-task-specific steps.				
Student successfully completed all five of the non-task-specific steps.				
Total Score: <total # of points/4 = %>				

Supervisor/Instructor:

Supervisor/instructor signature _____ Date _____

Comments:

Retest supervisor/instructor signature _____ Date _____

Comments:

CDX Tasksheet Number: MHT1A005

Student/Intern Information

Name _____ Date _____ Class _____

Vehicle, Customer, and Service Information

Vehicle used for this activity:

Year _____ Make _____ Model _____

Odometer _____ VIN _____

Materials Required

- Vehicle with possible engine concern
- Engine manufacturer's workshop materials
- Manufacturer-specific tools depending on the concern/procedure(s)
- Vehicle/component lifting equipment, if applicable

Task-Specific Safety Considerations

- Activities may require test-driving the vehicle on the school grounds or on a hoist, both of which carry severe risks. Attempt this task only with full permission from your supervisor/instructor, and follow all the guidelines exactly.
- Lifting equipment and machines such as vehicle jacks and stands, vehicle hoists, and engine hoists are important tools that increase productivity and make the job easier. However, they can also cause severe injury or death if used improperly. Make sure you follow the manufacturer's operation procedures. Also make sure you have your supervisor's/instructor's permission to use any particular type of lifting equipment.
- Comply with personal and environmental safety practices associated with clothing; eye protection; hand tools; power equipment; proper ventilation; and the handling, storage, and disposal of chemicals/materials in accordance with federal, state, and local regulations.
- Always wear the correct protective eyewear and clothing and use the appropriate safety equipment, as well as wheel chocks, fender covers, seat protectors, and floor mat protectors.
- Make sure you understand and observe all legislative and personal safety procedures when carrying out practical assignments. If you are unsure of what these are, ask your supervisor/instructor.

▶ **TASK** Use appropriate electronic service tool(s) and procedures to diagnose problems; check, record, and clear diagnostic codes; check and record trip/operational data; reset maintenance monitor (if applicable); and interpret digital multimeter (DMM) readings. *MTST* **I.A.5; P1**

Time off_____

Time on_____

Total time_____

Student Instructions: Read through the entire procedure prior to starting. Prepare your workspace and any tools or parts that may be needed to complete the task. When directed by your supervisor/instructor, begin the procedure to complete the task and check the box as each step is finished.

Note: This tasksheet may require the student to check the condition of miscellaneous vehicle fluids, some of which may be flammable and could damage the environment or cause health problems if not handled properly. Observe all safety precautions and follow local regulations for the proper disposal of fluids.

Procedure:	Step Completed
1. Start the engine and observe warning lights and gauges.	
a. List any warning lights (other than low air) that come on and stay on after the engine is started: (**Note:** The low-air light should go out after the truck's air system has reached 60 psi.)	☐
2. Check operation of all vehicle electrical accessories.	
a. List any electrical accessory that fails to operate or operates in an erratic manner:	☐
3. Using a diagnostic tool or the on-board diagnostic system, extract and record the engine monitoring information:	
a. Are there any fault codes listed in the diagnostic tester? Yes: ☐ No: ☐	☐
If Yes, list the codes:	
4. Using the diagnostic tool's monitoring function, record the following.	
a. Engine RPM: _____ RPM	☐
b. Engine temperature _____ degrees	☐
c. Throttle position, percent at idle: _____ %	☐
d. Throttle position: voltage at governed RPM _____ volts	☐

e. Key on time HH:MM:SS:	☐
f. Total idle time HH:MM:SS:	☐
g. Gallons of fuel used at idle: _____ gallons	☐
h. Turbo speed at governed RPM: _____ RPM	☐
i. Number of diesel particulate filter (DPF) regens:	☐
j. Exhaust system temperature _____ degrees	☐
5. Reference the vehicle manufacturer's specifications.	
a. Are all the results within the manufacturer's specifications? Yes: ☐ No: ☐	☐
b. If No, list the results that are outside the manufacturer's specifications:	☐
6. If directed by your supervisor/instructor:	
a. Clear any stored codes.	☐
b. Investigate and rectify where possible any of the "out of specifications" recorded.	☐
7. Return the vehicle to its beginning condition, and return any tools you used to their proper locations.	☐
8. Discuss your findings with your supervisor/instructor.	☐

Non-Task-Specific Evaluations:	Step Completed
1. Tools and equipment were used as directed and returned in good working order.	☐
2. Complied with all general and task-specific safety standards, including proper use of any personal protection equipment.	☐
3. Completed the task in an appropriate time frame (recommendation: 1.5 or 2 times the flat rate).	☐
4. Left the workspace clean and orderly.	☐
5. Cared for customer property and returned it undamaged.	☐

Student signature _____ Date _____

Comments:

Have your supervisor/instructor verify satisfactory completion of this procedure, any observations made, and any necessary action(s) recommended.

Evaluation Instructions: The scoring box below is intended to act as a guide for both student and supervisor/instructor. Each criterion listed will help students to understand what is expected of them and help supervisors/instructors articulate the level of success at a particular task. The scoring is set up to allow a second attempt at each task (see the Test and Retest columns). Scoring is also designed to award students points only for task criteria that were completed correctly. Points are lost for failure to complete the employability requirements (see Non-Task-Specific Evaluation criteria). When all criteria are evaluated, tally the points for a total at the bottom of each column.

Tasksheet Scoring

	Test		Retest	
Evaluation Items	**Pass**	**Fail**	**Pass**	**Fail**
Task-Specific Evaluation	**(1 pt)**	**(0 pts)**	**(1 pt)**	**(0 pts)**
Student started the engine and observed warning lights and gauges.				
Student checked operation of all vehicle electrical accessories.				
Using a diagnostic tool (or on-board diagnostic system), student extracted the engine monitoring information and recorded miscellaneous engine/system functions.				
Student reinstalled all removed components undamaged and in working order.				
Non-Task-Specific Evaluation	**(0 pts)**	**(−1 pt)**	**(0 pts)**	**(−1 pt)**
Student successfully completed at least three of the non-task-specific steps.				
Student successfully completed all five of the non-task-specific steps.				
Total Score: <total # of points/4 = %>				

Supervisor/Instructor:

Supervisor/instructor signature _____ Date _____

Comments:

Retest supervisor/instructor signature _____ Date _____

Comments:

CDX Tasksheet Number: MHT1A006

Student/Intern Information

Name _____ Date _____ Class _____

Vehicle, Customer, and Service Information

Vehicle used for this activity:

Year _____ Make _____ Model _____

Odometer _____ VIN _____

> ## Materials Required
> - Vehicle with possible engine concern
> - Engine manufacturer's workshop materials
> - Manufacturer-specific tools depending on the concern/procedure(s)
> - Vehicle/component lifting equipment, if applicable

Task-Specific Safety Considerations

- Activities may require test-driving the vehicle on the school grounds or on a hoist, both of which carry severe risks. Attempt this task only with full permission from your supervisor/instructor, and follow all the guidelines exactly.
- Lifting equipment and machines such as vehicle jacks and stands, vehicle hoists, and engine hoists are important tools that increase productivity and make the job easier. However, they can also cause severe injury or death if used improperly. Make sure you follow the manufacturer's operation procedures. Also make sure you have your supervisor's/instructor's permission to use any particular type of lifting equipment.
- Comply with personal and environmental safety practices associated with clothing; eye protection; hand tools; power equipment; proper ventilation; and the handling, storage, and disposal of chemicals/materials in accordance with federal, state, and local regulations.
- Always wear the correct protective eyewear and clothing and use the appropriate safety equipment, as well as wheel chocks, fender covers, seat protectors, and floor mat protectors.
- Make sure you understand and observe all legislative and personal safety procedures when carrying out practical assignments. If you are unsure of what these are, ask your supervisor/instructor.

▶ **TASK** Identify system components, configurations, and types of the following: cylinder head(s), valve train, engine block, engine lubrication, engine cooling, air induction, exhaust, fuel, and engine braking.

MTST
I.A.6; P1

Time off _____

Time on _____

Student Instructions: Read through the entire procedure prior to starting. Prepare your workspace and any tools or parts that may be needed to complete the task. When directed by your supervisor/instructor, begin the procedure to complete the task and check the box as each step is finished.

Total time _____

© 2021 Jones & Bartlett Learning, LLC, an Ascend Learning Company

General 149

Note: This tasksheet may require the student to check the condition of miscellaneous vehicle fluids, some of which may be flammable and could damage the environment or cause health problems if not handled properly. Observe all safety precautions and follow local regulations for the proper disposal of fluids.

Procedure:	Step Completed
1. Reference the manufacturer's workshop materials, and record miscellaneous engine/vehicle information.	
a. Engine configuration and number of cylinders (inline, V-type):	☐
b. Engine cylinder head type (e.g., one piece, individual, dual):	☐
c. Valve train (e.g., overhead, mid-block):	☐
d. Block/cylinder design (e.g., liner, parent bore):	☐
e. Oil pump type (e.g., gear, gerotor):	☐
f. Water pump type (e.g., belt driven, gear driven): _____ driven	☐
g. Air induction type (e.g., turbo, blower, naturally aspirated):	☐
h. Charge air cooling type (e.g., ATA, JWAC, N/A):	☐

	Step Completed
i. Exhaust system type (e.g., DPF, SCR)	☐
j. Fuel system type (e.g., common rail, HEUI):	☐
k. Engine brake system (e.g., compression, exhaust brake):	☐
l. Record any miscellaneous component(s) unique to vehicle:	☐
2. Discuss your findings with your supervisor/instructor.	☐

Non-Task-Specific Evaluations:	Step Completed
1. Tools and equipment were used as directed and returned in good working order.	☐
2. Complied with all general and task-specific safety standards, including proper use of any personal protection equipment.	☐
3. Completed the task in an appropriate time frame (recommendation: 1.5 or 2 times the flat rate)	☐
4. Left the workspace clean and orderly.	☐
5. Cared for customer property and returned it undamaged.	☐

Student signature _____ Date _____

Comments:

Have your supervisor/instructor verify satisfactory completion of this procedure, any observations made, and any necessary action(s) recommended.

Evaluation Instructions: The scoring box below is intended to act as a guide for both student and supervisor/instructor. Each criterion listed will help students to understand what is expected of them and help supervisors/instructors articulate the level of success at a particular task. The scoring is set up to allow a second attempt at each task (see the Test and Retest columns). Scoring is also designed to award students points only for task criteria that were completed correctly. Points are lost for failure to complete the employability requirements (see Non-Task-Specific Evaluation criteria). When all criteria are evaluated, tally the points for a total at the bottom of each column.

Tasksheet Scoring

Evaluation Items	Test		Retest	
	Pass	**Fail**	**Pass**	**Fail**
Task-Specific Evaluation	**(1 pt)**	**(0 pts)**	**(1 pt)**	**(0 pts)**
Student referenced the appropriate service information.				
Student properly researched each system component, configuration, and type.				
Student properly recorded each system component, configuration, and type.				
Student properly recorded any miscellaneous component(s) unique to vehicle.				
Non-Task-Specific Evaluation	**(0 pts)**	**(−1 pt)**	**(0 pts)**	**(−1 pt)**
Student successfully completed at least three of the non-task-specific steps.				
Student successfully completed all five of the non-task-specific steps.				
Total Score: <total # of points/4 = %>				

Supervisor/Instructor:

Supervisor/instructor signature _____ Date _____

Comments:

Retest supervisor/instructor signature _____ Date _____

Comments:

CDX Tasksheet Number: MHT1A007

Student/Intern Information

Name _____ Date _____ Class _____

Vehicle, Customer, and Service Information

Vehicle used for this activity:

Year _____ Make _____ Model _____

Odometer _____ VIN _____

Materials Required

- Vehicle with possible engine concern
- Engine manufacturer's workshop materials
- Manufacturer-specific tools depending on the concern/procedure(s)
- Vehicle/component lifting equipment, if applicable

Task-Specific Safety Considerations

- Activities may require test-driving the vehicle on the school grounds or on a hoist, both of which carry severe risks. Attempt this task only with full permission from your supervisor/instructor, and follow all the guidelines exactly.
- Lifting equipment and machines such as vehicle jacks and stands, vehicle hoists, and engine hoists are important tools that increase productivity and make the job easier. However, they can also cause severe injury or death if used improperly. Make sure you follow the manufacturer's operation procedures. Also make sure you have your supervisor's/instructor's permission to use any particular type of lifting equipment.
- Comply with personal and environmental safety practices associated with clothing; eye protection; hand tools; power equipment; proper ventilation; and the handling, storage, and disposal of chemicals/materials in accordance with federal, state, and local regulations.
- Always wear the correct protective eyewear and clothing and use the appropriate safety equipment, as well as wheel chocks, fender covers, seat protectors, and floor mat protectors.
- Make sure you understand and observe all legislative and personal safety procedures when carrying out practical assignments. If you are unsure of what these are, ask your supervisor/instructor.

▶ **TASK** Diagnose engine no-crank, cranks but fails to start, hard starting, and starts but does not continue to run problems; determine needed action.

MTST
I.A.7; P2

Student Instructions: Read through the entire procedure prior to starting. Prepare your workspace and any tools or parts that may be needed to comple`te the task. When directed by your supervisor/instructor, begin the procedure to complete the task and check the box as each step is finished.

Note: This tasksheet may require the student to check the condition of miscellaneous vehicle fluids, some of which may be flammable and could damage the environment or cause health problems if not handled properly. Observe all safety precautions and follow local regulations for the proper disposal of fluids.

Procedure:	Step Completed
1. Reference the manufacturer's workshop materials for the common causes of an engine no-crank situation.	
a. List all possible causes of an engine no-crank situation (the engine will not turn over using the starter motor):	☐
b. Determine what action will be required for an engine no-crank situation:	☐
2. Reference the manufacturer's workshop materials for the common causes of the situation where an engine cranks but fails to start.	☐
a. List all possible causes of the situation where an engine cranks but fails to start (the engine turns over by the starter motor but fails to run):	☐
b. Determine what action will be required for the situation where an engine cranks but fails to start:	☐
3. Reference the manufacturer's workshop materials for the common causes of an engine hard-start situation (the engine will run but takes longer than usual to start).	
a. List all possible causes of an engine hard-start situation:	☐
b. Determine what action will be required for an engine hard-start situation:	☐

4. Reference the manufacturer's workshop materials for the common causes of the situation where an engine starts but does not continue to run.	
a. List all possible causes of the situation where an engine starts but does not continue to run:	☐
b. Determine what action will be required for the situation where an engine starts but does not continue to run:	☐
5. Return the vehicle to its beginning condition, and return any tools you used to their proper locations.	☐
6. Discuss your findings with your supervisor/instructor.	☐

Non-Task-Specific Evaluations:	Step Completed
1. Tools and equipment were used as directed and returned in good working order.	☐
2. Complied with all general and task-specific safety standards, including proper use of any personal protection equipment.	☐
3. Completed the task in an appropriate time frame (recommendation: 1.5 or 2 times the flat rate).	☐
4. Left the workspace clean and orderly.	☐
5. Cared for customer property and returned it undamaged.	☐

Student signature _____ Date _____

Comments:

Have your supervisor/instructor verify satisfactory completion of this procedure, any observations made, and any necessary action(s) recommended.

Evaluation Instructions: The scoring box below is intended to act as a guide for both student and supervisor/instructor. Each criterion listed will help students to understand what is expected of them and help supervisors/instructors articulate the level of success at a particular task. The scoring is set up to allow a second attempt at each task (see the Test and Retest columns). Scoring is also designed to award students points only for task criteria that were completed correctly. Points are lost for failure to complete the employability requirements (see Non-Task-Specific Evaluation criteria). When all criteria are evaluated, tally the points for a total at the bottom of each column.

Tasksheet Scoring

Evaluation Items	Test		Retest	
	Pass	Fail	Pass	Fail
Task-Specific Evaluation	**(1 pt)**	**(0 pts)**	**(1 pt)**	**(0 pts)**
Student referenced the manufacturer's workshop material for each engine problem.				
Student correctly listed the causes of each engine problem.				
Student correctly determined the correct action for each engine problem.				
Student reinstalled all removed components undamaged and in working order.				
Non-Task-Specific Evaluation	**(0 pts)**	**(−1 pt)**	**(0 pts)**	**(−1 pt)**
Student successfully completed at least three of the non-task-specific steps.				
Student successfully completed all five of the non-task-specific steps.				
Total Score: <total # of points/4 = %>				

Supervisor/Instructor:

Supervisor/instructor signature _____ Date _____

Comments:

Retest supervisor/instructor signature _____ Date _____

Comments:

CDX Tasksheet Number: MHT1A008

Student/Intern Information

Name _____ Date _____ Class _____

Vehicle, Customer, and Service Information

Vehicle used for this activity:

Year _____ Make _____ Model _____

Odometer _____ VIN _____

Materials Required

- Vehicle with possible engine concern
- Engine manufacturer's workshop materials
- Manufacturer-specific tools depending on the concern/procedure(s)
- Vehicle/component lifting equipment, if applicable

Task-Specific Safety Considerations

- Activities may require test-driving the vehicle on the school grounds or on a hoist, both of which carry severe risks. Attempt this task only with full permission from your supervisor/instructor, and follow all the guidelines exactly.
- Lifting equipment and machines such as vehicle jacks and stands, vehicle hoists, and engine hoists are important tools that increase productivity and make the job easier. However, they can also cause severe injury or death if used improperly. Make sure you follow the manufacturer's operation procedures. Also make sure you have your supervisor's/instructor's permission to use any particular type of lifting equipment.
- Comply with personal and environmental safety practices associated with clothing; eye protection; hand tools; power equipment; proper ventilation; and the handling, storage, and disposal of chemicals/materials in accordance with federal, state, and local regulations.
- Always wear the correct protective eyewear and clothing and use the appropriate safety equipment, as well as wheel chocks, fender covers, seat protectors, and floor mat protectors.
- Make sure you understand and observe all legislative and personal safety procedures when carrying out practical assignments. If you are unsure of what these are, ask your supervisor/instructor.

▶ **TASK** Diagnose engine surging, rough operation, misfiring, low power, slow deceleration, slow acceleration, and/or shutdown problems; determine needed action.

MTST
I.A.8; P2

Time off_____

Time on_____

Total time_____

Student Instructions: Read through the entire procedure prior to starting. Prepare your workspace and any tools or parts that may be needed to complete the task. When directed by your supervisor/instructor, begin the procedure to complete the task and check the box as each step is finished.

Note: This tasksheet may require the student to check the condition of miscellaneous vehicle fluids, some of which may be flammable and could damage the environment or cause health problems if not handled properly. Observe all safety precautions and follow local regulations for the proper disposal of fluids.

Procedure:	Step Completed
1. Reference the manufacturer's workshop materials for the common causes of engine surging.	
a. List all possible causes of engine surging (uneven or rolling idle):	☐
b. Determine what action will be required for engine surging:	☐
2. Reference the manufacturer's workshop materials for the common causes of rough engine operation.	
a. List all possible causes of rough engine operation:	☐
b. Determine what action will be required for rough engine operation:	☐
3. Reference the manufacturer's workshop materials for the common causes of engine misfiring.	
a. List all possible causes of engine misfiring:	☐
b. Determine what action will be required for engine misfiring:	☐

4. Reference the manufacturer's workshop materials for the common causes of low engine power.	
a. List all possible causes of low engine power:	☐
b. Determine what action will be required for low engine power:	☐
5. Reference the manufacturer's workshop materials for the common causes of slow engine deceleration and/or slow engine acceleration.	
a. List all possible causes of slow engine deceleration and/or slow engine acceleration:	☐
b. Determine what action will be required for slow engine deceleration and/or slow engine acceleration:	☐
6. Reference the manufacturer's workshop materials for the common causes of engine shutdown problems.	
a. List all possible causes of engine shutdown problems:	☐
b. Determine what action will be required for engine shutdown problems:	☐
7. Return the vehicle to its beginning condition, and return any tools you used to their proper locations.	☐
8. Discuss your findings with your supervisor/instructor.	☐

Non-Task-Specific Evaluations:	Step Completed
1. Tools and equipment were used as directed and returned in good working order.	☐
2. Complied with all general and task-specific safety standards, including proper use of any personal protection equipment.	☐
3. Completed the task in an appropriate time frame (recommendation: 1.5 or 2 times the flat rate).	☐
4. Left the workspace clean and orderly.	☐
5. Cared for customer property and returned it undamaged.	☐

Student signature _____ Date _____

Comments:

Have your supervisor/instructor verify satisfactory completion of this procedure, any observations found, and any necessary action(s) recommended.

Evaluation Instructions: The scoring box below is intended to act as a guide for both student and supervisor/instructor. Each criterion listed will help students to understand what is expected of them and help supervisors/instructors articulate the level of success at a particular task. The scoring is set up to allow a second attempt at each task (see the Test and Retest columns). Scoring is also designed to award students points only for task criteria that were completed correctly. Points are lost for failure to complete the employability requirements (see Non-Task-Specific Evaluation criteria). When all criteria are evaluated, tally the points for a total at the bottom of each column.

Tasksheet Scoring

	Test		Retest	
	Pass	**Fail**	**Pass**	**Fail**
Evaluation Items				
Task-Specific Evaluation	**(1 pt)**	**(0 pts)**	**(1 pt)**	**(0 pts)**
Student referenced the manufacturer's workshop materials for each engine problem.				
Student correctly listed the causes of each engine problem.				
Student correctly determined the correct action for each engine problem.				
Student reinstalled all removed components undamaged and in working order.				
Non-Task-Specific Evaluation	**(0 pts)**	**(−1 pt)**	**(0 pts)**	**(−1 pt)**
Student successfully completed at least three of the non-task-specific steps.				
Student successfully completed all five of the non-task-specific steps.				
Total Score: <total # of points/4 = %>				

Supervisor/Instructor:

Supervisor/instructor signature _____ Date _____

Comments:

Retest supervisor/instructor signature _____ Date _____

Comments:

I.B Diesel Engines: Cylinder Head and Valve Train

Learning Objective/Task	CDX Tasksheet Number	ASE Foundation MTST Reference Number; Priority Level
• Inspect electronic wiring harness and brackets for wear, bending, cracks, and proper securement; determine needed action.	MHT1B001	I.B.1; P-1
• Inspect cylinder head for cracks/damage; check mating surfaces for warpage; check condition of passages; inspect core/expansion and gallery plugs; determine needed action.	MHT1B002	I.B.2; P-2
• Inspect injector sleeves and seals; determine needed action.	MHT1B003	I.B.3; P-3
• Inspect valve train components; determine needed action.	MHT1B004	I.B.4; P-1
• Inspect, measure, and replace/reinstall camshaft; measure/adjust end play and backlash.	MHT1B005	I.B.5; P-3
• Adjust valve bridges (crossheads); adjust valve clearances and injector settings.	MHT1B006	I.B.6; P-2
• Disassemble cylinder head; inspect valves, guides, seats, springs, retainers, rotators, locks, and seals; determine needed action.	MHT1B007	I.B.7; P-3
• Measure valve head height relative to deck; measure valve face-to-seat contact; determine needed action.	MHT1B008	I.B.8; P-3
• Reassemble cylinder head.	MHT1B009	I.B.9; P-3
• Inspect, measure, and replace/reinstall camshaft; measure end play and backlash; determine needed action.	MHT1B010	I.B.10; P-3

Materials Required

- Vehicle with possible engine concern
- Engine manufacturer's workshop materials
- Manufacturer-specific tools depending on the concern/procedure(s)
- Vehicle/component lifting equipment, if applicable

Safety Considerations

- Activities may require test-driving the vehicle on the school grounds or on a hoist, both of which carry severe risks. Attempt this task only with full permission from your supervisor/instructor, and follow all the guidelines exactly.
- Lifting equipment and machines such as vehicle jacks and stands, vehicle hoists, and engine hoists are important tools that increase productivity and make the job easier. However, they can also cause severe injury or death if used improperly. Make sure you follow the manufacturer's operation procedures. Also make sure you have your supervisor's/instructor's permission to use any particular type of lifting equipment.

- Comply with personal and environmental safety practices associated with clothing; eye protection; hand tools; power equipment; proper ventilation; and the handling, storage, and disposal of chemicals/materials in accordance with federal, state, and local regulations.
- Always wear the correct protective eyewear and clothing and use the appropriate safety equipment, as well as fender covers, seat protectors, and floor mat protectors.
- Make sure you understand and observe all legislative and personal safety procedures when carrying out practical assignments. If you are unsure of what these are, ask your supervisor/instructor.

CDX Tasksheet Number: MHT1B001

Student/Intern Information

Name _____ Date _____ Class _____

Vehicle, Customer, and Service Information

Vehicle used for this activity:

Year _____ Make _____ Model _____

Odometer _____ VIN _____

Materials Required

- Vehicle with possible engine concern
- Engine manufacturer's workshop materials
- Manufacturer-specific tools depending on the concern/procedure(s)
- Vehicle/component lifting equipment, if applicable

Task-Specific Safety Considerations

- Activities may require test-driving the vehicle on the school grounds or on a hoist, both of which carry severe risks. Attempt this task only with full permission from your supervisor/instructor, and follow all the guidelines exactly.
- Lifting equipment and machines such as vehicle jacks and stands, vehicle hoists, and engine hoists are important tools that increase productivity and make the job easier. However, they can also cause severe injury or death if used improperly. Make sure you follow the manufacturer's operation procedures. Also make sure you have your supervisor's/instructor's permission to use any particular type of lifting equipment.
- Comply with personal and environmental safety practices associated with clothing; eye protection; hand tools; power equipment; proper ventilation; and the handling, storage, and disposal of chemicals/materials in accordance with federal, state, and local regulations.
- Always wear the correct protective eyewear and clothing and use the appropriate safety equipment, as well as wheel chocks, fender covers, seat protectors, and floor mat protectors.
- Make sure you understand and observe all legislative and personal safety procedures when carrying out practical assignments. If you are unsure of what these are, ask your supervisor/instructor.

▶ **TASK** Inspect electronic wiring harness and brackets for wear, bending, cracks, and proper securement; determine needed action.

MTST I.B.1; P1

Time off_____

Time on_____

Total time_____

Student Instructions: Read through the entire procedure prior to starting. Prepare your workspace and any tools or parts that may be needed to complete the task. When directed by your supervisor/instructor, begin the procedure to complete the task and check the box as each step is finished.

Note: This tasksheet will require the student to check the condition of miscellaneous vehicle fluids, some of which may be flammable and could damage the environment or cause health problems if not handled properly. Observe all safety precautions and follow local regulations for the proper disposal of fluids.

Procedure:	Step Completed
1. Reference the appropriate manufacturer's workshop material.	☐
2. Inspect wiring harness for missing brackets/securement, and record:	☐
3. Inspect wiring harness for cuts, breaks, broken connector/connector latches, and record:	☐
4. Remove harness and inspect connector pins and sockets for damage, and record:	☐
5. Following the proper original equipment manufacturer (OEM) procedures, make any repairs as determined by your supervisor/instructor.	☐
6. Unless you are to continue with the teardown of the engine, return the engine/vehicle to its beginning condition, and return any tools you used to their proper locations.	☐
7. Discuss your findings with your supervisor/instructor.	☐

Non-Task-Specific Evaluations:	Step Completed
1. Tools and equipment were used as directed and returned in good working order.	☐
2. Complied with all general and task-specific safety standards, including proper use of any personal protection equipment.	☐
3. Completed the task in an appropriate time frame (recommendation: 1.5 or 2 times the flat rate).	☐
4. Left the workspace clean and orderly.	☐
5. Cared for customer property and returned it undamaged.	☐

Student signature _____ Date _____

Comments:

Have your supervisor/instructor verify satisfactory completion of this procedure, any observations made, and any necessary action(s) recommended.

Evaluation Instructions: The scoring box below is intended to act as a guide for both student and supervisor/instructor. Each criterion listed will help students to understand what is expected of them and help supervisors/instructors articulate the level of success at a particular task. The scoring is set up to allow a second attempt at each task (see the Test and Retest columns). Scoring is also designed to award students points only for task criteria that were completed correctly. Points are lost for failure to complete the employability requirements (see Non-Task-Specific Evaluation criteria). When all criteria are evaluated, tally the points for a total at the bottom of each column.

Tasksheet Scoring

Evaluation Items	Test Pass (1 pt)	Test Fail (0 pts)	Retest Pass (1 pt)	Retest Fail (0 pts)
Task-Specific Evaluation	**(1 pt)**	**(0 pts)**	**(1 pt)**	**(0 pts)**
Student inspected the wiring harness for missing brackets/securement, cuts, breaks, and broken connector/connector latches.				
Student removed the harness, inspected connector pins and sockets for damage, and recorded damage.				
Following the proper OEM procedures, student made any repairs as determined by the supervisor/instructor.				
Student reinstalled all removed components undamaged and in working order, unless teardown was to continue.				
Non-Task-Specific Evaluation	**(0 pts)**	**(−1 pt)**	**(0 pts)**	**(−1 pt)**
Student successfully completed at least three of the non-task-specific steps.				
Student successfully completed all five of the non-task-specific steps.				
Total Score: <total # of points/4 = %>				

Supervisor/Instructor:

Supervisor/instructor signature _____ Date _____

Comments:

Retest supervisor/instructor signature _____ Date _____

Comments:

© 2021 Jones & Bartlett Learning, LLC, an Ascend Learning Company

168   Cylinder Head and Valve Train

CDX Tasksheet Number: MHT1B002

Student/Intern Information

Name _____ Date _____ Class _____

Vehicle, Customer, and Service Information

Vehicle used for this activity:

Year _____ Make _____ Model _____

Odometer _____ VIN _____

Materials Required

- Vehicle with possible engine concern
- Engine manufacturer's workshop materials
- Manufacturer-specific tools depending on the concern/procedure(s)
- Vehicle/component lifting equipment, if applicable

Task-Specific Safety Considerations

- Activities may require test-driving the vehicle on the school grounds or on a hoist, both of which carry severe risks. Attempt this task only with full permission from your supervisor/instructor, and follow all the guidelines exactly.
- Lifting equipment and machines such as vehicle jacks and stands, vehicle hoists, and engine hoists are important tools that increase productivity and make the job easier. However, they can also cause severe injury or death if used improperly. Make sure you follow the manufacturer's operation procedures. Also make sure you have your supervisor's/instructor's permission to use any particular type of lifting equipment.
- Comply with personal and environmental safety practices associated with clothing; eye protection; hand tools; power equipment; proper ventilation; and the handling, storage, and disposal of chemicals/materials in accordance with federal, state, and local regulations.
- Always wear the correct protective eyewear and clothing and use the appropriate safety equipment, as well as wheel chocks, fender covers, seat protectors, and floor mat protectors.
- Make sure you understand and observe all legislative and personal safety procedures when carrying out practical assignments. If you are unsure of what these are, ask your supervisor/instructor.

▶ **TASK** Inspect cylinder head for cracks/damage; check mating surfaces for warpage; check condition of passages; inspect core/expansion and gallery plugs; determine needed action.

MTST *I.B.2; P2*

Time off_____

Time on_____

Total time_____

Student Instructions: Read through the entire procedure prior to starting. Prepare your workspace and any tools or parts that may be needed to complete the task. When directed by your supervisor/instructor, begin the procedure to complete the task and check the box as each step is finished.

Note: This tasksheet will require the student to check the condition of miscellaneous vehicle fluids, some of which may be flammable and could damage the environment or cause health problems if not handled properly. Observe all safety precautions and follow local regulations for the proper disposal of fluids.

Procedure:	Step Completed
1. Reference the appropriate manufacturer's workshop materials.	☐
2. Determine the type of crack detention process(es) that your workshop utilizes:	
a. Magnetic particle inspection: Yes: ☐ No: ☐	☐
b. Penetrating dyes: Yes: ☐ No: ☐	☐
c. Pressure testing: Yes: ☐ No: ☐	☐
d. Vacuum testing: Yes: ☐ No: ☐	☐
e. Ultrasonic testing: Yes: ☐ No: ☐	☐
f. If none of the above describes the method that your workshop uses, explain the method that is used:	☐
g. Outsource testing and repairs: Yes: ☐ No: ☐	☐
If Yes, describe the procedure used:	
3. Referencing the manufacturer's workshop materials, list the procedure and all safety precautions that must be observed when carrying out an inspection of a cylinder head for cracks/damage:	☐

4. Determine what safety precautions must be observed when inspecting a cylinder head for cracks/damage:	☐
5. Discuss these procedures and safety precautions with your supervisor/instructor. Determine what method of testing will be carried out:	☐
6. If directed by your supervisor/instructor, commence crack testing of the cylinder head. Follow the procedures listed previously and reference the manufacturer's workshop materials:	
a. Meets the manufacturer's specifications: Yes: ☐ No: ☐	☐
b. If No, list the areas of cracking and your recommendations for any rectifications:	☐
7. Referencing the manufacturer's workshop materials, list the procedure for checking for warpage of the cylinder head mating surfaces:	
a. List the steps involved in checking the cylinder head for warpage:	☐
b. Determine what safety precautions must be observed when checking the cylinder head for warpage:	☐
8. Following the procedures listed previously, and while referencing the manufacturer's workshop materials, check for any warpage of the cylinder head mating surfaces:	
a. Meets the manufacturer's specifications: Yes: ☐ No: ☐	☐
b. If No, list your recommendations for any rectifications:	☐

	Step Completed
9. Referring to the manufacturer's workshop materials, check the condition of passages and inspect the core/expansion and gallery plugs:	
a. Meets the manufacturer's specifications: Yes: ☐ No: ☐	☐
b. If No, list the areas of concerns and your recommendations for any rectifications:	☐
10. Reinstall all removed components undamaged and in working order unless teardown is to continue.	☐
11. Discuss your findings with your supervisor/instructor.	☐

Non-Task-Specific Evaluations:	Step Completed
1. Tools and equipment were used as directed and returned in good working order.	☐
2. Complied with all general and task-specific safety standards, including proper use of any personal protection equipment.	☐
3. Completed the task in an appropriate time frame (recommendation: 1.5 or 2 times the flat rate).	☐
4. Left the workspace clean and orderly.	☐
5. Cared for customer property and returned it undamaged.	☐

Student signature _____ Date _____

Comments:

Have your supervisor/instructor verify satisfactory completion of this procedure, any observations made, and any necessary action(s) recommended.

Evaluation Instructions: The scoring box below is intended to act as a guide for both student and supervisor/instructor. Each criterion listed will help students to understand what is expected of them and help supervisors/instructors articulate the level of success at a particular task. The scoring is set up to allow a second attempt at each task (see the Test and Retest columns). Scoring is also designed to award students points only for task criteria that were completed correctly. Points are lost for failure to complete the employability requirements (see Non-Task-Specific Evaluation criteria). When all criteria are evaluated, tally the points for a total at the bottom of each column.

Tasksheet Scoring

	Test		Retest	
Evaluation Items	**Pass**	**Fail**	**Pass**	**Fail**
Task-Specific Evaluation	**(1 pt)**	**(0 pts)**	**(1 pt)**	**(0 pts)**
Student determined the type of crack detention process(es) that the workshop utilizes.				
Referencing the manufacturer's workshop materials, student listed the procedure and all safety precautions that must be observed when carrying out each check/inspection.				
Using the manufacturer's workshop materials, student performed each check/test using the workshop's method(s).				
Student reinstalled all removed components undamaged and in working order, unless tear-down is to continue.				
Non-Task-Specific Evaluation	**(0 pts)**	**(−1 pt)**	**(0 pts)**	**(−1 pt)**
Student successfully completed at least three of the non-task-specific steps.				
Student successfully completed all five of the non-task-specific steps.				
Total Score: <total # of points/4 = %>				

Supervisor/Instructor:

Supervisor/instructor signature _____ Date _____

Comments:

Retest supervisor/instructor signature _____ Date _____

Comments:

CDX Tasksheet Number: MHT1B003

Student/Intern Information

Name _____ Date _____ Class _____

Vehicle, Customer, and Service Information

Vehicle used for this activity:

Year _____ Make _____ Model _____

Odometer _____ VIN _____

Materials Required
- Vehicle with possible engine concern
- Engine manufacturer's workshop materials
- Manufacturer-specific tools depending on the concern/procedure(s)
- Vehicle/component lifting equipment, if applicable

Task-Specific Safety Considerations
- Activities may require test-driving the vehicle on the school grounds or on a hoist, both of which carry severe risks. Attempt this task only with full permission from your supervisor/instructor, and follow all the guidelines exactly.
- Lifting equipment and machines such as vehicle jacks and stands, vehicle hoists, and engine hoists are important tools that increase productivity and make the job easier. However, they can also cause severe injury or death if used improperly. Make sure you follow the manufacturer's operation procedures. Also make sure you have your supervisor's/instructor's permission to use any particular type of lifting equipment.
- Comply with personal and environmental safety practices associated with clothing; eye protection; hand tools; power equipment; proper ventilation; and the handling, storage, and disposal of chemicals/materials in accordance with federal, state, and local regulations.
- Always wear the correct protective eyewear and clothing and use the appropriate safety equipment, as well as wheel chocks, fender covers, seat protectors, and floor mat protectors.
- Make sure you understand and observe all legislative and personal safety procedures when carrying out practical assignments. If you are unsure of what these are, ask your supervisor/instructor.

▶ **TASK** Inspect injector sleeves and seals; determine needed action.

MTST
I.B.3; P3

Time off_____

Student Instructions: Read through the entire procedure prior to starting. Prepare your workspace and any tools or parts that may be needed to complete the task. When directed by your supervisor/instructor, begin the procedure to complete the task and check the box as each step is finished.

Time on_____

Note: This tasksheet will require the student to check the condition of miscellaneous vehicle fluids, some of which may be flammable and could damage the environment or cause health problems if not handled properly. Observe all safety precautions and follow local regulations for the proper disposal of fluids.

Total time_____

Procedure:	Step Completed
1. While referencing the appropriate manufacturer's workshop materials, inspect injector sleeves and seals:	
a. Meets the manufacturer's specifications: Yes: ☐ No: ☐	☐
b. If No, list the areas of concern and recommendations for correction:	☐
2. While referencing the appropriate manufacturer's workshop materials and using the recommended special tools, measure the injector tip or nozzle protrusion, and record your findings:	
a. Cylinder #1 injector tip/nozzle protrusion:	☐
b. Cylinder #2 injector tip/nozzle protrusion:	☐
c. Cylinder #3 injector tip/nozzle protrusion:	☐
d. Cylinder #4 injector tip/nozzle protrusion:	☐
e. Cylinder #5 injector tip/nozzle protrusion:	☐
f. Cylinder #6 injector tip/nozzle protrusion:	☐

	Step Completed
3. List the areas of concern and your recommendations for any rectifications:	☐
4. Outsource repairs: Yes: ☐ No: ☐	☐
If Yes, describe the required repairs needed:	
5. Reinstall all removed components undamaged and in working order, unless teardown is to continue.	☐
6. Discuss your findings with your supervisor/instructor.	☐

Non-Task-Specific Evaluations:	Step Completed
1. Tools and equipment were used as directed and returned in good working order.	☐
2. Complied with all general and task-specific safety standards, including proper use of any personal protection equipment.	☐
3. Completed the task in an appropriate time frame (recommendation: 1.5 or 2 times the flat rate).	☐
4. Left the workspace clean and orderly.	☐
5. Cared for customer property and returned it undamaged.	☐

Student signature _____ Date _____

Comments:

Have your supervisor/instructor verify satisfactory completion of this procedure, any observations made,

and any necessary action(s) recommended.

Evaluation Instructions: The scoring box below is intended to act as a guide for both student and supervisor/instructor. Each criterion listed will help students to understand what is expected of them and help supervisors/instructors articulate the level of success at a particular task. The scoring is set up to allow a second attempt at each task (see the Test and Retest columns). Scoring is also designed to award students points only for task criteria that were completed correctly. Points are lost for failure to complete the employability requirements (see Non-Task-Specific Evaluation criteria). When all criteria are evaluated, tally the points for a total at the bottom of each column.

Tasksheet Scoring

Evaluation Items	Test		Retest	
	Pass	**Fail**	**Pass**	**Fail**
Task-Specific Evaluation	**(1 pt)**	**(0 pts)**	**(1 pt)**	**(0 pts)**
While referencing the appropriate manufacturer's workshop materials, student inspected injector sleeves and seals.				
While referencing the appropriate manufacturer's workshop materials and using the recommended special tools, student measured the injector tip or nozzle protrusion and recorded the findings.				
Student listed the areas of concern and any recommendations for rectification.				
Student reinstalled all removed components undamaged and in working order, unless teardown was to continue.				
Non-Task-Specific Evaluation	**(0 pts)**	**(−1 pt)**	**(0 pts)**	**(−1 pt)**
Student successfully completed at least three of the non-task-specific steps.				
Student successfully completed all five of the non-task-specific steps.				
Total Score: <total # of points/4 = %>				

Supervisor/Instructor:

Supervisor/instructor signature _____ Date _____

Comments:

Retest supervisor/instructor signature _____ Date _____

Comments:

CDX Tasksheet Number: MHT1B004

Student/Intern Information

Name _____ Date _____ Class _____

Vehicle, Customer, and Service Information

Vehicle used for this activity:

Year _____ Make _____ Model _____

Odometer _____ VIN _____

Materials Required

- Vehicle with possible engine concern
- Engine manufacturer's workshop materials
- Manufacturer-specific tools depending on the concern/procedure(s)
- Vehicle/component lifting equipment, if applicable

Task-Specific Safety Considerations

- Activities may require test-driving the vehicle on the school grounds or on a hoist, both of which carry severe risks. Attempt this task only with full permission from your supervisor/instructor, and follow all the guidelines exactly.
- Lifting equipment and machines such as vehicle jacks and stands, vehicle hoists, and engine hoists are important tools that increase productivity and make the job easier. However, they can also cause severe injury or death if used improperly. Make sure you follow the manufacturer's operation procedures. Also make sure you have your supervisor's/instructor's permission to use any particular type of lifting equipment.
- Comply with personal and environmental safety practices associated with clothing; eye protection; hand tools; power equipment; proper ventilation; and the handling, storage, and disposal of chemicals/materials in accordance with federal, state, and local regulations.
- Always wear the correct protective eyewear and clothing and use the appropriate safety equipment, as well as wheel chocks, fender covers, seat protectors, and floor mat protectors.
- Make sure you understand and observe all legislative and personal safety procedures when carrying out practical assignments. If you are unsure of what these are, ask your supervisor/instructor.

▶ **TASK** Inspect valve train components; determine needed action.   **MTST** I.B.4; P1

Time off_____

Time on_____

Student Instructions: Read through the entire procedure prior to starting. Prepare your workspace and any tools or parts that may be needed to complete the task. When directed by your supervisor/instructor, begin the procedure to complete the task and check the box as each step is finished.

Total time_____

Note: This tasksheet will require the student to check the condition of miscellaneous vehicle fluids, some of which may be flammable and could damage the environment or cause health problems if not handled properly. Observe all safety precautions and follow local regulations for the proper disposal of fluids.

Procedure:	Step Completed
1. While referencing the appropriate manufacturer's workshop materials, inspect the valve train components:	

a. Camshaft/lobes
      Serviceable: ☐
      Repairable: ☐
      Unserviceable: ☐
	☐

b. Cam followers
      Serviceable: ☐
      Repairable: ☐
      Unserviceable: ☐
	☐

c. Bucket tappets
      Serviceable: ☐
      Repairable: ☐
      Unserviceable: ☐
	☐

d. Adjusting shims
      Serviceable: ☐
      Repairable: ☐
      Unserviceable: ☐
	☐

e. Rockers
      Serviceable: ☐
      Repairable: ☐
      Unserviceable: ☐
	☐

f. Camshaft gear(s)
      Serviceable: ☐
      Repairable: ☐
      Unserviceable: ☐
	☐

g. Camshaft retaining caps
      Serviceable: ☐
      Repairable: ☐
      Unserviceable: ☐
	☐

h. Timing belt/chains(s)
      Serviceable: ☐
      Repairable: ☐
      Unserviceable: ☐
	☐

i. Rocker shafts	☐
Serviceable: ☐	
Repairable: ☐	
Unserviceable: ☐	
j. Rocker shaft bushings	☐
Serviceable: ☐	
Repairable: ☐	
Unserviceable: ☐	
2. Inspect and assess valve springs. Test valve springs for compressed height and tension, and record your findings:	
a. Cylinder #1 intake valve(s) (in. or mm) and tension (ft-lb or N•m):	☐
b. Cylinder #1 exhaust valve(s) (in. or mm) and tension (ft-lb or N•m):	☐
c. Cylinder #2 intake valve(s) (in. or mm) and tension (ft-lb or N•m):	☐
d. Cylinder #2 exhaust valve(s) (in. or mm) and tension (ft-lb or N•m):	☐
e. Cylinder #3 intake valve(s) (in. or mm) and tension (ft-lb or N•m):	☐
f. Cylinder #3 exhaust valve(s) (in. or mm) and tension (ft-lb or N•m):	☐
g. Cylinder #4 intake valve(s) (in. or mm) and tension (ft-lb or N•m):	☐

h. Cylinder #4 exhaust valve(s) (in. or mm) and tension (ft-lb or N•m):	☐
i. Cylinder #5 intake valve(s) (in. or mm) and tension (ft-lb or N•m):	☐
j. Cylinder #5 exhaust valve(s) (in. or mm) and tension (ft-lb or N•m):	☐
k. Cylinder #6 intake valve(s) (in. or mm) and tension (ft-lb or N•m):	☐
l. Cylinder #6 exhaust valve(s) (in. or mm) and tension (ft-lb or N•m):	☐
3. List any component that does not meet the manufacturer's specifications:	☐
4. Reinstall all removed components undamaged and in working order unless teardown is to continue.	☐
5. Discuss your findings with your supervisor/instructor.	☐

Non-Task-Specific Evaluations:	Step Completed
1. Tools and equipment were used as directed and returned in good working order.	☐
2. Complied with all general and task-specific safety standards, including proper use of any personal protection equipment.	☐
3. Completed the task in an appropriate time frame (recommendation: 1.5 or 2 times the flat rate).	☐
4. Left the workspace clean and orderly.	☐
5. Cared for customer property and returned it undamaged.	☐

Student signature _____ Date _____

Comments:

Have your supervisor/instructor verify satisfactory completion of this procedure, any observations made,

and any necessary action(s) recommended.

Evaluation Instructions: The scoring box below is intended to act as a guide for both student and supervisor/instructor. Each criterion listed will help students to understand what is expected of them and help supervisors/instructors articulate the level of success at a particular task. The scoring is set up to allow a second attempt at each task (see the Test and Retest columns). Scoring is also designed to award students points only for task criteria that were completed correctly. Points are lost for failure to complete the employability requirements (see Non-Task-Specific Evaluation criteria). When all criteria are evaluated, tally the points for a total at the bottom of each column.

Tasksheet Scoring

Evaluation Items	Test		Retest	
	Pass	Fail	Pass	Fail
Task–Specific Evaluation	**(1 pt)**	**(0 pts)**	**(1 pt)**	**(0 pts)**
While referencing the appropriate manufacturer's workshop materials, student inspected the valve train components.				
While referencing the appropriate manufacturer's workshop materials, student inspected and tested valve springs for height and tension.				
Student listed areas of concern and any recommendations for rectification.				
Student reinstalled all removed components undamaged and in working order, unless teardown was to continue.				
Non-Task-Specific Evaluation	**(0 pts)**	**(−1 pt)**	**(0 pts)**	**(−1 pt)**
Student successfully completed at least three of the non-task-specific steps.				
Student successfully completed all five of the non-task-specific steps.				
Total Score: <total # of points/4 = %>				

Supervisor/Instructor:

Supervisor/instructor signature _____ Date _____

Comments:

Retest supervisor/instructor signature _____ Date _____

Comments:

CDX Tasksheet Number: MHT1B005

Student/Intern Information

Name _____ Date _____ Class _____

Vehicle, Customer, and Service Information

Vehicle used for this activity:

Year _____ Make _____ Model _____

Odometer _____ VIN _____

Materials Required

- Vehicle with possible engine concern
- Engine manufacturer's workshop materials
- Manufacturer-specific tools depending on the concern/procedure(s)
- Vehicle/component lifting equipment, if applicable

Task-Specific Safety Considerations

- Activities may require test-driving the vehicle on the school grounds or on a hoist, both of which carry severe risks. Attempt this task only with full permission from your supervisor/instructor, and follow all the guidelines exactly.
- Lifting equipment and machines such as vehicle jacks and stands, vehicle hoists, and engine hoists are important tools that increase productivity and make the job easier. However, they can also cause severe injury or death if used improperly. Make sure you follow the manufacturer's operation procedures. Also make sure you have your supervisor's/instructor's permission to use any particular type of lifting equipment.
- Comply with personal and environmental safety practices associated with clothing; eye protection; hand tools; power equipment; proper ventilation; and the handling, storage, and disposal of chemicals/materials in accordance with federal, state, and local regulations.
- Always wear the correct protective eyewear and clothing and use the appropriate safety equipment, as well as wheel chocks, fender covers, seat protectors, and floor mat protectors.
- Make sure you understand and observe all legislative and personal safety procedures when carrying out practical assignments. If you are unsure of what these are, ask your supervisor/instructor.

▶ TASK Inspect, measure, and replace/reinstall overhead camshaft; measure/adjust end play and backlash.

MTST
I.B.5; P3

Time off_____

Time on_____

Student Instructions: Read through the entire procedure prior to starting. Prepare your workspace and any tools or parts that may be needed to complete the task. When directed by your supervisor/instructor, begin the procedure to complete the task and check the box as each step is finished.

Total time_____

Note: This tasksheet will require the student to check the condition of miscellaneous vehicle fluids, some of which may be flammable and could damage the environment or cause health problems if not handled properly. Observe all safety precautions and follow local regulations for the proper disposal of fluids.

Procedure:	Step Completed
1. Follow the procedures listed in the manufacturer's workshop materials. Reassemble the camshaft into the cylinder head (applicable only to overhead-mounted camshafts). Continue if this is an overhead cam (OHC) assembly.	☐
2. Check the camshaft bearings for excessive wear; replace if necessary.	☐
3. Install the camshaft into the cylinder head. (**Note:** Use extreme care; camshaft lobes are very sharp.)	
a. Once the camshaft is installed, you should be able to turn it by hand with very little effort. Yes: ☐ No: ☐	☐
b. If No, remove the camshaft and check bearings for damage, misalignment, or debris. Discuss your findings with your supervisor/instructor and record them:	
4. Fit cam mounting brackets and torque to the manufacturer's specifications:	
a. Manufacturer's specified torque: _____ ft-lb (N•m)	☐
5. Following the procedures listed in the manufacturer's workshop materials, use the recommended special tools to measure/adjust end play and backlash (applicable only to overhead-mounted camshafts).	
a. Manufacturer's specification—end play: _____ in./mm	☐
b. Actual end play measurement: _____ in./mm	☐
c. Manufacturer's specification—backlash: _____ in./mm	☐
d. Actual backlash measurement: _____ in./mm	☐
6. Have your supervisor/instructor inspect your assembled camshaft to this point and discuss the findings.	☐

Non-Task-Specific Evaluations:	Step Completed
1. Tools and equipment were used as directed and returned in good working order.	☐
2. Complied with all general and task-specific safety standards, including proper use of any personal protection equipment.	☐
3. Completed the task in an appropriate time frame (recommendation: 1.5 or 2 times the flat rate).	☐
4. Left the workspace clean and orderly.	☐
5. Cared for customer property and returned it undamaged.	☐

Student signature _____ Date _____

Comments:

Have your supervisor/instructor verify satisfactory completion of this procedure, any observations made, and any necessary action(s) recommended.

Evaluation Instructions: The scoring box below is intended to act as a guide for both student and supervisor/instructor. Each criterion listed will help students to understand what is expected of them and help supervisors/instructors articulate the level of success at a particular task. The scoring is set up to allow a second attempt at each task (see the Test and Retest columns). Scoring is also designed to award students points only for task criteria that were completed correctly. Points are lost for failure to complete the employability requirements (see Non-Task-Specific Evaluation criteria). When all criteria are evaluated, tally the points for a total at the bottom of each column.

Tasksheet Scoring

Evaluation Items	Test		Retest	
	Pass	**Fail**	**Pass**	**Fail**
Task-Specific Evaluation	**(1 pt)**	**(0 pts)**	**(1 pt)**	**(0 pts)**
Student inspected all camshaft bearings and replaced if necessary.				
Student assembled camshaft(s), following the manufacturer's directions and using the proper tooling.				
Student set camshaft(s) end play to manufacturer's specifications.				
Student set camshaft backlash to manufacturer's specifications.				
Non-Task-Specific Evaluation	**(0 pts)**	**(−1 pt)**	**(0 pts)**	**(−1 pt)**
Student successfully completed at least three of the non-task-specific steps.				
Student successfully completed all five of the non-task-specific steps.				
Total Score: <total # of points/4 = %>				

Supervisor/Instructor:

Supervisor/instructor signature _____ Date _____

Comments:

Retest supervisor/instructor signature _____ Date _____

Comments:

CDX Tasksheet Number: MHT1BOO6

Student/Intern Information

Name _____ Date _____ Class _____

Vehicle, Customer, and Service Information

Vehicle used for this activity:

Year _____ Make _____ Model _____

Odometer _____ VIN _____

Materials Required
- Vehicle with possible engine concern
- Engine manufacturer's workshop materials
- Manufacturer-specific tools depending on the concern/procedure(s)
- Vehicle/component lifting equipment, if applicable

Task-Specific Safety Considerations
- Activities may require test-driving the vehicle on the school grounds or on a hoist, both of which carry severe risks. Attempt this task only with full permission from your supervisor/instructor, and follow all the guidelines exactly.
- Lifting equipment and machines such as vehicle jacks and stands, vehicle hoists, and engine hoists are important tools that increase productivity and make the job easier. However, they can also cause severe injury or death if used improperly. Make sure you follow the manufacturer's operation procedures. Also make sure you have your supervisor's/instructor's permission to use any particular type of lifting equipment.
- Comply with personal and environmental safety practices associated with clothing; eye protection; hand tools; power equipment; proper ventilation; and the handling, storage, and disposal of chemicals/materials in accordance with federal, state, and local regulations.
- Always wear the correct protective eyewear and clothing and use the appropriate safety equipment, as well as wheel chocks, fender covers, seat protectors, and floor mat protectors.
- Make sure you understand and observe all legislative and personal safety procedures when carrying out practical assignments. If you are unsure of what these are, ask your supervisor/instructor.

▶ **TASK** Adjust valve bridges (crossheads); adjust valve clearances and injector settings.

MTST
I.B.6; P2

Time off_____

Time on_____

Total time_____

Student Instructions: Read through the entire procedure prior to starting. Prepare your workspace and any tools or parts that may be needed to complete the task. When directed by your supervisor/instructor, begin the procedure to complete the task and check the box as each step is finished.

Note: This tasksheet will require the student to check the condition of miscellaneous vehicle fluids, some of which may be flammable and could damage the environment or cause health problems if not handled properly. Observe all safety precautions and follow local regulations for the proper disposal of fluids.

Procedure:	Step Completed
1. Referencing the manufacturer's workshop materials, list the procedure to adjust valve bridges (crossheads).	
a. List the steps involved to adjust valve bridges (crossheads):	☐
b. Determine what safety precautions must be observed when adjusting valve bridges (crossheads):	☐
2. Following the procedures listed above, and while referencing the manufacturer's workshop materials, adjust the valve bridges (crossheads).	
a. Meets the manufacturer's specifications: Yes: ☐ No: ☐	☐
b. If No, list your recommendations for any rectifications:	☐
3. Referencing the manufacturer's workshop materials, list the procedure to adjust the injectors.	
a. List the steps involved to adjust the injectors:	☐
b. Determine what safety precautions must be observed when adjusting the injectors:	☐
4. Following the procedures listed above, and while referencing the manufacturer's workshop materials, adjust the injectors.	
a. Meets the manufacturer's specifications: Yes: ☐ No: ☐	☐
b. If No, list your recommendations for any rectifications:	☐

5. Following the procedures listed previously, and while referencing the manufacturer's workshop materials, adjust the valves.	
a. List the steps involved in adjusting the valves:	☐
b. Determine what safety precautions must be observed when adjusting the valves:	☐
6. Following the procedures listed previously, and while referencing the manufacturer's workshop materials, adjust the valves.	
a. Meets the manufacturer's specifications: Yes: ☐ No: ☐	☐
b. If No, list your recommendations for any rectifications:	☐
7. Reinstall all removed components undamaged and in working order.	☐
8. Discuss your findings with your supervisor/instructor.	☐

Non-Task-Specific Evaluations:	Step Completed
1. Tools and equipment were used as directed and returned in good working order.	☐
2. Complied with all general and task-specific safety standards, including proper use of any personal protection equipment.	☐
3. Completed the task in an appropriate time frame (recommendation: 1.5 or 2 times the flat rate).	☐
4. Left the workspace clean and orderly.	☐
5. Cared for customer property and returned it undamaged.	☐

Student signature _____ Date _____

Comments:

Have your supervisor/instructor verify satisfactory completion of this procedure, any observations made, and any necessary action(s) recommended.

Evaluation Instructions: The scoring box below is intended to act as a guide for both student and supervisor/instructor. Each criterion listed will help students to understand what is expected of them and help supervisors/instructors articulate the level of success at a particular task. The scoring is set up to allow a second attempt at each task (see the Test and Retest columns). Scoring is also designed to award students points only for task criteria that were completed correctly. Points are lost for failure to complete the employability requirements (see Non-Task-Specific Evaluation criteria). When all criteria are evaluated, tally the points for a total at the bottom of each column.

Tasksheet Scoring

Evaluation Items	Test		Retest	
	Pass	**Fail**	**Pass**	**Fail**
Task-Specific Evaluation	**(1 pt)**	**(0 pts)**	**(1 pt)**	**(0 pts)**
Student adjusted valve bridges to manufacturer's specifications.				
Student adjusted injectors to manufacturer's specifications.				
Student adjusted valves to manufacturer's specifications.				
Student reinstalled all removed components undamaged and in working order, unless teardown was to continue.				
Non-Task-Specific Evaluation	**(0 pts)**	**(−1 pt)**	**(0 pts)**	**(−1 pt)**
Student successfully completed at least three of the non-task-specific steps.				
Student successfully completed all five of the non-task-specific steps.				
Total Score: <total # of points/4 = %>				

Supervisor/Instructor:

Supervisor/instructor signature _____ Date _____

Comments:

Retest supervisor/instructor signature _____ Date _____

Comments:

CDX Tasksheet Number: MHT1B007

Student/Intern Information

Name _____ Date _____ Class _____

Vehicle, Customer, and Service Information

Vehicle used for this activity:

Year _____ Make _____ Model _____

Odometer _____ VIN _____

Materials Required
- Vehicle with possible engine concern
- Engine manufacturer's workshop materials
- Manufacturer-specific tools depending on the concern/procedure(s)
- Vehicle/component lifting equipment, if applicable

Task-Specific Safety Considerations
- Activities may require test-driving the vehicle on the school grounds or on a hoist, both of which carry severe risks. Attempt this task only with full permission from your supervisor/instructor, and follow all the guidelines exactly.
- Lifting equipment and machines such as vehicle jacks and stands, vehicle hoists, and engine hoists are important tools that increase productivity and make the job easier. However, they can also cause severe injury or death if used improperly. Make sure you follow the manufacturer's operation procedures. Also make sure you have your supervisor's/instructor's permission to use any particular type of lifting equipment.
- Comply with personal and environmental safety practices associated with clothing; eye protection; hand tools; power equipment; proper ventilation; and the handling, storage, and disposal of chemicals/materials in accordance with federal, state, and local regulations.
- Always wear the correct protective eyewear and clothing and use the appropriate safety equipment, as well as wheel chocks, fender covers, seat protectors, and floor mat protectors.
- Make sure you understand and observe all legislative and personal safety procedures when carrying out practical assignments. If you are unsure of what these are, ask your supervisor/instructor.

▶ **TASK** Disassemble cylinder head; inspect valves, guides, seats, springs, retainers, rotators, locks, and seals; determine needed action. **MTST** I.B.7; P3

Time off_____

Time on_____

Total time_____

Student Instructions: Read through the entire procedure prior to starting. Prepare your workspace and any tools or parts that may be needed to complete the task. When directed by your supervisor/instructor, begin the procedure to complete the task and check the box as each step is finished.

Note: This tasksheet will require the student to check the condition of miscellaneous vehicle fluids, some of which may be flammable and could damage the environment or cause health problems if not handled properly. Observe all safety precautions and follow local regulations for the proper disposal of fluids.

Procedure:	Step Completed
1. While referencing the appropriate manufacturer's workshop materials, dismantle the cylinder head using the recommended special tools. When removing the components, store all the nuts and bolts in order in storage trays or in a suitable alternative. As you dismantle each valve assembly, keep it in its correct order so that all components can be evaluated as a unit.	
a. Lay out the components so as to identify their original position.	☐

b. Remove and inspect the retainers.
       Meets the manufacturer's specifications:
       Yes: ☐   No: ☐
	☐

c. Remove and inspect the rotators.
       Meets the manufacturer's specifications:
       Yes: ☐   No: ☐
	☐

d. Remove and inspect the springs for twists, distortions, and nicks.
       Meets the manufacturer's specifications:
       Yes: ☐   No: ☐
	☐

e. Remove and inspect the valves.
       Meets the manufacturer's specifications:
       Yes: ☐   No: ☐
	☐

f. Remove and inspect the seals.
       Meets the manufacturer's specifications:
       Yes: ☐   No: ☐
	☐

g. Inspect the valve seats.
       Meets the manufacturer's specifications:
       Yes: ☐   No: ☐
	☐

h. If No to any of the above, list the areas of concern and your recommendations for any rectifications:	☐
2. Reinstall all removed components undamaged and in working order.	☐

3. Discuss your findings with your supervisor/instructor.	☐

Non-Task-Specific Evaluations:	Step Completed
1. Tools and equipment were used as directed and returned in good working order.	☐
2. Complied with all general and task-specific safety standards, including proper use of any personal protection equipment.	☐
3. Completed the task in an appropriate time frame (recommendation: 1.5 or 2 times the flat rate).	☐
4. Left the workspace clean and orderly.	☐
5. Cared for customer property and returned it undamaged.	☐

Student signature _____ Date _____

Comments:

Have your supervisor/instructor verify satisfactory completion of this procedure, any observations made,

and any necessary action(s) recommended.

Evaluation Instructions: The scoring box below is intended to act as a guide for both student and supervisor/instructor. Each criterion listed will help students to understand what is expected of them and help supervisors/instructors articulate the level of success at a particular task. The scoring is set up to allow a second attempt at each task (see the Test and Retest columns). Scoring is also designed to award students points only for task criteria that were completed correctly. Points are lost for failure to complete the employability requirements (see Non-Task-Specific Evaluation criteria). When all criteria are evaluated, tally the points for a total at the bottom of each column.

Tasksheet Scoring

Evaluation Items	Test		Retest	
	Pass	**Fail**	**Pass**	**Fail**
Task-Specific Evaluation	**(1 pt)**	**(0 pts)**	**(1 pt)**	**(0 pts)**
Student referenced the appropriate manufacturer's workshop materials.				
Student inspected retainers, rotators, springs, valves, and valve seats.				
Student noted any areas of concern.				
Student reinstalled all removed components undamaged and in working order.				
Non-Task-Specific Evaluation	**(0 pts)**	**(−1 pt)**	**(0 pts)**	**(−1 pt)**
Student successfully completed at least three of the non-task-specific steps.				
Student successfully completed all five of the non-task-specific steps.				
Total Score: <total # of points/4 = %>				

Supervisor/Instructor:

Supervisor/instructor signature _____ Date _____

Comments:

Retest supervisor/instructor signature _____ Date _____

Comments:

CDX Tasksheet Number: MHT1B008

Student/Intern Information

Name _____ Date _____ Class _____

Vehicle, Customer, and Service Information

Vehicle used for this activity:

Year _____ Make _____ Model _____

Odometer _____ VIN _____

Materials Required

- Vehicle with possible engine concern
- Engine manufacturer's workshop materials
- Manufacturer-specific tools depending on the concern/procedure(s)
- Vehicle/component lifting equipment, if applicable

Task-Specific Safety Considerations

- Activities may require test-driving the vehicle on the school grounds or on a hoist, both of which carry severe risks. Attempt this task only with full permission from your supervisor/instructor, and follow all the guidelines exactly.
- Lifting equipment and machines such as vehicle jacks and stands, vehicle hoists, and engine hoists are important tools that increase productivity and make the job easier. However, they can also cause severe injury or death if used improperly. Make sure you follow the manufacturer's operation procedures. Also make sure you have your supervisor's/instructor's permission to use any particular type of lifting equipment.
- Comply with personal and environmental safety practices associated with clothing; eye protection; hand tools; power equipment; proper ventilation; and the handling, storage, and disposal of chemicals/materials in accordance with federal, state, and local regulations.
- Always wear the correct protective eyewear and clothing and use the appropriate safety equipment, as well as wheel chocks, fender covers, seat protectors, and floor mat protectors.
- Make sure you understand and observe all legislative and personal safety procedures when carrying out practical assignments. If you are unsure of what these are, ask your supervisor/instructor.

▶ TASK Measure valve head height relative to deck; measure valve face-to-seat contact; determine needed action.

MTST
I.B.8; P3

Time off_____

Time on_____

Total time_____

Student Instructions: Read through the entire procedure prior to starting. Prepare your workspace and any tools or parts that may be needed to complete the task. When directed by your instructor, begin the procedure to complete the task and check the box as each step is finished.

Note: This tasksheet will require the student to check the condition of miscellaneous vehicle fluids, some of which may be flammable and could damage the environment or cause health problems if not handled properly. Observe all safety precautions and follow local regulations for the proper disposal of fluids.

Procedure:	Step Completed
1. While referencing the appropriate manufacturer's workshop materials, measure valve head height relative to the deck and valve face-to-seat contact using the recommended special tools. Record your findings below.	☐
2. Measure valve head height relative to deck:	
a. Cylinder #1 intake valve(s):	☐
b. Cylinder #1 exhaust valve(s):	☐
c. Cylinder #2 intake valve(s):	☐
d. Cylinder #2 exhaust valve(s):	☐
e. Cylinder #3 intake valve(s):	☐
f. Cylinder #3 exhaust valve(s):	☐
g. Cylinder #4 intake valve(s):	☐

h. Cylinder #4 exhaust valve(s):	☐
i. Cylinder #5 intake valve(s):	☐
j. Cylinder #5 exhaust valve(s):	☐
k. Cylinder #6 intake valve(s):	☐
l. Cylinder #6 exhaust valve(s):	☐
3. List areas of concern and your recommendations for any rectifications:	☐
4. Check valve face-to-seat contact; use the following coding: Unserviceable = US; Requires Servicing = RS; Serviceable = S; Requires Replacement = RR.	
a. Cylinder #1 intake valve(s):	☐
b. Cylinder #1 exhaust valve(s):	☐
c. Cylinder #2 intake valve(s):	☐

d. Cylinder #2 exhaust valve(s):	☐
e. Cylinder #3 intake valve(s):	☐
f. Cylinder #3 exhaust valve(s):	☐
g. Cylinder #4 intake valve(s):	☐
h. Cylinder #4 exhaust valve(s):	☐
i. Cylinder #5 intake valve(s):	☐
j. Cylinder #5 exhaust valve(s):	☐
k. Cylinder #6 intake valve(s):	☐
l. Cylinder #6 exhaust valve(s):	☐

	Step Completed
5. List areas of concern and your recommendations for any rectifications:	☐
6. Reinstall all removed components undamaged and in working order.	☐
7. Discuss your findings with your supervisor/instructor.	☐

Non-Task-Specific Evaluations:	Step Completed
1. Tools and equipment were used as directed and returned in good working order.	☐
2. Complied with all general and task-specific safety standards, including proper use of any personal protection equipment.	☐
3. Completed the task in an appropriate time frame (recommendation: 1.5 or 2 times the flat rate).	☐
4. Left the workspace clean and orderly.	☐
5. Cared for customer property and returned it undamaged.	☐

Student signature _____ Date _____

Comments:

Have your supervisor/instructor verify satisfactory completion of this procedure, any observations made,

and any necessary action(s) recommended.

Evaluation Instructions: The scoring box below is intended to act as a guide for both student and supervisor/instructor. Each criterion listed will help students to understand what is expected of them and help supervisors/instructors articulate the level of success at a particular task. The scoring is set up to allow a second attempt at each task (see the Test and Retest columns). Scoring is also designed to award students points only for task criteria that were completed correctly. Points are lost for failure to complete the employability requirements (see Non-Task-Specific Evaluation criteria). When all criteria are evaluated, tally the points for a total at the bottom of each column.

Tasksheet Scoring

Evaluation Items	Test		Retest	
	Pass	**Fail**	**Pass**	**Fail**
Task-Specific Evaluation	**(1 pt)**	**(0 pts)**	**(1 pt)**	**(0 pts)**
Student referenced the appropriate manufacturer's workshop materials.				
Student checked valve head height relative to deck.				
Student checked valve face-to-seat contact.				
Student reinstalled all removed components undamaged and in working order.				
Non-Task-Specific Evaluation	**(0 pts)**	**(−1 pt)**	**(0 pts)**	**(−1 pt)**
Student successfully completed at least three of the non-task-specific steps.				
Student successfully completed all four of the non-task-specific steps.				
Total Score: <total # of points/4 = %>				

Supervisor/Instructor:

Supervisor/instructor signature _____ Date _____

Comments:

Retest supervisor/instructor signature _____ Date _____

Comments:

CDX Tasksheet Number: MHT1B009

Student/Intern Information

Name _____ Date _____ Class _____

Vehicle, Customer, and Service Information

Vehicle used for this activity:

Year _____ Make _____ Model _____

Odometer _____ VIN _____

Materials Required

- Vehicle with possible engine concern
- Engine manufacturer's workshop materials
- Manufacturer-specific tools depending on the concern/procedure(s)
- Vehicle/component lifting equipment, if applicable

Task-Specific Safety Considerations

- Activities may require test-driving the vehicle on the school grounds or on a hoist, both of which carry severe risks. Attempt this task only with full permission from your supervisor/instructor, and follow all the guidelines exactly.
- Lifting equipment and machines such as vehicle jacks and stands, vehicle hoists, and engine hoists are important tools that increase productivity and make the job easier. However, they can also cause severe injury or death if used improperly. Make sure you follow the manufacturer's operation procedures. Also make sure you have your supervisor's/instructor's permission to use any particular type of lifting equipment.
- Comply with personal and environmental safety practices associated with clothing; eye protection; hand tools; power equipment; proper ventilation; and the handling, storage, and disposal of chemicals/materials in accordance with federal, state, and local regulations.
- Always wear the correct protective eyewear and clothing and use the appropriate safety equipment, as well as wheel chocks, fender covers, seat protectors, and floor mat protectors.
- Make sure you understand and observe all legislative and personal safety procedures when carrying out practical assignments. If you are unsure of what these are, ask your supervisor/instructor.

▶ **TASK** Reassemble cylinder head. **MTST** *I.B.9; P3*

Time off_____

Student Instructions: Read through the entire procedure prior to starting. Prepare your workspace and any tools or parts that may be needed to complete the task. When directed by your supervisor/instructor, begin the procedure to complete the task and check the box as each step is finished.

Time on_____

Note: This tasksheet will require the student to check the condition of miscellaneous vehicle fluids, some of which may be flammable and could damage the environment or cause health problems if not handled properly. Observe all safety precautions and follow local regulations for the proper disposal of fluids.

Total time_____

Procedure:	Step Completed
1. Ensure that all cylinder-head parts and associated parts have been cleaned and dried.	☐
2. Secure the cylinder head to the bench to ensure it does not fall and is safe to work on.	☐
3. Have the valves been ground in accordance with the manufacturer's specifications? Yes: ☐ No: ☐	☐
a. If No, discuss with your supervisor/instructor if this action is to be undertaken.	☐
b. If Yes, list the steps involved in servicing the valves:	☐
4. Have the valve seats been ground in accordance with the manufacturer's specifications? Yes: ☐ No: ☐	☐
a. If No, discuss with your supervisor/instructor if this action is to be undertaken.	☐
b. If Yes, list the steps involved in servicing the valve seats:	☐

5. Have the valves been lapped into the valve seats in accordance with the manufacturer's specifications? Yes: ☐ No: ☐	☐
a. If No, discuss with your supervisor/instructor if this action is to be undertaken.	☐
b. If Yes, list the steps involved in lapping the valve faces onto the valve seats:	☐
6. Referencing the manufacturer's workshop materials, list the procedure and all safety precautions that must be observed when reassembling the cylinder head.	
a. List the steps involved in reassembling the cylinder head:	☐
b. Determine what safety precautions must be observed when reassembling the cylinder head:	☐
7. Discuss these procedures and safety precautions with your supervisor/instructor.	☐
8. If directed by your supervisor/instructor, source all the special tooling and necessary spare parts/repair kits and commence reassembling the cylinder head.	☐
9. Following the procedures listed previously, and while referencing the manufacturer's workshop materials, reassemble the cylinder head.	☐

10. While referencing the appropriate manufacturer's workshop materials, measure valve head height relative to the deck and valve face-to-seat contact using the recommended special tools. Record your findings below:	
a. Cylinder #1 intake valve(s):	☐
b. Cylinder #1 exhaust valve(s):	☐
c. Cylinder #2 intake valve(s):	☐
d. Cylinder #2 exhaust valve(s):	☐
e. Cylinder #3 intake valve(s):	☐
f. Cylinder #3 exhaust valve(s):	☐
g. Cylinder #4 intake valve(s):	☐
h. Cylinder #4 exhaust valve(s):	☐

i. Cylinder #5 intake valve(s):	☐
j. Cylinder #5 exhaust valve(s):	☐
k. Cylinder #6 intake valve(s):	☐
l. Cylinder #6 exhaust valve(s):	☐
11. Meets the manufacturer's specifications: Yes: ☐ No: ☐	☐
a. If No, list the recommended corrective action:	☐
12. Following the procedures outlined in the manufacturer's workshop materials, reassemble the injector sleeves and injectors into the cylinder head.	☐
13. While referencing the appropriate manufacturer's workshop materials and using the recommended special tools, measure the injector tip or nozzle protrusion. Record your findings below:	
a. Cylinder #1:	☐
b. Cylinder #2:	☐

c. Cylinder #3:	☐
d. Cylinder #4:	☐
e. Cylinder #5:	☐
f. Cylinder #6:	☐
14. Meets the manufacturer's specifications: Yes: ☐ No: ☐	☐
a. If No, list the recommended corrective action:	☐
15. If the correct tooling is available, conduct either a pressure or vacuum test of the newly installed valves for correct sealing under operating pressures. Refer to your supervisor/instructor for directions and assistance to carry out this operation, if applicable.	☐
16. Have your supervisor/instructor inspect your assembled cylinder head to this point and discuss the findings.	☐

Non-Task-Specific Evaluations:	Step Completed
1. Tools and equipment were used as directed and returned in good working order.	☐
2. Complied with all general and task-specific safety standards, including proper use of any personal protection equipment.	☐
3. Completed the task in an appropriate time frame (recommendation: 1.5 or 2 times the flat rate).	☐
4. Left the workspace clean and orderly.	☐
5. Cared for customer property and returned it undamaged.	☐

Student signature _____ Date _____

Comments:

Have your supervisor/instructor verify satisfactory completion of this procedure, any observations found, and any necessary action(s) recommended.

Evaluation Instructions: The scoring box below is intended to act as a guide for both student and supervisor/instructor. Each criterion listed will help students to understand what is expected of them and help supervisors/instructors articulate the level of success at a particular task. The scoring is set up to allow a second attempt at each task (see the Test and Retest columns). Scoring is also designed to award students points only for task criteria that were completed correctly. Points are lost for failure to complete the employability requirements (see Non-Task-Specific Evaluation criteria). When all criteria are evaluated, tally the points for a total at the bottom of each column.

Tasksheet Scoring

Evaluation Items	Test		Retest	
	Pass	Fail	Pass	Fail
Task-Specific Evaluation	**(1 pt)**	**(0 pts)**	**(1 pt)**	**(0 pts)**
Student cleaned and dried all cylinder-head parts and associated parts before assembly.				
Student assembled cylinder head(s), following the manufacturer's directions and using the proper tooling.				
Student took post-assembly valve and injector protrusion measurements.				
Student performed pressure and/or vacuum testing on each valve.				
Non-Task-Specific Evaluation	**(0 pts)**	**(−1 pt)**	**(0 pts)**	**(−1 pt)**
Student successfully completed at least three of the non-task-specific steps.				
Student successfully completed all five of the non-task-specific steps.				
Total Score: <total # of points/4 = %>				

Supervisor/Instructor:

Supervisor/instructor signature _____ Date _____

Comments:

Retest supervisor/instructor signature _____ Date _____

Comments:

CDX Tasksheet Number: MHT1B010

Student/Intern Information

Name _____ Date _____ Class _____

Vehicle, Customer, and Service Information

Vehicle used for this activity:

Year _____ Make _____ Model _____

Odometer _____ VIN _____

Materials Required

- Vehicle with possible engine concern
- Engine manufacturer's workshop materials
- Manufacturer-specific tools depending on the concern/procedure(s)
- Vehicle/component lifting equipment, if applicable

Task-Specific Safety Considerations

- Activities may require test-driving the vehicle on the school grounds or on a hoist, both of which carry severe risks. Attempt this task only with full permission from your supervisor/instructor, and follow all the guidelines exactly.
- Lifting equipment and machines such as vehicle jacks and stands, vehicle hoists, and engine hoists are important tools that increase productivity and make the job easier. However, they can also cause severe injury or death if used improperly. Make sure you follow the manufacturer's operation procedures. Also make sure you have your supervisor's/instructor's permission to use any particular type of lifting equipment.
- Comply with personal and environmental safety practices associated with clothing; eye protection; hand tools; power equipment; proper ventilation; and the handling, storage, and disposal of chemicals/materials in accordance with federal, state, and local regulations.
- Always wear the correct protective eyewear and clothing and use the appropriate safety equipment, as well as wheel chocks, fender covers, seat protectors, and floor mat protectors.
- Make sure you understand and observe all legislative and personal safety procedures when carrying out practical assignments. If you are unsure of what these are, ask your supervisor/instructor.

▶ **TASK** Inspect, measure, and replace/reinstall overhead camshaft; measure/adjust end play and backlash.

MTST
I.B.5; P3

Time off_____

Time on_____

Total time_____

Student Instructions: Read through the entire procedure prior to starting. Prepare your workspace and any tools or parts that may be needed to complete the task. When directed by your supervisor/instructor, begin the procedure to complete the task and check the box as each step is finished.

Note: This tasksheet may require the student to check the condition of miscellaneous vehicle fluids, some of which may be flammable and could damage the environment or cause health problems if not handled properly. Observe all safety precautions and follow local regulations for the proper disposal of fluids.

Procedure:	Step Completed
1. Reassemble the camshaft into the cylinder head as outlined in the manufacturer's workshop materials [applicable only to overhead-mounted camshaft(s)]. Continue if this is an overhead camshaft engine (OHC) assembly.	☐
2. Check the camshaft bearings for excessive wear; replace if necessary.	☐
3. Install the camshaft into the cylinder head. (**Note:** Use extreme care, as camshaft lobes are very sharp.)	
a. Once camshaft is installed, you should be able to turn camshaft by hand with very little effort. Yes: ☐ No: ☐	☐
b. If No, remove the camshaft and check the bearings for damage, misalignment, or debris. Discuss findings with your supervisor/instructor and record your findings:	☐
4. Fit cam mounting brackets and torque to the manufacturer's specifications.	
a. Manufacturer's specified torque: _____ ft/lbs (Nm)	☐
5. Use the recommended special tools to measure/adjust end play and backlash as outlined in the manufacturer's workshop materials [applicable only to overhead-mounted camshaft(s)].	☐
a. Manufacturer's specification—end play: _____ in./mm	☐
b. Actual end play measurement: _____ in./mm	☐
c. Manufacturer's specification—backlash: _____ in./mm	☐
d. Actual backlash measurement: _____ in./mm	☐
6. Have your supervisor/instructor inspect your assembled camshaft to this point and discuss your findings.	☐

Non-Task-Specific Evaluations:	Step Completed
1. Tools and equipment were used as directed and returned in good working order.	☐
2. Complied with all general and task-specific safety standards, including proper use of any personal protection equipment.	☐
3. Completed the task in an appropriate time frame (recommendation: 1.5 or 2 times flat rate).	☐
4. Left the workspace clean and orderly.	☐
5. Cared for customer property and returned it undamaged.	☐

Student signature _____ Date _____

Comments:

Have your supervisor/instructor verify satisfactory completion of this procedure, any observations made, and any necessary action(s) recommended.

Evaluation Instructions: The scoring box below is intended to act as a guide for both student and supervisor/instructor. Each criterion listed will help students to understand what is expected of them and help supervisors/instructors articulate the level of success at a particular task. The scoring is set up to allow a second attempt at each task (see the Test and Retest columns). Scoring is also designed to award students points only for task criteria that were completed correctly. Points are lost for failure to complete the employability requirements (see Non-Task-Specific Evaluation criteria). When all criteria are evaluated, tally the points for a total at the bottom of each column.

Tasksheet Scoring

Evaluation Items	Test Pass (1 pt)	Test Fail (0 pts)	Retest Pass (1 pt)	Retest Fail (0 pts)
Task-Specific Evaluation	**(1 pt)**	**(0 pts)**	**(1 pt)**	**(0 pts)**
Student properly inspected all camshaft bearings and replaced them if necessary.				
Student properly assembled camshaft(s) following the manufacturer's directions using the proper tooling.				
Student correctly set camshaft(s) end play to the manufacturer's specifications.				
Student correctly set camshaft backlash to manufacturer's specifications.				
Non-Task-Specific Evaluation	**(0 pts)**	**(−1 pt)**	**(0 pts)**	**(−1 pt)**
Student successfully completed at least three of the non-task-specific steps.				
Student successfully completed all five of the non-task-specific steps.				
Total Score: <total # of points/4 = %>				

Supervisor/Instructor:

Supervisor/instructor signature _____ Date _____

Comments:

Retest supervisor/instructor signature _____ Date _____

Comments:

I.C Diesel Engines: Engine Block

Learning Objective/Task	CDX Tasksheet Number	ASE Foundation MTST Reference Number; Priority Level
• Inspect crankshaft vibration damper; inspect engine mounts; determine needed action.	MHT1C001	I.C.1; P-1
• Remove, inspect, service, and install pans, covers, gaskets, seals, wear rings, and crankcase ventilation components; determine needed action.	MHT1C002	I.C.2; P-1
• Perform crankcase pressure test; determine needed action.	MHT1C003	I.C.3; P-1
• Install and align flywheel housing; inspect flywheel housing(s) to transmission housing/engine mating surface(s); measure flywheel housing face and bore runout; determine needed action.	MHT1C004	I.C.4; P-2
• Inspect flywheel/flexplate (including ring gear) and mounting surfaces for cracks and wear; measure runout; determine needed action.	MHT1C005	I.C.5; P-2
• Disassemble and clean engine block; inspect engine block for cracks/damage; measure mating surfaces for warpage; check condition of passages, core/expansion plugs, and gallery plugs; inspect threaded holes, studs, dowel pins, and bolts for serviceability; determine needed action.	MHT1C006	I.C.6; P-2
• Inspect cylinder sleeve counter bore and lower bore; check bore distortion; determine needed action.	MHT1C007	I.C.7; P-2
• Clean, inspect, and measure cylinder walls or liners for wear and damage; determine needed action.	MHT1C008	I.C.8; P-2
• Replace/reinstall cylinder liners and seals; check and adjust liner height (protrusion).	MHT1C009	I.C.9; P-2
• Inspect in-block camshaft bearings for wear and damage; determine needed action.	MHT1C010	I.C.10; P-3
• Inspect, measure, and replace/reinstall in-block camshaft; measure end play and backlash; determine needed action.	MHT1C011	I.C.11; P-3
• Clean and inspect crankshaft for surface cracks and journal damage; check condition of oil passages; check passage plugs; measure journal diameter; determine needed action.	MHT1C012	I.C.12; P-2
• Inspect main bearings for wear patterns and damage; replace as needed; check bearing clearances; check and correct crankshaft end play.	MHT1C013	I.C.13; P-2
• Inspect, install, and time gear train; measure gear backlash; determine needed action.	MHT1C014	I.C.14; P-2
• Inspect connecting rod and bearings for wear patterns; measure pistons, pins, retainers, and bushings; determine needed action.	MHT1C015	I.C.15; P-3

Learning Objective/Task	CDX Tasksheet Number	ASE Foundation MTST Reference Number; Priority Level
• Determine piston-to-cylinder wall clearance; check ring-to-groove fit and end gap; install rings on pistons.	MHT1C016	I.C.16; P-3
• Assemble pistons and connecting rods and install them in the engine block; install rod bearings; and check clearances.	MHT1C017	I.C.17; P-2
• Check condition of piston cooling jets (nozzles); determine needed action.	MHT1C018	I.C.18; P-2

Materials Required

- Vehicle with possible engine concern
- Engine manufacturer's workshop materials
- Manufacturer-specific tools depending on the concern/procedure(s)
- Vehicle/component lifting equipment, if applicable

Safety Considerations

- Activities may require test-driving the vehicle on the school grounds or on a hoist, both of which carry severe risks. Attempt this task only with full permission from your supervisor/instructor, and follow all the guidelines exactly.
- Lifting equipment and machines such as vehicle jacks and stands, vehicle hoists, and engine hoists are important tools that increase productivity and make the job easier. However, they can also cause severe injury or death if used improperly. Make sure you follow the manufacturer's operation procedures. Also make sure you have your supervisor's/instructor's permission to use any particular type of lifting equipment.
- Comply with personal and environmental safety practices associated with clothing; eye protection; hand tools; power equipment; proper ventilation; and the handling, storage, and disposal of chemicals/materials in accordance with federal, state, and local regulations.
- Always wear the correct protective eyewear and clothing and use the appropriate safety equipment, as well as fender covers, seat protectors, and floor mat protectors.
- Make sure you understand and observe all legislative and personal safety procedures when carrying out practical assignments. If you are unsure of what these are, ask your supervisor/instructor.
- While working on a vehicle, wheel chocks must be placed on both sides of one set of tires or as directed by your supervisor/instructor.
- Exhaust evacuation hoses must be placed over exhaust outlets while the engine is used in a confined shop space.

CDX Tasksheet Number: MHT1C001

Student/Intern Information

Name _____ Date _____ Class _____

Vehicle, Customer, and Service Information

Vehicle used for this activity:

Year _____ Make _____ Model _____

Odometer _____ VIN _____

Materials Required

- Vehicle with possible engine concern
- Engine manufacturer's workshop materials
- Manufacturer-specific tools depending on the concern/procedure(s)
- Vehicle/component lifting equipment, if applicable

Task-Specific Safety Considerations

- Activities may require test-driving the vehicle on the school grounds or on a hoist, both of which carry severe risks. Attempt this task only with full permission from your supervisor/ instructor, and follow all the guidelines exactly.
- Lifting equipment and machines such as vehicle jacks and stands, vehicle hoists, and engine hoists are important tools that increase productivity and make the job easier. However, they can also cause severe injury or death if used improperly. Make sure you follow the manufacturer's operation procedures. Also make sure you have your supervisor's/ instructor's permission to use any particular type of lifting equipment.
- Comply with personal and environmental safety practices associated with clothing; eye protection; hand tools; power equipment; proper ventilation; and the handling, storage, and disposal of chemicals/materials in accordance with federal, state, and local regulations.
- Always wear the correct protective eyewear and clothing and use the appropriate safety equipment, as well as wheel chocks, fender covers, seat protectors, and floor mat protectors.
- Make sure you understand and observe all legislative and personal safety procedures when carrying out practical assignments. If you are unsure of what these are, ask your supervisor/ instructor.

▶ **TASK** Inspect crankshaft vibration damper; inspect engine mounts; determine needed action.

MTST
I.C.1; P1

Time off_____

Time on_____

Total time_____

Student Instructions: Read through the entire procedure prior to starting. Prepare your workspace and any tools or parts that may be needed to complete the task. When directed by your supervisor/instructor, begin the procedure to complete the task and check the box as each step is finished.

Note: This tasksheet will require the student to check the condition of miscellaneous vehicle fluids, some of which may be flammable and could damage the environment or cause health problems if not handled properly. Observe all safety precautions and follow local regulations for the proper disposal of fluids.

Procedure:	Step Completed
1. Record the type of crankshaft vibration dampener that is used:	☐
a. If viscous, inspect for dents or leaks to the outer shell, and record:	☐
b. If elastomer, inspect for missing, damaged, or swollen rubber between inner hub and outer ring, verify that index marks are aligned, and record:	☐
2. Using dial indicator, check for runout, and record reading:	☐
a. Is dampener within manufacturer's specifications? Yes: ☐ No: ☐	☐
3. Discuss the findings with your supervisor/instructor.	☐

Non-Task-Specific Evaluations:	Step Completed
1. Tools and equipment were used as directed and returned in good working order.	☐
2. Complied with all general and task-specific safety standards, including proper use of any personal protection equipment.	☐
3. Completed the task in an appropriate time frame (recommendation: 1.5 or 2 times the flat rate).	☐
4. Left the workspace clean and orderly.	☐
5. Cared for customer property and returned it undamaged.	☐

Student signature _____ Date _____

Comments:

Have your supervisor/instructor verify satisfactory completion of this procedure, any observations made, and any necessary action(s) recommended.

Evaluation Instructions: The scoring box below is intended to act as a guide for both student and supervisor/instructor. Each criterion listed will help students to understand what is expected of them and help supervisors/instructors articulate the level of success at a particular task. The scoring is set up to allow a second attempt at each task (see the Test and Retest columns). Scoring is also designed to award students points only for task criteria that were completed correctly. Points are lost for failure to complete the employability requirements (see Non-Task-Specific Evaluation criteria). When all criteria are evaluated, tally the points for a total at the bottom of each column.

Tasksheet Scoring

	Test		Retest	
Evaluation Items	**Pass**	**Fail**	**Pass**	**Fail**
Task-Specific Evaluation	**(1 pt)**	**(0 pts)**	**(1 pt)**	**(0 pts)**
Student referenced the appropriate manufacturer's workshop materials.				
Student correctly identified dampener type.				
Student correctly inspected dampener.				
Student reinstalled all removed components undamaged and in working order.				
Non-Task-Specific Evaluation	**(0 pts)**	**(−1 pt)**	**(0 pts)**	**(−1 pt)**
Student successfully completed at least three of the non-task-specific steps.				
Student successfully completed all five of the non-task-specific steps.				
Total Score: <total # of points/4 = %>				

Supervisor/Instructor:

Supervisor/instructor signature _____ Date _____

Comments:

Retest supervisor/instructor signature _____ Date _____

Comments:

CDX Tasksheet Number: MHT1C002

Student/Intern Information

Name _____ Date _____ Class _____

Vehicle, Customer, and Service Information

Vehicle used for this activity:

Year _____ Make _____ Model _____

Odometer _____ VIN _____

Materials Required
- Vehicle with possible engine concern
- Engine manufacturer's workshop materials
- Manufacturer-specific tools depending on the concern/procedure(s)
- Vehicle/component lifting equipment, if applicable

Task-Specific Safety Considerations
- Activities may require test-driving the vehicle on the school grounds or on a hoist, both of which carry severe risks. Attempt this task only with full permission from your supervisor/instructor, and follow all the guidelines exactly.
- Lifting equipment and machines such as vehicle jacks and stands, vehicle hoists, and engine hoists are important tools that increase productivity and make the job easier. However, they can also cause severe injury or death if used improperly. Make sure you follow the manufacturer's operation procedures. Also make sure you have your supervisor's/instructor's permission to use any particular type of lifting equipment.
- Comply with personal and environmental safety practices associated with clothing; eye protection; hand tools; power equipment; proper ventilation; and the handling, storage, and disposal of chemicals/materials in accordance with federal, state, and local regulations.
- Always wear the correct protective eyewear and clothing and use the appropriate safety equipment, as well as wheel chocks, fender covers, seat protectors, and floor mat protectors.
- Make sure you understand and observe all legislative and personal safety procedures when carrying out practical assignments. If you are unsure of what these are, ask your supervisor/instructor.

▶ **TASK** Remove, inspect, service, and install pans, covers, gaskets, seals, wear rings, and crankcase ventilation components; determine needed action.

MTST
I.C.2; P1

Time off_____

Time on_____

Total time_____

Student Instructions: Read through the entire procedure prior to starting. Prepare your workspace and any tools or parts that may be needed to complete the task. When directed by your supervisor/instructor, begin the procedure to complete the task and check the box as each step is finished.

Note: This tasksheet will require the student to check the condition of miscellaneous vehicle fluids, some of which may be flammable and could damage the environment or cause health problems if not handled properly. Observe all safety precautions and follow local regulations for the proper disposal of fluids.

Procedure:	Step Completed
1. Referencing the manufacturer's workshop materials, list the procedures and any special tooling that is to be used to remove the engine oil seals and wear rings:	☐
2. Using the proper tooling and procedures, remove engine oil seals and wear rings.	
a. If wear rings were not used, inspect seal wear surfaces for excessive wear. Discuss this with your supervisor/instructor, and record any special instructions:	☐
3. Using the proper tooling and procedures, install new wear rings and seals.	
a. Wear rings/seals correctly installed: Yes: ☐ No: ☐	☐
b. If No, record special instructions:	☐
4. Remove all external covers/pans and inspect for internal/external damage. Record any findings below:	☐
5. Inspect all external cover seals and gaskets. Record findings below:	☐
6. Clean and reinstall all external covers/pans.	☐

7. Referencing the manufacturer's workshop materials, remove and inspect the crankcase ventilation components.	
a. Meets the manufacturer's specifications: Yes: ☐ No: ☐	☐
b. If No, list the manufacturer's recommendations:	☐
8. Service and reinstall all crankcase ventilation components.	☐
9. If possible, start engine and bring up to operating temperature.	
a. Inspect for oil leaks, and record findings:	☐
b. Using an electronic service tool (EST), check for any crankcase ventilation codes, and record findings:	☐
10. Discuss findings with your supervisor/instructor and list any further instructions:	☐

Non-Task-Specific Evaluations:	Step Completed
1. Tools and equipment were used as directed and returned in good working order.	☐
2. Complied with all general and task-specific safety standards, including proper use of any personal protection equipment.	☐
3. Completed the task in an appropriate time frame (recommendation: 1.5 or 2 times the flat rate).	☐
4. Left the workspace clean and orderly.	☐
5. Cared for customer property and returned it undamaged.	☐

Student signature _____ Date _____

Comments:

Have your supervisor/instructor verify satisfactory completion of this procedure, any observations found, and any necessary action(s) recommended.

Evaluation Instructions: The scoring box below is intended to act as a guide for both student and supervisor/instructor. Each criterion listed will help students to understand what is expected of them and help supervisors/instructors articulate the level of success at a particular task. The scoring is set up to allow a second attempt at each task (see the Test and Retest columns). Scoring is also designed to award students points only for task criteria that were completed correctly. Points are lost for failure to complete the employability requirements (see Non-Task-Specific Evaluation criteria). When all criteria are evaluated, tally the points for a total at the bottom of each column.

Tasksheet Scoring

	Test		Retest	
	Pass	Fail	Pass	Fail
Evaluation Items				
Task-Specific Evaluation	**(1 pt)**	**(0 pts)**	**(1 pt)**	**(0 pts)**
Student removed, inspected, and reinstalled seals and wear rings using the proper tooling and procedures.				
Student removed, inspected, and reinstalled external covers/pans using the correct fasteners.				
Student removed, inspected, and reinstalled crankcase ventilation components using the correct fasteners.				
Student inspected the engine for oil leaks and crankcase ventilation codes.				
Non-Task-Specific Evaluation	**(0 pts)**	**(−1 pt)**	**(0 pts)**	**(−1 pt)**
Student successfully completed at least three of the non-task-specific steps.				
Student successfully completed all five of the non-task-specific steps.				
Total Score: <total # of points/4 = %>				

Supervisor/Instructor:

Supervisor/instructor signature _____ Date _____

Comments:

Retest supervisor/instructor signature _____ Date _____

Comments:

CDX Tasksheet Number: MHT1C003

Student/Intern Information

Name _____ Date _____ Class _____

Vehicle, Customer, and Service Information

Vehicle used for this activity:

Year _____ Make _____ Model _____

Odometer _____ VIN _____

Materials Required

- Vehicle with possible engine concern
- Engine manufacturer's workshop materials
- Manufacturer-specific tools depending on the concern/procedure(s)
- Vehicle/component lifting equipment, if applicable

Task-Specific Safety Considerations

- Activities may require test-driving the vehicle on the school grounds or on a hoist, both of which carry severe risks. Attempt this task only with full permission from your supervisor/instructor, and follow all the guidelines exactly.
- Lifting equipment and machines such as vehicle jacks and stands, vehicle hoists, and engine hoists are important tools that increase productivity and make the job easier. However, they can also cause severe injury or death if used improperly. Make sure you follow the manufacturer's operation procedures. Also make sure you have your supervisor's/instructor's permission to use any particular type of lifting equipment.
- Comply with personal and environmental safety practices associated with clothing; eye protection; hand tools; power equipment; proper ventilation; and the handling, storage, and disposal of chemicals/materials in accordance with federal, state, and local regulations.
- Always wear the correct protective eyewear and clothing and use the appropriate safety equipment, as well as wheel chocks, fender covers, seat protectors, and floor mat protectors.
- Make sure you understand and observe all legislative and personal safety procedures when carrying out practical assignments. If you are unsure of what these are, ask your supervisor/instructor.

▶ **TASK** Perform crankcase pressure test; determine needed action. **MTST** *I.C.3; P1*

Time off_____

Student Instructions: Read through the entire procedure prior to starting. Prepare your workspace and any tools or parts that may be needed to complete the task. When directed by your supervisor/instructor, begin the procedure to complete the task and check the box as each step is finished.

Time on_____

Note: This tasksheet will require the student to check the condition of miscellaneous vehicle fluids, some of which may be flammable and could damage the environment or cause health problems if not handled properly. Observe all safety precautions and follow local regulations for the proper disposal of fluids.

Total time_____

© 2021 Jones & Bartlett Learning, LLC, an Ascend Learning Company

Engine Block **229**

Procedure:	Step Completed
1. Referring to the manufacturer's workshop materials, list the procedures and all safety precautions that must be observed when performing a crankcase pressure test.	
a. List the steps involved when performing a crankcase pressure test:	☐
b. Determine what safety precautions must be observed when performing a crankcase pressure test:	☐
2. Discuss these procedures and safety precautions with your supervisor/ instructor, and record any special instructions:	☐
3. If directed by your supervisor/instructor, perform a crankcase pressure test following the procedures listed above and while referencing the manufacturer's workshop materials. Record percentage of leakage below.	
a. Cylinder #1: _____ % Meets the manufacturer's specifications: Yes: ☐ No: ☐	☐
b. Cylinder #2: _____ % Meets the manufacturer's specifications: Yes: ☐ No: ☐	☐
c. Cylinder #3: _____ % Meets the manufacturer's specifications: Yes: ☐ No: ☐	☐
d. Cylinder #4: _____ % Meets the manufacturer's specifications: Yes: ☐ No: ☐	☐
e. Cylinder #5: _____ % Meets the manufacturer's specifications: Yes: ☐ No: ☐	☐
f. Cylinder #6: _____ % Meets the manufacturer's specifications: Yes: ☐ No: ☐	☐

	Step Completed
4. For any cylinder that does not meet the manufacturer's specifications, describe the recommended correction:	☐
5. Discuss findings with your supervisor/instructor and list any further instructions:	☐

Non-Task-Specific Evaluations:	Step Completed
1. Tools and equipment were used as directed and returned in good working order.	☐
2. Complied with all general and task-specific safety standards, including proper use of any personal protection equipment.	☐
3. Completed the task in an appropriate time frame (recommendation: 1.5 or 2 times the flat rate).	☐
4. Left the workspace clean and orderly.	☐
5. Cared for customer property and returned it undamaged.	☐

Student signature _____ Date _____

Comments:

Have your supervisor/instructor verify satisfactory completion of this procedure, any observations made, and any necessary action(s) recommended.

Evaluation Instructions: The scoring box below is intended to act as a guide for both student and supervisor/instructor. Each criterion listed will help students to understand what is expected of them and help supervisors/instructors articulate the level of success at a particular task. The scoring is set up to allow a second attempt at each task (see the Test and Retest columns). Scoring is also designed to award students points only for task criteria that were completed correctly. Points are lost for failure to complete the employability requirements (see Non-Task-Specific Evaluation criteria). When all criteria are evaluated, tally the points for a total at the bottom of each column.

Tasksheet Scoring

Evaluation Items	Test		Retest	
	Pass	**Fail**	**Pass**	**Fail**
Task-Specific Evaluation	**(1 pt)**	**(0 pts)**	**(1 pt)**	**(0 pts)**
Student recorded specifications and precautions correctly.				
Student performed the test following the manufacturer's instructions.				
Student accurately and clearly recorded the results.				
Student accurately described the recommended correction for any cylinder that did not meet the manufacturer's specifications.				
Non-Task-Specific Evaluation	**(0 pts)**	**(−1 pt)**	**(0 pts)**	**(−1 pt)**
Student successfully completed at least three of the non-task-specific steps.				
Student successfully completed all five of the non-task-specific steps.				
Total Score: <total # of points/4 = %>				

CDX Tasksheet Number: MHT1C004

Student/Intern Information

Name _____ Date _____ Class _____

Vehicle, Customer, and Service Information

Vehicle used for this activity:

Year _____ Make _____ Model _____

Odometer _____ VIN _____

Materials Required
- Vehicle with possible engine concern
- Engine manufacturer's workshop materials
- Manufacturer-specific tools depending on the concern/procedure(s)
- Vehicle/component lifting equipment, if applicable

Task-Specific Safety Considerations
- Activities may require test-driving the vehicle on the school grounds or on a hoist, both of which carry severe risks. Attempt this task only with full permission from your supervisor/instructor, and follow all the guidelines exactly.
- Lifting equipment and machines such as vehicle jacks and stands, vehicle hoists, and engine hoists are important tools that increase productivity and make the job easier. However, they can also cause severe injury or death if used improperly. Make sure you follow the manufacturer's operation procedures. Also make sure you have your supervisor's/instructor's permission to use any particular type of lifting equipment.
- Comply with personal and environmental safety practices associated with clothing; eye protection; hand tools; power equipment; proper ventilation; and the handling, storage, and disposal of chemicals/materials in accordance with federal, state, and local regulations.
- Always wear the correct protective eyewear and clothing and use the appropriate safety equipment, as well as wheel chocks, fender covers, seat protectors, and floor mat protectors.
- Make sure you understand and observe all legislative and personal safety procedures when carrying out practical assignments. If you are unsure of what these are, ask your supervisor/instructor.

▶ **TASK** Install and align flywheel housing; inspect flywheel housing(s) to transmission housing/engine mating surface(s); measure flywheel housing face and bore runout; determine needed action.

MTST
I.C.4; P2

Time off_____

Time on_____

Total time_____

Student Instructions: Read through the entire procedure prior to starting. Prepare your workspace and any tools or parts that may be needed to complete the task. When directed by your supervisor/instructor, begin the procedure to complete the task and check the box as each step is finished.

Note: This tasksheet will require the student to check the condition of miscellaneous vehicle fluids, some of which may be flammable and could damage the environment or cause health problems if not handled properly. Observe all safety precautions and follow local regulations for the proper disposal of fluids.

Procedure:	Step Completed
1. Reference the manufacturer's workshop materials; install and align the flywheel housing.	
a. Meets the manufacturer's specifications: Yes: ☐ No: ☐	☐
b. If No, list recommendations for any rectifications:	☐
2. Reference the manufacturer's workshop materials; inspect the flywheel housing(s) to the transmission housing/engine mating surface(s) for damage and threaded holes for damaged/stripped threads.	
a. Make any repairs if directed by your supervisor/instructor:	☐
3. While referring to the manufacturer's workshop materials, measure the flywheel housing face and bore runout.	
a. Specification: _____ in./mm	☐
b. Actual: _____ in./mm	☐
c. Meets the manufacturer's specifications: Yes: ☐ No: ☐	☐
d. If No, list recommendations for rectification:	☐
4. Discuss the findings with your supervisor/instructor.	☐

Non-Task-Specific Evaluations:	Step Completed
1. Tools and equipment were used as directed and returned in good working order.	☐
2. Complied with all general and task-specific safety standards, including proper use of any personal protection equipment.	☐
3. Completed the task in an appropriate time frame (recommendation: 1.5 or 2 times the flat rate).	☐
4. Left the workspace clean and orderly.	☐
5. Cared for customer property and returned it undamaged.	☐

Student signature _____ Date _____

Comments:

Have your supervisor/instructor verify satisfactory completion of this procedure, any observations made, and any necessary action(s) recommended.

Evaluation Instructions: The scoring box below is intended to act as a guide for both student and supervisor/instructor. Each criterion listed will help students to understand what is expected of them and help supervisors/instructors articulate the level of success at a particular task. The scoring is set up to allow a second attempt at each task (see the Test and Retest columns). Scoring is also designed to award students points only for task criteria that were completed correctly. Points are lost for failure to complete the employability requirements (see Non-Task-Specific Evaluation criteria). When all criteria are evaluated, tally the points for a total at the bottom of each column.

Tasksheet Scoring

Evaluation Items	Test		Retest	
	Pass	Fail	Pass	Fail
Task-Specific Evaluation	**(1 pt)**	**(0 pts)**	**(1 pt)**	**(0 pts)**
Student referenced the appropriate manufacturer's workshop materials.				
Student installed the flywheel housing correctly using the correct procedure and tools.				
Student inspected the flywheel housing for damage.				
Student measured the flywheel housing face and bore runout.				
Non-Task-Specific Evaluation	**(0 pts)**	**(−1 pt)**	**(0 pts)**	**(−1 pt)**
Student successfully completed at least three of the non-task-specific steps.				
Student successfully completed all five of the non-task-specific steps.				
Total Score: <total # of points/4 = %>				

Supervisor/Instructor:

Supervisor/instructor signature _____ Date _____

Comments:

Retest supervisor/instructor signature _____ Date _____

Comments:

CDX Tasksheet Number: MHT1C005

Student/Intern Information

Name _____ Date _____ Class _____

Vehicle, Customer, and Service Information

Vehicle used for this activity:

Year _____ Make _____ Model _____

Odometer _____ VIN _____

Materials Required

- Vehicle with possible engine concern
- Engine manufacturer's workshop materials
- Manufacturer-specific tools depending on the concern/procedure(s)
- Vehicle/component lifting equipment, if applicable

Task-Specific Safety Considerations

- Activities may require test-driving the vehicle on the school grounds or on a hoist, both of which carry severe risks. Attempt this task only with full permission from your supervisor/instructor, and follow all the guidelines exactly.
- Lifting equipment and machines such as vehicle jacks and stands, vehicle hoists, and engine hoists are important tools that increase productivity and make the job easier. However, they can also cause severe injury or death if used improperly. Make sure you follow the manufacturer's operation procedures. Also make sure you have your supervisor's/instructor's permission to use any particular type of lifting equipment.
- Comply with personal and environmental safety practices associated with clothing; eye protection; hand tools; power equipment; proper ventilation; and the handling, storage, and disposal of chemicals/materials in accordance with federal, state, and local regulations.
- Always wear the correct protective eyewear and clothing and use the appropriate safety equipment, as well as wheel chocks, fender covers, seat protectors, and floor mat protectors.
- Make sure you understand and observe all legislative and personal safety procedures when carrying out practical assignments. If you are unsure of what these are, ask your supervisor/instructor.

▶ **TASK** Inspect flywheel/flexplate (including ring gear) and mounting surfaces for cracks and wear; measure runout; determine needed action. **MTST** *I.C.5; P2*

Time off_____

Time on_____

Total time_____

Student Instructions: Read through the entire procedure prior to starting. Prepare your workspace and any tools or parts that may be needed to complete the task. When directed by your supervisor/instructor, begin the procedure to complete the task and check the box as each step is finished.

Note: This tasksheet will require the student to check the condition of miscellaneous vehicle fluids, some of which may be flammable and could damage the environment or cause health problems if not handled properly. Observe all safety precautions and follow local regulations for the proper disposal of fluids.

Procedure:	Step Completed
1. Reference the manufacturer's workshop materials; inspect the flywheel/flexplate (including the ring gear) and mounting surfaces for cracks and wear.	
a. Meets the manufacturer's specifications: Yes: ☐ No: ☐	☐
b. If No, list recommendations for any rectifications:	☐
2. If applicable, inspect pilot bearing bore for proper diameter and bearing fit.	
a. Specification: _____ in./mm	☐
b. Actual: _____ in./mm	☐
c. Meets the manufacturer's specifications: Yes: ☐ No: ☐	☐
d. If No, list recommendations for rectification:	☐
3. While referring to the manufacturer's workshop materials, measure the runout using a dial indicator.	
a. Specification: _____ in./mm	☐
b. Actual: _____ in./mm	☐
c. Meets the manufacturer's specifications: Yes: ☐ No: ☐	☐
d. If No, list recommendations for rectification:	☐
4. Discuss the findings with your supervisor/instructor.	☐

Non-Task-Specific Evaluations:	Step Completed
1. Tools and equipment were used as directed and returned in good working order.	☐
2. Complied with all general and task-specific safety standards, including proper use of any personal protection equipment.	☐
3. Completed the task in an appropriate time frame (recommendation: 1.5 or 2 times the flat rate).	☐
4. Left the workspace clean and orderly.	☐
5. Cared for customer property and returned it undamaged.	☐

Student signature _____ Date _____

Comments:

Have your supervisor/instructor verify satisfactory completion of this procedure, any observations made,

and any necessary action(s) recommended.

Evaluation Instructions: The scoring box below is intended to act as a guide for both student and supervisor/instructor. Each criterion listed will help students to understand what is expected of them and help supervisors/instructors articulate the level of success at a particular task. The scoring is set up to allow a second attempt at each task (see the Test and Retest columns). Scoring is also designed to award students points only for task criteria that were completed correctly. Points are lost for failure to complete the employability requirements (see Non-Task-Specific Evaluation criteria). When all criteria are evaluated, tally the points for a total at the bottom of each column.

Tasksheet Scoring

Evaluation Items	Test		Retest	
	Pass	Fail	Pass	Fail
Task-Specific Evaluation	**(1 pt)**	**(0 pts)**	**(1 pt)**	**(0 pts)**
Student properly inspected the flywheel/flexplate.				
Student properly checked the pilot bearing bore.				
Student properly checked the flywheel/flexplate runout.				
Student properly inspected mounting surfaces.				
Non-Task-Specific Evaluation	**(0 pts)**	**(−1 pt)**	**(0 pts)**	**(−1 pt)**
Student successfully completed at least three of the non-task-specific steps.				
Student successfully completed all five of the non-task-specific steps.				
Total Score: <total # of points/4 = %>				

Supervisor/Instructor:

Supervisor/instructor signature _____ Date _____

Comments:

Retest supervisor/instructor signature _____ Date _____

Comments:

CDX Tasksheet Number: MHT1C006

Student/Intern Information

Name _____ Date _____ Class _____

Vehicle, Customer, and Service Information

Vehicle used for this activity:

Year _____ Make _____ Model _____

Odometer _____ VIN _____

Materials Required

- Vehicle with possible engine concern
- Engine manufacturer's workshop materials
- Manufacturer-specific tools depending on the concern/procedure(s)
- Vehicle/component lifting equipment, if applicable

Task-Specific Safety Considerations

- Activities may require test-driving the vehicle on the school grounds or on a hoist, both of which carry severe risks. Attempt this task only with full permission from your supervisor/instructor, and follow all the guidelines exactly.
- Lifting equipment and machines such as vehicle jacks and stands, vehicle hoists, and engine hoists are important tools that increase productivity and make the job easier. However, they can also cause severe injury or death if used improperly. Make sure you follow the manufacturer's operation procedures. Also make sure you have your supervisor's/instructor's permission to use any particular type of lifting equipment.
- Comply with personal and environmental safety practices associated with clothing; eye protection; hand tools; power equipment; proper ventilation; and the handling, storage, and disposal of chemicals/materials in accordance with federal, state, and local regulations.
- Always wear the correct protective eyewear and clothing and use the appropriate safety equipment, as well as wheel chocks, fender covers, seat protectors, and floor mat protectors.
- Make sure you understand and observe all legislative and personal safety procedures when carrying out practical assignments. If you are unsure of what these are, ask your supervisor/instructor.

▶ **TASK** Disassemble and clean engine block; inspect engine block for cracks/damage; measure mating surfaces for warpage; check condition of passages, core/expansion plugs, and gallery plugs; inspect threaded holes, studs, dowel pins, and bolts for serviceability; determine needed action.

MTST
I.C.6; P2

Time off_____

Time on_____

Total time_____

Student Instructions: Read through the entire procedure prior to starting. Prepare your workspace and any tools or parts that may be needed to complete the task. When directed by your supervisor/instructor, begin the procedure to complete the task and check the box as each step is finished.

Note: This tasksheet will require the student to check the condition of miscellaneous vehicle fluids, some of which may be flammable and could damage the environment or cause health problems if not handled properly. Observe all safety precautions and follow local regulations for the proper disposal of fluids.

Procedure:	Step Completed
1. Reference the manufacturer's workshop materials; list the procedures and any special tooling that is to be used when disassembling an engine assembly:	☐
a. Determine what safety precautions must be observed during the disassembly of the engine block:	☐
2. Discuss these procedures and safety precautions with your supervisor/instructor; record any special instructions:	☐
a. If available, mount the engine to the engine rebuild stand. (**Note:** Drain engine oil and coolant, and steam clean/pressure wash the engine if needed before installing on the stand.)	☐
3. Using the proper tools and procedures, disassemble the engine. (**Note:** Store all fasteners in labeled storage trays/bins. Store any component that may contain oil or other fluids in a manner to prevent spillage on the workshop floor, which is a safety requirement.)	☐
4. Before removing the connecting rod caps, mark their location and position.	☐
5. Inspect the cylinder liner/bore for a wear ridge at the top of the piston travel. Record findings and method for removing wear ridge:	☐

6. Remove piston/connecting rod assemblies and store in a safe location. (**Note:** Install the correct connecting rod cap onto the connecting rod immediately after removing from engine.)	☐
7. Remove flywheel and flywheel housing from engine.	☐
8. Remove front timing cover from engine.	☐
9. Remove main bearing caps. (**Note:** Mark position of crankshaft main bearing caps before removal.)	☐
10. Carefully remove crankshaft from engine and store in a safe location. (**Note:** Damage can occur if crankshaft is stored lying down; store in an upright position.) (**Hint:** Reinstall flywheel onto crankshaft to help keep it in an upright position for storage.)	☐
11. Reinstall main crankshaft main bearing caps onto engine.	☐
12. Using the correct tooling, remove the cylinder liners (if applicable). (**Note:** Damage can occur if liners are not stored in an upright position.)	☐
13. While observing all lifting safety precautions, transport the disassembled block and disassembled components to the designated cleaning bay.	☐

14. Clean and dry the engine block and all related components; have your supervisor/instructor inspect parts for cleanliness. ☐ Clean ☐ Further cleaning needed	☐
15. Remount clean engine block to the engine rebuild stand.	☐
16. Lay out all components in an orderly manner to assist in reassembly.	☐
17. Reference the manufacturer's workshop materials; describe the procedure for measuring mating surfaces for warpage:	☐
18. Following the procedures listed previously, and while referencing the manufacturer's workshop materials, measure mating surfaces for warpage.	
a. Meets the manufacturer's specifications: Yes: ☐ No: ☐	☐
b. If No, list any procedure(s) for rectification:	☐
19. Referring to the manufacturer's workshop materials, check the condition of passages, core/expansion plugs, and gallery plugs; inspect threaded holes, studs, dowel pins, and bolts for serviceability.	
a. Meets the manufacturer's specifications: Yes: ☐ No: ☐	☐
b. If No, list any procedure(s) for rectification:	☐
20. Discuss the findings with your supervisor/instructor.	☐

Non-Task-Specific Evaluations:	Step Completed
1. Tools and equipment were used as directed and returned in good working order.	☐
2. Complied with all general and task-specific safety standards, including proper use of any personal protection equipment.	☐
3. Completed the task in an appropriate time frame (recommendation: 1.5 or 2 times the flat rate).	☐
4. Left the workspace clean and orderly.	☐
5. Cared for customer property and returned it undamaged.	☐

Student signature _____ Date _____

Comments:

Have your supervisor/instructor verify satisfactory completion of this procedure, any observations made,

and any necessary action(s) recommended.

Evaluation Instructions: The scoring box below is intended to act as a guide for both student and supervisor/instructor. Each criterion listed will help students to understand what is expected of them and help supervisors/instructors articulate the level of success at a particular task. The scoring is set up to allow a second attempt at each task (see the Test and Retest columns). Scoring is also designed to award students points only for task criteria that were completed correctly. Points are lost for failure to complete the employability requirements (see Non-Task-Specific Evaluation criteria). When all criteria are evaluated, tally the points for a total at the bottom of each column.

Tasksheet Scoring

Evaluation Items	Test		Retest	
	Pass	**Fail**	**Pass**	**Fail**
Task-Specific Evaluation	**(1 pt)**	**(0 pts)**	**(1 pt)**	**(0 pts)**
Student sorted and labeled small parts and fasteners during disassembly.				
Student properly cleaned and neatly laid out all parts.				
Student checked surfaces for warpage using the proper tools and techniques.				
Student properly inspected threaded holes, dowel pins, core/expansion plugs, and gallery plugs.				
Non-Task-Specific Evaluation	**(0 pts)**	**(−1 pt)**	**(0 pts)**	**(−1 pt)**
Student successfully completed at least three of the non-task-specific steps.				
Student successfully completed all five of the non-task-specific steps.				
Total Score: <total # of points/4 = %>				

Supervisor/Instructor:

Supervisor/instructor signature _____ Date _____

Comments:

Retest supervisor/instructor signature _____ Date _____
Comments:

CDX Tasksheet Number: MHT1C007

Student/Intern Information

Name _____ Date _____ Class _____

Vehicle, Customer, and Service Information

Vehicle used for this activity:

Year _____ Make _____ Model _____

Odometer _____ VIN _____

Materials Required

- Vehicle with possible engine concerns
- Engine manufacturer's repair information
- Manufacturer-specific tools depending on the concern

Task-Specific Safety Considerations

- Activities may require test-driving the vehicle on the school grounds or on a hoist, both of which carry severe risks. Attempt this task only with full permission from your supervisor/instructor, and follow all the guidelines exactly.
- Comply with personal and environmental safety practices associated with clothing; eye protection; hand tools; power equipment; proper ventilation; and the handling, storage, and disposal of chemicals/materials in accordance with federal, state, and local regulations.
- Always wear the correct protective eyewear and clothing and use the appropriate safety equipment, as well as fender covers, seat protectors, and floor mat protectors.
- Make sure you understand and observe all legislative and personal safety procedures when carrying out practical assignments. If you are unsure of what these are, ask your supervisor/instructor.
- While working on a vehicle, wheel chocks must be placed on both sides of one set of tires or as directed by your supervisor/instructor.
- Exhaust evacuation hoses must be placed over exhaust outlets while the engine is used in a confined shop space.

▶ TASK Inspect cylinder sleeve counter bore and lower bore; check bore distortion; determine needed action.

MTST
I.C.7; P2

Time off_____

Time on_____

Total time_____

Student Instructions: Read through the entire procedure prior to starting. Prepare your workspace and any tools or parts that may be needed to complete the task. When directed by your supervisor/instructor, begin the procedure to complete the task and check the box as each step is finished.

Note: This tasksheet will require the student to check the condition of miscellaneous vehicle fluids, some of which may be flammable and could damage the environment or cause health problems if not handled properly. Observe all safety precautions and follow local regulations for the proper disposal of fluids.

Procedure:	Step Completed
1. Inspect the cylinder sleeve counter bore and check bore distortion as outlined in the manufacturer's workshop materials.	☐
2. Cylinder sleeve counter bore inspection:	
a. Thoroughly clean the liner and counter bores. Any dirt or other material will prevent the liner from seating properly.	☐
b. Inspect the liner counter bores for squareness, cracks, and galling from loose liner condition.	☐
i. Within manufacturer's specifications: Yes: ☐ No: ☐	☐
c. Measure counter bore in multiple spots for concentricity and depth according to the manufacturer's specification.	☐
i. Record the measurements:	☐
3. Inspect lower counter bore.	
a. Inspect for pitting or water damage due to improper pH or alkalinity levels.	☐
i. Within manufacturer's specifications: Yes: ☐ No: ☐	☐

b. Measure lower bore in multiple spots for concentricity as outlined in the manufacturer's workshop materials.	☐
i. Record the measurements:	☐
ii. Within manufacturer's specifications: Yes: ☐ No: ☐	☐
4. Return the vehicle/simulator to its beginning condition, and return any tools you used to their proper locations.	☐
5. Discuss your findings with your supervisor/instructor.	☐

Non-Task-Specific Evaluations:	Step Completed
1. Tools and equipment were used as directed and returned in good working order.	
2. Complied with all general and task-specific safety standards, including proper use of any personal protection equipment.	
3. Completed the task in an appropriate time frame (recommendation: 1.5 or 2 times the flat rate).	
4. Left the workspace clean and orderly.	
5. Cared for customer property and returned it undamaged.	

Student signature _____ Date _____

Comments:

Have your supervisor/instructor verify satisfactory completion of this procedure, any observations made, and any necessary action(s) recommended.

Evaluation Instructions: The scoring box below is intended to act as a guide for both student and supervisor/instructor. Each criterion listed will help students to understand what is expected of them and help supervisors/instructors articulate the level of success at a particular task. The scoring is set up to allow a second attempt at each task (see the Test and Retest columns). Scoring is also designed to award students points only for task criteria that were completed correctly. Points are lost for failure to complete the employability requirements (see Non-Task-Specific Evaluation criteria). When all criteria are evaluated, tally the points for a total at the bottom of each column.

Tasksheet Scoring

Evaluation Items	Test		Retest	
	Pass	**Fail**	**Pass**	**Fail**
Task-Specific Evaluation	**(1 pt)**	**(0 pts)**	**(1 pt)**	**(0 pts)**
Student detailed the 3Cs on the submitted repair order.				
Student displayed use of manufacturer's repair information.				
Student properly performed diagnostic measurements.				
Student developed appropriate conclusions based on diagnostics and completed repairs as directed by the supervisor/instructor.				
Non-Task-Specific Evaluation	**(0 pts)**	**(−1 pt)**	**(0 pts)**	**(−1 pt)**
Student successfully completed at least three of the non-task-specific steps.				
Student successfully completed all five of the non-task-specific steps.				
Total Score: <total # of points/4 = %>				

Supervisor/Instructor:

Supervisor/instructor signature _____ Date _____

Comments:

Retest supervisor/instructor signature _____ Date _____

Comments:

CDX Tasksheet Number: MHT1C008

Student/Intern Information

Name _____ Date _____ Class _____

Vehicle, Customer, and Service Information

Vehicle used for this activity:

Year _____ Make _____ Model _____

Odometer _____ VIN _____

Task-Specific Safety Considerations

- Activities may require test-driving the vehicle on the school grounds or on a hoist, both of which carry severe risks. Attempt this task only with full permission from your supervisor/instructor, and follow all the guidelines exactly.
- Lifting equipment and machines such as vehicle jacks and stands, vehicle hoists, and engine hoists are important tools that increase productivity and make the job easier. However, they can also cause severe injury or death if used improperly. Make sure you follow the manufacturer's operation procedures. Also make sure you have your supervisor's/instructor's permission to use any particular type of lifting equipment.
- Comply with personal and environmental safety practices associated with clothing; eye protection; hand tools; power equipment; proper ventilation; and the handling, storage, and disposal of chemicals/materials in accordance with federal, state, and local regulations.
- Always wear the correct protective eyewear and clothing and use the appropriate safety equipment, as well as wheel chocks, fender covers, seat protectors, and floor mat protectors.
- Make sure you understand and observe all legislative and personal safety procedures when carrying out practical assignments. If you are unsure of what these are, ask your supervisor/instructor.

▶ **TASK** Clean, inspect, and measure cylinder walls or liners for wear and damage; determine needed action.

MTST
I.C.8; P2

Time off_____

Time on_____

Total time_____

Student Instructions: Read through the entire procedure prior to starting. Prepare your workspace and any tools or parts that may be needed to complete the task. When directed by your supervisor/instructor, begin the procedure to complete the task and check the box as each step is finished.

Note: This tasksheet will require the student to check the condition of miscellaneous vehicle fluids, some of which may be flammable and could damage the environment or cause health problems if not handled properly. Observe all safety precautions and follow local regulations for the proper disposal of fluids.

Procedure:	Step Completed
1. Referring to the manufacturer's workshop materials, inspect and measure liners/cylinder walls for wear and damage; record specifications below.	
a. Cylinder diameter: _____ in./mm	☐
b. Cylinder taper: _____ in./mm	☐
c. Cylinder out-of-round: _____ in./mm	☐
d. Minimum wall thickness: _____ in./mm	☐
2. Visually inspect the liners/cylinder walls for damage such as pitting and cracks.	
a. Meets the manufacturer's specifications: Yes: ☐ No: ☐	☐
b. If No, list the recommendations for rectification:	☐
3. Referring to the manufacturer's workshop materials and using the correct recommended tools, measure and record the reading for each engine's liners/cylinder walls; record your findings below.	

a. #1
   Diameter (top) _____ in./mm
   Diameter @ 90° (top) _____ in./mm
   Diameter (bottom) _____ in./mm
   Diameter @ 90° (bottom) _____ in./mm
   Taper _____ in./mm
   Out-of-round _____ in./mm
	☐

b. #2
   Diameter (top) _____ in./mm
   Diameter @ 90° (top) _____ in./mm
   Diameter (bottom) _____ in./mm
   Diameter @ 90° (bottom) _____ in./mm
   Taper _____ in./mm
   Out-of-round _____ in./mm
	☐

c. #3
   Diameter (top) _____ in./mm
   Diameter @ 90° (top) _____ in./mm
   Diameter (bottom) _____ in./mm
   Diameter @ 90° (bottom) _____ in./mm
   Taper _____ in./mm
   Out-of-round _____ in./mm
	☐

d. #4
    Diameter (top) _____ in./mm
    Diameter @ 90° (top) _____ in./mm
    Diameter (bottom) _____ in./mm
    Diameter @ 90° (bottom) _____ in./mm
    Taper _____ in./mm
    Out-of-round _____ in./mm
	☐

e. #5
    Diameter (top) _____ in./mm
    Diameter @ 90° (top) _____ in./mm
    Diameter (bottom) _____ in./mm
    Diameter @ 90° (bottom) _____ in./mm
    Taper _____ in./mm
    Out-of-round _____ in./mm
	☐

f. #6
    Diameter (top) _____ in./mm
    Diameter @ 90° (top) _____ in./mm
    Diameter (bottom) _____ in./mm
    Diameter @ 90° (bottom) _____ in./mm
    Taper _____ in./mm
    Out-of-round _____ in./mm
	☐

4. Meets the manufacturer's specifications: Yes: ☐ No: ☐	☐
a. If No, list the recommendations for rectification:	☐
5. Discuss your findings with your supervisor/instructor.	☐

Non-Task-Specific Evaluations:	Step Completed
1. Tools and equipment were used as directed and returned in good working order.	☐
2. Complied with all general and task-specific safety standards, including proper use of any personal protection equipment.	☐
3. Completed the task in an appropriate time frame (recommendation: 1.5 or 2 times the flat rate).	☐
4. Left the workspace clean and orderly.	☐
5. Cared for customer property and returned it undamaged.	☐

Student signature _____ Date _____

Comments:

Have your supervisor/instructor verify satisfactory completion of this procedure, any observations made, and any necessary action(s) recommended.

Evaluation Instructions: The scoring box below is intended to act as a guide for both student and supervisor/instructor. Each criterion listed will help students to understand what is expected of them and help supervisors/instructors articulate the level of success at a particular task. The scoring is set up to allow a second attempt at each task (see the Test and Retest columns). Scoring is also designed to award students points only for task criteria that were completed correctly. Points are lost for failure to complete the employability requirements (see Non-Task-Specific Evaluation criteria). When all criteria are evaluated, tally the points for a total at the bottom of each column.

Tasksheet Scoring

	Test		Retest	
Evaluation Items	**Pass**	**Fail**	**Pass**	**Fail**
Task-Specific Evaluation	**(1 pt)**	**(0 pts)**	**(1 pt)**	**(0 pts)**
Student properly inspected cylinder condition.				
Student properly inspected cylinder diameter.				
Student properly inspected cylinder taper.				
Student properly inspected cylinder out-of-round.				
Non-Task-Specific Evaluation	**(0 pts)**	**(−1 pt)**	**(0 pts)**	**(−1 pt)**
Student successfully completed at least three of the non-task-specific steps.				
Student successfully completed all five of the non-task-specific steps.				
Total Score: <total # of points/4 = %>				

Supervisor/Instructor:

Supervisor/instructor signature _____ Date _____

Comments:

Retest supervisor/instructor signature _____ Date _____

Comments:

CDX Tasksheet Number: MHT1C009

Student/Intern Information

Name _____ Date _____ Class _____

Vehicle, Customer, and Service Information

Vehicle used for this activity:

Year _____ Make _____ Model _____

Odometer _____ VIN _____

Materials Required
- Vehicle with possible engine concern
- Engine manufacturer's workshop materials
- Manufacturer-specific tools depending on the concern/procedure(s)
- Vehicle/component lifting equipment, if applicable

Task-Specific Safety Considerations
- Activities may require test-driving the vehicle on the school grounds or on a hoist, both of which carry severe risks. Attempt this task only with full permission from your supervisor/instructor, and follow all the guidelines exactly.
- Lifting equipment and machines such as vehicle jacks and stands, vehicle hoists, and engine hoists are important tools that increase productivity and make the job easier. However, they can also cause severe injury or death if used improperly. Make sure you follow the manufacturer's operation procedures. Also make sure you have your supervisor's/instructor's permission to use any particular type of lifting equipment.
- Comply with personal and environmental safety practices associated with clothing; eye protection; hand tools; power equipment; proper ventilation; and the handling, storage, and disposal of chemicals/materials in accordance with federal, state, and local regulations.
- Always wear the correct protective eyewear and clothing and use the appropriate safety equipment, as well as wheel chocks, fender covers, seat protectors, and floor mat protectors.
- Make sure you understand and observe all legislative and personal safety procedures when carrying out practical assignments. If you are unsure of what these are, ask your supervisor/instructor.

▶ **TASK** Replace/reinstall cylinder liners and seals; check and adjust liner height (protrusion). **MTST** *I.C.9; P2*

Time off_____

Time on_____

Student Instructions: Read through the entire procedure prior to starting. Prepare your workspace and any tools or parts that may be needed to complete the task. When directed by your supervisor/instructor, begin the procedure to complete the task and check the box as each step is finished.

Total time_____

Note: This tasksheet will require the student to check the condition of miscellaneous vehicle fluids, some of which may be flammable and could damage the environment or cause health problems if not handled properly. Observe all safety precautions and follow local regulations for the proper disposal of fluids.

Procedure:	Step Completed
1. Reference the manufacturer's workshop materials; record the procedure for checking liner height (protrusion):	☐
2. Reference the manufacturer's workshop materials; record the manufacturer's specification for liner height (protrusion): _____ in./mm	☐
3. Install cylinder liners and record protrusion.	☐
a. #1 Liner height (protrusion) _____ in./mm	☐
b. #2 Liner height (protrusion) _____ in./mm	☐
c. #3 Liner height (protrusion) _____ in./mm	☐
d. #4 Liner height (protrusion) _____ in./mm	☐
e. #5 Liner height (protrusion) _____ in./mm	☐
f. #6 Liner height (protrusion) _____ in./mm	☐
4. Meets the manufacturer's specifications: Yes: ☐ No: ☐	☐
a. If No, list the recommendations for rectification:	☐
5. Discuss the findings with your supervisor/instructor.	☐

Non-Task-Specific Evaluations:	Step Completed
1. Tools and equipment were used as directed and returned in good working order.	
2. Complied with all general and task-specific safety standards, including proper use of any personal protection equipment.	
3. Completed the task in an appropriate time frame (recommendation: 1.5 or 2 times the flat rate).	
4. Left the workspace clean and orderly.	
5. Cared for customer property and returned it undamaged.	

Student signature _____ Date _____

Comments:

Have your supervisor/instructor verify satisfactory completion of this procedure, any observations made, and any necessary action(s) recommended.

Evaluation Instructions: The scoring box below is intended to act as a guide for both student and supervisor/instructor. Each criterion listed will help students to understand what is expected of them and help supervisors/instructors articulate the level of success at a particular task. The scoring is set up to allow a second attempt at each task (see the Test and Retest columns). Scoring is also designed to award students points only for task criteria that were completed correctly. Points are lost for failure to complete the employability requirements (see Non-Task-Specific Evaluation criteria). When all criteria are evaluated, tally the points for a total at the bottom of each column.

Tasksheet Scoring

Evaluation Items	Test Pass	Test Fail	Retest Pass	Retest Fail
Task-Specific Evaluation	**(1 pt)**	**(0 pts)**	**(1 pt)**	**(0 pts)**
Student accurately recorded the procedure for checking liner height (protrusion).				
Student accurately recorded the manufacturer's specifications.				
Student properly installed cylinder liners.				
Student properly checked cylinder liner height (protrusion).				
Non-Task-Specific Evaluation	**(0 pts)**	**(−1 pt)**	**(0 pts)**	**(−1 pt)**
Student successfully completed at least three of the non-task-specific steps.				
Student successfully completed all five of the non-task-specific steps.				
Total Score: <total # of points/4 = %>				

CDX Tasksheet Number: MHT1C010

Student/Intern Information

Name _____ Date _____ Class _____

Vehicle, Customer, and Service Information

Vehicle used for this activity:

Year _____ Make _____ Model _____

Odometer _____ VIN _____

Materials Required
- Vehicle with possible engine concern
- Engine manufacturer's workshop materials
- Manufacturer-specific tools depending on the concern/procedure(s)
- Vehicle/component lifting equipment, if applicable

Task-Specific Safety Considerations
- Activities may require test-driving the vehicle on the school grounds or on a hoist, both of which carry severe risks. Attempt this task only with full permission from your supervisor/instructor, and follow all the guidelines exactly.
- Lifting equipment and machines such as vehicle jacks and stands, vehicle hoists, and engine hoists are important tools that increase productivity and make the job easier. However, they can also cause severe injury or death if used improperly. Make sure you follow the manufacturer's operation procedures. Also make sure you have your supervisor's/instructor's permission to use any particular type of lifting equipment.
- Comply with personal and environmental safety practices associated with clothing; eye protection; hand tools; power equipment; proper ventilation; and the handling, storage, and disposal of chemicals/materials in accordance with federal, state, and local regulations.
- Always wear the correct protective eyewear and clothing and use the appropriate safety equipment, as well as wheel chocks, fender covers, seat protectors, and floor mat protectors.
- Make sure you understand and observe all legislative and personal safety procedures when carrying out practical assignments. If you are unsure of what these are, ask your supervisor/instructor.

▶ **TASK** Inspect in-block camshaft bearings for wear and damage; determine needed action.

MTST I.C.10; P3

Time off_____

Time on_____

Student Instructions: Read through the entire procedure prior to starting. Prepare your workspace and any tools or parts that may be needed to complete the task. When directed by your supervisor/instructor, begin the procedure to complete the task and check the box as each step is finished.

Total time_____

Note: This tasksheet will require the student to check the condition of miscellaneous vehicle fluids, some of which may be flammable and could damage the environment or cause health problems if not handled properly. Observe all safety precautions and follow local regulations for the proper disposal of fluids.

Procedure:	Step Completed
1. While referring to the manufacturer's workshop materials, record the in-block camshaft bearings specifications.	
a. Bearing diameter (inner): _____ in./mm	☐
b. Bearing taper (inner): _____ in./mm	☐
c. Bearing out-of-round (inner): _____ in./mm	☐
d. Minimum wall thickness: _____ in./mm	☐
2. Referring to the manufacturer's workshop materials and using the correct recommended tools, measure and record the reading for each engine's in-block camshaft bearing; record your findings below.	☐
a. #1 Diameter (inner) front _____ in./mm Diameter @ 90° (inner) front _____ in./mm Diameter (inner) rear _____ in./mm Diameter @ 90° (inner) rear _____ in./mm Taper _____ in./mm Out-of-round _____ in./mm	☐
b. #2 Diameter (inner) front _____ in./mm Diameter @ 90° (inner) front _____ in./mm Diameter (inner) rear _____ in./mm Diameter @ 90° (inner) rear _____ in./mm Taper _____ in./mm Out-of-round _____ in./mm	☐
c. #3 Diameter (inner) front _____ in./mm Diameter @ 90° (inner) front _____ in./mm Diameter (inner) rear _____ in./mm Diameter @ 90° (inner) rear _____ in./mm Taper _____ in./mm Out-of-round _____ in./mm	☐
d. #4 Diameter (inner) front _____ in./mm Diameter @ 90° (inner) front _____ in./mm Diameter (inner) rear _____ in./mm Diameter @ 90° (inner) rear _____ in./mm Taper _____ in./mm Out-of-round _____ in./mm	☐

e. #5
    Diameter (inner) front _____ in./mm
    Diameter @ 90° (inner) front _____ in./mm
    Diameter (inner) rear _____ in./mm
    Diameter @ 90° (inner) rear _____ in./mm
    Taper _____ in./mm
    Out-of-round _____ in./mm
	☐

f. #6
    Diameter (inner) front _____ in./mm
    Diameter @ 90° (inner) front _____ in./mm
    Diameter (inner) rear _____ in./mm
    Diameter @ 90° (inner) rear _____ in./mm
    Taper _____ in./mm
    Out-of-round _____ in./mm
	☐

g. #7
    Diameter (inner) front _____ in./mm
    Diameter @ 90° (inner) front _____ in./mm
    Diameter (inner) rear _____ in./mm
    Diameter @ 90° (inner) rear _____ in./mm
    Taper _____ in./mm
    Out-of-round _____ in./mm
	☐

h. #8
    Diameter (inner) front _____ in./mm
    Diameter @ 90° (inner) front _____ in./mm
    Diameter (inner) rear _____ in./mm
    Diameter @ 90° (inner) rear _____ in./mm
    Taper _____ in./mm
    Out-of-round _____ in./mm
	☐

3. Meets the manufacturer's specifications: Yes: ☐ No: ☐	☐
a. If No, list recommendations for rectification:	☐
4. Discuss your findings with your supervisor/instructor.	☐

Non-Task-Specific Evaluations:	Step Completed
1. Tools and equipment were used as directed and returned in good working order.	☐
2. Complied with all general and task-specific safety standards, including proper use of any personal protection equipment.	☐
3. Completed the task in an appropriate time frame (recommendation: 1.5 or 2 times the flat rate).	☐
4. Left the workspace clean and orderly.	☐
5. Cared for customer property and returned it undamaged.	☐

Student signature _____ Date _____

Comments:

Have your supervisor/instructor verify satisfactory completion of this procedure, any observations made, and any necessary action(s) recommended.

Evaluation Instructions: The scoring box below is intended to act as a guide for both student and supervisor/instructor. Each criterion listed will help students to understand what is expected of them and help supervisors/instructors articulate the level of success at a particular task. The scoring is set up to allow a second attempt at each task (see the Test and Retest columns). Scoring is also designed to award students points only for task criteria that were completed correctly. Points are lost for failure to complete the employability requirements (see Non-Task-Specific Evaluation criteria). When all criteria are evaluated, tally the points for a total at the bottom of each column.

Tasksheet Scoring

Evaluation Items	Test		Retest	
	Pass	Fail	Pass	Fail
Task-Specific Evaluation	**(1 pt)**	**(0 pts)**	**(1 pt)**	**(0 pts)**
Student properly inspected bearing condition.				
Student properly inspected bearing diameter.				
Student properly inspected bearing taper.				
Student properly inspected bearing out-of-round.				
Non-Task-Specific Evaluation	**(0 pts)**	**(−1 pt)**	**(0 pts)**	**(−1 pt)**
Student successfully completed at least three of the non-task-specific steps.				
Student successfully completed all five of the non-task-specific steps.				
Total Score: <total # of points/4 = %>				

Supervisor/Instructor:

Supervisor/instructor signature _____ Date _____

Comments:

[ ]

Retest supervisor/instructor signature _____ Date _____

Comments:

[ ]

CDX Tasksheet Number: MHT1C011

Student/Intern Information

Name _____ Date _____ Class _____

Vehicle, Customer, and Service Information

Vehicle used for this activity:

Year _____ Make _____ Model _____

Odometer _____ VIN _____

Materials Required

- Vehicle with possible engine concern
- Engine manufacturer's workshop materials
- Manufacturer-specific tools depending on the concern/procedure(s)
- Vehicle/component lifting equipment, if applicable

Task-Specific Safety Considerations

- Activities may require test-driving the vehicle on the school grounds or on a hoist, both of which carry severe risks. Attempt this task only with full permission from your supervisor/instructor, and follow all the guidelines exactly.
- Lifting equipment and machines such as vehicle jacks and stands, vehicle hoists, and engine hoists are important tools that increase productivity and make the job easier. However, they can also cause severe injury or death if used improperly. Make sure you follow the manufacturer's operation procedures. Also make sure you have your supervisor's/instructor's permission to use any particular type of lifting equipment.
- Comply with personal and environmental safety practices associated with clothing; eye protection; hand tools; power equipment; proper ventilation; and the handling, storage, and disposal of chemicals/materials in accordance with federal, state, and local regulations.
- Always wear the correct protective eyewear and clothing and use the appropriate safety equipment, as well as wheel chocks, fender covers, seat protectors, and floor mat protectors.
- Make sure you understand and observe all legislative and personal safety procedures when carrying out practical assignments. If you are unsure of what these are, ask your supervisor/instructor.

▶ **TASK** Inspect, measure, and replace/reinstall in-block camshaft; measure/adjust end play and backlash; determine needed action.

MTST
I.C.1; P3

Time off_____

Time on_____

Total time_____

Student Instructions: Read through the entire procedure prior to starting. Prepare your workspace and any tools or parts that may be needed to complete the task. When directed by your supervisor/instructor, begin the procedure to complete the task and check the box as each step is finished.

Note: This tasksheet will require the student to check the condition of miscellaneous vehicle fluids, some of which may be flammable and could damage the environment or cause health problems if not handled properly. Observe all safety precautions and follow local regulations for the proper disposal of fluids.

Procedure:	Step Completed
1. Following the manufacturer's workshop materials; list the procedures for installing the camshaft in the engine block:	☐
2. Install the camshaft in the engine block. (**Note:** Use extreme care; camshaft lobes are very sharp.)	
a. Once the camshaft is installed, you should be able to turn it by hand with very little effort. Yes: ☐ No: ☐	☐
b. If No, remove camshaft and check bearings for damage, misalignment, or debris. Discuss findings with your supervisor/instructor and record them:	☐
3. Install all retaining brackets and torque to the manufacturer's specifications.	
a. Manufacturer's specified torque: _____ ft-lb (N•m)	☐
4. Following the procedures listed in the manufacturer's workshop materials, use the recommended special tools to measure/adjust end play and backlash.	
a. Manufacturer's specified end play: _____ in./mm	☐
b. Actual end play measurement: _____ in./mm	☐
c. Manufacturer's specified backlash: _____ in./mm	☐
d. Actual backlash measurement: _____ in./mm	☐
5. Meets the manufacturer's specifications: Yes: ☐ No: ☐	☐
a. If No, list the recommendations for any rectifications:	☐

	Step Completed
6. Have your supervisor/instructor inspect your assembled camshaft to this point and discuss the findings.	☐

Non-Task-Specific Evaluations:	Step Completed
1. Tools and equipment were used as directed and returned in good working order.	☐
2. Complied with all general and task-specific safety standards, including proper use of any personal protection equipment.	☐
3. Completed the task in an appropriate time frame (recommendation: 1.5 or 2 times the flat rate).	☐
4. Left the workspace clean and orderly.	☐
5. Cared for customer property and returned it undamaged.	☐

Student signature _____ Date _____

Comments:

Have your supervisor/instructor verify satisfactory completion of this procedure, any observations made, and any necessary action(s) recommended.

Evaluation Instructions: The scoring box below is intended to act as a guide for both student and supervisor/instructor. Each criterion listed will help students to understand what is expected of them and help supervisors/instructors articulate the level of success at a particular task. The scoring is set up to allow a second attempt at each task (see the Test and Retest columns). Scoring is also designed to award students points only for task criteria that were completed correctly. Points are lost for failure to complete the employability requirements (see Non-Task-Specific Evaluation criteria). When all criteria are evaluated, tally the points for a total at the bottom of each column.

Tasksheet Scoring

Evaluation Items	Test		Retest	
	Pass	**Fail**	**Pass**	**Fail**
Task-Specific Evaluation	**(1 pt)**	**(0 pts)**	**(1 pt)**	**(0 pts)**
Student assembled camshaft, following the manufacturer's directions and using the proper tooling.				
Student properly installed and torqued all retaining brackets.				
Student set camshaft end play to manufacturer's specifications.				
Student set camshaft backlash to manufacturer's specifications.				
Non-Task-Specific Evaluation	**(0 pts)**	**(−1 pt)**	**(0 pts)**	**(−1 pt)**
Student successfully completed at least three of the non-task-specific steps.				
Student successfully completed all five of the non-task-specific steps.				
Total Score: <total # of points/4 = %>				

CDX Tasksheet Number: MHT1C012

Student/Intern Information

Name _____ Date _____ Class _____

Vehicle, Customer, and Service Information

Vehicle used for this activity:

Year _____ Make _____ Model _____

Odometer _____ VIN _____

Materials Required

- Vehicle with possible engine concern
- Engine manufacturer's workshop materials
- Manufacturer-specific tools depending on the concern/procedure(s)
- Vehicle/component lifting equipment, if applicable

Task-Specific Safety Considerations

- Activities may require test-driving the vehicle on the school grounds or on a hoist, both of which carry severe risks. Attempt this task only with full permission from your supervisor/instructor, and follow all the guidelines exactly.
- Lifting equipment and machines such as vehicle jacks and stands, vehicle hoists, and engine hoists are important tools that increase productivity and make the job easier. However, they can also cause severe injury or death if used improperly. Make sure you follow the manufacturer's operation procedures. Also make sure you have your supervisor's/instructor's permission to use any particular type of lifting equipment.
- Comply with personal and environmental safety practices associated with clothing; eye protection; hand tools; power equipment; proper ventilation; and the handling, storage, and disposal of chemicals/materials in accordance with federal, state, and local regulations.
- Always wear the correct protective eyewear and clothing and use the appropriate safety equipment, as well as wheel chocks, fender covers, seat protectors, and floor mat protectors.
- Make sure you understand and observe all legislative and personal safety procedures when carrying out practical assignments. If you are unsure of what these are, ask your supervisor/instructor.

▶ **TASK** Clean and inspect crankshaft for surface cracks and journal damage; check condition of oil passages; check passage plugs; measure journal diameter; determine needed action.

MTST
I.C.12; P2

Time off_____

Time on_____

Total time_____

Student Instructions: Read through the entire procedure prior to starting. Prepare your workspace and any tools or parts that may be needed to complete the task. When directed by your supervisor/instructor, begin the procedure to complete the task and check the box as each step is finished.

Note: This tasksheet will require the student to check the condition of miscellaneous vehicle fluids, some of which may be flammable and could damage the environment or cause health problems if not handled properly. Observe all safety precautions and follow local regulations for the proper disposal of fluids.

Procedure:	Step Completed
1. Visually inspect the crankshaft for surface cracks and damage.	
a. Meets the manufacturer's specifications: Yes: ☐ No: ☐	☐
b. If No, list the recommendations for rectification:	☐
2. Check all oil passages and plugs.	
a. Meets the manufacturer's specifications: Yes: ☐ No: ☐	☐
b. If No, list the recommendations for rectification:	☐
3. While referring to the manufacturer's workshop materials, measure the crankshaft main journal diameter.	
a. Main journal #1: Diameter (front of journal) _____ in./mm Diameter @ 90° (front of journal) _____ in./mm Diameter (rear of journal) _____ in./mm Diameter @ 90° (rear of journal) _____ in./mm Taper _____ in./mm Out-of-round _____ in./mm	☐
b. Main journal #2: Diameter (front of journal) _____ in./mm Diameter @ 90° (front of journal) _____ in./mm Diameter (rear of journal) _____ in./mm Diameter @ 90° (rear of journal) _____ in./mm Taper _____ in./mm Out-of-round _____ in./mm	☐
c. Main journal #3: Diameter (front of journal) _____ in./mm Diameter @ 90° (front of journal) _____ in./mm Diameter (rear of journal) _____ in./mm Diameter @ 90° (rear of journal) _____ in./mm Taper _____ in./mm Out-of-round _____ in./mm	☐

d. Main journal #4: Diameter (front of journal) _____ in./mm Diameter @ 90° (front of journal) _____ in./mm Diameter (rear of journal) _____ in./mm Diameter @ 90° (rear of journal) _____ in./mm Taper _____ in./mm Out-of-round _____ in./mm	☐
e. Main journal #5: Diameter (front of journal) _____ in./mm Diameter @ 90° (front of journal) _____ in./mm Diameter (rear of journal) _____ in./mm Diameter @ 90° (rear of journal) _____ in./mm Taper _____ in./mm Out-of-round _____ in./mm	☐
f. Main journal #6: Diameter (front of journal) _____ in./mm Diameter @ 90° (front of journal) _____ in./mm Diameter (rear of journal) _____ in./mm Diameter @ 90° (rear of journal) _____ in./mm Taper _____ in./mm Out-of-round _____ in./mm	☐
g. Main journal #7: Diameter (front of journal) _____ in./mm Diameter @ 90° (front of journal) _____ in./mm Diameter (rear of journal) _____ in./mm Diameter @ 90° (rear of journal) _____ in./mm Taper _____ in./mm Out-of-round _____ in./mm	☐
4. Meets the manufacturer's specifications: Yes: ☐ No: ☐	☐
a. If No, list the recommendations for rectification:	☐
5. While referring to the manufacturer's workshop materials, measure the crankshaft rod journal diameter:	
a. #1: Diameter (front of journal) _____ in./mm Diameter @ 90° (front of journal) _____ in./mm Diameter (rear of journal) _____ in./mm Diameter @ 90° (rear of journal) _____ in./mm Taper _____ in./mm Out-of-round _____ in./mm	☐

b. #2: Diameter (front of journal) _____ in./mm Diameter @ 90° (front of journal) _____ in./mm Diameter (rear of journal) _____ in./mm Diameter @ 90° (rear of journal) _____ in./mm Taper _____ in./mm Out-of-round _____ in./mm	☐
c. #3: Diameter (front of journal) _____ in./mm Diameter @ 90° (front of journal) _____ in./mm Diameter (rear of journal) _____ in./mm Diameter @ 90° (rear of journal) _____ in./mm Taper _____ in./mm Out-of-round _____ in./mm	☐
d. #4: Diameter (front of journal) _____ in./mm Diameter @ 90° (front of journal) _____ in./mm Diameter (rear of journal) _____ in./mm Diameter @ 90° (rear of journal) _____ in./mm Taper _____ in./mm Out-of-round _____ in./mm	☐
e. #5: Diameter (front of journal) _____ in./mm Diameter @ 90° (front of journal) _____ in./mm Diameter (rear of journal) _____ in./mm Diameter @ 90° (rear of journal) _____ in./mm Taper _____ in./mm Out-of-round _____ in./mm	☐
f. #6: Diameter (front of journal) _____ in./mm Diameter @ 90° (front of journal) _____ in./mm Diameter (rear of journal) _____ in./mm Diameter @ 90° (rear of journal) _____ in./mm Taper _____ in./mm Out-of-round _____ in./mm	☐
6. Meets the manufacturer's specifications: Yes: ☐ No: ☐	☐
a. If No, list the recommendations for rectification:	☐
7. Discuss the findings with your supervisor/instructor.	☐

Non-Task-Specific Evaluations:	Step Completed
1. Tools and equipment were used as directed and returned in good working order.	
2. Complied with all general and task-specific safety standards, including proper use of any personal protection equipment.	
3. Completed the task in an appropriate time frame (recommendation: 1.5 or 2 times the flat rate).	
4. Left the workspace clean and orderly.	
5. Cared for customer property and returned it undamaged.	

Student signature _____ Date _____

Comments:

Have your supervisor/instructor verify satisfactory completion of this procedure, any observations made, and any necessary action(s) recommended.

Evaluation Instructions: The scoring box below is intended to act as a guide for both student and supervisor/instructor. Each criterion listed will help students to understand what is expected of them and help supervisors/instructors articulate the level of success at a particular task. The scoring is set up to allow a second attempt at each task (see the Test and Retest columns). Scoring is also designed to award students points only for task criteria that were completed correctly. Points are lost for failure to complete the employability requirements (see Non-Task-Specific Evaluation criteria). When all criteria are evaluated, tally the points for a total at the bottom of each column.

Tasksheet Scoring

Evaluation Items	Test		Retest	
	Pass	**Fail**	**Pass**	**Fail**
Task-Specific Evaluation	**(1 pt)**	**(0 pts)**	**(1 pt)**	**(0 pts)**
Student properly inspected journal (main and rod) condition.				
Student properly inspected journal (main and rod) diameter.				
Student properly inspected journal (main and rod) taper.				
Student properly inspected journal (main and rod) out-of-round.				
Non-Task-Specific Evaluation	**(0 pts)**	**(−1 pt)**	**(0 pts)**	**(−1 pt)**
Student successfully completed at least three of the non-task-specific steps.				
Student successfully completed all five of the non-task-specific steps.				
Total Score: <total # of points/4 = %>				

CDX Tasksheet Number: MHT1C013

Student/Intern Information

Name _____ Date _____ Class _____

Vehicle, Customer, and Service Information

Vehicle used for this activity:

Year _____ Make _____ Model _____

Odometer _____ VIN _____

Task-Specific Safety Considerations

- Activities may require test-driving the vehicle on the school grounds or on a hoist, both of which carry severe risks. Attempt this task only with full permission from your supervisor/instructor, and follow all the guidelines exactly.
- Lifting equipment and machines such as vehicle jacks and stands, vehicle hoists, and engine hoists are important tools that increase productivity and make the job easier. However, they can also cause severe injury or death if used improperly. Make sure you follow the manufacturer's operation procedures. Also make sure you have your supervisor's/instructor's permission to use any particular type of lifting equipment.
- Comply with personal and environmental safety practices associated with clothing; eye protection; hand tools; power equipment; proper ventilation; and the handling, storage, and disposal of chemicals/materials in accordance with federal, state, and local regulations.
- Always wear the correct protective eyewear and clothing and use the appropriate safety equipment, as well as wheel chocks, fender covers, seat protectors, and floor mat protectors.
- Make sure you understand and observe all legislative and personal safety procedures when carrying out practical assignments. If you are unsure of what these are, ask your supervisor/instructor.

▶ **TASK** Inspect main bearings for wear patterns and damage; replace as needed; check bearing clearances; check and correct crankshaft end play. **MTST** I.C.13; P2

Time off _____

Time on _____

Total time _____

Student Instructions: Read through the entire procedure prior to starting. Prepare your workspace and any tools or parts that may be needed to complete the task. When directed by your supervisor/instructor, begin the procedure to complete the task and check the box as each step is finished.

Note: This tasksheet will require the student to check the condition of miscellaneous vehicle fluids, some of which may be flammable and could damage the environment or cause health problems if not handled properly. Observe all safety precautions and follow local regulations for the proper disposal of fluids.

Procedure:	Step Completed
1. Reference the manufacturer's workshop materials; inspect the main bearings for wear patterns and damage.	
a. Meets the manufacturer's specifications: Yes: ☐ No: ☐	☐
b. If No, list the recommendations for rectification:	☐
2. Referring to the manufacturer's workshop materials and using the correct recommended tools, measure and record the reading for each crankshaft main bearing clearance. Manufacturer's specification: _____ in./mm	☐
a. #1: _____ in./mm	☐
b. #2: _____ in./mm	☐
c. #3: _____ in./mm	☐
d. #4: _____ in./mm	☐
e. #5: _____ in./mm	☐
f. #6: _____ in./mm	☐
g. #7: _____ in./mm	☐
3. Meets the manufacturer's specifications: Yes: ☐ No: ☐	☐
a. If No, list the recommendations for rectification:	☐
4. While referring to the manufacturer's workshop materials, install the crankshaft and torque the main bearing caps. (**Note:** The crankshaft should turn by hand after installation. If not, remove the crankshaft and check for misaligned bearings or contamination.)	
a. Manufacturer's torque specification/procedure:	☐

	Step Completed
5. While referring to the manufacturer's workshop materials, measure the crankshaft end play. Manufacturer's specification: _____ in./mm	☐
a. Actual crankshaft end play: _____ in./mm	☐
b. Meets the manufacturer's specifications: Yes: ☐ No: ☐	☐
c. If No, list the recommendations for rectification:	☐
6. Discuss the findings with your supervisor/instructor.	☐

Non-Task-Specific Evaluations:	Step Completed
1. Tools and equipment were used as directed and returned in good working order.	☐
2. Complied with all general and task-specific safety standards, including proper use of any personal protection equipment.	☐
3. Completed the task in an appropriate time frame (recommendation: 1.5 or 2 times the flat rate).	☐
4. Left the workspace clean and orderly.	☐
5. Cared for customer property and returned it undamaged.	☐

Student signature _____ Date _____

Comments:

Have your supervisor/instructor verify satisfactory completion of this procedure, any observations made, and any necessary action(s) recommended.

Evaluation Instructions: The scoring box below is intended to act as a guide for both student and supervisor/instructor. Each criterion listed will help students to understand what is expected of them and help supervisors/instructors articulate the level of success at a particular task. The scoring is set up to allow a second attempt at each task (see the Test and Retest columns). Scoring is also designed to award students points only for task criteria that were completed correctly. Points are lost for failure to complete the employability requirements (see Non-Task-Specific Evaluation criteria). When all criteria are evaluated, tally the points for a total at the bottom of each column.

Tasksheet Scoring

Evaluation Items	Test		Retest	
	Pass	Fail	Pass	Fail
Task-Specific Evaluation	**(1 pt)**	**(0 pts)**	**(1 pt)**	**(0 pts)**
Student properly inspected bearings.				
Student properly checked crankshaft main bearing clearance.				
Student properly installed/torqued crankshaft.				
Student properly checked crankshaft end play.				
Non-Task-Specific Evaluation	**(0 pts)**	**(−1 pt)**	**(0 pts)**	**(−1 pt)**
Student successfully completed at least three of the non-task-specific steps.				
Student successfully completed all five of the non-task-specific steps.				
Total Score: <total # of points/4 = %>				

Supervisor/Instructor:

Supervisor/instructor signature _____ Date _____

Comments:

[ ]

Retest supervisor/instructor signature _____ Date _____

Comments:

[ ]

CDX Tasksheet Number: MHT1C014

Student/Intern Information

Name _____ Date _____ Class _____

Vehicle, Customer, and Service Information

Vehicle used for this activity:

Year _____ Make _____ Model _____

Odometer _____ VIN _____

Materials Required

- Vehicle with possible engine concern
- Engine manufacturer's workshop materials
- Manufacturer-specific tools depending on the concern/procedure(s)
- Vehicle/component lifting equipment, if applicable

Task-Specific Safety Considerations

- Activities may require test-driving the vehicle on the school grounds or on a hoist, both of which carry severe risks. Attempt this task only with full permission from your supervisor/instructor, and follow all the guidelines exactly.
- Lifting equipment and machines such as vehicle jacks and stands, vehicle hoists, and engine hoists are important tools that increase productivity and make the job easier. However, they can also cause severe injury or death if used improperly. Make sure you follow the manufacturer's operation procedures. Also make sure you have your supervisor's/instructor's permission to use any particular type of lifting equipment.
- Comply with personal and environmental safety practices associated with clothing; eye protection; hand tools; power equipment; proper ventilation; and the handling, storage, and disposal of chemicals/materials in accordance with federal, state, and local regulations.
- Always wear the correct protective eyewear and clothing and use the appropriate safety equipment, as well as wheel chocks, fender covers, seat protectors, and floor mat protectors.
- Make sure you understand and observe all legislative and personal safety procedures when carrying out practical assignments. If you are unsure of what these are, ask your supervisor/instructor.

▶ **TASK** Inspect, install, and time gear train; measure gear backlash; determine needed action.

MTST
I.C.14; P2

Time off_____

Time on_____

Total time_____

Student Instructions: Read through the entire procedure prior to starting. Prepare your workspace and any tools or parts that may be needed to complete the task. When directed by your supervisor/instructor, begin the procedure to complete the task and check the box as each step is finished.

Note: This tasksheet will require the student to check the condition of miscellaneous vehicle fluids, some of which may be flammable and could damage the environment or cause health problems if not handled properly. Observe all safety precautions and follow local regulations for the proper disposal of fluids.

Procedure:	Step Completed
1. Reference the manufacturer's workshop materials; install gear train; have your supervisor/instructor verify correct timing.	
a. Meets the manufacturer's specifications: Yes: ☐ No: ☐	☐
b. If No, list the recommendations for rectification:	☐
2. Referring to the manufacturer's workshop materials and using the correct recommended tools, measure and record timing gear backlash. Manufacturer's specification: _____ in./mm	☐
a. Actual timing gear backlash: _____ in./mm	☐
3. Meets the manufacturer's specifications: Yes: ☐ No: ☐	☐
a. If No, list the recommendations for rectification:	☐
4. Discuss the findings with your supervisor/instructor.	☐

Non-Task-Specific Evaluations:	Step Completed
1. Tools and equipment were used as directed and returned in good working order.	
2. Complied with all general and task-specific safety standards, including proper use of any personal protection equipment.	
3. Completed the task in an appropriate time frame (recommendation: 1.5 or 2 times the flat rate).	
4. Left the workspace clean and orderly.	
5. Cared for customer property and returned it undamaged.	

Student signature _____ Date _____

Comments:

Have your supervisor/instructor verify satisfactory completion of this procedure, any observations made,

and any necessary action(s) recommended.

Evaluation Instructions: The scoring box below is intended to act as a guide for both student and supervisor/instructor. Each criterion listed will help students to understand what is expected of them and help supervisors/instructors articulate the level of success at a particular task. The scoring is set up to allow a second attempt at each task (see the Test and Retest columns). Scoring is also designed to award students points only for task criteria that were completed correctly. Points are lost for failure to complete the employability requirements (see Non-Task-Specific Evaluation criteria). When all criteria are evaluated, tally the points for a total at the bottom of each column.

Tasksheet Scoring

Evaluation Items	Test		Retest	
	Pass	**Fail**	**Pass**	**Fail**
Task-Specific Evaluation	**(1 pt)**	**(0 pts)**	**(1 pt)**	**(0 pts)**
Student properly inspected timing components.				
Student properly installed timing components.				
Student properly used recommended measuring tools.				
Student properly recorded timing gear backlash.				
Non-Task-Specific Evaluation	**(0 pts)**	**(−1 pt)**	**(0 pts)**	**(−1 pt)**
Student successfully completed at least three of the non-task-specific steps.				
Student successfully completed all five of the non-task-specific steps.				
Total Score: <total # of points/4 = %>				

CDX Tasksheet Number: MHT1C015

Student/Intern Information

Name _____ Date _____ Class _____

Vehicle, Customer, and Service Information

Vehicle used for this activity:

Year _____ Make _____ Model _____

Odometer _____ VIN _____

Materials Required

- Vehicle with possible engine concern
- Engine manufacturer's workshop materials
- Manufacturer-specific tools depending on the concern/procedure(s)
- Vehicle/component lifting equipment, if applicable

Task-Specific Safety Considerations

- Activities may require test-driving the vehicle on the school grounds or on a hoist, both of which carry severe risks. Attempt this task only with full permission from your supervisor/instructor, and follow all the guidelines exactly.
- Lifting equipment and machines such as vehicle jacks and stands, vehicle hoists, and engine hoists are important tools that increase productivity and make the job easier. However, they can also cause severe injury or death if used improperly. Make sure you follow the manufacturer's operation procedures. Also make sure you have your supervisor's/instructor's permission to use any particular type of lifting equipment.
- Comply with personal and environmental safety practices associated with clothing; eye protection; hand tools; power equipment; proper ventilation; and the handling, storage, and disposal of chemicals/materials in accordance with federal, state, and local regulations.
- Always wear the correct protective eyewear and clothing and use the appropriate safety equipment, as well as wheel chocks, fender covers, seat protectors, and floor mat protectors.
- Make sure you understand and observe all legislative and personal safety procedures when carrying out practical assignments. If you are unsure of what these are, ask your supervisor/instructor.

▶ **TASK** Inspect connecting rod and bearings for wear patterns; measure pistons, pins, retainers, and bushings; determine needed action. **MTST** *I.C.15; P3*

Time off_____

Time on_____

Total time_____

Student Instructions: Read through the entire procedure prior to starting. Prepare your workspace and any tools or parts that may be needed to complete the task. When directed by your supervisor/instructor, begin the procedure to complete the task and check the box as each step is finished.

Note: This tasksheet will require the student to check the condition of miscellaneous vehicle fluids, some of which may be flammable and could damage the environment or cause health problems if not handled properly. Observe all safety precautions and follow local regulations for the proper disposal of fluids.

Procedure:	Step Completed
1. Referencing the manufacturer's workshop materials, inspect connecting rod, pistons, and bearings for damage and abnormal wear patterns.	
a. Meets the manufacturer's specifications: Yes: ☐ No: ☐	☐
b. If No, list the recommendations for rectification:	☐
2. Referencing the manufacturer's workshop materials, record piston and pin specifications.	
a. Piston diameter: _____ in./mm	☐
b. Piston pin diameter: _____ in./mm	☐
3. Referring to the manufacturer's workshop materials and using the correct recommended tools, measure and record the reading for each piston and pin.	

a. #1 Piston:
    Diameter (top) _____ in./mm
    Diameter @ 90° (top) _____ in./mm
    Diameter (bottom) _____ in./mm
    Diameter @ 90° (bottom) _____ in./mm
    Taper _____ in./mm
    Out-of-round _____ in./mm
    Piston pin diameter (outside) _____ in./mm
	☐

b. #2 Piston:
    Diameter (top) _____ in./mm
    Diameter @ 90° (top) _____ in./mm
    Diameter (bottom) _____ in./mm
    Diameter @ 90° (bottom) _____ in./mm
    Taper _____ in./mm
    Out-of-round _____ in./mm
    Piston pin diameter (outside) _____ in./mm
	☐

c. #3 Piston:
    Diameter (top) _____ in./mm
    Diameter @ 90° (top) _____ in./mm
    Diameter (bottom) _____ in./mm
    Diameter @ 90° (bottom) _____ in./mm
    Taper _____ in./mm
    Out-of-round _____ in./mm
    Piston pin diameter (outside) _____ in./mm
	☐

© 2021 Jones & Bartlett Learning, LLC, an Ascend Learning Company

d. #4 Piston: Diameter (top) _____ in./mm Diameter @ 90° (top) _____ in./mm Diameter (bottom) _____ in./mm Diameter @ 90° (bottom) _____ in./mm Taper _____ in./mm Out-of-round _____ in./mm Piston pin diameter (outside) _____ in./mm	☐
e. #5 Piston: Diameter (top) _____ in./mm Diameter @ 90° (top) _____ in./mm Diameter (bottom) _____ in./mm Diameter @ 90° (bottom) _____ in./mm Taper _____ in./mm Out-of-round _____ in./mm Piston pin diameter (outside) _____ in./mm	☐
f. #6 Piston: Diameter (top) _____ in./mm Diameter @ 90° (top) _____ in./mm Diameter (bottom) _____ in./mm Diameter @ 90° (bottom) _____ in./mm Taper _____ in./mm Out-of-round _____ in./mm Piston pin diameter (outside) _____ in./mm	☐
4. Meets the manufacturer's specifications: Yes: ☐ No: ☐	☐
a. If No, list the recommendations for rectification:	☐
5. Referencing the manufacturer's workshop materials, record connecting rod bearing bore and pin bushing specifications:	☐
6. Referring to the manufacturer's workshop materials and using the correct recommended tools, measure and record the reading for each connecting rod bearing bore and pin bushing.	☐
a. #1 Connecting rod: Diameter _____ in./mm Diameter @ 90° _____ in./mm Out-of-round _____ in./mm Pin bushing diameter _____ in./mm Pin bushing diameter @ 90° _____ in./mm Out-of-round _____ in./mm	☐

b. #2 Connecting rod: Diameter _____ in./mm Diameter @ 90° _____ in./mm Out-of-round _____ in./mm Pin bushing diameter _____ in./mm Pin bushing diameter @ 90° _____ in./mm Out-of-round _____ in./mm	☐
c. #3 Connecting rod: Diameter _____ in./mm Diameter @ 90° _____ in./mm Out-of-round _____ in./mm Pin bushing diameter _____ in./mm Pin bushing diameter @ 90° _____ in./mm Out-of-round _____ in./mm	☐
d. #4 Connecting rod: Diameter _____ in./mm Diameter @ 90° _____ in./mm Out-of-round _____ in./mm Pin bushing diameter _____ in./mm Pin bushing diameter @ 90° _____ in./mm Out-of-round _____ in./mm	☐
e. #5 Connecting rod: Diameter _____ in./mm Diameter @ 90° _____ in./mm Out-of-round _____ in./mm Pin bushing diameter _____ in./mm Pin bushing diameter @ 90° _____ in./mm Out-of-round _____ in./mm	☐
f. #6 Connecting rod: Diameter _____ in./mm Diameter @ 90° _____ in./mm Out-of-round _____ in./mm Pin bushing diameter _____ in./mm Pin bushing diameter @ 90° _____ in./mm Out-of-round _____ in./mm	☐
7. Meets the manufacturer's specifications: Yes: ☐ No: ☐	☐
a. If No, list the recommendations for rectification:	
8. Discuss your findings with your supervisor/instructor.	☐

Non-Task-Specific Evaluations:	Step Completed
1. Tools and equipment were used as directed and returned in good working order.	☐
2. Complied with all general and task-specific safety standards, including proper use of any personal protection equipment.	☐
3. Completed the task in an appropriate time frame (recommendation: 1.5 or 2 times the flat rate).	☐
4. Left the workspace clean and orderly.	☐
5. Cared for customer property and returned it undamaged.	☐

Student signature _____ Date _____

Comments:

Have your supervisor/instructor verify satisfactory completion of this procedure, any observations made, and any necessary action(s) recommended.

Evaluation Instructions: The scoring box below is intended to act as a guide for both student and supervisor/instructor. Each criterion listed will help students to understand what is expected of them and help supervisors/instructors articulate the level of success at a particular task. The scoring is set up to allow a second attempt at each task (see the Test and Retest columns). Scoring is also designed to award students points only for task criteria that were completed correctly. Points are lost for failure to complete the employability requirements (see Non-Task-Specific Evaluation criteria). When all criteria are evaluated, tally the points for a total at the bottom of each column.

Tasksheet Scoring

Evaluation Items	Test		Retest	
	Pass	Fail	Pass	Fail
Task-Specific Evaluation	**(1 pt)**	**(0 pts)**	**(1 pt)**	**(0 pts)**
Student properly inspected pistons, pins, and connecting rod conditions.				
Student properly inspected piston diameter.				
Student properly inspected piston pin diameter.				
Student properly inspected connecting rod bearing and bushing bore.				
Non-Task-Specific Evaluation	**(0 pts)**	**(−1 pt)**	**(0 pts)**	**(−1 pt)**
Student successfully completed at least three of the non-task-specific steps.				
Student successfully completed all five of the non-task-specific steps.				
Total Score: <total # of points/4 = %>				

Supervisor/Instructor:

Supervisor/instructor signature _____ Date _____

Comments:

Retest supervisor/instructor signature _____ Date _____

Comments:

CDX Tasksheet Number: MHT1CO16

Student/Intern Information

Name _____ Date _____ Class _____

Vehicle, Customer, and Service Information

Vehicle used for this activity:

Year _____ Make _____ Model _____

Odometer _____ VIN _____

Materials Required
- Vehicle with possible engine concern
- Engine manufacturer's workshop materials
- Manufacturer-specific tools depending on the concern/procedure(s)
- Vehicle/component lifting equipment, if applicable

Task-Specific Safety Considerations
- Activities may require test-driving the vehicle on the school grounds or on a hoist, both of which carry severe risks. Attempt this task only with full permission from your supervisor/instructor, and follow all the guidelines exactly.
- Lifting equipment and machines such as vehicle jacks and stands, vehicle hoists, and engine hoists are important tools that increase productivity and make the job easier. However, they can also cause severe injury or death if used improperly. Make sure you follow the manufacturer's operation procedures. Also make sure you have your supervisor's/instructor's permission to use any particular type of lifting equipment.
- Comply with personal and environmental safety practices associated with clothing; eye protection; hand tools; power equipment; proper ventilation; and the handling, storage, and disposal of chemicals/materials in accordance with federal, state, and local regulations.
- Always wear the correct protective eyewear and clothing and use the appropriate safety equipment, as well as wheel chocks, fender covers, seat protectors, and floor mat protectors.
- Make sure you understand and observe all legislative and personal safety procedures when carrying out practical assignments. If you are unsure of what these are, ask your supervisor/instructor.

▶ **TASK** Determine piston-to-cylinder wall clearance; check ring-to-groove fit and end gap; install rings on pistons. **MTST** *I.C.16; P3*

Time off_____

Time on_____

Student Instructions: Read through the entire procedure prior to starting. Prepare your workspace and any tools or parts that may be needed to complete the task. When directed by your supervisor/instructor, begin the procedure to complete the task and check the box as each step is finished.

Total time_____

Note: This tasksheet will require the student to check the condition of miscellaneous vehicle fluids, some of which may be flammable and could damage the environment or cause health problems if not handled properly. Observe all safety precautions and follow local regulations for the proper disposal of fluids.

Procedure:	Step Completed
1. Referencing the manufacturer's workshop materials, record piston-to-cylinder wall clearance specification below.	
a. Piston-to-cylinder wall clearance: _____ in./mm	☐
2. Referring to the manufacturer's workshop materials and using the correct recommended tools, measure and record the reading for each piston-to-cylinder wall clearance.	
a. #1 Piston/Cylinder clearance _____ in./mm	☐
b. #2 Piston/Cylinder clearance _____ in./mm	☐
c. #3 Piston/Cylinder clearance _____ in./mm	☐
d. #4 Piston/Cylinder clearance _____ in./mm	☐
e. #5 Piston/Cylinder clearance _____ in./mm	☐
f. #6 Piston/Cylinder clearance _____ in./mm	☐
3. Meets the manufacturer's specifications: Yes: ☐ No: ☐	☐
a. If No, list the recommendations for rectification:	☐
4. Referencing the manufacturer's workshop materials, record piston ring end gap: Specification: _____ in./mm	☐
5. Referring to the manufacturer's workshop material and using the correct recommended tools, measure and record the piston ring end gap for each of the piston ring.	☐
a. #1 Cylinder: Compression ring #1 _____ in./mm Compression ring #2 _____ in./mm Compression ring #3 _____ in./mm Oil control ring #1 _____ in./mm Oil control ring #2 _____ in./mm	☐

b. #2 Cylinder: Compression ring #1 _____ in./mm Compression ring #2 _____ in./mm Compression ring #3 _____ in./mm Oil control ring #1 _____ in./mm Oil control ring #2 _____ in./mm	☐
c. #3 Cylinder: Compression ring #1 _____ in./mm Compression ring #2 _____ in./mm Compression ring #3 _____ in./mm Oil control ring #1 _____ in./mm Oil control ring #2 _____ in./mm	☐
d. #4 Cylinder: Compression ring #1 _____ in./mm Compression ring #2 _____ in./mm Compression ring #3 _____ in./mm Oil control ring #1 _____ in./mm Oil control ring #2 _____ in./mm	☐
e. #5 Cylinder: Compression ring #1 _____ in./mm Compression ring #2 _____ in./mm Compression ring #3 _____ in./mm Oil control ring #1 _____ in./mm Oil control ring #2 _____ in./mm	☐
f. #6 Cylinder: Compression ring #1 _____ in./mm Compression ring #2 _____ in./mm Compression ring #3 _____ in./mm Oil control ring #1 _____ in./mm Oil control ring #2 _____ in./mm	☐
6. Meets the manufacturer's specifications: Yes: ☐ No: ☐	☐
a. If No, list the recommendations for rectification:	☐
7. Referencing the manufacturer's workshop materials, install rings on pistons.	☐
8. Discuss your findings with your supervisor/instructor.	☐

Non-Task-Specific Evaluations:	Step Completed
1. Tools and equipment were used as directed and returned in good working order.	☐
2. Complied with all general and task-specific safety standards, including proper use of any personal protection equipment.	☐
3. Completed the task in an appropriate time frame (recommendation: 1.5 or 2 times the flat rate).	☐
4. Left the workspace clean and orderly.	☐
5. Cared for customer property and returned it undamaged.	☐

Student signature _____ Date _____

Comments:

Have your supervisor/instructor verify satisfactory completion of this procedure, any observations made, and any necessary action(s) recommended.

Evaluation Instructions: The scoring box below is intended to act as a guide for both student and supervisor/instructor. Each criterion listed will help students to understand what is expected of them and help supervisors/instructors articulate the level of success at a particular task. The scoring is set up to allow a second attempt at each task (see the Test and Retest columns). Scoring is also designed to award students points only for task criteria that were completed correctly. Points are lost for failure to complete the employability requirements (see Non-Task-Specific Evaluation criteria). When all criteria are evaluated, tally the points for a total at the bottom of each column.

Tasksheet Scoring

Evaluation Items	Test Pass (1 pt)	Test Fail (0 pts)	Retest Pass (1 pt)	Retest Fail (0 pts)
Task-Specific Evaluation	**(1 pt)**	**(0 pts)**	**(1 pt)**	**(0 pts)**
Student properly recorded piston-to-cylinder wall clearance.				
Student properly inspected piston-to-cylinder wall clearance.				
Student properly inspected piston ring end gap.				
Student properly installed piston rings on pistons.				
Non-Task-Specific Evaluation	**(0 pts)**	**(−1 pt)**	**(0 pts)**	**(−1 pt)**
Student successfully completed at least three of the non-task-specific steps.				
Student successfully completed all five of the non-task-specific steps.				
Total Score: <total # of points/4 = %>				

Supervisor/Instructor:

Supervisor/instructor signature _____ Date _____

Comments:

Retest supervisor/instructor signature _____ Date _____

Comments:

CDX Tasksheet Number: MHT1C017

Student/Intern Information

Name _____ Date _____ Class _____

Vehicle, Customer, and Service Information

Vehicle used for this activity:

Year _____ Make _____ Model _____

Odometer _____ VIN _____

Materials Required

- Vehicle with possible engine concern
- Engine manufacturer's workshop materials
- Manufacturer-specific tools depending on the concern/procedure(s)
- Vehicle/component lifting equipment, if applicable

Task-Specific Safety Considerations

- Activities may require test-driving the vehicle on the school grounds or on a hoist, both of which carry severe risks. Attempt this task only with full permission from your supervisor/instructor, and follow all the guidelines exactly.
- Lifting equipment and machines such as vehicle jacks and stands, vehicle hoists, and engine hoists are important tools that increase productivity and make the job easier. However, they can also cause severe injury or death if used improperly. Make sure you follow the manufacturer's operation procedures. Also make sure you have your supervisor's/instructor's permission to use any particular type of lifting equipment.
- Comply with personal and environmental safety practices associated with clothing; eye protection; hand tools; power equipment; proper ventilation; and the handling, storage, and disposal of chemicals/materials in accordance with federal, state, and local regulations.
- Always wear the correct protective eyewear and clothing and use the appropriate safety equipment, as well as wheel chocks, fender covers, seat protectors, and floor mat protectors.
- Make sure you understand and observe all legislative and personal safety procedures when carrying out practical assignments. If you are unsure of what these are, ask your supervisor/instructor.

▶ **TASK** Assemble pistons and connecting rods and install them in the engine block; install rod bearings; and check clearances.

MTST I.C.17; P2

Time off_____

Time on_____

Total time_____

Student Instructions: Read through the entire procedure prior to starting. Prepare your workspace and any tools or parts that may be needed to complete the task. When directed by your supervisor/instructor, begin the procedure to complete the task and check the box as each step is finished.

Note: This tasksheet will require the student to check the condition of miscellaneous vehicle fluids, some of which may be flammable and could damage the environment or cause health problems if not handled properly. Observe all safety precautions and follow local regulations for the proper disposal of fluids.

Procedure:	Step Completed
1. Referring to the manufacturer's workshop materials, assemble pistons and connecting rods.	
a. Meets the manufacturer's specifications: Yes: ☐ No: ☐	☐
b. If No, list the recommendations for rectification:	☐
2. Referring to the manufacturer's workshop materials and using the correct recommended tools, measure and record the reading for each connecting rod bearing clearance. Manufacturer's specification: _____ in./mm	☐
a. Connecting rod bearing #1: _____ in./mm	☐
b. Connecting rod bearing #2: _____ in./mm	☐
c. Connecting rod bearing #3: _____ in./mm	☐
d. Connecting rod bearing #4: _____ in./mm	☐
e. Connecting rod bearing #5: _____ in./mm	☐
f. Connecting rod bearing #6: _____ in./mm	☐
3. Meets the manufacturer's specifications: Yes: ☐ No: ☐	☐
a. If No, list the recommendations for rectification:	☐
4. While referring to the manufacturer's workshop materials, install the pistons and torque connecting rod caps. (**Note:** The connecting rods should move freely front to back by hand after torqueing. If not, remove piston/connecting rod assembly and check for misaligned bearings or contamination.) Describe the manufacturer's torque specifications and the procedure for installing the pistons and torque connecting rod caps:	☐
a. Meets the manufacturer's specifications: Yes: ☐ No: ☐	☐

	Step Completed
b. If No, list the recommendations for rectification:	☐
5. Discuss your findings with your supervisor/instructor.	☐

Non-Task-Specific Evaluations:	Step Completed
1. Tools and equipment were used as directed and returned in good working order.	☐
2. Complied with all general and task-specific safety standards, including proper use of any personal protection equipment.	☐
3. Completed the task in an appropriate time frame (recommendation: 1.5 or 2 times the flat rate).	☐
4. Left the workspace clean and orderly.	☐
5. Cared for customer property and returned it undamaged.	☐

Student signature _____ Date _____

Comments:

Have your supervisor/instructor verify satisfactory completion of this procedure, any observations made, and any necessary action(s) recommended.

Evaluation Instructions: The scoring box below is intended to act as a guide for both student and supervisor/instructor. Each criterion listed will help students to understand what is expected of them and help supervisors/instructors articulate the level of success at a particular task. The scoring is set up to allow a second attempt at each task (see the Test and Retest columns). Scoring is also designed to award students points only for task criteria that were completed correctly. Points are lost for failure to complete the employability requirements (see Non-Task-Specific Evaluation criteria). When all criteria are evaluated, tally the points for a total at the bottom of each column.

Tasksheet Scoring

Evaluation Items	Test		Retest	
	Pass	**Fail**	**Pass**	**Fail**
Task-Specific Evaluation	**(1 pt)**	**(0 pts)**	**(1 pt)**	**(0 pts)**
Student properly installed pistons on the connecting rods.				
Student properly inspected connecting rod bearing clearance.				
Student properly installed pistons.				
Student properly installed connecting rods.				
Non-Task-Specific Evaluation	**(0 pts)**	**(−1 pt)**	**(0 pts)**	**(−1 pt)**
Student successfully completed at least three of the non-task-specific steps.				
Student successfully completed all five of the non-task-specific steps.				
Total Score: <total # of points/4 = %>				

Supervisor/Instructor:

Supervisor/instructor signature _____ Date _____

Comments:

_____

Retest supervisor/instructor signature _____ Date _____

Comments:

_____

CDX Tasksheet Number: MHT1C018

Student/Intern Information

Name _____ Date _____ Class _____

Vehicle, Customer, and Service Information

Vehicle used for this activity:

Year _____ Make _____ Model _____

Odometer _____ VIN _____

Materials Required

- Vehicle with possible engine concern
- Engine manufacturer's workshop materials
- Manufacturer-specific tools depending on the concern/procedure(s)
- Vehicle/component lifting equipment, if applicable

Task-Specific Safety Considerations

- Activities may require test-driving the vehicle on the school grounds or on a hoist, both of which carry severe risks. Attempt this task only with full permission from your supervisor/instructor, and follow all the guidelines exactly.
- Lifting equipment and machines such as vehicle jacks and stands, vehicle hoists, and engine hoists are important tools that increase productivity and make the job easier. However, they can also cause severe injury or death if used improperly. Make sure you follow the manufacturer's operation procedures. Also make sure you have your supervisor's/instructor's permission to use any particular type of lifting equipment.
- Comply with personal and environmental safety practices associated with clothing; eye protection; hand tools; power equipment; proper ventilation; and the handling, storage, and disposal of chemicals/materials in accordance with federal, state, and local regulations.
- Always wear the correct protective eyewear and clothing and use the appropriate safety equipment, as well as wheel chocks, fender covers, seat protectors, and floor mat protectors.
- Make sure you understand and observe all legislative and personal safety procedures when carrying out practical assignments. If you are unsure of what these are, ask your supervisor/instructor.

▶ **TASK** Check condition of piston cooling jets (nozzles); determine needed action.

MTST
I.C.18; P2

Time off_____

Time on_____

Total time_____

Student Instructions: Read through the entire procedure prior to starting. Prepare your workspace and any tools or parts that may be needed to complete the task. When directed by your supervisor/instructor, begin the procedure to complete the task and check the box as each step is finished.

Note: This tasksheet will require the student to check the condition of miscellaneous vehicle fluids, some of which may be flammable and could damage the environment or cause health problems if not handled properly. Observe all safety precautions and follow local regulations for the proper disposal of fluids.

Procedure:	Step Completed
1. Reference the manufacturer's workshop materials; check the condition of the piston cooling jets (nozzles).	
a. Meets the manufacturer's specifications: Yes: ☐ No: ☐	☐
b. If No, list the recommendations for rectification:	☐
2. Referring to the manufacturer's workshop materials and using the correct recommended tools, install piston cooling jets (nozzles).	
a. Meets the manufacturer's specifications: Yes: ☐ No: ☐	☐
b. If No, list the recommendations for rectification:	☐
3. Discuss your findings with your supervisor/instructor.	☐

Non-Task-Specific Evaluations:	Step Completed
1. Tools and equipment were used as directed and returned in good working order.	☐
2. Complied with all general and task-specific safety standards, including proper use of any personal protection equipment.	☐
3. Completed the task in an appropriate time frame (recommendation: 1.5 or 2 times the flat rate).	☐
4. Left the workspace clean and orderly.	☐
5. Cared for customer property and returned it undamaged.	☐

Student signature _____ Date _____

Comments:

Have your supervisor/instructor verify satisfactory completion of this procedure, any observations made, and any necessary action(s) recommended.

Evaluation Instructions: The scoring box below is intended to act as a guide for both student and supervisor/instructor. Each criterion listed will help students to understand what is expected of them and help supervisors/instructors articulate the level of success at a particular task. The scoring is set up to allow a second attempt at each task (see the Test and Retest columns). Scoring is also designed to award students points only for task criteria that were completed correctly. Points are lost for failure to complete the employability requirements (see Non-Task-Specific Evaluation criteria). When all criteria are evaluated, tally the points for a total at the bottom of each column.

Tasksheet Scoring

Evaluation Items	Test		Retest	
	Pass	**Fail**	**Pass**	**Fail**
Task-Specific Evaluation	**(1 pt)**	**(0 pts)**	**(1 pt)**	**(0 pts)**
Student properly inspected piston cooling jets (nozzles).				
Student properly installed piston cooling jets (nozzles).				
Student used recommended tools properly.				
Student met the manufacturer's specifications.				
Non-Task-Specific Evaluation	**(0 pts)**	**(−1 pt)**	**(0 pts)**	**(−1 pt)**
Student successfully completed at least three of the non-task-specific steps.				
Student successfully completed all five of the non-task-specific steps.				
Total Score: <total # of points/4 = %>				

I.D Diesel Engines: Lubrication Systems

Learning Objective/Task	CDX Tasksheet Number	ASE Foundation MTST Reference Number; Priority Level
• Test engine oil pressure; check operation of pressure sensor, gauge, and/or sending unit; test engine oil temperature; check operation of temperature sensor; determine needed action.	MHT1D001	I.D.1; P-1
• Check engine oil level, condition, and consumption; take engine oil sample; determine needed action.	MHT1D002	I.D.2; P-1
• Determine proper lubricant; perform oil and filter service.	MHT1D003	I.D.3; P-1
• Inspect, clean, and test oil cooler and its components; determine needed action.	MHT1D004	I.D.4; P-2
• Inspect turbocharger lubrication systems; determine needed action.	MHT1D005	I.D.5; P-2
• Inspect and measure oil pump, drives, inlet pipes, and pick-up screens; check drive gear clearances; determine needed action.	MHT1D006	I.D.6; P-2
• Inspect oil pressure regulator valve(s), bypass and pressure relief valve(s), oil thermostat, and filters; determine needed action.	MHT1D007	I.D.7; P-2

Materials Required

- Vehicle with possible engine concern
- Engine manufacturer's workshop materials
- Manufacturer-specific tools depending on the concern/procedure(s)
- Vehicle/component lifting equipment, if applicable

Safety Considerations

- Activities may require test-driving the vehicle on the school grounds or on a hoist, both of which carry severe risks. Attempt this task only with full permission from your supervisor/instructor, and follow all the guidelines exactly.
- Lifting equipment and machines such as vehicle jacks and stands, vehicle hoists, and engine hoists are important tools that increase productivity and make the job easier. However, they can also cause severe injury or death if used improperly. Make sure you follow the manufacturer's operation procedures. Also make sure you have your supervisor's/instructor's permission to use any particular type of lifting equipment.
- Comply with personal and environmental safety practices associated with clothing; eye protection; hand tools; power equipment; proper ventilation; and the handling, storage, and disposal of chemicals/materials in accordance with federal, state, and local regulations.
- Always wear the correct protective eyewear and clothing and use the appropriate safety equipment, as well as fender covers, seat protectors, and floor mat protectors.
- Make sure you understand and observe all legislative and personal safety procedures when carrying out practical assignments. If you are unsure of what these are, ask your supervisor/instructor.

CDX Tasksheet Number: MHT1D001

Student/Intern Information

Name _____ Date _____ Class _____

Vehicle, Customer, and Service Information

Vehicle used for this activity:

Year _____ Make _____ Model _____

Odometer _____ VIN _____

> ## Materials Required
>
> - Vehicle with possible engine concern
> - Engine manufacturer's workshop materials
> - Manufacturer-specific tools depending on the concern/procedure(s)
> - Vehicle/component lifting equipment, if applicable

Task-Specific Safety Considerations

- Activities may require test-driving the vehicle on the school grounds or on a hoist, both of which carry severe risks. Attempt this task only with full permission from your supervisor/instructor, and follow all the guidelines exactly.
- Lifting equipment and machines such as vehicle jacks and stands, vehicle hoists, and engine hoists are important tools that increase productivity and make the job easier. However, they can also cause severe injury or death if used improperly. Make sure you follow the manufacturer's operation procedures. Also make sure you have your supervisor's/instructor's permission to use any particular type of lifting equipment.
- Comply with personal and environmental safety practices associated with clothing; eye protection; hand tools; power equipment; proper ventilation; and the handling, storage, and disposal of chemicals/materials in accordance with federal, state, and local regulations.
- Always wear the correct protective eyewear and clothing and use the appropriate safety equipment, as well as wheel chocks, fender covers, seat protectors, and floor mat protectors.
- Make sure you understand and observe all legislative and personal safety procedures when carrying out practical assignments. If you are unsure of what these are, ask your supervisor/instructor.

▶ **TASK** Test engine oil pressure; check operation of the pressure sensor, gauge, and/or sending unit; test engine oil temperature; check operation of the temperature sensor; and determine needed action.

MTST
I.D.1; P1

Time off_____

Time on_____

Total time_____

Student Instructions: Read through the entire procedure prior to starting. Prepare your workspace and any tools or parts that may be needed to complete the task. When directed by your supervisor/instructor, begin the procedure to complete the task and check the box as each step is finished.

Note: This tasksheet may require the student to check the condition of miscellaneous vehicle fluids, some of which may be flammable and could damage the environment or cause health problems if not handled properly. Observe all safety precautions and follow local regulations for the proper disposal of fluids.

Procedure:	Step Completed
1. Test the engine oil pressure with a manual pressure gauge as outlined in the manufacturer's workshop materials. Compare this reading with the operation of the original equipment manufacturer (OEM) pressure sensor, gauge, and/or sending unit.	
a. Within manufacturer's specifications: Yes: ☐ No: ☐	☐
b. If No, describe the recommended corrective action(s):	☐
2. Test the engine oil temperature with an infrared thermometer as outlined in the manufacturer's workshop materials. Compare this reading with the operation of the OEM temperature sensor and gauge.	
a. Within manufacturer's specifications: Yes: ☐ No: ☐	☐
b. If No, describe the recommended corrective action(s):	☐
3. Discuss your findings with your supervisor/instructor.	☐

Non-Task-Specific Evaluations:	Step Completed
1. Tools and equipment were used as directed and returned in good working order.	☐
2. Complied with all general and task-specific safety standards, including proper use of any personal protection equipment.	☐
3. Completed the task in an appropriate time frame (recommendation: 1.5 or 2 times the flat rate).	☐
4. Left the workspace clean and orderly.	☐
5. Cared for customer property and returned it undamaged.	☐

Student signature _____ Date _____

Comments:

Have your supervisor/instructor verify satisfactory completion of this procedure, any observations made,

and any necessary action(s) recommended.

Evaluation Instructions: The scoring box below is intended to act as a guide for both student and supervisor/instructor. Each criterion listed will help students to understand what is expected of them and help supervisors/instructors articulate the level of success at a particular task. The scoring is set up to allow a second attempt at each task (see the Test and Retest columns). Scoring is also designed to award students points only for task criteria that were completed correctly. Points are lost for failure to complete the employability requirements (see Non-Task-Specific Evaluation criteria). When all criteria are evaluated, tally the points for a total at the bottom of each column.

Tasksheet Scoring

Evaluation Items	Test		Retest	
	Pass	Fail	Pass	Fail
Task-Specific Evaluation	**(1 pt)**	**(0 pts)**	**(1 pt)**	**(0 pts)**
Student properly checked engine oil pressure.				
Student properly compared the pressure reading with the operation of the OEM pressure sensor, gauge, and/or sending unit.				
Student properly checked engine oil temperature.				
Student properly compared the temperature reading with the operation of the OEM temperature sensor and gauge.				
Non-Task-Specific Evaluation	**(0 pts)**	**(−1 pt)**	**(0 pts)**	**(−1 pt)**
Student successfully completed at least three of the non-task-specific steps.				
Student successfully completed all five of the non-task-specific steps.				
Total Score: <total # of points/4 = %>				

Supervisor/Instructor:

Supervisor/instructor signature _____ Date _____

Comments:

[ ]

Retest supervisor/instructor signature _____ Date _____

Comments:

[ ]

CDX Tasksheet Number: MHT1D002

Student/Intern Information

Name _____ Date _____ Class _____

Vehicle, Customer, and Service Information

Vehicle used for this activity:

Year _____ Make _____ Model _____

Odometer _____ VIN _____

Materials Required

- Vehicle with possible engine concern
- Engine manufacturer's workshop materials
- Manufacturer-specific tools depending on the concern/procedure(s)
- Vehicle/component lifting equipment, if applicable

Task-Specific Safety Considerations

- Activities may require test-driving the vehicle on the school grounds or on a hoist, both of which carry severe risks. Attempt this task only with full permission from your supervisor/instructor, and follow all the guidelines exactly.
- Lifting equipment and machines such as vehicle jacks and stands, vehicle hoists, and engine hoists are important tools that increase productivity and make the job easier. However, they can also cause severe injury or death if used improperly. Make sure you follow the manufacturer's operation procedures. Also make sure you have your supervisor's/instructor's permission to use any particular type of lifting equipment.
- Comply with personal and environmental safety practices associated with clothing; eye protection; hand tools; power equipment; proper ventilation; and the handling, storage, and disposal of chemicals/materials in accordance with federal, state, and local regulations.
- Always wear the correct protective eyewear and clothing and use the appropriate safety equipment, as well as wheel chocks, fender covers, seat protectors, and floor mat protectors.
- Make sure you understand and observe all legislative and personal safety procedures when carrying out practical assignments. If you are unsure of what these are, ask your supervisor/instructor.

▶ TASK Check engine oil level, condition, and consumption; take engine oil sample; determine needed action.

MTST *I.D.2; P1*

Time off _____

Time on _____

Total time _____

Student Instructions: Read through the entire procedure prior to starting. Prepare your workspace and any tools or parts that may be needed to complete the task. When directed by your supervisor/instructor, begin the procedure to complete the task and check the box as each step is finished.

Note: This tasksheet may require the student to check the condition of miscellaneous vehicle fluids, some of which may be flammable and could damage the environment or cause health problems if not handled properly. Observe all safety precautions and follow local regulations for the proper disposal of fluids.

Procedure:	Step Completed
1. Check the engine oil level as outlined in the manufacturer's workshop materials.	
a. Within the manufacturer's specifications: Yes: ☐ No: ☐	☐
b. If No, describe the recommended corrective action(s):	☐
2. Using the proper equipment, take an engine oil sample. Record all information needed for analysis:	☐
3. Determine conditions needed to conduct a proper oil consumption test:	☐
4. Discuss your findings with your supervisor/instructor.	☐

Non-Task-Specific Evaluations:	Step Completed
1. Tools and equipment were used as directed and returned in good working order.	☐
2. Complied with all general and task-specific safety standards, including proper use of any personal protection equipment.	☐
3. Completed the task in an appropriate time frame (recommendation: 1.5 or 2 times the flat rate).	☐
4. Left the workspace clean and orderly.	☐
5. Cared for customer property and returned it undamaged.	☐

Student signature _____ Date _____

Comments:

Have your supervisor/instructor verify satisfactory completion of this procedure, any observations made, and any necessary action(s) recommended.

Evaluation Instructions: The scoring box below is intended to act as a guide for both student and supervisor/instructor. Each criterion listed will help students to understand what is expected of them and help supervisors/instructors articulate the level of success at a particular task. The scoring is set up to allow a second attempt at each task (see the Test and Retest columns). Scoring is also designed to award students points only for task criteria that were completed correctly. Points are lost for failure to complete the employability requirements (see Non-Task-Specific Evaluation criteria). When all criteria are evaluated, tally the points for a total at the bottom of each column.

Tasksheet Scoring

Evaluation Items	Test		Retest	
	Pass	**Fail**	**Pass**	**Fail**
Task-Specific Evaluation	**(1 pt)**	**(0 pts)**	**(1 pt)**	**(0 pts)**
Student properly checked the engine oil level.				
Student properly took an engine oil sample.				
Student recorded information about the engine oil consumption test.				
Student correctly determined conditions needed to conduct a proper oil consumption test.				
Non-Task-Specific Evaluation	**(0 pts)**	**(−1 pt)**	**(0 pts)**	**(−1 pt)**
Student successfully completed at least three of the non-task-specific steps.				
Student successfully completed all five of the non-task-specific steps.				
Total Score: <total # of points/4 = %>				

Supervisor/Instructor:

Supervisor/instructor signature _____ Date _____

Comments:

Retest supervisor/instructor signature _____ Date _____

Comments:

CDX Tasksheet Number: MHT1D003

Student/Intern Information

Name _____ Date _____ Class _____

Vehicle, Customer, and Service Information

Vehicle used for this activity:

Year _____ Make _____ Model _____

Odometer _____ VIN _____

Materials Required
- Vehicle with possible engine concern
- Engine manufacturer's workshop materials
- Manufacturer-specific tools depending on the concern/procedure(s)
- Vehicle/component lifting equipment, if applicable

Task-Specific Safety Considerations
- Activities may require test-driving the vehicle on the school grounds or on a hoist, both of which carry severe risks. Attempt this task only with full permission from your supervisor/instructor, and follow all the guidelines exactly.
- Lifting equipment and machines such as vehicle jacks and stands, vehicle hoists, and engine hoists are important tools that increase productivity and make the job easier. However, they can also cause severe injury or death if used improperly. Make sure you follow the manufacturer's operation procedures. Also make sure you have your supervisor's/instructor's permission to use any particular type of lifting equipment.
- Comply with personal and environmental safety practices associated with clothing; eye protection; hand tools; power equipment; proper ventilation; and the handling, storage, and disposal of chemicals/materials in accordance with federal, state, and local regulations.
- Always wear the correct protective eyewear and clothing and use the appropriate safety equipment, as well as wheel chocks, fender covers, seat protectors, and floor mat protectors.
- Make sure you understand and observe all legislative and personal safety procedures when carrying out practical assignments. If you are unsure of what these are, ask your supervisor/instructor.

▶ **TASK** Determine proper lubricant; perform oil and filter service.

MTST
I.D.3; P1

Time off_____

Time on_____

Total time_____

Student Instructions: Read through the entire procedure prior to starting. Prepare your workspace and any tools or parts that may be needed to complete the task. When directed by your supervisor/instructor, begin the procedure to complete the task and check the box as each step is finished.

Note: This tasksheet may require the student to check the condition of miscellaneous vehicle fluids, some of which may be flammable and could damage the environment or cause health problems if not handled properly. Observe all safety precautions and follow local regulations for the proper disposal of fluids.

Procedure:	Step Completed
1. Record the proper engine oil type and quantity as outlined in the manufacturer's workshop materials.	
a. Type:	☐
b. Quantity: _____ quarts/liters	☐
2. Using the proper equipment, drain the engine oil and remove the filter(s). Place them in proper container(s) for disposal. List the steps of the procedure that you followed:	☐
3. Install the new filter(s). List the steps of the procedure that you followed:	☐
4. Determine how much oil is to be added to bring the oil level from the ADD mark to the FULL mark on the engine oil dipstick: _____ quarts/liters/gallons	☐
5. Fill the engine with the appropriate amount of engine oil minus the amount of oil needed to bring the level from the ADD to the FULL mark on the engine oil dipstick. (**Note:** This is the procedure used to determine the proper calibration of the engine oil dipstick.)	☐
6. Allow a sufficient amount of time for the engine oil to drain into the engine oil pan, and then check the oil level on the dipstick. (**Note:** The oil level should be at the ADD mark on the dipstick.)	
a. Within manufacturer's specifications: Yes: ☐ No: ☐	☐
b. If No, describe the recommended corrective action(s):	☐

7. Add the appropriate amount of engine oil to bring the level from the ADD mark to the FULL mark on the engine oil dipstick.	☐
8. Allow a sufficient amount of time for the engine oil to drain into the engine oil pan, and then check the oil level on the dipstick. (**Note:** The oil level should be at the FULL mark on the dipstick.)	
a. Within manufacturer's specifications: Yes: ☐ No: ☐	☐
b. If No, describe the recommended corrective action(s):	☐
9. Discuss your findings with your supervisor/instructor.	☐

Non-Task-Specific Evaluations:	Step Completed
1. Tools and equipment were used as directed and returned in good working order.	
2. Complied with all general and task-specific safety standards, including proper use of any personal protection equipment.	
3. Completed the task in an appropriate time frame (recommendation: 1.5 or 2 times the flat rate).	
4. Left the workspace clean and orderly.	
5. Cared for customer property and returned it undamaged.	

Student signature _____ Date _____

Comments:

Have your supervisor/instructor verify satisfactory completion of this procedure, any observations made, and any necessary action(s) recommended.

Evaluation Instructions: The scoring box below is intended to act as a guide for both student and supervisor/instructor. Each criterion listed will help students to understand what is expected of them and help supervisors/instructors articulate the level of success at a particular task. The scoring is set up to allow a second attempt at each task (see the Test and Retest columns). Scoring is also designed to award students points only for task criteria that were completed correctly. Points are lost for failure to complete the employability requirements (see Non-Task-Specific Evaluation criteria). When all criteria are evaluated, tally the points for a total at the bottom of each column.

Tasksheet Scoring

Evaluation Items	Test Pass	Test Fail	Retest Pass	Retest Fail
Task-Specific Evaluation	**(1 pt)**	**(0 pts)**	**(1 pt)**	**(0 pts)**
Student drained engine oil and placed it in suitable container(s) for disposal.				
Student determined appropriate amount of engine oil to add.				
Student properly changed the engine oil filter(s).				
Student properly checked the engine oil dipstick calibration.				
Non-Task-Specific Evaluation	**(0 pts)**	**(−1 pt)**	**(0 pts)**	**(−1 pt)**
Student successfully completed at least three of the non-task-specific steps.				
Student successfully completed all five of the non-task-specific steps.				
Total Score: <total # of points/4 = %>				

Supervisor/Instructor:

Supervisor/instructor signature _____ Date _____

Comments:

Retest supervisor/instructor signature _____ Date _____

Comments:

CDX Tasksheet Number: MHT1D004

Student/Intern Information

Name _____ Date _____ Class _____

Vehicle, Customer, and Service Information

Vehicle used for this activity:

Year _____ Make _____ Model _____

Odometer _____ VIN _____

Materials Required

- Vehicle with possible engine concern
- Engine manufacturer's workshop materials
- Manufacturer-specific tools depending on the concern/procedure(s)
- Vehicle/component lifting equipment, if applicable

Task-Specific Safety Considerations

- Activities may require test-driving the vehicle on the school grounds or on a hoist, both of which carry severe risks. Attempt this task only with full permission from your supervisor/instructor, and follow all the guidelines exactly.
- Lifting equipment and machines such as vehicle jacks and stands, vehicle hoists, and engine hoists are important tools that increase productivity and make the job easier. However, they can also cause severe injury or death if used improperly. Make sure you follow the manufacturer's operation procedures. Also make sure you have your supervisor's/instructor's permission to use any particular type of lifting equipment.
- Comply with personal and environmental safety practices associated with clothing; eye protection; hand tools; power equipment; proper ventilation; and the handling, storage, and disposal of chemicals/materials in accordance with federal, state, and local regulations.
- Always wear the correct protective eyewear and clothing and use the appropriate safety equipment, as well as wheel chocks, fender covers, seat protectors, and floor mat protectors.
- Make sure you understand and observe all legislative and personal safety procedures when carrying out practical assignments. If you are unsure of what these are, ask your supervisor/instructor.

▶ **TASK** Inspect, clean, and test oil cooler and its components; determine needed action.

MTST I.D.4; P2

Time off_____

Time on_____

Total time_____

Student Instructions: Read through the entire procedure prior to starting. Prepare your workspace and any tools or parts that may be needed to complete the task. When directed by your instructor, begin the procedure to complete the task and check the box as each step is finished.

Note: This tasksheet may require the student to check the condition of miscellaneous vehicle fluids, some of which may be flammable and could damage the environment or cause health problems if not handled properly. Observe all safety precautions and follow local regulations for the proper disposal of fluids.

Procedure:	Step Completed
1. Record the manufacturer's recommendation(s) for replacing an engine oil cooler:	☐
2. Using the proper equipment, test the engine oil cooler.	
a. Within manufacturer's specifications: Yes: ☐ No: ☐	☐
b. If No, describe the recommended corrective action(s):	☐
3. Discuss your findings with your supervisor/instructor.	☐

Non-Task-Specific Evaluations:	Step Completed
1. Tools and equipment were used as directed and returned in good working order.	☐
2. Complied with all general and task-specific safety standards, including proper use of any personal protection equipment.	☐
3. Completed the task in an appropriate time frame (recommendation: 1.5 or 2 times the flat rate).	☐
4. Left the workspace clean and orderly.	☐
5. Cared for customer property and returned it undamaged.	☐

Student signature _____ Date _____

Comments:

Have your supervisor/instructor verify satisfactory completion of this procedure, any observations made, and any necessary action(s) recommended.

Evaluation Instructions: The scoring box below is intended to act as a guide for both student and supervisor/instructor. Each criterion listed will help students to understand what is expected of them and help supervisors/instructors articulate the level of success at a particular task. The scoring is set up to allow a second attempt at each task (see the Test and Retest columns). Scoring is also designed to award students points only for task criteria that were completed correctly. Points are lost for failure to complete the employability requirements (see Non-Task-Specific Evaluation criteria). When all criteria are evaluated, tally the points for a total at the bottom of each column.

Tasksheet Scoring

	Test		Retest	
Evaluation Items	Pass	Fail	Pass	Fail
Task-Specific Evaluation	**(1 pt)**	**(0 pts)**	**(1 pt)**	**(0 pts)**
Student properly cleaned the engine oil cooler.				
Student properly inspected the engine oil cooler.				
Student properly recorded the criteria for engine oil cooler replacement.				
Student properly tested the engine oil cooler.				
Non-Task-Specific Evaluation	**(0 pts)**	**(−1 pt)**	**(0 pts)**	**(−1 pt)**
Student successfully completed at least three of the non-task-specific steps.				
Student successfully completed all five of the non-task-specific steps.				
Total Score: <total # of points/4 = %>				

Supervisor/Instructor:

Supervisor/instructor signature _____ Date _____

Comments:

Retest supervisor/instructor signature _____ Date _____

Comments:

CDX Tasksheet Number: MHT1D005

Student/Intern Information

Name _____ Date _____ Class _____

Vehicle, Customer, and Service Information

Vehicle used for this activity:

Year _____ Make _____ Model _____

Odometer _____ VIN _____

Materials Required
- Vehicle with possible engine concern
- Engine manufacturer's workshop materials
- Manufacturer-specific tools depending on the concern/procedure(s)
- Vehicle/component lifting equipment, if applicable

Task-Specific Safety Considerations
- Activities may require test-driving the vehicle on the school grounds or on a hoist, both of which carry severe risks. Attempt this task only with full permission from your supervisor/instructor, and follow all the guidelines exactly.
- Lifting equipment and machines such as vehicle jacks and stands, vehicle hoists, and engine hoists are important tools that increase productivity and make the job easier. However, they can also cause severe injury or death if used improperly. Make sure you follow the manufacturer's operation procedures. Also make sure you have your supervisor's/instructor's permission to use any particular type of lifting equipment.
- Comply with personal and environmental safety practices associated with clothing; eye protection; hand tools; power equipment; proper ventilation; and the handling, storage, and disposal of chemicals/materials in accordance with federal, state, and local regulations.
- Always wear the correct protective eyewear and clothing and use the appropriate safety equipment, as well as wheel chocks, fender covers, seat protectors, and floor mat protectors.
- Make sure you understand and observe all legislative and personal safety procedures when carrying out practical assignments. If you are unsure of what these are, ask your supervisor/instructor.

▶ **TASK** Inspect turbocharger lubrication systems; determine needed action.

MTST
I.D.5; P2

Time off_____

Time on_____

Total time_____

Student Instructions: Read through the entire procedure prior to starting. Prepare your workspace and any tools or parts that may be needed to complete the task. When directed by your supervisor/instructor, begin the procedure to complete the task and check the box as each step is finished.

Note: This tasksheet may require the student to check the condition of miscellaneous vehicle fluids, some of which may be flammable and could damage the environment or cause health problems if not handled properly. Observe all safety precautions and follow local regulations for the proper disposal of fluids.

Procedure:	Step Completed
1. Inspect the turbocharger oil pressure inlet line for damage as outlined in the manufacturer's workshop materials, as well as for loose or leaking fittings.	
a. Within manufacturer's specifications: Yes: ☐ No: ☐	☐
b. If No, describe the recommended corrective action(s):	☐
2. Inspect the turbocharger oil drain line for damage as outlined in the manufacturer's workshop materials, as well as for loose or leaking fittings.	
a. Within manufacturer's specifications: Yes: ☐ No: ☐	☐
b. If No, describe the recommended corrective action(s):	☐
3. Discuss your findings with your supervisor/instructor.	☐

Non-Task-Specific Evaluations:	Step Completed
1. Tools and equipment were used as directed and returned in good working order.	☐
2. Complied with all general and task-specific safety standards, including proper use of any personal protection equipment.	☐
3. Completed the task in an appropriate time frame (recommendation: 1.5 or 2 times the flat rate).	☐
4. Left the workspace clean and orderly.	☐
5. Cared for customer property and returned it undamaged.	☐

Student signature _____ Date _____

Comments:

Have your supervisor/instructor verify satisfactory completion of this procedure, any observations made, and any necessary action(s) recommended.

Evaluation Instructions: The scoring box below is intended to act as a guide for both student and supervisor/instructor. Each criterion listed will help students to understand what is expected of them and help supervisors/instructors articulate the level of success at a particular task. The scoring is set up to allow a second attempt at each task (see the Test and Retest columns). Scoring is also designed to award students points only for task criteria that were completed correctly. Points are lost for failure to complete the employability requirements (see Non-Task-Specific Evaluation criteria). When all criteria are evaluated, tally the points for a total at the bottom of each column.

Tasksheet Scoring

Evaluation Items	Test		Retest	
	Pass	**Fail**	**Pass**	**Fail**
Task-Specific Evaluation	**(1 pt)**	**(0 pts)**	**(1 pt)**	**(0 pts)**
Student properly inspected turbocharger oil pressure inlet line.				
Student properly inspected the fittings for the turbocharger oil pressure inlet line.				
Student properly inspected turbocharger oil drain line.				
Student properly inspected the fittings for the turbocharger oil drain line.				
Non-Task-Specific Evaluation	**(0 pts)**	**(−1 pt)**	**(0 pts)**	**(−1 pt)**
Student successfully completed at least three of the non-task-specific steps.				
Student successfully completed all five of the non-task-specific steps.				
Total Score: <total # of points/4 = %>				

CDX Tasksheet Number: MHT1D006

Student/Intern Information

Name _____ Date _____ Class _____

Vehicle, Customer, and Service Information

Vehicle used for this activity:

Year _____ Make _____ Model _____

Odometer _____ VIN _____

Materials Required
- Vehicle with possible engine concern
- Engine manufacturer's workshop materials
- Manufacturer-specific tools depending on the concern/procedure(s)
- Vehicle/component lifting equipment, if applicable

Task-Specific Safety Considerations
- Activities may require test-driving the vehicle on the school grounds or on a hoist, both of which carry severe risks. Attempt this task only with full permission from your supervisor/instructor, and follow all the guidelines exactly.
- Lifting equipment and machines such as vehicle jacks and stands, vehicle hoists, and engine hoists are important tools that increase productivity and make the job easier. However, they can also cause severe injury or death if used improperly. Make sure you follow the manufacturer's operation procedures. Also make sure you have your supervisor's/instructor's permission to use any particular type of lifting equipment.
- Comply with personal and environmental safety practices associated with clothing; eye protection; hand tools; power equipment; proper ventilation; and the handling, storage, and disposal of chemicals/materials in accordance with federal, state, and local regulations.
- Always wear the correct protective eyewear and clothing and use the appropriate safety equipment, as well as wheel chocks, fender covers, seat protectors, and floor mat protectors.
- Make sure you understand and observe all legislative and personal safety procedures when carrying out practical assignments. If you are unsure of what these are, ask your supervisor/instructor.

▶ TASK Inspect and measure oil pump, drives, inlet pipes, and pick-up screens; check drive gear clearances; and determine needed action.

MTST I.D.6; P2

Time off_____

Time on_____

Total time_____

Student Instructions: Read through the entire procedure prior to starting. Prepare your workspace and any tools or parts that may be needed to complete the task. When directed by your supervisor/instructor, begin the procedure to complete the task and check the box as each step is finished.

Note: This tasksheet may require the student to check the condition of miscellaneous vehicle fluids, some of which may be flammable and could damage the environment or cause health problems if not handled properly. Observe all safety precautions and follow local regulations for the proper disposal of fluids.

Procedure:	Step Completed
1. List the type of oil pump (e.g., gear, gerotor) as outlined in the manufacturer's workshop materials:	☐
2. While referencing the manufacturer's workshop materials, disassemble the oil pump, and clean and inspect for damage/wear.	
a. Within manufacturer's specifications: Yes: ☐ No: ☐	☐
b. If No, describe the recommended corrective action(s):	☐
3. Check gear to pump body end clearance as outlined in the manufacturer's workshop materials: Specification: _____ in./mm Measured: _____ in./mm	
a. Within manufacturer's specifications: Yes: ☐ No: ☐	☐
b. If No, describe the recommended corrective action(s):	☐
4. Check gear inner tip clearance as outlined in the manufacturer's workshop materials: Specification: _____ in./mm Measured: _____ in./mm	☐
a. Within manufacturer's specifications: Yes: ☐ No: ☐	☐
b. If No, describe the recommended corrective action(s):	☐
5. Check pressure regulator bore and piston for wear/damage as outlined in the manufacturer's workshop materials: Specification: _____ in./mm Measured: _____ in./mm	☐

a. Bore measurement:
Specification: _____ in./mm
Measured: _____ in./mm
  i. Within manufacturer's specifications:
    Yes: ☐ No: ☐
	☐

ii. If No, describe the recommended corrective action(s):	☐

b. Piston measurement:
Specification: _____ in./mm
Measured: _____ in./mm
  i. Within manufacturer's specifications:
    Yes: ☐ No: ☐
	☐

ii. If No, describe the recommended corrective action(s):	☐
6. Reassemble the oil pump as outlined in the manufacturer's workshop materials. Place the oil pump in a clean plastic bag until installed on the engine. (**Note:** Apply a coating of lithium grease to all rotating components during assembly.)	☐
7. Inspect the oil pickup tube for damage [e.g., cracks, broken mount(s)] as outlined in the manufacturer's workshop materials.	☐
8. Discuss your findings with your supervisor/instructor.	☐

Non-Task-Specific Evaluations:	Step Completed
1. Tools and equipment were used as directed and returned in good working order.	☐
2. Complied with all general and task-specific safety standards, including proper use of any personal protection equipment.	☐
3. Completed the task in an appropriate time frame (recommendation: 1.5 or 2 times the flat rate).	☐
4. Left the workspace clean and orderly.	☐
5. Cared for customer property and returned it undamaged.	☐

Student signature _____ Date _____

Comments:

Have your supervisor/instructor verify satisfactory completion of this procedure, any observations made, and any necessary action(s) recommended.

Evaluation Instructions: The scoring box below is intended to act as a guide for both student and supervisor/instructor. Each criterion listed will help students to understand what is expected of them and help supervisors/instructors articulate the level of success at a particular task. The scoring is set up to allow a second attempt at each task (see the Test and Retest columns). Scoring is also designed to award students points only for task criteria that were completed correctly. Points are lost for failure to complete the employability requirements (see Non-Task-Specific Evaluation criteria). When all criteria are evaluated, tally the points for a total at the bottom of each column.

Tasksheet Scoring

	Test		Retest	
Evaluation Items	**Pass**	**Fail**	**Pass**	**Fail**
Task-Specific Evaluation	**(1 pt)**	**(0 pts)**	**(1 pt)**	**(0 pts)**
Student correctly identified oil pump type.				
Student properly inspected oil pump, end clearance, and inner tip clearance.				
Student properly cleaned and reassembled oil pick pump.				
Student properly inspected oil pickup tube and screen.				
Non-Task-Specific Evaluation	**(0 pts)**	**(−1 pt)**	**(0 pts)**	**(−1 pt)**
Student successfully completed at least three of the non-task-specific steps.				
Student successfully completed all five of the non-task-specific steps.				
Total Score: <total # of points/4 = %>				

Supervisor/Instructor:

Supervisor/instructor signature _____ Date _____

Comments:

Retest supervisor/instructor signature _____ Date _____

Comments:

CDX Tasksheet Number: MHT1D007

Student/Intern Information

Name _____ Date _____ Class _____

Vehicle, Customer, and Service Information

Vehicle used for this activity:

Year _____ Make _____ Model _____

Odometer _____ VIN _____

> ## Materials Required
> - Vehicle with possible engine concern
> - Engine manufacturer's workshop materials
> - Manufacturer-specific tools depending on the concern/procedure(s)
> - Vehicle/component lifting equipment, if applicable

Task-Specific Safety Considerations

- Activities may require test-driving the vehicle on the school grounds or on a hoist, both of which carry severe risks. Attempt this task only with full permission from your supervisor/instructor, and follow all the guidelines exactly.
- Lifting equipment and machines such as vehicle jacks and stands, vehicle hoists, and engine hoists are important tools that increase productivity and make the job easier. However, they can also cause severe injury or death if used improperly. Make sure you follow the manufacturer's operation procedures. Also make sure you have your supervisor's/instructor's permission to use any particular type of lifting equipment.
- Comply with personal and environmental safety practices associated with clothing; eye protection; hand tools; power equipment; proper ventilation; and the handling, storage, and disposal of chemicals/materials in accordance with federal, state, and local regulations.
- Always wear the correct protective eyewear and clothing and use the appropriate safety equipment, as well as wheel chocks, fender covers, seat protectors, and floor mat protectors.
- Make sure you understand and observe all legislative and personal safety procedures when carrying out practical assignments. If you are unsure of what these are, ask your supervisor/instructor.

▶ **TASK** Inspect oil pressure regulator valve(s), bypass and pressure relief valve(s), oil thermostat, and filters; determine needed action.

MTST
I.D.7; P2

Time off_____

Time on_____

Total time_____

Student Instructions: Read through the entire procedure prior to starting. Prepare your workspace and any tools or parts that may be needed to complete the task. When directed by your supervisor/instructor, begin the procedure to complete the task and check the box as each step is finished.

Note: This tasksheet may require the student to check the condition of miscellaneous vehicle fluids, some of which may be flammable and could damage the environment if not handled properly or cause health problems. Observe all safety precautions and follow local regulations for the proper disposal of fluids.

Procedure:	Step Completed
1. Inspect the external oil pressure regulator bore and piston for wear/damage as outlined in the manufacturer's workshop materials. Specification: _____ in./mm Measured: _____ in./mm	
a. Within manufacturer's specifications: Yes: ☐ No: ☐	☐
b. If No, describe the recommended corrective action(s):	☐
2. Inspect the oil pressure bypass valve and piston for wear/damage as outlined in the manufacturer's workshop materials. Specification: _____ in./mm Measured: _____ in./mm	
a. Within manufacturer's specifications: Yes: ☐ No: ☐	☐
b. If No, describe the recommended corrective action(s):	☐
3. Inspect the pressure relief valve and piston for wear/damage as outlined in the manufacturer's workshop materials: Specification: _____ in./mm Measured: _____ in./mm	
a. Within manufacturer's specifications: Yes: ☐ No: ☐	☐
b. If No, describe the recommended corrective action(s):	☐
4. Inspect the oil cooler thermostat as outlined in the manufacturer's workshop materials.	
a. Within manufacturer's specifications: Yes: ☐ No: ☐	☐

b. If No, describe the recommended corrective action(s):	☐
5. Remove the oil filter and, using the appropriate tools, remove the filter media. (**Note**: Use extreme caution; cut edges on filter canisters are extremely sharp.) Cut a section of media loose from the core and place it in a clean rag. Using a shop vise, squeeze the oil out of the filter media. Inspect the filter media for metal particles/contamination, and record your findings:	☐
6. Discuss your findings with your supervisor/instructor.	☐

Non-Task-Specific Evaluations:	Step Completed
1. Tools and equipment were used as directed and returned in good working order.	☐
2. Complied with all general and task-specific safety standards, including proper use of any personal protection equipment.	☐
3. Completed the task in an appropriate time frame (recommendation: 1.5 or 2 times the flat rate).	☐
4. Left the workspace clean and orderly.	☐
5. Cared for customer property and returned it undamaged.	☐

Student signature _____ Date _____

Comments:

Have your supervisor/instructor verify satisfactory completion of this procedure, any observations made, and any necessary action(s) recommended.

Evaluation Instructions: The scoring box below is intended to act as a guide for both student and supervisor/instructor. Each criterion listed will help students to understand what is expected of them and help supervisors/instructors articulate the level of success at a particular task. The scoring is set up to allow a second attempt at each task (see the Test and Retest columns). Scoring is also designed to award students points only for task criteria that were completed correctly. Points are lost for failure to complete the employability requirements (see Non-Task-Specific Evaluation criteria). When all criteria are evaluated, tally the points for a total at the bottom of each column.

Tasksheet Scoring

Evaluation Items	Test		Retest	
	Pass	Fail	Pass	Fail
Task-Specific Evaluation	**(1 pt)**	**(0 pts)**	**(1 pt)**	**(0 pts)**
Student properly inspected the external oil pressure regulator bore and piston.				
Student properly inspected the oil pressure bypass valve and piston.				
Student properly inspected the oil pressure relief valve and piston.				
Student properly inspected the oil cooler thermostat and the oil filter.				
Non-Task-Specific Evaluation	**(0 pts)**	**(−1 pt)**	**(0 pts)**	**(−1 pt)**
Student successfully completed at least three of the non-task-specific steps.				
Student successfully completed all five of the non-task-specific steps.				
Total Score: <total # of points/4 = %>				

Supervisor/Instructor:

Supervisor/instructor signature _____ Date _____

Comments:

Retest supervisor/instructor signature _____ Date _____

Comments:

I.E Diesel Engines: Cooling System

Learning Objective/Task	CDX Tasksheet Number	ASE Foundation MTST Reference Number; Priority Level
• Check engine coolant type, level, and condition; test coolant for freeze protection and additive package concentration.	MHT1E001	I.E.1; P-1
• Test coolant temperature; test operation of temperature and level sensors, gauge, and/or sending unit; determine needed action.	MHT1E002	I.E.2; P-1
• Inspect and reinstall/replace pulleys, tensioners, and drive belts; adjust drive belts and check alignment.	MHT1E003	I.E.3; P-1
• Recover coolant; flush and refill with recommended coolant/additive package; bleed cooling system.	MHT1E004	I.E.4; P-1
• Inspect coolant conditioner/filter assembly for leaks; inspect valves, lines, and fittings; replace as needed.	MHT1E005	I.E.5; P-1
• Inspect water pump, hoses, and clamps; determine needed action.	MHT1E006	I.E.6; P-1
• Inspect and pressure test cooling system(s); pressure test cap, tank(s), and recovery systems; inspect radiator and mountings; determine needed action.	MHT1E007	I.E.7; P-1
• Inspect, test, and repair thermostatic cooling fan system (hydraulic, pneumatic, and electronic) and fan shroud; determine needed action.	MHT1E008	I.E.8; P-1
• Test engine block heater(s); determine needed action.	MHT1E009	I.E.9; P-2
• Diagnose engine coolant consumption; determine needed action.	MHT1E010	I.E.10; P-1
• Inspect thermostat(s), bypasses, housing(s), and seals; replace as needed.	MHT1E011	I.E.11; P-1
• Inspect turbocharger cooling systems; determine needed action.	MHT1E012	I.E.12; P-2

Materials Required

- Vehicle with possible engine concern
- Engine manufacturer's workshop materials
- Manufacturer-specific tools depending on the concern/procedure(s)
- Vehicle/component lifting equipment, if applicable

Safety Considerations

- Activities may require test-driving the vehicle on the school grounds or on a hoist, both of which carry severe risks. Attempt this task only with full permission from your supervisor/instructor, and follow all the guidelines exactly.

- Lifting equipment and machines such as vehicle jacks and stands, vehicle hoists, and engine hoists are important tools that increase productivity and make the job easier. However, they can also cause severe injury or death if used improperly. Make sure you follow the manufacturer's operation procedures. Also make sure you have your supervisor's/instructor's permission to use any particular type of lifting equipment.
- Comply with personal and environmental safety practices associated with clothing; eye protection; hand tools; power equipment; proper ventilation; and the handling, storage, and disposal of chemicals/materials in accordance with federal, state, and local regulations.
- Always wear the correct protective eyewear and clothing and use the appropriate safety equipment, as well as fender covers, seat protectors, and floor mat protectors.
- Make sure you understand and observe all legislative and personal safety procedures when carrying out practical assignments. If you are unsure of what these are, ask your supervisor/instructor.

CDX Tasksheet Number: MHT1E001

Student/Intern Information

Name _____ Date _____ Class _____

Vehicle, Customer, and Service Information

Vehicle used for this activity:

Year _____ Make _____ Model _____

Odometer _____ VIN _____

Materials Required

- Vehicle with possible engine concern
- Engine manufacturer's workshop materials
- Manufacturer-specific tools depending on the concern/procedure(s)
- Vehicle/component lifting equipment, if applicable

Task-Specific Safety Considerations

- Activities may require test-driving the vehicle on the school grounds or on a hoist, both of which carry severe risks. Attempt this task only with full permission from your supervisor/instructor, and follow all the guidelines exactly.
- Lifting equipment and machines such as vehicle jacks and stands, vehicle hoists, and engine hoists are important tools that increase productivity and make the job easier. However, they can also cause severe injury or death if used improperly. Make sure you follow the manufacturer's operation procedures. Also make sure you have your supervisor's/instructor's permission to use any particular type of lifting equipment.
- Comply with personal and environmental safety practices associated with clothing; eye protection; hand tools; power equipment; proper ventilation; and the handling, storage, and disposal of chemicals/materials in accordance with federal, state, and local regulations.
- Always wear the correct protective eyewear and clothing and use the appropriate safety equipment, as well as wheel chocks, fender covers, seat protectors, and floor mat protectors.
- Make sure you understand and observe all legislative and personal safety procedures when carrying out practical assignments. If you are unsure of what these are, ask your supervisor/instructor.

▶ TASK Check engine coolant type, level, and condition; test coolant for freeze protection and additive package concentration.

MTST
I.E.1; P1

Time off_____

Time on_____

Total time_____

Student Instructions: Read through the entire procedure prior to starting. Prepare your workspace and any tools or parts that may be needed to complete the task. When directed by your supervisor/instructor, begin the procedure to complete the task and check the box as each step is finished.

Note: This tasksheet may require the student to check the condition of miscellaneous vehicle fluids, some of which may be flammable and could damage the environment or cause health problems if not handled properly. Observe all safety precautions and follow local regulations for the proper disposal of fluids.

Procedure:	Step Completed
1. Check engine coolant type as outlined in the manufacturer's workshop materials.	
a. Coolant type:	☐
b. Coolant quantity: _____ quarts/gallons	☐
c. Cooling system pressure cap: _____ psi/kPa	☐
2. Check the coolant level.	
a. Within manufacturer's specifications: Yes: ☐ No: ☐	☐
b. If No, describe the recommended corrective action(s):	☐
3. Pressure test cooling system pressure cap. Actual _____ psi/kPa	
a. Within manufacturer's specifications: Yes: ☐ No: ☐	☐
b. If No, describe the recommended corrective action(s):	☐
4. Pressure test cooling system.	
a. Within manufacturer's specifications: Yes: ☐ No: ☐	☐
b. If No, describe the recommended corrective action(s):	☐
5. Retrieve a coolant sample for analysis.	☐

6. Test coolant for proper freeze protection.	
a. Within manufacturer's specifications: Yes: ☐ No: ☐	☐
b. If No, describe the recommended corrective action(s):	☐
7. Test the coolant for proper additive package concentration.	
a. Within manufacturer's specifications: Yes: ☐ No: ☐	☐
b. If No, describe the recommended corrective action(s):	☐
8. Test the cooling system for proper pH.	
a. Within manufacturer's specifications: Yes: ☐ No: ☐	☐
b. If No, describe the recommended corrective action(s):	☐
9. List possible causes for excessive coolant consumption as outlined in the manufacturer's workshop materials:	☐
10. Discuss your findings with your supervisor/instructor.	☐

Non-Task–Specific Evaluations:	Step Completed
1. Tools and equipment were used as directed and returned in good working order.	☐
2. Complied with all general and task-specific safety standards, including proper use of any personal protection equipment.	☐
3. Completed the task in an appropriate time frame (recommendation: 1.5 or 2 times the flat rate).	☐
4. Left the workspace clean and orderly.	☐
5. Cared for customer property and returned it undamaged.	☐

Student signature _____ Date _____

Comments:

Have your supervisor/instructor verify satisfactory completion of this procedure, any observations made, and any necessary action(s) recommended.

Evaluation Instructions: The scoring box below is intended to act as a guide for both student and supervisor/instructor. Each criterion listed will help students to understand what is expected of them and help supervisors/instructors articulate the level of success at a particular task. The scoring is set up to allow a second attempt at each task (see the Test and Retest columns). Scoring is also designed to award students points only for task criteria that were completed correctly. Points are lost for failure to complete the employability requirements (see Non-Task-Specific Evaluation criteria). When all criteria are evaluated, tally the points for a total at the bottom of each column.

Tasksheet Scoring

	Test		Retest	
	Pass	**Fail**	**Pass**	**Fail**
Evaluation Items				
Task-Specific Evaluation	**(1 pt)**	**(0 pts)**	**(1 pt)**	**(0 pts)**
Student properly checked the coolant level.				
Student properly checked the cooling system pressure cap and performed the cooling system pressure test.				
Student properly took a cooling system sample.				
Student properly checked the cooling system freeze protection, cooling system additive package, and cooling system pH.				
Non-Task-Specific Evaluation	**(0 pts)**	**(−1 pt)**	**(0 pts)**	**(−1 pt)**
Student successfully completed at least three of the non-task-specific steps.				
Student successfully completed all five of the non-task-specific steps.				
Total Score: <total # of points/4 = %>				

CDX Tasksheet Number: MHT1E002

Student/Intern Information

Name _____ Date _____ Class _____

Vehicle, Customer, and Service Information

Vehicle used for this activity:

Year _____ Make _____ Model _____

Odometer _____ VIN _____

Materials Required

- Vehicle with possible engine concern
- Engine manufacturer's workshop materials
- Manufacturer-specific tools depending on the concern/procedure(s)
- Vehicle/component lifting equipment, if applicable

Task-Specific Safety Considerations

- Activities may require test-driving the vehicle on the school grounds or on a hoist, both of which carry severe risks. Attempt this task only with full permission from your supervisor/instructor, and follow all the guidelines exactly.
- Lifting equipment and machines such as vehicle jacks and stands, vehicle hoists, and engine hoists are important tools that increase productivity and make the job easier. However, they can also cause severe injury or death if used improperly. Make sure you follow the manufacturer's operation procedures. Also make sure you have your supervisor's/instructor's permission to use any particular type of lifting equipment.
- Comply with personal and environmental safety practices associated with clothing; eye protection; hand tools; power equipment; proper ventilation; and the handling, storage, and disposal of chemicals/materials in accordance with federal, state, and local regulations.
- Always wear the correct protective eyewear and clothing and use the appropriate safety equipment, as well as wheel chocks, fender covers, seat protectors, and floor mat protectors.
- Make sure you understand and observe all legislative and personal safety procedures when carrying out practical assignments. If you are unsure of what these are, ask your supervisor/instructor.

▶ **TASK** Test coolant temperature; test operation of temperature and level sensors, gauge, and/or sending unit; determine needed action.

MTST **I.E.2; P1**

Time off_____

Time on_____

Total time_____

Student Instructions: Read through the entire procedure prior to starting. Prepare your workspace and any tools or parts that may be needed to complete the task. When directed by your supervisor/instructor, begin the procedure to complete the task and check the box as each step is finished.

Note: This tasksheet may require the student to check the condition of miscellaneous vehicle fluids, some of which may be flammable and could damage the environment or cause health problems if not handled properly. Observe all safety precautions and follow local regulations for the proper disposal of fluids.

Procedure:	Step Completed
1. Record engine coolant operating temperature as outlined in the manufacturer's workshop materials:	
a. Engine coolant operating temperature: _____ °F/°C	☐
2. Test the engine temperature with an infrared thermometer at or near the coolant temperature sensor while cold. Compare this reading with the operation of the original equipment manufacturer (OEM) temperature sensor and gauge.	
a. Engine coolant temperature cold: _____ °F/°C	☐
b. Within manufacturer's specifications: Yes: ☐ No: ☐	☐
c. If No, describe the recommended corrective action(s):	☐
3. Bring the engine to operating temperature and test the engine temperature with an infrared thermometer at or near the coolant temperature sensor. Compare this reading with the operation of the OEM temperature sensor and gauge.	
a. Engine coolant temperature hot: _____ °F/°C	☐
b. Within manufacturer's specifications: Yes: ☐ No: ☐	☐
c. If No, describe the recommended corrective action(s):	☐
4. Check the operation of the coolant level sensors as outlined in the manufacturer's workshop materials.	
a. Within manufacturer's specifications: Yes: ☐ No: ☐	☐
b. If No, describe the recommended corrective action(s):	☐

5. Discuss your findings with your supervisor/instructor.	☐

Non-Task-Specific Evaluations:	Step Completed
1. Tools and equipment were used as directed and returned in good working order.	☐
2. Complied with all general and task-specific safety standards, including proper use of any personal protection equipment.	☐
3. Completed the task in an appropriate time frame (recommendation: 1.5 or 2 times the flat rate).	☐
4. Left the workspace clean and orderly.	☐
5. Cared for customer property and returned it undamaged.	☐

Student signature _____ Date _____

Comments:

Have your supervisor/instructor verify satisfactory completion of this procedure, any observations made,

and any necessary action(s) recommended.

Evaluation Instructions: The scoring box below is intended to act as a guide for both student and supervisor/instructor. Each criterion listed will help students to understand what is expected of them and help supervisors/instructors articulate the level of success at a particular task. The scoring is set up to allow a second attempt at each task (see the Test and Retest columns). Scoring is also designed to award students points only for task criteria that were completed correctly. Points are lost for failure to complete the employability requirements (see Non-Task-Specific Evaluation criteria). When all criteria are evaluated, tally the points for a total at the bottom of each column.

Tasksheet Scoring

Evaluation Items	Test		Retest	
	Pass	**Fail**	**Pass**	**Fail**
Task-Specific Evaluation	**(1 pt)**	**(0 pts)**	**(1 pt)**	**(0 pts)**
Student correctly recorded the engine coolant operating temperature.				
Student properly checked the cooling system temperature (cold).				
Student properly checked the cooling system temperature (hot).				
Student properly checked the cooling system level sensor.				
Non-Task-Specific Evaluation	**(0 pts)**	**(−1 pt)**	**(0 pts)**	**(−1 pt)**
Student successfully completed at least three of the non-task-specific steps.				
Student successfully completed all five of the non-task-specific steps.				
Total Score: <total # of points/4 = %>				

Supervisor/Instructor:

Supervisor/instructor signature _____ Date _____

Comments:

Retest supervisor/instructor signature _____ Date _____

Comments:

CDX Tasksheet Number: MHT1E003

Student/Intern Information

Name _____ Date _____ Class _____

Vehicle, Customer, and Service Information

Vehicle used for this activity:

Year _____ Make _____ Model _____

Odometer _____ VIN _____

Materials Required

- Vehicle with possible engine concern
- Engine manufacturer's workshop materials
- Manufacturer-specific tools depending on the concern/procedure(s)
- Vehicle/component lifting equipment, if applicable

Task-Specific Safety Considerations

- Activities may require test-driving the vehicle on the school grounds or on a hoist, both of which carry severe risks. Attempt this task only with full permission from your supervisor/instructor, and follow all the guidelines exactly.
- Lifting equipment and machines such as vehicle jacks and stands, vehicle hoists, and engine hoists are important tools that increase productivity and make the job easier. However, they can also cause severe injury or death if used improperly. Make sure you follow the manufacturer's operation procedures. Also make sure you have your supervisor's/instructor's permission to use any particular type of lifting equipment.
- Comply with personal and environmental safety practices associated with clothing; eye protection; hand tools; power equipment; proper ventilation; and the handling, storage, and disposal of chemicals/materials in accordance with federal, state, and local regulations.
- Always wear the correct protective eyewear and clothing and use the appropriate safety equipment, as well as wheel chocks, fender covers, seat protectors, and floor mat protectors.
- Make sure you understand and observe all legislative and personal safety procedures when carrying out practical assignments. If you are unsure of what these are, ask your supervisor/instructor.

▶ **TASK** Inspect and reinstall/replace pulleys, tensioners, and drive belts; adjust drive belts and check alignment.   *MTST* *I.E.3; P1*

Time off_____

Time on_____

Total time_____

Student Instructions: Read through the entire procedure prior to starting. Prepare your workspace and any tools or parts that may be needed to complete the task. When directed by your supervisor/instructor, begin the procedure to complete the task and check the box as each step is finished.

Note: This tasksheet may require the student to check the condition of miscellaneous vehicle fluids, some of which may be flammable and could damage the environment or cause health problems if not handled properly. Observe all safety precautions and follow local regulations for the proper disposal of fluids.

Procedure:	Step Completed
1. Reference the appropriate manufacturer's workshop materials.	

a. Identify belt type(s).
   i. Serpentine: ☐
   ii. V-belt: ☐
	☐

b. Identify tensioner type(s).
   i. Self-tensioner: ☐
   ii. Manual: ☐
	☐

c. Drive-belt tension: _____ ft-lb/N·m	☐
2. Inspect all drive belts and pulleys for proper alignment as outlined in the manufacturer's workshop materials.	
a. Within manufacturer's specifications: Yes: ☐ No: ☐	☐
b. If No, describe the recommended corrective action(s):	☐
3. Remove all drive belts and inspect them for wear/damage as outlined in the manufacturer's workshop materials.	
a. Within manufacturer's specifications: Yes: ☐ No: ☐	☐
b. If No, describe the recommended corrective action(s):	☐
4. Inspect all drive pulleys for wear/damage as outlined in the manufacturer's workshop materials.	
a. Within manufacturer's specifications: Yes: ☐ No: ☐	☐
b. If No, describe the recommended corrective action(s):	☐

5. Inspect all tensioners for wear/damage as outlined in the manufacturer's workshop materials.	
a. Within manufacturer's specifications: Yes: ☐ No: ☐	☐
b. If No, describe the recommended corrective action(s):	☐
6. If instructed by your supervisor/instructor, repair any pulley(s) that are out of alignment. List the steps of your procedure:	☐
7. Reinstall the drive belt(s) and adjust them to proper tension as outlined in the manufacturer's workshop materials.	
a. Within manufacturer's specifications: Yes: ☐ No: ☐	☐
b. If No, describe the recommended corrective action(s):	☐
8. Discuss your findings with your supervisor/instructor.	☐

Non-Task-Specific Evaluations:	Step Completed
1. Tools and equipment were used as directed and returned in good working order.	☐
2. Complied with all general and task-specific safety standards, including proper use of any personal protection equipment.	☐
3. Completed the task in an appropriate time frame (recommendation: 1.5 or 2 times the flat rate).	☐
4. Left the workspace clean and orderly.	☐
5. Cared for customer property and returned it undamaged.	☐

Student signature _____ Date _____

Comments:

Have your supervisor/instructor verify satisfactory completion of this procedure, any observations made, and any necessary action(s) recommended.

Evaluation Instructions: The scoring box below is intended to act as a guide for both student and supervisor/instructor. Each criterion listed will help students to understand what is expected of them and help supervisors/instructors articulate the level of success at a particular task. The scoring is set up to allow a second attempt at each task (see the Test and Retest columns). Scoring is also designed to award students points only for task criteria that were completed correctly. Points are lost for failure to complete the employability requirements (see Non-Task-Specific Evaluation criteria). When all criteria are evaluated, tally the points for a total at the bottom of each column.

Tasksheet Scoring

Evaluation Items	Test		Retest	
	Pass	**Fail**	**Pass**	**Fail**
Task-Specific Evaluation	**(1 pt)**	**(0 pts)**	**(1 pt)**	**(0 pts)**
Student properly removed and inspected the drive belts.				
Student properly checked and corrected pulley alignment.				
Student properly inspected pulleys and tensioners.				
Student reinstalled all removed components undamaged and in working order.				
Non-Task-Specific Evaluation	**(0 pts)**	**(−1 pt)**	**(0 pts)**	**(−1 pt)**
Student successfully completed at least three of the non-task-specific steps.				
Student successfully completed all five of the non-task-specific steps.				
Total Score: <total # of points/4 = %>				

Supervisor/Instructor:

Supervisor/instructor signature _____ Date _____

Comments:

Retest supervisor/instructor signature _____ Date _____

Comments:

CDX Tasksheet Number: MHT1E004

Student/Intern Information

Name _____ Date _____ Class _____

Vehicle, Customer, and Service Information

Vehicle used for this activity:

Year _____ Make _____ Model _____

Odometer _____ VIN _____

Materials Required

- Vehicle with possible engine concern
- Engine manufacturer's workshop materials
- Manufacturer-specific tools depending on the concern/procedure(s)
- Vehicle/component lifting equipment, if applicable

Task-Specific Safety Considerations

- Activities may require test-driving the vehicle on the school grounds or on a hoist, both of which carry severe risks. Attempt this task only with full permission from your supervisor/instructor, and follow all the guidelines exactly.
- Lifting equipment and machines such as vehicle jacks and stands, vehicle hoists, and engine hoists are important tools that increase productivity and make the job easier. However, they can also cause severe injury or death if used improperly. Make sure you follow the manufacturer's operation procedures. Also make sure you have your supervisor's/instructor's permission to use any particular type of lifting equipment.
- Comply with personal and environmental safety practices associated with clothing; eye protection; hand tools; power equipment; proper ventilation; and the handling, storage, and disposal of chemicals/materials in accordance with federal, state, and local regulations.
- Always wear the correct protective eyewear and clothing and use the appropriate safety equipment, as well as wheel chocks, fender covers, seat protectors, and floor mat protectors.
- Make sure you understand and observe all legislative and personal safety procedures when carrying out practical assignments. If you are unsure of what these are, ask your supervisor/instructor.

▶ **TASK** Recover coolant; flush and refill with the recommended coolant/additive package; bleed cooling system.

MTST
I.E.4; P1

Time off_____

Time on_____

Total time_____

Student Instructions: Read through the entire procedure prior to starting. Prepare your workspace and any tools or parts that may be needed to complete the task. When directed by your supervisor/instructor, begin the procedure to complete the task and check the box as each step is finished.

Note: This tasksheet may require the student to check the condition of miscellaneous vehicle fluids, some of which may be flammable and could damage the environment or cause health problems if not handled properly. Observe all safety precautions and follow local regulations for the proper disposal of fluids.

Procedure:	Step Completed
1. Reference the appropriate manufacturer's workshop materials.	
a. Coolant type:	☐
b. Coolant quantity: _____ quarts/gallons	☐
2. Using a collection container of an adequate size, drain the coolant.	☐
3. Ensure that the discarded coolant is disposed of in accordance with all environmental and government regulations.	☐
4. Flush the cooling system as outlined in the manufacturer's workshop materials. Use a coolant flush machine to make sure the entire system is adequately flushed.	☐
5. Refill the cooling system with the manufacturer's recommended coolant and quantity. List any original equipment manufacturer (OEM) recommended procedures for bleeding the cooling system:	☐
6. Once the cooling system has been properly filled and bled, start the engine and bring it to operating temperature.	☐
7. Shut down the engine and allow it to cool. Check for proper coolant level.	
a. Within manufacturer's specifications: Yes: ☐ No: ☐	☐
b. If No, describe the recommended corrective action(s):	☐

8. Discuss your findings with your supervisor/instructor.	☐

Non-Task-Specific Evaluations:	Step Completed
1. Tools and equipment were used as directed and returned in good working order.	
2. Complied with all general and task-specific safety standards, including proper use of any personal protection equipment.	
3. Completed the task in an appropriate time frame (recommendation: 1.5 or 2 times the flat rate).	
4. Left the workspace clean and orderly.	
5. Cared for customer property and returned it undamaged.	

Student signature _____ Date _____

Comments:

Have your supervisor/instructor verify satisfactory completion of this procedure, any observations made, and any necessary action(s) recommended.

Evaluation Instructions: The scoring box below is intended to act as a guide for both student and supervisor/instructor. Each criterion listed will help students to understand what is expected of them and help supervisors/instructors articulate the level of success at a particular task. The scoring is set up to allow a second attempt at each task (see the Test and Retest columns). Scoring is also designed to award students points only for task criteria that were completed correctly. Points are lost for failure to complete the employability requirements (see Non-Task-Specific Evaluation criteria). When all criteria are evaluated, tally the points for a total at the bottom of each column.

Tasksheet Scoring

Evaluation Items	Test		Retest	
	Pass	Fail	Pass	Fail
Task-Specific Evaluation	**(1 pt)**	**(0 pts)**	**(1 pt)**	**(0 pts)**
Student properly drained coolant and disposed of it.				
Student properly flushed the cooling system.				
Student properly refilled and bled the cooling system.				
Student properly checked the cooling system level.				
Non-Task-Specific Evaluation	**(0 pts)**	**(−1 pt)**	**(0 pts)**	**(−1 pt)**
Student successfully completed at least three of the non-task-specific steps.				
Student successfully completed all five of the non-task-specific steps.				
Total Score: <total # of points/4 = %>				

Supervisor/Instructor:

Supervisor/instructor signature _____ Date _____

Comments:

[ ]

Retest supervisor/instructor signature _____ Date _____

Comments:

[ ]

CDX Tasksheet Number: MHT1E005

Student/Intern Information

Name _____ Date _____ Class _____

Vehicle, Customer, and Service Information

Vehicle used for this activity:

Year _____ Make _____ Model _____

Odometer _____ VIN _____

Materials Required

- Vehicle with possible engine concern
- Engine manufacturer's workshop materials
- Manufacturer-specific tools depending on the concern/procedure(s)
- Vehicle/component lifting equipment, if applicable

Task-Specific Safety Considerations

- Activities may require test-driving the vehicle on the school grounds or on a hoist, both of which carry severe risks. Attempt this task only with full permission from your supervisor/instructor, and follow all the guidelines exactly.
- Lifting equipment and machines such as vehicle jacks and stands, vehicle hoists, and engine hoists are important tools that increase productivity and make the job easier. However, they can also cause severe injury or death if used improperly. Make sure you follow the manufacturer's operation procedures. Also make sure you have your supervisor's/instructor's permission to use any particular type of lifting equipment.
- Comply with personal and environmental safety practices associated with clothing; eye protection; hand tools; power equipment; proper ventilation; and the handling, storage, and disposal of chemicals/materials in accordance with federal, state, and local regulations.
- Always wear the correct protective eyewear and clothing and use the appropriate safety equipment, as well as wheel chocks, fender covers, seat protectors, and floor mat protectors.
- Make sure you understand and observe all legislative and personal safety procedures when carrying out practical assignments. If you are unsure of what these are, ask your supervisor/instructor.

▶ TASK Inspect coolant conditioner/filter assembly for leaks; inspect valves, lines, and fittings; replace as needed.

MTST
I.E.5; P1

Time off_____

Time on_____

Total time_____

Student Instructions: Read through the entire procedure prior to starting. Prepare your workspace and any tools or parts that may be needed to complete the task. When directed by your supervisor/instructor, begin the procedure to complete the task and check the box as each step is finished.

Note: This tasksheet may require the student to check the condition of miscellaneous vehicle fluids, some of which may be flammable and could damage the environment or cause health problems if not handled properly. Observe all safety precautions and follow local regulations for the proper disposal of fluids.

Procedure:	Step Completed
1. Reference the appropriate manufacturer's workshop materials.	
a. Coolant conditioner/filter type:	☐
2. Check and inspect the coolant conditioner/filter assembly for leaks.	☐
3. Pressurize the cooling system and recheck and inspect the coolant conditioner/filter assembly, lines, and valves for leaks.	
a. Filter assembly: Yes: ☐ No: ☐	☐
b. Coolant filter lines: Yes: ☐ No: ☐	☐
c. Coolant filter valves: Yes: ☐ No: ☐	☐
d. If Yes for any of the items above, describe the recommended corrective action(s):	☐
4. Check the coolant for the proper additive level. List any original equipment manufacturer (OEM) recommended procedures for bleeding the cooling system:	
a. Within manufacturer's specifications: Yes: ☐ No: ☐	☐
b. If No, describe the recommended corrective action(s):	☐
5. Retrieve a coolant sample for analysis.	☐

	Step Completed
6. If directed by your supervisor/instructor, remove and replace coolant system filter.	☐
7. Discuss your findings with your supervisor/instructor.	☐

Non-Task-Specific Evaluations:	Step Completed
1. Tools and equipment were used as directed and returned in good working order.	☐
2. Complied with all general and task-specific safety standards, including proper use of any personal protection equipment.	☐
3. Completed the task in an appropriate time frame (recommendation: 1.5 or 2 times the flat rate).	☐
4. Left the workspace clean and orderly.	☐
5. Cared for customer property and returned it undamaged.	☐

Student signature _____ Date _____

Comments:

Have your supervisor/instructor verify satisfactory completion of this procedure, any observations made, and any necessary action(s) recommended.

Evaluation Instructions: The scoring box below is intended to act as a guide for both student and supervisor/instructor. Each criterion listed will help students to understand what is expected of them and help supervisors/instructors articulate the level of success at a particular task. The scoring is set up to allow a second attempt at each task (see the Test and Retest columns). Scoring is also designed to award students points only for task criteria that were completed correctly. Points are lost for failure to complete the employability requirements (see Non-Task-Specific Evaluation criteria). When all criteria are evaluated, tally the points for a total at the bottom of each column.

Tasksheet Scoring

Evaluation Items	Test		Retest	
	Pass	Fail	Pass	Fail
Task-Specific Evaluation	**(1 pt)**	**(0 pts)**	**(1 pt)**	**(0 pts)**
Student properly inspected the coolant filter, lines, and valves.				
Student properly checked the coolant additive package.				
Student properly took the coolant sample.				
Student properly changed the coolant filter.				
Non-Task-Specific Evaluation	**(0 pts)**	**(−1 pt)**	**(0 pts)**	**(−1 pt)**
Student successfully completed at least three of the non-task-specific steps.				
Student successfully completed all five of the non-task-specific steps.				
Total Score: <total # of points/4 = %>				

Supervisor/Instructor:

Supervisor/instructor signature _____ Date _____

Comments:

```

```

Retest supervisor/instructor signature _____ Date _____

Comments:

```

```

CDX Tasksheet Number: MHT1E006

Student/Intern Information

Name _____ Date _____ Class _____

Vehicle, Customer, and Service Information

Vehicle used for this activity:

Year _____ Make _____ Model _____

Odometer _____ VIN _____

Materials Required

- Vehicle with possible engine concern
- Engine manufacturer's workshop materials
- Manufacturer-specific tools depending on the concern/procedure(s)
- Vehicle/component lifting equipment, if applicable

Task-Specific Safety Considerations

- Activities may require test-driving the vehicle on the school grounds or on a hoist, both of which carry severe risks. Attempt this task only with full permission from your supervisor/instructor, and follow all the guidelines exactly.
- Lifting equipment and machines such as vehicle jacks and stands, vehicle hoists, and engine hoists are important tools that increase productivity and make the job easier. However, they can also cause severe injury or death if used improperly. Make sure you follow the manufacturer's operation procedures. Also make sure you have your supervisor's/instructor's permission to use any particular type of lifting equipment.
- Comply with personal and environmental safety practices associated with clothing; eye protection; hand tools; power equipment; proper ventilation; and the handling, storage, and disposal of chemicals/materials in accordance with federal, state, and local regulations.
- Always wear the correct protective eyewear and clothing and use the appropriate safety equipment, as well as wheel chocks, fender covers, seat protectors, and floor mat protectors.
- Make sure you understand and observe all legislative and personal safety procedures when carrying out practical assignments. If you are unsure of what these are, ask your supervisor/instructor.

▶ **TASK** Inspect water pump, hoses, and clamps; determine needed action. **MTST** *I.E.6; P1*

Time off_____

Time on_____

Student Instructions: Read through the entire procedure prior to starting. Prepare your workspace and any tools or parts that may be needed to complete the task. When directed by your supervisor/instructor, begin the procedure to complete the task and check the box as each step is finished.

Total time_____

Note: This tasksheet may require the student to check the condition of miscellaneous vehicle fluids, some of which may be flammable and could damage the environment or cause health problems if not handled properly. Observe all safety precautions and follow local regulations for the proper disposal of fluids.

Procedure:	Step Completed
1. Check and inspect the water pump for leaks as outlined in the manufacturer's workshop materials. (**Note:** Look closely at the weep hole in the bottom of the pump for dried coolant residue. Always replace upon engine overhaul.)	
a. Within manufacturer's specifications: Yes: ☐ No: ☐	☐
b. If No, describe the recommended corrective action(s):	☐
2. Check and inspect all hoses for leaks, damage, swelling, or soft spots.	
a. Within manufacturer's specifications: Yes: ☐ No: ☐	☐
b. If No, describe the recommended corrective action(s):	☐
3. Check all hose clamps for proper tightness/damage.	
a. Within manufacturer's specifications: Yes: ☐ No: ☐	☐
b. If No, describe the recommended corrective action(s):	☐
4. If directed by your supervisor/instructor, replace the water pump, hoses, and/or clamps. List the steps of your procedure:	☐
5. Discuss your findings with your supervisor/instructor.	☐

Non-Task-Specific Evaluations:	Step Completed
1. Tools and equipment were used as directed and returned in good working order.	☐
2. Complied with all general and task-specific safety standards, including proper use of any personal protection equipment.	☐
3. Completed the task in an appropriate time frame (recommendation: 1.5 or 2 times the flat rate).	☐
4. Left the workspace clean and orderly.	☐
5. Cared for customer property and returned it undamaged.	☐

Student signature _____ Date _____

Comments:

Have your supervisor/instructor verify satisfactory completion of this procedure, any observations made, and any necessary action(s) recommended.

Evaluation Instructions: The scoring box below is intended to act as a guide for both student and supervisor/instructor. Each criterion listed will help students to understand what is expected of them and help supervisors/instructors articulate the level of success at a particular task. The scoring is set up to allow a second attempt at each task (see the Test and Retest columns). Scoring is also designed to award students points only for task criteria that were completed correctly. Points are lost for failure to complete the employability requirements (see Non-Task-Specific Evaluation criteria). When all criteria are evaluated, tally the points for a total at the bottom of each column.

Tasksheet Scoring

Evaluation Items	Test		Retest	
	Pass	**Fail**	**Pass**	**Fail**
Task-Specific Evaluation	**(1 pt)**	**(0 pts)**	**(1 pt)**	**(0 pts)**
Student properly inspected the water pump.				
Student properly inspected the cooling system hoses and clamps.				
Student properly replaced the water pump, hoses, and/or clamps.				
Student properly changed the coolant filter.				
Non-Task-Specific Evaluation	**(0 pts)**	**(−1 pt)**	**(0 pts)**	**(−1 pt)**
Student successfully completed at least three of the non-task-specific steps.				
Student successfully completed all five of the non-task-specific steps.				
Total Score: <total # of points/4 = %>				

Supervisor/Instructor:

Supervisor/instructor signature _____ Date _____

Comments:

Retest supervisor/instructor signature _____ Date _____

Comments:

CDX Tasksheet Number: MHT1E007

Student/Intern Information

Name _____ Date _____ Class _____

Vehicle, Customer, and Service Information

Vehicle used for this activity:

Year _____ Make _____ Model _____

Odometer _____ VIN _____

Materials Required

- Vehicle with possible engine concern
- Engine manufacturer's workshop materials
- Manufacturer-specific tools depending on the concern/procedure(s)
- Vehicle/component lifting equipment, if applicable

Task-Specific Safety Considerations

- Activities may require test-driving the vehicle on the school grounds or on a hoist, both of which carry severe risks. Attempt this task only with full permission from your supervisor/instructor, and follow all the guidelines exactly.
- Lifting equipment and machines such as vehicle jacks and stands, vehicle hoists, and engine hoists are important tools that increase productivity and make the job easier. However, they can also cause severe injury or death if used improperly. Make sure you follow the manufacturer's operation procedures. Also make sure you have your supervisor's/instructor's permission to use any particular type of lifting equipment.
- Comply with personal and environmental safety practices associated with clothing; eye protection; hand tools; power equipment; proper ventilation; and the handling, storage, and disposal of chemicals/materials in accordance with federal, state, and local regulations.
- Always wear the correct protective eyewear and clothing and use the appropriate safety equipment, as well as wheel chocks, fender covers, seat protectors, and floor mat protectors.
- Make sure you understand and observe all legislative and personal safety procedures when carrying out practical assignments. If you are unsure of what these are, ask your supervisor/instructor.

▶ **TASK** Inspect and pressure test cooling system(s); pressure test cap, tank(s), and recovery systems; inspect radiator and mountings; determine needed action.

MTST
I.E.7; P1

Time off_____

Time on_____

Total time_____

Student Instructions: Read through the entire procedure prior to starting. Prepare your workspace and any tools or parts that may be needed to complete the task. When directed by your supervisor/instructor, begin the procedure to complete the task and check the box as each step is finished.

Note: This tasksheet may require the student to check the condition of miscellaneous vehicle fluids, some of which may be flammable and could damage the environment or cause health problems if not handled properly. Observe all safety precautions and follow local regulations for the proper disposal of fluids.

Procedure:	Step Completed
1. Inspect the radiator and recovery tanks for signs of leakage.	
a. Within manufacturer's specifications: Yes: ☐ No: ☐	☐
b. If No, describe the recommended corrective action(s):	☐
2. Inspect the radiator mounts for loose, missing, or damaged components.	
a. Within manufacturer's specifications: Yes: ☐ No: ☐	☐
b. If No, describe the recommended corrective action(s):	☐
3. Test the cooling system pressure cap as outlined in the manufacturer's workshop materials, and record the pressure cap rating.	
a. Cooling system pressure cap rating: _____ psi/kPa	☐
b. Within manufacturer's specifications: Yes: ☐ No: ☐	☐
c. If No, describe the recommended corrective action(s):	☐
4. Record the manufacturer's pressure recommendation for pressure testing the cooling system, and perform the test.	
a. Cooling system pressure test specification: _____ psi/kPa	☐
b. Within manufacturer's specifications: Yes: ☐ No: ☐	☐
c. If No, describe the recommended corrective action(s):	☐

5. Start the engine and bring it to operating temperature. Using an infrared thermometer, check the radiator core in multiple locations for hot and cold areas.	
a. Within manufacturer's specifications: Yes: ☐ No: ☐	☐
b. If No, describe the recommended corrective action(s):	☐
6. Discuss your findings with your supervisor/instructor.	☐

Non-Task-Specific Evaluations:	Step Completed
1. Tools and equipment were used as directed and returned in good working order.	☐
2. Complied with all general and task-specific safety standards, including proper use of any personal protection equipment.	☐
3. Completed the task in an appropriate time frame (recommendation: 1.5 or 2 times the flat rate).	☐
4. Left the workspace clean and orderly.	☐
5. Cared for customer property and returned it undamaged.	☐

Student signature _____ Date _____

Comments:

Have your supervisor/instructor verify satisfactory completion of this procedure, any observations made, and any necessary action(s) recommended.

Evaluation Instructions: The scoring box below is intended to act as a guide for both student and supervisor/instructor. Each criterion listed will help students to understand what is expected of them and help supervisors/instructors articulate the level of success at a particular task. The scoring is set up to allow a second attempt at each task (see the Test and Retest columns). Scoring is also designed to award students points only for task criteria that were completed correctly. Points are lost for failure to complete the employability requirements (see Non-Task-Specific Evaluation criteria). When all criteria are evaluated, tally the points for a total at the bottom of each column.

Tasksheet Scoring

Evaluation Items	Test		Retest	
	Pass	Fail	Pass	Fail
Task-Specific Evaluation	**(1 pt)**	**(0 pts)**	**(1 pt)**	**(0 pts)**
Student properly inspected the radiator, recovery tank, radiator mounts, and brackets.				
Student properly tested the cooling system.				
Student properly performed the cooling system pressure test.				
Student properly inspected the radiator for hot and cold spots.				
Non-Task-Specific Evaluation	**(0 pts)**	**(−1 pt)**	**(0 pts)**	**(−1 pt)**
Student successfully completed at least three of the non-task-specific steps.				
Student successfully completed all five of the non-task-specific steps.				
Total Score: <total # of points/4 = %>				

Supervisor/Instructor:

Supervisor/instructor signature _____ Date _____

Comments:

Retest supervisor/instructor signature _____ Date _____

Comments:

CDX Tasksheet Number: MHT1E008

Student/Intern Information

Name _____ Date _____ Class _____

Vehicle, Customer, and Service Information

Vehicle used for this activity:

Year _____ Make _____ Model _____

Odometer _____ VIN _____

Materials Required

- Vehicle with possible engine concern
- Engine manufacturer's workshop materials
- Manufacturer-specific tools depending on the concern/procedure(s)
- Vehicle/component lifting equipment, if applicable

Task-Specific Safety Considerations

- Activities may require test-driving the vehicle on the school grounds or on a hoist, both of which carry severe risks. Attempt this task only with full permission from your supervisor/instructor, and follow all the guidelines exactly.
- Lifting equipment and machines such as vehicle jacks and stands, vehicle hoists, and engine hoists are important tools that increase productivity and make the job easier. However, they can also cause severe injury or death if used improperly. Make sure you follow the manufacturer's operation procedures. Also make sure you have your supervisor's/instructor's permission to use any particular type of lifting equipment.
- Comply with personal and environmental safety practices associated with clothing; eye protection; hand tools; power equipment; proper ventilation; and the handling, storage, and disposal of chemicals/materials in accordance with federal, state, and local regulations.
- Always wear the correct protective eyewear and clothing and use the appropriate safety equipment, as well as wheel chocks, fender covers, seat protectors, and floor mat protectors.
- Make sure you understand and observe all legislative and personal safety procedures when carrying out practical assignments. If you are unsure of what these are, ask your supervisor/instructor.

▶ **TASK** Inspect, test, and repair thermostatic cooling fan system (hydraulic, pneumatic, and electronic) and fan shroud; determine needed action.

MTST
I.E.8; P1

Time off_____

Time on_____

Total time_____

Student Instructions: Read through the entire procedure prior to starting. Prepare your workspace and any tools or parts that may be needed to complete the task. When directed by your supervisor/instructor, begin the procedure to complete the task and check the box as each step is finished.

Note: This tasksheet may require the student to check the condition of miscellaneous vehicle fluids, some of which may be flammable and could damage the environment or cause health problems if not handled properly. Observe all safety precautions and follow local regulations for the proper disposal of fluids.

Procedure:	Step Completed
1. Identify the type of cooling fan drive (viscous, hydraulic, pneumatic, electric, or Visctronic©):	☐
2. List any issues of concern for the applicable fan drive as outlined in the manufacturer's workshop:	☐
3. Inspect the fan drive for loose, missing, or damaged components.	
a. Within manufacturer's specifications: Yes: ☐ No: ☐	☐
b. If No, describe the recommended corrective action(s):	☐
4. Inspect the engine cooling fan for loose, missing, or damaged blades/mounting.	
a. Within manufacturer's specifications: Yes: ☐ No: ☐	☐
b. If No, describe the recommended corrective action(s):	☐
5. Inspect the radiator shroud for loose, missing, or damaged components.	
a. Within manufacturer's specifications: Yes: ☐ No: ☐	☐
b. If No, describe the recommended corrective action(s):	☐

	Step Completed
6. Start the engine and, using the appropriate electronic service tool (EST), command the cooling fan to engage.	
a. Within manufacturer's specifications: Yes: ☐ No: ☐	☐
b. If No, describe the recommended corrective action(s):	☐
7. If directed by your supervisor/instructor, remove/reinstall the fan drive. List the steps of your procedure:	☐
8. Discuss your findings with your supervisor/instructor.	☐

Non-Task-Specific Evaluations:	Step Completed
1. Tools and equipment were used as directed and returned in good working order.	☐
2. Complied with all general and task-specific safety standards, including proper use of any personal protection equipment.	☐
3. Completed the task in an appropriate time frame (recommendation: 1.5 or 2 times the flat rate).	☐
4. Left the workspace clean and orderly.	☐
5. Cared for customer property and returned it undamaged.	☐

Student signature _____ Date _____

Comments:

Have your supervisor/instructor verify satisfactory completion of this procedure, any observations made, and any necessary action(s) recommended.

Evaluation Instructions: The scoring box below is intended to act as a guide for both student and supervisor/instructor. Each criterion listed will help students to understand what is expected of them and help supervisors/instructors articulate the level of success at a particular task. The scoring is set up to allow a second attempt at each task (see the Test and Retest columns). Scoring is also designed to award students points only for task criteria that were completed correctly. Points are lost for failure to complete the employability requirements (see Non-Task-Specific Evaluation criteria). When all criteria are evaluated, tally the points for a total at the bottom of each column.

Tasksheet Scoring

Evaluation Items	Test		Retest	
	Pass	Fail	Pass	Fail
Task-Specific Evaluation	**(1 pt)**	**(0 pts)**	**(1 pt)**	**(0 pts)**
Student properly identified and inspected the fan drive.				
Student properly inspected the cooling fan.				
Student properly inspected the fan shroud.				
Student properly used the EST to engage the fan drive.				
Non-Task-Specific Evaluation	**(0 pts)**	**(−1 pt)**	**(0 pts)**	**(−1 pt)**
Student successfully completed at least three of the non-task-specific steps.				
Student successfully completed all five of the non-task-specific steps.				
Total Score: <total # of points/4 = %>				

Supervisor/Instructor:

Supervisor/instructor signature _____ Date _____

Comments:

Retest supervisor/instructor signature _____ Date _____

Comments:

CDX Tasksheet Number: MHT1E009

Student/Intern Information

Name _____ Date _____ Class _____

Vehicle, Customer, and Service Information

Vehicle used for this activity:

Year _____ Make _____ Model _____

Odometer _____ VIN _____

Materials Required

- Vehicle with possible engine concern
- Engine manufacturer's workshop materials
- Manufacturer-specific tools depending on the concern/procedure(s)
- Vehicle/component lifting equipment, if applicable

Task-Specific Safety Considerations

- Activities may require test-driving the vehicle on the school grounds or on a hoist, both of which carry severe risks. Attempt this task only with full permission from your supervisor/instructor, and follow all the guidelines exactly.
- Lifting equipment and machines such as vehicle jacks and stands, vehicle hoists, and engine hoists are important tools that increase productivity and make the job easier. However, they can also cause severe injury or death if used improperly. Make sure you follow the manufacturer's operation procedures. Also make sure you have your supervisor's/instructor's permission to use any particular type of lifting equipment.
- Comply with personal and environmental safety practices associated with clothing; eye protection; hand tools; power equipment; proper ventilation; and the handling, storage, and disposal of chemicals/materials in accordance with federal, state, and local regulations.
- Always wear the correct protective eyewear and clothing and use the appropriate safety equipment, as well as wheel chocks, fender covers, seat protectors, and floor mat protectors.
- Make sure you understand and observe all legislative and personal safety procedures when carrying out practical assignments. If you are unsure of what these are, ask your supervisor/instructor.

▶ **TASK** Test engine block heater(s); determine needed action. _____ **MTST** **I.E.9; P2**

Time off_____

Time on_____

Student Instructions: Read through the entire procedure prior to starting. Prepare your workspace and any tools or parts that may be needed to complete the task. When directed by your supervisor/instructor, begin the procedure to complete the task and check the box as each step is finished.

Total time_____

Note: This tasksheet may require the student to check the condition of miscellaneous vehicle fluids, some of which may be flammable and could damage the environment or cause health problems if not handled properly. Observe all safety precautions and follow local regulations for the proper disposal of fluids.

Procedure:	Step Completed
1. Identify the type of engine block heater rating as outlined in the manufacturer's workshop materials:	☐
2. Inspect the block heater cord/connections for burnt or damaged wires.	☐
3. Inspect the block heater for signs of coolant leakage.	☐
4. With the engine cold and using an infrared thermometer, record the temperature of the engine block at or near the engine block heater: _____ °F/°C	☐
5. With the engine cold, plug in the block heater for one hour. Using an infrared thermometer, record the temperature of the engine block at or near the engine block heater: _____ °F/°C	☐
6. Using a digital volt-ohmmeter (DVOM), record the block heater ohms. A reading of OL (meaning "open loop") indicates an open block heater cord or heating element. _____ ohms	
a. Within manufacturer's specifications: Yes: ☐ No: ☐	☐
b. If No, describe the recommended corrective action(s):	☐
7. If directed by your supervisor/instructor, replace the block heater and/or cord.	☐
8. Discuss your findings with your supervisor/instructor.	☐

Non-Task-Specific Evaluations:	Step Completed
1. Tools and equipment were used as directed and returned in good working order.	☐
2. Complied with all general and task-specific safety standards, including proper use of any personal protection equipment.	☐
3. Completed the task in an appropriate time frame (recommendation: 1.5 or 2 times the flat rate).	☐
4. Left the workspace clean and orderly.	☐
5. Cared for customer property and returned it undamaged.	☐

Student signature _____ Date _____

Comments:

Have your supervisor/instructor verify satisfactory completion of this procedure, any observations made,

and any necessary action(s) recommended.

Evaluation Instructions: The scoring box below is intended to act as a guide for both student and supervisor/instructor. Each criterion listed will help students to understand what is expected of them and help supervisors/instructors articulate the level of success at a particular task. The scoring is set up to allow a second attempt at each task (see the Test and Retest columns). Scoring is also designed to award students points only for task criteria that were completed correctly. Points are lost for failure to complete the employability requirements (see Non-Task-Specific Evaluation criteria). When all criteria are evaluated, tally the points for a total at the bottom of each column.

Tasksheet Scoring

Evaluation Items	Test		Retest	
	Pass	**Fail**	**Pass**	**Fail**
Task-Specific Evaluation	**(1 pt)**	**(0 pts)**	**(1 pt)**	**(0 pts)**
Student properly inspected the block heater cord.				
Student properly inspected the block heater for signs of coolant leakage.				
Student properly checked the block heater function and ohms.				
Student properly replaced the block heater and/or cord.				
Non-Task-Specific Evaluation	**(0 pts)**	**(−1 pt)**	**(0 pts)**	**(−1 pt)**
Student successfully completed at least three of the non-task-specific steps.				
Student successfully completed all five of the non-task-specific steps.				
Total Score: <total # of points/4 = %>				

Supervisor/Instructor:

Supervisor/instructor signature _____ Date _____

Comments:

Retest supervisor/instructor signature _____ Date _____

Comments:

CDX Tasksheet Number: MHT1E010

Student/Intern Information

Name _____ Date _____ Class _____

Vehicle, Customer, and Service Information

Vehicle used for this activity:

Year _____ Make _____ Model _____

Odometer _____ VIN _____

Materials Required
- Vehicle with possible engine concern
- Engine manufacturer's workshop materials
- Manufacturer-specific tools depending on the concern/procedure(s)
- Vehicle/component lifting equipment, if applicable

Task-Specific Safety Considerations
- Activities may require test-driving the vehicle on the school grounds or on a hoist, both of which carry severe risks. Attempt this task only with full permission from your supervisor/instructor, and follow all the guidelines exactly.
- Lifting equipment and machines such as vehicle jacks and stands, vehicle hoists, and engine hoists are important tools that increase productivity and make the job easier. However, they can also cause severe injury or death if used improperly. Make sure you follow the manufacturer's operation procedures. Also make sure you have your supervisor's/instructor's permission to use any particular type of lifting equipment.
- Comply with personal and environmental safety practices associated with clothing; eye protection; hand tools; power equipment; proper ventilation; and the handling, storage, and disposal of chemicals/materials in accordance with federal, state, and local regulations.
- Always wear the correct protective eyewear and clothing and use the appropriate safety equipment, as well as wheel chocks, fender covers, seat protectors, and floor mat protectors.
- Make sure you understand and observe all legislative and personal safety procedures when carrying out practical assignments. If you are unsure of what these are, ask your supervisor/instructor.

▶ **TASK** Diagnose engine coolant consumption; determine needed action. **MTST** *I.E.10; P1*

Time off_____

Time on_____

Student Instructions: Read through the entire procedure prior to starting. Prepare your workspace and any tools or parts that may be needed to complete the task. When directed by your supervisor/instructor, begin the procedure to complete the task and check the box as each step is finished.

Total time_____

Note: This tasksheet may require the student to check the condition of miscellaneous vehicle fluids, some of which may be flammable and could damage the environment or cause health problems if not handled properly. Observe all safety precautions and follow local regulations for the proper disposal of fluids.

Procedure:	Step Completed
1. Research and record different causes of engine coolant consumption:	☐
2. Research signs of engine coolant entering the lube oil system of a diesel engine, and perform an inspection.	
a. Within manufacturer's specifications: Yes: ☐ No: ☐	☐
b. If No, describe the recommended corrective action(s):	☐
3. Research signs of engine coolant leaking into the air brake system, and perform an inspection.	
a. Within manufacturer's specifications: Yes: ☐ No: ☐	☐
b. If No, describe the recommended corrective action(s):	☐
4. Research signs of an exhaust gas recirculation (EGR) cooler leaking coolant, and perform an inspection.	
a. Within manufacturer's specifications: Yes: ☐ No: ☐	☐
b. If No, describe the recommended corrective action(s):	☐
5. Research signs of a head gasket external engine coolant leak, and perform an inspection.	
a. Within manufacturer's specifications: Yes: ☐ No: ☐	☐
b. If No, describe the recommended corrective action(s):	☐

	Step Completed
6. Research signs of engine coolant leaking into the combustion area of a diesel engine, and perform an inspection.	
a. Within manufacturer's specifications: Yes: ☐ No: ☐	☐
b. If No, describe the recommended corrective action(s):	☐
7. Research signs of engine coolant leaking into the passenger compartment, and perform an inspection.	
a. Within manufacturer's specifications: Yes: ☐ No: ☐	☐
b. If No, describe the recommended corrective action(s):	☐
8. Discuss your findings with your supervisor/instructor.	☐

Non-Task-Specific Evaluations:	Step Completed
1. Tools and equipment were used as directed and returned in good working order.	☐
2. Complied with all general and task-specific safety standards, including proper use of any personal protection equipment.	☐
3. Completed the task in an appropriate time frame (recommendation: 1.5 or 2 times the flat rate).	☐
4. Left the workspace clean and orderly.	☐
5. Cared for customer property and returned it undamaged.	☐

Student signature _____ Date _____

Comments:

Have your supervisor/instructor verify satisfactory completion of this procedure, any observations made,

and any necessary action(s) recommended.

Evaluation Instructions: The scoring box below is intended to act as a guide for both student and supervisor/instructor. Each criterion listed will help students to understand what is expected of them and help supervisors/instructors articulate the level of success at a particular task. The scoring is set up to allow a second attempt at each task (see the Test and Retest columns). Scoring is also designed to award students points only for task criteria that were completed correctly. Points are lost for failure to complete the employability requirements (see Non-Task-Specific Evaluation criteria). When all criteria are evaluated, tally the points for a total at the bottom of each column.

Tasksheet Scoring

Evaluation Items	Test		Retest	
	Pass	**Fail**	**Pass**	**Fail**
Task-Specific Evaluation	**(1 pt)**	**(0 pts)**	**(1 pt)**	**(0 pts)**
Student researched the causes of coolant consumption.				
Student properly researched and inspected signs of coolant leaking into lube oil, the air brake system, and the EGR cooler.				
Student properly researched and inspected signs of a head gasket external coolant leak.				
Student properly researched and inspected signs of coolant leaking into the combustion area and passenger compartment.				
Non-Task-Specific Evaluation	**(0 pts)**	**(−1 pt)**	**(0 pts)**	**(−1 pt)**
Student successfully completed at least three of the non-task-specific steps.				
Student successfully completed all five of the non-task-specific steps.				
Total Score: <total # of points/4 = %>				

CDX Tasksheet Number: MHT1EO11

Student/Intern Information

Name _____ Date _____ Class _____

Vehicle, Customer, and Service Information

Vehicle used for this activity:

Year _____ Make _____ Model _____

Odometer _____ VIN _____

Materials Required

- Vehicle with possible engine concern
- Engine manufacturer's workshop materials
- Manufacturer-specific tools depending on the concern/procedure(s)
- Vehicle/component lifting equipment, if applicable

Task-Specific Safety Considerations

- Activities may require test-driving the vehicle on the school grounds or on a hoist, both of which carry severe risks. Attempt this task only with full permission from your supervisor/instructor, and follow all the guidelines exactly.
- Lifting equipment and machines such as vehicle jacks and stands, vehicle hoists, and engine hoists are important tools that increase productivity and make the job easier. However, they can also cause severe injury or death if used improperly. Make sure you follow the manufacturer's operation procedures. Also make sure you have your supervisor's/instructor's permission to use any particular type of lifting equipment.
- Comply with personal and environmental safety practices associated with clothing; eye protection; hand tools; power equipment; proper ventilation; and the handling, storage, and disposal of chemicals/materials in accordance with federal, state, and local regulations.
- Always wear the correct protective eyewear and clothing and use the appropriate safety equipment, as well as wheel chocks, fender covers, seat protectors, and floor mat protectors.
- Make sure you understand and observe all legislative and personal safety procedures when carrying out practical assignments. If you are unsure of what these are, ask your supervisor/instructor.

▶ **TASK** Inspect thermostat(s), by passes, housing(s), and seals; replace as needed.

MTST
I.E.11; P1

Time off_____

Time on_____

Total time_____

Student Instructions: Read through the entire procedure prior to starting. Prepare your workspace and any tools or parts that may be needed to complete the task. When directed by your supervisor/instructor, begin the procedure to complete the task and check the box as each step is finished.

Note: This tasksheet may require the student to check the condition of miscellaneous vehicle fluids, some of which may be flammable and could damage the environment or cause health problems if not handled properly. Observe all safety precautions and follow local regulations for the proper disposal of fluids.

Procedure:	Step Completed
1. Reference the manufacturer's workshop materials, and record the engine thermostat setting: _____ °F/°C	☐
2. Reference the manufacturer's workshop materials, record the procedure for an in-chassis thermostat seal test, and perform the test.	
a. Within manufacturer's specifications: Yes: ☐ No: ☐	☐
b. If No, describe the recommended corrective action(s):	☐
3. Record the procedure for an in-chassis thermostat-opening temperature test as outlined in the manufacturer's workshop materials, and perform test:	
a. Within manufacturer's specifications: Yes: ☐ No: ☐	☐
b. If No, describe the recommended corrective action(s):	☐
4. If directed by your supervisor/instructor, remove the thermostat and seal.	☐
5. Record the procedure for an out-of-chassis thermostat-opening temperature test as outlined in the manufacturer's workshop materials, and perform test:	
a. Within manufacturer's specifications: Yes: ☐ No: ☐	☐

b. If No, describe the recommended corrective action(s):	☐
6. If directed by your supervisor/instructor, reinstall the thermostat and seal.	☐
7. Start the engine, bring it to operating temperature, and inspect the thermostat housing for leaks.	
a. Within manufacturer's specifications: Yes: ☐ No: ☐	☐
b. If No, describe the recommended corrective action(s):	☐
8. Discuss your findings with your supervisor/instructor.	☐

Non-Task-Specific Evaluations:	Step Completed
1. Tools and equipment were used as directed and returned in good working order.	☐
2. Complied with all general and task-specific safety standards, including proper use of any personal protection equipment.	☐
3. Completed the task in an appropriate time frame (recommendation: 1.5 or 2 times the flat rate).	☐
4. Left the workspace clean and orderly.	☐
5. Cared for customer property and returned it undamaged.	☐

Student signature _____ Date _____

Comments:

Have your supervisor/instructor verify satisfactory completion of this procedure, any observations made, and any necessary action(s) recommended.

Evaluation Instructions: The scoring box below is intended to act as a guide for both student and supervisor/instructor. Each criterion listed will help students to understand what is expected of them and help supervisors/instructors articulate the level of success at a particular task. The scoring is set up to allow a second attempt at each task (see the Test and Retest columns). Scoring is also designed to award students points only for task criteria that were completed correctly. Points are lost for failure to complete the employability requirements (see Non-Task-Specific Evaluation criteria). When all criteria are evaluated, tally the points for a total at the bottom of each column.

Tasksheet Scoring

Evaluation Items	Test		Retest	
	Pass	**Fail**	**Pass**	**Fail**
Task-Specific Evaluation	**(1 pt)**	**(0 pts)**	**(1 pt)**	**(0 pts)**
Student properly researched and inspected engine thermostat setting.				
Student properly researched and inspected the procedure for in-chassis thermostat seal test and thermostat-opening temperature test.				
Student properly researched and inspected the procedure for an out-of-chassis thermostat-opening temperature test.				
Student properly researched and inspected the procedure for checking operating temperature and inspecting the thermostat housing for leaks.				
Non-Task-Specific Evaluation	**(0 pts)**	**(−1 pt)**	**(0 pts)**	**(−1 pt)**
Student successfully completed at least three of the non-task-specific steps.				
Student successfully completed all five of the non-task-specific steps.				
Total Score: <total # of points/4 = %>				

Supervisor/Instructor:

Supervisor/instructor signature _____ Date _____

Comments:

Retest supervisor/instructor signature _____ Date _____

Comments:

CDX Tasksheet Number: MHT1EO12

Student/Intern Information

Name _____ Date _____ Class _____

Vehicle, Customer, and Service Information

Vehicle used for this activity:

Year _____ Make _____ Model _____

Odometer _____ VIN _____

Materials Required

- Vehicle with possible engine concern
- Engine manufacturer's workshop materials
- Manufacturer-specific tools depending on the concern/procedure(s)
- Vehicle/component lifting equipment, if applicable

Task-Specific Safety Considerations

- Activities may require test-driving the vehicle on the school grounds or on a hoist, both of which carry severe risks. Attempt this task only with full permission from your supervisor/instructor, and follow all the guidelines exactly.
- Lifting equipment and machines such as vehicle jacks and stands, vehicle hoists, and engine hoists are important tools that increase productivity and make the job easier. However, they can also cause severe injury or death if used improperly. Make sure you follow the manufacturer's operation procedures. Also make sure you have your supervisor's/instructor's permission to use any particular type of lifting equipment.
- Comply with personal and environmental safety practices associated with clothing; eye protection; hand tools; power equipment; proper ventilation; and the handling, storage, and disposal of chemicals/materials in accordance with federal, state, and local regulations.
- Always wear the correct protective eyewear and clothing and use the appropriate safety equipment, as well as wheel chocks, fender covers, seat protectors, and floor mat protectors.
- Make sure you understand and observe all legislative and personal safety procedures when carrying out practical assignments. If you are unsure of what these are, ask your supervisor/instructor.

▶ **TASK** Inspect turbocharger cooling systems; determine needed action. | **MTST** I.E.12; P2

Time off_____

Time on_____

Student Instructions: Read through the entire procedure prior to starting. Prepare your workspace and any tools or parts that may be needed to complete the task. When directed by your supervisor/instructor, begin the procedure to complete the task and check the box as each step is finished.

Total time_____

Note: This tasksheet may require the student to check the condition of miscellaneous vehicle fluids, some of which may be flammable and could damage the environment or cause health problems if not handled properly. Observe all safety precautions and follow local regulations for the proper disposal of fluids.

Procedure:	Step Completed
1. Inspect the turbocharger oil supply line for leaks, damage, or loose fittings as outlined in the manufacturer's workshop materials.	
a. Within manufacturer's specifications: Yes: ☐ No: ☐	☐
b. If No, describe the recommended corrective action(s):	☐
2. Inspect the turbocharger oil return/drain line for leaks, damage, or loose fittings as outlined in the manufacturer's workshop materials.	
a. Within manufacturer's specifications: Yes: ☐ No: ☐	☐
b. If No, describe the recommended corrective action(s):	☐
3. Remove oil return/drain line and inspect for any obstruction as outlined in the manufacturer's workshop materials.	
a. Within manufacturer's specifications: Yes: ☐ No: ☐	☐
b. If No, describe the recommended corrective action(s):	☐
4. Install a tee fitting into the turbocharger oil pressure supply, and record the oil pressure while the engine is running as outlined in the manufacturer's workshop materials: _____ lbs/kPa	
a. Within manufacturer's specifications: Yes: ☐ No: ☐	☐
b. If No, describe the recommended corrective action(s):	☐
5. Start the engine and bring it to operating temperature. Inspect variable geometry actuator (VGT) coolant lines for leaks and missing or damaged components.	

	Step Completed
a. Within manufacturer's specifications Yes: ☐ No: ☐	☐
b. If No, describe the recommended corrective action(s):	☐
6. Discuss your findings with your supervisor/instructor.	☐

Non-Task-Specific Evaluations:	Step Completed
1. Tools and equipment were used as directed and returned in good working order.	☐
2. Complied with all general and task-specific safety standards, including proper use of any personal protection equipment.	☐
3. Completed the task in an appropriate time frame (recommendation: 1.5 or 2 times the flat rate).	☐
4. Left the workspace clean and orderly.	☐
5. Cared for customer property and returned it undamaged.	☐

Student signature _____ Date _____

Comments:

Have your supervisor/instructor verify satisfactory completion of this procedure, any observations made, and any necessary action(s) recommended.

Evaluation Instructions: The scoring box below is intended to act as a guide for both student and supervisor/instructor. Each criterion listed will help students to understand what is expected of them and help supervisors/instructors articulate the level of success at a particular task. The scoring is set up to allow a second attempt at each task (see the Test and Retest columns). Scoring is also designed to award students points only for task criteria that were completed correctly. Points are lost for failure to complete the employability requirements (see Non-Task-Specific Evaluation criteria). When all criteria are evaluated, tally the points for a total at the bottom of each column.

Tasksheet Scoring

Evaluation Items	Test		Retest	
	Pass	Fail	Pass	Fail
Task-Specific Evaluation	**(1 pt)**	**(0 pts)**	**(1 pt)**	**(0 pts)**
Student properly inspected the turbocharger oil supply line.				
Student properly inspected the turbocharger oil return/drain line.				
Student properly checked the oil pressure at the turbocharger supply line.				
Student properly inspected coolant lines to the VGT actuator.				
Non-Task-Specific Evaluation	**(0 pts)**	**(−1 pt)**	**(0 pts)**	**(−1 pt)**
Student successfully completed at least three of the non-task-specific steps.				
Student successfully completed all five of the non-task-specific steps.				
Total Score: <total # of points/4 = %>				

Supervisor/Instructor:

Supervisor/instructor signature _____ Date _____

Comments:

Retest supervisor/instructor signature _____ Date _____

Comments:

Section 3: Diesel Fuel and Fuel Systems

I.G Diesel Engines: Fuel System

Learning Objective/Task	CDX Tasksheet Number	ASE Foundation MTST Reference Number; Priority Level
• Check fuel level and condition; determine needed action.	MHT1G001	I.G.1; P-1
• Inspect fuel tanks, vents, caps, mounts, valves, screens, crossover system, hoses, lines, and fittings; determine needed action.	MHT1G002	I.G.2; P-1
• Inspect low-pressure fuel system components, including fuel pump, pump drives, screens, fuel water separators/indicators, hoses, lines, filters, heaters, coolers, engine control module (ECM) cooling plates, check valves, pressure regulator valves, restrictive fittings, and mounting hardware; determine needed action.	MHT1G003	I.G.3; P-1
• Replace fuel filter(s); prime and bleed fuel system.	MHT1G004	I.G.4; P-1
• Inspect high-pressure fuel system components, including fuel pump, pump drives, hoses, injection lines, filters, hold downs, fittings, seals, and mounting hardware.	MHT1G005	I.G.5; P-1
• Demonstrate knowledge and understanding of the different types of fuel systems.	MHT1G006	I.G.6; P-1
• Perform fuel supply and return system tests; determine needed action.	MHT1G007	I.G.7; P-1
• Perform cylinder contribution test using electronic service tool(s); determine needed action.	MHT1G008	I.G.8; P-1
• Demonstrate knowledge of how to set performance parameters using electronic service tools (ESTs) and service information system access.	MHT1G009	I.G.9; P-2

Materials Required

- Vehicle with possible engine concern
- Engine manufacturer's workshop materials
- Manufacturer-specific tools depending on the concern/procedure(s)
- Vehicle/component lifting equipment, if applicable

Safety Considerations

- Activities may require test-driving the vehicle on the school grounds or on a hoist, both of which carry severe risks. Attempt this task only with full permission from your supervisor/instructor, and follow all the guidelines exactly.

- Lifting equipment and machines such as vehicle jacks and stands, vehicle hoists, and engine hoists are important tools that increase productivity and make the job easier. However, they can also cause severe injury or death if used improperly. Make sure you follow the manufacturer's operation procedures. Also make sure you have your supervisor's/instructor's permission to use any particular type of lifting equipment.

- Comply with personal and environmental safety practices associated with clothing; eye protection; hand tools; power equipment; proper ventilation; and the handling, storage, and disposal of chemicals/materials in accordance with federal, state, and local regulations.

- Always wear the correct protective eyewear and clothing and use the appropriate safety equipment, as well as fender covers, seat protectors, and floor mat protectors.

- Make sure you understand and observe all legislative and personal safety procedures when carrying out practical assignments. If you are unsure of what these are, ask your supervisor/instructor.

CDX Tasksheet Number: MHT1G001

Student/Intern Information

Name _____ Date _____ Class _____

Vehicle, Customer, and Service Information

Vehicle used for this activity:

Year _____ Make _____ Model _____

Odometer _____ VIN _____

Materials Required

- Vehicle with possible engine concern
- Engine manufacturer's workshop materials
- Manufacturer-specific tools depending on the concern/procedure(s)
- Vehicle/component lifting equipment, if applicable

Task-Specific Safety Considerations

- Activities may require test-driving the vehicle on the school grounds or on a hoist, both of which carry severe risks. Attempt this task only with full permission from your supervisor/instructor, and follow all the guidelines exactly.
- Lifting equipment and machines such as vehicle jacks and stands, vehicle hoists, and engine hoists are important tools that increase productivity and make the job easier. However, they can also cause severe injury or death if used improperly. Make sure you follow the manufacturer's operation procedures. Also make sure you have your supervisor's/instructor's permission to use any particular type of lifting equipment.
- Comply with personal and environmental safety practices associated with clothing; eye protection; hand tools; power equipment; proper ventilation; and the handling, storage, and disposal of chemicals/materials in accordance with federal, state, and local regulations.
- Always wear the correct protective eyewear and clothing and use the appropriate safety equipment, as well as wheel chocks, fender covers, seat protectors, and floor mat protectors.
- Make sure you understand and observe all legislative and personal safety procedures when carrying out practical assignments. If you are unsure of what these are, ask your supervisor/instructor.

▶ **TASK** Check fuel level and condition; determine needed action. _____ **MTST** *I.G.1; P1*

Time off_____

Student Instructions: Read through the entire procedure prior to starting. Prepare your workspace and any tools or parts that may be needed to complete the task. When directed by your supervisor/instructor, begin the procedure to complete the task and check the box as each step is finished.

Time on_____

Note: This tasksheet may require the student to check the condition of miscellaneous vehicle fluids, some of which may be flammable and could damage the environment or cause health problems if not handled properly. Observe all safety precautions and follow local regulations for the proper disposal of fluids.

Total time_____

Procedure:	Step Completed
1. Record the fuel level as it is shown on the manufacturer's electronic fuel gauge:	☐
2. Manually check the fuel level. Insert a clean yardstick or some other measuring instrument in the fuel tank and compare the fuel level shown with the manufacturer's electronic fuel gauge.	
a. Within manufacturer's specifications: Yes: ☐ No: ☐	☐
b. If No, describe the recommended corrective action(s):	☐
3. Draw off a clean fuel sample for testing as outlined in the manufacturer's workshop materials.	
a. Within manufacturer's specifications: Yes: ☐ No: ☐	☐
b. If No, describe the recommended corrective action(s):	☐
4. Record the procedure for using a water test paste to check the fuel supply for contamination, and perform the test. List any issues:	
a. Within manufacturer's specifications: Yes: ☐ No: ☐	☐
b. If No, describe the recommended corrective action(s):	☐
5. Discuss your findings with your supervisor/instructor.	☐

Non-Task-Specific Evaluations:	Step Completed
1. Tools and equipment were used as directed and returned in good working order.	
2. Complied with all general and task-specific safety standards, including proper use of any personal protection equipment.	
3. Completed the task in an appropriate time frame (recommendation: 1.5 or 2 times the flat rate).	
4. Left the workspace clean and orderly.	
5. Cared for customer property and returned it undamaged.	

Student signature _____ Date _____

Comments:

Have your supervisor/instructor verify satisfactory completion of this procedure, any observations made, and any necessary action(s) recommended.

Evaluation Instructions: The scoring box below is intended to act as a guide for both student and supervisor/instructor. Each criterion listed will help students to understand what is expected of them and help supervisors/instructors articulate the level of success at a particular task. The scoring is set up to allow a second attempt at each task (see the Test and Retest columns). Scoring is also designed to award students points only for task criteria that were completed correctly. Points are lost for failure to complete the employability requirements (see Non-Task-Specific Evaluation criteria). When all criteria are evaluated, tally the points for a total at the bottom of each column.

Tasksheet Scoring

Evaluation Items	Test Pass	Test Fail	Retest Pass	Retest Fail
Task-Specific Evaluation	**(1 pt)**	**(0 pts)**	**(1 pt)**	**(0 pts)**
Student properly checked the fuel system level using the manufacturer's electronic fuel gauge.				
Student properly checked the fuel system level using a clean yardstick or some other measuring instrument and compared this with the electronic fuel system gauge.				
Student properly obtained a fuel system sample for testing.				
Student properly tested the fuel system storage tank for water contamination.				
Non-Task-Specific Evaluation	**(0 pts)**	**(−1 pt)**	**(0 pts)**	**(−1 pt)**
Student successfully completed at least three of the non-task-specific steps.				
Student successfully completed all five of the non-task-specific steps.				
Total Score: <total # of points/4 = %>				

Supervisor/Instructor:

Supervisor/instructor signature _____ Date _____

Comments:

Retest supervisor/instructor signature _____ Date _____

Comments:

CDX Tasksheet Number: MHT1G002

Student/Intern Information

Name _____ Date _____ Class _____

Vehicle, Customer, and Service Information

Vehicle used for this activity:

Year _____ Make _____ Model _____

Odometer _____ VIN _____

Materials Required
- Vehicle with possible engine concern
- Engine manufacturer's workshop materials
- Manufacturer-specific tools depending on the concern/procedure(s)
- Vehicle/component lifting equipment, if applicable

Task-Specific Safety Considerations
- Activities may require test-driving the vehicle on the school grounds or on a hoist, both of which carry severe risks. Attempt this task only with full permission from your supervisor/instructor, and follow all the guidelines exactly.
- Lifting equipment and machines such as vehicle jacks and stands, vehicle hoists, and engine hoists are important tools that increase productivity and make the job easier. However, they can also cause severe injury or death if used improperly. Make sure you follow the manufacturer's operation procedures. Also make sure you have your supervisor's/instructor's permission to use any particular type of lifting equipment.
- Comply with personal and environmental safety practices associated with clothing; eye protection; hand tools; power equipment; proper ventilation; and the handling, storage, and disposal of chemicals/materials in accordance with federal, state, and local regulations.
- Always wear the correct protective eyewear and clothing and use the appropriate safety equipment, as well as wheel chocks, fender covers, seat protectors, and floor mat protectors.
- Make sure you understand and observe all legislative and personal safety procedures when carrying out practical assignments. If you are unsure of what these are, ask your supervisor/instructor.

▶ **TASK** Inspect fuel tanks, vents, caps, mounts, valves, screens, crossover system, hoses, lines, and fittings; determine needed action.

MTST
I.G.2; P1

Time off_____

Time on_____

Total time_____

Student Instructions: Read through the entire procedure prior to starting. Prepare your workspace and any tools or parts that may be needed to complete the task. When directed by your supervisor/instructor, begin the procedure to complete the task and check the box as each step is finished.

Note: This tasksheet may require the student to check the condition of miscellaneous vehicle fluids, some of which may be flammable and could damage the environment or cause health problems if not handled properly. Observe all safety precautions and follow local regulations for the proper disposal of fluids.

Procedure:	Step Completed
1. While referencing the manufacturer's workshop materials, inspect the fuel tank for any signs of structural damage or leakage.	
a. Within manufacturer's specifications: Yes: ☐ No: ☐	☐
b. If No, describe the recommended corrective action(s):	☐
2. While referencing the manufacturer's workshop materials, inspect the fuel tank cap/vents for signs of damage or blockage.	
a. Within manufacturer's specifications: Yes: ☐ No: ☐	☐
b. If No, describe the recommended corrective action(s):	☐
3. Inspect the fuel tank mounts for any signs of damage (e.g., loose bolts, damaged straps, missing or damaged strap isolators, damaged/loose frame mounts).	
a. Within manufacturer's specifications: Yes: ☐ No: ☐	☐
b. If No, describe the recommended corrective action(s):	☐
4. Record the fuel tank strap torque, and then check the tank strap torque: _____ ft-lb/N·m	
a. Within manufacturer's specifications: Yes: ☐ No: ☐	☐
b. If No, describe the recommended corrective action(s):	☐
5. Record the fuel tank mount-bolt torque, and then check the mount-bolt torque: _____ ft-lb/N·m	

a. Within manufacturer's specifications: Yes: ☐ No: ☐	☐
b. If No, describe the recommended corrective action(s):	☐
6. Inspect the fuel tank valves for signs of leakage and proper operation.	
a. Within manufacturer's specifications: Yes: ☐ No: ☐	☐
b. If No, describe the recommended corrective action(s):	☐
7. Inspect the fuel tank for missing or damaged filler screens.	
a. Within manufacturer's specifications: Yes: ☐ No: ☐	☐
b. If No, describe the recommended corrective action(s):	☐
8. Inspect the fuel tank crossover line/pipe (if applicable) for leaks, damage, and proper securement.	
a. Within manufacturer's specifications: Yes: ☐ No: ☐	☐
b. If No, describe the recommended corrective action(s):	☐
9. Inspect the fuel supply and return lines for damage, leaks, and proper securement.	
a. Within manufacturer's specifications: Yes: ☐ No: ☐	☐
b. If No, describe the recommended corrective action(s):	☐
10. Discuss your findings with your supervisor/instructor.	☐

Non-Task-Specific Evaluations:	Step Completed
1. Tools and equipment were used as directed and returned in good working order.	☐
2. Complied with all general and task-specific safety standards, including proper use of any personal protection equipment.	☐
3. Completed the task in an appropriate time frame (recommendation: 1.5 or 2 times the flat rate)	☐
4. Left the workspace clean and orderly.	☐
5. Cared for customer property and returned it undamaged.	☐

Student signature _____ Date _____

Comments:

Have your supervisor/instructor verify satisfactory completion of this procedure, any observations made, and any necessary action(s) recommended.

Evaluation Instructions: The scoring box below is intended to act as a guide for both student and supervisor/instructor. Each criterion listed will help students to understand what is expected of them and help supervisors/instructors articulate the level of success at a particular task. The scoring is set up to allow a second attempt at each task (see the Test and Retest columns). Scoring is also designed to award students points only for task criteria that were completed correctly. Points are lost for failure to complete the employability requirements (see Non-Task-Specific Evaluation criteria). When all criteria are evaluated, tally the points for a total at the bottom of each column.

Tasksheet Scoring

Evaluation Items	Test Pass (1 pt)	Test Fail (0 pts)	Retest Pass (1 pt)	Retest Fail (0 pts)
Task-Specific Evaluation	**(1 pt)**	**(0 pts)**	**(1 pt)**	**(0 pts)**
Student properly inspected the fuel tank for damage and leaks.				
Student properly inspected the fuel tank cap and vents for damage or blockage.				
Student properly checked the fuel tank mounts, fuel tank strap torque, and fuel tank mount-bolt torque.				
Student properly inspected the fuel tank valves, fuel tank crossover line/pipe, and fuel tank supply and return lines.				
Non-Task-Specific Evaluation	**(0 pts)**	**(−1 pt)**	**(0 pts)**	**(−1 pt)**
Student successfully completed at least three of the non-task-specific steps.				
Student successfully completed all five of the non-task-specific steps.				
Total Score: <total # of points/4 = %>				

Supervisor/Instructor:

Supervisor/instructor signature _____ Date _____

Comments:

Retest supervisor/instructor signature _____ Date _____

Comments:

CDX Tasksheet Number: MHT1G003

Student/Intern Information

Name _____ Date _____ Class _____

Vehicle, Customer, and Service Information

Vehicle used for this activity:

Year _____ Make _____ Model _____

Odometer _____ VIN _____

Materials Required

- Vehicle with possible engine concern
- Engine manufacturer's workshop materials
- Manufacturer-specific tools depending on the concern/procedure(s)
- Vehicle/component lifting equipment, if applicable

Task-Specific Safety Considerations

- Activities may require test-driving the vehicle on the school grounds or on a hoist, both of which carry severe risks. Attempt this task only with full permission from your supervisor/instructor, and follow all the guidelines exactly.
- Lifting equipment and machines such as vehicle jacks and stands, vehicle hoists, and engine hoists are important tools that increase productivity and make the job easier. However, they can also cause severe injury or death if used improperly. Make sure you follow the manufacturer's operation procedures. Also make sure you have your supervisor's/instructor's permission to use any particular type of lifting equipment.
- Comply with personal and environmental safety practices associated with clothing; eye protection; hand tools; power equipment; proper ventilation; and the handling, storage, and disposal of chemicals/materials in accordance with federal, state, and local regulations.
- Always wear the correct protective eyewear and clothing and use the appropriate safety equipment, as well as wheel chocks, fender covers, seat protectors, and floor mat protectors.
- Make sure you understand and observe all legislative and personal safety procedures when carrying out practical assignments. If you are unsure of what these are, ask your supervisor/instructor.

▶ **TASK** Inspect low-pressure fuel system components, including fuel pump, pump drives, screens, fuel water separators/indicators, hoses, lines, filters, heaters, coolers, engine control module (ECM) cooling plates, check valves, pressure regulator valves, restrictive fittings, and mounting hardware; determine needed action.

MTST
I.G.3; P1

Time off_____

Time on_____

Total time_____

Student Instructions: Read through the entire procedure prior to starting. Prepare your workspace and any tools or parts that may be needed to complete the task. When directed by your supervisor/instructor, begin the procedure to complete the task and check the box as each step is finished.

Note: This tasksheet may require the student to check the condition of miscellaneous vehicle fluids, some of which may be flammable and could damage the environment or cause health problems if not handled properly. Observe all safety precautions and follow local regulations for the proper disposal of fluids.

Procedure:	Step Completed
1. Inspect the fuel supply and return lines for damage, leaks, and proper securement as outlined in the manufacturer's workshop materials.	
a. Within manufacturer's specifications: Yes: ☐ No: ☐	☐
b. If No, describe the recommended corrective action(s):	☐
2. Inspect the ECM cooling plate for proper mounting, damage, or signs of leakage as outlined in the manufacturer's workshop materials.	
a. Within manufacturer's specifications: Yes: ☐ No: ☐	☐
b. If No, describe the recommended corrective action(s):	☐
3. Inspect the water fuel separator/primary fuel filter for proper mounting, damage, or signs of leakage as outlined in the manufacturer's workshop materials.	
a. Within manufacturer's specifications: Yes: ☐ No: ☐	☐
b. If No, describe the recommended corrective action(s):	☐
4. Drain any water from the water fuel separator and properly dispose of it.	☐
5. Disconnect the wiring harness from the water fuel separator and observe the operation of the water in the fuel light. If the light does not come on with the harness disconnected, place a jumper wire across the harness connections and observe the operation of the water in the fuel light. (**Note:** For wiring harnesses other than a 2-wire harness/connector, refer to the manufacturer's workshop materials/wiring diagrams[s] for proper testing.)	
a. Within manufacturer's specifications: Yes: ☐ No: ☐	☐

b. If No, describe the recommended collective action(s):	☐
6. Inspect the fuel cooler for proper mounting, damage, or signs of leakage as outlined in the manufacturer's workshop materials.	
a. Within manufacturer's specifications: Yes: ☐ No: ☐	☐
b. If No, describe the recommended collective action(s):	☐
7. Record the procedure for performing a fuel heater test as outlined in the manufacturer's workshop materials, and then perform the test:	
a. Within manufacturer's specifications: Yes: ☐ No: ☐	☐
b. If No, describe the recommended collective action(s):	☐
8. Inspect the electric/mechanical fuel transfer/lift pump for proper mounting, damage, or signs of leakage as outlined in the manufacturer's workshop materials.	
a. Within manufacturer's specifications: Yes: ☐ No: ☐	☐
b. If No, describe the recommended collective action(s):	☐
9. Remove the manual transfer/lift pump and inspect the pump drive for damage as outlined in the manufacturer's workshop materials. (**Note:** This procedure is only for engines with mechanical lift pumps.)	
a. Within manufacturer's specifications: Yes: ☐ No: ☐	☐
b. If No, describe the recommended collective action(s):	☐

10. Record the procedure for performing a transfer/lift pump flow-rate test as outlined in the manufacturer's workshop materials, and then perform the test:	
a. Within manufacturer's specifications: Yes: ☐ No: ☐	☐
b. If No, describe the recommended collective action(s):	☐
11. Record the procedure for performing a transfer/lift pump pressure test as outlined in the manufacturer's workshop materials, and then perform the test:	
a. Within the manufacturer's specifications: Yes: ☐ No: ☐	☐
b. If No, describe the recommended collective action(s):	☐
12. Discuss your findings with your supervisor/instructor.	☐

Non-Task-Specific Evaluations:	Step Completed
1. Tools and equipment were used as directed and returned in good working order.	☐
2. Complied with all general and task-specific safety standards, including proper use of any personal protection equipment.	☐
3. Completed the task in an appropriate time frame (recommendation: 1.5 or 2 times the flat rate).	☐
4. Left the workspace clean and orderly.	☐
5. Cared for customer property and returned it undamaged.	☐

Student signature _____ Date _____

Comments:

Have your supervisor/instructor verify satisfactory completion of this procedure, any observations made,

and any necessary action(s) recommended.

Evaluation Instructions: The scoring box below is intended to act as a guide for both student and supervisor/instructor. Each criterion listed will help students to understand what is expected of them and help supervisors/instructors articulate the level of success at a particular task. The scoring is set up to allow a second attempt at each task (see the Test and Retest columns). Scoring is also designed to award students points only for task criteria that were completed correctly. Points are lost for failure to complete the employability requirements (see Non-Task-Specific Evaluation criteria). When all criteria are evaluated, tally the points for a total at the bottom of each column.

Tasksheet Scoring

Evaluation Items	Test		Retest	
	Pass	Fail	Pass	Fail
Task-Specific Evaluation	**(1 pt)**	**(0 pts)**	**(1 pt)**	**(0 pts)**
Student properly inspected the fuel tank supply, return lines, ECM cooling plate, water fuel separator, and water in the fuel light's operation.				
Student properly inspected the fuel cooler and fuel heater.				
Student properly removed and inspected the fuel transfer/lift pump.				
Student properly performed the fuel transfer/lift pump flow-rate test and pressure test.				
Non-Task-Specific Evaluation	**(0 pts)**	**(−1 pt)**	**(0 pts)**	**(−1 pt)**
Student successfully completed at least three of the non-task-specific steps.				
Student successfully completed all five of the non-task-specific steps.				
Total Score: <total # of points/4 = %>				

Supervisor/Instructor:

Supervisor/instructor signature _____ Date _____

Comments:

Retest supervisor/instructor signature _____ Date _____

Comments:

CDX Tasksheet Number: MHT1G004

Student/Intern Information

Name _____ Date _____ Class _____

Vehicle, Customer, and Service Information

Vehicle used for this activity:

Year _____ Make _____ Model _____

Odometer _____ VIN _____

Materials Required

- Vehicle with possible engine concern
- Engine manufacturer's workshop materials
- Manufacturer-specific tools depending on the concern/procedure(s)
- Vehicle/component lifting equipment, if applicable

Task-Specific Safety Considerations

- Activities may require test-driving the vehicle on the school grounds or on a hoist, both of which carry severe risks. Attempt this task only with full permission from your supervisor/instructor, and follow all the guidelines exactly.
- Lifting equipment and machines such as vehicle jacks and stands, vehicle hoists, and engine hoists are important tools that increase productivity and make the job easier. However, they can also cause severe injury or death if used improperly. Make sure you follow the manufacturer's operation procedures. Also make sure you have your supervisor's/instructor's permission to use any particular type of lifting equipment.
- Comply with personal and environmental safety practices associated with clothing; eye protection; hand tools; power equipment; proper ventilation; and the handling, storage, and disposal of chemicals/materials in accordance with federal, state, and local regulations.
- Always wear the correct protective eyewear and clothing and use the appropriate safety equipment, as well as wheel chocks, fender covers, seat protectors, and floor mat protectors.
- Make sure you understand and observe all legislative and personal safety procedures when carrying out practical assignments. If you are unsure of what these are, ask your supervisor/instructor.

▶ **TASK** Replace fuel filter(s); prime and bleed fuel system.   **MTST** *I.G.4; P1*

Time off_____

Time on_____

Student Instructions: Read through the entire procedure prior to starting. Prepare your workspace and any tools or parts that may be needed to complete the task. When directed by your supervisor/instructor, begin the procedure to complete the task and check the box as each step is finished.

Total time_____

Note: This tasksheet may require the student to check the condition of miscellaneous vehicle fluids, some of which may be flammable and could damage the environment or cause health problems if not handled properly. Observe all safety precautions and follow local regulations for the proper disposal of fluids.

Procedure:	Step Completed
1. Inspect the fuel filter(s) and mounts for damage, leaks, and proper securement as outlined in the manufacturer's workshop materials.	
a. Within manufacturer's specifications: Yes: ☐ No: ☐	☐
b. If No, describe the recommended corrective action(s):	☐
2. Close fuel supply valve(s), start engine, and allow to run out of fuel as outlined in the manufacturer's workshop materials. (**Note:** This procedure is to allow you to learn the proper procedure for bleeding the air from a fuel system.)	☐
3. Remove fuel filter(s), and drain filter(s) in appropriate container for proper disposal as outlined in the manufacturer's workshop materials. Install new filter(s).	☐
4. Record the procedure for bleeding air from the fuel system as outlined in the manufacturer's workshop materials:	☐
5. Bleed the air from the fuel system as outlined in the manufacturer's workshop materials.	
a. Within manufacturer's specifications: Yes: ☐ No: ☐	☐
b. If No, describe the recommended corrective action(s):	☐
6. Start the engine and bring it up to operating temperature as outlined in the manufacturer's workshop materials. (**Note:** Don't crank engine for more than 30 seconds, and wait at least 2 minutes between cranking attempts.)	
a. Within manufacturer's specifications: Yes: ☐ No: ☐	☐
b. If No, describe the recommended corrective action(s):	☐

7. Inspect new fuel filters for signs of leakage as outlined in the manufacturer's workshop materials.	
a. Within manufacturer's specifications: Yes: ☐ No: ☐	☐
b. If No, describe the recommended corrective action(s):	☐
8. Discuss your findings with your supervisor/instructor.	☐

Non-Task-Specific Evaluations:	Step Completed
1. Tools and equipment were used as directed and returned in good working order.	☐
2. Complied with all general and task-specific safety standards, including proper use of any personal protection equipment.	☐
3. Completed the task in an appropriate time frame (recommendation: 1.5 or 2 times the flat rate).	☐
4. Left the workspace clean and orderly.	☐
5. Cared for customer property and returned it undamaged.	☐

Student signature _____ Date _____

Comments:

Have your supervisor/instructor verify satisfactory completion of this procedure, any observations made, and any necessary action(s) recommended.

Evaluation Instructions: The scoring box below is intended to act as a guide for both student and supervisor/instructor. Each criterion listed will help students to understand what is expected of them and help supervisors/instructors articulate the level of success at a particular task. The scoring is set up to allow a second attempt at each task (see the Test and Retest columns). Scoring is also designed to award students points only for task criteria that were completed correctly. Points are lost for failure to complete the employability requirements (see Non-Task-Specific Evaluation criteria). When all criteria are evaluated, tally the points for a total at the bottom of each column.

Tasksheet Scoring

Evaluation Items	Test		Retest	
	Pass	Fail	Pass	Fail
Task-Specific Evaluation	**(1 pt)**	**(0 pts)**	**(1 pt)**	**(0 pts)**
Student properly inspected fuel filter(s) and mounts.				
Student closed fuel supply valve(s), allowing the engine to run out of fuel.				
Student properly replaced filter(s) and bled air from the fuel system.				
Student properly inspected new filter(s) for leaks.				
Non-Task-Specific Evaluation	**(0 pts)**	**(−1 pt)**	**(0 pts)**	**(−1 pt)**
Student successfully completed at least three of the non-task-specific steps.				
Student successfully completed all five of the non-task-specific steps.				
Total Score: <total # of points/4 = %>				

Supervisor/Instructor:

Supervisor/instructor signature _____ Date _____

Comments:

Retest supervisor/instructor signature _____ Date _____

Comments:

CDX Tasksheet Number: MHT1G005

Student/Intern Information

Name _____ Date _____ Class _____

Vehicle, Customer, and Service Information

Vehicle used for this activity:

Year _____ Make _____ Model _____

Odometer _____ VIN _____

Materials Required

- Vehicle with possible engine concern
- Engine manufacturer's workshop materials
- Manufacturer-specific tools depending on the concern/procedure(s)
- Vehicle/component lifting equipment, if applicable

Task-Specific Safety Considerations

- Activities may require test-driving the vehicle on the school grounds or on a hoist, both of which carry severe risks. Attempt this task only with full permission from your supervisor/ instructor, and follow all the guidelines exactly.
- Lifting equipment and machines such as vehicle jacks and stands, vehicle hoists, and engine hoists are important tools that increase productivity and make the job easier. However, they can also cause severe injury or death if used improperly. Make sure you follow the manufacturer's operation procedures. Also make sure you have your supervisor's/ instructor's permission to use any particular type of lifting equipment.
- Comply with personal and environmental safety practices associated with clothing; eye protection; hand tools; power equipment; proper ventilation; and the handling, storage, and disposal of chemicals/materials in accordance with federal, state, and local regulations.
- Always wear the correct protective eyewear and clothing and use the appropriate safety equipment, as well as wheel chocks, fender covers, seat protectors, and floor mat protectors.
- Make sure you understand and observe all legislative and personal safety procedures when carrying out practical assignments. If you are unsure of what these are, ask your supervisor/ instructor.

▶ **TASK** Inspect high-pressure fuel system components, including fuel pump, pump drives, hoses, injection lines, filters, hold downs, fittings, seals, and mounting hardware; determine needed action.

MTST
I.G.5; P1

Time off_____

Time on_____

Student Instructions: Read through the entire procedure prior to starting. Prepare your workspace and any tools or parts that may be needed to complete the task. When directed by your supervisor/instructor, begin the procedure to complete the task and check the box as each step is finished.

Total time_____

Note: This tasksheet may require the student to check the condition of miscellaneous vehicle fluids, some of which may be flammable and could damage the environment or cause health problems if not handled properly. Observe all safety precautions and follow local regulations for the proper disposal of fluids.

Procedure:	Step Completed
1. Inspect the high-pressure fuel system for damage, leaks, and proper securement as outlined in the manufacturer's workshop materials.	
a. Within manufacturer's specifications: Yes: ☐ No: ☐	☐
b. If No, describe the recommended corrective action(s):	☐
2. List all special precautions to be used before servicing the high-pressure fuel system as outlined in the manufacturer's workshop materials:	☐
3. List all safety precautions when servicing the high-pressure fuel system as outlined in the manufacturer's workshop materials:	☐
4. List the inspection procedure for high-pressure fuel lines as outlined in the manufacturer's workshop materials, and inspect:	
a. Within manufacturer's specifications: Yes: ☐ No: ☐	☐
b. If No, describe the recommended corrective action(s):	☐

5. List the inspection procedure for the fuel pressure relief valve as outlined in the manufacturer's workshop materials, and inspect:	
a. Within manufacturer's specifications: Yes: ☐ No: ☐	☐
b. If No, describe the recommended corrective action(s):	☐
6. List the procedure for inspecting the fuel injector feed tubes as outlined in the manufacturer's workshop materials, and inspect:	
a. Within manufacturer's specifications: Yes: ☐ No: ☐	☐
b. If No, describe the recommended corrective action(s):	☐
7. Record the procedure for performing a high-pressure system leak-down test as outlined in the manufacturer's workshop materials, and perform the test:	
a. Within manufacturer's specifications: Yes: ☐ No: ☐	☐
b. If No, describe the recommended corrective action(s):	☐

8. Record the procedure for performing a high-pressure fuel pump return flow test as outlined in the manufacturer's workshop materials, and perform the test:	
a. Within manufacturer's specifications: Yes: ☐ No: ☐	☐
b. If No, describe the recommended corrective action(s):	☐
9. Record the procedure for performing a high-pressure injector return flow test as outlined in the manufacturer's workshop materials, and perform the test:	
a. Within manufacturer's specifications: Yes: ☐ No: ☐	☐
b. If No, describe the recommended corrective action(s):	☐
10. Record the procedure for performing a high-pressure fuel pump performance test as outlined in the manufacturer's workshop materials, and perform the test:	
a. Within manufacturer's specifications: Yes: ☐ No: ☐	☐
b. If No, describe the recommended corrective action(s):	☐

11. Record the procedure for performing a high-pressure injector return flow isolation test as outlined in the manufacturer's workshop materials, and perform the test:	
a. Within manufacturer's specifications: Yes: ☐ No: ☐	☐
b. If No, describe the recommended corrective action(s):	☐
12. Record the procedure for performing a fuel pressure relief valve return flow test as outlined in the manufacturer's workshop materials, and perform the test:	
a. Within manufacturer's specifications: Yes: ☐ No: ☐	☐
b. If No, describe the recommended corrective action(s):	☐
13. Discuss your findings with your supervisor/instructor.	☐

Non-Task-Specific Evaluations:	Step Completed
1. Tools and equipment were used as directed and returned in good working order.	☐
2. Complied with all general and task-specific safety standards, including proper use of any personal protection equipment.	☐
3. Completed the task in an appropriate time frame (recommendation: 1.5 or 2 times the flat rate).	☐
4. Left the workspace clean and orderly.	☐
5. Cared for customer property and returned it undamaged.	☐

Student signature _____ Date _____

Comments:

Have your supervisor/instructor verify satisfactory completion of this procedure, any observations made, and any necessary action(s) recommended.

Evaluation Instructions: The scoring box below is intended to act as a guide for both student and supervisor/instructor. Each criterion listed will help students to understand what is expected of them and help supervisors/instructors articulate the level of success at a particular task. The scoring is set up to allow a second attempt at each task (see the Test and Retest columns). Scoring is also designed to award students points only for task criteria that were completed correctly. Points are lost for failure to complete the employability requirements (see Non-Task-Specific Evaluation criteria). When all criteria are evaluated, tally the points for a total at the bottom of each column.

Tasksheet Scoring

	Test		Retest	
Evaluation Items	**Pass**	**Fail**	**Pass**	**Fail**
Task-Specific Evaluation	**(1 pt)**	**(0 pts)**	**(1 pt)**	**(0 pts)**
Student properly inspected high-pressure fuel system for damage, leaks, and proper securement.				
Student properly inspected high-pressure fuel lines, the fuel pressure relief valve, and injector feed tubes.				
Student properly performed high-pressure leak-down test, fuel pump return flow test, injector return flow test, fuel pump performance test, and injector return flow isolation test.				
Student properly performed fuel pressure relief valve return flow test.				
Non-Task-Specific Evaluation	**(0 pts)**	**(−1 pt)**	**(0 pts)**	**(−1 pt)**
Student successfully completed at least three of the non-task-specific steps.				
Student successfully completed all five of the non-task-specific steps.				
Total Score: <total # of points/4 = %>				

Supervisor/Instructor:

Supervisor/instructor signature _____ Date _____

Comments:

Retest supervisor/instructor signature _____ Date _____

Comments:

CDX Tasksheet Number: MHT1G006

Student/Intern Information

Name _____ Date _____ Class _____

Vehicle, Customer, and Service Information

Vehicle used for this activity:

Year _____ Make _____ Model _____

Odometer _____ VIN _____

Materials Required

- Vehicle with possible engine concern
- Engine manufacturer's workshop materials
- Manufacturer-specific tools depending on the concern/procedure(s)
- Vehicle/component lifting equipment, if applicable

Task-Specific Safety Considerations

- Activities may require test-driving the vehicle on the school grounds or on a hoist, both of which carry severe risks. Attempt this task only with full permission from your supervisor/instructor, and follow all the guidelines exactly.
- Lifting equipment and machines such as vehicle jacks and stands, vehicle hoists, and engine hoists are important tools that increase productivity and make the job easier. However, they can also cause severe injury or death if used improperly. Make sure you follow the manufacturer's operation procedures. Also make sure you have your supervisor's/instructor's permission to use any particular type of lifting equipment.
- Comply with personal and environmental safety practices associated with clothing; eye protection; hand tools; power equipment; proper ventilation; and the handling, storage, and disposal of chemicals/materials in accordance with federal, state, and local regulations.
- Always wear the correct protective eyewear and clothing and use the appropriate safety equipment, as well as wheel chocks, fender covers, seat protectors, and floor mat protectors.
- Make sure you understand and observe all legislative and personal safety procedures when carrying out practical assignments. If you are unsure of what these are, ask your supervisor/instructor.

▶ **TASK** Demonstrate knowledge and understanding of the different fuel systems.

MTST
I.G.6; P1

Time off_____

Time on_____

Total time_____

Student Instructions: Read through the entire procedure prior to starting. Prepare your workspace and any tools or parts that may be needed to complete the task. When directed by your supervisor/instructor, begin the procedure to complete the task and check the box as each step is finished.

Note: This tasksheet may require the student to check the condition of miscellaneous vehicle fluids, some of which may be flammable and could damage the environment or cause health problems if not handled properly. Observe all safety precautions and follow local regulations for the proper disposal of fluids.

Procedure:	Step Completed
1. While researching different manufacturers, explain the operation of an indirect diesel fuel injection system (IDI).	
a. Manufacturer type:	☐
b. Special service precautions:	☐
c. Disadvantages:	☐
2. While researching different manufacturers, explain the operation of a multiple-plunger diesel fuel injection system.	
a. Manufacturer type:	☐
b. Special service precautions:	☐
c. Disadvantages:	☐
3. While researching different manufacturers, explain the operation of a mechanical distributor diesel fuel injection system.	
a. Manufacturer type:	☐
b. Special service precautions:	☐

c. Disadvantages:	☐
4. While researching different manufacturers, explain the operation of an electronic distributor diesel fuel injection system.	
a. Manufacturer type:	☐
b. Special service precautions:	☐
c. Disadvantages:	☐
5. While researching different manufacturers, explain the operation of an electronic unit injector (EUI) diesel fuel injection system.	
a. Manufacturer type:	☐
b. Special service precautions:	☐
c. Disadvantages:	☐
6. While researching different manufacturers, explain the operation of a hydraulic electronic unit injector (HEUI) diesel fuel injection system.	
a. Manufacturer type:	☐

b. Special service precautions:	☐
c. Disadvantages:	☐
7. While researching different manufacturers, explain the operation of a unit injector diesel fuel injection system.	
a. Manufacturer type:	☐
b. Special service precautions:	☐
c. Disadvantages:	☐
8. While researching different manufacturers, explain the operation of a common rail diesel fuel injection system.	
a. Manufacturer type:	☐
b. Special service precautions:	☐
c. Disadvantages:	☐

	Step Completed
9. Describe some of the characteristics that the different fuel injection systems have in common:	☐
10. Discuss your findings with your supervisor/instructor.	☐

Non-Task-Specific Evaluations:	Step Completed
1. Tools and equipment were used as directed and returned in good working order.	☐
2. Complied with all general and task-specific safety standards, including proper use of any personal protection equipment.	☐
3. Completed the task in an appropriate time frame (recommendation: 1.5 or 2 times the flat rate).	☐
4. Left the workspace clean and orderly.	☐
5. Cared for customer property and returned it undamaged.	☐

Student signature _____ Date _____

Comments:

Have your supervisor/instructor verify satisfactory completion of this procedure, any observations made, and any necessary action(s) recommended.

Evaluation Instructions: The scoring box below is intended to act as a guide for both student and supervisor/instructor. Each criterion listed will help students to understand what is expected of them and help supervisors/instructors articulate the level of success at a particular task. The scoring is set up to allow a second attempt at each task (see the Test and Retest columns). Scoring is also designed to award students points only for task criteria that were completed correctly. Points are lost for failure to complete the employability requirements (see Non-Task-Specific Evaluation criteria). When all criteria are evaluated, tally the points for a total at the bottom of each column.

Tasksheet Scoring

Evaluation Items	Test Pass	Test Fail	Retest Pass	Retest Fail
Task-Specific Evaluation	**(1 pt)**	**(0 pts)**	**(1 pt)**	**(0 pts)**
Student properly explained the operation of an indirect fuel system, multiple-plunger fuel system, and mechanical and electronic distributor fuel system.				
Student properly explained the operation of a mechanical and electronic distributor fuel system.				
Student properly explained the operation of an electronic unit fuel system and a hydraulic electronic fuel injection system.				
Student properly explained the operation of a unit injector fuel system and common rail fuel system.				
Non-Task-Specific Evaluation	**(0 pts)**	**(−1 pt)**	**(0 pts)**	**(−1 pt)**
Student successfully completed at least three of the non-task-specific steps.				
Student successfully completed all five of the non-task-specific steps.				
Total Score: <total # of points/4 = %>				

Supervisor/Instructor:

Supervisor/instructor signature _____ Date _____

Comments:

Retest supervisor/instructor signature _____ Date _____

Comments:

CDX Tasksheet Number: MHT1G007

Student/Intern Information

Name _____ Date _____ Class _____

Vehicle, Customer, and Service Information

Vehicle used for this activity:

Year _____ Make _____ Model _____

Odometer _____ VIN _____

Materials Required

- Vehicle with possible engine concern
- Engine manufacturer's workshop materials
- Manufacturer-specific tools depending on the concern/procedure(s)
- Vehicle/component lifting equipment, if applicable

Task-Specific Safety Considerations

- Activities may require test-driving the vehicle on the school grounds or on a hoist, both of which carry severe risks. Attempt this task only with full permission from your supervisor/instructor, and follow all the guidelines exactly.
- Lifting equipment and machines such as vehicle jacks and stands, vehicle hoists, and engine hoists are important tools that increase productivity and make the job easier. However, they can also cause severe injury or death if used improperly. Make sure you follow the manufacturer's operation procedures. Also make sure you have your supervisor's/instructor's permission to use any particular type of lifting equipment.
- Comply with personal and environmental safety practices associated with clothing; eye protection; hand tools; power equipment; proper ventilation; and the handling, storage, and disposal of chemicals/materials in accordance with federal, state, and local regulations.
- Always wear the correct protective eyewear and clothing and use the appropriate safety equipment, as well as wheel chocks, fender covers, seat protectors, and floor mat protectors.
- Make sure you understand and observe all legislative and personal safety procedures when carrying out practical assignments. If you are unsure of what these are, ask your supervisor/instructor.

▶ **TASK** Perform fuel supply and return system tests; determine needed action.

MTST
I.G.7; P1

Time off_____

Time on_____

Total time_____

Student Instructions: Read through the entire procedure prior to starting. Prepare your workspace and any tools or parts that may be needed to complete the task. When directed by your supervisor/instructor, begin the procedure to complete the task and check the box as each step is finished.

Note: This tasksheet may require the student to check the condition of miscellaneous vehicle fluids, some of which may be flammable and could damage the environment or cause health problems if not handled properly. Observe all safety precautions and follow local regulations for the proper disposal of fluids.

Procedure:	Step Completed
1. Inspect the fuel supply and return lines for damage, leaks, and proper securement as outlined in the manufacturer's workshop materials.	
a. Within manufacturer's specifications: Yes: ☐ No: ☐	☐
b. If No, describe the recommended corrective action(s):	☐
2. Record the procedure for performing a supply-side air in fuel system test as outlined in the manufacturer's workshop materials, and perform the test:	
a. Within manufacturer's specifications: Yes: ☐ No: ☐	☐
b. If No, describe the recommended corrective action(s):	☐
3. Record the procedure for performing a low-pressure supply pump flow test as outlined in the manufacturer's workshop materials, and perform the test:	
a. Manufacturer's specification: _____ GPM	☐
b. Within manufacturer's specifications: Yes: ☐ No: ☐	☐
c. If No, describe the recommended corrective action(s):	☐

4. Record the procedure for performing a low-pressure supply pump pressure test as outlined in the manufacturer's workshop materials, and perform the test:	
a. Manufacturer's specification: _____ psi/kpa	☐
b. Within manufacturer's specifications: Yes: ☐ No: ☐	☐
c. If No, describe the recommended corrective action(s):	☐
5. Record the procedure for performing a fuel drain line restriction test as outlined in the manufacturer's workshop materials, and perform the test:	
a. Manufacturer's specification: _____ mm/in-hg	☐
b. Within manufacturer's specifications: Yes: ☐ No: ☐	☐
c. If No, describe the recommended corrective action(s):	☐
6. Discuss your findings with your supervisor/instructor.	☐

Non-Task–Specific Evaluations:	Step Completed
1. Tools and equipment were used as directed and returned in good working order.	☐
2. Complied with all general and task-specific safety standards, including proper use of any personal protection equipment.	☐
3. Completed the task in an appropriate time frame (recommendation: 1.5 or 2 times the flat rate).	☐
4. Left the workspace clean and orderly.	☐
5. Cared for customer property and returned it undamaged.	☐

Student signature _____ Date _____

Comments:

Have your supervisor/instructor verify satisfactory completion of this procedure, any observations made, and any necessary action(s) recommended.

Evaluation Instructions: The scoring box below is intended to act as a guide for both student and supervisor/instructor. Each criterion listed will help students to understand what is expected of them and help supervisors/instructors articulate the level of success at a particular task. The scoring is set up to allow a second attempt at each task (see the Test and Retest columns). Scoring is also designed to award students points only for task criteria that were completed correctly. Points are lost for failure to complete the employability requirements (see Non-Task-Specific Evaluation criteria). When all criteria are evaluated, tally the points for a total at the bottom of each column.

Tasksheet Scoring

	Test		Retest	
	Pass	Fail	Pass	Fail
Evaluation Items				
Task-Specific Evaluation	**(1 pt)**	**(0 pts)**	**(1 pt)**	**(0 pts)**
Student properly inspected fuel supply and return lines for damage, leaks, and proper securement.				
Student properly performed supply-side air in fuel system test.				
Student properly performed low-pressure supply pump flow and pressure tests.				
Student properly performed fuel drain line restriction test.				
Non-Task-Specific Evaluation	**(0 pts)**	**(−1 pt)**	**(0 pts)**	**(−1 pt)**
Student successfully completed at least three of the non-task-specific steps.				
Student successfully completed all five of the non-task-specific steps.				
Total Score: <total # of points/4 = %>				

Supervisor/Instructor:

Supervisor/instructor signature _____ Date _____

Comments:

_____

Retest supervisor/instructor signature _____ Date _____

Comments:

_____

CDX Tasksheet Number: MHT1G008

Student/Intern Information

Name _____ Date _____ Class _____

Vehicle, Customer, and Service Information

Vehicle used for this activity:

Year _____ Make _____ Model _____

Odometer _____ VIN _____

Materials Required

- Vehicle with possible engine concern
- Engine manufacturer's workshop materials
- Manufacturer-specific tools depending on the concern/procedure(s)
- Vehicle/component lifting equipment, if applicable

Task-Specific Safety Considerations

- Activities may require test-driving the vehicle on the school grounds or on a hoist, both of which carry severe risks. Attempt this task only with full permission from your supervisor/instructor, and follow all the guidelines exactly.
- Lifting equipment and machines such as vehicle jacks and stands, vehicle hoists, and engine hoists are important tools that increase productivity and make the job easier. However, they can also cause severe injury or death if used improperly. Make sure you follow the manufacturer's operation procedures. Also make sure you have your supervisor's/instructor's permission to use any particular type of lifting equipment.
- Comply with personal and environmental safety practices associated with clothing; eye protection; hand tools; power equipment; proper ventilation; and the handling, storage, and disposal of chemicals/materials in accordance with federal, state, and local regulations.
- Always wear the correct protective eyewear and clothing and use the appropriate safety equipment, as well as wheel chocks, fender covers, seat protectors, and floor mat protectors.
- Make sure you understand and observe all legislative and personal safety procedures when carrying out practical assignments. If you are unsure of what these are, ask your supervisor/instructor.

▶ TASK Perform cylinder contribution test using electronic service tool(s); determine needed action.

MTST
I.G.8; P1

Time off_____

Time on_____

Total time_____

Student Instructions: Read through the entire procedure prior to starting. Prepare your workspace and any tools or parts that may be needed to complete the task. When directed by your supervisor/instructor, begin the procedure to complete the task and check the box as each step is finished.

Note: This tasksheet may require the student to check the condition of miscellaneous vehicle fluids, some of which may be flammable and could damage the environment or cause health problems if not handled properly. Observe all safety precautions and follow local regulations for the proper disposal of fluids.

Procedure:	Step Completed
1. Record the procedure for performing a cylinder contribution test as outlined in the manufacturer's workshop materials:	☐
2. Record any safety precautions to be observed when performing a cylinder contribution test as outlined in the manufacturer's workshop materials:	☐
3. Record any special instructions and/or conditions that must be met before performing a cylinder contribution test as outlined in the manufacturer's workshop materials:	☐
4. Connect the electronic service tool and record any fault codes that may prohibit the performing of a cylinder contribution test as outlined in the manufacturer's workshop materials:	
a. If directed by your supervisor/instructor, repair the above fault codes.	☐
5. While using the electronic service tool, perform a cylinder contribution test.	
a. Within manufacturer's specifications: Yes: ☐ No: ☐	☐
b. If No, describe the recommended corrective action(s):	☐
6. Record the procedure for performing a cylinder cut-out test as outlined in the manufacturer's workshop materials:	☐
7. Record any safety precautions to be observed when performing a cylinder cut-out test as outlined in the manufacturer's workshop materials:	☐

8. Record any special instructions and/or conditions that must be met before performing a cylinder cut-out test as outlined in the manufacturer's workshop materials:	☐
9. Connect the electronic service tool and record any fault codes that may prohibit the performing of a cylinder cut-out test as outlined in the manufacturer's workshop materials:	
a. If directed by the supervisor/instructor, repair the above fault codes.	☐
10. While using the electronic service tool, perform a cylinder cut-out test.	
a. Within manufacturer's specifications: Yes: ☐ No: ☐	☐
b. If No, describe the recommended corrective action(s):	☐
11. Discuss your findings with your supervisor/instructor.	☐

Non-Task-Specific Evaluations:	Step Completed
1. Tools and equipment were used as directed and returned in good working order.	☐
2. Complied with all general and task-specific safety standards, including proper use of any personal protection equipment.	☐
3. Completed the task in an appropriate time frame (recommendation: 1.5 or 2 times the flat rate).	☐
4. Left the workspace clean and orderly.	☐
5. Cared for customer property and returned it undamaged.	☐

Student signature _____ Date _____

Comments:

Have your supervisor/instructor verify satisfactory completion of this procedure, any observations made, and any necessary action(s) recommended.

Evaluation Instructions: The scoring box below is intended to act as a guide for both student and supervisor/instructor. Each criterion listed will help students to understand what is expected of them and help supervisors/instructors articulate the level of success at a particular task. The scoring is set up to allow a second attempt at each task (see the Test and Retest columns). Scoring is also designed to award students points only for task criteria that were completed correctly. Points are lost for failure to complete the employability requirements (see Non-Task-Specific Evaluation criteria). When all criteria are evaluated, tally the points for a total at the bottom of each column.

Tasksheet Scoring

Evaluation Items	Test		Retest	
	Pass	**Fail**	**Pass**	**Fail**
Task-Specific Evaluation	**(1 pt)**	**(0 pts)**	**(1 pt)**	**(0 pts)**
Student properly recorded and repaired fault codes that would prohibit the performing of a cylinder contribution test.				
Student properly performed a cylinder contribution test.				
Student properly recorded and repaired fault codes that would prohibit the performing of a cylinder cut-out test.				
Student properly performed a cylinder cut-out test.				
Non-Task-Specific Evaluation	**(0 pts)**	**(−1 pt)**	**(0 pts)**	**(−1 pt)**
Student successfully completed at least three of the non-task-specific steps.				
Student successfully completed all five of the non-task-specific steps.				
Total Score: <total # of points/4 = %>				

Supervisor/Instructor:

Supervisor/instructor signature _____ Date _____

Comments:

Retest supervisor/instructor signature _____ Date _____

Comments:

CDX Tasksheet Number: MHT1G009

Student/Intern Information

Name _____ Date _____ Class _____

Vehicle, Customer, and Service Information

Vehicle used for this activity:

Year _____ Make _____ Model _____

Odometer _____ VIN _____

Materials Required
- Vehicle with possible engine concern
- Engine manufacturer's workshop materials
- Manufacturer-specific tools depending on the concern/procedure(s)
- Vehicle/component lifting equipment, if applicable

Task-Specific Safety Considerations
- Activities may require test-driving the vehicle on the school grounds or on a hoist, both of which carry severe risks. Attempt this task only with full permission from your supervisor/instructor, and follow all the guidelines exactly.
- Lifting equipment and machines such as vehicle jacks and stands, vehicle hoists, and engine hoists are important tools that increase productivity and make the job easier. However, they can also cause severe injury or death if used improperly. Make sure you follow the manufacturer's operation procedures. Also make sure you have your supervisor's/instructor's permission to use any particular type of lifting equipment.
- Comply with personal and environmental safety practices associated with clothing; eye protection; hand tools; power equipment; proper ventilation; and the handling, storage, and disposal of chemicals/materials in accordance with federal, state, and local regulations.
- Always wear the correct protective eyewear and clothing and use the appropriate safety equipment, as well as wheel chocks, fender covers, seat protectors, and floor mat protectors.
- Make sure you understand and observe all legislative and personal safety procedures when carrying out practical assignments. If you are unsure of what these are, ask your supervisor/instructor.

▶ **TASK** Demonstrate knowledge of how to set performance parameters using its electronic service tools (ESTs) and service information system access.

MTST
I.G.9; P2

Time off_____

Time on_____

Total time_____

Student Instructions: Read through the entire procedure prior to starting. Prepare your workspace and any tools or parts that may be needed to complete the task. When directed by your supervisor/instructor, begin the procedure to complete the task and check the box as each step is finished.

Note: This tasksheet may require the student to check the condition of miscellaneous vehicle fluids, some of which may be flammable and could damage the environment or cause health problems if not handled properly. Observe all safety precautions and follow local regulations for the proper disposal of fluids.

Procedure:	Step Completed
1. Connect the electronic service tool as outlined in the manufacturer's workshop materials, and record any fault codes that may prohibit the changing of any engine parameters:	
a. If directed by your supervisor/instructor, repair the above fault codes.	☐
2. Record the procedure for changing fuel injector trim codes as outlined in the manufacturer's workshop materials:	☐
3. Connect the electronic service tool and swap fuel injector trim codes 1-3 with those of 4-6 and 4-6 with those of 1-3. (**Note:** If directed by your supervisor/instructor, replace the fuel injectors with new trim codes.)	
a. Was the above procedure successful? Yes: ☐ No: ☐	☐
b. If No, describe the recommended corrective action(s):	☐
4. If new injectors were not installed and trim codes for cylinders 1-3 and 4-6 were swapped, return trim codes back to their original cylinder positions.	
a. Was the above procedure successful? Yes: ☐ No: ☐	☐
b. If No, describe the recommended corrective action(s):	☐

5. Record the procedure for adjusting engine idle as outlined in the manufacturer's workshop materials, and adjust to maximum setting:	
a. Was the above procedure successful? Yes: ☐ No: ☐	☐
b. If Yes, return idle back to original setting.	☐
c. If No, describe the recommended corrective action(s):	☐
6. Record the procedure for adjusting engine idle timer as outlined in the manufacturer's workshop materials, and adjust to maximum setting:	
a. Was the above procedure successful? Yes: ☐ No: ☐	☐
b. If Yes, return idle back to original setting.	☐
c. If No, describe the recommended corrective action(s):	☐
7. Record the procedure for adjusting vehicle top speed as outlined in the manufacturer's workshop materials, and adjust to maximum setting:	
a. Was the above procedure successful? Yes: ☐ No: ☐	☐
b. If Yes, return idle back to original setting.	☐
c. If No, describe the recommended corrective action(s):	☐

8. Record the procedure for adjusting vehicle tire size to the correct speedometer reading as outlined in the manufacturer's workshop materials, and adjust tire size to 496 revolutions per mile: (**Note:** If current setting is 496, see supervisor/instructor for different setting.)	
a. Was the above procedure successful? Yes: ☐ No: ☐	☐
b. If Yes, return tire revolutions per mile back to original setting.	☐
c. If No, describe the recommended corrective action(s):	☐
9. Record the procedure for reflashing an engine control module (ECM) as outlined in the manufacturer's workshop materials:	
a. If directed by your supervisor/instructor, reflash the engine ECM.	☐
b. Was the above procedure successful? Yes: ☐ No: ☐	☐
c. If No, describe the recommended corrective action(s):	☐
10. Discuss your findings with your supervisor/instructor.	☐

Non-Task-Specific Evaluations:	Step Completed
1. Tools and equipment were used as directed and returned in good working order.	
2. Complied with all general and task-specific safety standards, including proper use of any personal protection equipment.	
3. Completed the task in an appropriate time frame (recommendation: 1.5 or 2 times the flat rate).	
4. Left the workspace clean and orderly.	
5. Cared for customer property and returned it undamaged.	

Student signature _____ Date _____

Comments:

Have your supervisor/instructor verify satisfactory completion of this procedure, any observations made,

and any necessary action(s) recommended.

Evaluation Instructions: The scoring box below is intended to act as a guide for both student and supervisor/instructor. Each criterion listed will help students to understand what is expected of them and help supervisors/instructors articulate the level of success at a particular task. The scoring is set up to allow a second attempt at each task (see the Test and Retest columns). Scoring is also designed to award students points only for task criteria that were completed correctly. Points are lost for failure to complete the employability requirements (see Non-Task-Specific Evaluation criteria). When all criteria are evaluated, tally the points for a total at the bottom of each column.

Tasksheet Scoring

Evaluation Items	Test		Retest	
	Pass	Fail	Pass	Fail
Task-Specific Evaluation	**(1 pt)**	**(0 pts)**	**(1 pt)**	**(0 pts)**
Student properly retrieved and corrected fault codes.				
Student properly changed fuel injector trim codes.				
Student properly adjusted engine idle, engine idle timer, vehicle top speed, and vehicle tire size.				
Student properly reflashed ECM.				
Non-Task-Specific Evaluation	**(0 pts)**	**(−1 pt)**	**(0 pts)**	**(−1 pt)**
Student successfully completed at least three of the non-task-specific steps.				
Student successfully completed all five of the non-task-specific steps.				
Total Score: <total # of points/4 = %>				

Supervisor/Instructor:

Supervisor/instructor signature _____ Date _____

Comments:

```



```

Retest supervisor/instructor signature _____ Date _____

Comments:

```



```

Section 4: Air Induction and Exhaust Systems

I.F Diesel Engines: General

Learning Objective/Task	CDX Tasksheet Number	ASE Foundation MTST Reference Number; Priority Level
• Inspect turbocharger(s), wastegate(s), and piping systems; determine needed action.	MHT1F001	I.F.1; P-2
• Diagnose air induction system problems; inspect, clean, and/or replace cooler assembly, piping, hoses, clamps, and mountings; replace air filter as needed; reset restriction indicator (if applicable).	MHT1F002	I.F.2; P-1
• Inspect intake manifold, gaskets, and connections; determine needed action.	MHT1F003	I.F.3; P-1
• Inspect engine exhaust system, exhaust gas recirculation (EGR) system, and exhaust aftertreatment system for leaks, mounting, proper routing, and damaged or missing components; determine needed action.	MHT1F004	I.F.4; P-1
• Inspect crankcase ventilation system; service as needed.	MHT1F005	I.F.5; P-1
• Diagnose problems/faults in the exhaust gas recirculation (EGR) system, including EGR valve, cooler, piping, filter, electronic sensors, controls, and wiring; determine needed action.	MHT1F006	I.F.6; P-1
• Perform air intake system restriction and leakage tests; determine needed action.	MHT1F007	I.F.7; P-1
• Perform air intake manifold pressure (boost) test; determine needed action.	MHT1F008	I.F.8; P-3
• Check exhaust backpressure; determine needed action.	MHT1F009	I.F.9; P-3
• Inspect variable-ratio geometry turbocharger (VGT), controls, and actuators (pneumatic, hydraulic, and electronic); determine needed action.	MHT1F010	I.F.10; P-2
• Demonstrate knowledge of charge air cooler operation and testing.	MHT1F011	I.F.11; P-1
• Diagnose exhaust aftertreatment system performance problems; determine needed action.	MHT1F012	I.F.12; P-1
• Diagnose preheater/inlet air heater or glow plug system and controls; determine needed action.	MHT1F013	I.F.13; P-2

Materials Required

- Vehicle with possible engine concern
- Engine manufacturer's workshop materials
- Manufacturer-specific tools depending on the concern/procedure(s)
- Vehicle/component lifting equipment, if applicable

Safety Considerations

- Activities may require test-driving the vehicle on the school grounds or on a hoist, both of which carry severe risks. Attempt this task only with full permission from your supervisor/instructor, and follow all the guidelines exactly.
- Lifting equipment and machines such as vehicle jacks and stands, vehicle hoists, and engine hoists are important tools that increase productivity and make the job easier. However, they can also cause severe injury or death if used improperly. Make sure you follow the manufacturer's operation procedures. Also make sure you have your supervisor's/instructor's permission to use any particular type of lifting equipment.
- Comply with personal and environmental safety practices associated with clothing; eye protection; hand tools; power equipment; proper ventilation; and the handling, storage, and disposal of chemicals/materials in accordance with federal, state, and local regulations.
- Always wear the correct protective eyewear and clothing and use the appropriate safety equipment, as well as wheel chocks, fender covers, seat protectors, and floor mat protectors.
- Make sure you understand and observe all legislative and personal safety procedures when carrying out practical assignments. If you are unsure of what these are, ask your supervisor/instructor.

CDX Tasksheet Number: MHT1F001

Student/Intern Information

Name _____ Date _____ Class _____

Vehicle, Customer, and Service Information

Vehicle used for this activity:

Year _____ Make _____ Model _____

Odometer _____ VIN _____

Materials Required

- Vehicle with possible engine concern
- Engine manufacturer's workshop materials
- Manufacturer-specific tools depending on the concern/procedure(s)
- Vehicle/component lifting equipment, if applicable

Task-Specific Safety Considerations

- Activities may require test-driving the vehicle on the school grounds or on a hoist, both of which carry severe risks. Attempt this task only with full permission from your supervisor/instructor, and follow all the guidelines exactly.
- Lifting equipment and machines such as vehicle jacks and stands, vehicle hoists, and engine hoists are important tools that increase productivity and make the job easier. However, they can also cause severe injury or death if used improperly. Make sure you follow the manufacturer's operation procedures. Also make sure you have your supervisor's/instructor's permission to use any particular type of lifting equipment.
- Comply with personal and environmental safety practices associated with clothing; eye protection; hand tools; power equipment; proper ventilation; and the handling, storage, and disposal of chemicals/materials in accordance with federal, state, and local regulations.
- Always wear the correct protective eyewear and clothing and use the appropriate safety equipment, as well as wheel chocks, fender covers, seat protectors, and floor mat protectors.
- Make sure you understand and observe all legislative and personal safety procedures when carrying out practical assignments. If you are unsure of what these are, ask your supervisor/instructor.

▶ **TASK** Inspect turbocharger(s), wastegate(s), and piping systems; determine needed action.

MTST
I.F.1; P2

Time off_____

Time on_____

Total time_____

Student Instructions: Read through the entire procedure prior to starting. Prepare your workspace and any tools or parts that may be needed to complete the task. When directed by your supervisor/instructor, begin the procedure to complete the task and check the box as each step is finished.

Note: This tasksheet may require the student to check the condition of miscellaneous vehicle fluids, some of which may be flammable and could damage the environment or cause health problems if not handled properly. Observe all safety precautions and follow local regulations for the proper disposal of fluids.

Procedure:	Step Completed
1. Inspect turbocharger mounting for missing, loose, or damaged components as outlined in the manufacturer's workshop materials.	
a. Within manufacturer's specifications: Yes: ☐ No: ☐	☐
b. If No, describe the recommended corrective action(s):	☐
2. Check turbocharger shaft for radial and axial clearance as outlined in the manufacturer's workshop materials.	

a. Radial clearance specification: _____ thousands/mm
     i. Within manufacturer's specifications:
     Yes: ☐ No: ☐
	☐

ii. If No, describe the recommended corrective action(s):	☐

b. Axial clearance specification: _____ thousands/mm
     i. Within manufacturer's specifications:
     Yes: ☐ No: ☐
	☐

ii. If No, describe the recommended corrective action(s):	☐
3. Inspect wastegate linkage for binding, loose, missing, or damaged parts.	
a. Within manufacturer's specifications: Yes: ☐ No: ☐	☐
b. If No, describe the recommended corrective action(s):	☐
4. Record method of wastegate operation (e.g., pressure, vacuum, or electronic) as outlined in the manufacturer's workshop materials:	☐

5. Record procedure for testing wastegate operation as outlined in the manu- facturer's workshop materials, and perform the test:	
a. Within manufacturer's specifications: Yes: ☐ No: ☐	☐
b. If No, describe the recommended corrective action(s):	☐
6. Inspect the turbocharger air inlet and exhaust piping for loose, missing, or damaged parts.	
a. Within manufacturer's specifications: Yes: ☐ No: ☐	☐
b. If No, describe the recommended corrective action(s):	☐
7. Discuss your findings with your supervisor/instructor.	☐

Non-Task-Specific Evaluations:	Step Completed
1. Tools and equipment were used as directed and returned in good working order.	☐
2. Complied with all general and task-specific safety standards, including proper use of any personal protection equipment.	☐
3. Completed the task in an appropriate time frame (recommendation: 1.5 or 2 times the flat rate).	☐
4. Left the workspace clean and orderly.	☐
5. Cared for customer property and returned it undamaged.	☐

Student signature _____ Date _____

Comments:

Have your supervisor/instructor verify satisfactory completion of this procedure, any observations made, and any necessary action(s) recommended.

Evaluation Instructions: The scoring box below is intended to act as a guide for both student and supervisor/instructor. Each criterion listed will help students to understand what is expected of them and help supervisors/instructors articulate the level of success at a particular task. The scoring is set up to allow a second attempt at each task (see the Test and Retest columns). Scoring is also designed to award students points only for task criteria that were completed correctly. Points are lost for failure to complete the employability requirements (see Non-Task-Specific Evaluation criteria). When all criteria are evaluated, tally the points for a total at the bottom of each column.

Tasksheet Scoring

Evaluation Items	Test		Retest	
	Pass	**Fail**	**Pass**	**Fail**
Task-Specific Evaluation	**(1 pt)**	**(0 pts)**	**(1 pt)**	**(0 pts)**
Student properly inspected turbocharger mounting.				
Student properly checked turbocharger radial and axial clearances.				
Student properly inspected turbocharger wastegate.				
Student properly checked turbocharger wastegate operation, air inlet, and exhaust piping.				
Non-Task-Specific Evaluation	**(0 pts)**	**(−1 pt)**	**(0 pts)**	**(−1 pt)**
Student successfully completed at least three of the non-task-specific steps.				
Student successfully completed all five of the non-task-specific steps.				
Total Score: <total # of points/4 = %>				

Supervisor/Instructor:

Supervisor/instructor signature _____ Date _____

Comments:

```



```

Retest supervisor/instructor signature _____ Date _____

Comments:

```



```

CDX Tasksheet Number: MHT1F002

Student/Intern Information

Name _____ Date _____ Class _____

Vehicle, Customer, and Service Information

Vehicle used for this activity:

Year _____ Make _____ Model _____

Odometer _____ VIN _____

> ## Materials Required
> - Vehicle with possible engine concern
> - Engine manufacturer's workshop materials
> - Manufacturer-specific tools depending on the concern/procedure(s)
> - Vehicle/component lifting equipment, if applicable

Task-Specific Safety Considerations
- Activities may require test-driving the vehicle on the school grounds or on a hoist, both of which carry severe risks. Attempt this task only with full permission from your supervisor/instructor, and follow all the guidelines exactly.
- Lifting equipment and machines such as vehicle jacks and stands, vehicle hoists, and engine hoists are important tools that increase productivity and make the job easier. However, they can also cause severe injury or death if used improperly. Make sure you follow the manufacturer's operation procedures. Also make sure you have your supervisor's/instructor's permission to use any particular type of lifting equipment.
- Comply with personal and environmental safety practices associated with clothing; eye protection; hand tools; power equipment; proper ventilation; and the handling, storage, and disposal of chemicals/materials in accordance with federal, state, and local regulations.
- Always wear the correct protective eyewear and clothing and use the appropriate safety equipment, as well as wheel chocks, fender covers, seat protectors, and floor mat protectors.
- Make sure you understand and observe all legislative and personal safety procedures when carrying out practical assignments. If you are unsure of what these are, ask your supervisor/instructor.

▶ **TASK** Diagnose air induction system problems; inspect, clean, and/or replace cooler assembly, piping, hoses, clamps, and mountings; replace air filter as needed; reset restriction indicator (if applicable).

MTST
I.F.2; P1

Time off_____

Time on_____

Total time_____

Student Instructions: Read through the entire procedure prior to starting. Prepare your workspace and any tools or parts that may be needed to complete the task. When directed by your supervisor/instructor, begin the procedure to complete the task and check the box as each step is finished.

Note: This tasksheet may require the student to check the condition of miscellaneous vehicle fluids, some of which may be flammable and could damage the environment or cause health problems if not handled properly. Observe all safety precautions and follow local regulations for the proper disposal of fluids.

Procedure:	Step Completed
1. Inspect the charge air cooler tubes, fins, welds, and mounts for missing, loose, or damaged components as outlined in the manufacturer's workshop materials.	
a. Within manufacturer's specifications: Yes: ☐ No: ☐	☐
b. If No, describe the recommended corrective action(s):	☐
2. Inspect the charge air cooler inlet and outlet piping, hoses, and clamps for missing, loose, or damaged components as outlined in the manufacturer's workshop materials.	
a. Within manufacturer's specifications: Yes: ☐ No: ☐	☐
b. If No, describe the recommended corrective action(s):	☐
3. Record the procedure for performing a charge air cooler leak test as outlined in the manufacturer's workshop materials, and perform the test:	
a. List any special precautions when performing a charge air cooler leak test:	
b. Within manufacturer's specifications: Yes: ☐ No: ☐	☐
c. If No, describe the recommended corrective action(s):	☐

4. Record the procedure for performing a charge air cooler temperature differential test as outlined in the manufacturer's workshop materials, and perform the test:	
a. Within manufacturer's specifications: Yes: ☐ No: ☐	☐
b. If No, describe the recommended corrective action(s):	☐
5. Record the procedure for performing a charge air cooler pressure differential test as outlined in the manufacturer's workshop materials, and perform the test:	
a. Within manufacturer's specifications: Yes: ☐ No: ☐	☐
b. If No, describe the recommended corrective action(s):	☐
6. If directed by your supervisor/instructor, remove and reinstall the charge air cooler. List any special precautions for removing and reinstalling the charge air cooler:	☐
7. Remove the air cleaner as outlined in the manufacturer's workshop materials, and inspect for reuse. List any special precautions when replacing the air cleaner:	
a. Within manufacturer's specifications: Yes: ☐ No: ☐	☐

b. If No, describe the recommended corrective action(s):	☐
8. Inspect the air cleaner restriction gauge for missing, loose, or damaged components as outlined in the manufacturer's workshop materials, and reset.	
a. Within manufacturer's specifications: Yes: ☐ No: ☐	☐
b. If No, describe the recommended corrective action(s):	☐
9. Discuss your findings with your supervisor/instructor.	☐

Non-Task-Specific Evaluations:	Step Completed
1. Tools and equipment were used as directed and returned in good working order.	☐
2. Complied with all general and task-specific safety standards, including proper use of any personal protection equipment.	☐
3. Completed the task in an appropriate time frame (recommendation: 1.5 or 2 times the flat rate).	☐
4. Left the workspace clean and orderly.	☐
5. Cared for customer property and returned it undamaged.	☐

Student signature _____ Date _____

Comments:

Have your supervisor/instructor verify satisfactory completion of this procedure, any observations made, and any necessary action(s) recommended.

© 2021 Jones & Bartlett Learning, LLC, an Ascend Learning Company

Evaluation Instructions: The scoring box below is intended to act as a guide for both student and supervisor/instructor. Each criterion listed will help students to understand what is expected of them and help supervisors/instructors articulate the level of success at a particular task. The scoring is set up to allow a second attempt at each task (see the Test and Retest columns). Scoring is also designed to award students points only for task criteria that were completed correctly. Points are lost for failure to complete the employability requirements (see Non-Task-Specific Evaluation criteria). When all criteria are evaluated, tally the points for a total at the bottom of each column.

Tasksheet Scoring

Evaluation Items	Test		Retest	
	Pass	Fail	Pass	Fail
Task-Specific Evaluation	**(1 pt)**	**(0 pts)**	**(1 pt)**	**(0 pts)**
Student properly inspected charge air cooler tubes, fins, welds, and mounts.				
Student properly inspected charge air cooler inlet and outlet piping, hoses, and clamps.				
Student properly performed charge air cooler leak, temperature differential, and pressure differential tests.				
Student properly removed and reinstalled charge air cooler, air cleaner, and air cleaner restriction gauge.				
Non-Task-Specific Evaluation	**(0 pts)**	**(−1 pt)**	**(0 pts)**	**(−1 pt)**
Student successfully completed at least three of the non-task-specific steps.				
Student successfully completed all five of the non-task-specific steps.				
Total Score: <total # of points/4 = %>				

Supervisor/Instructor:

Supervisor/instructor signature _____ Date _____

Comments:

Retest supervisor/instructor signature _____ Date _____

Comments:

CDX Tasksheet Number: MHT1F003

Student/Intern Information

Name _____ Date _____ Class _____

Vehicle, Customer, and Service Information

Vehicle used for this activity:

Year _____ Make _____ Model _____

Odometer _____ VIN _____

Materials Required

- Vehicle with possible engine concern
- Engine manufacturer's workshop materials
- Manufacturer-specific tools depending on the concern/procedure(s)
- Vehicle/component lifting equipment, if applicable

Task-Specific Safety Considerations

- Activities may require test-driving the vehicle on the school grounds or on a hoist, both of which carry severe risks. Attempt this task only with full permission from your supervisor/ instructor, and follow all the guidelines exactly.
- Lifting equipment and machines such as vehicle jacks and stands, vehicle hoists, and engine hoists are important tools that increase productivity and make the job easier. However, they can also cause severe injury or death if used improperly. Make sure you follow the manufacturer's operation procedures. Also make sure you have your supervisor's/ instructor's permission to use any particular type of lifting equipment.
- Comply with personal and environmental safety practices associated with clothing; eye protection; hand tools; power equipment; proper ventilation; and the handling, storage, and disposal of chemicals/materials in accordance with federal, state, and local regulations.
- Always wear the correct protective eyewear and clothing and use the appropriate safety equipment, as well as wheel chocks, fender covers, seat protectors, and floor mat protectors.
- Make sure you understand and observe all legislative and personal safety procedures when carrying out practical assignments. If you are unsure of what these are, ask your supervisor/ instructor.

▶ TASK Inspect intake manifold, gaskets, and connections; determine needed action.

MTST I.F.3; P1

Time off_____

Time on_____

Total time_____

Student Instructions: Read through the entire procedure prior to starting. Prepare your workspace and any tools or parts that may be needed to complete the task. When directed by your supervisor/instructor, begin the procedure to complete the task and check the box as each step is finished.

Note: This tasksheet may require the student to check the condition of miscellaneous vehicle fluids, some of which may be flammable and could damage the environment or cause health problems if not handled properly. Observe all safety precautions and follow local regulations for the proper disposal of fluids.

Procedure:	Step Completed
1. Inspect the intake manifold for missing, loose, or damaged components as outlined in the manufacturer's workshop materials.	
a. Within manufacturer's specifications: Yes: ☐ No: ☐	☐
b. If No, describe the recommended corrective action(s):	☐
2. Inspect the intake manifold gaskets for signs of leakage or damage as outlined in the manufacturer's workshop materials.	
a. Within manufacturer's specifications: Yes: ☐ No: ☐	☐
b. If No, describe the recommended corrective action(s):	☐
3. Inspect the intake manifold connections for missing, loose, or damaged components as outlined in the manufacturer's workshop materials.	
a. Within manufacturer's specifications: Yes: ☐ No: ☐	☐
b. If No, describe the recommended corrective action(s):	☐
4. Record the procedure and torque specification(s) for tightening the intake manifold bolts, and check intake manifold bolt torque:	
a. Within manufacturer's specifications: Yes: ☐ No: ☐	☐
b. If No, describe the recommended corrective action(s):	☐
5. Discuss your findings with your supervisor/instructor.	☐

Non-Task-Specific Evaluations:	Step Completed
1. Tools and equipment were used as directed and returned in good working order.	☐
2. Complied with all general and task-specific safety standards, including proper use of any personal protection equipment.	☐
3. Completed the task in an appropriate time frame (recommendation: 1.5 or 2 times the flat rate).	☐
4. Left the workspace clean and orderly.	☐
5. Cared for customer property and returned it undamaged.	☐

Student signature _____ Date _____

Comments:

Have your supervisor/instructor verify satisfactory completion of this procedure, any observations made, and any necessary action(s) recommended.

Evaluation Instructions: The scoring box below is intended to act as a guide for both student and supervisor/instructor. Each criterion listed will help students to understand what is expected of them and help supervisors/instructors articulate the level of success at a particular task. The scoring is set up to allow a second attempt at each task (see the Test and Retest columns). Scoring is also designed to award students points only for task criteria that were completed correctly. Points are lost for failure to complete the employability requirements (see Non-Task-Specific Evaluation criteria). When all criteria are evaluated, tally the points for a total at the bottom of each column.

Tasksheet Scoring

Evaluation Items	Test		Retest	
	Pass	**Fail**	**Pass**	**Fail**
Task-Specific Evaluation	**(1 pt)**	**(0 pts)**	**(1 pt)**	**(0 pts)**
Student properly inspected intake manifold for missing, loose, or damaged components.				
Student properly inspected intake manifold gaskets.				
Student properly inspected intake manifold connections for missing, loose, or damaged components.				
Student properly checked intake manifold bolt torque.				
Non-Task-Specific Evaluation	**(0 pts)**	**(−1 pt)**	**(0 pts)**	**(−1 pt)**
Student successfully completed at least three of the non-task-specific steps.				
Student successfully completed all five of the non-task-specific steps.				
Total Score: <total # of points/4 = %>				

CDX Tasksheet Number: MHT1F004

Student/Intern Information

Name _____ Date _____ Class _____

Vehicle, Customer, and Service Information

Vehicle used for this activity:

Year _____ Make _____ Model _____

Odometer _____ VIN _____

Materials Required

- Vehicle with possible engine concern
- Engine manufacturer's workshop materials
- Manufacturer-specific tools depending on the concern/procedure(s)
- Vehicle/component lifting equipment, if applicable

Task-Specific Safety Considerations

- Activities may require test-driving the vehicle on the school grounds or on a hoist, both of which carry severe risks. Attempt this task only with full permission from your supervisor/instructor, and follow all the guidelines exactly.
- Lifting equipment and machines such as vehicle jacks and stands, vehicle hoists, and engine hoists are important tools that increase productivity and make the job easier. However, they can also cause severe injury or death if used improperly. Make sure you follow the manufacturer's operation procedures. Also make sure you have your supervisor's/instructor's permission to use any particular type of lifting equipment.
- Comply with personal and environmental safety practices associated with clothing; eye protection; hand tools; power equipment; proper ventilation; and the handling, storage, and disposal of chemicals/materials in accordance with federal, state, and local regulations.
- Always wear the correct protective eyewear and clothing and use the appropriate safety equipment, as well as wheel chocks, fender covers, seat protectors, and floor mat protectors.
- Make sure you understand and observe all legislative and personal safety procedures when carrying out practical assignments. If you are unsure of what these are, ask your supervisor/instructor.

▶ **TASK** Inspect engine exhaust system, exhaust gas recirculation (EGR) system, and exhaust aftertreatment system for leaks, mounting, proper routing, and damaged or missing components; determine needed action. **MTST** *I.F.4; P1*

Time off_____

Time on_____

Student Instructions: Read through the entire procedure prior to starting. Prepare your workspace and any tools or parts that may be needed to complete the task. When directed by your supervisor/instructor, begin the procedure to complete the task and check the box as each step is finished.

Total time_____

Note: This tasksheet may require the student to check the condition of miscellaneous vehicle fluids, some of which may be flammable and could damage the environment or cause health problems if not handled properly. Observe all safety precautions and follow local regulations for the proper disposal of fluids.

Procedure:	Step Completed
1. Inspect the exhaust manifold for missing, loose, or damaged components.	
a. Within manufacturer's specifications: Yes: ☐ No: ☐	☐
b. If No, describe the recommended corrective action(s):	☐
2. Inspect the exhaust manifold gaskets/sections for signs of leakage or damage.	
a. Within manufacturer's specifications: Yes: ☐ No: ☐	☐
b. If No, describe the recommended corrective action(s):	☐
3. Record the procedure and torque specification(s) for tightening the exhaust manifold bolts as outlined in the manufacturer's workshop materials, and check the exhaust manifold bolt torque:	
a. Within manufacturer's specifications: Yes: ☐ No: ☐	☐
b. If No, describe the recommended corrective action(s):	☐
4. Inspect the EGR cooler for missing, loose, or damaged components.	
a. Within manufacturer's specifications: Yes: ☐ No: ☐	☐
b. If No, describe the recommended corrective action(s):	☐

5. Record the procedure for performing an engine EGR cooler coolant strip test as outlined in the manufacturer's workshop materials, and perform the test:	
a. Within manufacturer's specifications: Yes: ☐ No: ☐	☐
b. If No, decribe the recommended corrective action(s):	☐
6. Record the procedure for performing an EGR cooler pressure test as outlined in the manufacturer's workshop materials, and perform the test:	
a. Within manufacturer's specifications: Yes: ☐ No: ☐	☐
b. If No, describe the recommended corrective action(s):	☐
7. Inspect the exhaust pipe and muffler for missing, loose, or damaged components, leaks, and proper routing.	
a. Within manufacturer's specifications: Yes: ☐ No: ☐	☐
b. If No, describe the recommended corrective action(s):	☐
8. Inspect the aftertreatment system for missing, loose, or damaged components and leaks.	
a. Within manufacturer's specifications: Yes: ☐ No: ☐	☐
b. If No, describe the recommended corrective action(s):	☐

9. Record the procedure for removing and inspecting the aftertreatment selective catalytic reduction (SCR) catalyst as outlined in the manufacturer's workshop materials. Remove the SCR catalyst, inspect, and reinstall:	
a. Within manufacturer's specifications: Yes: ☐ No: ☐	☐
b. If No, describe the recommended corrective action(s):	☐
10. Record the procedure for removing and inspecting the diesel particulate filter (DPF) as outlined in the manufacturer's workshop materials. Remove the DPF, inspect, and reinstall:	
a. Within manufacturer's specifications: Yes: ☐ No: ☐	☐
b. If No, describe the recommended corrective action(s):	☐
11. Discuss your findings with your supervisor/instructor.	☐

Non-Task-Specific Evaluations:	Step Completed
1. Tools and equipment were used as directed and returned in good working order.	☐
2. Complied with all general and task-specific safety standards, including proper use of any personal protection equipment.	☐
3. Completed the task in an appropriate time frame (recommendation: 1.5 or 2 times the flat rate).	☐
4. Left the workspace clean and orderly.	☐
5. Cared for customer property and returned it undamaged.	☐

Student signature _____ Date _____

Comments:

Have your supervisor/instructor verify satisfactory completion of this procedure, any observations made,

and any necessary action(s) recommended.

Evaluation Instructions: The scoring box below is intended to act as a guide for both student and supervisor/instructor. Each criterion listed will help students to understand what is expected of them and help supervisors/instructors articulate the level of success at a particular task. The scoring is set up to allow a second attempt at each task (see the Test and Retest columns). Scoring is also designed to award students points only for task criteria that were completed correctly. Points are lost for failure to complete the employability requirements (see Non-Task-Specific Evaluation criteria). When all criteria are evaluated, tally the points for a total at the bottom of each column.

Tasksheet Scoring

Evaluation Items	Test		Retest	
	Pass	Fail	Pass	Fail
Task-Specific Evaluation	**(1 pt)**	**(0 pts)**	**(1 pt)**	**(0 pts)**
Student properly inspected exhaust manifold, gaskets/sections, and EGR cooler for missing, loose, or damaged components.				
Student properly performed engine EGR cooler test strip and cooler pressure tests.				
Student properly inspected exhaust pipe, muffler, and aftertreatment system for missing, loose, or damaged components.				
Student properly removed, inspected, and reinstalled SCR catalyst and DPF.				
Non-Task-Specific Evaluation	**(0 pts)**	**(−1 pt)**	**(0 pts)**	**(−1 pt)**
Student successfully completed at least three of the non-task-specific steps.				
Student successfully completed all five of the non-task-specific steps.				
Total Score: <total # of points/4 = %>				

Supervisor/Instructor:

Supervisor/instructor signature _____ Date _____

Comments:

Retest supervisor/instructor signature _____ Date _____

Comments:

CDX Tasksheet Number: MHT1F005

Student/Intern Information

Name _____ Date _____ Class _____

Vehicle, Customer, and Service Information

Vehicle used for this activity:

Year _____ Make _____ Model _____

Odometer _____ VIN _____

Materials Required

- Vehicle with possible engine concern
- Engine manufacturer's workshop materials
- Manufacturer-specific tools depending on the concern/procedure(s)
- Vehicle/component lifting equipment, if applicable

Task-Specific Safety Considerations

- Activities may require test-driving the vehicle on the school grounds or on a hoist, both of which carry severe risks. Attempt this task only with full permission from your supervisor/instructor, and follow all the guidelines exactly.
- Lifting equipment and machines such as vehicle jacks and stands, vehicle hoists, and engine hoists are important tools that increase productivity and make the job easier. However, they can also cause severe injury or death if used improperly. Make sure you follow the manufacturer's operation procedures. Also make sure you have your supervisor's/instructor's permission to use any particular type of lifting equipment.
- Comply with personal and environmental safety practices associated with clothing; eye protection; hand tools; power equipment; proper ventilation; and the handling, storage, and disposal of chemicals/materials in accordance with federal, state, and local regulations.
- Always wear the correct protective eyewear and clothing and use the appropriate safety equipment, as well as wheel chocks, fender covers, seat protectors, and floor mat protectors.
- Make sure you understand and observe all legislative and personal safety procedures when carrying out practical assignments. If you are unsure of what these are, ask your supervisor/instructor.

▶ **TASK** Inspect crankcase ventilation system; service as needed. _____ **MTST** *I.F.5; P1*

Time off_____

Time on_____

Student Instructions: Read through the entire procedure prior to starting. Prepare your workspace and any tools or parts that may be needed to complete the task. When directed by your supervisor/instructor, begin the procedure to complete the task and check the box as each step is finished.

Total time_____

Note: This tasksheet may require the student to check the condition of miscellaneous vehicle fluids, some of which may be flammable and could damage the environment or cause health problems if not handled properly. Observe all safety precautions and follow local regulations for the proper disposal of fluids.

Procedure:	Step Completed
1. Identify the crankcase ventilation filter/insert type as outlined in the manufacturer's workshop materials:	☐
2. Inspect the crankcase ventilation system for missing, loose, or damaged components.	
a. Within manufacturer's specifications: Yes: ☐ No: ☐	☐
b. If No, describe the recommended corrective action(s):	☐
3. Record the procedure for inspecting the crankcase breather tube as outlined in the manufacturer's workshop materials, and perform the inspection:	
a. Within manufacturer's specifications: Yes: ☐ No: ☐	☐
b. If No, describe the recommended corrective action(s):	☐
4. Record the procedure for inspecting the crankcase breather filter element/breather insert as outlined in the manufacturer's workshop materials, and perform the inspection:	
a. Within manufacturer's specifications: Yes: ☐ No: ☐	☐
b. If No, describe the recommended corrective action(s):	☐

5. Discuss your findings with your supervisor/instructor.	☐

Non-Task-Specific Evaluations:	Step Completed
1. Tools and equipment were used as directed and returned in good working order.	☐
2. Complied with all general and task-specific safety standards, including proper use of any personal protection equipment.	☐
3. Completed the task in an appropriate time frame (recommendation: 1.5 or 2 times the flat rate).	☐
4. Left the workspace clean and orderly.	☐
5. Cared for customer property and returned it undamaged.	☐

Student signature _____ Date _____

Comments:

Have your supervisor/instructor verify satisfactory completion of this procedure, any observations made,

and any necessary action(s) recommended.

Evaluation Instructions: The scoring box below is intended to act as a guide for both student and supervisor/instructor. Each criterion listed will help students to understand what is expected of them and help supervisors/instructors articulate the level of success at a particular task. The scoring is set up to allow a second attempt at each task (see the Test and Retest columns). Scoring is also designed to award students points only for task criteria that were completed correctly. Points are lost for failure to complete the employability requirements (see Non-Task-Specific Evaluation criteria). When all criteria are evaluated, tally the points for a total at the bottom of each column.

Tasksheet Scoring

Evaluation Items	Test		Retest	
	Pass	**Fail**	**Pass**	**Fail**
Task-Specific Evaluation	**(1 pt)**	**(0 pts)**	**(1 pt)**	**(0 pts)**
Student correctly identified crankcase ventilation system filter/insert type.				
Student properly inspected crankcase ventilation system for missing, loose, or damaged components.				
Student properly inspected crankcase ventilation system breather tube.				
Student properly removed, inspected, and reinstalled crankcase ventilation filter/insert.				
Non-Task-Specific Evaluation	**(0 pts)**	**(−1 pt)**	**(0 pts)**	**(−1 pt)**
Student successfully completed at least three of the non-task-specific steps.				
Student successfully completed all five of the non-task-specific steps.				
Total Score: <total # of points/4 = %>				

Supervisor/Instructor:

Supervisor/instructor signature _____ Date _____

Comments:

Retest supervisor/instructor signature _____ Date _____

Comments:

CDX Tasksheet Number: MHT1F006

Student/Intern Information

Name _____ Date _____ Class _____

Vehicle, Customer, and Service Information

Vehicle used for this activity:

Year _____ Make _____ Model _____

Odometer _____ VIN _____

Materials Required

- Vehicle with possible engine concern
- Engine manufacturer's workshop materials
- Manufacturer-specific tools depending on the concern/procedure(s)
- Vehicle/component lifting equipment, if applicable

Task-Specific Safety Considerations

- Activities may require test-driving the vehicle on the school grounds or on a hoist, both of which carry severe risks. Attempt this task only with full permission from your supervisor/instructor, and follow all the guidelines exactly.
- Lifting equipment and machines such as vehicle jacks and stands, vehicle hoists, and engine hoists are important tools that increase productivity and make the job easier. However, they can also cause severe injury or death if used improperly. Make sure you follow the manufacturer's operation procedures. Also make sure you have your supervisor's/instructor's permission to use any particular type of lifting equipment.
- Comply with personal and environmental safety practices associated with clothing; eye protection; hand tools; power equipment; proper ventilation; and the handling, storage, and disposal of chemicals/materials in accordance with federal, state, and local regulations.
- Always wear the correct protective eyewear and clothing and use the appropriate safety equipment, as well as wheel chocks, fender covers, seat protectors, and floor mat protectors.
- Make sure you understand and observe all legislative and personal safety procedures when carrying out practical assignments. If you are unsure of what these are, ask your supervisor/instructor.

▶ **TASK** Diagnose problems/faults in the exhaust gas recirculation (EGR) system, including EGR valve, cooler, piping, filter, electronic sensors, controls, and wiring; determine needed action.

MTST
I.F.6; P1

Time off_____

Time on_____

Student Instructions: Read through the entire procedure prior to starting. Prepare your workspace and any tools or parts that may be needed to complete the task. When directed by your supervisor/instructor, begin the procedure to complete the task and check the box as each step is finished.

Total time_____

Note: This tasksheet may require the student to check the condition of miscellaneous vehicle fluids, some of which may be flammable and could damage the environment or cause health problems if not handled properly. Observe all safety precautions and follow local regulations for the proper disposal of fluids.

Procedure:	Step Completed
1. Check for and record EGR fault codes as outlined in the manufacturer's workshop materials:	☐
2. Inspect the EGR electronic controls and wiring for missing or broken connectors or damaged wiring.	
a. Within manufacturer's specifications: Yes: ☐ No: ☐	☐
b. If No, describe the recommended corrective action(s):	☐
3. Inspect the EGR valve, piping, and cooler for missing, loose, or damaged components.	
a. Within manufacturer's specifications: Yes: ☐ No: ☐	☐
b. If No, describe the recommended corrective action(s):	☐
4. Record the procedure for removing and inspecting the EGR valve as outlined in the manufacturer's workshop materials. Remove, inspect, and reinstall the EGR valve:	
a. Within manufacturer's specifications: Yes: ☐ No: ☐	☐
b. If No, describe the recommended corrective action(s):	☐
5. Check for and record any new EGR fault codes after the EGR valve has been removed, inspected, and reinstalled:	☐

6. If directed by your supervisor/instructor, perform any task necessary to troubleshoot and repair any active or pending EGR fault code.	☐
7. Inspect the EGR cooler for missing, loose, or damaged components.	
a. Within manufacturer's specifications: Yes: ☐ No: ☐	☐
b. If No, describe the recommended corrective action(s):	☐
8. Record the procedure for performing an on-engine EGR cooler coolant strip test as outlined in the manufacturer's workshop materials, and perform the test:	
a. Within manufacturer's specifications: Yes: ☐ No: ☐	☐
b. If No, describe the recommended corrective action(s):	☐
9. Record the procedure for performing an EGR cooler pressure test as outlined in the manufacturer's workshop materials, and perform the test:	
a. Within manufacturer's specifications: Yes: ☐ No: ☐	☐
b. If No, describe the recommended corrective action(s):	☐
10. Discuss your findings with your supervisor/instructor.	☐

Non-Task-Specific Evaluations:	Step Completed
1. Tools and equipment were used as directed and returned in good working order.	☐
2. Complied with all general and task-specific safety standards, including proper use of any personal protection equipment.	☐
3. Completed the task in an appropriate time frame (recommendation: 1.5 or 2 times the flat rate).	☐
4. Left the workspace clean and orderly.	☐
5. Cared for customer property and returned it undamaged.	☐

Student signature _____ Date _____

Comments:

Have your supervisor/instructor verify satisfactory completion of this procedure, any observations made, and any necessary action(s) recommended.

Evaluation Instructions: The scoring box below is intended to act as a guide for both student and supervisor/instructor. Each criterion listed will help students to understand what is expected of them and help supervisors/instructors articulate the level of success at a particular task. The scoring is set up to allow a second attempt at each task (see the Test and Retest columns). Scoring is also designed to award students points only for task criteria that were completed correctly. Points are lost for failure to complete the employability requirements (see Non-Task-Specific Evaluation criteria). When all criteria are evaluated, tally the points for a total at the bottom of each column.

Tasksheet Scoring

Evaluation Items	Test		Retest	
	Pass	**Fail**	**Pass**	**Fail**
Task-Specific Evaluation	**(1 pt)**	**(0 pts)**	**(1 pt)**	**(0 pts)**
Student properly checked EGR system for fault codes and properly performed troubleshooting and repair of EGR codes.				
Student properly inspected EGR electronic controls, wiring, EGR valve, piping, and cooler.				
Student properly removed, inspected, and reinstalled the EGR valve.				
Student properly performed on engine EGR cooler test strip test and EGR cooler pressure test.				
Non-Task-Specific Evaluation	**(0 pts)**	**(−1 pt)**	**(0 pts)**	**(−1 pt)**
Student successfully completed at least three of the non-task-specific steps.				
Student successfully completed all five of the non-task-specific steps.				
Total Score: <total # of points/4 = %>				

Supervisor/Instructor:

Supervisor/instructor signature _____ Date _____

Comments:

Retest supervisor/instructor signature _____ Date _____

Comments:

CDX Tasksheet Number: MHT1F007

Student/Intern Information

Name _____ Date _____ Class _____

Vehicle, Customer, and Service Information

Vehicle used for this activity:

Year _____ Make _____ Model _____

Odometer _____ VIN _____

Materials Required

- Vehicle with possible engine concern
- Engine manufacturer's workshop materials
- Manufacturer-specific tools depending on the concern/procedure(s)
- Vehicle/component lifting equipment, if applicable

Task-Specific Safety Considerations

- Activities may require test-driving the vehicle on the school grounds or on a hoist, both of which carry severe risks. Attempt this task only with full permission from your supervisor/instructor, and follow all the guidelines exactly.
- Lifting equipment and machines such as vehicle jacks and stands, vehicle hoists, and engine hoists are important tools that increase productivity and make the job easier. However, they can also cause severe injury or death if used improperly. Make sure you follow the manufacturer's operation procedures. Also make sure you have your supervisor's/instructor's permission to use any particular type of lifting equipment.
- Comply with personal and environmental safety practices associated with clothing; eye protection; hand tools; power equipment; proper ventilation; and the handling, storage, and disposal of chemicals/materials in accordance with federal, state, and local regulations.
- Always wear the correct protective eyewear and clothing and use the appropriate safety equipment, as well as wheel chocks, fender covers, seat protectors, and floor mat protectors.
- Make sure you understand and observe all legislative and personal safety procedures when carrying out practical assignments. If you are unsure of what these are, ask your supervisor/instructor.

▶ TASK: Perform air intake system restriction and leakage tests; determine needed action.

MTST
I.F.7; P1

Time off_____

Time on_____

Total time_____

Student Instructions: Read through the entire procedure prior to starting. Prepare your workspace and any tools or parts that may be needed to complete the task. When directed by your supervisor/instructor, begin the procedure to complete the task and check the box as each step is finished.

Note: This tasksheet may require the student to check the condition of miscellaneous vehicle fluids, some of which may be flammable and could damage the environment or cause health problems if not handled properly. Observe all safety precautions and follow local regulations for the proper disposal of fluids.

Procedure:	Step Completed
1. Inspect the air intake system for missing, loose, or damaged components.	
a. Within manufacturer's specifications: Yes: ☐ No: ☐	☐
b. If No, describe the recommended corrective action(s):	☐
2. Record the procedure for performing an air intake restriction test as outlined in the manufacturer's workshop materials, and perform the test:	
a. Maximum restriction/leakage permissible:	☐
b. Within manufacturer's specifications: Yes: ☐ No: ☐	☐
c. If No, describe the recommended corrective action(s):	☐
3. Record the procedure for checking for high-pressure air leaks in the air intake system as outlined in the manufacturer's workshop materials, and perform the test:	
a. Within manufacturer's specifications: Yes: ☐ No: ☐	☐
b. If No, describe the recommended corrective action(s):	☐
4. Discuss your findings with your supervisor/instructor.	☐

Non-Task-Specific Evaluations:	Step Completed
1. Tools and equipment were used as directed and returned in good working order.	☐
2. Complied with all general and task-specific safety standards, including proper use of any personal protection equipment.	☐
3. Completed the task in an appropriate time frame (recommendation: 1.5 or 2 times the flat rate).	☐
4. Left the workspace clean and orderly.	☐
5. Cared for customer property and returned it undamaged.	☐

Student signature _____ Date _____

Comments:

Have your supervisor/instructor verify satisfactory completion of this procedure, any observations made,

and any necessary action(s) recommended.

Evaluation Instructions: The scoring box below is intended to act as a guide for both student and supervisor/instructor. Each criterion listed will help students to understand what is expected of them and help supervisors/instructors articulate the level of success at a particular task. The scoring is set up to allow a second attempt at each task (see the Test and Retest columns). Scoring is also designed to award students points only for task criteria that were completed correctly. Points are lost for failure to complete the employability requirements (see Non-Task-Specific Evaluation criteria). When all criteria are evaluated, tally the points for a total at the bottom of each column.

Tasksheet Scoring

Evaluation Items	Test		Retest	
	Pass	**Fail**	**Pass**	**Fail**
Task-Specific Evaluation	**(1 pt)**	**(0 pts)**	**(1 pt)**	**(0 pts)**
Student properly inspected air intake system for missing, loose, or damaged components.				
Student properly performed air intake system restriction test.				
Student properly performed air intake system high-pressure leak test.				
Student reinstalled all removed components undamaged and in working order.				
Non-Task-Specific Evaluation	**(0 pts)**	**(−1 pt)**	**(0 pts)**	**(−1 pt)**
Student successfully completed at least three of the non-task-specific steps.				
Student successfully completed all five of the non-task-specific steps.				
Total Score: <total # of points/4 = %>				

Supervisor/Instructor:

Supervisor/instructor signature _____ Date _____

Comments:

Retest supervisor/instructor signature _____ Date _____

Comments:

CDX Tasksheet Number: MHT1F008

Student/Intern Information

Name _____ Date _____ Class _____

Vehicle, Customer, and Service Information

Vehicle used for this activity:

Year _____ Make _____ Model _____

Odometer _____ VIN _____

Materials Required

- Vehicle with possible engine concern
- Engine manufacturer's workshop materials
- Manufacturer-specific tools depending on the concern/procedure(s)
- Vehicle/component lifting equipment, if applicable

Task-Specific Safety Considerations

- Activities may require test-driving the vehicle on the school grounds or on a hoist, both of which carry severe risks. Attempt this task only with full permission from your supervisor/instructor, and follow all the guidelines exactly.
- Lifting equipment and machines such as vehicle jacks and stands, vehicle hoists, and engine hoists are important tools that increase productivity and make the job easier. However, they can also cause severe injury or death if used improperly. Make sure you follow the manufacturer's operation procedures. Also make sure you have your supervisor's/instructor's permission to use any particular type of lifting equipment.
- Comply with personal and environmental safety practices associated with clothing; eye protection; hand tools; power equipment; proper ventilation; and the handling, storage, and disposal of chemicals/materials in accordance with federal, state, and local regulations.
- Always wear the correct protective eyewear and clothing and use the appropriate safety equipment, as well as wheel chocks, fender covers, seat protectors, and floor mat protectors.
- Make sure you understand and observe all legislative and personal safety procedures when carrying out practical assignments. If you are unsure of what these are, ask your supervisor/instructor.

▶ **TASK** Perform air intake manifold pressure (boost) test; determine needed action.

MTST
I.F.8; P3

Time off_____

Time on_____

Total time_____

Student Instructions: Read through the entire procedure prior to starting. Prepare your workspace and any tools or parts that may be needed to complete the task. When directed by your supervisor/instructor, begin the procedure to complete the task and check the box as each step is finished.

Note: This tasksheet may require the student to check the condition of miscellaneous vehicle fluids, some of which may be flammable and could damage the environment or cause health problems if not handled properly. Observe all safety precautions and follow local regulations for the proper disposal of fluids.

Procedure:	Step Completed
1. Inspect the air intake system for missing, loose, or damaged components.	
a. Within manufacturer's specifications: Yes: ☐ No: ☐	☐
b. If No, describe the recommended corrective action(s):	☐
2. Record the procedure for performing an air intake manifold pressure (boost) test as outlined in the manufacturer's workshop materials, and perform the test:	
a. Manufacturer's air intake manifold pressure (boost) specification: _____ psi	☐
b. Within manufacturer's specifications: Yes: ☐ No: ☐	☐
c. If No, describe the recommended corrective action(s):	☐
3. Discuss your findings with your supervisor/instructor.	☐

Non-Task-Specific Evaluations:	Step Completed
1. Tools and equipment were used as directed and returned in good working order.	☐
2. Complied with all general and task-specific safety standards, including proper use of any personal protection equipment.	☐
3. Completed the task in an appropriate time frame (recommendation: 1.5 or 2 times the flat rate).	☐
4. Left the workspace clean and orderly.	☐
5. Cared for customer property and returned it undamaged.	☐

Student signature _____ Date _____

Comments:

Have your supervisor/instructor verify satisfactory completion of this procedure, any observations made, and any necessary action(s) recommended.

Evaluation Instructions: The scoring box below is intended to act as a guide for both student and supervisor/instructor. Each criterion listed will help students to understand what is expected of them and help supervisors/instructors articulate the level of success at a particular task. The scoring is set up to allow a second attempt at each task (see the Test and Retest columns). Scoring is also designed to award students points only for task criteria that were completed correctly. Points are lost for failure to complete the employability requirements (see Non-Task-Specific Evaluation criteria). When all criteria are evaluated, tally the points for a total at the bottom of each column.

Tasksheet Scoring

Evaluation Items	Test		Retest	
	Pass	Fail	Pass	Fail
Task-Specific Evaluation	**(1 pt)**	**(0 pts)**	**(1 pt)**	**(0 pts)**
Student properly inspected air intake system for missing, loose, or damaged components.				
Student properly recorded the procedure for performing an air intake manifold pressure (boost) test.				
Student properly performed air intake manifold pressure (boost) system test.				
Student reinstalled all removed components undamaged and in working order.				
Non-Task-Specific Evaluation	**(0 pts)**	**(−1 pt)**	**(0 pts)**	**(−1 pt)**
Student successfully completed at least three of the non-task-specific steps.				
Student successfully completed all five of the non-task-specific steps.				
Total Score: <total # of points/4 = %>				

CDX Tasksheet Number: MHT1F009

Student/Intern Information

Name _____ Date _____ Class _____

Vehicle, Customer, and Service Information

Vehicle used for this activity:

Year _____ Make _____ Model _____

Odometer _____ VIN _____

Materials Required

- Vehicle with possible engine concern
- Engine manufacturer's workshop materials
- Manufacturer-specific tools depending on the concern/procedure(s)
- Vehicle/component lifting equipment, if applicable

Task-Specific Safety Considerations

- Activities may require test-driving the vehicle on the school grounds or on a hoist, both of which carry severe risks. Attempt this task only with full permission from your supervisor/instructor, and follow all the guidelines exactly.
- Lifting equipment and machines such as vehicle jacks and stands, vehicle hoists, and engine hoists are important tools that increase productivity and make the job easier. However, they can also cause severe injury or death if used improperly. Make sure you follow the manufacturer's operation procedures. Also make sure you have your supervisor's/instructor's permission to use any particular type of lifting equipment.
- Comply with personal and environmental safety practices associated with clothing; eye protection; hand tools; power equipment; proper ventilation; and the handling, storage, and disposal of chemicals/materials in accordance with federal, state, and local regulations.
- Always wear the correct protective eyewear and clothing and use the appropriate safety equipment, as well as wheel chocks, fender covers, seat protectors, and floor mat protectors.
- Make sure you understand and observe all legislative and personal safety procedures when carrying out practical assignments. If you are unsure of what these are, ask your supervisor/instructor.

▶ TASK Check exhaust backpressure; determine needed action.   **MTST** I.F.9; P3

Time off_____

Time on_____

Student Instructions: Read through the entire procedure prior to starting. Prepare your workspace and any tools or parts that may be needed to complete the task. When directed by your instructor, begin the procedure to complete the task, and check the box as each step is finished.

Total time_____

Note: This tasksheet may require the student to check the condition of miscellaneous vehicle fluids, some of which may be flammable and could damage the environment or cause health problems if not handled properly. Observe all safety precautions and follow local regulations for the proper disposal of fluids.

Procedure:	Step Completed
1. Inspect the exhaust system for missing, loose, or damaged components.	
a. Within manufacturer's specifications: Yes: ☐ No: ☐	☐
b. If No, describe the recommended corrective action(s):	☐
2. Record the procedure for performing a stationary regen of the aftertreatment system as outlined in the manufacturer's workshop materials, and perform the regen. (**Note:** This procedure is to be done prior to testing for exhaust system backpressure [exhaust restriction].)	☐
3. Record the procedure for performing an exhaust backpressure (restriction) test as outlined in the manufacturer's workshop materials, and perform the test:	
a. Manufacturer's maximum allowable exhaust system backpressure specification: _____ in-Hg	☐
b. Within manufacturer's specifications: Yes: ☐ No: ☐	☐
c. If No, describe the recommended corrective action(s):	☐
4. Discuss your findings with your supervisor/instructor.	☐

Non-Task-Specific Evaluations:	Step Completed
1. Tools and equipment were used as directed and returned in good working order.	☐
2. Complied with all general and task-specific safety standards, including proper use of any personal protection equipment.	☐
3. Completed the task in an appropriate time frame (recommendation: 1.5 or 2 times the flat rate).	☐
4. Left the workspace clean and orderly.	☐
5. Cared for customer property and returned it undamaged.	☐

Student signature _____ Date _____

Comments:

Have your supervisor/instructor verify satisfactory completion of this procedure, any observations made,

and any necessary action(s) recommended.

Evaluation Instructions: The scoring box below is intended to act as a guide for both student and supervisor/instructor. Each criterion listed will help students to understand what is expected of them and help supervisors/instructors articulate the level of success at a particular task. The scoring is set up to allow a second attempt at each task (see the Test and Retest columns). Scoring is also designed to award students points only for task criteria that were completed correctly. Points are lost for failure to complete the employability requirements (see Non-Task-Specific Evaluation criteria). When all criteria are evaluated, tally the points for a total at the bottom of each column.

Tasksheet Scoring

Evaluation Items	Test		Retest	
	Pass	**Fail**	**Pass**	**Fail**
Task-Specific Evaluation	**(1 pt)**	**(0 pts)**	**(1 pt)**	**(0 pts)**
Student properly inspected exhaust system for missing, loose, or damaged components.				
Student properly performed stationary regen.				
Student properly performed exhaust system backpressure (exhaust restriction) test.				
Student reinstalled all removed components undamaged and in working order.				
Non-Task-Specific Evaluation	**(0 pts)**	**(−1 pt)**	**(0 pts)**	**(−1 pt)**
Student successfully completed at least three of the non-task-specific steps.				
Student successfully completed all five of the non-task-specific steps.				
Total Score: <total # of points/4 = %>				

CDX Tasksheet Number: MHT1FO10

Student/Intern Information

Name _____ Date _____ Class _____

Vehicle, Customer, and Service Information

Vehicle used for this activity:

Year _____ Make _____ Model _____

Odometer _____ VIN _____

Materials Required

- Vehicle with possible engine concern
- Engine manufacturer's workshop materials
- Manufacturer-specific tools depending on the concern/procedure(s)
- Vehicle/component lifting equipment, if applicable

Task-Specific Safety Considerations

- Activities may require test-driving the vehicle on the school grounds or on a hoist, both of which carry severe risks. Attempt this task only with full permission from your supervisor/instructor, and follow all the guidelines exactly.
- Lifting equipment and materials such as vehicle jacks and stands, vehicle hoists, and engine hoists are important tools that increase productivity and make the job easier. However, they can also cause severe injury or death if used improperly. Make sure you follow the manufacturer's operation procedures. Also make sure you have your supervisor's/instructor's permission to use any particular type of lifting equipment.
- Comply with personal and environmental safety practices associated with clothing; eye protection; hand tools; power equipment; proper ventilation; and the handling, storage, and disposal of chemicals/materials in accordance with federal, state, and local regulations.
- Always wear the correct protective eyewear and clothing and use the appropriate safety equipment, as well as wheel chocks, fender covers, seat protectors, and floor mat protectors.
- Make sure you understand and observe all legislative and personal safety procedures when carrying out practical assignments. If you are unsure of what these are, ask your supervisor/instructor.

▶ TASK Inspect variable-ratio geometry turbocharger (VGT), controls, and actuators (pneumatic, hydraulic, and electronic); determine needed action.

MTST I.F.10; P2

Time off _____

Time on _____

Total time _____

Student Instructions: Read through the entire procedure prior to starting. Prepare your workspace and any tools or parts that may be needed to complete the task. When directed by your supervisor/instructor, begin the procedure to complete the task and check the box as each step is finished.

Note: This tasksheet may require the student to check the condition of miscellaneous vehicle fluids, some of which may be flammable and could damage the environment or cause health problems if not handled properly. Observe all safety precautions and follow local regulations for the proper disposal of fluids.

© 2021 Jones & Bartlett Learning, LLC, an Ascend Learning Company

Procedure:	Step Completed
1. Inspect the turbocharger and actuator/control for missing, loose, or damaged components.	
a. Within manufacturer's specifications: Yes: ☐ No: ☐	☐
b. If No, describe the recommended corrective action(s):	☐
2. Record the type of VGT turbocharger actuator/control installed (pneumatic, hydraulic, electronic) as outlined in the manufacturer's workshop materials:	☐
3. Record the procedure for replacing a VGT turbocharger actuator as outlined in the manufacturer's workshop materials:	☐
4. Record the procedure for performing a VGT turbocharger actuator/control calibration as outlined in the manufacturer's workshop materials:	☐
5. If directed by your supervisor/instructor, remove, reinstall, and perform a VGT turbocharger actuator/control calibration.	
a. Within manufacturer's specifications: Yes: ☐ No: ☐	☐
b. If No, describe the recommended corrective action(s):	☐
6. Discuss your findings with your supervisor/instructor.	☐

Non-Task-Specific Evaluations:	Step Completed
1. Tools and equipment were used as directed and returned in good working order.	☐
2. Complied with all general and task-specific safety standards, including proper use of any personal protection equipment.	☐
3. Completed the task in an appropriate time frame (recommendation: 1.5 or 2 times the flat rate).	☐
4. Left the workspace clean and orderly.	☐
5. Cared for customer property and returned it undamaged.	☐

Student signature _____ Date _____

Comments:

Have your supervisor/instructor verify satisfactory completion of this procedure, any observations made,

and any necessary action(s) recommended.

Evaluation Instructions: The scoring box below is intended to act as a guide for both student and supervisor/instructor. Each criterion listed will help students to understand what is expected of them and help supervisors/instructors articulate the level of success at a particular task. The scoring is set up to allow a second attempt at each task (see the Test and Retest columns). Scoring is also designed to award students points only for task criteria that were completed correctly. Points are lost for failure to complete the employability requirements (see Non-Task-Specific Evaluation criteria). When all criteria are evaluated, tally the points for a total at the bottom of each column.

Tasksheet Scoring

Evaluation Items	Test		Retest	
	Pass	Fail	Pass	Fail
Task-Specific Evaluation	**(1 pt)**	**(0 pts)**	**(1 pt)**	**(0 pts)**
Student properly inspected VGT turbocharger and actuator/control for missing, loose, or damaged components.				
Student properly recorded VGT turbocharger actuator/control removal/installation procedure.				
Student properly recorded VGT turbocharger actuator/control calibration procedure.				
Student properly performed VGT turbocharger actuator/control removal, installation, and calibration.				
Non-Task-Specific Evaluation	**(0 pts)**	**(−1 pt)**	**(0 pts)**	**(−1 pt)**
Student successfully completed at least three of the non-task-specific steps.				
Student successfully completed all five of the non-task-specific steps.				
Total Score: <total # of points/4 = %>				

Supervisor/Instructor:

Supervisor/instructor signature _____ Date _____

Comments:

Retest supervisor/instructor signature _____ Date _____

Comments:

CDX Tasksheet Number: MHT1FO11

Student/Intern Information

Name _____ Date _____ Class _____

Vehicle, Customer, and Service Information

Vehicle used for this activity:

Year _____ Make _____ Model _____

Odometer _____ VIN _____

Materials Required

- Vehicle with possible engine concern
- Engine manufacturer's workshop materials
- Manufacturer-specific tools depending on the concern/procedure(s)
- Vehicle/component lifting equipment, if applicable

Task-Specific Safety Considerations

- Activities may require test-driving the vehicle on the school grounds or on a hoist, both of which carry severe risks. Attempt this task only with full permission from your supervisor/instructor, and follow all the guidelines exactly.
- Lifting equipment and machines such as vehicle jacks and stands, vehicle hoists, and engine hoists are important tools that increase productivity and make the job easier. However, they can also cause severe injury or death if used improperly. Make sure you follow the manufacturer's operation procedures. Also make sure you have your supervisor's/instructor's permission to use any particular type of lifting equipment.
- Comply with personal and environmental safety practices associated with clothing; eye protection; hand tools; power equipment; proper ventilation; and the handling, storage, and disposal of chemicals/materials in accordance with federal, state, and local regulations.
- Always wear the correct protective eyewear and clothing and use the appropriate safety equipment, as well as wheel chocks, fender covers, seat protectors, and floor mat protectors.
- Make sure you understand and observe all legislative and personal safety procedures when carrying out practical assignments. If you are unsure of what these are, ask your supervisor/instructor.

▶ **TASK** Demonstrate knowledge of charge air cooler operation and testing.

MTST *I.F.11; P1*

Time off _____

Time on _____

Total time _____

Student Instructions: Read through the entire procedure prior to starting. Prepare your workspace and any tools or parts that may be needed to complete the task. When directed by your supervisor/instructor, begin the procedure to complete the task and check the box as each step is finished.

Note: This tasksheet may require the student to check the condition of miscellaneous vehicle fluids, some of which may be flammable and could damage the environment or cause health problems if not handled properly. Observe all safety precautions and follow local regulations for the proper disposal of fluids.

Procedure:	Step Completed
1. Inspect the charge air cooler tubes, fins, welds, and mounts for missing, loose, or damaged components.	
a. Within manufacturer's specifications: Yes: ☐ No: ☐	☐
b. If No, describe the recommended corrective action(s):	☐
2. Inspect the charge air cooler inlet and outlet piping, hoses, and clamps for missing, loose, or damaged components.	
a. Within manufacturer's specifications: Yes: ☐ No: ☐	☐
b. If No, describe the recommended corrective action(s):	☐
3. Record the procedure for performing a charge air cooler leak test as outlined in the manufacturer's workshop materials, and perform the test:	
a. List any special precautions when performing a charge air cooler leak test:	☐
b. Within manufacturer's specifications: Yes: ☐ No: ☐	☐
c. If No, describe the recommended corrective action(s):	☐

4. Record the procedure for performing a charge air cooler temperature differential test as outlined in the manufacturer's workshop materials, and perform the test:	
a. Within manufacturer's specifications: Yes: ☐ No: ☐	☐
b. If No, describe the recommended corrective action(s):	☐
5. Record the procedure for performing a charge air cooler pressure differential test as outlined in the manufacturer's workshop materials, and perform the test:	
a. Within manufacturer's specifications: Yes: ☐ No: ☐	☐
b. If No, describe the recommended corrective action(s):	☐
6. If equipped, inspect the aftercooler assembly (JWAC) connections, weld, and mounts for missing, loose, or damaged components.	
a. Within manufacturer's specifications: Yes: ☐ No: ☐	☐
b. If No, describe the recommended corrective action(s):	☐

7. Record the procedure for performing an aftercooler pressure test as outlined in the manufacturer's workshop materials, and perform the test:	
a. List any special precautions when performing an aftercooler pressure test:	☐
b. Within manufacturer's specifications: Yes: ☐ No: ☐	☐
c. If No, describe the recommended corrective action(s):	☐
8. Discuss your findings with your supervisor/instructor.	☐

Non-Task-Specific Evaluations:	Step Completed
1. Tools and equipment were used as directed and returned in good working order.	☐
2. Complied with all general and task-specific safety standards, including proper use of any personal protection equipment.	☐
3. Completed the task in an appropriate time frame (recommendation: 1.5 or 2 times the flat rate).	☐
4. Left the workspace clean and orderly.	☐
5. Cared for customer property and returned it undamaged.	☐

Student signature _____ Date _____

Comments:

Have your supervisor/instructor verify satisfactory completion of this procedure, any observations made, and any necessary action(s) recommended.

Evaluation Instructions: The scoring box below is intended to act as a guide for both student and supervisor/instructor. Each criterion listed will help students to understand what is expected of them and help supervisors/instructors articulate the level of success at a particular task. The scoring is set up to allow a second attempt at each task (see the Test and Retest columns). Scoring is also designed to award students points only for task criteria that were completed correctly. Points are lost for failure to complete the employability requirements (see Non-Task-Specific Evaluation criteria). When all criteria are evaluated, tally the points for a total at the bottom of each column.

Tasksheet Scoring

Evaluation Items	Test		Retest	
	Pass	**Fail**	**Pass**	**Fail**
Task-Specific Evaluation	**(1 pt)**	**(0 pts)**	**(1 pt)**	**(0 pts)**
Student properly inspected charge air cooler connection, welds, and mounts and charge air cooler inlet and outlet piping, hoses, and clamps.				
Student properly performed charge air cooler leak and temperature differential tests.				
Student properly inspected aftercooler tubes, fins, welds, and mounts.				
Student properly performed aftercooler pressure test.				
Non-Task-Specific Evaluation	**(0 pts)**	**(−1 pt)**	**(0 pts)**	**(−1 pt)**
Student successfully completed at least three of the non-task-specific steps.				
Student successfully completed all five of the non-task-specific steps.				
Total Score: <total # of points/4 = %>				

Supervisor/Instructor:

Supervisor/instructor signature _____ Date _____

Comments:

Retest supervisor/instructor signature _____ Date _____

Comments:

CDX Tasksheet Number: MHT1F012

Student/Intern Information

Name _____ Date _____ Class _____

Vehicle, Customer, and Service Information

Vehicle used for this activity:

Year _____ Make _____ Model _____

Odometer _____ VIN _____

Materials Required

- Vehicle with possible engine concern
- Engine manufacturer's workshop materials
- Manufacturer-specific tools depending on the concern/procedure(s)
- Vehicle/component lifting equipment, if applicable

Task-Specific Safety Considerations

- Activities may require test-driving the vehicle on the school grounds or on a hoist, both of which carry severe risks. Attempt this task only with full permission from your supervisor/instructor, and follow all the guidelines exactly.
- Lifting equipment and machines such as vehicle jacks and stands, vehicle hoists, and engine hoists are important tools that increase productivity and make the job easier. However, they can also cause severe injury or death if used improperly. Make sure you follow the manufacturer's operation procedures. Also make sure you have your supervisor's/instructor's permission to use any particular type of lifting equipment.
- Comply with personal and environmental safety practices associated with clothing; eye protection; hand tools; power equipment; proper ventilation; and the handling, storage, and disposal of chemicals/materials in accordance with federal, state, and local regulations.
- Always wear the correct protective eyewear and clothing and use the appropriate safety equipment, as well as wheel chocks, fender covers, seat protectors, and floor mat protectors.
- Make sure you understand and observe all legislative and personal safety procedures when carrying out practical assignments. If you are unsure of what these are, ask your supervisor/instructor.

▶ **TASK** Diagnose exhaust aftertreatment system performance problems; determine needed action.

MTST
I.F.12; P1

Time off_____

Time on_____

Student Instructions: Read through the entire procedure prior to starting. Prepare your workspace and any tools or parts that may be needed to complete the task. When directed by your supervisor/instructor, begin the procedure to complete the task and check the box as each step is finished.

Total time_____

Note: This tasksheet may require the student to check the condition of miscellaneous vehicle fluids, some of which may be flammable and could damage the environment or cause health problems if not handled properly. Observe all safety precautions and follow local regulations for the proper disposal of fluids.

Procedure:	Step Completed
1. Using the appropriate electronic service tool (EST), record any aftertreatment codes as outlined in the manufacturer's workshop materials:	☐
2. Inspect the exhaust aftertreatment system for missing, loose, or damaged components.	
a. Within manufacturer's specifications: Yes: ☐ No: ☐	☐
b. If No, describe the recommended corrective action(s):	☐
3. If equipped, inspect the aftertreatment fuel injector connections for signs of fuel (and coolant, if equipped) leakage.	
a. Within manufacturer's specifications: Yes: ☐ No: ☐	☐
b. If No, describe the recommended corrective action(s):	☐
4. Record the procedure for removing and inspecting the aftertreatment fuel injector (if equipped) as outlined in the manufacturer's workshop materials:	☐
5. If directed by your supervisor/instructor, remove, inspect, and reinstall the aftertreatment fuel injector.	
a. Within manufacturer's specifications: Yes: ☐ No: ☐	☐
b. If No, describe the recommended corrective action(s):	☐
6. Record the procedure for removing and inspecting the aftertreatment selective catalytic reduction (SCR) catalyst as outlined in the manufacturer's workshop materials:	☐

7. If directed by your supervisor/instructor, remove, inspect, and reinstall the aftertreatment SCR catalyst.	
a. Within manufacturer's specifications: Yes: ☐ No: ☐	☐
b. If No, describe the recommended corrective action(s):	☐
8. Record the procedure for removing and inspecting the diesel particulate filter (DPF) as outlined in the manufacturer's workshop materials:	☐
9. If directed by your supervisor/instructor, remove, inspect, and reinstall the DPF.	
a. Within manufacturer's specifications: Yes: ☐ No: ☐	☐
b. If No, describe the recommended corrective action(s):	☐
10. Inspect the diesel exhaust fluid (DEF) reservoir, lines, and connections for missing, loose, or damaged components.	
a. Within manufacturer's specifications: Yes: ☐ No: ☐	☐
b. If No, describe the recommended corrective action(s):	☐
11. Record the procedure for removing, inspecting, and reinstalling the aftertreatment decomposition tube as outlined in the manufacturer's workshop materials:	☐
12. If directed by your supervisor/instructor, remove, inspect, and reinstall the aftertreatment decomposition tube.	
a. Within manufacturer's specifications: Yes: ☐ No: ☐	☐

b. If No, describe the recommended corrective action(s):	☐
13. Using the appropriate EST, record any aftertreatment codes that may have become active after the aftertreatment components were removed, inspected, and reinstalled:	☐
14. If directed by your supervisor/instructor, repair any active aftertreatment code(s).	
a. Within manufacturer's specifications: Yes: ☐ No: ☐	☐
b. If No, describe the recommended corrective action(s):	☐
15. Record the procedure and any special precautions for performing a stationary regen as outlined in the manufacturer's workshop materials:	☐
16. If directed by your supervisor/instructor, perform a stationary regen.	
a. Within manufacturer's specifications: Yes: ☐ No: ☐	☐
b. If No, describe the recommended corrective action(s):	☐
17. Discuss your findings with your supervisor/instructor.	☐

Non-Task-Specific Evaluations:	Step Completed
1. Tools and equipment were used as directed and returned in good working order.	☐
2. Complied with all general and task-specific safety standards, including proper use of any personal protection equipment.	☐
3. Completed the task in an appropriate time frame (recommendation: 1.5 or 2 times the flat rate).	☐
4. Left the workspace clean and orderly.	☐
5. Cared for customer property and returned it undamaged.	☐

Student signature _____ Date _____

Comments:

Have your supervisor/instructor verify satisfactory completion of this procedure, any observations made, and any necessary action(s) recommended.

Evaluation Instructions: The scoring box below is intended to act as a guide for both student and supervisor/instructor. Each criterion listed will help students to understand what is expected of them and help supervisors/instructors articulate the level of success at a particular task. The scoring is set up to allow a second attempt at each task (see the Test and Retest columns). Scoring is also designed to award students points only for task criteria that were completed correctly. Points are lost for failure to complete the employability requirements (see Non-Task-Specific Evaluation criteria). When all criteria are evaluated, tally the points for a total at the bottom of each column.

Tasksheet Scoring

Evaluation Items	Test		Retest	
	Pass	**Fail**	**Pass**	**Fail**
Task-Specific Evaluation	**(1 pt)**	**(O pts)**	**(1 pt)**	**(O pts)**
Student properly retrieved, diagnosed, and repaired exhaust aftertreatment codes.				
Student properly inspected aftertreatment fuel injector and DEF reservoir lines and connections.				
Student properly removed, inspected, and reinstalled aftertreatment fuel injector, SCR catalyst, DPF, and decomposition tube.				
Student properly performed stationary regen.				
Non-Task-Specific Evaluation	**(O pts)**	**(−1 pt)**	**(O pts)**	**(−1 pt)**
Student successfully completed at least three of the non-task-specific steps.				
Student successfully completed all five of the non-task-specific steps.				
Total Score: <total # of points/4 = %>				

CDX Tasksheet Number: MHT1F013

Student/Intern Information

Name _____ Date _____ Class _____

Vehicle, Customer, and Service Information

Vehicle used for this activity:

Year _____ Make _____ Model _____

Odometer _____ VIN _____

Materials Required

- Vehicle with possible engine concern
- Engine manufacturer's workshop materials
- Manufacturer-specific tools depending on the concern/procedure(s)
- Vehicle/component lifting equipment, if applicable

Task-Specific Safety Considerations

- Activities may require test-driving the vehicle on the school grounds or on a hoist, both of which carry severe risks. Attempt this task only with full permission from your supervisor/instructor, and follow all the guidelines exactly.
- Lifting equipment and materials such as vehicle jacks and stands, vehicle hoists, and engine hoists are important tools that increase productivity and make the job easier. However, they can also cause severe injury or death if used improperly. Make sure you follow the manufacturer's operation procedures. Also make sure you have your supervisor's/instructor's permission to use any particular type of lifting equipment.
- Comply with personal and environmental safety practices associated with clothing; eye protection; hand tools; power equipment; proper ventilation; and the handling, storage, and disposal of chemicals/materials in accordance with federal, state, and local regulations.
- Always wear the correct protective eyewear and clothing and use the appropriate safety equipment, as well as wheel chocks, fender covers, seat protectors, and floor mat protectors.
- Make sure you understand and observe all legislative and personal safety procedures when carrying out practical assignments. If you are unsure of what these are, ask your supervisor/instructor.

▶ **TASK** Diagnose preheater/inlet air heater or glow plug system and controls; determine needed action.

MTST
I.F.13; P2

Time off_____

Time on_____

Total time_____

Student Instructions: Read through the entire procedure prior to starting. Prepare your workspace and any tools or parts that may be needed to complete the task. When directed by your supervisor/instructor, begin the procedure to complete the task and check the box as each step is finished.

Note: This tasksheet may require the student to check the condition of miscellaneous vehicle fluids, some of which may be flammable and could damage the environment or cause health problems if not handled properly. Observe all safety precautions and follow local regulations for the proper disposal of fluids.

Procedure:	Step Completed
1. Record the type of air induction system heating device as outlined in the manufacturer's workshop materials:	☐
2. Inspect the air induction system heating system for missing, loose, or damaged components.	
a. Within manufacturer's specifications: Yes: ☐ No: ☐	☐
b. If No, describe the recommended corrective action(s):	☐
3. Inspect the air induction system heating system wiring and controls for damaged wiring and connections.	
a. Within manufacturer's specifications: Yes: ☐ No: ☐	☐
b. If No, describe the recommended corrective action(s):	☐
4. Using the appropriate electronic service tool (EST), record any air induction heating system codes:	☐
5. If directed by your supervisor/instructor, repair any active air induction heating system codes.	
a. Within manufacturer's specifications: Yes: ☐ No: ☐	☐
b. If No, describe the recommended corrective action(s):	☐
6. Using the appropriate EST, perform a grid heater override test (if equipped).	
a. Within manufacturer's specifications: Yes: ☐ No: ☐	☐

b. If No, describe the recommended corrective action(s):	☐
7. Remove all electrical connections from the glow plugs (if equipped). Using a test light with an incandescent bulb, connect the alligator clip to source voltage and touch the probe end of the test light to the electrical connection on each glow plug. The test light should light when touched to each connection at the glow plug (not the glow plug electrical harness). For any glow plug that is tested and the test light does not light, the glow plug is open and needs to be replaced. Record the test result for each glow plug: (**Note:** This test can only be done with a test light with an incandescent bulb.)	☐
8. If directed by your supervisor/instructor, replace any defective glow plug(s).	
a. Within manufacturer's specifications: Yes: ☐ No: ☐	☐
b. If No, describe the recommended corrective action(s):	☐
9. Discuss your findings with your supervisor/instructor.	☐

Non-Task-Specific Evaluations:	Step Completed
1. Tools and equipment were used as directed and returned in good working order.	☐
2. Complied with all general and task-specific safety standards, including proper use of any personal protection equipment.	☐
3. Completed the task in an appropriate time frame (recommendation: 1.5 or 2 times the flat rate).	☐
4. Left the workspace clean and orderly.	☐
5. Cared for customer property and returned it undamaged.	☐

Student signature _____ Date _____

Comments:

Have your supervisor/instructor verify satisfactory completion of this procedure, any observations made, and any necessary action(s) recommended.

Evaluation Instructions: The scoring box below is intended to act as a guide for both student and supervisor/instructor. Each criterion listed will help students to understand what is expected of them and help supervisors/instructors articulate the level of success at a particular task. The scoring is set up to allow a second attempt at each task (see the Test and Retest columns). Scoring is also designed to award students points only for task criteria that were completed correctly. Points are lost for failure to complete the employability requirements (see Non-Task-Specific Evaluation criteria). When all criteria are evaluated, tally the points for a total at the bottom of each column.

Tasksheet Scoring

Evaluation Items	Test		Retest	
	Pass	**Fail**	**Pass**	**Fail**
Task-Specific Evaluation	**(1 pt)**	**(0 pts)**	**(1 pt)**	**(0 pts)**
Student properly identified air induction system heating device.				
Student properly inspected air induction system heating device wiring and controls for damaged wiring and connections and for missing, loose, or damaged components.				
Student properly retrieved, diagnosed, and repaired active air induction heating system codes.				
Student properly tested grid heater override and tested and repaired glow plugs.				
Non-Task-Specific Evaluation	**(0 pts)**	**(−1 pt)**	**(0 pts)**	**(−1 pt)**
Student successfully completed at least three of the non-task-specific steps.				
Student successfully completed all five of the non-task-specific steps.				
Total Score: <total # of points/4 = %>				

Supervisor/instructor:

Supervisor/instructor signature _____ Date _____

Comments:

Retest supervisor/instructor signature _____ Date _____

Comments:

I.H Diesel Engines: Engine Brakes

Learning Objective/Task	CDX Tasksheet Number	ASE Foundation MTST Reference Number; Priority Level
• Inspect engine compression and/or exhaust brake housing, valves, seals, lines, and fittings; determine needed action.	MHT1H001	I.H.1; P-1
• Inspect and adjust engine compression and/or exhaust brake systems; determine needed action.	MHT1H002	I.H.2; P-2
• Inspect, test, and adjust engine compression and/or exhaust brake control circuits, switches, and solenoids; determine needed action.	MHT1H003	I.H.3; P-2

Materials Required

- Vehicle with possible engine concern
- Engine manufacturer's workshop materials
- Manufacturer-specific tools depending on the concern/procedure(s)
- Vehicle/component lifting equipment, if applicable

Safety Considerations

- Activities may require test-driving the vehicle on the school grounds or on a hoist, both of which carry severe risks. Attempt this task only with full permission from your supervisor/instructor, and follow all the guidelines exactly.
- Lifting equipment and machines such as vehicle jacks and stands, vehicle hoists, and engine hoists are important tools that increase productivity and make the job easier. However, they can also cause severe injury or death if used improperly. Make sure you follow the manufacturer's operation procedures. Also make sure you have your supervisor's/instructor's permission to use any particular type of lifting equipment.
- Comply with personal and environmental safety practices associated with clothing; eye protection; hand tools; power equipment; proper ventilation; and the handling, storage, and disposal of chemicals/materials in accordance with federal, state, and local regulations.
- Always wear the correct protective eyewear and clothing and use the appropriate safety equipment, as well as wheel chocks, fender covers, seat protectors, and floor mat protectors.
- Make sure you understand and observe all legislative and personal safety procedures when carrying out practical assignments. If you are unsure of what these are, ask your supervisor/instructor.

CDX Tasksheet Number: MHT1H001

Student/Intern Information

Name _____ Date _____ Class _____

Vehicle, Customer, and Service Information

Vehicle used for this activity:

Year _____ Make _____ Model _____

Odometer _____ VIN _____

Materials Required

- Vehicle with possible engine concern
- Engine manufacturer's workshop materials
- Manufacturer-specific tools depending on the concern/procedure(s)
- Vehicle/component lifting equipment, if applicable

Task-Specific Safety Considerations

- Activities may require test-driving the vehicle on the school grounds or on a hoist, both of which carry severe risks. Attempt this task only with full permission from your supervisor/instructor, and follow all the guidelines exactly.
- Lifting equipment and machines such as vehicle jacks and stands, vehicle hoists, and engine hoists are important tools that increase productivity and make the job easier. However, they can also cause severe injury or death if used improperly. Make sure you follow the manufacturer's operation procedures. Also make sure you have your supervisor's/instructor's permission to use any particular type of lifting equipment.
- Comply with personal and environmental safety practices associated with clothing; eye protection; hand tools; power equipment; proper ventilation; and the handling, storage, and disposal of chemicals/materials in accordance with federal, state, and local regulations.
- Always wear the correct protective eyewear and clothing and use the appropriate safety equipment, as well as wheel chocks, fender covers, seat protectors, and floor mat protectors.
- Make sure you understand and observe all legislative and personal safety procedures when carrying out practical assignments. If you are unsure of what these are, ask your supervisor/instructor.

▶ **TASK** Inspect engine compression and/or exhaust brake housing, valves, seals, lines, and fittings; determine needed action.

MTST
I.H.1; P1

Time off_____

Time on_____

Total time_____

Student Instructions: Read through the entire procedure prior to starting. Prepare your workspace and any tools or parts that may be needed to complete the task. When directed by your supervisor/instructor, begin the procedure to complete the task and check the box as each step is finished.

Note: This tasksheet may require the student to check the condition of miscellaneous vehicle fluids, some of which may be flammable and could damage the environment or cause health problems if not handled properly. Observe all safety precautions and follow local regulations for the proper disposal of fluids.

Procedure:	Step Completed
1. Record the make and model of the compression/exhaust brake as outlined in the manufacturer's workshop materials:	☐
2. Inspect the compression/exhaust brake housing(s) for damage, leaks, and proper securement.	
a. Within manufacturer's specifications: Yes: ☐ No: ☐	☐
b. If No, describe the recommended corrective action(s):	☐
3. Record the type of exhaust brake activation method (e.g., vacuum, air pressure) as outlined in the manufacturer's workshop materials: (**Note:** Steps 3–6 are for engines with an exhaust brake only.)	☐
4. Inspect the exhaust brake lines and fittings for damage, leaks, and proper securement.	☐
5. Engage the exhaust brake and inspect the linkage for signs of binding and full movement.	
a. Within manufacturer's specifications: Yes: ☐ No: ☐	☐
b. If No, describe the recommended corrective action(s):	☐

6. Record the procedure for testing exhaust brake application pressure/vacuum as outlined in the manufacturer's workshop materials, and perform the test:	
a. Within manufacturer's specifications: Yes: ☐ No: ☐	☐
b. If No, describe the recommended corrective action(s):	☐
7. Remove the engine valve covers, turn the compression brake to the on position, and observe the operation of the oil control solenoid armatures. (**Note:** Steps 7 and 8 are for engines with a compression brake only.)	
a. Within manufacturer's specifications: Yes: ☐ No: ☐	☐
b. If No, describe the recommended corrective action(s):	☐
8. Record the procedure for conducting a control valve oil pressure test as outlined in the manufacturer's workshop materials, and perform the test:	
a. Within the manufacturer's specifications: Yes: ☐ No: ☐	☐
b. If No, describe the recommended corrective action(s):	☐
9. Discuss your findings with your supervisor/instructor.	

Non-Task-Specific Evaluations:	Step Completed
1. Tools and equipment were used as directed and returned in good working order.	☐
2. Complied with all general and task-specific safety standards, including proper use of any personal protection equipment.	☐
3. Completed the task in an appropriate time frame (recommendation: 1.5 or 2 times the flat rate).	☐
4. Left the workspace clean and orderly.	☐
5. Cared for customer property and returned it undamaged.	☐

Student signature _____ Date _____

Comments:

Have your supervisor/instructor verify satisfactory completion of this procedure, any observations made,

and any necessary action(s) recommended.

Evaluation Instructions: The scoring box below is intended to act as a guide for both student and supervisor/instructor. Each criterion listed will help students to understand what is expected of them and help supervisors/instructors articulate the level of success at a particular task. The scoring is set up to allow a second attempt at each task (see the Test and Retest columns). Scoring is also designed to award students points only for task criteria that were completed correctly. Points are lost for failure to complete the employability requirements (see Non-Task-Specific Evaluation criteria). When all criteria are evaluated, tally the points for a total at the bottom of each column.

Tasksheet Scoring

	Test		Retest	
	Pass	**Fail**	**Pass**	**Fail**
Evaluation Items				
Task-Specific Evaluation	**(1 pt)**	**(0 pts)**	**(1 pt)**	**(0 pts)**
Student properly recorded compression/ exhaust brake make and model and exhaust brake activation method.				
Student properly inspected compression/ exhaust brake housings and exhaust brake lines and fittings for damage, leaks, and proper securement.				
Student properly inspected exhaust brake linkage for binding and full engagement and tested the exhaust brake application pressure/vacuum.				
Student inspected compression brake solenoids for proper operation and tested the compression brake control valve oil pressure.				
Non-Task-Specific Evaluation	**(0 pts)**	**(−1 pt)**	**(0 pts)**	**(−1 pt)**
Student successfully completed at least three of the non-task-specific steps.				
Student successfully completed all five of the non-task-specific steps.				
Total Score: <total # of points/4 = %>				

Supervisor/Instructor:

Supervisor/instructor signature _____ Date _____

Comments:

[ ]

Retest supervisor/instructor signature _____ Date _____

Comments:

[ ]

CDX Tasksheet Number: MHT1H002

Student/Intern Information

Name _____ Date _____ Class _____

Vehicle, Customer, and Service Information

Vehicle used for this activity:

Year _____ Make _____ Model _____

Odometer _____ VIN _____

Materials Required

- Vehicle with possible engine concern
- Engine manufacturer's workshop materials
- Manufacturer-specific tools depending on the concern/procedure(s)
- Vehicle/component lifting equipment, if applicable

Task-Specific Safety Considerations

- Activities may require test-driving the vehicle on the school grounds or on a hoist, both of which carry severe risks. Attempt this task only with full permission from your supervisor/instructor, and follow all the guidelines exactly.
- Lifting equipment and machines such as vehicle jacks and stands, vehicle hoists, and engine hoists are important tools that increase productivity and make the job easier. However, they can also cause severe injury or death if used improperly. Make sure you follow the manufacturer's operation procedures. Also make sure you have your supervisor's/instructor's permission to use any particular type of lifting equipment.
- Comply with personal and environmental safety practices associated with clothing; eye protection; hand tools; power equipment; proper ventilation; and the handling, storage, and disposal of chemicals/materials in accordance with federal, state, and local regulations.
- Always wear the correct protective eyewear and clothing and use the appropriate safety equipment, as well as wheel chocks, fender covers, seat protectors, and floor mat protectors.
- Make sure you understand and observe all legislative and personal safety procedures when carrying out practical assignments. If you are unsure of what these are, ask your supervisor/instructor.

▶**TASK** Inspect and adjust engine compression and/or exhaust brake systems; determine needed action.

MTST
I.H.2; P2

Time off_____

Time on_____

Total time_____

Student Instructions: Read through the entire procedure prior to starting. Prepare your workspace and any tools or parts that may be needed to complete the task. When directed by your supervisor/instructor, begin the procedure to complete the task and check the box as each step is finished.

Note: This tasksheet may require the student to check the condition of miscellaneous vehicle fluids, some of which may be flammable and could damage the environment or cause health problems if not handled properly. Observe all safety precautions and follow local regulations for the proper disposal of fluids.

Procedure:	Step Completed
1. Record any special instructions/procedures required before adjusting compression/exhaust brakes as outlined in the manufacturer's workshop materials:	☐
2. Record the procedure for adjusting compression brakes as outlined in the manufacturer's workshop materials, and perform the adjustment(s): (**Note:** Steps 2 and 3 are for engines with a compression brake only.)	
a. Slave piston lash setting: _____ in./mm	☐
b. Within manufacturer's specifications: Yes: ☐ No: ☐	☐
c. If No, describe the recommended corrective action(s):	☐
3. Start the engine, and engage the compression brake at different settings to check operation.	
a. Within manufacturer's specifications: Yes: ☐ No: ☐	☐
b. If No, describe the recommended corrective action(s):	☐
4. Record the type of exhaust brake activation method (e.g., vacuum, air pressure) as outlined in the manufacturer's workshop materials: (**Note:** Steps 4 to 6 are for engines with an exhaust brake only.)	☐
5. Record the procedure for testing exhaust brake application pressure/ vacuum as outlined in the manufacturer's workshop materials, and perform the test:	

	Step Completed
a. Within manufacturer's specifications: Yes: ☐ No: ☐	☐
b. If No, describe the recommended corrective action(s):	☐
6. Record the procedure for testing exhaust system backpressure when the exhaust brake is applied as outlined in the manufacturer's workshop materials, and perform the test:	
a. Exhaust backpressure specification: _____ psi	☐
b. Within manufacturer's specifications: Yes: ☐ No: ☐	☐
c. If No, describe the recommended corrective action(s):	☐
7. Discuss your findings with your supervisor/instructor.	☐

Non-Task-Specific Evaluations:	Step Completed
1. Tools and equipment were used as directed and returned in good working order.	☐
2. Complied with all general and task-specific safety standards, including proper use of any personal protection equipment.	☐
3. Completed the task in an appropriate time frame (recommendation: 1.5 or 2 times the flat rate).	☐
4. Left the workspace clean and orderly.	☐
5. Cared for customer property and returned it undamaged.	☐

Student signature _____ Date _____

Comments:

Have your supervisor/instructor verify satisfactory completion of this procedure, any observations made,

and any necessary action(s) recommended.

Evaluation Instructions: The scoring box below is intended to act as a guide for both student and supervisor/instructor. Each criterion listed will help students to understand what is expected of them and help supervisors/instructors articulate the level of success at a particular task. The scoring is set up to allow a second attempt at each task (see the Test and Retest columns). Scoring is also designed to award students points only for task criteria that were completed correctly. Points are lost for failure to complete the employability requirements (see Non-Task-Specific Evaluation criteria). When all criteria are evaluated, tally the points for a total at the bottom of each column.

Tasksheet Scoring

Evaluation Items	Test		Retest	
	Pass	**Fail**	**Pass**	**Fail**
Task-Specific Evaluation	**(1 pt)**	**(0 pts)**	**(1 pt)**	**(0 pts)**
Student properly recorded special instructions/procedures before adjusting compression/exhaust brake.				
Student properly performed compression brake adjustment and tested compression brake operation				
Student properly tested exhaust brake application pressure/vacuum.				
Student properly tested exhaust system backpressure.				
Non-Task-Specific Evaluation	**(0 pts)**	**(−1 pt)**	**(0 pts)**	**(−1 pt)**
Student successfully completed at least three of the non-task-specific steps.				
Student successfully completed all five of the non-task-specific steps.				
Total Score: <total # of points/4 = %>				

Supervisor/Instructor:

Supervisor/instructor signature _____ Date _____

Comments:

Retest supervisor/instructor signature _____ Date _____

Comments:

CDX Tasksheet Number: MHT1H003

Student/Intern Information

Name _____ Date _____ Class _____

Vehicle, Customer, and Service Information

Vehicle used for this activity:

Year _____ Make _____ Model _____

Odometer _____ VIN _____

Materials Required

- Vehicle with possible engine concern
- Engine manufacturer's workshop materials
- Manufacturer-specific tools depending on the concern/procedure(s)
- Vehicle/component lifting equipment, if applicable

Task-Specific Safety Considerations

- Activities may require test-driving the vehicle on the school grounds or on a hoist, both of which carry severe risks. Attempt this task only with full permission from your supervisor/instructor, and follow all the guidelines exactly.
- Lifting equipment and machines such as vehicle jacks and stands, vehicle hoists, and engine hoists are important tools that increase productivity and make the job easier. However, they can also cause severe injury or death if used improperly. Make sure you follow the manufacturer's operation procedures. Also make sure you have your supervisor's/instructor's permission to use any particular type of lifting equipment.
- Comply with personal and environmental safety practices associated with clothing; eye protection; hand tools; power equipment; proper ventilation; and the handling, storage, and disposal of chemicals/materials in accordance with federal, state, and local regulations.
- Always wear the correct protective eyewear and clothing and use the appropriate safety equipment, as well as wheel chocks, fender covers, seat protectors, and floor mat protectors.
- Make sure you understand and observe all legislative and personal safety procedures when carrying out practical assignments. If you are unsure of what these are, ask your supervisor/instructor.

▶ **TASK** Inspect, test, and adjust engine compression and/or exhaust brake control circuits, switches, and solenoids; determine needed action. **MTST** I.H.3; P2

Time off_____

Time on_____

Student Instructions: Read through the entire procedure prior to starting. Prepare your workspace and any tools or parts that may be needed to complete the task. When directed by your supervisor/instructor, begin the procedure to complete the task and check the box as each step is finished.

Total time_____

Note: This tasksheet may require the student to check the condition of miscellaneous vehicle fluids, some of which may be flammable and could damage the environment or cause health problems if not handled properly. Observe all safety precautions and follow local regulations for the proper disposal of fluids.

Procedure:	Step Completed
1. Record the procedure for testing continuity and resistance in engine brake control switches as outlined in the manufacturer's workshop materials, and perform the test:	
a. Within manufacturer's specifications: Yes: ☐ No: ☐	☐
b. If No, describe the recommended corrective action(s):	☐
2. Record the procedure for testing for short to ground in engine brake control circuits as outlined in the manufacturer's workshop materials, and perform the test:	
a. Within manufacturer's specifications: Yes: ☐ No: ☐	☐
b. If No, describe the recommended corrective action(s):	☐
3. Record the procedure for testing for short to power in engine brake control circuits as outlined in the manufacturer's workshop materials, and perform the test:	
a. Within manufacturer's specifications: Yes: ☐ No: ☐	☐
b. If No, describe the recommended corrective action(s):	☐

4. Record the procedure for testing for a short between engine brake control circuits as outlined in the manufacturer's workshop materials, and perform the test:	
a. Within manufacturer's specifications: Yes: ☐ No: ☐	☐
b. If No, describe the recommended corrective action(s):	☐
5. Record the procedure for testing engine brake application voltage at solenoids/control valves as outlined in the manufacturer's workshop materials, and perform the test:	
a. Within manufacturer's specifications: Yes: ☐ No: ☐	☐
b. If No, describe the recommended corrective action(s):	☐
6. Record the procedure for checking/adjusting engine brake control switches as outlined in the manufacturer's workshop materials. Check adjustment of switches:	
a. Within manufacturer's specifications: Yes: ☐ No: ☐	☐
b. If No, describe the recommended corrective action(s):	☐
7. Discuss your findings with your supervisor/instructor.	☐

Non-Task-Specific Evaluations:	Step Completed
1. Tools and equipment were used as directed and returned in good working order.	☐
2. Complied with all general and task-specific safety standards, including proper use of any personal protection equipment.	☐
3. Completed the task in an appropriate time frame (recommendation: 1.5 or 2 times the flat rate).	☐
4. Left the workspace clean and orderly.	☐
5. Cared for customer property and returned it undamaged.	☐

Student signature _____ Date _____

Comments:

Have your supervisor/instructor verify satisfactory completion of this procedure, any observations made, and any necessary action(s) recommended.

Evaluation Instructions: The scoring box below is intended to act as a guide for both student and supervisor/instructor. Each criterion listed will help students to understand what is expected of them and help supervisors/instructors articulate the level of success at a particular task. The scoring is set up to allow a second attempt at each task (see the Test and Retest columns). Scoring is also designed to award students points only for task criteria that were completed correctly. Points are lost for failure to complete the employability requirements (see Non-Task-Specific Evaluation criteria). When all criteria are evaluated, tally the points for a total at the bottom of each column.

Tasksheet Scoring

	Test		Retest	
Evaluation Items	**Pass**	**Fail**	**Pass**	**Fail**
Task-Specific Evaluation	**(1 pt)**	**(0 pts)**	**(1 pt)**	**(0 pts)**
Student properly checked continuity and resistance in engine brake control switches.				
Student properly tested short to ground and short to power in engine brake control circuits and short between engine brake control circuits.				
Student properly tested engine brake application voltage at solenoids/control valves.				
Student properly performed checking/adjusting of engine brake control switches.				
Non-Task-Specific Evaluation	**(0 pts)**	**(−1 pt)**	**(0 pts)**	**(−1 pt)**
Student successfully completed at least three of the non-task-specific steps.				
Student successfully completed all five of the non-task-specific steps.				
Total Score: <total # of points/4 = %>				

Supervisor/Instructor:

Supervisor/instructor signature _____ Date _____

Comments:

Retest supervisor/instructor signature _____ Date _____

Comments:

Section 5: Engine Electrical

V.A Electrical/Electronic Systems: General

Learning Objective/Task	CDX Tasksheet Number	ASE Foundation MTST Reference Number; Priority Level
• Research vehicle service information, including vehicle service history, service precautions, and technical service bulletins.	MHT5A001	V.A.1; P-1
• Demonstrate knowledge of electrical/electronic series, parallel, and series-parallel circuits using principles of electricity (Ohm's law).	MHT5A002	V.A.2; P-1
• Demonstrate proper use of test equipment when measuring source voltage, voltage drop (including grounds), current flow, continuity, and resistance.	MHT5A003	V.A.3; P-1
• Demonstrate knowledge of the causes and effects of shorts, grounds, opens, and resistance problems in electrical/electronic circuits; identify and locate faults in electrical/electronic circuits.	MHT5A004	V.A.4; P-1
• Use wiring diagrams during the diagnosis (troubleshooting) of electrical/electronic circuit problems.	MHT5A005	V.A.5; P-1
• Measure parasitic (key-off) battery drain; determine needed action.	MHT5A006	V.A.6; P-1
• Demonstrate knowledge of the function, operation, and testing of fusible links, circuit breakers, relays, solenoids, diodes, and fuses; perform inspection and testing; determine needed action.	MHT5A007	V.A.7; P-1
• Inspect, test, repair (including solder repair), and/or replace components, connectors, seals, terminal ends, harnesses, and wiring; verify proper routing and securement; determine needed action.	MHT5A008	V.A.8; P-1

Learning Objective/Task	CDX Tasksheet Number	ASE Foundation MTST Reference Number; Priority Level
• Use appropriate electronic service tool(s) (EST) and procedures to diagnose problems; check, record, and clear diagnostic codes; interpret digital multimeter (DMM) readings.	MHT5A009	V.A.9; P-1
• Diagnose faults in the data bus communications network; determine needed action.	MHT5A010	V.A.10; P-2
• Identify electrical/electronic system components and configuration.	MHT5A011	V.A.11; P-1
• Check frequency, pulse width, and waveforms of electrical/ electronic signals using appropriate test equipment; interpret readings; determine needed repairs.	MHT5A012	V.A.12; P-2
• Understand the process for software transfer, software updates, and/or reprogramming of electronic modules.	MHT5A013	V.A.13; P-3

Materials Required

- Vehicle or simulator with possible electrical concerns
- Vehicle manufacturer's repair information, including schematic wiring diagrams
- Vehicle with possible engine concern
- Engine manufacturer's workshop materials
- Digital multimeter (DMM)
- Digital volt-ohmmeter (DVOM), current clamp
- Digital storage oscilloscope (DSO)
- Manufacturer-specific tools depending on the concern/procedure(s)
- Vehicle/component lifting equipment, if applicable

Safety Considerations

- Activities require you to measure electrical values. Always ensure that your supervisor/ instructor checks test instrument connections prior to connecting power or taking measurements. High current flows can be dangerous; avoid accidental short circuits or grounding a battery's positive connections.
- Activities may require test-driving the vehicle on the school grounds or on a hoist, both of which carry severe risks. Attempt this task only with full permission from your supervisor/ instructor, and follow all the guidelines exactly.
- Lifting equipment and machines such as vehicle jacks and stands, vehicle hoists, and engine hoists are important tools that increase productivity and make the job easier. However, they can also cause severe injury or death if used improperly. Make sure you follow the manufacturer's operation procedures. Also make sure you have your supervisor's/ instructor's permission to use any particular type of lifting equipment.
- Comply with personal and environmental safety practices associated with clothing; eye protection; hand tools; power equipment; proper ventilation; and the handling, storage, and disposal of chemicals/materials in accordance with federal, state, and local regulations.
- Always wear the correct protective eyewear and clothing and use the appropriate safety equipment, as well as wheel chocks, fender covers, seat protectors, and floor mat protectors.
- Make sure you understand and observe all legislative and personal safety procedures when carrying out practical assignments. If you are unsure of what these are, ask your supervisor/instructor.

CDX Tasksheet Number: MHT5A001

Student/Intern Information

Name _____ Date _____ Class _____

Vehicle, Customer, and Service Information

Vehicle used for this activity:

Year _____ Make _____ Model _____

Odometer _____ VIN _____

Materials Required

- Vehicle with possible engine concern
- Engine manufacturer's workshop materials
- Manufacturer-specific tools depending on the concern/procedure(s)
- Vehicle/component lifting equipment, if applicable

Task-Specific Safety Considerations

- Activities may require test-driving the vehicle on the school grounds or on a hoist, both of which carry severe risks. Attempt this task only with full permission from your supervisor/instructor, and follow all the guidelines exactly.
- Lifting equipment and machines such as vehicle jacks and stands, vehicle hoists, and engine hoists are important tools that increase productivity and make the job easier. However, they can also cause severe injury or death if used improperly. Make sure you follow the manufacturer's operation procedures. Also make sure you have your supervisor's/instructor's permission to use any particular type of lifting equipment.
- Comply with personal and environmental safety practices associated with clothing; eye protection; hand tools; power equipment; proper ventilation; and the handling, storage, and disposal of chemicals/materials in accordance with federal, state, and local regulations.
- Always wear the correct protective eyewear and clothing and use the appropriate safety equipment, as well as wheel chocks, fender covers, seat protectors, and floor mat protectors.
- Make sure you understand and observe all legislative and personal safety procedures when carrying out practical assignments. If you are unsure of what these are, ask your supervisor/instructor.

▶TASK Research vehicle service information, including vehicle service history, service precautions, and technical service bulletins.

Time off_____

Time on_____

Student Instructions: Read through the entire procedure prior to starting. Prepare your workspace and any tools or parts that may be needed to complete the task. When directed by your supervisor/instructor, begin the procedure to complete the task and check the box as each step is finished.

Total time_____

Note: This tasksheet may require the student to check the condition of miscellaneous vehicle fluids, some of which may be flammable and could damage the environment and cause health problems if not handled properly. Observe all safety precautions and follow local regulations for the proper disposal of fluids.

Procedure:	Step Completed
1. Reference the manufacturer's vehicle data plate, and record the vehicle identification number (VIN):	☐
2. Reference the manufacturer's engine data plate, and record the engine serial number and model:	☐
3. Reference the manufacturer's transmission data plate, and record the transmission serial number and model:	☐
4. Reference the manufacturer's rear end(s) data plate, and record the rear end(s) serial number(s) and model:	☐
5. Record the recommended oil change intervals for the engine, transmission, and rear ends, as well as oil type and quantity, as outlined in the manufacturer's workshop materials. Include information for any miscellaneous manufacturer's specific fluid(s).	
a. Engine oil change interval: _____ miles/km	☐
b. Engine oil type:	☐
c. Engine oil quantity: _____ qts/gallons	☐
d. Transmission oil change interval: _____ miles/km	☐
e. Transmission oil type:	☐

f. Transmission oil quantity: _____ qts/gallons	☐
g. Rear end oil change interval: _____ miles/km	☐
h. Rear end oil type:	☐
i. Rear end oil quantity: _____ qts/gallons	☐
j. Misc. oil change interval: _____ miles/km	☐
k. Misc. oil type:	☐
l. Misc. oil quantity: _____ qts/gallons	☐
6. Record any special service precautions or conditions as outlined in the manufacturer's workshop materials:	☐
7. Reference the manufacturer's online information, and record any recent technical service bulletins (TSBs):	☐
8. Discuss your findings with your supervisor/instructor.	☐

Non-Task–Specific Evaluations:	Step Completed
1. Tools and equipment were used as directed and returned in good working order.	☐
2. Complied with all general and task-specific safety standards, including proper use of any personal protection equipment.	☐
3. Completed the task in an appropriate time frame (recommendation: 1.5 or 2 times the flat rate).	☐
4. Left the workspace clean and orderly.	☐
5. Cared for customer property and returned it undamaged.	☐

Student signature _____ Date _____

Comments:

Have your supervisor/instructor verify satisfactory completion of this procedure, any observations made, and any necessary action(s) recommended.

Evaluation Instructions: The scoring box below is intended to act as a guide for both student and supervisor/instructor. Each criterion listed will help students to understand what is expected of them and help supervisors/instructors articulate the level of success at a particular task. The scoring is set up to allow a second attempt at each task (see the Test and Retest columns). Scoring is also designed to award students points only for task criteria that were completed correctly. Points are lost for failure to complete the employability requirements (see Non-Task-Specific Evaluation criteria). When all criteria are evaluated, tally the points for a total at the bottom of each column.

Tasksheet Scoring

Evaluation Items	Test		Retest	
	Pass	**Fail**	**Pass**	**Fail**
Task-Specific Evaluation	**(1 pt)**	**(0 pts)**	**(1 pt)**	**(0 pts)**
Student properly recorded VIN, drivetrain component serial, and model numbers.				
Student properly researched and recorded engine oil change, transmission oil change, rear end(s), and miscellaneous oil change interval, fluid type, and quantity.				
Student properly researched and recorded special service precautions and conditions.				
Student properly researched and recorded TSBs.				
Non-Task-Specific Evaluation	**(0 pts)**	**(−1 pt)**	**(0 pts)**	**(−1 pt)**
Student successfully completed at least three of the non-task-specific steps.				
Student successfully completed all five of the non-task-specific steps.				
Total Score: <total # of points/4 = %>				

Supervisor/Instructor:

Supervisor/instructor signature _____ Date _____

Comments:

Retest supervisor/instructor signature _____ Date _____

Comments:

CDX Tasksheet Number: MHT5A002

Student/Intern Information

Name _____ Date _____ Class _____

Vehicle, Customer, and Service Information

Vehicle used for this activity:

Year _____ Make _____ Model _____

Odometer _____ VIN _____

Materials Required

- Vehicle with possible engine concern
- Engine manufacturer's workshop materials
- Manufacturer-specific tools depending on the concern/procedure(s)
- Vehicle/component lifting equipment, if applicable

Task-Specific Safety Considerations

- Activities may require test-driving the vehicle on the school grounds or on a hoist, both of which carry severe risks. Attempt this task only with full permission from your supervisor/instructor, and follow all the guidelines exactly.
- Lifting equipment and machines such as vehicle jacks and stands, vehicle hoists, and engine hoists are important tools that increase productivity and make the job easier. However, they can also cause severe injury or death if used improperly. Make sure you follow the manufacturer's operation procedures. Also make sure you have your supervisor's/instructor's permission to use any particular type of lifting equipment.
- Comply with personal and environmental safety practices associated with clothing; eye protection; hand tools; power equipment; proper ventilation; and the handling, storage, and disposal of chemicals/materials in accordance with federal, state, and local regulations.
- Always wear the correct protective eyewear and clothing and use the appropriate safety equipment, as well as wheel chocks, fender covers, seat protectors, and floor mat protectors.
- Make sure you understand and observe all legislative and personal safety procedures when carrying out practical assignments. If you are unsure of what these are, ask your supervisor/instructor.

▶ **TASK** Demonstrate knowledge of electrical/electronic series, as well as parallel and series-parallel circuits, using principles of electricity (Ohm's law).

MTST
V.A.2; P1

Time off_____

Time on_____

Total time_____

Student Instructions: Read through the entire procedure prior to starting. Prepare your workspace and any tools or parts that may be needed to complete the task. When directed by your supervisor/instructor, begin the procedure to complete the task and check the box as each step is finished.

Note: This tasksheet may require the student to check the condition of miscellaneous vehicle fluids, some of which may be flammable and could damage the environment or cause health problems if not handled properly. Observe all safety precautions and follow local regulations for the proper disposal of fluids.

Procedure:	Step Completed
OHM'S LAW V / A R VOLTS = AMPS X OHMS SERIES CIRCUIT FORMULAS $R_T = R1 + R2 + R3 \dots$ PARALLEL CIRCUIT FORMULAS $R_T = \dfrac{1}{\dfrac{1}{R1} + \dfrac{1}{R2} + \dfrac{1}{R3} \dots + \dfrac{1}{RN}}$	
1. Calculate the amperage in the circuit shown: V = 14v A = ? R = 2Ω	☐
2. Calculate the voltage in the circuit shown: V = ? A = 4A R = 3Ω	☐
3. Calculate the resistance in the circuit shown: V = 12v A = 1.5A R = Ω?	☐
4. Calculate the amperage in the circuit shown: V = 12v = ?A R = 4Ω R = 6Ω R = 2Ω	☐

5. Calculate the voltage in the circuit shown:

V = ?

= 10A   R = 3Ω   R = 4Ω   R = 1Ω

---

6. Calculate the missing resistance value in the circuit shown:

V = 50v

= 5A   R = 4Ω   R = 2Ω   R = Ω?

---

7. Calculate the amperage in the circuit shown:

R1 = 10Ω

V = 15

A = ?A

R2 = 10Ω

---

8. Calculate the voltage in the circuit shown:

R1 = 4Ω

V = ?

A = 5A

R2 = 4Ω

---

9. Calculate the amperage and voltage drop across R2 in the circuit shown:

R1 = 6Ω

V = 24v

A

R2 = 4Ω

V

10. Determine the missing values in the circuit shown:

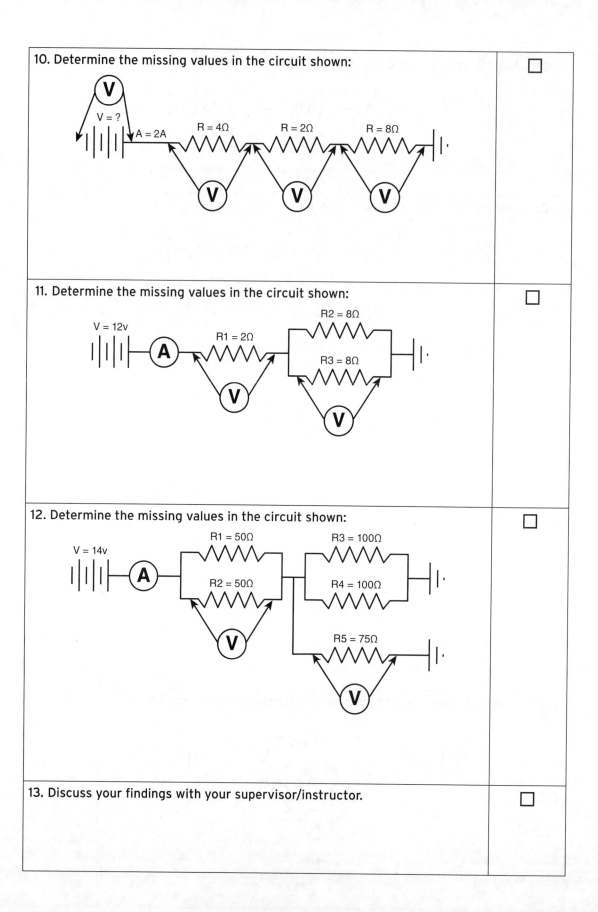

V = ?

A = 2A

R = 4Ω   R = 2Ω   R = 8Ω

11. Determine the missing values in the circuit shown:

V = 12v

A

R1 = 2Ω

R2 = 8Ω

R3 = 8Ω

12. Determine the missing values in the circuit shown:

V = 14v

A

R1 = 50Ω

R2 = 50Ω

R3 = 100Ω

R4 = 100Ω

R5 = 75Ω

13. Discuss your findings with your supervisor/instructor.

Non-Task-Specific Evaluations:	Step Completed
1. Tools and equipment were used as directed and returned in good working order.	☐
2. Complied with all general and task-specific safety standards, including proper use of any personal protection equipment.	☐
3. Completed the task in an appropriate time frame (recommendation: 1.5 or 2 times the flat rate).	☐
4. Left the workspace clean and orderly.	☐
5. Cared for customer property and returned it undamaged.	☐

Student signature _____ Date _____

Comments:

Have your supervisor/instructor verify satisfactory completion of this procedure, any observations made,

and any necessary action(s) recommended.

Evaluation Instructions: The scoring box below is intended to act as a guide for both student and supervisor/instructor. Each criterion listed will help students to understand what is expected of them and help supervisors/instructors articulate the level of success at a particular task. The scoring is set up to allow a second attempt at each task (see the Test and Retest columns). Scoring is also designed to award students points only for task criteria that were completed correctly. Points are lost for failure to complete the employability requirements (see Non-Task-Specific Evaluation criteria). When all criteria are evaluated, tally the points for a total at the bottom of each column.

Tasksheet Scoring

Evaluation Items	Test Pass	Test Fail	Retest Pass	Retest Fail
Task-Specific Evaluation	**(1 pt)**	**(0 pts)**	**(1 pt)**	**(0 pts)**
Student properly calculated circuit amperage, voltage, and resistance.				
Student properly calculated series circuit amperage, voltage, and resistance.				
Student properly calculated parallel circuit amperage, voltage, and amperage and voltage drop.				
Student properly calculated circuit amperage and voltage drops.				
Non-Task-Specific Evaluation	**(0 pts)**	**(−1 pt)**	**(0 pts)**	**(−1 pt)**
Student successfully completed at least three of the non-task-specific steps.				
Student successfully completed all five of the non-task-specific steps.				
Total Score: <total # of points/4 = %>				

CDX Tasksheet Number: MHT5A003

Student/Intern Information

Name _____ Date _____ Class _____

Vehicle, Customer, and Service Information

Vehicle used for this activity:

Year _____ Make _____ Model _____

Odometer _____ VIN _____

Materials Required

- Vehicle or simulator with possible electrical concerns
- Vehicle manufacturer's repair information, including schematic wiring diagrams
- Digital volt-ohmmeter (DVOM), current clamp
- Vehicle/component lifting equipment, if applicable

Task-Specific Safety Considerations

- Activities require you to measure electrical values. Always ensure that the supervisor/instructor checks test instrument connections prior to connecting power or taking measurements. High current flows can be dangerous; avoid accidental short circuits or grounding a battery's positive connections.
- Activities may require test-driving the vehicle on the school grounds or on a hoist, both of which carry severe risks. Attempt this task only with full permission from your supervisor/instructor, and follow all the guidelines exactly.
- Lifting equipment and machines such as vehicle jacks and stands, vehicle hoists, and engine hoists are important tools that increase productivity and make the job easier. However, they can also cause severe injury or death if used improperly. Make sure you follow the manufacturer's operation procedures. Also make sure you have your supervisor's/instructor's permission to use any particular type of lifting equipment.
- Comply with personal and environmental safety practices associated with clothing; eye protection; hand tools; power equipment; proper ventilation; and the handling, storage, and disposal of chemicals/materials in accordance with federal, state, and local regulations.
- Always wear the correct protective eyewear and clothing and use the appropriate safety equipment, as well as fender covers, seat protectors, and floor mat protectors.
- Make sure you understand and observe all legislative and personal safety procedures when carrying out practical assignments. If you are unsure of what these are, ask your supervisor/instructor.

▶ **TASK** Demonstrate proper use of test equipment when measuring source voltage, voltage drop (including grounds), current flow, continuity, and resistance.

MTST
V.A.3; P1

Time off_____

Time on_____

Total time_____

Student Instructions: Read through the entire procedure prior to starting. Prepare your workspace and any tools or parts that may be needed to complete the task. When directed by your supervisor/instructor, begin the procedure to complete the task and check the box as each step is finished.

Note: This tasksheet will require the use of a vehicle or simulator with an electrical fault. Ask your supervisor/instructor which vehicle or simulator you are to use. Be sure to follow the correct steps for connecting your DVOM or ammeter to check for amperage/current flow. Have your supervisor/instructor check your connections. Improper connection of the DVOM may damage your meter.

Procedure:	Step Completed
1. Using the appropriate service information for the vehicle you are working on, research how to check applied voltages, circuit voltages, and voltage drops in electrical/electronic circuits. List the circuits, including the lead connections.	
a. Applied voltages:	☐
b. Circuit voltages:	☐
c. Voltage drops:	☐
2. Prepare the DVOM to measure DC volts.	
a. List the steps necessary in preparing your DVOM to measure voltage:	☐
3. Have your supervisor/instructor verify your research. Supervisor's/instructor's initials:	☐
4. Using the appropriate service information, check applied voltages, circuit voltages, and voltage drops in electrical/electronic circuits. Ask your supervisor/instructor for a vehicle and circuits to check.	
a. Applied voltages: List the circuit being checked:	☐
i. Within manufacturer's specifications: Yes: ☐ No: ☐	☐

ii. If No, describe the recommended corrective action(s):	☐
b. Circuit voltages: List the circuit being checked:	☐
i. Within manufacturer's specifications: Yes: ☐ No: ☐	☐
ii. If No, describe the recommended corrective action(s):	☐
c. Voltage drops: List the circuit being checked:	☐
i. Within manufacturer's specifications: Yes: ☐ No: ☐	☐
ii. If No, describe the recommended corrective action(s):	☐
5. Research how to measure current flow in electrical/electronic circuits and components as outlined in the manufacturer's workshop materials. List the circuits, including the lead connections:	
a. DVOM current measurements: Draw a diagram showing the lead connection and circuit.	☐

b. DVOM with inductive clamp current measurements: Draw a diagram showing the lead connection and circuit.	☐
6. Prepare the DVOM to measure DC current.	
a. List the steps necessary in preparing your DVOM to measure current:	☐
7. Have your supervisor/instructor verify your research. Supervisor's/instructor's initials:	☐
8. Check current flow in electrical/electronic circuits and components as outlined in the manufacturer's workshop materials. Ask your supervisor/instructor for a vehicle and circuits to check. (**Note:** Ensure that the meter is connected correctly when measuring current draw. Damage may occur to circuits and the test equipment if connections are made incorrectly.)	
a. List the circuit being checked:	☐
i. Within manufacturer's specifications: Yes: ☐ No: ☐	☐
ii. If No, describe the recommended corrective action(s):	☐
b. List the circuit being checked:	☐
i. Within manufacturer's specifications: Yes: ☐ No: ☐	☐
ii. If No, describe the recommended corrective action(s):	☐

c. List the circuit being checked:	☐
i. Within manufacturer's specifications: Yes: ☐ No: ☐	☐
ii. If No, describe the recommended corrective action(s):	☐
9. Research how to check resistance in electrical/electronic circuits and components as outlined in the manufacturer's workshop materials. List the circuits, including the lead connections:	
a. DVOM resistance measurements: Draw a diagram showing the lead connection and circuit.	☐
10. Prepare the DVOM to measure resistance.	
a. List the steps necessary in preparing your DVOM to measure resistance:	☐
11. Explain why resistance measurements should only be undertaken without power connected to the circuit under test:	☐
12. Have your supervisor/instructor verify your research. Supervisor's/instructor's initials:	☐

13. Using the appropriate service information, check resistance in electrical/ electronic circuits and components. Ask your supervisor/instructor for a vehicle and circuits to check. (**Note:** Ensure that the meter is correctly connected and no power is applied to the circuit under test when measuring resistance.)	
a. List the circuit/component being checked:	☐
i. Within manufacturer's specifications: Yes: ☐ No: ☐	☐
ii. If No, describe the recommended corrective action(s):	☐
b. List the circuit/component being checked:	☐
i. Within manufacturer's specifications: Yes: ☐ No: ☐	☐
ii. If No, describe the recommended corrective action(s):	☐
c. List the circuit/component being checked:	☐
i. Within manufacturer's specifications: Yes: ☐ No: ☐	☐
ii. If No, describe the recommended corrective action(s):	☐

14. Prepare the DVOM to measure continuity. Continuity is measured using the Ohms scale on the DVOM.	
a. List the steps necessary in preparing your DVOM to measure continuity:	☐
b. Explain how to connect the meter leads:	☐
c. What readings would you expect the DVOM to indicate when the circuit has the following?	
i. Good continuity:	☐
ii. Poor continuity:	☐
15. Check for circuit continuity in electrical/electronic circuits as outlined in the manufacturer's workshop materials. Ask your supervisor/instructor for a vehicle and circuits to check continuity.	

a. Circuit 1:
      i. Within manufacturer's specifications:
      Yes: ☐ No: ☐
	☐

ii. If No, describe the recommended corrective action(s):	☐

b. Circuit 2:
      i. Within manufacturer's specifications:
      Yes: ☐ No: ☐
	☐

ii. If No, describe the recommended corrective action(s):	☐

	Step Completed

c. Circuit 3:
    i. Within manufacturer's specifications:
 	
      Yes: ☐ No: ☐
	☐

ii. If No, describe the recommended corrective action(s):	☐
16. Return the vehicle to its beginning condition, and return any tools you used to their proper locations.	☐
17. Discuss your findings with your supervisor/instructor.	☐

Non-Task-Specific Evaluations:	Step Completed
1. Tools and equipment were used as directed and returned in good working order.	☐
2. Complied with all general and task-specific safety standards, including proper use of any personal protection equipment.	☐
3. Completed the task in an appropriate time frame (recommendation: 1.5 or 2 times the flat rate).	☐
4. Left the workspace clean and orderly.	☐
5. Cared for customer property and returned it undamaged.	☐

Student signature _____ Date _____

Comments:

Have your supervisor/instructor verify satisfactory completion of this procedure, any observations made, and any necessary action(s) recommended.

Evaluation Instructions: The scoring box below is intended to act as a guide for both student and supervisor/instructor. Each criterion listed will help students to understand what is expected of them and help supervisors/instructors articulate the level of success at a particular task. The scoring is set up to allow a second attempt at each task (see the Test and Retest columns). Scoring is also designed to award students points only for task criteria that were completed correctly. Points are lost for failure to complete the employability requirements (see Non-Task-Specific Evaluation criteria). When all criteria are evaluated, tally the points for a total at the bottom of each column.

Tasksheet Scoring

Evaluation Items	Test		Retest	
	Pass	Fail	Pass	Fail
Task-Specific Evaluation	**(1 pt)**	**(0 pts)**	**(1 pt)**	**(0 pts)**
Student used the appropriate service information to research how to check applied voltage, circuit voltage, voltage drop, current flow, resistance, and continuity.				
Student successfully checked applied voltage, circuit voltage, voltage drop, current flow, resistance, and continuity.				
Student used a DVOM and current clamp as directed and required.				
Student reinstalled all removed components undamaged and in working order.				
Non-Task-Specific Evaluation	**(0 pts)**	**(−1 pt)**	**(0 pts)**	**(−1 pt)**
Student successfully completed at least three of the non-task-specific steps.				
Student successfully completed all five of the non-task-specific steps.				
Total Score: <total # of points/4 = %>				

Supervisor/Instructor:

Supervisor/instructor signature _____ Date _____

Comments:

Retest supervisor/instructor signature _____ Date _____

Comments:

CDX Tasksheet Number: MHT5A004

Student/Intern Information

Name _____ Date _____ Class _____

Vehicle, Customer, and Service Information

Vehicle used for this activity:

Year _____ Make _____ Model _____

Odometer _____ VIN _____

Materials Required

- Vehicle or simulator with electrical concerns
- Vehicle manufacturer's repair information, including schematic wiring diagrams
- Digital multimeter (DMM)
- Vehicle/component lifting equipment, if applicable

Task-Specific Safety Considerations

- Activities require you to measure electrical values. Always ensure that the supervisor/ instructor checks test instrument connections prior to connecting power or taking measurements. High current flows can be dangerous; avoid accidental short circuits or grounding a battery's positive connections.
- Activities may require test-driving the vehicle on the school grounds or on a hoist, both of which carry severe risks. Attempt this task only with full permission from your supervisor/ instructor, and follow all the guidelines exactly.
- Lifting equipment and machines such as vehicle jacks and stands, vehicle hoists, and engine hoists are important tools that increase productivity and make the job easier. However, they can also cause severe injury or death if used improperly. Make sure you follow the manufacturer's operation procedures. Also make sure you have your supervisor's/ instructor's permission to use any particular type of lifting equipment.
- Comply with personal and environmental safety practices associated with clothing; eye protection; hand tools; power equipment; proper ventilation; and the handling, storage, and disposal of chemicals/materials in accordance with federal, state, and local regulations.
- Always wear the correct protective eyewear and clothing and use the appropriate safety equipment, as well as fender covers, seat protectors, and floor mat protectors.
- Make sure you understand and observe all legislative and personal safety procedures when carrying out practical assignments. If you are unsure of what these are, ask your supervisor/ instructor.

▶ **TASK** Demonstrate knowledge of the causes and effects of shorts, grounds, opens, and resistance problems in electrical/electronic circuits; identify and locate faults in electrical/electronic circuits.

MTST
V.A.4; P1

Time off_____

Time on_____

Total time_____

Student Instructions: Read through the entire procedure prior to starting. Prepare your workspace and any tools or parts that may be needed to complete the task. When directed by your supervisor/instructor, begin the procedure to complete the task and check the box as each step is finished.

Note: This tasksheet will require the use of a vehicle or simulator with an electrical fault. Ask your instructor which vehicle or simulator you are to use.

Procedure:	Step Completed
1. List the complaints or concerns for this tasksheet:	☐
2. Identify or isolate the circuit or circuits involved.	
a. List circuit components that are not working as designed:	☐
3. Locate the wiring diagram for the circuit(s) you identified in Step 2.	☐
4. Identify the short circuit present with this vehicle/simulator.	
a. List your findings:	☐
5. Identify the open circuit present with this vehicle/simulator.	
a. List your findings:	☐
6. Identify the high-resistance fault present with this vehicle/simulator.	
a. List your findings:	☐
7. Return the vehicle to its beginning condition, and return any tools you used to their proper locations.	☐
8. Discuss your findings with your supervisor/instructor.	☐

Non-Task-Specific Evaluations:	Step Completed
1. Tools and equipment were used as directed and returned in good working order.	☐
2. Complied with all general and task-specific safety standards, including proper use of any personal protection equipment.	☐
3. Completed the task in an appropriate time frame (recommendation: 1.5 or 2 times the flat rate).	☐
4. Left the workspace clean and orderly.	☐
5. Cared for customer property and returned it undamaged.	☐

Student signature _____ Date _____

Comments:

Have your supervisor/instructor verify satisfactory completion of this procedure, any observations made,

and any necessary action(s) recommended.

Evaluation Instructions: The scoring box below is intended to act as a guide for both student and supervisor/instructor. Each criterion listed will help students to understand what is expected of them and help supervisors/instructors articulate the level of success at a particular task. The scoring is set up to allow a second attempt at each task (see the Test and Retest columns). Scoring is also designed to award students points only for task criteria that were completed correctly. Points are lost for failure to complete the employability requirements (see Non-Task-Specific Evaluation criteria). When all criteria are evaluated, tally the points for a total at the bottom of each column.

Tasksheet Scoring

Evaluation Items	Test		Retest	
	Pass	**Fail**	**Pass**	**Fail**
Task-Specific Evaluation	**(1 pt)**	**(0 pts)**	**(1 pt)**	**(0 pts)**
Student correctly identified the circuit(s) involved.				
Student used the appropriate service information to locate necessary wiring diagrams.				
Student successfully identified circuit faults, including shorts, opens, and high resistance.				
Student reinstalled all removed components undamaged and in working order.				
Non-Task-Specific Evaluation	**(0 pts)**	**(−1 pt)**	**(0 pts)**	**(−1 pt)**
Student successfully completed at least three of the non-task-specific steps.				
Student successfully completed all five of the non-task-specific steps.				
Total Score: <total # of points/4 = %>				

Supervisor/Instructor:

Supervisor/instructor signature _____ Date _____

Comments:

Retest supervisor/instructor signature _____ Date _____

Comments:

CDX Tasksheet Number: MHT5A005

Student/Intern Information

Name _____ Date _____ Class _____

Vehicle, Customer, and Service Information

Vehicle used for this activity:

Year _____ Make _____ Model _____

Odometer _____ VIN _____

Materials Required

- Vehicle with possible engine concern
- Engine manufacturer's workshop materials
- Manufacturer-specific tools depending on the concern/procedure(s)
- Vehicle/component lifting equipment, if applicable

Task-Specific Safety Considerations

- Activities may require test-driving the vehicle on the school grounds or on a hoist, both of which carry severe risks. Attempt this task only with full permission from your supervisor/instructor, and follow all the guidelines exactly.
- Lifting equipment and machines such as vehicle jacks and stands, vehicle hoists, and engine hoists are important tools that increase productivity and make the job easier. However, they can also cause severe injury or death if used improperly. Make sure you follow the manufacturer's operation procedures. Also make sure you have your supervisor's/instructor's permission to use any particular type of lifting equipment.
- Comply with personal and environmental safety practices associated with clothing; eye protection; hand tools; power equipment; proper ventilation; and the handling, storage, and disposal of chemicals/materials in accordance with federal, state, and local regulations.
- Always wear the correct protective eyewear and clothing and use the appropriate safety equipment, as well as wheel chocks, fender covers, seat protectors, and floor mat protectors.
- Make sure you understand and observe all legislative and personal safety procedures when carrying out practical assignments. If you are unsure of what these are, ask your supervisor/instructor.

▶ **TASK** Use wiring diagrams during the diagnosis (troubleshooting) of electrical/electronic circuit problems.

MTST
V.A.5; P1

Time off_____

Time on_____

Total time_____

Student Instructions: Read through the entire procedure prior to starting. Prepare your workspace and any tools or parts that may be needed to complete the task. When directed by your supervisor/instructor, begin the procedure to complete the task and check the box as each step is finished.

Note: This tasksheet may require the student to check the condition of miscellaneous vehicle fluids, some of which may be flammable and could damage the environment or cause health problems if not handled properly. Observe all safety precautions and follow local regulations for the proper disposal of fluids.

Procedure:	Step Completed
1. Locate the wiring diagram(s) as outlined in the manufacturer's workshop materials.	☐
2. If a vehicle with an electrical problem is not available, have your supervisor/instructor install a bug in the electrical system. Bug/Complaint:	☐
3. Record the following for the above bug/complaint as outlined in the manufacturer's workshop materials and wiring diagram.	
a. Circuit #(s):	☐
b. Circuit protection type and rating:	☐
c. Wire(s) color(s):	☐
d. Wire(s) size(s):	☐
e. Circuit(s) control(s):	☐
f. Number of connections for affected component/circuit:	☐

g. Types of connections for affected component/circuit:	☐
h. Length of conductor(s):	☐
4. Troubleshoot the bug/complaint using the manufacturer's workshop materials, wiring diagram(s), and proper techniques.	
a. Is this a power-side problem? Yes: ☐ No: ☐	☐
b. Describe the process for determining your conclusion in step a:	☐
c. Is this a ground-side problem? Yes: ☐ No: ☐	☐
d. Describe the process for determining your conclusion in step c:	☐
e. Is this a component problem? Yes: ☐ No: ☐	☐
f. Describe the process for determining your conclusion in step e:	☐
5. Discuss your findings with your supervisor/instructor.	☐

Non-Task-Specific Evaluations:	Step Completed
1. Tools and equipment were used as directed and returned in good working order.	☐
2. Complied with all general and task-specific safety standards, including proper use of any personal protection equipment.	☐
3. Completed the task in an appropriate time frame (recommendation: 1.5 or 2 times the flat rate).	☐
4. Left the workspace clean and orderly.	☐
5. Cared for customer property and returned it undamaged.	☐

Student signature _____ Date _____

Comments:

Have your supervisor/instructor verify satisfactory completion of this procedure, any observations made, and any necessary action(s) recommended.

Evaluation Instructions: The scoring box below is intended to act as a guide for both student and supervisor/instructor. Each criterion listed will help students to understand what is expected of them and help supervisors/instructors articulate the level of success at a particular task. The scoring is set up to allow a second attempt at each task (see the Test and Retest columns). Scoring is also designed to award students points only for task criteria that were completed correctly. Points are lost for failure to complete the employability requirements (see Non-Task-Specific Evaluation criteria). When all criteria are evaluated, tally the points for a total at the bottom of each column.

Tasksheet Scoring

	Test		Retest	
Evaluation Items	**Pass**	**Fail**	**Pass**	**Fail**
Task-Specific Evaluation	**(1 pt)**	**(0 pts)**	**(1 pt)**	**(0 pts)**
Student properly identified circuit #(s), control(s), protection type, and rating.				
Student properly identified wire color(s) and size(s).				
Student properly identified number and types of connections and conductor(s) length.				
Student properly performed process for determining power-side, ground-side, and component problems.				
Non-Task-Specific Evaluation	**(0 pts)**	**(−1 pt)**	**(0 pts)**	**(−1 pt)**
Student successfully completed at least three of the non-task-specific steps.				
Student successfully completed all five of the non-task-specific steps.				
Total Score: <total # of points/4 = %>				

Supervisor/Instructor:

Supervisor/instructor signature _____ Date _____

Comments:

Retest supervisor/instructor signature _____ Date _____

Comments:

CDX Tasksheet Number: MHT5A006

Student/Intern Information

Name _____ Date _____ Class _____

Vehicle, Customer, and Service Information

Vehicle used for this activity:

Year _____ Make _____ Model _____

Odometer _____ VIN _____

Materials Required

- Vehicle with possible electrical concerns
- Vehicle manufacturer's repair information, including schematic wiring diagrams
- Digital multimeter (DMM)
- Vehicle/component lifting equipment, if applicable

Task-Specific Safety Considerations

- Activities require you to measure electrical values. Always ensure that the supervisor/ instructor checks test instrument connections prior to connecting power or taking measurements. High current flows can be dangerous; avoid accidental short circuits or grounding a battery's positive connections.
- Activities may require test-driving the vehicle on the school grounds or on a hoist, both of which carry severe risks. Attempt this task only with full permission from your supervisor/ instructor, and follow all the guidelines exactly.
- Lifting equipment and machines such as vehicle jacks and stands, vehicle hoists, and engine hoists are important tools that increase productivity and make the job easier. However, they can also cause severe injury or death if used improperly. Make sure you follow the manufacturer's operation procedures. Also make sure you have your supervisor's/ instructor's permission to use any particular type of lifting equipment.
- Comply with personal and environmental safety practices associated with clothing; eye protection; hand tools; power equipment; proper ventilation; and the handling, storage, and disposal of chemicals/materials in accordance with federal, state, and local regulations.
- Always wear the correct protective eyewear and clothing and use the appropriate safety equipment, as well as wheel chocks, fender covers, seat protectors, and floor mat protectors.
- Make sure you understand and observe all legislative and personal safety procedures when carrying out practical assignments. If you are unsure of what these are, ask your supervisor/ instructor.

▶ **TASK** Measure parasitic (key-off) battery drain; determine needed action. **MTST** *V.A.6; P1*

Time off_____

Time on_____

Student Instructions: Read through the entire procedure prior to starting. Prepare your workspace and any tools or parts that may be needed to complete the task. When directed by your supervisor/instructor, begin the procedure to complete the task and check the box as each step is finished.

Total time_____

Note: This tasksheet will require the use of a vehicle or simulator with an electrical fault. Ask your supervisor/instructor which vehicle or simulator you are to use. Be sure to follow the correct steps for connecting your DVOM to check for amperage/current flow. Have your supervisor/instructor check your connections. Improper connection of the DVOM may damage your meter.

Procedure:	Step Completed
1. Using the appropriate service information, research key-off battery drain (parasitic drain) checks. **(Note:** Parasitic drain is current draw that is present when the key is in the off position. Too much current draw can drain the vehicle's battery over a period of time.)	☐
2. Determine the maximum key-off battery drain (parasitic drain) for the vehicle/simulator that has been assigned to you.	
a. Maximum drain: _____ mA	☐
3. List the appropriate steps to check for key-off battery drain (parasitic drain) for the vehicle/simulator that has been assigned to you:	☐
4. Using the steps listed, check the key-off battery drain (parasitic drain) for the vehicle/simulator that has been assigned to you.	
a. Maximum drain: _____ mA	☐
b. Within manufacturer's specifications: Yes: ☐ No: ☐	☐
5. If the reading is more than the allowable maximum drain, determine what is causing the excessive drain.	
a. List any item(s) that you found at fault:	☐
6. Use the appropriate service procedures to determine the necessary repair(s). List any repairs:	☐

	Step Completed
7. Return the vehicle/simulator to its beginning condition, and return any tools you used to their proper locations.	☐
8. Discuss your findings with your supervisor/instructor.	☐

Non-Task-Specific Evaluations:	Step Completed
1. Tools and equipment were used as directed and returned in good working order.	☐
2. Complied with all general and task-specific safety standards, including proper use of any personal protection equipment.	☐
3. Completed the task in an appropriate time frame (recommendation: 1.5 or 2 times the flat rate).	☐
4. Left the workspace clean and orderly.	☐
5. Cared for customer property and returned it undamaged.	☐

Student signature _____ Date _____

Comments:

Have your supervisor/instructor verify satisfactory completion of this procedure, any observations made,

and any necessary action(s) recommended.

Evaluation Instructions: The scoring box below is intended to act as a guide for both student and supervisor/instructor. Each criterion listed will help students to understand what is expected of them and help supervisors/instructors articulate the level of success at a particular task. The scoring is set up to allow a second attempt at each task (see the Test and Retest columns). Scoring is also designed to award students points only for task criteria that were completed correctly. Points are lost for failure to complete the employability requirements (see Non-Task-Specific Evaluation criteria). When all criteria are evaluated, tally the points for a total at the bottom of each column.

Tasksheet Scoring

Evaluation Items	Test		Retest	
	Pass	**Fail**	**Pass**	**Fail**
Task-Specific Evaluation	**(1 pt)**	**(0 pts)**	**(1 pt)**	**(0 pts)**
Student used the appropriate service information to determine the maximum key-off battery drain.				
Student properly measured parasitic (key-off) battery drain and determined any necessary actions.				
Student used the appropriate service procedures to determine the necessary repair(s).				
Student reinstalled all removed components undamaged and in working order.				
Non-Task-Specific Evaluation	**(0 pts)**	**(−1 pt)**	**(0 pts)**	**(−1 pt)**
Student successfully completed at least three of the non-task-specific steps.				
Student successfully completed all five of the non-task-specific steps.				
Total Score: <total # of points/4 = %>				

Supervisor/Instructor:

Supervisor/instructor signature _____ Date _____

Comments:

Retest supervisor/instructor signature _____ Date _____

Comments:

CDX Tasksheet Number: MHT5A007

Student/Intern Information

Name _____ Date _____ Class _____

Vehicle, Customer, and Service Information

Vehicle used for this activity:

Year _____ Make _____ Model _____

Odometer _____ VIN _____

Materials Required

- Vehicle with possible electrical concerns
- Vehicle manufacturer's repair information including schematic wiring diagrams
- Digital multimeter (DMM)
- Vehicle/component lifting equipment, if applicable

Task-Specific Safety Considerations

- Activities require you to measure electrical values. Always ensure that the supervisor/instructor checks test instrument connections prior to connecting power or taking measurements. High current flows can be dangerous; avoid accidental short circuits or grounding a battery's positive connections.
- Activities may require test-driving the vehicle on the school grounds or on a hoist, both of which carry severe risks. Attempt this task only with full permission from your supervisor/instructor, and follow all the guidelines exactly.
- Lifting equipment and machines such as vehicle jacks and stands, vehicle hoists, and engine hoists are important tools that increase productivity and make the job easier. However, they can also cause severe injury or death if used improperly. Make sure you follow the manufacturer's operation procedures. Also make sure you have your supervisor's/instructor's permission to use any particular type of lifting equipment.
- Comply with personal and environmental safety practices associated with clothing; eye protection; hand tools; power equipment; proper ventilation; and the handling, storage, and disposal of chemicals/materials in accordance with federal, state, and local regulations.
- Always wear the correct protective eyewear and clothing and use the appropriate safety equipment, as well as wheel chocks, fender covers, seat protectors, and floor mat protectors.
- Make sure you understand and observe all legislative and personal safety procedures when carrying out practical assignments. If you are unsure of what these are, ask your supervisor/instructor.

▶ **TASK** Demonstrate knowledge of the function, operation, and testing of fusible links, circuit breakers, relays, solenoids and diodes, and fuses; perform inspection and testing; determine needed action. *MTST* V.A.7; P1

Time off_____

Time on_____

Student Instructions: Read through the entire procedure prior to starting. Prepare your workspace and any tools or parts that may be needed to complete the task. When directed by your supervisor/instructor, begin the procedure to complete the task and check the box as each step is finished.

Total time_____

Note: This tasksheet will require the use of a vehicle or simulator with an electrical fault. Ask your supervisor/instructor which vehicle or simulator you are to use.

Procedure:	Step Completed
1. Using the appropriate service information, locate the fuse panel(s), circuit breakers, fusible links, relays, solenoids, and diodes for the vehicle/simulator you are assigned to.	
a. List the fuse panel, circuit breaker, fusible link, relay, and solenoid locations for this vehicle/simulator:	☐
2. Determine and list any fuses, fusible links, or circuit breakers that are defective (open): (**Note:** Circuit protection devices [fuses, fusible links, and circuit breakers] do not normally wear out. If a circuit protection device is found to be faulty, too much current was/is present.)	☐
3. Determine and list the rating (size) of the circuit protection device for this circuit:	☐
4. Is the correct size installed? Yes: ☐ No: ☐	☐
5. Determine the cause for the circuit protection device to fail. List your findings:	☐
6. Determine and list any relays, solenoids, or diodes that are defective:	☐
7. Return the vehicle/simulator to its beginning condition, and return any tools you used to their proper locations.	☐

8. Discuss your findings with your supervisor/instructor.	☐

Non-Task-Specific Evaluations:	Step Completed
1. Tools and equipment were used as directed and returned in good working order.	☐
2. Complied with all general and task-specific safety standards, including proper use of any personal protection equipment.	☐
3. Completed the task in an appropriate time frame (recommendation: 1.5 or 2 times the flat rate).	☐
4. Left the workspace clean and orderly.	☐
5. Cared for customer property and returned it undamaged.	☐

Student signature _____ Date _____

Comments:

Have your supervisor/instructor verify satisfactory completion of this procedure, any observations made, and any necessary action(s) recommended.

Evaluation Instructions: The scoring box below is intended to act as a guide for both student and supervisor/instructor. Each criterion listed will help students to understand what is expected of them and help supervisors/instructors articulate the level of success at a particular task. The scoring is set up to allow a second attempt at each task (see the Test and Retest columns). Scoring is also designed to award students points only for task criteria that were completed correctly. Points are lost for failure to complete the employability requirements (see Non-Task-Specific Evaluation criteria). When all criteria are evaluated, tally the points for a total at the bottom of each column.

Tasksheet Scoring

Evaluation Items	Test		Retest	
	Pass	**Fail**	**Pass**	**Fail**
Task-Specific Evaluation	**(1 pt)**	**(0 pts)**	**(1 pt)**	**(0 pts)**
Student used the appropriate service information to locate fuse panel(s), circuit breakers, fusible links, relays, solenoids, and diodes.				
Student correctly determined any defective circuit breakers, fusible links, relays, solenoids, or diodes.				
Student correctly determined any and all necessary repairs.				
Student reinstalled all removed components undamaged and in working order.				
Non-Task-Specific Evaluation	**(0 pts)**	**(−1 pt)**	**(0 pts)**	**(−1 pt)**
Student successfully completed at least three of the non-task-specific steps.				
Student successfully completed all five of the non-task-specific steps.				
Total Score: <total # of points/4 = %>				

Supervisor/Instructor:

Supervisor/instructor signature _____ Date _____

Comments:

Retest supervisor/instructor signature _____ Date _____

Comments:

CDX Tasksheet Number: MHT5A008

Student/Intern Information

Name _____ Date _____ Class _____

Vehicle, Customer, and Service Information

Vehicle used for this activity:

Year _____ Make _____ Model _____

Odometer _____ VIN _____

Materials Required

- Vehicle with possible engine concern
- Engine manufacturer's workshop materials
- Manufacturer-specific tools depending on the concern/procedure(s)
- Vehicle/component lifting equipment, if applicable

Task-Specific Safety Considerations

- Activities may require test-driving the vehicle on the school grounds or on a hoist, both of which carry severe risks. Attempt this task only with full permission from your supervisor/instructor, and follow all the guidelines exactly.
- Lifting equipment and machines such as vehicle jacks and stands, vehicle hoists, and engine hoists are important tools that increase productivity and make the job easier. However, they can also cause severe injury or death if used improperly. Make sure you follow the manufacturer's operation procedures. Also make sure you have your supervisor's/instructor's permission to use any particular type of lifting equipment.
- Comply with personal and environmental safety practices associated with clothing; eye protection; hand tools; power equipment; proper ventilation; and the handling, storage, and disposal of chemicals/materials in accordance with federal, state, and local regulations.
- Always wear the correct protective eyewear and clothing and use the appropriate safety equipment, as well as wheel chocks, fender covers, seat protectors, and floor mat protectors.
- Make sure you understand and observe all legislative and personal safety procedures when carrying out practical assignments. If you are unsure of what these are, ask your supervisor/instructor.

▶ **TASK** Inspect, test, repair (including solder repair), and/or replace components, connectors, seals, terminal ends, harnesses, and wiring; verify proper routing and securement; determine needed action.

MTST
V.A.8; P1

Time off_____

Time on_____

Total time_____

Student Instructions: Read through the entire procedure prior to starting. Prepare your workspace and any tools or parts that may be needed to complete the task. When directed by your supervisor/instructor, begin the procedure to complete the task and check the box as each step is finished.

Note: This tasksheet may require the student to check the condition of miscellaneous vehicle fluids, some of which may be flammable and could damage the environment cause health problems if not handled properly. Observe all safety precautions and follow local regulations for the proper disposal of fluids.

Procedure:	Step Completed
1. Perform solderless crimp connector repair. If vehicle harness is not available, perform repair on bulk wiring.	
a. Wire size: _____ awg/mm	☐
b. Type of connector (e.g., butt, ring):	☐
c. Research proper tooling/techniques and record, and perform the crimp connector repair:	☐
d. Perform pull test on installed connector and have your supervisor/ instructor inspect.	☐
e. Within manufacturer's specifications: Yes: ☐ No: ☐	☐
f. If No, describe the recommended corrective action(s):	☐
2. Perform heat-shrink solder crimp connector repair. If vehicle harness is not available, perform repair on bulk wiring.	
a. Wire size: _____ awg/mm	☐
b. Type of connector (e.g., butt, ring):	☐

c. Research and record proper tooling/techniques, and perform the heat shrink solder crimp connector repair:	☐
d. Perform pull test on installed connector, and have your supervisor/instructor inspect.	☐
e. Within manufacturer's specifications: Yes: ☐ No: ☐	☐
f. If No, describe the recommended corrective action(s):	☐
3. Perform solder/heat-shrink repair. If vehicle harness is not available, perform repair on bulk wiring.	
a. Wire size: _____ awg/mm	☐
b. Type of connector (e.g., butt, ring, splice):	☐
c. Research proper tooling/techniques and record, and solder/heat-shrink the connector repair:	☐
d. Have your supervisor/instructor inspect soldered connection before installing heat shrink.	☐
e. Within manufacturer's specifications: Yes: ☐ No: ☐	☐

f. If No, describe the recommended corrective action(s):	☐
4. Perform battery cable repair. If vehicle is not available, perform repair on bulk cable.	
a. Cable size: _____ awg/mm	☐
b. Type of connector (e.g., butt, ring):	☐
c. Research and record proper tooling/techniques, and perform the battery cable repair:	☐
d. Have your supervisor/instructor inspect connection.	☐
e. Within manufacturer's specifications: Yes: ☐ No: ☐	☐
f. If No, describe the recommended corrective action(s):	☐
5. Perform Delphi Weather Pack connector repair. If vehicle is not available, perform repair on bulk wire.	
a. Wire size: _____ awg/mm	☐
b. Type of connector:	☐
c. Research and record proper tooling/techniques, and perform the Delphi Weather Pack connector repair:	☐

d. Perform pull test on installed connector, and have your supervisor/instructor inspect.	☐
e. Within manufacturer's specifications: Yes: ☐ No: ☐	☐
f. If No, describe the recommended corrective action(s):	☐
6. Perform Deutsch connector repair. If vehicle is not available, perform repair on bulk wire.	
a. Wire size: _____ awg/mm	☐
b. Type of connector:	☐
c. Research and record proper tooling/techniques, and perform the Deutsch connector repair:	☐
d. Perform pull test on installed connector, and have your supervisor/instructor inspect.	☐
e. Within manufacturer's specifications: Yes: ☐ No: ☐	☐
f. If No, describe the recommended corrective action(s):	☐
7. Inspect vehicle harnesses for proper securement and routing.	
a. Vehicle make/model:	☐

© 2021 Jones & Bartlett Learning, LLC, an Ascend Learning Company

	Step Completed
b. VIN/serial number:	☐
c. Component harness inspected (e.g., engine, transmission):	☐
d. Within manufacturer's specifications: Yes: ☐ No: ☐	☐
e. If No, describe the recommended corrective action(s):	☐
8. Discuss your findings with your supervisor/instructor.	☐

Non-Task-Specific Evaluations:	Step Completed
1. Tools and equipment were used as directed and returned in good working order.	☐
2. Complied with all general and task-specific safety standards, including proper use of any personal protection equipment.	☐
3. Completed the task in an appropriate time frame (recommendation: 1.5 or 2 times the flat rate).	☐
4. Left the workspace clean and orderly.	☐
5. Cared for customer property and returned it undamaged.	☐

Student signature _____ Date _____

Comments:

Have your supervisor/instructor verify satisfactory completion of this procedure, any observations made, and any necessary action(s) recommended.

Evaluation Instructions: The scoring box below is intended to act as a guide for both student and supervisor/instructor. Each criterion listed will help students to understand what is expected of them and help supervisors/instructors articulate the level of success at a particular task. The scoring is set up to allow a second attempt at each task (see the Test and Retest columns). Scoring is also designed to award students points only for task criteria that were completed correctly. Points are lost for failure to complete the employability requirements (see Non-Task-Specific Evaluation criteria). When all criteria are evaluated, tally the points for a total at the bottom of each column.

Tasksheet Scoring

Evaluation Items	Test		Retest	
	Pass	**Fail**	**Pass**	**Fail**
Task-Specific Evaluation	**(1 pt)**	**(0 pts)**	**(1 pt)**	**(0 pts)**
Student properly performed solderless crimp, heat-shrink solder crimp, and solder/heat-shrink connector repairs.				
Student properly performed battery cable repair.				
Student properly performed Delphi Weather Pack and Deutsch connector repairs.				
Student properly performed harness inspection.				
Non-Task-Specific Evaluation	**(0 pts)**	**(−1 pt)**	**(0 pts)**	**(−1 pt)**
Student successfully completed at least three of the non-task-specific steps.				
Student successfully completed all five of the non-task-specific steps.				
Total Score: <total # of points/4 = %>				

CDX Tasksheet Number: MHT5A009

Student/Intern Information

Name _____ Date _____ Class _____

Vehicle, Customer, and Service Information

Vehicle used for this activity:

Year _____ Make _____ Model _____

Odometer _____ VIN _____

> ## Materials Required
>
> - Vehicle with possible engine concern
> - Engine manufacturer's workshop materials
> - Manufacturer-specific tools depending on the concern/procedure(s)
> - Vehicle/component lifting equipment, if applicable

Task-Specific Safety Considerations

- Activities may require test-driving the vehicle on the school grounds or on a hoist, both of which carry severe risks. Attempt this task only with full permission from your supervisor/instructor, and follow all the guidelines exactly.
- Lifting equipment and machines such as vehicle jacks and stands, vehicle hoists, and engine hoists are important tools that increase productivity and make the job easier. However, they can also cause severe injury or death if used improperly. Make sure you follow the manufacturer's operation procedures. Also make sure you have your supervisor's/instructor's permission to use any particular type of lifting equipment.
- Comply with personal and environmental safety practices associated with clothing; eye protection; hand tools; power equipment; proper ventilation; and the handling, storage, and disposal of chemicals/materials in accordance with federal, state, and local regulations.
- Always wear the correct protective eyewear and clothing and use the appropriate safety equipment, as well as wheel chocks, fender covers, seat protectors, and floor mat protectors.
- Make sure you understand and observe all legislative and personal safety procedures when carrying out practical assignments. If you are unsure of what these are, ask your supervisor/instructor.

▶ **TASK** Use appropriate electronic service tool(s) (EST) and procedures to diagnose problems; check, record, and clear diagnostic codes; interpret digital multimeter (DMM) readings.

MTST
V.A.9; P1

Time off _____

Time on _____

Total time _____

Student Instructions: Read through the entire procedure prior to starting. Prepare your workspace and any tools or parts that may be needed to complete the task. When directed by your supervisor/instructor, begin the procedure to complete the task and check the box as each step is finished.

Note: This tasksheet may require the student to check the condition of miscellaneous vehicle fluids, some of which may be flammable and could damage the environment or cause health problems if not handled properly. Observe all safety precautions and follow local regulations for the proper disposal of fluids.

Procedure:	Step Completed
1. Connect the EST(s) and check for active codes as outlined in the manufacturer's workshop materials. (**Note:** If no codes are active, have instructor install a bug.)	
a. EST type:	☐
b. Code description:	☐
c. Lamp color associated with active code:	☐
d. Parameter identifier (PID) associated with active code:	☐
e. Suspect parameter number (SPN) associated with active code:	☐
f. Failure mode identifier (FMI) associated with active code:	☐
g. Occurrence count(s) (OC) associated with active code:	☐
h. List condition(s) present at the time code became active (e.g., temperature, rpm, pressure):	☐

i. Condition(s) for setting fault code:	☐
j. Action(s) taken when the fault code is active:	☐
k. Condition(s) for clearing fault code:	☐
2. Diagnose the active fault code using the EST and a digital volt-ohmmeter (DVOM) as outlined in the manufacturer's workshop materials.	
a. Step 1, record procedure and results:	☐
b. Step 2, record procedure and results:	☐
c. Step 3, record procedure and results:	☐
d. Step 4, record procedure and results:	☐
e. Step 5, record procedure and results:	☐
f. Step 6, record procedure and results:	☐

	Step Completed
g. Step 7, record procedure and results:	☐
h. Step 8, record procedure and results:	☐
i. Step 9, record procedure and results:	☐
j. Step 10, record procedure and results:	☐
3. Discuss your findings with your supervisor/instructor.	☐

Non-Task-Specific Evaluations:	Step Completed
1. Tools and equipment were used as directed and returned in good working order.	☐
2. Complied with all general and task-specific safety standards, including proper use of any personal protection equipment.	☐
3. Completed the task in an appropriate time frame (recommendation: 1.5 or 2 times the flat rate).	☐
4. Left the workspace clean and orderly.	☐
5. Cared for customer property and returned it undamaged.	☐

Student signature _____ Date _____

Comments:

Have your supervisor/instructor verify satisfactory completion of this procedure, any observations made, and any necessary action(s) recommended.

Evaluation Instructions: The scoring box below is intended to act as a guide for both student and supervisor/instructor. Each criterion listed will help students to understand what is expected of them and help supervisors/instructors articulate the level of success at a particular task. The scoring is set up to allow a second attempt at each task (see the Test and Retest columns). Scoring is also designed to award students points only for task criteria that were completed correctly. Points are lost for failure to complete the employability requirements (see Non-Task-Specific Evaluation criteria). When all criteria are evaluated, tally the points for a total at the bottom of each column.

Tasksheet Scoring

Evaluation Items	Test		Retest	
	Pass	Fail	Pass	Fail
Task-Specific Evaluation	**(1 pt)**	**(0 pts)**	**(1 pt)**	**(0 pts)**
Student properly connected EST.				
Student properly identified code description, lamp color, PID, SPN, FMI, and OC.				
Student properly identified condition(s) for setting and clearing code.				
Student properly diagnosed fault code.				
Non-Task-Specific Evaluation	**(0 pts)**	**(−1 pt)**	**(0 pts)**	**(−1 pt)**
Student successfully completed at least three of the non-task-specific steps.				
Student successfully completed all five of the non-task-specific steps.				
Total Score: <total # of points/4 = %>				

Supervisor/Instructor:

Supervisor/instructor signature _____ Date _____

Comments:

```



```

Retest supervisor/instructor signature _____ Date _____

Comments:

```



```

CDX Tasksheet Number: MHT5A010

Student/Intern Information

Name _____ Date _____ Class _____

Vehicle, Customer, and Service Information

Vehicle used for this activity:

Year _____ Make _____ Model _____

Odometer _____ VIN _____

Materials Required

- Vehicle with possible engine concern
- Engine manufacturer's workshop materials
- Manufacturer-specific tools depending on the concern/procedure(s)
- Vehicle/component lifting equipment, if applicable

Task-Specific Safety Considerations

- Activities may require test-driving the vehicle on the school grounds or on a hoist, both of which carry severe risks. Attempt this task only with full permission from your supervisor/instructor, and follow all the guidelines exactly.
- Lifting equipment and machines such as vehicle jacks and stands, vehicle hoists, and engine hoists are important tools that increase productivity and make the job easier. However, they can also cause severe injury or death if used improperly. Make sure you follow the manufacturer's operation procedures. Also make sure you have your supervisor's/instructor's permission to use any particular type of lifting equipment.
- Comply with personal and environmental safety practices associated with clothing; eye protection; hand tools; power equipment; proper ventilation; and the handling, storage, and disposal of chemicals/materials in accordance with federal, state, and local regulations.
- Always wear the correct protective eyewear and clothing and use the appropriate safety equipment, as well as wheel chocks, fender covers, seat protectors, and floor mat protectors.
- Make sure you understand and observe all legislative and personal safety procedures when carrying out practical assignments. If you are unsure of what these are, ask your supervisor/instructor.

▶ **TASK** Diagnose faults in the data bus communication network; determine needed action.

MTST
V.A.10; P2

Time off_____

Time on_____

Total time_____

Student Instructions: Read through the entire procedure prior to starting. Prepare your workspace and any tools or parts that may be needed to complete the task. When directed by your supervisor/instructor, begin the procedure to complete the task and check the box as each step is finished.

Note: This tasksheet may require the student to check the condition of miscellaneous vehicle fluids, some of which may be flammable and could damage the environment or cause health problems if not handled properly. Observe all safety precautions and follow local regulations for the proper disposal of fluids.

Procedure:	Step Completed
1. Perform the following voltage checks of a vehicle's data bus at the 9-pin data-link connector (DLC) with a digital volt-ohmmeter (DVOM) as outlined in the manufacturer's workshop materials.	☐
2. Pin A to Pin B Specification: _____ volts Results: _____ volts	
a. Within manufacturer's specifications: Yes: ☐ No: ☐	☐
b. If No, describe the recommended corrective action(s):	☐
3. Pin A to Pin D Specification: _____ volts Results: _____ volts	
a. Within manufacturer's specifications: Yes: ☐ No: ☐	☐
b. If No, describe the recommended corrective action(s):	☐
4. Pin A to Pin C Specification: _____ volts Results: _____ volts	
a. Within manufacturer's specifications: Yes: ☐ No: ☐	☐
b. If No, describe the recommended corrective action(s):	☐
5. Pin A to Pin E Specification: _____ volts Results: _____ volts	
a. Within manufacturer's specifications: Yes: ☐ No: ☐	☐

b. If No, describe the recommended corrective action(s):	☐
6. Pin A to Pin F Specification: _____ volts Results: _____ volts	
a. Within manufacturer's specifications: Yes: ☐ No: ☐	☐
b. If No, describe the recommended corrective action(s):	☐
7. Pin A to Pin G Specification: _____ volts Results: _____ volts	
a. Within manufacturer's specifications: Yes: ☐ No: ☐	☐
b. If No, describe the recommended corrective action(s):	☐
8. Pin A to Pin H Specification: _____ volts Results: _____ volts	
a. Within manufacturer's specifications: Yes: ☐ No: ☐	☐
b. If No, describe the recommended corrective action(s):	☐
9. Perform the following resistance checks of a vehicle's data bus at the 9-pin DLC with a DVOM as outlined in the manufacturer's workshop materials. (**Note:** Disconnect battery[ies] before performing the following tests.)	
10. Pin F to Pin G Specification: _____ ohms Results: _____ ohms	

a. Within manufacturer's specifications: Yes: ☐ No: ☐	☐
b. If No, describe the recommended corrective action(s):	☐
11. Pin F to Pin A Specification: _____ ohms Results: _____ ohms	
a. Within manufacturer's specifications: Yes: ☐ No: ☐	☐
b. If No, describe the recommended corrective action(s):	☐
12. Pin G to Pin A Specification: _____ ohms Results: _____ ohms	
a. Within manufacturer's specifications: Yes: ☐ No: ☐	☐
b. If No, describe the recommended corrective action(s):	☐
13. Pin C to Pin D Specification: _____ ohms Results: _____ ohms	
a. Within manufacturer's specifications: Yes: ☐ No: ☐	☐
b. If No, describe the recommended corrective action(s):	☐
14. Pin C to Pin A Specification: _____ ohms Results: _____ ohms	
a. Within manufacturer's specifications: Yes: ☐ No: ☐	☐

	Step Completed
b. If No, describe the recommended corrective action(s):	☐

15. Pin D to Pin A
    Specification: _____ ohms
    Results: _____ ohms	

a. Within manufacturer's specifications: Yes: ☐ No: ☐	☐
b. If No, describe the recommended corrective action(s):	☐
16. Discuss your findings with your supervisor/instructor.	☐

Non-Task-Specific Evaluations:	Step Completed
1. Tools and equipment were used as directed and returned in good working order.	☐
2. Complied with all general and task-specific safety standards, including proper use of any personal protection equipment.	☐
3. Completed the task in an appropriate time frame (recommendation: 1.5 or 2 times the flat rate).	☐
4. Left the workspace clean and orderly.	☐
5. Cared for customer property and returned it undamaged.	☐

Student signature _____ Date _____

Comments:

Have your supervisor/instructor verify satisfactory completion of this procedure, any observations made, and any necessary action(s) recommended.

Evaluation Instructions: The scoring box below is intended to act as a guide for both student and supervisor/instructor. Each criterion listed will help students to understand what is expected of them and help supervisors/instructors articulate the level of success at a particular task. The scoring is set up to allow a second attempt at each task (see the Test and Retest columns). Scoring is also designed to award students points only for task criteria that were completed correctly. Points are lost for failure to complete the employability requirements (see Non-Task-Specific Evaluation criteria). When all criteria are evaluated, tally the points for a total at the bottom of each column.

Tasksheet Scoring

Evaluation Items	Test		Retest	
	Pass	Fail	Pass	Fail
Task-Specific Evaluation	**(1 pt)**	**(0 pts)**	**(1 pt)**	**(0 pts)**
Student properly used a DVOM.				
Student properly performed data-link voltage tests.				
Student properly performed data-link resistance tests.				
Student properly reconnected all disconnected batteries undamaged and in working order.				
Non-Task-Specific Evaluation	**(0 pts)**	**(−1 pt)**	**(0 pts)**	**(−1 pt)**
Student successfully completed at least three of the non-task-specific steps.				
Student successfully completed all five of the non-task-specific steps.				
Total Score: <total # of points/4 = %>				

Supervisor/Instructor:

Supervisor/instructor signature _____ Date _____

Comments:

Retest supervisor/instructor signature _____ Date _____

Comments:

CDX Tasksheet Number: MHT5A011

Student/Intern Information

Name _____ Date _____ Class _____

Vehicle, Customer, and Service Information

Vehicle used for this activity:

Year _____ Make _____ Model _____

Odometer _____ VIN _____

Materials Required
- Vehicle with possible engine concern
- Engine manufacturer's workshop materials
- Manufacturer-specific tools depending on the concern/procedure(s)
- Vehicle/component lifting equipment, if applicable

Task-Specific Safety Considerations
- Activities may require test-driving the vehicle on the school grounds or on a hoist, both of which carry severe risks. Attempt this task only with full permission from your supervisor/instructor, and follow all the guidelines exactly.
- Lifting equipment and machines such as vehicle jacks and stands, vehicle hoists, and engine hoists are important tools that increase productivity and make the job easier. However, they can also cause severe injury or death if used improperly. Make sure you follow the manufacturer's operation procedures. Also make sure you have your supervisor's/instructor's permission to use any particular type of lifting equipment.
- Comply with personal and environmental safety practices associated with clothing; eye protection; hand tools; power equipment; proper ventilation; and the handling, storage, and disposal of chemicals/materials in accordance with federal, state, and local regulations.
- Always wear the correct protective eyewear and clothing and use the appropriate safety equipment, as well as wheel chocks, fender covers, seat protectors, and floor mat protectors.
- Make sure you understand and observe all legislative and personal safety procedures when carrying out practical assignments. If you are unsure of what these are, ask your supervisor/instructor.

▶ **TASK** Identify electrical/electronic system components and configuration.

MTST V.A.11; P1

Time off_____

Time on_____

Total time_____

Student Instructions: Read through the entire procedure prior to starting. Prepare your workspace and any tools or parts that may be needed to complete the task. When directed by your supervisor/instructor, begin the procedure to complete the task and check the box as each step is finished.

Note: This tasksheet may require the student to check the condition of miscellaneous vehicle fluids, some of which may be flammable and could damage the environment or cause health problems if not handled properly. Observe all safety precautions and follow local regulations for the proper disposal of fluids.

Procedure:	Step Completed
1. Locate and record the location of the data-link connector (DLC) as out-lined in the manufacturer's workshop materials:	☐
2. Record the Society of Automotive Engineers (SAE) number of the DLC. SAE:	☐
3. Connect the electronic service tool (EST) as outlined in the manufacturer's workshop materials, and record the engine control module (ECM) serial number:	
a. Engine ECM location:☐	☐
b. Communication protocol:	☐
4. Record the location of the following sensors/actuators as outlined in the manufacturer's workshop materials.	
a. Engine coolant temperature sensor:	☐
b. Engine speed sensor temperature sensor:	☐
c. Variable-geometry turbo actuator:	☐

5. Connect the EST and record the transmission ECM serial number:	
a. Transmission ECM location:	☐
b. Communication protocol:	☐
6. Record the location of the following sensors as outlined in the manufacturer's workshop materials.	
a. Transmission temperature sensor:	☐
b. Transmission output speed sensor:	☐
c. Transmission main shaft speed sensor:	☐
7. Connect the EST and record the chassis/body ECM(s) serial number(s):	
a. Chassis(s) ECM(s) location(s):	☐
b. Communication protocol:	☐

8. Record the location of the following sensors/components as outlined in the manufacturer's workshop materials.	
a. Outside ambient air temperature sensor:	☐
b. Cab air temperature sensor:	☐
c. J1939 terminating resistors:	☐
9. Connect the EST and record any miscellaneous ECM(s) serial number(s):	
a. Miscellaneous ECM(s) location(s):	☐
b. Communication protocol:	☐
10. While referencing the manufacturer's workshop materials, inspect the vehicle's charging system and record the following:	
a. Alternator make/model:	☐
b. Alternator rating:	☐

11. While referencing the manufacturer's workshop materials, inspect the vehicle's starting system and record the following:	
a. Starter make/model:	☐
b. Battery size and rating:	☐
c. Battery configuration Series: ☐ Parallel: ☐	☐
12. Discuss your findings with your supervisor/instructor.	☐

Non-Task-Specific Evaluations:	Step Completed
1. Tools and equipment were used as directed and returned in good working order.	☐
2. Complied with all general and task-specific safety standards, including proper use of any personal protection equipment.	☐
3. Completed the task in an appropriate time frame (recommendation: 1.5 or 2 times the flat rate).	☐
4. Left the workspace clean and orderly.	☐
5. Cared for customer property and returned it undamaged.	☐

Student signature _____ Date _____

Comments:

Have your supervisor/instructor verify satisfactory completion of this procedure, any observations made, and any necessary action(s) recommended.

Evaluation Instructions: The scoring box below is intended to act as a guide for both student and supervisor/instructor. Each criterion listed will help students to understand what is expected of them and help supervisors/instructors articulate the level of success at a particular task. The scoring is set up to allow a second attempt at each task (see the Test and Retest columns). Scoring is also designed to award students points only for task criteria that were completed correctly. Points are lost for failure to complete the employability requirements (see Non-Task-Specific Evaluation criteria). When all criteria are evaluated, tally the points for a total at the bottom of each column.

Tasksheet Scoring

Evaluation Items	Test		Retest	
	Pass	**Fail**	**Pass**	**Fail**
Task-Specific Evaluation	**(1 pt)**	**(0 pts)**	**(1 pt)**	**(0 pts)**
Student properly recorded DLC location and SAE number.				
Student properly recorded engine, transmission, and chassis/body ECM serial numbers, location, and communication protocol.				
Student properly identified engine, transmission, and chassis/body sensors, engine actuator, and terminating resistors.				
Student properly identified alternator make/model/rating, starter make/model, and battery size/rating and configuration.				
Non-Task-Specific Evaluation	**(0 pts)**	**(−1 pt)**	**(0 pts)**	**(−1 pt)**
Student successfully completed at least three of the non-task-specific steps.				
Student successfully completed all five of the non-task-specific steps.				
Total Score: <total # of points/4 = %>				

CDX Tasksheet Number: MHT5A012

Student/Intern Information

Name _____ Date _____ Class _____

Vehicle, Customer, and Service Information

Vehicle used for this activity:

Year _____ Make _____ Model _____

Odometer _____ VIN _____

Materials Required

- Vehicle or simulator with electrical concerns
- Vehicle manufacturer's repair information, including schematic wiring diagrams
- Digital storage oscilloscope (DSO)

Task-Specific Safety Considerations

- Activities require you to measure electrical values. Always ensure that the supervisor/instructor checks test instrument connections prior to connecting power or taking measurements. High current flows can be dangerous; avoid accidental short circuits or grounding a battery's positive connections.
- Activities may require test-driving the vehicle on the school grounds or on a hoist, both of which carry severe risks. Attempt this task only with full permission from your supervisor/instructor, and follow all the guidelines exactly.
- Lifting equipment and machines such as vehicle jacks and stands, vehicle hoists, and engine hoists are important tools that increase productivity and make the job easier. However, they can also cause severe injury or death if used improperly. Make sure you follow the manufacturer's operation procedures. Also make sure you have your supervisor's/instructor's permission to use any particular type of lifting equipment.
- Comply with personal and environmental safety practices associated with clothing; eye protection; hand tools; power equipment; proper ventilation; and the handling, storage, and disposal of chemicals/materials in accordance with federal, state, and local regulations.
- Always wear the correct protective eyewear and clothing and use the appropriate safety equipment, as well as wheel chocks, fender covers, seat protectors, and floor mat protectors.
- Make sure you understand and observe all legislative and personal safety procedures when carrying out practical assignments. If you are unsure of what these are, ask your supervisor/instructor.

▶ **TASK** Check frequency, pulse width, and waveforms of electrical/electronic signals using appropriate test equipment; interpret readings; determine needed repairs.

MTST
V.A.12; P2

Time off_____

Time on_____

Total time_____

Student Instructions: Read through the entire procedure prior to starting. Prepare your workspace and any tools or parts that may be needed to complete the task. When directed by your supervisor/instructor, begin the procedure to complete the task and check the box as each step is finished.

Note: This tasksheet will require the use of a vehicle or simulator with an electrical fault. Ask your supervisor/instructor which vehicle or simulator you are to use.

Procedure:	Step Completed
1. Prepare the vehicle and/or circuit for the tests to be carried out.	☐
2. Using the appropriate service manual, research the correct procedures and list the steps:	☐
3. Carry out the tests using digital storage oscilloscope (DSO). The tests should include: • Frequency data • Pulse width • Output signal	

a. What are the frequency and pulse width?
 	
   Frequency: _____
 	
   Pulse width: _____
	☐

b. Within manufacturer's specifications: Yes: ☐ No: ☐	☐
c. List your findings:	☐
4. Determine any necessary action(s):	☐
5. Return the vehicle and/or circuit to its beginning condition, and return any tools you used to their proper locations.	☐
6. Discuss your findings with your supervisor/instructor.	☐

Non-Task-Specific Evaluations:	Step Completed
1. Tools and equipment were used as directed and returned in good working order.	☐
2. Complied with all general and task-specific safety standards, including proper use of any personal protection equipment.	☐
3. Completed the task in an appropriate time frame (recommendation: 1.5 or 2 times the flat rate).	☐
4. Left the workspace clean and orderly.	☐
5. Cared for customer property and returned it undamaged.	☐

Student signature _____ Date _____

Comments:

Have your supervisor/instructor verify satisfactory completion of this procedure, any observations made, and any necessary action(s) recommended.

Evaluation Instructions: The scoring box below is intended to act as a guide for both student and supervisor/instructor. Each criterion listed will help students to understand what is expected of them and help supervisors/instructors articulate the level of success at a particular task. The scoring is set up to allow a second attempt at each task (see the Test and Retest columns). Scoring is also designed to award students points only for task criteria that were completed correctly. Points are lost for failure to complete the employability requirements (see Non-Task-Specific Evaluation criteria). When all criteria are evaluated, tally the points for a total at the bottom of each column.

Tasksheet Scoring

Evaluation Items	Test		Retest	
	Pass	**Fail**	**Pass**	**Fail**
Task-Specific Evaluation	**(1 pt)**	**(0 pts)**	**(1 pt)**	**(0 pts)**
Student used the appropriate service information to research the correct procedures and list the steps.				
Student correctly carried out frequency data, pulse width, and output signal tests using a DSO.				
Student accurately determined any necessary actions.				
Student reinstalled all removed components undamaged and in working order.				
Non-Task-Specific Evaluation	**(0 pts)**	**(−1 pt)**	**(0 pts)**	**(−1 pt)**
Student successfully completed at least three of the non-task-specific steps.				
Student successfully completed all five of the non-task-specific steps.				
Total Score: <total # of points/4 = %>				

CDX Tasksheet Number: MHT5A013

Student/Intern Information

Name _____ Date _____ Class _____

Vehicle, Customer, and Service Information

Vehicle used for this activity:

Year _____ Make _____ Model _____

Odometer _____ VIN _____

Materials Required

- Vehicle with possible engine concern
- Engine manufacturer's workshop materials
- Manufacturer-specific tools depending on the concern/procedure(s)
- Vehicle/component lifting equipment, if applicable

Task-Specific Safety Considerations

- Activities may require test-driving the vehicle on the school grounds or on a hoist, both of which carry severe risks. Attempt this task only with full permission from your supervisor/instructor, and follow all the guidelines exactly.
- Lifting equipment and machines such as vehicle jacks and stands, vehicle hoists, and engine hoists are important tools that increase productivity and make the job easier. However, they can also cause severe injury or death if used improperly. Make sure you follow the manufacturer's operation procedures. Also make sure you have your supervisor's/instructor's permission to use any particular type of lifting equipment.
- Comply with personal and environmental safety practices associated with clothing; eye protection; hand tools; power equipment; proper ventilation; and the handling, storage, and disposal of chemicals/materials in accordance with federal, state, and local regulations.
- Always wear the correct protective eyewear and clothing and use the appropriate safety equipment, as well as wheel chocks, fender covers, seat protectors, and floor mat protectors.
- Make sure you understand and observe all legislative and personal safety procedures when carrying out practical assignments. If you are unsure of what these are, ask your supervisor/instructor.

▶ **TASK** CUnderstand the process for software transfer, software updates, and/or reprogramming of electronic modules.

MTST
V.A.13; P3

Student Instructions: Read through the entire procedure prior to starting. Prepare your workspace and any tools or parts that may be needed to complete the task. When directed by your supervisor/instructor, begin the procedure to complete the task and check the box as each step is finished.

Time off_____

Time on_____

Total time_____

© 2021 Jones & Bartlett Learning, LLC, an Ascend Learning Company

Note: This tasksheet may require the student to check the condition of miscellaneous vehicle fluids, some of which may be flammable and could damage the environment or cause health problems if not handled properly. Observe all safety precautions and follow local regulations for the proper disposal of fluids.

Procedure:	Step Completed
1. List the control module to be updated/reprogrammed as outlined in the manufacturer's workshop materials:	☐
2. Connect the electronic service tool (EST) as outlined in the manufacturer's workshop materials, and check for any diagnostic trouble codes (DTC) that may prevent a control module update or reprogram.	
a. Within manufacturer's specifications Yes: ☐ No: ☐	☐
b. If No, describe the recommended corrective action(s):	☐
3. Record the procedure for updating/reprogramming the selected control module as outlined in the manufacturer's workshop materials:	☐
4. Record any special precautions when updating/reprogramming the selected control module:	☐
5. Record any customer-specific settings/parameters in the control module to be updated/reprogrammed:	☐
6. Record the current calibration code:	☐

7. Record the new calibration code:	☐
8. While referencing the EST, perform a control module update/reprogram.	
a. Within manufacturer's specifications: Yes: ☐ No: ☐	☐
b. If No, describe the recommended corrective action(s):	☐
9. Check for any DTCs that may have occurred after the control module was updated/reprogrammed as outlined in the manufacturer's workshop materials.	
a. Within manufacturer's specifications: Yes: ☐ No: ☐	☐
b. If No, describe the recommended corrective action(s):	☐
10. Reset any customer-specific settings/parameters as outlined in the manufacturer's workshop materials.	
a. Within manufacturer's specifications: Yes: ☐ No: ☐	☐
b. If No, describe the recommended corrective action(s):	☐
11. Discuss your findings with your supervisor/instructor.	☐

Non-Task-Specific Evaluations:	Step Completed
1. Tools and equipment were used as directed and returned in good working order.	☐
2. Complied with all general and task-specific safety standards, including proper use of any personal protection equipment.	☐
3. Completed the task in an appropriate time frame (recommendation: 1.5 or 2 times the flat rate).	☐
4. Left the workspace clean and orderly.	☐
5. Cared for customer property and returned it undamaged.	☐

Student signature _____ Date _____

Comments:

Have your supervisor/instructor verify satisfactory completion of this procedure, any observations made, and any necessary action(s) recommended.

Evaluation Instructions: The scoring box below is intended to act as a guide for both student and supervisor/instructor. Each criterion listed will help students to understand what is expected of them and help supervisors/instructors articulate the level of success at a particular task. The scoring is set up to allow a second attempt at each task (see the Test and Retest columns). Scoring is also designed to award students points only for task criterion that were completed correctly. Points are lost for failure to complete the employability requirements (see Non-Task-Specific Evaluation criteria). When all criteria are evaluated, tally the points for a total at the bottom of each column.

Tasksheet Scoring

Evaluation Items	Test		Retest	
	Pass	Fail	Pass	Fail
Task-Specific Evaluation	**(1 pt)**	**(0 pts)**	**(1 pt)**	**(0 pts)**
Student properly retrieved DTCs before and after control module was updated/reprogrammed.				
Student properly recorded control module update/reprogram procedure and special precautions.				
Student properly recorded current and new calibration codes and preformed control module update/reprogramming.				
Student properly recorded and reset customer-specific settings/parameters after update/reprogram.				
Non-Task-Specific Evaluation	**(0 pts)**	**(−1 pt)**	**(0 pts)**	**(−1 pt)**
Student successfully completed at least three of the non-task-specific steps.				
Student successfully completed all five of the non-task-specific steps.				
Total Score: <total # of points/4 = %>				

Supervisor/Instructor:

Supervisor/instructor signature _____ Date _____

Comments:

Retest supervisor/instructor signature _____ Date _____

Comments:

V.B Electrical/Electronic Systems: Battery System

Learning Objective/Task	CDX Tasksheet Number	ASE Foundation MTST Reference Number; Priority Level
• Identify battery type and system configuration.	MHT5B001	V.B.1; P-1
• Confirm proper battery capacity for application; perform battery state-of-charge test; perform battery capacity test; determine needed action.	MHT5B002	V.B.2; P-1
• Inspect battery, battery cables, connectors, battery boxes, mounts, and hold-downs; determine needed action.	MHT5B003	V.B.3; P-1
• Charge battery using appropriate method for battery type.	MHT5B004	V.B.4; P-1
• Jump-start vehicle using a booster battery and jumper cables or using an appropriate auxiliary power supply.	MHT5B005	V.B.5; P-1
• Check low-voltage disconnect (LVD) systems; determine needed action.	MHT5B006	V.B.6; P-1
• Inspect, clean, and service battery; replace as needed.	MHT5B007	V.B.7; P-1
• Inspect and clean battery boxes, mounts, and hold-downs; repair or replace as needed.	MHT5B008	V.B.8; P-1
• Inspect, test and clean battery cables and connectors; repair or replace as needed.	MHT5B009	V.B.9; P-1
• Identify electrical/electronic modules, radios, and other accessories that require reinitialization or code entry after reconnecting vehicle battery.	MHT5B010	V.B.10; P-2

Materials Required

- Vehicle with possible battery concern
- Vehicle manufacturer's workshop materials
- Battery load tester, Digital volt-ohmmeter (DVOM), conductance/capacitance tester, slow and fast chargers, jumper cables, and booster battery
- Manufacturer-specific tools depending on the concern/procedure(s)
- Personal protection equipment (PPE)
- Vehicle manufacturer's repair information
- Vehicle/component lifting equipment, if applicable

Safety Considerations

- Activities may require test-driving the vehicle on the school grounds or on a hoist, both of which carry severe risks. Attempt this task only with full permission from your supervisor/instructor, and follow all the guidelines exactly.
- Lifting equipment and machines such as vehicle jacks and stands, vehicle hoists, and engine hoists are important tools that increase productivity and make the job easier. However, they can also cause severe injury or death if used improperly. Make sure you follow the manufacturer's operation procedures. Also make sure you have your supervisor's/instructor's permission to use any particular type of lifting equipment.

- While working on the vehicle, wheel chocks must be placed on both sides of one set of tires or as directed by your supervisor/instructor.
- Exhaust evacuation hoses must be placed over the exhaust outlets while the engine is used in a confined shop space.
- Diagnosis of this fault may require running the engine and managing an environment of dangerous gases and chemicals that carry severe risks. Attempt this task only with full permission from your supervisor/instructor, and follow all the guidelines exactly.
- Use extreme caution when working around batteries. Immediately remove any electrolyte that may come in contact with you. Electrolyte is a mixture of sulfuric acid and water. Batteries may produce explosive mixtures of gas containing hydrogen; avoid creating any sparks around batteries. Please consult with the shop safety and emergency procedures when working with or around batteries.
- Make sure you follow the manufacturer's operation procedures. Also make sure you have your supervisor's/instructor's permission to use any particular type of lifting equipment.
- Comply with personal and environmental safety practices associated with clothing; eye protection; hand tools; power equipment; proper ventilation; and the handling, storage, and disposal of chemicals/materials in accordance with federal, state, and local regulations.
- Always wear the correct protective eyewear and clothing and use the appropriate safety equipment, as well as wheel chocks, fender covers, seat protectors, and floor mat protectors.
- Make sure you understand and observe all legislative and personal safety procedures when carrying out practical assignments. If you are unsure of what these are, ask your supervisor/instructor.

CDX Tasksheet Number: MHT5B001

Student/Intern Information

Name _____ Date _____ Class _____

Vehicle, Customer, and Service Information

Vehicle used for this activity:

Year _____ Make _____ Model _____

Odometer _____ VIN _____

Materials Required
- Vehicle with possible battery concern
- Vehicle manufacturer's repair information
- Manufacturer-specific tools depending on the concern/procedure(s)

Task-Specific Safety Considerations
- Activities may require test-driving the vehicle on the school grounds or on a hoist, both of which carry severe risks. Attempt this task only with full permission from your supervisor/instructor, and follow all the guidelines exactly.
- Comply with personal and environmental safety practices associated with clothing; eye protection; hand tools; power equipment; proper ventilation; and the handling, storage, and disposal of chemicals/materials in accordance with federal, state, and local regulations.
- Always wear the correct protective eyewear and clothing and use the appropriate safety equipment, as well as fender covers, seat protectors, and floor mat protectors.
- Make sure you understand and observe all legislative and personal safety procedures when carrying out practical assignments. If you are unsure of what these are, ask your supervisor/instructor.
- While working on the vehicle, wheel chocks must be placed on both sides of one set of tires or as directed by your supervisor/instructor.
- Exhaust evacuation hoses must be placed over the exhaust outlets while the engine is used in a confined shop space.

▶ **TASK** Identify battery type and system configuration. **MTST** *V.B.1; P 1*

Time off_____

Time on_____

Student Instructions: Read through the entire procedure prior to starting. Prepare your workspace and any tools or parts that may be needed to complete the task. When directed by your supervisor/instructor, begin the procedure to complete the task and check the box as each step is finished.

Total time_____

Procedure:	Step Completed
1. Using the appropriate service manual, research and confirm proper battery type and system configuration for the vehicle application.	
a. List the specifications:	☐
2. Identify battery type.	
a. Flooded cell, including low-maintenance or maintenance-free and deep-cycle flooded cell.	☐
b. Sealed lead-acid (SLA) or recombinant battery.	☐
c. Flooded, gel cell, absorbed glass mat (AGM), and spiral cell (Optima batteries) are classified as sealed batteries.	☐
3. Identify battery system configuration.	
a. Manufacturers build their batteries to an internationally adopted Battery Council International (BCI) group number. BCI group numbers are established according to the physical case size, terminal placement, terminal type, and polarity. See Figures 1 and 2.	☐

LPT

Low Profile Terminal

HPT

High Profile Terminal

WNT

Wingnut Terminal

AP

Automotive Post Terminal

UT

Universal Terminal

DT

Automotive Post and Stud Terminal

ST

Stud Terminal

DWNT

Dual Wingnut Terminal

LT

L - Terminal

BCI Group Size	Length (mm)	Width (mm)	Height (mm)	Length (inches)	Width (inches)	Height (inches)	
4D	527	222	250	20 3/4	8 3/4	9 7/8	
6D	527	254	260	20 3/4	10	10 1/4	
8D	527	283	250	20 3/4	11 1/8	9 7/8	
28	261	173	240	10 5/16	6 13/16	9 7/16	
29H	334	171	232	13 1/8	6 3/4	9 1/8 10	
30H	343	173	235	13 1/2	6 13/16	9 1/4 10	
31	330	173	240	13	6 13/18	9 7/16	
4. Within manufacturer's specifications: Yes: ☐ No: ☐							
5. Return the vehicle/simulator to its beginning condition, and return any tools you used to their proper locations.							☐
6. Discuss your findings with your supervisor/instructor.							☐

Non-Task-Specific Evaluations:	Step Completed
1. Tools and equipment were used as directed and returned in good working order.	☐
2. Complied with all general and task-specific safety standards, including proper use of any personal protection equipment.	☐
3. Completed the task in an appropriate time frame (recommendation: 1.5 or 2 times the flat rate).	☐
4. Left the workspace clean and orderly.	☐
5. Cared for customer property and returned it undamaged.	☐

Student signature _____ Date _____

Comments:

Have your supervisor/instructor verify satisfactory completion of this procedure, any observations made, and any necessary action(s) recommended.

Evaluation Instructions: The scoring box below is intended to act as a guide for both student and supervisor/instructor. Each criterion listed will help students to understand what is expected of them and help supervisors/instructors articulate the level of success at a particular task. The scoring is set up to allow a second attempt at each task (see the Test and Retest columns). Scoring is also designed to award students points only for task criteria that were completed correctly. Points are lost for failure to complete the employability requirements (see Non-Task-Specific Evaluation criteria). When all criteria are evaluated, tally the points for a total at the bottom of each column.

Tasksheet Scoring

Evaluation Items	Test		Retest	
	Pass	**Fail**	**Pass**	**Fail**
Task-Specific Evaluation	**(1 pt)**	**(0 pts)**	**(1 pt)**	**(0 pts)**
Student detailed the 3 Cs on the submitted repair order.				
Student correctly displayed use of manufacturer's repair information.				
Student properly performed diagnostic measurements and drew appropriate conclusions based on diagnostics.				
Student completed repairs as directed by instructor.				
Non-Task-Specific Evaluation	**(0 pts)**	**(−1 pt)**	**(0 pts)**	**(−1 pt)**
Student successfully completed at least three of the non-task-specific steps.				
Student successfully completed all five of the non-task-specific steps.				
Total Score: <total # of points/4 = %>				

Supervisor/Instructor:

Supervisor/instructor signature _____ Date _____

Comments:

Retest supervisor/instructor signature _____ Date _____

Comments:

CDX Tasksheet Number: MHT5B002

Student/Intern Information

Name _____ Date _____ Class _____

Vehicle, Customer, and Service Information

Vehicle used for this activity:

Year _____ Make _____ Model _____

Odometer _____ VIN _____

Materials Required

- Vehicle with possible battery concern
- Vehicle manufacturer's workshop materials
- Digital volt-ohmmeter (DVOM), conductance/capacitance tester
- Personal protection equipment (PPE)

Task-Specific Safety Considerations

- Diagnosis of this fault may require running the engine and managing an environment of dangerous gases and chemicals that carry severe risks. Attempt this task only with full permission from your supervisor/instructor, and follow all the guidelines exactly.
- Use extreme caution when working around batteries. Immediately remove any electrolyte that may come in contact with you. Electrolyte is a mixture of sulfuric acid and water. Batteries may produce explosive mixtures of gas containing hydrogen; avoid creating any sparks around batteries. Please consult with the shop safety and emergency procedures when working with or around batteries.
- Make sure you follow the manufacturer's operation procedures. Also make sure you have your supervisor's/instructor's permission to use any particular type of lifting equipment.
- Comply with personal and environmental safety practices associated with clothing; eye protection; hand tools; power equipment; proper ventilation; and the handling, storage, and disposal of chemicals/materials in accordance with federal, state, and local regulations.
- Always wear the correct protective eyewear and clothing, and use the appropriate safety equipment, as well as wheel chocks, fender covers, seat protectors, and floor mat protectors.
- Make sure you understand and observe all legislative and personal safety procedures when carrying out practical assignments. If you are unsure of what these are, ask your supervisor/instructor.

▶ TASK   Confirm proper battery capacity for application; perform battery state-of-charge test; perform battery capacity test; determine needed action.

MTST *V.B.2; P1*

Time off_____

Time on_____

Student Instructions: Read through the entire procedure prior to starting. Prepare your workspace and any tools or parts that may be needed to complete the task. When directed by your supervisor/instructor, begin the procedure to complete the task and check the box as each step is finished.

Total time_____

Note: This tasksheet will require the use of a vehicle or simulator with an electrical fault. Ask your supervisor/instructor which vehicle or simulator you are to use.

Procedure:	Step Completed
1. Locate "Open-Circuit Voltage Test" (to measure battery state-of-charge) in the assigned vehicle service manual. List the steps for this procedure: (**Note:** Open-circuit voltage testing should not be used to make a final determination for battery replacement.)	☐
2. Make sure the engine is off and the battery is stabilized. If the battery has just been recharged, you must load test the battery to remove the surface charge. Turning the headlights on for 30 seconds can be used to remove the surface charge of a battery. Wait at least 10 minutes after the load test before measuring the open-circuit voltage. Follow the manufacturer's recommendations closely.	☐
3. Prepare the DVOM to measure voltage.	☐
4. Measure the battery voltage with the meter. Place the red lead on the positive post/terminal and the black lead on the negative post/terminal.	
a. Measured voltage (state-of-charge) of the battery: _____ volts	☐
5. The chart below represents the state-of-charge of the battery. Please mark the state of charge of the battery as it relates to the voltage measured.	☐

12.6V or greater	100% charge	
12.4–12.6V	75–100% charge	
12.2–12.4V	50–75% charge	
12.0–12.2V	25–50% charge	
11.7–12.0V	0–25% charge	
11.7–0.0V	0% or no charge	

6. Connect the digital battery analyzer to the vehicle. Place the red lead on the positive post/terminal and the black lead on the negative post/terminal. Follow the on-screen prompts to test battery conductance.	
a. Describe test results:	☐
7. Determine any necessary action(s):	☐

	Step Completed
8. Return the vehicle/simulator to its beginning condition, and return any tools you used to their proper locations.	☐
9. Discuss your findings with your supervisor/instructor.	☐

Non-Task-Specific Evaluations:	Step Completed
1. Tools and equipment were used as directed and returned in good working order.	☐
2. Complied with all general and task-specific safety standards, including proper use of any personal protection equipment.	☐
3. Completed the task in an appropriate time frame (recommendation: 1.5 or 2 times the flat rate).	☐
4. Left the workspace clean and orderly.	☐
5. Cared for customer property and returned it undamaged.	☐

Student signature _____ Date _____

Comments:

Have your supervisor/instructor verify satisfactory completion of this procedure, any observations made, and any necessary action(s) recommended.

Evaluation Instructions: The scoring box below is intended to act as a guide for both student and supervisor/instructor. Each criterion listed will help students to understand what is expected of them and help supervisors/instructors articulate the level of success at a particular task. The scoring is set up to allow a second attempt at each task (see the Test and Retest columns). Scoring is also designed to award students points only for task criteria that were completed correctly. Points are lost for failure to complete the employability requirements (see Non-Task-Specific Evaluation criteria). When all criteria are evaluated, tally the points for a total at the bottom of each column.

Tasksheet Scoring

Evaluation Items	Test		Retest	
	Pass	**Fail**	**Pass**	**Fail**
Task-Specific Evaluation	**(1 pt)**	**(0 pts)**	**(1 pt)**	**(0 pts)**
Student used the appropriate service information to research how to conduct "Open-Circuit Voltage Test" and measure battery state-of-charge.				
Student successfully performed battery capacitance test.				
Student used a digital multimeter (DMM) and digital battery analyzer as directed and required.				
Student reinstalled all removed components undamaged and in working order.				
Non-Task-Specific Evaluation	**(0 pts)**	**(−1 pt)**	**(0 pts)**	**(−1 pt)**
Student successfully completed at least three of the non-task-specific steps.				
Student successfully completed all five of the non-task-specific steps.				
Total Score: <total # of points/4 = %>				

Supervisor/Instructor:

Supervisor/instructor signature _____ Date _____

Comments:

Retest supervisor/instructor signature _____ Date _____

Comments:

CDX Tasksheet Number: MHT5BOO3

Student/Intern Information

Name _____ Date _____ Class _____

Vehicle, Customer, and Service Information

Vehicle used for this activity:

Year _____ Make _____ Model _____

Odometer _____ VIN _____

Materials Required

- Vehicle with possible battery concern
- Vehicle manufacturer's workshop materials
- Personal protection equipment (PPE)

Task-Specific Safety Considerations

- Diagnosis of this fault may require running the engine and managing an environment of dangerous gases and chemicals that carry severe risks. Attempt this task only with full permission from your supervisor/instructor, and follow all the guidelines exactly.
- Use extreme caution when working around batteries. Immediately remove any electrolyte that may come in contact with you. Electrolyte is a mixture of sulfuric acid and water. Batteries may produce explosive mixtures of gas containing hydrogen; avoid creating any sparks around batteries. Please consult with the shop safety and emergency procedures when working with or around batteries.
- Make sure you follow the manufacturer's operation procedures. Also make sure you have your supervisor's/instructor's permission to use any particular type of lifting equipment.
- Comply with personal and environmental safety practices associated with clothing; eye protection; hand tools; power equipment; proper ventilation; and the handling, storage, and disposal of chemicals/materials in accordance with federal, state, and local regulations.
- Always wear the correct protective eyewear and clothing, and use the appropriate safety equipment, as well as wheel chocks, fender covers, seat protectors, and floor mat protectors.
- Make sure you understand and observe all legislative and personal safety procedures when carrying out practical assignments. If you are unsure of what these are, ask your supervisor/instructor.

▶ **TASK** Inspect battery, battery cables, connectors, battery boxes, mounts, and hold-downs; determine needed action.

MTST
V.B.3; P1

Time off_____

Time on_____

Total time_____

Student Instructions: Read through the entire procedure prior to starting. Prepare your workspace and any tools or parts that may be needed to complete the task. When directed by your supervisor/instructor, begin the procedure to complete the task and check the box as each step is finished.

Procedure:	Step Completed
1. Research the recommended inspection processes in the appropriate service manual or other available data.	☐
2. Inspect the battery. Note your observations:	☐
3. Inspect the battery cables and connectors. Note your observations:	☐
4. Inspect the battery boxes, mounts, and hold-downs. Note your observations:	☐
5. Discuss your findings with your supervisor/instructor.	☐

Non-Task-Specific Evaluations:	Step Completed
1. Tools and equipment were used as directed and returned in good working order.	☐
2. Complied with all general and task-specific safety standards, including proper use of any personal protection equipment.	☐
3. Completed the task in an appropriate time frame (recommendation: 1.5 or 2 times the flat rate).	☐
4. Left the workspace clean and orderly.	☐
5. Cared for customer property and returned it undamaged.	☐

Student signature _____ Date _____

Comments:

Have your supervisor/instructor verify satisfactory completion of this procedure, any observations made,

and any necessary action(s) recommended.

Evaluation Instructions: The scoring box below is intended to act as a guide for both student and supervisor/instructor. Each criterion listed will help students to understand what is expected of them and help supervisors/instructors articulate the level of success at a particular task. The scoring is set up to allow a second attempt at each task (see the Test and Retest columns). Scoring is also designed to award students points only for task criteria that were completed correctly. Points are lost for failure to complete the employability requirements (see Non-Task-Specific Evaluation criteria). When all criteria are evaluated, tally the points for a total at the bottom of each column.

Tasksheet Scoring

Evaluation Items	Test		Retest	
	Pass	**Fail**	**Pass**	**Fail**
Task-Specific Evaluation	**(1 pt)**	**(0 pts)**	**(1 pt)**	**(0 pts)**
Student used the appropriate service information to research how to inspect the battery, battery cables, connectors, battery boxes, mounts, and hold-downs.				
Student accurately inspected the battery.				
Student accurately inspected the battery cables, connectors, battery boxes, mounts, and hold-downs.				
Student reinstalled all removed components undamaged and in working order.				
Non-Task-Specific Evaluation	**(0 pts)**	**(−1 pt)**	**(0 pts)**	**(−1 pt)**
Student successfully completed at least three of the non-task-specific steps.				
Student successfully completed all five of the non-task-specific steps.				
Total Score: <total # of points/4 = %>				

Supervisor/Instructor:

Supervisor/instructor signature _____ Date _____

Comments:

Retest supervisor/instructor signature _____ Date _____

Comments:

CDX Tasksheet Number: MHT5B004

Student/Intern Information

Name _____ Date _____ Class _____

Vehicle, Customer, and Service Information

Vehicle used for this activity:

Year _____ Make _____ Model _____

Odometer _____ VIN _____

Materials Required
- Vehicle with possible battery concern
- Vehicle manufacturer's workshop materials
- Slow and fast chargers
- Personal protection equipment (PPE)

Task-Specific Safety Considerations
- Diagnosis of this fault may require running the engine and managing an environment of dangerous gases and chemicals that carry severe risks. Attempt this task only with full permission from your supervisor/instructor, and follow all the guidelines exactly.
- Use extreme caution when working around batteries. Immediately remove any electrolyte that may come in contact with you. Electrolyte is a mixture of sulfuric acid and water. Batteries may produce explosive mixtures of gas containing hydrogen; avoid creating any sparks around batteries. Please consult with the shop safety and emergency procedures when working with or around batteries.
- Make sure you follow the manufacturer's operation procedures. Also make sure you have your supervisor's/instructor's permission to use any particular type of lifting equipment.
- Comply with personal and environmental safety practices associated with clothing; eye protection; hand tools; power equipment; proper ventilation; and the handling, storage, and disposal of chemicals/materials in accordance with federal, state, and local regulations.
- Always wear the correct protective eyewear and clothing, and use the appropriate safety equipment, as well as wheel chocks, fender covers, seat protectors, and floor mat protectors.
- Make sure you understand and observe all legislative and personal safety procedures when carrying out practical assignments. If you are unsure of what these are, ask your supervisor/instructor.

▶TASK Charge battery using appropriate method for battery type. **MTST** V.B.4; P1

Time off_____

Time on_____

Student Instructions: Read through the entire procedure prior to starting. Prepare your workspace and any tools or parts that may be needed to complete the task. When directed by your supervisor/instructor, begin the procedure to complete the task and check the box as each step is finished.

Total time_____

Note: You may use either a vehicle with a discharged battery or an assigned battery that is out of a vehicle. Recharging a battery differs from manufacturer to manufacturer. It is important that you follow the recharging steps recommended by the manufacturer of the battery that is assigned to you. Be careful when attempting to charge a battery. Hooking the charger up incorrectly could cause injury to the eyes and skin.

Procedure:	Step Completed
1. Using the appropriate service manual, research slow and/or fast battery charging for this vehicle. Follow all directions.	
a. List the steps for recharging the battery:	☐
2. Method required for recharging the battery (slow charge or fast charge):	☐
3. List the steps for charging at the rate determined in Step 2:	☐
4. Have your supervisor/instructor check your steps for recharging the battery. Supervisor's/instructor's initials:	☐
5. Charge the battery according to the manufacturer's recommendations.	
a. Time battery took to charge:	☐
b. Highest amperage setting during charging: _____ amps	☐
c. Lowest amperage setting during charging: _____ amps	☐
d. Describe how you determined the battery was fully charged:	☐

6. Determine any necessary action(s):	☐
7. Return any tools you used to their proper locations.	☐
8. Discuss your findings with your supervisor/instructor.	☐

Non-Task-Specific Evaluations:	Step Completed
1. Tools and equipment were used as directed and returned in good working order.	☐
2. Complied with all general and task-specific safety standards, including proper use of any personal protection equipment.	☐
3. Completed the task in an appropriate time frame (recommendation: 1.5 or 2 times the flat rate).	☐
4. Left the workspace clean and orderly.	☐
5. Cared for customer property and returned it undamaged.	☐

Student signature _____ Date _____

Comments:

Have your supervisor/instructor verify satisfactory completion of this procedure, any observations made,

and any necessary action(s) recommended.

Evaluation Instructions: The scoring box below is intended to act as a guide for both student and supervisor/instructor. Each criterion listed will help students to understand what is expected of them and help supervisors/instructors articulate the level of success at a particular task. The scoring is set up to allow a second attempt at each task (see the Test and Retest columns). Scoring is also designed to award students points only for task criteria that were completed correctly. Points are lost for failure to complete the employability requirements (see Non-Task-Specific Evaluation criteria). When all criteria are evaluated, tally the points for a total at the bottom of each column.

Tasksheet Scoring

Evaluation Items	Test		Retest	
	Pass	Fail	Pass	Fail
Task-Specific Evaluation	**(1 pt)**	**(0 pts)**	**(1 pt)**	**(0 pts)**
Student used the appropriate service information to research how to charge the battery.				
Student properly charged the battery using the specified method.				
Student accurately determined any necessary actions.				
Student reinstalled all removed components undamaged and in working order.				
Non-Task-Specific Evaluation	**(0 pts)**	**(−1 pt)**	**(0 pts)**	**(−1 pt)**
Student successfully completed at least three of the non-task-specific steps.				
Student successfully completed all five of the non-task-specific steps.				
Total Score: <total # of points/4 = %>				

CDX Tasksheet Number: MHT5B005

Student/Intern Information

Name _____ Date _____ Class _____

Vehicle, Customer, and Service Information

Vehicle used for this activity:

Year _____ Make _____ Model _____

Odometer _____ VIN _____

Materials Required

- Vehicle with possible battery concern
- Vehicle manufacturer's workshop materials
- Jumper cables and booster battery
- Personal protection equipment (PPE)

Task-Specific Safety Considerations

- Diagnosis of this fault may require running the engine and managing an environment of dangerous gases and chemicals that carry severe risks. Attempt this task only with full permission from your supervisor/instructor, and follow all the guidelines exactly.
- Use extreme caution when working around batteries. Immediately remove any electrolyte that may come in contact with you. Electrolyte is a mixture of sulfuric acid and water. Batteries may produce explosive mixtures of gas containing hydrogen; avoid creating any sparks around batteries. Please consult with the shop safety and emergency procedures when working with or around batteries.
- Make sure you follow the manufacturer's operation procedures. Also make sure you have your supervisor's/instructor's permission to use any particular type of lifting equipment.
- Comply with personal and environmental safety practices associated with clothing; eye protection; hand tools; power equipment; proper ventilation; and the handling, storage, and disposal of chemicals/materials in accordance with federal, state, and local regulations.
- Always wear the correct protective eyewear and clothing, and use the appropriate safety equipment, as well as wheel chocks, fender covers, seat protectors, and floor mat protectors.
- Make sure you understand and observe all legislative and personal safety procedures when carrying out practical assignments. If you are unsure of what these are, ask your supervisor/instructor.

▶ TASK Jump-start vehicle using a booster battery and jumper cables or using an appropriate auxiliary power supply.   **MTST** *V.B.5; P1*

Time off _____

Time on _____

Student Instructions: Read through the entire procedure prior to starting. Prepare your workspace and any tools or parts that may be needed to complete the task. When directed by your supervisor/instructor, begin the procedure to complete the task and check the box as each step is finished.

Total time _____

Procedure:	Step Completed
1. Locate "Starting a Vehicle With a Dead Battery" or "Jump-Starting Procedures" in the appropriate service information for the vehicle you are working on. (**Note:** Some vehicle manufacturers prohibit jump-starting of their vehicles. If this is the case, inform your supervisor/instructor.)	☐
2. List the steps as outlined in the service information:	☐
3. Have your supervisor/instructor verify the steps for the vehicle assigned to you. Supervisor's/instructor's initials:	☐
4. Connect the jumper cables as outlined in the service information, or connect the auxiliary power supply (jump box) as outlined in the service information.	☐
5. Explain why the last connection to the dead battery is away from the battery, preferably on a nonpainted metal component on the engine:	☐
6. Start the engine.	☐
7. Remove the cables in the reverse order as they were installed.	☐
8. Return the vehicle/simulator to its beginning condition, and return any tools you used to their proper locations.	☐
9. Discuss your findings with your supervisor/instructor.	☐

Non-Task-Specific Evaluations:	Step Completed
1. Tools and equipment were used as directed and returned in good working order.	☐
2. Complied with all general and task-specific safety standards, including proper use of any personal protection equipment.	☐
3. Completed the task in an appropriate time frame (recommendation: 1.5 or 2 times the flat rate).	☐
4. Left the workspace clean and orderly.	☐
5. Cared for customer property and returned it undamaged.	☐

Student signature _____ Date _____

Comments:

Have your supervisor/instructor verify satisfactory completion of this procedure, any observations made, and any necessary action(s) recommended.

Evaluation Instructions: The scoring box below is intended to act as a guide for both student and supervisor/instructor. Each criterion listed will help students to understand what is expected of them and help supervisors/instructors articulate the level of success at a particular task. The scoring is set up to allow a second attempt at each task (see the Test and Retest columns). Scoring is also designed to award students points only for task criteria that were completed correctly. Points are lost for failure to complete the employability requirements (see Non-Task-Specific Evaluation criteria). When all criteria are evaluated, tally the points for a total at the bottom of each column.

Tasksheet Scoring

Evaluation Items	Test		Retest	
	Pass	**Fail**	**Pass**	**Fail**
Task-Specific Evaluation	**(1 pt)**	**(0 pts)**	**(1 pt)**	**(0 pts)**
Student used the appropriate service information to research how to jump-start a vehicle.				
Student connected the jumper cables as outlined in the service information or connected the auxiliary power supply (jump box) as was outlined in the service information.				
Student successfully jump-started the vehicle using a booster battery and jumper cables or using an appropriate auxiliary power supply.				
Student reinstalled all removed components undamaged and in working order.				
Non-Task-Specific Evaluation	**(0 pts)**	**(−1 pt)**	**(0 pts)**	**(−1 pt)**
Student successfully completed at least three of the non-task-specific steps.				
Student successfully completed all five of the non-task-specific steps.				
Total Score: <total # of points/4 = %>				

CDX Tasksheet Number: MHT5B006

Student/Intern Information

Name _____ Date _____ Class _____

Vehicle, Customer, and Service Information

Vehicle used for this activity:

Year _____ Make _____ Model _____

Odometer _____ VIN _____

Task-Specific Safety Considerations

- Diagnosis of this fault may require running the engine and managing an environment of dangerous gases and chemicals that carry severe risks. Attempt this task only with full permission from your supervisor/instructor, and follow all the guidelines exactly.
- Use extreme caution when working around batteries. Immediately remove any electrolyte that may come in contact with you. Electrolyte is a mixture of sulfuric acid and water. Batteries may produce explosive mixtures of gas containing hydrogen; avoid creating any sparks around batteries. Please consult with the shop safety and emergency procedures when working with or around batteries.
- Make sure you follow the manufacturer's operation procedures. Also make sure you have your supervisor's/instructor's permission to use any particular type of lifting equipment.
- Comply with personal and environmental safety practices associated with clothing; eye protection; hand tools; power equipment; proper ventilation; and the handling, storage, and disposal of chemicals/materials in accordance with federal, state, and local regulations.
- Always wear the correct protective eyewear and clothing, and use the appropriate safety equipment, as well as wheel chocks, fender covers, seat protectors, and floor mat protectors.
- Make sure you understand and observe all legislative and personal safety procedures when carrying out practical assignments. If you are unsure of what these are, ask your supervisor/instructor.

▶ **TASK** Check low-voltage disconnect (LVD) systems; determine needed action.

MTST
V.B.6; P1

Time off_____

Time on_____

Student Instructions: Read through the entire procedure prior to starting. Prepare your workspace and any tools or parts that may be needed to complete the task. When directed by your supervisor/instructor, begin the procedure to complete the task and check the box as each step is finished.

Note: LVDs are designed to protect batteries from excessive voltage draw.

Total time_____

Procedure:	Step Completed
1. Check to make sure that a corrosion inhibitor is present to prevent battery acid from corroding the connections. The corrosion inhibitor is usually mounted in the battery box.	
a. Inhibitor present? Yes: ☐ No: ☐	☐
b. If the inhibitor is not present, consult manufacturer's guidelines for the correct inhibitor to use.	☐
2. Connect a digital volt-ohmmeter (DVOM) or voltmeter to the sense terminal (depending on the model of the LVD) and the ground terminal.	☐
3. Connect a carbon pile or some way of creating a parasitic load to the battery. Monitor the voltage for a decrease and observe the set-point indicator light.	☐
4. When the indicator light switches from off to on, record the reading of the set point.	
a. Voltage recorded: _____ volts	☐
b. Manufacturer recommended set-point voltage: _____ volts	☐
c. If adjustment is necessary, consult and record manufacturer's guidelines for adjusting to the proper set-point voltage:	☐
5. Discuss your findings with your supervisor/instructor, and record any recommendations necessary:	☐

Non-Task-Specific Evaluations:	Step Completed
1. Tools and equipment were used as directed and returned in good working order.	☐
2. Complied with all general and task-specific safety standards, including proper use of any personal protection equipment.	☐
3. Completed the task in an appropriate time frame (recommendation: 1.5 or 2 times the flat rate).	☐
4. Left the workspace clean and orderly.	☐
5. Cared for customer property and returned it undamaged.	☐

Student signature _____ Date _____

Comments:

Have your supervisor/instructor verify satisfactory completion of this procedure, any observations made,

and any necessary action(s) recommended.

Evaluation Instructions: The scoring box below is intended to act as a guide for both student and supervisor/instructor. Each criterion listed will help students to understand what is expected of them and help supervisors/instructors articulate the level of success at a particular task. The scoring is set up to allow a second attempt at each task (see the Test and Retest columns). Scoring is also designed to award students points only for task criteria that were completed correctly. Points are lost for failure to complete the employability requirements (see Non-Task-Specific Evaluation criteria). When all criteria are evaluated, tally the points for a total at the bottom of each column.

Tasksheet Scoring

Evaluation Items	Test		Retest	
	Pass	**Fail**	**Pass**	**Fail**
Task-Specific Evaluation	**(1 pt)**	**(0 pts)**	**(1 pt)**	**(0 pts)**
Student checked for a corrosion inhibitor.				
Student successfully tested the LVD system using a DVOM and carbon pile tester.				
Student used the appropriate service information to research voltage set points and make adjustments as necessary.				
Student reinstalled all removed components undamaged and in working order.				
Non-Task-Specific Evaluation	**(0 pts)**	**(−1 pt)**	**(0 pts)**	**(−1 pt)**
Student successfully completed at least three of the non-task-specific steps.				
Student successfully completed all five of the non-task-specific steps.				
Total Score: <total # of points/4 = %>				

Supervisor/Instructor:

Supervisor/instructor signature _____ Date _____

Comments:

Retest supervisor/instructor signature _____ Date _____

Comments:

Student/Intern Information

Name _____ Date _____ Class _____

Vehicle, Customer, and Service Information

Vehicle used for this activity:

Year _____ Make _____ Model _____

Odometer _____ VIN _____

Materials Required

- Vehicle with possible battery concern
- Vehicle manufacturer's workshop materials
- Personal protection equipment (PPE)

Task-Specific Safety Considerations

- Diagnosis of this fault may require running the engine and managing an environment of dangerous gases and chemicals that carry severe risks. Attempt this task only with full permission from your supervisor/instructor, and follow all the guidelines exactly.
- Use extreme caution when working around batteries. Immediately remove any electrolyte that may come in contact with you. Electrolyte is a mixture of sulfuric acid and water. Batteries may produce explosive mixtures of gas containing hydrogen; avoid creating any sparks around batteries. Please consult with the shop safety and emergency procedures when working with or around batteries.
- Make sure you follow the manufacturer's operation procedures. Also make sure you have your supervisor's/instructor's permission to use any particular type of lifting equipment.
- Comply with personal and environmental safety practices associated with clothing; eye protection; hand tools; power equipment; proper ventilation; and the handling, storage, and disposal of chemicals/materials in accordance with federal, state, and local regulations.
- Always wear the correct protective eyewear and clothing, and use the appropriate safety equipment, as well as wheel chocks, fender covers, seat protectors, and floor mat protectors.
- Make sure you understand and observe all legislative and personal safety procedures when carrying out practical assignments. If you are unsure of what these are, ask your supervisor/instructor.

▶ **TASK** Inspect, clean, and service battery; replace as needed. **MTST** *V.B.7; P1*

Time off_____

Student Instructions: Read through the entire procedure prior to starting. Prepare your workspace and any tools or parts that may be needed to complete the task. When directed by your supervisor/instructor, begin the procedure to complete the task and check the box as each step is finished.

Time on_____

Total time_____

Procedure:	Step Completed
1. Prepare the vehicle/simulator for the task.	☐
2. Research the recommended process in the appropriate service manual or other available data. List the steps:	☐
3. Inspect, clean, and/or replace battery, as required. Note your observations:	☐
4. Determine any necessary further action(s):	☐
5. Return the vehicle/simulator to its beginning condition, and return any tools you used to their proper locations.	☐
6. Discuss your findings with your supervisor/instructor.	☐

Non-Task-Specific Evaluations:	Step Completed
1. Tools and equipment were used as directed and returned in good working order.	☐
2. Complied with all general and task-specific safety standards, including proper use of any personal protection equipment.	☐
3. Completed the task in an appropriate time frame (recommendation: 1.5 or 2 times the flat rate).	☐
4. Left the workspace clean and orderly.	☐
5. Cared for customer property and returned it undamaged.	☐

Student signature _____ Date _____

Comments:

Have your supervisor/instructor verify satisfactory completion of this procedure, any observations made,

and any necessary action(s) recommended.

Evaluation Instructions: The scoring box below is intended to act as a guide for both student and supervisor/instructor. Each criterion listed will help students to understand what is expected of them and help supervisors/instructors articulate the level of success at a particular task. The scoring is set up to allow a second attempt at each task (see the Test and Retest columns). Scoring is also designed to award students points only for task criteria that were completed correctly. Points are lost for failure to complete the employability requirements (see Non-Task-Specific Evaluation criteria). When all criteria are evaluated, tally the points for a total at the bottom of each column.

Tasksheet Scoring

Evaluation Items	Test		Retest	
	Pass	**Fail**	**Pass**	**Fail**
Task-Specific Evaluation	**(1 pt)**	**(0 pts)**	**(1 pt)**	**(0 pts)**
Student used the appropriate service information to research the recommended process in the appropriate service manual or other available data.				
Student successfully cleaned or replaced the battery as needed.				
Student accurately determined any necessary further actions.				
Student reinstalled all removed components undamaged and in working order.				
Non-Task-Specific Evaluation	**(0 pts)**	**(−1 pt)**	**(0 pts)**	**(−1 pt)**
Student successfully completed at least three of the non-task-specific steps.				
Student successfully completed all five of the non-task-specific steps.				
Total Score: <total # of points/4 = %>				

Supervisor/Instructor:

Supervisor/instructor signature _____ Date _____

Comments:

Retest supervisor/instructor signature _____ Date _____

Comments:

CDX Tasksheet Number: MHT5B008

Student/Intern Information

Name _____ Date _____ Class _____

Vehicle, Customer, and Service Information

Vehicle used for this activity:

Year _____ Make _____ Model _____

Odometer _____ VIN _____

> ## Materials Required
> - Vehicle with possible battery concern
> - Vehicle manufacturer's workshop materials
> - Personal protection equipment (PPE)

Task-Specific Safety Considerations
- Diagnosis of this fault may require running the engine and managing an environment of dangerous gases and chemicals that carry severe risks. Attempt this task only with full permission from your supervisor/instructor, and follow all the guidelines exactly.
- Use extreme caution when working around batteries. Immediately remove any electrolyte that may come in contact with you. Electrolyte is a mixture of sulfuric acid and water. Batteries may produce explosive mixtures of gas containing hydrogen; avoid creating any sparks around batteries. Please consult with the shop safety and emergency procedures when working with or around batteries.
- Make sure you follow the manufacturer's operation procedures. Also make sure you have your supervisor's/instructor's permission to use any particular type of lifting equipment.
- Comply with personal and environmental safety practices associated with clothing; eye protection; hand tools; power equipment; proper ventilation; and the handling, storage, and disposal of chemicals/materials in accordance with federal, state, and local regulations.
- Always wear the correct protective eyewear and clothing, and use the appropriate safety equipment, as well as wheel chocks, fender covers, seat protectors, and floor mat protectors.
- Make sure you understand and observe all legislative and personal safety procedures when carrying out practical assignments. If you are unsure of what these are, ask your supervisor/instructor.

▶ **TASK** Inspect and clean battery boxes, mounts, and hold-downs; repair or replace as needed. **MTST** *V.B.8; P1*

Time off_____

Time on_____

Student Instructions: Read through the entire procedure prior to starting. Prepare your workspace and any tools or parts that may be needed to complete the task. When directed by your supervisor/instructor, begin the procedure to complete the task and check the box as each step is finished.

Total time_____

© 2021 Jones & Bartlett Learning, LLC, an Ascend Learning Company

Procedure:	Step Completed
1. Research inspecting and cleaning battery boxes, mounts, and hold-downs.	☐
2. List the steps for inspecting and cleaning battery boxes, mounts, and hold-downs:	☐
3. Determine whether the battery should be removed to allow this task to be performed. Follow the manufacturer's recommendations.	☐
4. Inspect the battery hold-down hardware and the battery tray. List your findings and any recommendations you have:	☐
5. Clean the battery, battery tray, and hold-down hardware with a suitable cleaner or by mixing baking soda and water. Be careful when using baking soda as it is an acid neutralizer if introduced into the cells. (**Note:** The consistency of the baking soda and water should be like a paste. The use of a small brush will help the cleaning process.)	
a. Have your supervisor/instructor check your work. Supervisor's/instructor's initials:	☐
6. Rinse the components with clean water. Wipe the components dry. Do not use compressed air.	☐
7. Install the battery (if removed) and hold-down hardware. Reconnect the cables as outlined in the service information.	☐
8. Return any tools you used to their proper locations.	☐

Non-Task-Specific Evaluations:	Step Completed
1. Tools and equipment were used as directed and returned in good working order.	☐
2. Complied with all general and task-specific safety standards, including proper use of any personal protection equipment.	☐
3. Completed the task in an appropriate time frame (recommendation: 1.5 or 2 times the flat rate).	☐
4. Left the workspace clean and orderly.	☐
5. Cared for customer property and returned it undamaged.	☐

Student signature _____ Date _____

Comments:

Have your supervisor/instructor verify satisfactory completion of this procedure, any observations made, and any necessary action(s) recommended.

Evaluation Instructions: The scoring box below is intended to act as a guide for both student and supervisor/instructor. Each criterion listed will help students to understand what is expected of them and help supervisors/instructors articulate the level of success at a particular task. The scoring is set up to allow a second attempt at each task (see the Test and Retest columns). Scoring is also designed to award students points only for task criteria that were completed correctly. Points are lost for failure to complete the employability requirements (see Non-Task-Specific Evaluation criteria). When all criteria are evaluated, tally the points for a total at the bottom of each column.

Tasksheet Scoring

Evaluation Items	Test		Retest	
	Pass	Fail	Pass	Fail
Task-Specific Evaluation	**(1 pt)**	**(0 pts)**	**(1 pt)**	**(0 pts)**
Student used the appropriate service information to research inspecting and cleaning battery boxes, mounts, and hold-downs.				
Student accurately inspected the battery hold-down hardware and the battery tray.				
Student successfully cleaned the battery, battery tray, and hold-down hardware with a suitable cleaner or by mixing baking soda and water.				
Student reinstalled all removed components undamaged and in working order.				
Non-Task-Specific Evaluation	**(0 pts)**	**(−1 pt)**	**(0 pts)**	**(−1 pt)**
Student successfully completed at least three of the non-task-specific steps.				
Student successfully completed all five of the non-task-specific steps.				
Total Score: <total # of points/4 = %>				

Supervisor/Instructor:

Supervisor/instructor signature _____ Date _____

Comments:

Retest supervisor/instructor signature _____ Date _____

Comments:

CDX Tasksheet Number: MHT5B009

Student/Intern Information

Name _____ Date _____ Class _____

Vehicle, Customer, and Service Information

Vehicle used for this activity:

Year _____ Make _____ Model _____

Odometer _____ VIN _____

> ## Materials Required
> - Vehicle with possible battery concern
> - Vehicle manufacturer's workshop materials
> - Personal protection equipment (PPE)

Task-Specific Safety Considerations

- Diagnosis of this fault may require running the engine and managing an environment of dangerous gases and chemicals that carry severe risks. Attempt this task only with full permission from your supervisor/instructor, and follow all the guidelines exactly.
- Use extreme caution when working around batteries. Immediately remove any electrolyte that may come in contact with you. Electrolyte is a mixture of sulfuric acid and water. Batteries may produce explosive mixtures of gas containing hydrogen; avoid creating any sparks around batteries. Please consult with the shop safety and emergency procedures when working with or around batteries.
- Make sure you follow the manufacturer's operation procedures. Also make sure you have your supervisor's/instructor's permission to use any particular type of lifting equipment.
- Comply with personal and environmental safety practices associated with clothing; eye protection; hand tools; power equipment; proper ventilation; and the handling, storage, and disposal of chemicals/materials in accordance with federal, state, and local regulations.
- Always wear the correct protective eyewear and clothing, and use the appropriate safety equipment, as well as wheel chocks, fender covers, seat protectors, and floor mat protectors.
- Make sure you understand and observe all legislative and personal safety procedures when carrying out practical assignments. If you are unsure of what these are, ask your supervisor/instructor.

▶ **TASK** Inspect, test, and clean battery cables and connectors; repair or replace as needed.

MTST
V.B.9; P1

Time off_____

Time on_____

Total time_____

Student Instructions: Read through the entire procedure prior to starting. Prepare your workspace and any tools or parts that may be needed to complete the task. When directed by your supervisor/instructor, begin the procedure to complete the task and check the box as each step is finished.

Procedure:	Step Completed
1. Research inspecting, testing, cleaning, and repair or replacement of battery cables and connectors. List the steps:	☐
2. Determine whether the battery should be removed to allow this task to be performed. Follow the manufacturer's recommendations.	☐
3. Inspect the battery cables and connectors. List your findings and any recommendations you have:	☐
4. Clean the battery cables and connectors with a suitable cleaner or by mixing baking soda and water. (**Note:** The consistency of the baking soda and water should be like a paste. The use of a small brush will help the cleaning process.)	☐
5. Repair or replace the battery cables and connectors with suitable replacements as per the manufacturer's specifications.	☐
6. Have your supervisor/instructor check your work. Supervisor's/instructor's initials:	☐
7. Install the battery (if removed) and hold-down hardware. Reconnect the cables as outlined in the service information.	☐
8. Return any tools you used to their proper locations.	☐
9. Discuss your findings with your supervisor/the instructor.	☐

Non-Task-Specific Evaluations:	Step Completed
1. Tools and equipment were used as directed and returned in good working order.	☐
2. Complied with all general and task-specific safety standards, including proper use of any personal protection equipment.	☐
3. Completed the task in an appropriate time frame (recommendation: 1.5 or 2 times the flat rate).	☐
4. Left the workspace clean and orderly.	☐
5. Cared for customer property and returned it undamaged.	☐

Student signature _____ Date _____

Comments:

Have your supervisor/instructor verify satisfactory completion of this procedure, any observations made, and any necessary action(s) recommended.

Evaluation Instructions: The scoring box below is intended to act as a guide for both student and supervisor/instructor. Each criterion listed will help students to understand what is expected of them and help supervisors/instructors articulate the level of success at a particular task. The scoring is set up to allow a second attempt at each task (see the Test and Retest columns). Scoring is also designed to award students points only for task criteria that were completed correctly. Points are lost for failure to complete the employability requirements (see Non-Task-Specific Evaluation criteria). When all criteria are evaluated, tally the points for a total at the bottom of each column.

Tasksheet Scoring

Evaluation Items	Test		Retest	
	Pass	Fail	Pass	Fail
Task-Specific Evaluation	**(1 pt)**	**(0 pts)**	**(1 pt)**	**(0 pts)**
Student used the appropriate service information to research inspecting, testing, cleaning, and repair or replacement of battery cables and connectors.				
Student successfully cleaned the battery cables and connectors with a suitable cleaner or by mixing baking soda and water.				
Student properly repaired or replaced the battery cables and connectors with suitable replacements as per the manufacturer's specifications.				
Student reinstalled all removed components undamaged and in working order.				
Non-Task-Specific Evaluation	**(0 pts)**	**(−1 pt)**	**(0 pts)**	**(−1 pt)**
Student successfully completed at least three of the non-task-specific steps.				
Student successfully completed all five of the non-task-specific steps.				
Total Score: <total # of points/4 = %>				

Supervisor/Instructor:

Supervisor/instructor signature _____ Date _____

Comments:

Retest supervisor/instructor signature _____ Date _____

Comments:

CDX Tasksheet Number: MHT5B010

Student/Intern Information

Name _____ Date _____ Class _____

Vehicle, Customer, and Service Information

Vehicle used for this activity:

Year _____ Make _____ Model _____

Odometer _____ VIN _____

Materials Required

- Vehicle with possible battery concern
- Vehicle manufacturer's workshop materials
- Manufacturer-specific tools depending on the concern/procedure(s)
- Vehicle/component lifting equipment, if applicable

Task-Specific Safety Considerations

- Activities may require test-driving the vehicle on the school grounds or on a hoist, both of which carry severe risks. Attempt this task only with full permission from your supervisor/instructor, and follow all the guidelines exactly.
- Lifting equipment and machines such as vehicle jacks and stands, vehicle hoists, and engine hoists are important tools that increase productivity and make the job easier. However, they can also cause severe injury or death if used improperly. Make sure you follow the manufacturer's operation procedures. Also make sure you have your supervisor's/instructor's permission to use any particular type of lifting equipment.
- Comply with personal and environmental safety practices associated with clothing; eye protection; hand tools; power equipment; proper ventilation; and the handling, storage, and disposal of chemicals/materials in accordance with federal, state, and local regulations.
- Always wear the correct protective eyewear and clothing and use the appropriate safety equipment, as well as wheel chocks, fender covers, seat protectors, and floor mat protectors.
- Make sure you understand and observe all legislative and personal safety procedures when carrying out practical assignments. If you are unsure of what these are, ask your supervisor/instructor.

▶ **TASK** Identify electrical/electronic modules, radios, and other accessories that require reinitialization or code entry after reconnecting the vehicle battery.

MTST
V.B.10; P2

Time off_____

Time on_____

Student Instructions: Read through the entire procedure prior to starting. Prepare your workspace and any tools or parts that may be needed to complete the task. When directed by your supervisor/instructor, begin the procedure to complete the task and check the box as each step is finished.

Total time_____

Procedure:	Step Completed
1. While referencing the manufacturer's workshop materials, record any special precautions/procedures for module/component reinitialization or code entry before and after the vehicle's batteries have been disconnected:	☐
2. Record audio system presets before batteries are disconnected:	☐
3. Record power seat settings before batteries are disconnected:	☐
4. Record any vehicle door access codes before batteries are disconnected:	☐
5. Record any miscellaneous codes or parameters that will not be saved when the batteries are disconnected:	☐
6. Disconnect the vehicle's batteries as outlined in the manufacturer's workshop materials.	☐
7. After waiting an appropriate amount of time, reconnect the vehicle's batteries.	☐
8. Reprogram the audio system presets as outlined in the manufacturer's workshop materials.	
a. Within manufacturer's specifications: Yes: ☐ No: ☐	☐
b. If No, describe the recommended corrective action(s):	☐

9. Reprogram the power seat presets as outlined in the manufacturer's workshop materials.	
a. Within manufacturer's specifications: Yes: ☐ No: ☐	☐
b. If No, describe the recommended corrective actions(s):	☐
10. Reprogram the vehicle door access codes as outlined in the manufacturer's workshop materials.	
a. Within manufacturer's specifications: Yes: ☐ No: ☐	☐
b. If No, describe the recommended corrective action(s):	☐
11. Reprogram any miscellaneous codes or parameters as outlined in the manufacturer's workshop materials.	
a. Within manufacturer's specifications: Yes: ☐ No: ☐	☐
b. If No, describe the recommended corrective action(s):	☐
12. Discuss your findings with your supervisor/instructor.	☐

Non-Task-Specific Evaluations:	Step Completed
1. Tools and equipment were used as directed and returned in good working order.	☐
2. Complied with all general and task-specific safety standards, including proper use of any personal protection equipment.	☐
3. Completed the task in an appropriate time frame (recommendation: 1.5 or 2 times the flat rate).	☐
4. Left the workspace clean and orderly.	☐
5. Cared for customer property and returned it undamaged.	☐

Student signature _____ Date _____

Comments:

Have your supervisor/instructor verify satisfactory completion of this procedure, any observations made,

and any necessary action(s) recommended.

Evaluation Instructions: The scoring box below is intended to act as a guide for both student and supervisor/instructor. Each criterion listed will help students to understand what is expected of them and help supervisors/instructors articulate the level of success at a particular task. The scoring is set up to allow a second attempt at each task (see the Test and Retest columns). Scoring is also designed to award students points only for task criteria that were completed correctly. Points are lost for failure to complete the employability requirements (see Non-Task-Specific Evaluation criteria). When all criteria are evaluated, tally the points for a total at the bottom of each column.

Tasksheet Scoring

Evaluation Items	Test		Retest	
	Pass	Fail	Pass	Fail
Task-Specific Evaluation	**(1 pt)**	**(0 pts)**	**(1 pt)**	**(0 pts)**
Student properly recorded special precautions/procedures for module/component reinitialization or code reentry.				
Student properly recorded audio system presets, power seat settings, door access codes, and miscellaneous codes/parameters.				
Student properly disconnected and reconnected vehicle batteries.				
Student properly reset audio system settings, power seat settings, vehicle door settings, and miscellaneous codes/parameters.				
Non-Task-Specific Evaluation	**(0 pts)**	**(−1 pt)**	**(0 pts)**	**(−1 pt)**
Student successfully completed at least three of the non-task-specific steps.				
Student successfully completed all five of the non-task-specific steps.				
Total Score: <total # of points/4 = %>				

Supervisor/Instructor:

Supervisor/instructor signature _____ Date _____

Comments:

Retest supervisor/instructor signature _____ Date _____

Comments:

V.C Electrical/Electronic Systems: Starting System

Learning Objective/Task	CDX Tasksheet Number	ASE Foundation MTST Reference Number; Priority Level
• Demonstrate understanding of starter system operation.	MHT5C001	V.C.1; P-1
• Perform starter circuit cranking voltage and voltage-drop tests; determine needed action.	MHT5C002	V.C.2; P-1
• Inspect and test starter control circuit switches (key switch, push button, and/or magnetic switch), relays, connectors, terminals, wires, and harnesses (including over-crank protection); determine needed action.	MHT5C003	V.C.3; P-1
• Diagnose causes of no-crank or slow-crank condition; differentiate between electrical and engine mechanical problems; determine needed action.	MHT5C004	V.C.4; P-1
• Perform starter current-draw test; determine needed action.	MHT5C005	V.C.5; P-2
• Remove and replace starter; inspect flywheel ring gear or flexplate.	MHT5C006	V.C.6; P-1

Materials Required

- Vehicle with possible engine concern
- Engine/vehicle manufacturer's workshop materials
- Digital volt-ohmmeter (DVOM)
- Manufacturer-specific tools depending on the concern/procedure(s)
- Personal protection equipment (PPE)

Safety Considerations

- Activities may require test-driving the vehicle on the school grounds or on a hoist, both of which carry severe risks. Attempt this task only with full permission from your supervisor/instructor, and follow all the guidelines exactly.
- Lifting equipment and machines such as vehicle jacks and stands, vehicle hoists, and engine hoists are important tools that increase productivity and make the job easier. However, they can also cause severe injury or death if used improperly. Make sure you follow the manufacturer's operation procedures. Also make sure you have your supervisor's/instructor's permission to use any particular type of lifting equipment.
- Activities may require running the engine and managing an environment of rotating equipment and large current draw, which carry severe risks. Attempt this task only with full permission from your supervisor/instructor, and follow all the guidelines exactly.
- Use extreme caution when working around batteries. Immediately remove any electrolyte that may come in contact with you. Electrolyte is a mixture of sulfuric acid and water. Batteries may produce explosive mixtures of gas containing hydrogen; avoid creating any sparks around batteries. Consult with the shop safety and emergency procedures when working with or around batteries.

- Make sure you follow the manufacturer's operation procedures. Also make sure you have your supervisor's/instructor's permission to use any particular type of lifting equipment.
- Comply with personal and environmental safety practices associated with clothing; eye protection; hand tools; power equipment; proper ventilation; and the handling, storage, and disposal of chemicals/materials in accordance with federal, state, and local regulations.
- Always wear the correct protective eyewear and clothing and use the appropriate safety equipment, as well as wheel chocks, fender covers, seat protectors, and floor mat protectors.
- Make sure you understand and observe all legislative and personal safety procedures when carrying out practical assignments. If you are unsure of what these are, ask your supervisor/instructor.

CDX Tasksheet Number: MHT5C001

Student/Intern Information

Name _____ Date _____ Class _____

Vehicle, Customer, and Service Information

Vehicle used for this activity:

Year _____ Make _____ Model _____

Odometer _____ VIN _____

Materials Required

- Vehicle with possible engine concern
- Engine manufacturer's workshop materials
- Manufacturer-specific tools depending on the concern/procedure(s)
- Vehicle/component lifting equipment, if applicable

Task-Specific Safety Considerations

- Activities may require test-driving the vehicle on the school grounds or on a hoist, both of which carry severe risks. Attempt this task only with full permission from your supervisor/instructor, and follow all the guidelines exactly.
- Lifting equipment and machines such as vehicle jacks and stands, vehicle hoists, and engine hoists are important tools that increase productivity and make the job easier. However, they can also cause severe injury or death if used improperly. Make sure you follow the manufacturer's operation procedures. Also make sure you have your supervisor's/instructor's permission to use any particular type of lifting equipment.
- Comply with personal and environmental safety practices associated with clothing; eye protection; hand tools; power equipment; proper ventilation; and the handling, storage, and disposal of chemicals/materials in accordance with federal, state, and local regulations.
- Always wear the correct protective eyewear and clothing and use the appropriate safety equipment, as well as wheel chocks, fender covers, seat protectors, and floor mat protectors.
- Make sure you understand and observe all legislative and personal safety procedures when carrying out practical assignments. If you are unsure of what these are, ask your supervisor/instructor.

▶ TASK Demonstrate understanding of starter system operation. _____ **MTST** V.C.1; P1

Time off_____

Student Instructions: Read through the entire procedure prior to starting. Prepare your workspace and any tools or parts that may be needed to complete the task. When directed by your supervisor/instructor, begin the procedure to complete the task and check the box as each step is finished.

Time on_____

Note: This tasksheet may require the student to check the condition of miscellaneous vehicle fluids, some of which may be flammable and could damage the environment or cause health problems if not handled properly. Observe all safety precautions and follow local regulations for the proper disposal of fluids.

Total time_____

Procedure:	Step Completed
1. Record the cranking system configuration as outlined in the manufacturer's workshop materials. 12 Volt: _____ 24 Volt: _____	☐
2. Record the size and rating of the battery(ies) as outlined in the manufacturer's workshop materials:	☐
3. Record any cranking system interlocks as outlined in the manufacturer's workshop materials:	☐
4. Record any special precautions/procedures for cranking/starting the vehicle as outlined in the manufacturer's workshop materials:	☐
5. Draw a schematic on a separate piece of paper of the vehicle's cranking system, labeling each component. (**Note:** Schematic must be drawn using straight lines, 90° corners, and proper symbols.)	☐
6. Discuss your findings with your supervisor/instructor.	☐

Non-Task-Specific Evaluations:	Step Completed
1. Tools and equipment were used as directed and returned in good working order.	☐
2. Complied with all general and task-specific safety standards, including proper use of any personal protection equipment.	☐
3. Completed the task in an appropriate time frame (recommendation: 1.5 or 2 times the flat rate).	☐
4. Left the workspace clean and orderly.	☐
5. Cared for customer property and returned it undamaged.	☐

Student signature _____ Date _____

Comments:

Have your supervisor/instructor verify satisfactory completion of this procedure, any observations made, and any necessary action(s) recommended.

Evaluation Instructions: The scoring box below is intended to act as a guide for both student and supervisor/instructor. Each criterion listed will help students to understand what is expected of them and help supervisors/instructors articulate the level of success at a particular task. The scoring is set up to allow a second attempt at each task (see the Test and Retest columns). Scoring is also designed to award students points only for task criteria that were completed correctly. Points are lost for failure to complete the employability requirements (see Non-Task-Specific Evaluation criteria). When all criteria are evaluated, tally the points for a total at the bottom of each column.

Tasksheet Scoring

Evaluation Items	Test		Retest	
	Pass	**Fail**	**Pass**	**Fail**
Task-Specific Evaluation	**(1 pt)**	**(0 pts)**	**(1 pt)**	**(0 pts)**
Student properly identified starting system configuration.				
Student properly identified battery size and rating.				
Student properly identified starting system interlocks and precautions/procedures.				
Student properly drew starting system schematic.				
Non-Task-Specific Evaluation	**(0 pts)**	**(−1 pt)**	**(0 pts)**	**(−1 pt)**
Student successfully completed at least three of the non-task-specific steps.				
Student successfully completed all five of the non-task-specific steps.				
Total Score: <total # of points/4 = %>				

Supervisor/Instructor:

Supervisor/instructor signature _____ Date _____

Comments:

Retest supervisor/instructor signature _____ Date _____

Comments:

CDX Tasksheet Number: MHT5C002

Student/Intern Information

Name _____ Date _____ Class _____

Vehicle, Customer, and Service Information

Vehicle used for this activity:

Year _____ Make _____ Model _____

Odometer _____ VIN _____

Materials Required

- Vehicle with possible engine concern
- Vehicle manufacturer's workshop materials
- Digital volt-ohmmeter (DVOM)
- Personal protection equipment (PPE)

Task-Specific Safety Considerations

- Activities may require running the engine and managing an environment of rotating equipment and large current draw, which carry severe risks. Attempt this task only with full permission from your supervisor/instructor, and follow all the guidelines exactly.
- Use extreme caution when working around batteries. Immediately remove any electrolyte that may come in contact with you. Electrolyte is a mixture of sulfuric acid and water. Batteries may produce explosive mixtures of gas containing hydrogen; avoid creating any sparks around batteries. Consult with the shop safety and emergency procedures when working with or around batteries.
- Make sure you follow the manufacturer's operation procedures. Also make sure you have your supervisor's/instructor's permission to use any particular type of lifting equipment.
- Comply with personal and environmental safety practices associated with clothing; eye protection; hand tools; power equipment; proper ventilation; and the handling, storage, and disposal of chemicals/materials in accordance with federal, state, and local regulations.
- Always wear the correct protective eyewear and clothing, and use the appropriate safety equipment, as well as wheel chocks, fender covers, seat protectors, and floor mat protectors.
- Make sure you understand and observe all legislative and personal safety procedures when carrying out practical assignments. If you are unsure of what these are, ask your supervisor/instructor.

▶ TASK Perform starter circuit cranking voltage and voltage drop tests; determine needed action.

MTST
V.C.2; P1

Time off_____

Time on_____

Student Instructions: Read through the entire procedure prior to starting. Prepare your workspace and any tools or parts that may be needed to complete the task. When directed by your supervisor/instructor, begin the procedure to complete the task and check the box as each step is finished.

Total time_____

Procedure:	Step Completed
1. Locate "Cranking Voltage Test" in the assigned vehicle service manual, and list the steps for this procedure:	☐
2. Prepare the DVOM to measure voltage.	☐
3. Measure the battery voltage at the starter motor with the meter while the engine is cranking. Place the red lead on the main battery terminal of the solenoid and the black lead on the ground terminal of the starter motor. (**Note:** If the starter is not easily accessible, cranking voltage may be measured at the battery. Remember that any voltage drop between the battery and the starter may affect the test results.)	
a. Measured voltage (cranking circuit voltage): _____ volts	☐
4. Determine any necessary action(s).	
a. Within manufacturer's specifications: Yes: ☐ No: ☐	☐
b. If No, describe the recommended corrective action(s):	☐
c. Have your supervisor/instructor verify these steps. Supervisor's/instructor's initials:	☐
5. Using the appropriate service information for the vehicle you are working on, locate the starter circuit voltage-drop tests. List the steps outlined:	☐
6. What is (are) the maximum voltage-drop specification(s) for this test?	
a. Positive side: _____ volts	☐
b. Negative side, if specified: _____ volts	☐

7. To conduct this test, it will be required that the engine cranks but does not start. Follow the manufacturer's recommendations for disabling the engine so that it does not start. Identify the steps you will take to prevent the engine from starting:	
a. Have your supervisor/instructor verify these steps. Supervisor's/instructor's initials:	☐
8. Starter circuit voltage-drop test: Positive/feed side.	
a. List the voltmeter connection points in the circuit.	☐
i. Black lead: _____	☐
ii. Red lead: _____	☐
b. Conduct the starter circuit voltage-drop test.	☐
i. Voltage drop on positive side: _____ volts	☐
ii. Within manufacturer's specifications: Yes: ☐ No: ☐	☐
9. Starter circuit voltage-drop test: Ground side.	
a. List the voltmeter connection points in the circuit.	☐
i. Black lead: _____	☐
ii. Red lead: _____	☐
b. Conduct the starter circuit voltage-drop test.	☐
i. Voltage drop on negative side: _____ volts	☐
ii. Within manufacturer's specifications: Yes: ☐ No: ☐	☐
iii. If No, describe recommended corrective action(s):	☐
10. Return the vehicle engine to normal operating condition.	☐
11. Start the vehicle and verify proper operation of the starting system and engine.	☐

12. Return any tools you used to their proper locations.	☐
13. Discuss your findings with your supervisor/instructor.	☐

Non-Task-Specific Evaluations:	Step Completed
1. Tools and equipment were used as directed and returned in good working order.	☐
2. Complied with all general and task-specific safety standards, including proper use of any personal protection equipment.	☐
3. Completed the task in an appropriate time frame (recommendation: 1.5 or 2 times the flat rate).	☐
4. Left the workspace clean and orderly.	☐
5. Cared for customer property and returned it undamaged.	☐

Student signature _____ Date _____

Comments:

Have your supervisor/instructor verify satisfactory completion of this procedure, any observations made, and any necessary action(s) recommended.

Evaluation Instructions: The scoring box below is intended to act as a guide for both student and supervisor/instructor. Each criterion listed will help students to understand what is expected of them and help supervisors/instructors articulate the level of success at a particular task. The scoring is set up to allow a second attempt at each task (see the Test and Retest columns). Scoring is also designed to award students points only for task criteria that were completed correctly. Points are lost for failure to complete the employability requirements (see Non-Task-Specific Evaluation criteria). When all criteria are evaluated, tally the points for a total at the bottom of each column.

Tasksheet Scoring

	Test		Retest	
Evaluation Items	**Pass**	**Fail**	**Pass**	**Fail**
Task-Specific Evaluation	**(1 pt)**	**(0 pts)**	**(1 pt)**	**(0 pts)**
Student used the appropriate service information to research how to perform a starter circuit cranking voltage test and starter circuit voltage-drop test.				
Student properly used a DVOM to measure starter cranking voltage and measure voltage drop on both sides of the starter circuit.				
Student accurately compared readings to the manufacturer's specifications and determined any necessary actions.				
Student reinstalled all removed components undamaged and in working order.				
Non-Task-Specific Evaluation	**(0 pts)**	**(−1 pt)**	**(0 pts)**	**(−1 pt)**
Student successfully completed at least three of the non-task-specific steps.				
Student successfully completed all five of the non-task-specific steps.				
Total Score: <total # of points/4 = %>				

Supervisor/Instructor:

Supervisor/instructor signature _____ Date _____

Comments:

Retest supervisor/instructor signature _____ Date _____

Comments:

CDX Tasksheet Number: MHT5C003

Student/Intern Information

Name _____ Date _____ Class _____

Vehicle, Customer, and Service Information

Vehicle used for this activity:

Year _____ Make _____ Model _____

Odometer _____ VIN _____

Materials Required

- Vehicle with possible engine concern
- Engine manufacturer's workshop materials
- Manufacturer-specific tools depending on the concern/procedure(s)
- Vehicle/component lifting equipment, if applicable

Task-Specific Safety Considerations

- Activities may require test-driving the vehicle on the school grounds or on a hoist, both of which carry severe risks. Attempt this task only with full permission from your supervisor/instructor, and follow all the guidelines exactly.
- Lifting equipment and machines such as vehicle jacks and stands, vehicle hoists, and engine hoists are important tools that increase productivity and make the job easier. However, they can also cause severe injury or death if used improperly. Make sure you follow the manufacturer's operation procedures. Also make sure you have your supervisor's/instructor's permission to use any particular type of lifting equipment.
- Comply with personal and environmental safety practices associated with clothing; eye protection; hand tools; power equipment; proper ventilation; and the handling, storage, and disposal of chemicals/materials in accordance with federal, state, and local regulations.
- Always wear the correct protective eyewear and clothing and use the appropriate safety equipment, as well as wheel chocks, fender covers, seat protectors, and floor mat protectors.
- Make sure you understand and observe all legislative and personal safety procedures when carrying out practical assignments. If you are unsure of what these are, ask your supervisor/instructor.

▶ **TASK** Inspect and test starter control circuit switches (key switch, push button, and/or magnetic switch), relays, connectors, terminals, wires, and harnesses (including over-crank protection); determine needed action.

MTST
V.C.3; P1

Time off_____

Time on_____

Total time_____

Student Instructions: Read through the entire procedure prior to starting. Prepare your workspace and any tools or parts that may be needed to complete the task. When directed by your supervisor/instructor, begin the procedure to complete the task and check the box as each step is finished.

Note: This tasksheet may require the student to check the condition of miscellaneous vehicle fluids, some of which may be flammable and could damage the environment or cause health problems if not handled properly. Observe all safety precautions and follow local regulations for the proper disposal of fluids.

Procedure:	Step Completed

1. Record the cranking system configuration.
   12 Volt: _____
   24 Volt: _____
	☐

2. Record the size and rating of the battery(ies):	☐
3. Record any starter system interlocks:	☐
4. Record any special precautions/procedures for cranking/starting the vehicle as outlined in the manufacturer's workshop materials:	☐
5. Inspect key switch, push-button switch, magnetic relay, and starter solenoid for burnt, loose, or damaged wiring/connections, proper securement, and wire routing.	
a. Within manufacturer's specifications: Yes: ☐ No: ☐	☐
b. If No, describe the recommended corrective action(s):	☐
6. Before the following tests can be performed, the engine will be required to crank but not start. Follow the manufacturer's recommendation for disabling the engine so that it cranks but does not start, and record the required steps:	☐
7. Test operation of the key switch for binding/sticking and correct operation.	
a. Within manufacturer's specifications: Yes: ☐ No: ☐	☐

b. If No, describe the recommended corrective action(s):	☐
8. Test operation of push-button switch for sticking and correct operation.	
a. Within manufacturer's specifications: Yes: ☐ No: ☐	☐
b. If No, describe the recommended corrective action(s):	☐
9. Record signal voltage at magnetic relay while cranking: _____ Volts	
a. Within manufacturer's specifications: Yes: ☐ No: ☐	☐
b. If No, describe the recommended corrective action(s):	☐
10. Record voltage drop across magnetic relay: _____ Volts	
a. Within manufacturer's specifications: Yes: ☐ No: ☐	☐
b. If No, describe the recommended corrective action(s):	☐
11. Record voltage at S terminal on starter solenoid while cranking: _____ Volts	
a. Within manufacturer's specifications: Yes: ☐ No: ☐	☐
b. If No, describe the recommended corrective action(s):	☐
12. Record voltage drop on the conductor from magnetic relay to S terminal on starter: _____ Volts	
a. Within manufacturer's specifications: Yes: ☐ No: ☐	☐

b. If No, describe the recommended corrective action(s):	☐
13. Record voltage drop across the starter solenoid battery to motor terminals: _____ Volts	
a. Within manufacturer's specifications: Yes: ☐ No: ☐	☐
b. If No, describe the recommended corrective action(s):	☐
14. Record procedure for testing starter over-crank protection, and perform the test:	
a. Within manufacturer's specifications: Yes: ☐ No: ☐	☐
b. If No, describe the recommended corrective action(s):	☐
15. Record procedure for testing cranking system safety interlock(s), and perform the test(s):	☐
a. Within manufacturer's specifications: Yes: ☐ No: ☐	☐
b. If No, describe the recommended corrective action(s):	☐
16. Return the engine to a normal operating condition, and test the cranking system/engine for normal operation.	☐
17. Discuss your findings with your supervisor/instructor.	☐

Non-Task-Specific Evaluations:	Step Completed
1. Tools and equipment were used as directed and returned in good working order.	☐
2. Complied with all general and task-specific safety standards, including proper use of any personal protection equipment.	☐
3. Completed the task in an appropriate time frame (recommendation: 1.5 or 2 times the flat rate).	☐
4. Left the workspace clean and orderly.	☐
5. Cared for customer property and returned it undamaged.	☐

Student signature _____ Date _____

Comments:

Have your supervisor/instructor verify satisfactory completion of this procedure, any observations made,

and any necessary action(s) recommended.

Evaluation Instructions: The scoring box below is intended to act as a guide for both student and supervisor/instructor. Each criterion listed will help students to understand what is expected of them and help supervisors/instructors articulate the level of success at a particular task. The scoring is set up to allow a second attempt at each task (see the Test and Retest columns). Scoring is also designed to award students points only for task criteria that were completed correctly. Points are lost for failure to complete the employability requirements (see Non-Task-Specific Evaluation criteria). When all criteria are evaluated, tally the points for a total at the bottom of each column.

Tasksheet Scoring

	Test		Retest	
Evaluation Items	**Pass**	**Fail**	**Pass**	**Fail**
Task-Specific Evaluation	**(1 pt)**	**(0 pts)**	**(1 pt)**	**(0 pts)**
Student correctly identified cranking system configuration, battery size and rating, starter system interlocks, and precautions/procedures.				
Student properly inspected wiring and connectors and disabled engine so as to create a crank but no-start condition.				
Student correctly tested key switch and push-button operation, magnetic relay signal voltage and voltage drop, voltage as S terminal at starter solenoid, and voltage drop from magnetic relay to starter solenoid S terminal and across starter solenoid battery to motor terminal.				
Student properly tested starter over-crank protection and starter interlocks and made sure engine was returned to normal operation and cranking system.				
Non-Task-Specific Evaluation	**(0 pts)**	**(−1 pt)**	**(0 pts)**	**(−1 pt)**
Student successfully completed at least three of the non-task-specific steps.				
Student successfully completed all five of the non-task-specific steps.				
Total Score: <total # of points/4 = %>				

CDX Tasksheet Number: MHT5C004

Student/Intern Information

Name _____ Date _____ Class _____

Vehicle, Customer, and Service Information

Vehicle used for this activity:

Year _____ Make _____ Model _____

Odometer _____ VIN _____

Materials Required

- Vehicle with possible engine concern
- Engine manufacturer's workshop materials
- Manufacturer-specific tools depending on the concern/procedure(s)
- Vehicle/component lifting equipment, if applicable

Task-Specific Safety Considerations

- Activities may require test-driving the vehicle on the school grounds or on a hoist, both of which carry severe risks. Attempt this task only with full permission from your supervisor/instructor, and follow all the guidelines exactly.
- Lifting equipment and machines such as vehicle jacks and stands, vehicle hoists, and engine hoists are important tools that increase productivity and make the job easier. However, they can also cause severe injury or death if used improperly. Make sure you follow the manufacturer's operation procedures. Also make sure you have your supervisor's/instructor's permission to use any particular type of lifting equipment.
- Comply with personal and environmental safety practices associated with clothing; eye protection; hand tools; power equipment; proper ventilation; and the handling, storage, and disposal of chemicals/materials in accordance with federal, state, and local regulations.
- Always wear the correct protective eyewear and clothing and use the appropriate safety equipment, as well as wheel chocks, fender covers, seat protectors, and floor mat protectors.
- Make sure you understand and observe all legislative and personal safety procedures when carrying out practical assignments. If you are unsure of what these are, ask your supervisor/instructor.

▶ **TASK** Diagnose causes of no-crank or slow-crank condition; differentiate between electrical and engine mechanical problems; determine needed action.

MTST
V.C.4; P1

Time off_____

Time on_____

Total time_____

Student Instructions: Read through the entire procedure prior to starting. Prepare your workspace and any tools or parts that may be needed to complete the task. When directed by your supervisor/instructor, begin the procedure to complete the task and check the box as each step is finished.

Note: This tasksheet may require the student to check the condition of miscellaneous vehicle fluids, some of which may be flammable and could damage the environment or cause health problems if not handled properly. Observe all safety precautions and follow local regulations for the proper disposal of fluids.

Procedure:	Step Completed

1. Record the cranking system configuration.
   12 Volt: _____
   24 Volt: _____
	☐

2. Record the size and rating of the battery(ies):	☐
3. Record any cranking system interlocks:	☐
4. Record any special precautions/procedures for cranking/starting the vehicle as outlined in the manufacturer's workshop materials:	☐
5. Test the cranking system for normal operation.	
a. Within manufacturer's specifications: Yes: ☐ No: ☐	☐
b. If No, describe the recommended corrective action(s):	☐
6. Record the possible causes and procedures for troubleshooting a slow-crank condition in severely cold temperatures:	☐
7. Record the possible causes and procedures for troubleshooting a slow-crank low-amperage-draw condition:	☐

8. Record the possible causes and procedures for troubleshooting a slow-crank high-amperage-draw condition: (**Note:** In this scenario, there are no mechanical engine/transmission problems present.)	☐
9. Record the possible causes and procedures for troubleshooting a slow-crank high-amperage-draw condition: (**Note:** In this scenario, there are mechanical engine/transmission problems present.)	☐
10. Record the possible causes and procedures for troubleshooting a starter that repeatedly clicks but does not crank condition:	☐
11. Record the possible causes and procedures for troubleshooting a starter that does nothing or makes a single click condition:	☐
12. Record the possible causes and procedures for troubleshooting a starter that makes a spinning or grinding sound but does not crank condition:	☐
13. Discuss your findings with your supervisor/instructor.	☐

Non-Task-Specific Evaluations:	Step Completed
1. Tools and equipment were used as directed and returned in good working order.	☐
2. Complied with all general and task-specific safety standards, including proper use of any personal protection equipment.	☐
3. Completed the task in an appropriate time frame (recommendation: 1.5 or 2 times the flat rate).	☐
4. Left the workspace clean and orderly.	☐
5. Cared for customer property and returned it undamaged.	☐

Student signature _____ Date _____

Comments:

Have your supervisor/instructor verify satisfactory completion of this procedure, any observations made, and any necessary action(s) recommended.

Evaluation Instructions: The scoring box below is intended to act as a guide for both student and supervisor/instructor. Each criterion listed will help students to understand what is expected of them and help supervisors/instructors articulate the level of success at a particular task. The scoring is set up to allow a second attempt at each task (see the Test and Retest columns). Scoring is also designed to award students points only for task criteria that were completed correctly. Points are lost for failure to complete the employability requirements (see Non-Task-Specific Evaluation criteria). When all criteria are evaluated, tally the points for a total at the bottom of each column.

Tasksheet Scoring

	Test		Retest	
	Pass	**Fail**	**Pass**	**Fail**
Evaluation Items				
Task-Specific Evaluation	**(1 pt)**	**(0 pts)**	**(1 pt)**	**(0 pts)**
Student correctly identified cranking system configuration, battery size and rating, starter system interlocks, and precautions/procedures.				
Student properly tested cranking system for normal operation.				
Student properly identified causes and troubleshooting procedures for a slow-crank condition in severely low temperatures, slow-crank low-amperage condition, and slow-crank high-amperage condition with or without mechanical problems.				
Student properly identified causes and trouble-shooting procedures for a starter that repeatedly clicks but does not crank condition, does nothing or makes a single click condition, or makes a spinning or grinding sound but does not crank condition.				

Non-Task-Specific Evaluation	(0 pts)	(−1 pt)	(0 pts)	(−1 pt)
Student successfully completed at least three of the non-task-specific steps.				
Student successfully completed all five of the non-task-specific steps.				
Total Score: <total # of points/4 = %>				

CDX Tasksheet Number: MHT5C005

Student/Intern Information

Name _____ Date _____ Class _____

Vehicle, Customer, and Service Information

Vehicle used for this activity:

Year _____ Make _____ Model _____

Odometer _____ VIN _____

Materials Required
- Vehicle with possible engine concern
- Engine manufacturer's workshop materials
- Manufacturer-specific tools depending on the concern/procedure(s)
- Vehicle/component lifting equipment, if applicable

Task-Specific Safety Considerations
- Activities may require test-driving the vehicle on the school grounds or on a hoist, both of which carry severe risks. Attempt this task only with full permission from your supervisor/instructor, and follow all the guidelines exactly.
- Lifting equipment and machines such as vehicle jacks and stands, vehicle hoists, and engine hoists are important tools that increase productivity and make the job easier. However, they can also cause severe injury or death if used improperly. Make sure you follow the manufacturer's operation procedures. Also make sure you have your supervisor's/instructor's permission to use any particular type of lifting equipment.
- Comply with personal and environmental safety practices associated with clothing; eye protection; hand tools; power equipment; proper ventilation; and the handling, storage, and disposal of chemicals/materials in accordance with federal, state, and local regulations.
- Always wear the correct protective eyewear and clothing and use the appropriate safety equipment, as well as wheel chocks, fender covers, seat protectors, and floor mat protectors.
- Make sure you understand and observe all legislative and personal safety procedures when carrying out practical assignments. If you are unsure of what these are, ask your supervisor/instructor.

▶ **TASK** Perform starter current draw test; determine needed action. **MTST** **V.C.5; P2**

Time off_____

Time on_____

Student Instructions: Read through the entire procedure prior to starting. Prepare your workspace and any tools or parts that may be needed to complete the task. When directed by your supervisor/instructor, begin the procedure to complete the task and check the box as each step is finished.

Total time_____

Note: This tasksheet may require the student to check the condition of miscellaneous vehicle fluids, some of which may be flammable and could damage the environment or cause health problems if not handled properly. Observe all safety precautions and follow local regulations for the proper disposal of fluids.

Procedure:	Step Completed
1. Record the cranking system configuration. 12 Volt: _____ 24 Volt: _____	☐
2. Record the size and rating of the battery(ies):	☐
3. Record any cranking system interlocks:	☐
4. Record any special precautions/procedures for cranking/starting the vehicle as outlined in the manufacturer's workshop materials:	☐
5. Test the cranking system for normal operation.	
a. Within manufacturer's specifications: Yes: ☐ No: ☐	☐
b. If No, describe the recommended corrective action(s):	☐
6. Record the procedure for performing a starter on-engine current draw/cranking rpm test, and perform the test:	
a. Manufacturer's specification: _____ cranking rpm	☐
b. Manufacturer's specification: _____ cranking amps	☐
c. Within manufacturer's specifications: Yes: ☐ No: ☐	☐
d. If No, describe the recommended corrective action(s):	☐

7. Record the procedure for performing a starter off-engine current draw/cranking rpm test, and perform the test:	
a. Manufacturer's specification: _____ cranking rpm	☐
b. Manufacturer's specification: _____ cranking amps	☐
c. Within manufacturer's specifications: Yes: ☐ No: ☐	☐
d. If No, describe the recommended corrective action(s)	☐
8. Discuss your findings with your supervisor/instructor.	☐

Non-Task-Specific Evaluations:	Step Completed
1. Tools and equipment were used as directed and returned in good working order.	☐
2. Complied with all general and task-specific safety standards, including proper use of any personal protection equipment.	☐
3. Completed the task in an appropriate time frame (recommendation: 1.5 or 2 times the flat rate).	☐
4. Left the workspace clean and orderly.	☐
5. Cared for customer property and returned it undamaged.	☐

Student signature _____ Date _____

Comments:

Have your supervisor/instructor verify satisfactory completion of this procedure, any observations made, and any necessary action(s) recommended.

Evaluation Instructions: The scoring box below is intended to act as a guide for both student and supervisor/instructor. Each criterion listed will help students to understand what is expected of them and help supervisors/instructors articulate the level of success at a particular task. The scoring is set up to allow a second attempt at each task (see the Test and Retest columns). Scoring is also designed to award students points only for task criteria that were completed correctly. Points are lost for failure to complete the employability requirements (see Non-Task-Specific Evaluation criteria). When all criteria are evaluated, tally the points for a total at the bottom of each column.

Tasksheet Scoring

Evaluation Items	Test		Retest	
	Pass	**Fail**	**Pass**	**Fail**
Task-Specific Evaluation	**(1 pt)**	**(0 pts)**	**(1 pt)**	**(0 pts)**
Student correctly identified cranking system configuration, battery size and rating, starter system interlocks, and precautions/procedures.				
Student properly tested cranking system for normal operation.				
Student properly performed starter on-engine current draw/cranking rpm procedure and test.				
Student properly performed starter off-engine current draw/cranking rpm procedure and test.				
Non-Task-Specific Evaluation	**(0 pts)**	**(−1 pt)**	**(0 pts)**	**(−1 pt)**
Student successfully completed at least three of the non-task-specific steps.				
Student successfully completed all five of the non-task-specific steps.				
Total Score: <total # of points/4 = %>				

Supervisor/Instructor:

Supervisor/instructor signature _____ Date _____

Comments:

Retest supervisor/instructor signature _____ Date _____

Comments:

CDX Tasksheet Number: MHT5C006

Student/Intern Information

Name _____ Date _____ Class _____

Vehicle, Customer, and Service Information

Vehicle used for this activity:

Year _____ Make _____ Model _____

Odometer _____ VIN _____

Materials Required

- Vehicle with possible engine concern
- Vehicle manufacturer's workshop materials
- Personal protection equipment (PPE)

Task-Specific Safety Considerations

- Activities may require running the engine and managing an environment of rotating equipment and large current draw, which carry severe risks. Attempt this task only with full permission from your supervisor/instructor, and follow all the guidelines exactly.
- Use extreme caution when working around batteries. Immediately remove any electrolyte that may come in contact with you. Electrolyte is a mixture of sulfuric acid and water. Batteries may produce explosive mixtures of gas containing hydrogen; avoid creating any sparks around batteries. Consult with the shop safety and emergency procedures when working with or around batteries.
- Make sure you follow the manufacturer's operation procedures. Also make sure you have your supervisor's/instructor's permission to use any particular type of lifting equipment.
- Comply with personal and environmental safety practices associated with clothing; eye protection; hand tools; power equipment; proper ventilation; and the handling, storage, and disposal of chemicals/materials in accordance with federal, state, and local regulations.
- Always wear the correct protective eyewear and clothing, and use the appropriate safety equipment, as well as fender covers, seat protectors, and floor mat protectors.
- Make sure you understand and observe all legislative and personal safety procedures when carrying out practical assignments. If you are unsure of what these are, ask your supervisor/instructor.

▶ TASK Remove and replace starter; inspect flywheel ring gear or flex plate.

MTST
V.C.6; P1

Time off_____

Time on_____

Total time_____

Student Instructions: Read through the entire procedure prior to starting. Prepare your workspace and any tools or parts that may be needed to complete the task. When directed by your supervisor/instructor, begin the procedure to complete the task and check the box as each step is finished.

Procedure:	Step Completed
1. Using the appropriate service manual, research the starter removal and installation procedure for this vehicle.	
a. List the procedures and tools required to perform this task:	☐
b. List any torque specifications for this procedure: _____ (ft-lb/N•m)	☐
c. Have your supervisor/instructor verify this information. Supervisor's/instructor's initials:	☐
2. Remove the starter, following the manufacturer's procedures. (**Note:** Manufacturers may require that the vehicle cab or hood be lifted to remove the starter. Follow the manufacturer's recommendations regarding the correct procedure.)	
a. Have your supervisor/instructor verify the starter removal. Supervisor's/instructor's initials:	☐
3. Using the appropriate service manual, research the manufacturer's procedure for inspection of the flywheel ring gear or flexplate for this vehicle.	
a. List the checks that should be made:	☐
b. List the result of the inspection:	☐
c. Have your supervisor/instructor verify this information. Supervisor's/instructor's initials:	☐
4. Install the starter as outlined in the manufacturer's workshop materials.	
a. Have your supervisor/instructor verify the starter installation. Supervisor/instructor's initials:	☐
5. Return the vehicle/simulator to its beginning condition, and return any tools you used to their proper locations.	☐
6. Discuss your findings with your supervisor/instructor.	☐

Non-Task-Specific Evaluations:	Step Completed
1. Tools and equipment were used as directed and returned in good working order.	☐
2. Complied with all general and task-specific safety standards, including proper use of any personal protection equipment.	☐
3. Completed the task in an appropriate time frame (recommendation: 1.5 or 2 times the flat rate).	☐
4. Left the workspace clean and orderly.	☐
5. Cared for customer property and returned it undamaged.	☐

Student signature _____ Date _____

Comments:

Have your supervisor/instructor verify satisfactory completion of this procedure, any observations made, and any necessary action(s) recommended.

Evaluation Instructions: The scoring box below is intended to act as a guide for both student and supervisor/instructor. Each criterion listed will help students to understand what is expected of them and help supervisors/instructors articulate the level of success at a particular task. The scoring is set up to allow a second attempt at each task (see the Test and Retest columns). Scoring is also designed to award students points only for task criteria that were completed correctly. Points are lost for failure to complete the employability requirements (see Non-Task-Specific Evaluation criteria). When all criteria are evaluated, tally the points for a total at the bottom of each column.

Tasksheet Scoring

Evaluation Items	Test		Retest	
	Pass	**Fail**	**Pass**	**Fail**
Task-Specific Evaluation	**(1 pt)**	**(0 pts)**	**(1 pt)**	**(0 pts)**
Student used the appropriate service information to research how to remove the starter and inspect the flywheel ring gear or flexplate ring gear.				
Student removed the starter and properly inspected the flywheel ring gear or flexplate ring gear in accordance with the manufacturer's recommendations.				
Student installed the starter correctly and torqued fasteners to specification.				
Student reinstalled all removed components undamaged and in working order.				
Non-Task-Specific Evaluation	**(0 pts)**	**(−1 pt)**	**(0 pts)**	**(−1 pt)**
Student successfully completed at least three of the non-task-specific steps.				
Student successfully completed all five of the non-task-specific steps.				
Total Score: <total # of points/4 = %>				

Supervisor/Instructor:

Supervisor/instructor signature _____ Date _____

Comments:

Retest supervisor/instructor signature _____ Date _____

Comments:

V.D Electrical/Electronic Systems: Charging System

Learning Objective/Task	CDX Tasksheet Number	ASE Foundation MTST Reference Number; Priority Level
• Identify and understand the operation of the generator (alternator).	MHT5D001	V.D.1; P-1
• Test instrument-panel-mounted voltmeters and/or indicator lamps; determine needed action.	MHT5D002	V.D.2; P-1
• Inspect, adjust, and/or replace generator (alternator) drive belt; check pulleys and tensioners for wear; check fans and mounting brackets; verify proper belt alignment; determine needed action.	MHT5D003	V.D.3; P-1
• Inspect cables, wires, and connectors in the charging circuit.	MHT5D004	V.D.4; P-1
• Perform charging system voltage and amperage output tests; perform AC ripple test; determine needed action.	MHT5D005	V.D.5; P-1
• Perform charging circuit voltage-drop tests; determine needed action.	MHT5D006	V.D.6; P-1
• Remove, inspect, and/or replace generator (alternator).	MHT5D007	V.D.7; P-1

Materials Required

- Vehicle with possible alternator concern, including cable, wiring, or connector faults
- Vehicle manufacturer's workshop materials
- Digital volt-ohmmeter (DVOM); ammeters; test lamp; and alternator testing equipment such as load banks, and oscilloscope
- Manufacturer-specific tools depending on the concern/procedure(s)
- Exhaust hoses
- Personal protection equipment (PPE)
- Belt tension gauge

Safety Considerations

- Activities may require running the engine and managing an environment of rotating equipment and large current draw, which carry severe risks. Attempt this task only with full permission from your supervisor/instructor, and follow all the guidelines exactly.
- Ensure that your supervisor/instructor checks the connectors of any test equipment.
- Do not run the alternator without a load connected or allow the output voltage to exceed the manufacturer's specified maximum.
- Use extreme caution when working around batteries. Immediately remove any electrolyte that may come in contact with you. Electrolyte is a mixture of sulfuric acid and water. Batteries may produce explosive mixtures of gas containing hydrogen; avoid creating any sparks around batteries. Consult with the shop safety and emergency procedures when working with or around batteries.
- Make sure you follow the manufacturer's operation procedures. Also make sure you have your supervisor's/instructor's permission to use any particular type of lifting equipment.

- Comply with personal and environmental safety practices associated with clothing; eye protection; hand tools; power equipment; proper ventilation; and the handling, storage, and disposal of chemicals/materials in accordance with federal, state, and local regulations.
- Always wear the correct protective eyewear and clothing and use the appropriate safety equipment, as well as wheel chocks, fender covers, seat protectors, and floor mat protectors.
- Make sure you understand and observe all legislative and personal safety procedures when carrying out practical assignments. If you are unsure of what these are, ask your supervisor/instructor.

CDX Tasksheet Number: MHT5D001

Student/Intern Information

Name _____ Date _____ Class _____

Vehicle, Customer, and Service Information

Vehicle used for this activity:

Year _____ Make _____ Model _____

Odometer _____ VIN _____

Materials Required

- Vehicle with possible alternator concern, including cable, wiring, or connector faults
- Vehicle manufacturer's workshop materials
- Digital volt-ohmmeter (DVOM)
- Personal protection equipment (PPE)

Task-Specific Safety Considerations

- Activities may require running the engine and managing an environment of rotating equipment and large current draw, which carry severe risks. Attempt this task only with full permission from your supervisor/instructor, and follow all the guidelines exactly.
- Ensure that your supervisor/instructor checks the connectors of any test equipment.
- Do not run the alternator without a load connected or allow the output voltage to exceed the manufacturer's specified maximum.
- Use extreme caution when working around batteries. Immediately remove any electrolyte that may come in contact with you. Electrolyte is a mixture of sulfuric acid and water. Batteries may produce explosive mixtures of gas containing hydrogen; avoid creating any sparks around batteries. Consult with the shop safety and emergency procedures when working with or around batteries.
- Make sure you follow the manufacturer's operation procedures. Also make sure you have your supervisor's/instructor's permission to use any particular type of lifting equipment.
- Comply with personal and environmental safety practices associated with clothing; eye protection; hand tools; power equipment; proper ventilation; and the handling, storage, and disposal of chemicals/materials in accordance with federal, state, and local regulations.
- Always wear the correct protective eyewear and clothing and use the appropriate safety equipment, as well as wheel chocks, fender covers, seat protectors, and floor mat protectors.
- Make sure you understand and observe all legislative and personal safety procedures when carrying out practical assignments. If you are unsure of what these are, ask your supervisor/instructor.

▶ **TASK** Identify and understand the operation of the generator (alternator). **MTST** *V.D.1; P1*

Time off_____

Time on_____

Student Instructions: Read through the entire procedure prior to starting. Prepare your workspace and any tools or parts that may be needed to complete the task. When directed by your supervisor/instructor, begin the procedure to complete the task and check the box as each step is finished.

Total time_____

Procedure:	Step Completed
1. While referencing the manufacturer's workshop materials, record the charging system configuration: 12 volt: _____ 24 volt: _____	☐
2. While referencing the manufacturer's workshop materials, record the alternator make/model/amperage rating:	☐
3. Does the alternator have a remote sensing wire? Yes: ☐ No: ☐	☐
4. Is the alternator a brushless design? Yes: ☐ No: ☐	☐
5. Start engine and record charging system no-load voltage at idle and 1500 rpm: _____ volts @ idle _____ volts @ 1500 rpm	
a. Meets the manufacturer's specifications: Yes: ☐ No: ☐	☐
b. If No, list the recommendations for rectification:	☐
6. With engine running, turn on all electrical accessories and record charging system voltage at idle and 1500 rpm: _____ volts @ idle _____ volts @ 1500 rpm	
a. Meets the manufacturer's specifications: Yes: ☐ No: ☐	☐
b. If No, list the recommendations for rectification:	☐
7. While referencing the manufacturer's workshop materials, record the procedure for removing and replacing the alternator:	☐

8. While referencing the manufacturer's workshop materials and the alternator manufacturer's material, describe the difference between an alternator with and without a remote sensing wire:	☐
9. While referencing the manufacturer's workshop materials and the alternator manufacturer's material, describe the difference between a brush-type and brushless alternator:	☐
10. While referencing the manufacturer's workshop materials and the alternator manufacturer's material, describe the difference between a Wye-wound alternator and a Delta-wound alternator:	☐
11. While referencing the manufacturer's workshop materials and the alternator manufacturer's material, describe the function of the rectifier:	☐
12. While referencing the manufacturer's workshop materials and the alternator manufacturer's material, describe the purpose of full-wave rectification:	☐
13. While referencing the manufacturer's workshop materials and the alternator manufacturer's material, describe the function of the smoothing capacitor:	☐
14. While referencing the manufacturer's workshop materials and the alternator manufacturer's material, describe the function of the voltage regulator:	☐

15. While referencing the manufacturer's workshop materials and the alternator manufacturer's material, describe the difference between an internally regulated and an externally regulated alternator:	☐
16. While referencing the manufacturer's workshop materials and the alternator manufacturer's material, describe the procedure for full field testing of an externally regulated alternator:	☐
17. While referencing the manufacturer's workshop materials and the alternator manufacturer's material, describe how an alternator regulates amperage output:	☐
18. While referencing the manufacturer's workshop materials and the alternator manufacturer's material, record the procedure for restoring residual magnetism:	☐
19. While referencing the manufacturer's workshop materials and the alternator manufacturer's material, describe the procedure for testing for excessive diode leakage:	☐
20. While referencing the manufacturer's workshop materials and the alternator manufacturer's material, describe the procedure for testing for excessive air-conditioner (A/C) leakage:	☐
21. While referencing the manufacturer's workshop materials and the alternator manufacturer's material, describe how and why a vehicle's charging system light is on when the alternator is not charging and off when the alternator is charging:	☐

22. While referencing the manufacturer's workshop materials and the alternator manufacturer's material, describe the difference between an alternator with an "A"-type regulator and a "B"-type regulator:	☐
23. While referencing the manufacturer's workshop materials and the alternator manufacturer's material, describe the purpose/function of the "R" terminal of an alternator:	☐
24. Describe the difference between an alternator and a generator:	☐
25. While referencing the manufacturer's workshop materials and electronic service tool (EST), check for any fault codes related to the charging system.	
a. Meets the manufacturer's specifications: Yes: ☐ No: ☐	☐
b. If No, list the recommendations for rectification:	☐
26. Discuss your findings with your supervisor/instructor.	☐

Non-Task-Specific Evaluations:	Step Completed
1. Tools and equipment were used as directed and returned in good working order.	☐
2. Complied with all general and task-specific safety standards, including proper use of any personal protection equipment.	☐
3. Completed the task in an appropriate time frame (recommendation: 1.5 or 2 times the flat rate).	☐
4. Left the workspace clean and orderly.	☐
5. Cared for customer property and returned it undamaged.	☐

Student signature _____ Date _____

Comments:

Have your supervisor/instructor verify satisfactory completion of this procedure, any observations made, and any necessary action(s) recommended.

Evaluation Instructions: The scoring box below is intended to act as a guide for both student and supervisor/instructor. Each criterion listed will help students understand what is expected of them and help supervisors/instructors articulate the level of success at a particular task. The scoring is set up to allow a second attempt at each task (see the Test and Retest columns). Scoring is also designed to award students points only for the task criteria that were completed correctly. Points are lost for failure to complete the employability requirements (see Non-Task-Specific Evaluation criteria). When all criteria are evaluated, tally the points for a total at the bottom of each column.

Tasksheet Scoring

	Test		Retest	
Evaluation Items	**Pass**	**Fail**	**Pass**	**Fail**
Task-Specific Evaluation	**(1 pt)**	**(0 pts)**	**(1 pt)**	**(0 pts)**
Student correctly identified charging system configuration, alternator make/model/ amperage rating, and alternator design (brushless/remote sensing).				
Student correctly tested charging system no-load voltage and charging system voltage with all accessories on, correctly described charging system light operation, and properly checked fault codes for the charging system.				
Student correctly recorded alternator removal and replacement; described amperage output regulation, wye-wound and Delta-wound alternator difference, voltage regulator function, and internally and externally regulated alternator; and described difference between an alternator and generator.				
Student correctly described rectifier function and full-wave rectification, smoothing capacitor function, full field testing, procedure for restoring residual magnetism, testing for excessive A/C and diode leakage, "A"-type and "B"-type /regulator operation, and the function of "R" terminal.				

Non-Task-Specific Evaluation	(0 pts)	(−1 pt)	(0 pts)	(−1 pt)
Student successfully completed at least three of the non-task-specific steps.				
Student successfully completed all five of the non-task-specific steps.				
Total Score: <total # of points/4 = %>				

Supervisor/Instructor:

Supervisor/instructor signature _____ Date _____

Comments:

Retest supervisor/instructor signature _____ Date _____

Comments:

CDX Tasksheet Number: MHT5D002

Student/Intern Information

Name _____ Date _____ Class _____

Vehicle, Customer, and Service Information

Vehicle used for this activity:

Year _____ Make _____ Model _____

Odometer _____ VIN _____

Materials Required

- Vehicle with possible alternator concern, including cable, wiring, or connector faults
- Vehicle manufacturer's workshop materials
- Digital volt-ohmmeter (DVOM)
- Personal protection equipment (PPE)

Task-Specific Safety Considerations

- Activities may require running the engine and managing an environment of rotating equipment and large current draw, which carry severe risks. Attempt this task only with full permission from your supervisor/instructor, and follow all the guidelines exactly.
- Ensure that your supervisor/instructor checks the connectors of any test equipment.
- Do not run the alternator without a load connected or allow the output voltage to exceed the manufacturer's specified maximum.
- Use extreme caution when working around batteries. Immediately remove any electrolyte that may come in contact with you. Electrolyte is a mixture of sulfuric acid and water. Batteries may produce explosive mixtures of gas containing hydrogen; avoid creating any sparks around batteries. Consult with the shop safety and emergency procedures when working with or around batteries.
- Make sure you follow the manufacturer's operation procedures. Also make sure you have your supervisor's/instructor's permission to use any particular type of lifting equipment.
- Comply with personal and environmental safety practices associated with clothing; eye protection; hand tools; power equipment; proper ventilation; and the handling, storage, and disposal of chemicals/materials in accordance with federal, state, and local regulations.
- Always wear the correct protective eyewear and clothing, and use the appropriate safety equipment, as well as wheel chocks fender covers, seat protectors, and floor mat protectors.
- Make sure you understand and observe all legislative and personal safety procedures when carrying out practical assignments. If you are unsure of what these are, ask your supervisor/instructor.

▶ **TASK** Test instrument-panel-mounted voltmeters and/or indicator lamps; determine needed action.

MTST
V.D.2; P1

Time off_____

Time on_____

Total time_____

Student Instructions: Read through the entire procedure prior to starting. Prepare your workspace and any tools or parts that may be needed to complete the task. When directed by your supervisor/instructor, begin the procedure to complete the task and check the box as each step is finished.

Procedure:	Step Completed
1. Using the appropriate service information for the vehicle you are working on, locate the test for panel-mounted voltmeters and/or indicator lamps.	☐
2. List the inspection and test procedures for panel-mounted voltmeters and/or indicator lamps:	☐
3. Check your documented procedures with your supervisor/instructor. Supervisor's/instructor's initials:	☐
4. Using the appropriate service information, inspect and test panel-mounted voltmeters and/or indicator lamps.	
a. List the results of conducting your tests:	☐
b. Determine and list any necessary corrective action(s):	☐
5. Check corrective actions with your supervisor/instructor. Supervisor's/instructor's initials:	☐
6. Return the vehicle to its beginning condition, and return any tools you used to their proper locations.	☐
7. Discuss your findings with your supervisor/instructor.	☐

Non-Task-Specific Evaluations:	Step Completed
1. Tools and equipment were used as directed and returned in good working order.	☐
2. Complied with all general and task-specific safety standards, including proper use of any personal protection equipment.	☐
3. Completed the task in an appropriate time frame (recommendation: 1.5 or 2 times the flat rate).	☐
4. Left the workspace clean and orderly.	☐
5. Cared for customer property and returned it undamaged.	☐

Student signature _____ Date _____

Comments:

Have your supervisor/instructor verify satisfactory completion of this procedure, any observations made,

and any necessary action(s) recommended.

Evaluation Instructions: The scoring box below is intended to act as a guide for both student and supervisor/instructor. Each criterion listed will help students understand what is expected of them and help supervisors/instructors articulate the level of success at a particular task. The scoring is set up to allow a second attempt at each task (see the Test and Retest columns). Scoring is also designed to award students points only for task criteria that were completed correctly. Points are lost for failure to complete the employability requirements (see Non-Task-Specific Evaluation criteria). When all criteria are evaluated, tally the points for a total at the bottom of each column.

Tasksheet Scoring

Evaluation Items	Test		Retest	
	Pass	**Fail**	**Pass**	**Fail**
Task-Specific Evaluation	**(1 pt)**	**(0 pts)**	**(1 pt)**	**(0 pts)**
Student used the appropriate service information to locate the test for panel-mounted voltmeters and/or indicator lamps.				
Student properly inspected and tested panel-mounted voltmeters and/or indicator lamps.				
Student determined any necessary corrective actions.				
Student reinstalled all removed components undamaged and in working order.				
Non-Task-Specific Evaluation	**(0 pts)**	**(−1 pt)**	**(0 pts)**	**(−1 pt)**
Student successfully completed at least three of the non-task-specific steps.				
Student successfully completed all five of the non-task-specific steps.				
Total Score: <total # of points/4 = %>				

Supervisor/Instructor:

Supervisor/instructor signature _____ Date _____

Comments:

Retest supervisor/instructor signature _____ Date _____

Comments:

CDX Tasksheet Number: MHT5D003

Student/Intern Information

Name _____ Date _____ Class _____

Vehicle, Customer, and Service Information

Vehicle used for this activity:

Year _____ Make _____ Model _____

Odometer _____ VIN _____

Materials Required

- Vehicle with possible alternator concern, including cable, wiring, or connector faults
- Vehicle manufacturer's workshop materials
- Belt tension gauge
- Personal protection equipment (PPE)

Task-Specific Safety Considerations

- Activities may require running the engine and managing an environment of rotating equipment and large current draw, which carry severe risks. Attempt this task only with full permission from your supervisor/instructor, and follow all the guidelines exactly.
- Ensure that your supervisor/instructor checks the connectors of any test equipment.
- Do not run the alternator without a load connected or allow the output voltage to exceed the manufacturer's specified maximum.
- Use extreme caution when working around batteries. Immediately remove any electrolyte that may come in contact with you. Electrolyte is a mixture of sulfuric acid and water. Batteries may produce explosive mixtures of gas containing hydrogen; avoid creating any sparks around batteries. Consult with the shop safety and emergency procedures when working with or around batteries.
- Make sure you follow the manufacturer's operation procedures. Also make sure you have your supervisor's/instructor's permission to use any particular type of lifting equipment.
- Comply with personal and environmental safety practices associated with clothing; eye protection; hand tools; power equipment; proper ventilation; and the handling, storage, and disposal of chemicals/materials in accordance with federal, state, and local regulations.
- Always wear the correct protective eyewear and clothing, and use the appropriate safety equipment, as well as wheel chocks, fender covers, seat protectors, and floor mat protectors.
- Make sure you understand and observe all legislative and personal safety procedures when carrying out practical assignments. If you are unsure of what these are, ask your supervisor/instructor.

▶ **TASK** Inspect, adjust, and/or replace generator (alternator) drive belt; check pulleys and tensioners for wear; check fans and mounting brackets; verify proper belt alignment; determine needed action. **MTST** *V.D.3; P1*

Time off _____

Time on _____

Total time _____

Student Instructions: Read through the entire procedure prior to starting. Prepare your workspace and any tools or parts that may be needed to complete the task. When directed by your supervisor/instructor, begin the procedure to complete the task and check the box as each step is finished.

Procedure:	Step Completed
1. Using the appropriate service information for the vehicle you are working on, locate "Inspecting, Adjusting, and/or Replacing Alternator Drive Belts, Pulleys, Fans, Tensioners, and Mounting Brackets; Check Pulley and Belt Alignment."	
a. List the steps outlined in the service information:	☐
b. Write down the specified tension of the alternator drive belt:	☐
c. List faults to look for when inspecting drive belts, pulleys, tensioners, fans, and mounting brackets:	☐
d. Describe how to check correct pulley and belt alignment:	☐
2. Remove the vehicle drive belt(s).	☐
3. Inspect the vehicle drive belts, pulleys, tensioners, fans, and mounting brackets for faults.	
a. List any faults identified on the vehicle drive belt(s), pulleys, tensioners, fans, and mounting brackets:	☐
4. Refit the vehicle drive belts using appropriate service information.	☐
5. Retension the drive belt(s) using appropriate service information.	☐

6. Check for correct pulley, tensioner, and drive belt alignment.	☐
7. Return the vehicle to a satisfactory condition, and return any tools you used to their proper locations.	☐
8. Discuss your findings with your supervisor/instructor.	☐

Non-Task-Specific Evaluations:	Step Completed
1. Tools and equipment were used as directed and returned in good working order.	☐
2. Complied with all general and task-specific safety standards, including proper use of any personal protection equipment.	☐
3. Completed the task in an appropriate time frame (recommendation: 1.5 or 2 times the flat rate).	☐
4. Left the workspace clean and orderly.	☐
5. Cared for customer property and returned it undamaged.	☐

Student signature _____ Date _____

Comments:

Have your supervisor/instructor verify satisfactory completion of this procedure, any observations made,

and any necessary action(s) recommended.

Evaluation Instructions: The scoring box below is intended to act as a guide for both student and supervisor/instructor. Each criterion listed will help students understand what is expected of them and help supervisors/instructors articulate the level of success at a particular task. The scoring is set up to allow a second attempt at each task (see the Test and Retest columns). Scoring is also designed to award students points only for task criteria that were completed correctly. Points are lost for failure to complete the employability requirements (see Non-Task-Specific Evaluation criteria). When all criteria are evaluated, tally the points for a total at the bottom of each column.

Tasksheet Scoring

Evaluation Items	Test Pass (1 pt)	Test Fail (0 pts)	Retest Pass (1 pt)	Retest Fail (0 pts)
Task-Specific Evaluation	**(1 pt)**	**(0 pts)**	**(1 pt)**	**(0 pts)**
Student used the appropriate service information to research "Inspecting, Adjusting, and/or Replacing Alternator Drive Belts, Pulleys, Fans, Tensioners, and Mounting Brackets; Check Pulley and Belt Alignment."				
Student correctly removed the vehicle belt and accurately inspected belts, pulleys, tensioners, fans, and mounting brackets for faults.				
Student properly reinstalled the vehicle drive belt, set the correct belt tension, and ensured proper belt alignment.				
Student reinstalled all removed components undamaged and in working order.				
Non-Task-Specific Evaluation	**(0 pts)**	**(−1 pt)**	**(0 pts)**	**(−1 pt)**
Student successfully completed at least three of the non-task-specific steps.				
Student successfully completed all five of the non-task-specific steps.				
Total Score: <total # of points/4 = %>				

Supervisor/Instructor:

Supervisor/instructor signature _____ Date _____

Comments:

Retest supervisor/instructor signature _____ Date _____

Comments:

CDX Tasksheet Number: MHT5D004

Student/Intern Information

Name _____ Date _____ Class _____

Vehicle, Customer, and Service Information

Vehicle used for this activity:

Year _____ Make _____ Model _____

Odometer _____ VIN _____

> ## Materials Required
> - Vehicle with possible alternator concern, including cable, wiring, or connector faults
> - Vehicle manufacturer's workshop materials
> - Digital volt-ohmmeter (DVOM)
> - Personal protection equipment (PPE)

Task-Specific Safety Considerations

- Activities may require running the engine and managing an environment of rotating equipment and large current draw, which carry severe risks. Attempt this task only with full permission from your supervisor/instructor, and follow all the guidelines exactly.
- Ensure that your supervisor/instructor checks the connectors of any test equipment.
- Do not run the alternator without a load connected or allow the output voltage to exceed the manufacturer's specified maximum.
- Use extreme caution when working around batteries. Immediately remove any electrolyte that may come in contact with you. Electrolyte is a mixture of sulfuric acid and water. Batteries may produce explosive mixtures of gas containing hydrogen; avoid creating any sparks around batteries. Consult with the shop safety and emergency procedures when working with or around batteries.
- Make sure you follow the manufacturer's operation procedures. Also make sure you have your supervisor's/instructor's permission to use any particular type of lifting equipment.
- Comply with personal and environmental safety practices associated with clothing; eye protection; hand tools; power equipment; proper ventilation; and the handling, storage, and disposal of chemicals/materials in accordance with federal, state, and local regulations.
- Always wear the correct protective eyewear and clothing, and use the appropriate safety equipment, as well as wheel chocks, fender covers, seat protectors, and floor mat protectors.
- Make sure you understand and observe all legislative and personal safety procedures when carrying out practical assignments. If you are unsure of what these are, ask your supervisor/instructor.

▶ **TASK** Inspect cables, wires, and connectors in the charging circuit. **MTST** V.D.4; P1

Time off_____

Time on_____

Student Instructions: Read through the entire procedure prior to starting. Prepare your workspace and any tools or parts that may be needed to complete the task. When directed by your supervisor/instructor, begin the procedure to complete the task and check the box as each step is finished.

Total time_____

Procedure:	Step Completed
1. Locate the wiring diagram for the charging system that you are testing.	☐
2. Research "Inspect Cables, Wires, and Connectors as Needed" for this vehicle in the appropriate service manual.	
a. List the steps outlined in the service information to inspect cables, wires, and connectors:	☐
3. Prepare the vehicle, tilt the cabin or lift the hood, and set the parking brake.	☐
4. Inspect the wires, cables, and connectors for the charging circuit as outlined in the appropriate service information or as listed in Step 2a.	☐
5. Determine and list any necessary corrective action(s):	☐
6. Return the vehicle to its beginning condition, and return any tools you used to their proper locations.	☐
7. Discuss your findings with your supervisor/instructor.	☐

Non-Task-Specific Evaluations:	Step Completed
1. Tools and equipment were used as directed and returned in good working order.	☐
2. Complied with all general and task-specific safety standards, including proper use of any personal protection equipment.	☐
3. Completed the task in an appropriate time frame (recommendation: 1.5 or 2 times the flat rate).	☐
4. Left the workspace clean and orderly.	☐
5. Cared for customer property and returned it undamaged.	☐

Student signature _____ Date _____

Comments:

Have your supervisor/instructor verify satisfactory completion of this procedure, any observations made,

and any necessary action(s) recommended.

Evaluation Instructions: The scoring box below is intended to act as a guide for both student and supervisor/instructor. Each criterion listed will help students understand what is expected of them and help supervisors/instructors articulate the level of success at a particular task. The scoring is set up to allow a second attempt at each task (see the Test and Retest columns). Scoring is also designed to award students points only for task criteria that were completed correctly. Points are lost for failure to complete the employability requirements (see Non-Task–Specific Evaluation criteria). When all criteria are evaluated, tally the points for a total at the bottom of each column.

Tasksheet Scoring

Evaluation Items	Test		Retest	
	Pass	Fail	Pass	Fail
Task-Specific Evaluation	**(1 pt)**	**(0 pts)**	**(1 pt)**	**(0 pts)**
Student used the appropriate service information to research "Inspect Cables, Wires, and Connectors as Needed" for this vehicle in the appropriate service manual.				
Student accurately inspected the wires, cables, and connectors for the charging circuit.				
Student determined any necessary corrective actions.				
Student reinstalled all removed components undamaged and in working order.				
Non-Task–Specific Evaluation	**(0 pts)**	**(−1 pt)**	**(0 pts)**	**(−1 pt)**
Student successfully completed at least three of the non-task-specific steps.				
Student successfully completed all five of the non-task-specific steps.				
Total Score: <total # of points/4 = %>				

Supervisor/Instructor:

Supervisor/instructor signature _____ Date _____

Comments:

Retest supervisor/instructor signature _____ Date _____

Comments:

CDX Tasksheet Number: MHT5D005

Student/Intern Information

Name _____ Date _____ Class _____

Vehicle, Customer, and Service Information

Vehicle used for this activity:

Year _____ Make _____ Model _____

Odometer _____ VIN _____

Materials Required

- Vehicle(s) with possible alternator concern, including cable, wiring, or connector faults
- Vehicle manufacturer's workshop materials
- Digital volt-ohmmeter (DVOM); ammeters; and alternator testing equipment, such as load banks and oscilloscope
- Exhaust hoses
- Personal protection equipment (PPE)

Task-Specific Safety Considerations

- Activities may require running the engine and managing an environment of rotating equipment and large current draw, which carry severe risks. Attempt this task only with full permission from your supervisor/instructor, and follow all the guidelines exactly.
- Ensure that your supervisor/instructor checks the connectors of any test equipment.
- Do not run the alternator without a load connected or allow the output voltage to exceed the manufacturer's specified maximum.
- Use extreme caution when working around batteries. Immediately remove any electrolyte that may come in contact with you. Electrolyte is a mixture of sulfuric acid and water. Batteries may produce explosive mixtures of gas containing hydrogen; avoid creating any sparks around batteries. Consult with the shop safety and emergency procedures when working with or around batteries.
- Make sure you follow the manufacturer's operation procedures. Also make sure you have your supervisor's/instructor's permission to use any particular type of lifting equipment.
- Comply with personal and environmental safety practices associated with clothing; eye protection; hand tools; power equipment; proper ventilation; and the handling, storage, and disposal of chemicals/materials in accordance with federal, state, and local regulations.
- Always wear the correct protective eyewear and clothing, and use the appropriate safety equipment, as well as wheel chocks, fender covers, seat protectors, and floor mat protectors.
- Make sure you understand and observe all legislative and personal safety procedures when carrying out practical assignments. If you are unsure of what these are, ask your supervisor/instructor.

Time off_____

Time on_____

▶ **TASK** Perform charging system voltage and amperage output tests; perform AC ripple test; determine needed action.

MTST
V.D.5; P1

Total time_____

Student Instructions: Read through the entire procedure prior to starting. Prepare your workspace and any tools or parts that may be needed to complete the task. When directed by your supervisor/instructor, begin the procedure to complete the task and check the box as each step is finished.

Procedure:	Step Completed
1. List the steps of the test for system voltage, amperage, and AC ripple as outlined in the service information:	☐
2. What is the specified charging system output? _____ amps at _____ volts at _____ rpm AC ripple: _____	☐
3. Install exhaust hose(s), set the parking brake, and lift the cabin or hood as necessary.	☐
4. Connect the test instruments as outlined in the appropriate service information or as listed in Step 1.	☐
5. Have your supervisor/instructor verify your test procedure and connections. Supervisor's/instructor's initials:	☐
6. Conduct the charging system output test. List the measured results at the maximum output: _____ amps at _____ volts at _____ rpm AC ripple: _____	☐
7. Compare your results to the manufacturer's specifications. List your observations:	☐
8. Determine and list any necessary corrective action(s):	☐

	Step Completed
9. Return the vehicle to its beginning condition, and return any tools you used to their proper locations.	☐
10. Discuss your findings with your supervisor/instructor.	☐

Non-Task-Specific Evaluations:	Step Completed
1. Tools and equipment were used as directed and returned in good working order.	☐
2. Complied with all general and task-specific safety standards, including proper use of any personal protection equipment.	☐
3. Completed the task in an appropriate time frame (4ecommendation: 1.5 or 2 times the flat rate).	☐
4. Left the workspace clean and orderly.	☐
5. Cared for customer property and returned it undamaged.	☐

Student signature _____ Date _____

Comments:

Have your supervisor/instructor verify satisfactory completion of this procedure, any observations made,

and any necessary action(s) recommended.

Evaluation Instructions: The scoring box below is intended to act as a guide for both student and supervisor/instructor. Each criterion listed will help students understand what is expected of them and help supervisors/instructors articulate the level of success at a particular task. The scoring is set up to allow a second attempt at each task (see the Test and Retest columns). Scoring is also designed to award students points only for task criteria that were completed correctly. Points are lost for failure to complete the employability requirements (see Non-Task-Specific Evaluation criteria). When all criteria are evaluated, tally the points for a total at the bottom of each column.

Tasksheet Scoring

Evaluation Items	Test		Retest	
	Pass	**Fail**	**Pass**	**Fail**
Task-Specific Evaluation	**(1 pt)**	**(0 pts)**	**(1 pt)**	**(0 pts)**
Student used the appropriate service information to research the testing system voltage, amperage, and AC ripple.				
Student accurately performed charging system voltage and amperage output tests, then performed the AC ripple test.				
Student compared results to the manufacturer's specifications, then determined any necessary actions.				
Student reinstalled all removed components undamaged and in working order.				
Non-Task-Specific Evaluation	**(0 pts)**	**(−1 pt)**	**(0 pts)**	**(−1 pt)**
Student successfully completed at least three of the non-task-specific steps.				
Student successfully completed all five of the non-task-specific steps.				
Total Score: <total # of points/4 = %>				

Supervisor/Instructor:

Supervisor/instructor signature _____ Date _____

Comments:

> [blank box]

Retest supervisor/instructor signature _____ Date _____

Comments:

> [blank box]

CDX Tasksheet Number: MHT5D006

Student/Intern Information

Name _____ Date _____ Class _____

Vehicle, Customer, and Service Information

Vehicle used for this activity:

Year _____ Make _____ Model _____

Odometer _____ VIN _____

Materials Required

- Vehicle with possible alternator concern, including cable, wiring, or connector faults
- Vehicle manufacturer's workshop materials
- Digital volt-ohmmeter (DVOM); ammeters; and alternator testing equipment, such as load banks and oscilloscope
- Exhaust hoses
- Personal protection equipment (PPE)

Task-Specific Safety Considerations

- Activities may require running the engine and managing an environment of rotating equipment and large current draw, which carry severe risks. Attempt this task only with full permission from your supervisor/instructor, and follow all the guidelines exactly.
- Ensure that your supervisor/instructor checks the connectors of any test equipment.
- Do not run the alternator without a load connected or allow the output voltage to exceed the manufacturer's specified maximum.
- Use extreme caution when working around batteries. Immediately remove any electrolyte that may come in contact with you. Electrolyte is a mixture of sulfuric acid and water. Batteries may produce explosive mixtures of gas containing hydrogen; avoid creating any sparks around batteries. Consult with the shop safety and emergency procedures when working with or around batteries.
- Make sure you follow the manufacturer's operation procedures. Also make sure you have your supervisor's/instructor's permission to use any particular type of lifting equipment.
- Comply with personal and environmental safety practices associated with clothing; eye protection; hand tools; power equipment; proper ventilation; and the handling, storage, and disposal of chemicals/materials in accordance with federal, state, and local regulations.
- Always wear the correct protective eyewear and clothing, and use the appropriate safety equipment, as well as wheel chocks, fender covers, seat protectors, and floor mat protectors.
- Make sure you understand and observe all legislative and personal safety procedures when carrying out practical assignments. If you are unsure of what these are, ask your supervisor/instructor.

Time off_____

Time on_____

▶ **TASK** Perform charging circuit voltage-drop tests; determine needed action.

MTST
V.D.6; P1

Total time_____

Student Instructions: Read through the entire procedure prior to starting. Prepare your workspace and any tools or parts that may be needed to complete the task. When directed by your supervisor/instructor, begin the procedure to complete the task and check the box as each step is finished.

Procedure:	Step Completed
1. Locate "Perform Charging Circuit Voltage-Drop Tests; Determine Necessary Action" in the service information for the vehicle you are working on.	
a. List the procedure as outlined in the service information to perform charging circuit voltage-drop tests:	☐
b. List the maximum specified allowable charging circuit voltage drop: _____ volts	☐
2. Prepare the vehicle, attach exhaust hose(s), tilt cabin or lift hood, and set the parking brake.	☐
3. Connect the tester as outlined in the appropriate service information or as listed in Step 1a.	☐
4. Have your supervisor/instructor verify your test procedure and connections. Supervisor's/instructor's initials:	☐
5. Conduct the charging system voltage-drop test. Repeat the tests as many times as required to test all parts of the charging circuit as described in Step 1. List the measured results.	
a. Voltage drop between _____ and _____ is _____ volts at _____ amps.	☐
b. Voltage drop between _____ and _____ is _____ volts at _____ amps.	☐
c. List the total voltage drop for the charging circuit: _____ volts	☐
6. Compare your results to the manufacturer's specifications.	
a. List your observations:	☐

7. Determine any necessary corrective action(s) and list them:	☐
8. Return any tools you used to their proper locations.	☐
9. Discuss your findings with your supervisor/instructor.	☐

Non-Task-Specific Evaluations:	Step Completed
1. Tools and equipment were used as directed and returned in good working order.	☐
2. Complied with all general and task-specific safety standards, including proper use of any personal protection equipment.	☐
3. Completed the task in an appropriate time frame (recommendation: 1.5 or 2 times the flat rate).	☐
4. Left the workspace clean and orderly.	☐
5. Cared for customer property and returned it undamaged.	☐

Student signature _____ Date _____

Comments:

Have your supervisor/instructor verify satisfactory completion of this procedure, any observations made,

and any necessary action(s) recommended.

Evaluation Instructions: The scoring box below is intended to act as a guide for both student and supervisor/instructor. Each criterion listed will help students understand what is expected of them and help supervisors/instructors articulate the level of success at a particular task. The scoring is set up to allow a second attempt at each task (see the Test and Retest columns). Scoring is also designed to award students points only for task criteria that were completed correctly. Points are lost for failure to complete the employability requirements (see Non-Task-Specific Evaluation criteria). When all criteria are evaluated, tally the points for a total at the bottom of each column.

Tasksheet Scoring

Evaluation Items	Test		Retest	
	Pass	Fail	Pass	Fail
Task-Specific Evaluation	**(1 pt)**	**(0 pts)**	**(1 pt)**	**(0 pts)**
Student used the appropriate service information to research charging system voltage-drop tests.				
Student accurately performed the charging system voltage-drop test on all necessary parts of the circuit.				
Student compared results to the manufacturer's specifications, then determined any necessary actions.				
Student reinstalled all removed components undamaged and in working order.				
Non-Task-Specific Evaluation	**(0 pts)**	**(−1 pt)**	**(0 pts)**	**(−1 pt)**
Student successfully completed at least three of the non-task-specific steps.				
Student successfully completed all five of the non-task-specific steps.				
Total Score: <total # of points/4 = %>				

Supervisor/Instructor:

Supervisor/instructor signature _____ Date _____

Comments:

Retest supervisor/instructor signature _____ Date _____

Comments:

CDX Tasksheet Number: MHT5D007

Student/Intern Information

Name _____ Date _____ Class _____

Vehicle, Customer, and Service Information

Vehicle used for this activity:

Year _____ Make _____ Model _____

Odometer _____ VIN _____

Materials Required

- Vehicle with possible alternator concern, including cable, wiring, or connector faults
- Vehicle manufacturer's workshop materials
- Digital volt-ohmmeter (DVOM); ammeters; and alternator testing equipment, such as load banks and oscilloscope
- Exhaust hoses
- Personal protection equipment (PPE)

Task-Specific Safety Considerations

- Activities may require running the engine and managing an environment of rotating equipment and large current draw, which carry severe risks. Attempt this task only with full permission from your supervisor/instructor, and follow all the guidelines exactly.
- Ensure that your supervisor/instructor checks the connectors of any test equipment.
- Do not run the alternator without a load connected or allow the output voltage to exceed the manufacturer's specified maximum.
- Use extreme caution when working around batteries. Immediately remove any electrolyte that may come in contact with you. Electrolyte is a mixture of sulfuric acid and water. Batteries may produce explosive mixtures of gas containing hydrogen; avoid creating any sparks around batteries. Consult with the shop safety and emergency procedures when working with or around batteries.
- Make sure you follow the manufacturer's operation procedures. Also make sure you have your supervisor's/instructor's permission to use any particular type of lifting equipment.
- Comply with personal and environmental safety practices associated with clothing; eye protection; hand tools; power equipment; proper ventilation; and the handling, storage, and disposal of chemicals/materials in accordance with federal, state, and local regulations.
- Always wear the correct protective eyewear and clothing, and use the appropriate safety equipment, as well as wheel chocks, fender covers, seat protectors, and floor mat protectors.
- Make sure you understand and observe all legislative and personal safety procedures when carrying out practical assignments. If you are unsure of what these are, ask your supervisor/instructor.

Time off_____

Time on_____

▶ **TASK** Remove, inspect, and/or replace generator (alternator).   **MTST** *V.D.7; P1*

Total time_____

© 2021 Jones & Bartlett Learning, LLC, an Ascend Learning Company

Charging System   721

Student Instructions: Read through the entire procedure prior to starting. Prepare your workspace and any tools or parts that may be needed to complete the task. When directed by your supervisor/instructor, begin the procedure to complete the task and check the box as each step is finished.

Procedure:	Step Completed
1. Locate "Remove and Replace Generator (Alternator)" in the appropriate service information for the vehicle you are working on.	
List the steps outlined in the service information to remove the alternator:	☐
2. Remove the alternator as per the service information.	☐
3. List the steps outlined in the service information to install the alternator:	☐
4. Install the alternator as per the service information.	☐
5. Start the vehicle and check the alternator output and voltage.	
a. Voltage output: _____ volts	☐
b. Amperage output: _____ amps	☐
6. Return any tools you used to their proper locations.	☐
7. Discuss your findings with your supervisor/instructor.	☐

Non-Task-Specific Evaluations:	Step Completed
1. Tools and equipment were used as directed and returned in good working order.	☐
2. Complied with all general and task-specific safety standards, including proper use of any personal protection equipment.	☐
3. Completed the task in an appropriate time frame (recommendation: 1.5 or 2 times the flat rate).	☐
4. Left the workspace clean and orderly.	☐
5. Cared for customer property and returned it undamaged.	☐

Student signature _____ Date _____

Comments:

Have your supervisor/instructor verify satisfactory completion of this procedure, any observations made,

and any necessary action(s) recommended.

Evaluation Instructions: The scoring box below is intended to act as a guide for both student and supervisor/instructor. Each criterion listed will help students understand what is expected of them and help supervisors/instructors articulate the level of success at a particular task. The scoring is set up to allow a second attempt at each task (see the Test and Retest columns). Scoring is also designed to award students points only for task criteria that were completed correctly. Points are lost for failure to complete the employability requirements (see Non-Task-Specific Evaluation criteria). When all criteria are evaluated, tally the points for a total at the bottom of each column.

Tasksheet Scoring

Evaluation Items	Test		Retest	
	Pass	**Fail**	**Pass**	**Fail**
Task-Specific Evaluation	**(1 pt)**	**(0 pts)**	**(1 pt)**	**(0 pts)**
Student used the appropriate service information to research alternator removal and replacement.				
Student properly removed and reinstalled the alternator per the service information.				
Student tested the alternator and compared results to the manufacturer's specifications, then determined any necessary actions.				
Student reinstalled all removed components undamaged and in working order.				
Non-Task-Specific Evaluation	**(0 pts)**	**(−1 pt)**	**(0 pts)**	**(−1 pt)**
Student successfully completed at least three of the non-task-specific steps.				
Student successfully completed all five of the non-task-specific steps.				
Total Score: <total # of points/4 = %>				

Supervisor/Instructor:

Supervisor/instructor signature _____ Date _____

Comments:

Retest supervisor/instructor signature _____ Date _____

Comments:

V.E Electrical/Electronic Systems: Lighting System

Learning Objective/Task	CDX Tasksheet Number	ASE Foundation MTST Reference Number; Priority Level
• Diagnose causes of brighter-than-normal, intermittent, dim, or no-light operation; determine needed action.	MHT5E001	V.E.1; P-1
• Test, replace, and aim headlights.	MHT5E002	V.E.2; P-1
• Inspect cables, wires, and connectors in the lighting systems.	MHT5E003	V.E.3; P-1
• Diagnose faults in tractor-to-trailer multiwire connector(s), cables, and holders; determine needed action.	MHT5E004	V.E.4; P-2
• Diagnose faults in switches, relays, bulbs/light-emitting diodes (LEDs), wires, terminals, connectors, sockets, and control components/modules of exterior lighting systems; determine needed action.	MHT5E005	V.E.5; P-2
• Diagnose faults in switches, relays, bulbs/light-emitting diodes (LEDs), wires, terminals, connectors, sockets, and control components/modules of interior lighting systems; determine needed action.	MHT5E006	V.E.6; P-2
• Diagnose faults in switches, relays, bulbs/light-emitting diodes (LEDs), wires, terminals, connectors, sockets, and control components/modules of auxiliary lighting circuits; determine needed action.	MHT5E007	V.E.7; P-2

Materials Required

- Vehicle or simulator with electrical lighting concern(s)
- Vehicle manufacturer's workshop materials, including schematic wiring diagrams
- Digital volt-ohmmeter (DVOM)
- Exhaust hoses
- Personal protection equipment (PPE)

Safety Considerations

- Activities require you to measure electrical values. Always ensure that your supervisor/instructor checks test instrument connections prior to connecting power or taking measurements. High current flows can be dangerous; avoid accidental short circuits or grounding the battery's positive connections.
- Activities may require test-driving the vehicle on the school grounds or on a hoist, both of which carry severe risks. Attempt this task only with full permission from your supervisor/instructor, and follow all the guidelines exactly.
- Comply with personal and environmental safety practices associated with clothing; eye protection; hand tools; power equipment; proper ventilation; and the handling, storage, and disposal of chemicals/materials in accordance with federal, state, and local regulations.

- Always wear the correct protective eyewear and clothing and use the appropriate safety equipment, as well as wheel chocks fender covers, seat protectors, and floor mat protectors.
- Make sure you understand and observe all legislative and personal safety procedures when carrying out practical assignments. If you are unsure of what these are, ask your supervisor/instructor.

CDX Tasksheet Number: MHT5E001

Student/Intern Information

Name _____ Date _____ Class _____

Vehicle, Customer, and Service Information

Vehicle used for this activity:

Year _____ Make _____ Model _____

Odometer _____ VIN _____

Materials Required

- Vehicle or simulator with electrical lighting concern(s)
- Vehicle manufacturer's workshop materials, including schematic wiring diagrams
- Digital volt-ohmmeter (DVOM)
- Exhaust hoses
- Personal protection equipment (PPE)

Task-Specific Safety Considerations

- Activities require you to measure electrical values. Always ensure that the instructor/supervisor checks test instrument connections prior to connecting power or taking measurements. High current flows can be dangerous; avoid accidental short circuits or grounding the battery's positive connections.
- Activities may require test-driving the vehicle on the school grounds or on a hoist, both of which carry severe risks. Attempt this task only with full permission from your supervisor/instructor and follow all the guidelines exactly.
- Comply with personal and environmental safety practices associated with clothing; eye protection; hand tools; power equipment; proper ventilation; and the handling, storage, and disposal of chemicals/materials in accordance with federal, state, and local regulations.
- Always wear the correct protective eyewear and clothing, and use the appropriate safety equipment, as well as wheel chocks, fender covers, seat protectors, and floor mat protectors.
- Make sure you understand and observe all legislative and personal safety procedures when carrying out practical assignments. If you are unsure of what these are, ask your supervisor/instructor.

▶ TASK Diagnose causes of brighter-than-normal, intermittent, dim, or no-light operation; determine needed action.

MTST
V.E.1; P1

Time off_____

Time on_____

Total time_____

Student Instructions: Read through the entire procedure prior to starting. Prepare your workspace and any tools or parts that may be needed to complete the task. When directed by your supervisor/instructor, begin the procedure to complete the task and check the box as each step is finished.

Procedure:	Step Completed
1. List the customer complaint regarding the lighting system fault:	☐
2. If the lights are dim or do not operate, go to Step 3. If the lights are too bright, go to Step 9.	☐
3. Research the affected lighting system troubleshooting section and the wiring diagram(s) in the appropriate manufacturer's service information for the vehicle you are working on.	☐
4. Turn on the affected lights(s), measure the battery voltage, and list it here: _____ volts	☐
5. Measure the voltage drop across the power and ground at the light while illuminated. List the voltage: _____ volts	
a. Calculate the total voltage drop in the circuit and list it here: _____ voltage drop	☐
b. Is the voltage drop excessive? Yes: ☐ No: ☐	☐
c. If Yes, go to Step 7. If No, go to Step 6.	☐
6. Inspect the bulb and connection for any faults (wrong bulb, corroded, or loose connection). List your observations below:	☐
7. Measure the voltage drop from the battery's positive post to the input terminal of the light.	
a. List the voltage drop: _____ volts	☐
b. Is this within specifications? Yes: ☐ No: ☐	☐
c. Determine any necessary actions and list them below:	☐

8. Measure the voltage drop from the bulb ground to the battery negative post.	
a. List the voltage drop: _____ volts	☐
b. Is this within specifications? Yes: ☐ No: ☐	☐
c. Determine any necessary actions and list them below:	☐
9. Install an exhaust hose(s) and wheel chocks, and set the parking brake. Start the vehicle.	☐
10. Measure the charging system voltage at the battery, with the engine running at 1500 rpm. If the battery voltage is too high, you will need to perform charging system checks to determine the cause of the overcharge: _____ volts	
a. Is this within specifications? Yes: ☐ No: ☐	☐
11. List your observations below:	☐
12. Determine any necessary action(s) and list them below:	☐
13. Have your supervisor/instructor verify satisfactory completion of this procedure, any observations found, and any necessary action(s) recommended.	☐

Non-Task–Specific Evaluations:	Step Completed
1. Tools and equipment were used as directed and returned in good working order.	☐
2. Complied with all general and task-specific safety standards, including proper use of any personal protection equipment.	☐
3. Completed the task in an appropriate time frame (recommendation: 1.5 or 2 times the flat rate).	☐
4. Left the workspace clean and orderly.	☐
5. Cared for customer property and returned it undamaged.	☐

Student signature _____ Date _____

Comments:

Have your supervisor/instructor verify satisfactory completion of this procedure, any observations made,

and any necessary action(s) recommended.

Evaluation Instructions: The scoring box below is intended to act as a guide for both student and supervisor/instructor. Each criterion listed will help students to understand what is expected of them and help supervisors/instructors articulate the level of success at a particular task. The scoring is set up to allow a second attempt at each task (see the Test and Retest columns). Scoring is also designed to award students points only for task criteria that were completed correctly. Points are lost for failure to complete the employability requirements (see Non-Task-Specific Evaluation criteria). When all criteria are evaluated, tally the points for a total at the bottom of each column.

Tasksheet Scoring

	Test		Retest	
Evaluation Items	**Pass**	**Fail**	**Pass**	**Fail**
Task-Specific Evaluation	**(1 pt)**	**(0 pts)**	**(1 pt)**	**(0 pts)**
Student used the appropriate service information to research the customer complaint.				
Student accurately performed measurements to diagnose the brighter-than-normal, intermittent, dim, or no-light condition.				
Student compared the results to the specifications, then correctly determined any necessary actions.				
Student reinstalled all removed components undamaged and in working order.				
Non-Task-Specific Evaluation	**(0 pts)**	**(−1 pt)**	**(0 pts)**	**(−1 pt)**
Student successfully completed at least three of the non-task-specific steps.				
Student successfully completed all five of the non-task-specific steps.				
Total Score: <total # of points/4 = %>				

Supervisor/Instructor:

Supervisor/instructor signature _____ Date _____

Comments:

Retest supervisor/instructor signature _____ Date _____

Comments:

CDX Tasksheet Number: MHT5E002

Student/Intern Information

Name _____ Date _____ Class _____

Vehicle, Customer, and Service Information

Vehicle used for this activity:

Year _____ Make _____ Model _____

Odometer _____ VIN _____

Materials Required

- Vehicle or simulator with electrical lighting concern(s)
- Vehicle manufacturer's workshop materials, including schematic wiring diagrams
- Digital volt-ohmmeter (DVOM)
- Personal protection equipment (PPE)

Task-Specific Safety Considerations

- Activities require you to measure electrical values. Always ensure that the instructor/ supervisor checks test instrument connections prior to connecting power or taking measurements. High current flows can be dangerous; avoid accidental short circuits or grounding the battery's positive connections.
- Activities may require test-driving the vehicle on the school grounds or on a hoist, both of which carry severe risks. Attempt this task only with full permission from your supervisor/ instructor and follow all the guidelines exactly.
- Comply with personal and environmental safety practices associated with clothing; eye protection; hand tools; power equipment; proper ventilation; and the handling, storage, and disposal of chemicals/materials in accordance with federal, state, and local regulations.
- Always wear the correct protective eyewear and clothing, and use the appropriate safety equipment, as well as wheel chocks, fender covers, seat protectors, and floor mat protectors.
- Make sure you understand and observe all legislative and personal safety procedures when carrying out practical assignments. If you are unsure of what these are, ask your supervisor/ instructor.

▶ TASK Test, replace, and aim headlights. **MTST** V.E.2; P1

Time off_____

Time on_____

Student Instructions: Read through the entire procedure prior to starting. Prepare your workspace and any tools or parts that may be needed to complete the task. When directed by your supervisor/instructor, begin the procedure to complete the task and check the box as each step is finished.

Total time_____

Procedure:	Step Completed
1. Research the headlight aiming procedure in the exterior lighting section in the appropriate manufacturer service manual for the vehicle you are working on.	
a. Type of headlights the vehicle is equipped with:	☐
b. High-beam bulb number:	☐
c. Low-beam bulb number:	☐
2. Research the headlamp aiming process in the appropriate manufacturer service manual for the vehicle you are working on. List (or print off and attach) the steps that are required to aim these headlights: (**Note:** Do not touch the bulb with your fingers. Some bulbs will prematurely due to the oils from your skin.)	☐
3. Aim the headlights following the specified procedure.	☐
4. List any problems you encountered performing this task:	☐
5. Consult with your supervisor/instructor and list any recommendations that may be necessary:	☐

Non-Task-Specific Evaluations:	Step Completed
1. Tools and equipment were used as directed and returned in good working order.	☐
2. Complied with all general and task-specific safety standards, including proper use of any personal protection equipment.	☐
3. Completed the task in an appropriate time frame (recommendation: 1.5 or 2 times the flat rate).	☐
4. Left the workspace clean and orderly.	☐
5. Cared for customer property and returned it undamaged.	☐

Student signature _____ Date _____

Comments:

Have your supervisor/instructor verify satisfactory completion of this procedure, any observations made,

and any necessary action(s) recommended.

Evaluation Instructions: The scoring box below is intended to act as a guide for both student and supervisor/instructor. Each criterion listed will help students to understand what is expected of them and help supervisors/instructors articulate the level of success at a particular task. The scoring is set up to allow a second attempt at each task (see the Test and Retest columns). Scoring is also designed to award students points only for task criteria that were completed correctly. Points are lost for failure to complete the employability requirements (see Non-Task-Specific Evaluation criteria). When all criteria are evaluated, tally the points for a total at the bottom of each column.

Tasksheet Scoring

Evaluation Items	Test		Retest	
	Pass	Fail	Pass	Fail
Task-Specific Evaluation	**(1 pt)**	**(0 pts)**	**(1 pt)**	**(0 pts)**
Student used the appropriate service information to research the headlight aiming procedure.				
Student successfully aimed the headlights following the specified instructions.				
Student noted any problems encountered during the process.				
Student reinstalled all removed components undamaged and in working order.				
Non-Task-Specific Evaluation	**(0 pts)**	**(−1 pt)**	**(0 pts)**	**(−1 pt)**
Student successfully completed at least three of the non-task-specific steps.				
Student successfully completed all five of the non-task-specific steps.				
Total Score: <total # of points/4 = %>				

Supervisor/Instructor:

Supervisor/instructor signature _____ Date _____

Comments:

Retest supervisor/instructor signature _____ Date _____

Comments:

CDX Tasksheet Number: MHT5E003

Student/Intern Information

Name _____ Date _____ Class _____

Vehicle, Customer, and Service Information

Vehicle used for this activity:

Year _____ Make _____ Model _____

Odometer _____ VIN _____

Materials Required

- Vehicle or simulator with electrical lighting concern(s)
- Vehicle manufacturer's workshop materials, including schematic wiring diagrams
- Digital volt-ohmmeter (DVOM)
- Personal protection equipment (PPE)

Task-Specific Safety Considerations

- Activities require you to measure electrical values. Always ensure that the instructor/ supervisor checks test instrument connections prior to connecting power or taking measurements. High current flows can be dangerous; avoid accidental short circuits or grounding the battery's positive connections.
- Activities may require test-driving the vehicle on the school grounds or on a hoist, both of which carry severe risks. Attempt this task only with full permission from your supervisor/ instructor, and follow all the guidelines exactly.
- Comply with personal and environmental safety practices associated with clothing; eye protection; hand tools; power equipment; proper ventilation; and the handling, storage, and disposal of chemicals/materials in accordance with federal, state, and local regulations.
- Always wear the correct protective eyewear and clothing and use the appropriate safety equipment, as well as wheel chocks, fender covers, seat protectors, and floor mat protectors.
- Make sure you understand and observe all legislative and personal safety procedures when carrying out practical assignments. If you are unsure of what these are, ask your supervisor/ instructor.

▶ **TASK** Inspect cables, wires, and connectors in the lighting systems. *MTST V.E.3; P1*

Time off_____

Time on_____

Student Instructions: Read through the entire procedure prior to starting. Prepare your workspace and any tools or parts that may be needed to complete the task. When directed by your supervisor/instructor, begin the procedure to complete the task and check the box as each step is finished.

Total time_____

Procedure:	Step Completed
1. While referencing the manufacturer's workshop materials, check the operation of all lighting.	
a. Within, manufacturer's specifications: Yes: ☐ No: ☐	☐
b. If No, list the recommended corrective action(s):	☐
2. While referencing the manufacturer's workshop materials, check the operation of all lighting switches for proper operation and sticking/binding.	
a. Within, manufacturer's specifications: Yes: ☐ No: ☐	☐
b. If No, list the recommended corrective action(s):	☐
3. While referencing the manufacturer's workshop materials, inspect the headlight wiring harness(s) for damage and proper securement.	
a. Within manufacturer's specifications: Yes: ☐ No: ☐	☐
b. If No, list the recommended corrective action(s):	☐
4. While referencing the manufacturer's workshop materials, check the headlight connections for loose/burnt/damaged connections.	
a. Within manufacturer's specifications: Yes: ☐ No: ☐	☐
b. If No, list the recommended corrective action(s):	☐
5. While referencing the manufacturer's workshop materials, inspect the front turn signal and marker wiring harness(es) for damage and proper securement.	
a. Within manufacturer's specifications: Yes: ☐ No: ☐	☐

b. If No, list the recommended corrective action(s):	☐
6. While referencing the manufacturer's workshop materials, check the front turn signal and marker light connections for loose/burnt/damaged connections.	
a. Within manufacturer's specifications: Yes: ☐ No: ☐	☐
b. If No, list the recommended corrective action(s):	☐
7. While referencing the manufacturer's workshop materials, inspect the rear turn signal and marker wiring harness(s) for damage and proper securement.	
a. Within manufacturer's specifications: Yes: ☐ No: ☐	☐
b. If No, list the recommended corrective action(s):	☐
8. While referencing the manufacturer's workshop materials, check the rear turn signal and marker light connections for loose/burnt/damaged connections.	
a. Within manufacturer's specifications: Yes: ☐ No: ☐	☐
b. If No, list the recommendations for rectification:	☐
9. While referencing the manufacturer's workshop materials, inspect any auxiliary/custom lighting wiring harness(s) for damage and proper securement.	
a. Within manufacturer's specifications: Yes: ☐ No: ☐	☐
b. If No, list the recommended corrective action(s):	☐

10. While referencing the manufacturer's workshop materials, inspect any auxiliary/custom lighting for loose/burnt/damaged connections.	
a. Within manufacturer's specifications: Yes: ☐ No: ☐	☐
b. If No, list the recommended corrective action(s):	☐
11. While referencing the manufacturer's workshop materials, inspect any miscellaneous lighting wiring harness(es) for damage and proper securement.	
a. Within manufacturer's specifications: Yes: ☐ No: ☐	☐
b. If No, list the recommended corrective action(s):	☐
12. While referencing the manufacturer's workshop materials, check any miscellaneous lighting connections for loose/burnt/damaged connections.	
a. Within manufacturer's specifications: Yes: ☐ No: ☐	☐
b. If No, list the recommended corrective action(s):	☐
13. While referencing the manufacturer's workshop materials and electronic service tool (EST), check for any diagnostic trouble codes (DTCs) that are associated with the vehicle lighting.	
a. Within manufacturer's specifications: Yes: ☐ No: ☐	☐
b. If No, list the recommended corrective action(s):	☐
14. While referencing the manufacturer's workshop materials and EST, check the operation of the lighting circuits.	
a. Within the manufacturer's specifications: Yes: ☐ No: ☐	☐

	Step Completed
b. If No, list the recommendations for rectification:	☐
15. Discuss your findings with your supervisor/instructor.	☐

Non-Task-Specific Evaluations:	Step Completed
1. Tools and equipment were used as directed and returned in good working order.	☐
2. Complied with all general and task-specific safety standards, including proper use of any personal protection equipment.	☐
3. Completed the task in an appropriate time frame (recommendation: 1.5 or 2 times the flat rate).	☐
4. Left the workspace clean and orderly.	☐
5. Cared for customer property and returned it undamaged.	☐

Student signature _____ Date _____

Comments:

Have your supervisor/instructor verify satisfactory completion of this procedure, any observations made, and any necessary action(s) recommended.

Evaluation Instructions: The scoring box below is intended to act as a guide for both student and supervisor/instructor. Each criterion listed will help students to understand what is expected of them and help supervisors/instructors articulate the level of success at a particular task. The scoring is set up to allow a second attempt at each task (see the Test and Retest columns). Scoring is also designed to award students points only for task criteria that were completed correctly. Points are lost for failure to complete the employability requirements (see Non-Task-Specific Evaluation criteria). When all criteria are evaluated, tally the points for a total at the bottom of each column.

Tasksheet Scoring

	Test		Retest	
Evaluation Items	**Pass**	**Fail**	**Pass**	**Fail**
Task-Specific Evaluation	**(1 pt)**	**(0 pts)**	**(1 pt)**	**(0 pts)**
Student properly inspected lighting operation and lighting system switches and checked lighting system using an EST.				
Student properly inspected headlight harness(es) and connections, auxiliary/custom harness(es) and connections, and miscellaneous harness(es) and connections.				
Student properly inspected front turn signal and marker light harness(es) and connections and rear turn signal and marker light harness(es) and connections.				
Student properly checked DTCs for the lighting system.				
Non-Task-Specific Evaluation	**(0 pts)**	**(−1 pt)**	**(0 pts)**	**(−1 pt)**
Student successfully completed at least three of the non-task-specific steps.				
Student successfully completed all five of the non-task-specific steps.				
Total Score: <total # of points/4 = %>				

Supervisor/Instructor:

Supervisor/instructor signature _____ Date _____

Comments:

Retest supervisor/instructor signature _____ Date _____

Comments:

CDX Tasksheet Number: MHT5E004

Student/Intern Information

Name _____ Date _____ Class _____

Vehicle, Customer, and Service Information

Vehicle used for this activity:

Year _____ Make _____ Model _____

Odometer _____ VIN _____

Materials Required

- Vehicle or simulator with electrical lighting concern(s)
- Vehicle manufacturer's workshop materials, including schematic wiring diagrams
- Digital volt-ohmmeter (DVOM)
- Personal protection equipment (PPE)

Task-Specific Safety Considerations

- Activities require you to measure electrical values. Always ensure that the instructor/supervisor checks test instrument connections prior to connecting power or taking measurements. High current flows can be dangerous; avoid accidental short circuits or grounding the battery's positive connections.
- Activities may require test-driving the vehicle on the school grounds or on a hoist, both of which carry severe risks. Attempt this task only with full permission from your supervisor/instructor and follow all the guidelines exactly.
- Comply with personal and environmental safety practices associated with clothing; eye protection; hand tools; power equipment; proper ventilation; and the handling, storage, and disposal of chemicals/materials in accordance with federal, state, and local regulations.
- Always wear the correct protective eyewear and clothing, and use the appropriate safety equipment, as well as wheel chocks, fender covers, seat protectors, and floor mat protectors.
- Make sure you understand and observe all legislative and personal safety procedures when carrying out practical assignments. If you are unsure of what these are, ask your supervisor/instructor.

▶ TASK Diagnose faults in tractor-to-trailer multiwire connector(s), cables, and holders; determine needed action.

MTST
V.E.4; P2

Time off_____

Time on_____

Student Instructions: Read through the entire procedure prior to starting. Prepare your workspace and any tools or parts that may be needed to complete the task. When directed by your supervisor/instructor, begin the procedure to complete the task and check the box as each step is finished.

Total time_____

Procedure:	Step Completed
1. List the customer complaint regarding the tractor-to-trailer connector fault:	☐
2. Consult the appropriate manufacturer workshop materials for the correct wiring diagram information to do this task.	☐
3. Test the trailer connector/International Standards Organization (ISO), utilizing a DVOM for continuity throughout each wire in the cable.	
a. Test and record connector continuity: _____ ohms	☐
4. Test and record the voltage at each pin.	
a.	☐
b.	☐
c.	☐
d.	☐
e.	☐
f.	☐
g.	☐

5. Check that none of the connector pins is damaged and that corrosion is not present in the connector, indicating water penetration.	☐
6. Is damage or corrosion present? Yes: ☐ No: ☐	
a. If damage is present, consult the appropriate service manual information on repairing or replacing the connectors or cable and record it below:	☐
7. Consult with your supervisor/instructor about any recommendations necessary to correct any existing problems and record them below:	☐

Non-Task-Specific Evaluations:	Step Completed
1. Tools and equipment were used as directed and returned in good working order.	☐
2. Complied with all general and task-specific safety standards, including proper use of any personal protection equipment.	☐
3. Completed the task in an appropriate time frame (recommendation: 1.5 or 2 times the flat rate).	☐
4. Left the workspace clean and orderly.	☐
5. Cared for customer property and returned it undamaged.	☐

Student signature _____ Date _____

Comments:

Have your supervisor/instructor verify satisfactory completion of this procedure, any observations made, and any necessary action(s) recommended.

Evaluation Instructions: The scoring box below is intended to act as a guide for both student and supervisor/instructor. Each criterion listed will help students to understand what is expected of them and help supervisors/instructors articulate the level of success at a particular task. The scoring is set up to allow a second attempt at each task (see the Test and Retest columns). Scoring is also designed to award students points only for task criteria that were completed correctly. Points are lost for failure to complete the employability requirements (see Non-Task-Specific Evaluation criteria). When all criteria are evaluated, tally the points for a total at the bottom of each column.

Tasksheet Scoring

Evaluation Items	Test		Retest	
	Pass	**Fail**	**Pass**	**Fail**
Task-Specific Evaluation	**(1 pt)**	**(0 pts)**	**(1 pt)**	**(0 pts)**
Student used the appropriate service information to research the customer complaint.				
Student accurately tested and inspected the tractor-to-trailer connector.				
Student compared the results to the specifications, then correctly determined any necessary actions.				
Student reinstalled all removed components undamaged and in working order.				
Non-Task-Specific Evaluation	**(0 pts)**	**(−1 pt)**	**(0 pts)**	**(−1 pt)**
Student successfully completed at least three of the non-task-specific steps.				
Student successfully completed all five of the non-task-specific steps.				
Total Score: <total # of points/4 = %>				

Supervisor/Instructor:

Supervisor/instructor signature _____ Date _____

Comments:

Retest supervisor/instructor signature _____ Date _____

Comments:

CDX Tasksheet Number: MHT5E005

Student/Intern Information

Name _____ Date _____ Class _____

Vehicle, Customer, and Service Information

Vehicle used for this activity:

Year _____ Make _____ Model _____

Odometer _____ VIN _____

Materials Required

- Vehicle or simulator with electrical lighting concern(s)
- Vehicle manufacturer's workshop materials, including schematic wiring diagrams
- Digital volt-ohmmeter (DVOM)
- Personal protection equipment (PPE)

Task-Specific Safety Considerations

- Activities require you to measure electrical values. Always ensure that the instructor/ supervisor checks test instrument connections prior to connecting power or taking measurements. High current flows can be dangerous; avoid accidental short circuits or grounding the battery's positive connections.
- Activities may require test-driving the vehicle on the school grounds or on a hoist, both of which carry severe risks. Attempt this task only with full permission from your supervisor/ instructor and follow all the guidelines exactly.
- Comply with personal and environmental safety practices associated with clothing; eye protection; hand tools; power equipment; proper ventilation; and the handling, storage, and disposal of chemicals/materials in accordance with federal, state, and local regulations.
- Always wear the correct protective eyewear and clothing, and use the appropriate safety equipment, as well as wheel chocks, fender covers, seat protectors, and floor mat protectors.
- Make sure you understand and observe all legislative and personal safety procedures when carrying out practical assignments. If you are unsure of what these are, ask your supervisor/ instructor.

▶ TASK Diagnose faults in switches, relays, bulbs/light-emitting diodes (LEDs), wires, terminals, connectors, sockets, and control components/modules of exterior lighting systems; determine needed action.

MTST
V.E.5; P2

Time off_____

Time on_____

Total time_____

Student Instructions: Read through the entire procedure prior to starting. Prepare your workspace and any tools or parts that may be needed to complete the task. When directed by your supervisor/instructor, begin the procedure to complete the task and check the box as each step is finished.

Procedure:	Step Completed
1. List the customer complaint regarding the exterior lighting fault:	☐
2. Consult the appropriate manufacturer service manual for the correct wiring diagram information to do this task.	☐
3. Inspect and test all switches associated with the circuit by operating them and checking for illumination of all lights in the circuit.	
a. Are the switches working? Yes: ☐ No: ☐	☐
b. If No, consult the appropriate service information to repair or replace faulty switches.	☐
4. Test relay(s) for proper operation.	
a. Consult manufacturer workshop materials and record the proper procedures to test these components:	☐
5. Inspect and test all bulbs/LEDs associated with the circuit.	
a. Are the bulbs/LEDs working? Yes: ☐ No: ☐	☐
b. If No, consult the appropriate service information to replace the bulbs/LEDs.	☐
6. Check all wiring that is present to that circuit for bare spots, cracked insulation, and no connection to the connector or component. Perform voltage-drop tests to the circuit if necessary.	
a. Condition of wiring: Good: ☐ Bad: ☐	☐
7. If the condition of the wiring is bad, make recommendations for repairing or replacing the wiring:	☐
8. Check all switch connections/terminals for corrosion and connector tightness.	☐

9. Check all connectors to relays and control modules for looseness, cracking, and burn marks that may cause the system to malfunction. Any burn marks or discoloration of the connectors may indicate excessive amperage running through them.	
a. Condition of connectors: Good: ☐ Bad: ☐	☐
10. If the connectors are bad, make recommendations for repairing or replacing the connections.	☐
11. Check all sockets for any water damage or burnt conditions.	
a. Condition of sockets: Good: ☐ Bad: ☐	☐
12. Test modules for proper operation.	
a. Consult manufacturer service manual and record the proper procedures to test these components:	☐
13. Return the vehicle to its beginning condition, and return any tools to their proper locations.	☐
14. Consult with your supervisor/instructor and record any recommendations to bring the circuit back to manufacturer specifications:	☐

Non-Task-Specific Evaluations:	Step Completed
1. Tools and equipment were used as directed and returned in good working order.	☐
2. Complied with all general and task-specific safety standards, including proper use of any personal protection equipment.	☐
3. Completed the task in an appropriate time frame (recommendation: 1.5 or 2 times the flat rate).	☐
4. Left the workspace clean and orderly.	☐
5. Cared for customer property and returned it undamaged.	☐

Student signature _____ Date _____

Comments:

Have your supervisor/instructor verify satisfactory completion of this procedure, any observations made, and any necessary action(s) recommended.

Evaluation Instructions: The scoring box below is intended to act as a guide for both student and supervisor/instructor. Each criterion listed will help students to understand what is expected of them and help supervisors/instructors articulate the level of success at a particular task. The scoring is set up to allow a second attempt at each task (see the Test and Retest columns). Scoring is also designed to award students points only for task criteria that were completed correctly. Points are lost for failure to complete the employability requirements (see Non-Task-Specific Evaluation criteria). When all criteria are evaluated, tally the points for a total at the bottom of each column.

Tasksheet Scoring

Evaluation Items	Test		Retest	
	Pass	**Fail**	**Pass**	**Fail**
Task-Specific Evaluation	**(1 pt)**	**(0 pts)**	**(1 pt)**	**(0 pts)**
Student used the appropriate service information to research the customer complaint.				
Student accurately tested and inspected the exterior lighting circuit.				
Student compared the results to the specifications, then correctly determined any necessary actions.				
Student reinstalled all removed components undamaged and in working order.				
Non-Task-Specific Evaluation	**(0 pts)**	**(−1 pt)**	**(0 pts)**	**(−1 pt)**
Student successfully completed at least three of the non-task-specific steps.				
Student successfully completed all five of the non-task-specific steps.				
Total Score: <total # of points/4 = %>				

Supervisor/Instructor:

Supervisor/instructor signature _____ Date _____

Comments:

Retest supervisor/instructor signature _____ Date _____

Comments:

CDX Tasksheet Number: MHT5E006

Student/Intern Information

Name _____ Date _____ Class _____

Vehicle, Customer, and Service Information

Vehicle used for this activity:

Year _____ Make _____ Model _____

Odometer _____ VIN _____

Materials Required
- Vehicle or simulator with electrical lighting concern(s)
- Vehicle manufacturer's workshop materials, including schematic wiring diagrams
- Digital volt-ohmmeter (DVOM)
- Personal protection equipment (PPE)

Task-Specific Safety Considerations
- Activities require you to measure electrical values. Always ensure that the instructor/ supervisor checks test instrument connections prior to connecting power or taking measurements. High current flows can be dangerous; avoid accidental short circuits or grounding the battery's positive connections.
- Activities may require test driving the vehicle on the school grounds or on a hoist, both of which carry severe risks. Attempt this task only with full permission from your supervisor/ instructor and follow all the guidelines exactly.
- Comply with personal and environmental safety practices associated with clothing; eye protection; hand tools; power equipment; proper ventilation; and the handling, storage, and disposal of chemicals/materials in accordance with federal, state, and local regulations.
- Always wear the correct protective eyewear and clothing, and use the appropriate safety equipment, as well as wheel chocks, fender covers, seat protectors, and floor mat protectors.
- Make sure you understand and observe all legislative and personal safety procedures when carrying out practical assignments. If you are unsure of what these are, ask your supervisor/ instructor.

▶ **TASK** Diagnose faults in switches, relays, bulbs/light-emitting diodes (LEDs), wires, terminals, connectors, sockets, and control components/modules of interior lighting systems; determine needed action. *MTST* V.E.6; P2

Time off_____

Time on_____

Total time_____

Student Instructions: Read through the entire procedure prior to starting. Prepare your workspace and any tools or parts that may be needed to complete the task. When directed by your supervisor/instructor, begin the procedure to complete the task and check the box as each step is finished.

Procedure:	Step Completed
1. List the customer complaint regarding the auxiliary lighting fault:	☐
2. Consult the appropriate manufacturer service manual for the correct wiring diagram information to do this task.	☐
3. Inspect and test all switches associated with the circuit by operating them and checking for illumination of all lights in the circuit.	
a. Are the switches working? Yes: ☐ No: ☐	☐
b. If No, consult the appropriate service information to repair or replace faulty switches.	☐
4. Test relay(s) for proper operation.	
a. Consult manufacturer workshop materials and record the proper procedures to test these components:	☐
5. Inspect and test all bulbs/LEDs associated with the circuit.	
a. Are the bulbs/LEDs working? Yes: ☐ No: ☐	☐
b. If No, consult the appropriate service information to replace the bulbs/LEDs.	☐
6. Check all wiring that is present to that circuit for bare spots, cracked insulation, and no connection to a connector or component. Perform voltage-drop tests to the circuit if necessary.	
a. Condition of wiring: Good: ☐ Bad: ☐	☐
7. If the condition of the wiring is bad, make recommendations for repairing or replacing the wiring:	☐
8. Check all switch connections/terminals for corrosion and connector tightness.	☐

754 Lighting System

9. Check all connectors to relays and control modules for looseness, cracking, and burn marks that may cause the system to malfunction. Any burn marks or discoloration of the connectors may indicate excessive amperage running through them.	
a. Condition of connectors: Good: ☐ Bad: ☐	☐
10. If the connectors are bad, make recommendations for repairing or replacing the connections:	☐
11. Check all sockets for any water damage or burnt conditions.	
a. Condition of sockets: Good: ☐ Bad: ☐	☐
12. Test modules for proper operation.	
a. Consult manufacturer service manual and record the proper procedures to test these components:	☐
13. Return the vehicle to its beginning condition, and return any tools to their proper locations.	☐
14. Consult with your supervisor/instructor and record any recommendations to bring the circuit back to manufacturer specifications:	☐

Non-Task-Specific Evaluations:	Step Completed
1. Tools and equipment were used as directed and returned in good working order.	☐
2. Complied with all general and task-specific safety standards, including proper use of any personal protection equipment.	☐
3. Completed the task in an appropriate time frame (recommendation: 1.5 or 2 times the flat rate).	☐
4. Left the workspace clean and orderly.	☐
5. Cared for customer property and returned it undamaged.	☐

Student signature _____ Date _____

Comments:

Have your supervisor/instructor verify satisfactory completion of this procedure, any observations made,

and any necessary action(s) recommended.

Evaluation Instructions: The scoring box below is intended to act as a guide for both student and supervisor/instructor. Each criterion listed will help students to understand what is expected of them and help supervisors/instructors articulate the level of success at a particular task. The scoring is set up to allow a second attempt at each task (see the Test and Retest columns). Scoring is also designed to award students points only for task criteria that were completed correctly. Points are lost for failure to complete the employability requirements (see Non-Task-Specific Evaluation criteria). When all criteria are evaluated, tally the points for a total at the bottom of each column.

Tasksheet Scoring

Evaluation Items	Test		Retest	
	Pass	**Fail**	**Pass**	**Fail**
Task-Specific Evaluation	**(1 pt)**	**(0 pts)**	**(1 pt)**	**(0 pts)**
Student successfully used the appropriate service information to research the customer complaint.				
Student accurately tested and inspected the interior lighting circuit.				
Student compared the results to the specifications, then correctly determined any necessary actions.				
Student reinstalled all removed components undamaged and in working order.				
Non-Task-Specific Evaluation	**(0 pts)**	**(−1 pt)**	**(0 pts)**	**(−1 pt)**
Student successfully completed at least three of the non-task-specific steps.				
Student successfully completed all five of the non-task-specific steps.				
Total Score: <total # of points/4 = %>				

CDX Tasksheet Number: MHT5E007

Student/Intern Information

Name _____ Date _____ Class _____

Vehicle, Customer, and Service Information

Vehicle used for this activity:

Year _____ Make _____ Model _____

Odometer _____ VIN _____

Materials Required

- Vehicle or simulator with electrical lighting concern(s)
- Vehicle manufacturer's workshop materials, including schematic wiring diagrams
- Digital volt-ohmmeter (DVOM)
- Personal protection equipment (PPE)

Task-Specific Safety Considerations

- Activities may require you to measure electrical values. Always ensure that the instructor/supervisor checks test instrument connections prior to connecting power or taking measurements. High current flows can be dangerous; avoid accidental short circuits or grounding the battery's positive connections.
- Activities may require test-driving the vehicle on the school grounds or on a hoist, both of which carry severe risks. Attempt this task only with full permission from your supervisor/instructor, and follow all the guidelines exactly.
- Comply with personal and environmental safety practices associated with clothing; eye protection; hand tools; power equipment; proper ventilation; and the handling, storage, and disposal of chemicals/materials in accordance with federal, state, and local regulations.
- Always wear the correct protective eyewear and clothing and use the appropriate safety equipment, as well as wheel chocks, fender covers, seat protectors, and floor mat protectors.
- Make sure you understand and observe all legislative and personal safety procedures when carrying out practical assignments. If you are unsure of what these are, ask your supervisor/instructor.

▶ **TASK** Diagnose faults in switches, relays, bulbs/light-emitting diodes (LEDs), wires, terminals, connectors, sockets, and control components/modules of auxiliary lighting circuits; determine needed action.

MTST
V.E.7; P2

Time off_____

Time on_____

Total time_____

Student Instructions: Read through the entire procedure prior to starting. Prepare your workspace and any tools or parts that may be needed to complete the task. When directed by your supervisor/instructor, begin the procedure to complete the task and check the box as each step is finished.

Procedure:	Step Completed
1. Inspect the vehicle and record the auxiliary lighting position(s) and type(s):	☐
2. While referencing the manufacturer's workshop materials, check the operation of all auxiliary lighting switches for proper operation, as well as binding/sticking.	☐
3. While referencing the manufacturer's workshop materials, check the operation of all auxiliary lighting.	
a. Within manufacturer's specifications: Yes: ☐ No: ☐	☐
b. If No, list the recommended corrective action(s):	☐
4. While referencing the manufacturer's workshop materials, inspect the auxiliary light wiring harness(es) for damage and proper securement.	
a. Within manufacturer's specifications: Yes: ☐ No: ☐	☐
b. If No, list the recommended corrective action(s):	☐
5. While referencing the manufacturer's workshop materials, check the auxiliary lighting connections for loose/burnt/damaged connections.	
a. Within manufacturer's specifications: Yes: ☐ No: ☐	☐
b. If No, list the recommended corrective action(s):	☐
6. While referencing the manufacturer's workshop materials, list the auxiliary lighting circuit protection type(s) and rating(s):	☐

7. While referencing the manufacturer's workshop materials, list the auxiliary light(s) that are controlled by a relay(s):	☐
8. While referencing the manufacturer's workshop materials, list the auxiliary light(s) relays that are ground-side controlled and power-side controlled. Ground-side controlled: Power-side controlled	☐
9. While referencing the manufacturer's workshop materials, list which auxiliary lighting is controller area network bus (CANbus) controlled:	☐
10. While referencing the manufacturer's workshop materials, list which control module(s) control any auxiliary lighting:	☐
11. While referencing the manufacturer's workshop materials, list the auxiliary light(s) that are controlled by a smart switch:	☐
12. While referencing the manufacturer's workshop materials and electronic service tool (EST), check for any diagnostic trouble codes (DTCs) that are associated with the auxiliary lighting.	
a. Within manufacturer's specifications: Yes: ☐ No: ☐	☐
b. If No, list the recommended corrective action(s):	☐

	Step Completed
13. While referencing the manufacturer's workshop materials and EST, check the operation of the auxiliary lighting.	
a. Within manufacturer's specifications: Yes: ☐ No: ☐	☐
b. If No, list the recommended corrective action(s):	☐
14. Discuss your findings with your supervisor/instructor.	☐

Non-Task-Specific Evaluations:	Step Completed
1. Tools and equipment were used as directed and returned in good working order.	☐
2. Complied with all general and task-specific safety standards, including proper use of any personal protection equipment.	☐
3. Completed the task in an appropriate time frame (recommendation: 1.5 or 2 times the flat rate).	☐
4. Left the workspace clean and orderly.	☐
5. Cared for customer property and returned it undamaged.	☐

Student signature _____ Date _____

Comments:

Have your supervisor/instructor verify satisfactory completion of this procedure, any observations made, and any necessary action(s) recommended.

Evaluation Instructions: The scoring box below is intended to act as a guide for both student and supervisor/instructor. Each criterion listed will help students to understand what is expected of them and help supervisors/instructors articulate the level of success at a particular task. The scoring is set up to allow a second attempt at each task (see the Test and Retest columns). Scoring is also designed to award students points only for task criteria that were completed correctly. Points are lost for failure to complete the employability requirements (see Non-Task-Specific Evaluation criteria). When all criteria are evaluated, tally the points for a total at the bottom of each column.

Tasksheet Scoring

Evaluation Items	Test		Retest	
	Pass	Fail	Pass	Fail
Task-Specific Evaluation	**(1 pt)**	**(0 pts)**	**(1 pt)**	**(0 pts)**
Student properly recorded auxiliary lighting position and type, auxiliary lighting circuit protection and relay(s), and auxiliary lighting harness(es).				
Student properly inspected auxiliary lighting switches, light operation, and auxiliary lighting connections and performed operation of auxiliary lighting using an EST.				
Student properly recorded auxiliary lighting relay controls and CANbus-controlled auxiliary lighting and modules.				
Student properly recorded auxiliary lighting smart switches and auxiliary lighting DTCs.				
Non-Task-Specific Evaluation	**(0 pts)**	**(−1 pt)**	**(0 pts)**	**(−1 pt)**
Student successfully completed at least three of the non-task-specific steps.				
Student successfully completed all five of the non-task-specific steps.				
Total Score: <total # of points/4 = %>				

Supervisor/Instructor:

Supervisor/instructor signature _____ Date _____

Comments:

Retest supervisor/instructor signature _____ Date _____

Comments:

V.F Electrical/Electronic Systems: Instrument Cluster and Driver Information Systems

Learning Objective/Task	CDX Tasksheet Number	ASE Foundation MTST Reference Number; Priority Level
• Check gauge and warning indicator operation.	MHT5F001	V.F.1; P-1
• Diagnose faults in the sensor/sending units, gauges, switches, relays, bulbs/light-emitting diodes (LEDs), wires, terminals, connectors, sockets, printed circuits, and control components/modules of the instrument cluster, driver information systems, and warning systems; determine needed action.	MHT5F002	V.F.2; P-2
• Inspect, test, replace, and calibrate (if applicable) electronic speedometer, odometer, and tachometer systems.	MHT5F003	V.F.3; P-3

Materials Required

- Vehicle or simulator with gauge and warning device concerns
- Vehicle manufacturer's workshop materials, including schematic wiring diagrams
- Test lamp, digital volt-ohmmeter (DVOM)
- Personal Protection Equipment (PPE)

• Safety Considerations

- Activities require you to measure electrical values. Always ensure that your supervisor/instructor checks test instrument connections prior to connecting power or taking measurements. High current flows can be dangerous; avoid accidental short circuits or grounding the battery's positive connections.
- Activities may require test-driving the vehicle on the school grounds or on a hoist, both of which carry severe risks. Attempt this task only with full permission from your supervisor/instructor, and follow all the guidelines exactly.
- Comply with personal and environmental safety practices associated with clothing; eye protection; hand tools; power equipment; proper ventilation; and the handling, storage, and disposal of chemicals/materials in accordance with federal, state, and local regulations.
- Always wear the correct protective eyewear and clothing and use the appropriate safety equipment, as well as wheel chocks, fender covers, seat protectors, and floor mat protectors.
- Make sure you understand and observe all legislative and personal safety procedures when carrying out practical assignments. If you are unsure of what these are, ask your supervisor/instructor.

CDX Tasksheet Number: MHT5F001

Student/Intern Information

Name _____ Date _____ Class _____

Vehicle, Customer, and Service Information

Vehicle used for this activity:

Year _____ Make _____ Model _____

Odometer _____ VIN _____

Materials Required

- Vehicle or simulator with gauge and warning device concerns
- Vehicle manufacturer's workshop materials including schematic wiring diagrams
- Test lamp, digital volt-ohmmeter (DVOM)
- Personal protection equipment (PPE)

Task-Specific Safety Considerations

- Activities require you to measure electrical values. Always ensure that the instructor/supervisor checks test instrument connections prior to connecting power or taking measurements. High current flows can be dangerous; avoid accidental short circuits or grounding the battery's positive connections.
- Activities may require test-driving the vehicle on the school grounds or on a hoist, both of which carry severe risks. Attempt this task only with full permission from your supervisor/instructor, and follow all the guidelines exactly.
- Comply with personal and environmental safety practices associated with clothing; eye protection; hand tools; power equipment; proper ventilation; and the handling, storage, and disposal of chemicals/materials in accordance with federal, state, and local regulations.
- Always wear the correct protective eyewear and clothing and use the appropriate safety equipment, as well as wheel chocks, fender covers, seat protectors, and floor mat protectors.
- Make sure you understand and observe all legislative and personal safety procedures when carrying out practical assignments. If you are unsure of what these are, ask your supervisor/instructor.

▶ **TASK** Check gauge and warning indicator operation. **MTST** *V.F.1; P1*

Time off_____

Student Instructions: Read through the entire procedure prior to starting. Prepare your workspace and any tools or parts that may be needed to complete the task. When directed by your supervisor/instructor, begin the procedure to complete the task and check the box as each step is finished.

Time on_____

Total time_____

Procedure:	Step Completed
1. While referencing the manufacturer's workshop materials, record the gauges that are manual, electric, and controller area network bus (CANbus) controlled.	
a. Manual gauge(s):	☐
b. Electric gauge(s):	☐
c. Electronic/CANbus controlled gauge(s):	☐
2. While referencing the manufacturer's workshop materials, record the warning light description(s):	☐
3. While referencing the manufacturer's workshop materials, describe the procedure for testing the manual gauges:	☐
4. While referencing the manufacturer's workshop materials, test the manual gauges for proper operation.	
a. Within, manufacturer's specifications: Yes: ☐ No: ☐	☐
b. If No, list the recommended corrective action(s):	☐
5. While referencing the manufacturer's workshop materials, record the operation of the electric gauges when the ignition switch is first turned on:	☐

6. While referencing the manufacturer's workshop materials, describe the procedure for testing the electric gauges:	☐
7. While referencing the manufacturer's workshop materials, test the electric gauges for proper operation.	
a. Within, manufacturer's specifications: Yes: ☐ No: ☐	☐
b. If No, list the recommended corrective action(s):	☐
8. While referencing the manufacturer's workshop materials, record the operation of the electronic/CANbus-controlled gauges when the ignition switch is first turned on:	☐
9. While referencing the manufacturer's workshop materials, turn the ignition switch to the on position and observe the operation of the electronic/CANbus-controlled gauges.	
a. Within, manufacturer's specifications: Yes: ☐ No: ☐	☐
b. If No, list the recommended corrective action(s):	☐
10. While referencing the manufacturer's workshop materials, record the operation of the warning lights when the ignition switch is first turned on:	☐
11. While referencing the manufacturer's workshop materials, turn the ignition switch to the on position and observe the operation of the warning lights.	
a. Within, manufacturer's specifications: Yes: ☐ No: ☐	☐

	Step Completed
b. If No, list the recommended corrective action(s):	☐
12. While referencing the manufacturer's workshop materials and electronic service tool (EST), check for any fault codes related to gauge/warning light operation.	
a. Within, manufacturer's specifications: Yes: ☐ No: ☐	☐
b. If No, list the recommended corrective action(s):	☐
13. Discuss your findings with your supervisor/instructor.	☐

Non-Task-Specific Evaluations:	Step Completed
1. Tools and equipment were used as directed and returned in good working order.	☐
2. Complied with all general and task-specific safety standards, including proper use of any personal protection equipment.	☐
3. Completed the task in an appropriate time frame (recommendation: 1.5 or 2 times the flat rate).	☐
4. Left the workspace clean and orderly.	☐
5. Cared for customer property and returned it undamaged.	☐

Student signature _____ Date _____

Comments:

Have your supervisor/instructor verify satisfactory completion of this procedure, any observations made, and any necessary action(s) recommended.

Evaluation Instructions: The scoring box below is intended to act as a guide for both student and supervisor/instructor. Each criterion listed will help students to understand what is expected of them and help supervisors/instructors articulate the level of success at a particular task. The scoring is set up to allow a second attempt at each task (see the Test and Retest columns). Scoring is also designed to award students points only for task criteria that were completed correctly. Points are lost for failure to complete the employability requirements (see Non-Task-Specific Evaluation criteria). When all criteria are evaluated, tally the points for a total at the bottom of each column.

Tasksheet Scoring

Evaluation Items	Test		Retest	
	Pass	Fail	Pass	Fail
Task-Specific Evaluation	**(1 pt)**	**(0 pts)**	**(1 pt)**	**(0 pts)**
Student properly identified manual, electric, and CANbus gauges and warning lights.				
Student properly checked operation of manual gauges and electrical gauges.				
Student properly checked operation of CANbus-controlled gauges and warning lights.				
Student properly checked fault codes related to gauge/warning light operation.				
Non-Task-Specific Evaluation	**(0 pts)**	**(−1 pt)**	**(0 pts)**	**(−1 pt)**
Student successfully completed at least three of the non-task-specific steps.				
Student successfully completed all five of the non-task-specific steps.				
Total Score: <total # of points/4 = %>				

Supervisor/Instructor:

Supervisor/instructor signature _____ Date _____

Comments:

Retest supervisor/instructor signature _____ Date _____

Comments:

CDX Tasksheet Number: MHT5F002

Student/Intern Information

Name _____ Date _____ Class _____

Vehicle, Customer, and Service Information

Vehicle used for this activity:

Year _____ Make _____ Model _____

Odometer _____ VIN _____

Materials Required

- Vehicle or simulator with gauge and warning device concerns
- Vehicle manufacturer's workshop materials including schematic wiring diagrams
- Test lamp, digital volt-ohmmeter (DVOM)
- Personal protection equipment (PPE)

Task-Specific Safety Considerations

- Activities require you to measure electrical values. Always ensure that the instructor/supervisor checks test instrument connections prior to connecting power or taking measurements. High current flows can be dangerous; avoid accidental short circuits or grounding the battery's positive connections.
- Activities may require test-driving the vehicle on the school grounds or on a hoist, both of which carry severe risks. Attempt this task only with full permission from your supervisor/instructor, and follow all the guidelines exactly.
- Comply with personal and environmental safety practices associated with clothing; eye protection; hand tools; power equipment; proper ventilation; and the handling, storage, and disposal of chemicals/materials in accordance with federal, state, and local regulations.
- Always wear the correct protective eyewear and clothing, and use the appropriate safety equipment, as well as wheel chocks, fender covers, seat protectors, and floor mat protectors.
- Make sure you understand and observe all legislative and personal safety procedures when carrying out practical assignments. If you are unsure of what these are, ask your supervisor/instructor.

▶ TASK Diagnose faults in the sensor/sending units, gauges, switches, relays, bulbs/light-emitting diodes (LEDs), wires, terminals, connectors, sockets, printed circuits, and control components/modules of the instrument cluster, driver information systems, and warning systems; determine needed action.

MTST
V.F.2; P2

Time off_____

Time on_____

Total time_____

Student Instructions: Read through the entire procedure prior to starting. Prepare your workspace and any tools or parts that may be needed to complete the task. When directed by your supervisor/instructor, begin the procedure to complete the task and check the box as each step is finished.

Procedure:	Step Completed
1. List the customer concern regarding the instrument cluster/driver information system:	☐
2. If the gauges are not operating correctly, go to Step 3. If the warning devices are not operating correctly, go to Step 9.	☐
3. Research the particular complaint/concern in the appropriate manufacturer's service manual.	
a. List the possible causes:	☐
b. List any relevant gauge or sending unit specifications:	☐
4. Diagnose the cause of the concern using the appropriate service information and wiring diagrams. List your tests and their results:	☐
5. Perform any voltage-drop tests necessary to diagnose any causes or concerns in the instrument cluster system.	☐
6. Check the conditions of all wiring, connectors, and terminals in the circuit.	
a. Condition of wiring: Good: ☐ Bad: ☐	☐
b. Condition of connectors: Good: ☐ Bad: ☐	☐
c. Condition of terminals: Good: ☐ Bad: ☐	☐
7. List the cause of the concern/complaint:	☐

8. Determine any necessary action(s) to correct the fault:	☐
9. Consult the appropriate manufacturer's service manual for the correct wiring diagram information to do this task.	☐
10. Inspect and test all warning devices (lights and audible sensor circuits) by operating them and checking for illumination of all lights in the circuit.	
a. Are the warning devices working? Yes: ☐ No: ☐	☐
b. If No, consult the appropriate service information to repair or replace the faulty components.	☐
11. Check all switch connections for corrosion and connector tightness.	☐
12. Check all connectors to sockets and control modules for looseness, cracking, and burn marks that may cause the system to malfunction.	
a. Condition of connectors: Good: ☐ Bad: ☐	☐
(Note: Any burn marks or discoloration of the connectors may indicate excessive amperage running through them.)	
13. If the connectors are found to be bad, make recommendations for repairing or replacing the connections:	☐
14. Test all modules for proper operation.	
a. Consult the manufacturer's workshop materials, and record the proper procedures to test these components:	☐
15. Check all wiring that is present to the circuit for bare spots, cracked insulation, and no connection to a connector or component. Perform voltage-drop tests to the circuit if necessary.	
a. Condition of wiring: Good: ☐ Bad: ☐	☐

16. If the wiring is found to be bad, make recommendations for repairing or replacing the wiring:	
a. Condition of wiring: Good: ☐ Bad: ☐	☐
17. If the condition of the wiring is bad, make recommendations for repairing or replacing the wiring:	☐
18. Return the vehicle to its beginning condition, and return any tools to their proper locations.	☐
19. Consult with your supervisor/instructor and record any recommendations to bring the circuit back to manufacturer specifications:	☐

Non-Task-Specific Evaluations:	Step Completed
1. Tools and equipment were used as directed and returned in good working order.	☐
2. Complied with all general and task-specific safety standards, including proper use of any personal protection equipment.	☐
3. Completed the task in an appropriate time frame (recommendation: 1.5 or 2 times the flat rate).	☐
4. Left the workspace clean and orderly.	☐
5. Cared for customer property and returned it undamaged.	☐

Student signature _____ Date _____

Comments:

Have your supervisor/instructor verify satisfactory completion of this procedure, any observations made, and any necessary action(s) recommended.

Evaluation Instructions: The scoring box below is intended to act as a guide for both student and supervisor/instructor. Each criterion listed will help students to understand what is expected of them and help supervisors/instructors articulate the level of success at a particular task. The scoring is set up to allow a second attempt at each task (see the Test and Retest columns). Scoring is also designed to award students points only for task criteria that were completed correctly. Points are lost for failure to complete the employability requirements (see Non-Task-Specific Evaluation criteria). When all criteria are evaluated, tally the points for a total at the bottom of each column.

Tasksheet Scoring

Evaluation Items	Test		Retest	
	Pass	**Fail**	**Pass**	**Fail**
Task-Specific Evaluation	**(1 pt)**	**(0 pts)**	**(1 pt)**	**(0 pts)**
Student used the appropriate service information to research the customer complaint.				
Student accurately tested and inspected the gauge or warning device circuit.				
Student compared the results to the specifications and correctly determined any necessary actions.				
Student reinstalled all removed components undamaged and in working order.				
Non-Task-Specific Evaluation	**(0 pts)**	**(−1 pt)**	**(0 pts)**	**(−1 pt)**
Student successfully completed at least three of the non-task-specific steps.				
Student successfully completed all five of the non-task-specific steps.				
Total Score: <total # of points/4 = %>				

Supervisor/Instructor:

Supervisor/instructor signature _____ Date _____

Comments:

Retest supervisor/instructor signature _____ Date _____

Comments:

CDX Tasksheet Number: MHT5F003

Student/Intern Information

Name _____ Date _____ Class _____

Vehicle, Customer, and Service Information

Vehicle used for this activity:

Year _____ Make _____ Model _____

Odometer _____ VIN _____

Materials Required

- Vehicle or simulator with gauge and warning device concerns
- Vehicle manufacturer's workshop materials including schematic wiring diagrams
- Test lamp, digital volt-ohmmeter (DVOM)
- Personal protection equipment (PPE)

Task-Specific Safety Considerations

- Activities require you to measure electrical values. Always ensure that the instructor/ supervisor checks test instrument connections prior to connecting power or taking measurements. High current flows can be dangerous; avoid accidental short circuits or grounding the battery's positive connections.
- Activities may require test-driving the vehicle on the school grounds or on a hoist, both of which carry severe risks. Attempt this task only with full permission from your supervisor/ instructor, and follow all the guidelines exactly.
- Comply with personal and environmental safety practices associated with clothing; eye protection; hand tools; power equipment; proper ventilation; and the handling, storage, and disposal of chemicals/materials in accordance with federal, state, and local regulations.
- Always wear the correct protective eyewear and clothing and use the appropriate safety equipment, as well as wheel chocks fender, covers, seat protectors, and floor mat protectors.
- Make sure you understand and observe all legislative and personal safety procedures when carrying out practical assignments. If you are unsure of what these are, ask your supervisor/ instructor.

▶ **TASK** Inspect, test, replace, and calibrate (if applicable) electronic speedometer, odometer, and tachometer systems.

MTST
V.F.3; P3

Time off_____

Time on_____

Total time_____

Student Instructions: Read through the entire procedure prior to starting. Prepare your workspace and any tools or parts that may be needed to complete the task. When directed by your supervisor/instructor, begin the procedure to complete the task and check the box as each step is finished.

Procedure:	Step Completed
1. While referencing the manufacturer's workshop materials, record the operation of the speedometer, odometer, and tachometer when the ignition switch is first turned on:	☐
2. While referencing the manufacturer's workshop materials, turn the ignition switch to the on position and observe the operation of the speedometer, odometer, and tachometer:	
a. Within, manufacturer's specifications: Yes: ☐ No: ☐	☐
b. If No, list the recommended corrective action(s):	☐
3. While referencing the manufacturer's workshop materials, record the procedure for removing the speedometer, odometer, and tachometer:	☐
4. If directed by your supervisor/instructor, remove and inspect the speedometer, odometer, and tachometer and inspect all connections for damaged, burnt, or loose connections.	☐
a. Within, manufacturer's specifications: Yes: ☐ No: ☐	☐
b. If No, list the recommended corrective action(s):	☐
5. If directed by your supervisor/instructor, reinstall the speedometer, odometer, and tachometer and check the operation.	
a. Within, manufacturer's specifications: Yes: ☐ No: ☐	☐
b. If No, list the recommended corrective action(s):	☐

6. While referencing the manufacturer's workshop materials, record the procedure for recalibrating the speedometer, odometer, and tachometer:	☐
7. If directed by your supervisor/instructor, recalibrate the speedometer, odometer, and tachometer and check the operation.	
a. Within manufacturer's specifications: Yes: ☐ No: ☐	☐
b. If No, list the recommended corrective action(s):	☐
8. While referencing the manufacturer's workshop materials and electronic service tool (EST), check for any fault codes related to the speedometer, odometer, and tachometer.	
a. Within, manufacturer's specifications: Yes: ☐ No: ☐	☐
b. If No, list the recommended corrective action(s):	☐
9. Discuss your findings with your supervisor/instructor.	☐

© 2021 Jones & Bartlett Learning, LLC, an Ascend Learning Company

Instrument Cluster and Driver Information Systems **781**

Non-Task-Specific Evaluations:	Step Completed
1. Tools and equipment were used as directed and returned in good working order.	☐
2. Complied with all general and task-specific safety standards, including proper use of any personal protection equipment.	☐
3. Completed the task in an appropriate time frame (recommendation: 1.5 or 2 times the flat rate).	☐
4. Left the workspace clean and orderly.	☐
5. Cared for customer property and returned it undamaged.	☐

Student signature _____ Date _____

Comments:

Have your supervisor/instructor verify satisfactory completion of this procedure, any observations made, and any necessary action(s) recommended.

Evaluation Instructions: The scoring box below is intended to act as a guide for both student and supervisor/instructor. Each criterion listed will help students to understand what is expected of them and help supervisors/instructors articulate the level of success at a particular task. The scoring is set up to allow a second attempt at each task (see the Test and Retest columns). Scoring is also designed to award students points only for task criteria that were completed correctly. Points are lost for failure to complete the employability requirements (see Non-Task-Specific Evaluation criteria). When all criteria are evaluated, tally the points for a total at the bottom of each column.

Tasksheet Scoring

Evaluation Items	Test		Retest	
	Pass	Fail	Pass	Fail
Task-Specific Evaluation	**(1 pt)**	**(0 pts)**	**(1 pt)**	**(0 pts)**
Student properly recorded and checked operation of speedometer, odometer, and tachometer when the ignition was first turned on.				
Student properly removed and inspected speedometer, odometer, and tachometer.				
Student properly reinstalled and performed speedometer, odometer, and tachometer recalibration.				
Student properly checked fault codes related to the speedometer, odometer, and tachometer.				
Non-Task-Specific Evaluation	**(0 pts)**	**(−1 pt)**	**(0 pts)**	**(−1 pt)**
Student successfully completed at least three of the non-task-specific steps.				
Student successfully completed all five of the non-task-specific steps.				
Total Score: <total # of points/4 = %>				

Supervisor/Instructor:

Supervisor/instructor signature _____ Date _____

Comments:

Retest supervisor/instructor signature _____ Date _____

Comments:

V.G Electrical/Electronic Systems: Cab and Chassis Electrical Systems

Learning Objective/Task	CDX Tasksheet Number	ASE Foundation MTST Reference Number; Priority Level
• Diagnose the operation of horn(s), wiper/washer, and occupant restraint systems.	MHT5G001	V.G.1; P-1
• Understand the operation of safety systems and related circuits, including speed control, collision avoidance, lane departure, and camera systems.	MHT5G002	V.G.2; P-3
• Understand the operation of comfort and convenience systems and related circuits, including power windows, power seats, power locks, remote keyless entry, steering wheel controls, and cruise control.	MHT5G003	V.G.3; P-3
• Understand the operation of entertainment systems and related circuits, including radio, DVD, navigation, speakers, antennas, and voice-activated accessories.	MHT5G004	V.G.4; P-3
• Understand the operation of power inverters, protection devices, connectors, terminals, wiring, and control components/modules of auxiliary power systems.	MHT5G005	V.G.5; P-3
• Understand the operation of telematics systems.	MHT5G006	V.G.6; P-3
• Diagnose faults in engine block and engine oil heater(s); determine needed action.	MHT5G007	V.G.7; P-2

Materials Required

- Vehicle with possible electrical/electronic concern
- Engine manufacturer's workshop materials
- Vehicles or simulators with electrical faults within the auxiliary power systems
- Vehicle manufacturer's workshop materials, including schematic wiring diagrams
- Digital volt-ohmmeter (DVOM), PC-based software, and/or data scan tools
- Manufacturer-specific tools depending on the concern/procedure(s)
- Vehicle/component lifting equipment if applicable

Safety Considerations

- Activities require you to measure electrical values. Always ensure that your supervisor/instructor checks test instrument connections prior to connecting power or taking measurements. High current flows can be dangerous; avoid accidental short circuits or grounding the battery's positive connections.
- Air-conditioning systems have refrigerant gas within the system. When the system is running, high-pressure gas and liquid refrigerant will be circulating in the system. Use extreme caution working around high-pressure hoses.

- This activity may require you to work with solenoid actuators. Actuators may create a crush injury hazard; keep fingers away from mechanisms.
- Electric motors may start up when you least expect it; keep fingers and clothing away from the mechanism.
- Activities may require test-driving the vehicle on the school grounds or on a hoist, both of which carry severe risks. Attempt this task only with full permission from your supervisor/instructor, and follow all the guidelines exactly.
- Comply with personal and environmental safety practices associated with clothing; eye protection; hand tools; power equipment; proper ventilation; and the handling, storage, and disposal of chemicals/materials in accordance with federal, state, and local regulations.
- Always wear the correct protective eyewear and clothing and use the appropriate safety equipment, as well as wheel chocks, fender covers, seat protectors, and floor mat protectors.
- Make sure you understand and observe all legislative and personal safety procedures when carrying out practical assignments. If you are unsure of what these are, ask your supervisor/instructor.

CDX Tasksheet Number: MHT5G001

Student/Intern Information

Name _____ Date _____ Class _____

Vehicle, Customer, and Service Information

Vehicle used for this activity:

Year _____ Make _____ Model _____

Odometer _____ VIN _____

Materials Required

- Vehicle with possible electrical/electronic system concerns
- Vehicle manufacturer's repair information
- Manufacturer-specific tools depending on the concern/procedure(s)

Task-Specific Safety Considerations

- Activities may require test-driving the vehicle on the school grounds or on a hoist, both of which carry severe risks. Attempt this task only with full permission from your supervisor/instructor, and follow all the guidelines exactly.
- Comply with personal and environmental safety practices associated with clothing; eye protection; hand tools; power equipment; proper ventilation; and the handling, storage, and disposal of chemicals/materials in accordance with federal, state, and local regulations.
- Always wear the correct protective eyewear and clothing and use the appropriate safety equipment, as well as wheel chocks, fender covers, seat protectors, and floor mat protectors.
- Make sure you understand and observe all legislative and personal safety procedures when carrying out practical assignments. If you are unsure of what these are, ask your supervisor/instructor.
- While working on the vehicle, wheel chocks must be placed on both sides of one set of tires or as directed by the instructor.
- Exhaust evacuation hoses must be placed over exhaust outlets while the engine is used in a confined shop space.

▶ **TASK** Diagnose the operation of horn(s), wiper/washer, and occupant restraint systems.

MTST
V.G.1; P1

Time off_____

Time on_____

Total time_____

Student Instructions: Read through the entire procedure prior to starting. Prepare your workspace and any tools or parts that may be needed to complete the task. When directed by your supervisor/instructor, begin the procedure to complete the task and check the box as each step is finished.

Procedure:	Step Completed
1. Research manufacturer's repair information for proper steps to diagnose operation of horn(s), wiper/washer, and occupant restraint systems.	☐
2. Diagnose operation of horn(s).	
a. Utilizing a digital volt-ohmmeter (DVOM), measure the voltage at the horn circuit fuse according to manufacturer guidelines. Record your findings:	☐
3. Consult the appropriate manufacturer service manual for the correct wiring diagram information to do this task.	☐
4. Inspect and test all switches associated with the horn circuits by operating them and checking for audible sounds in the circuit.	
a. Are the horn circuits working? Yes: ☐ No: ☐	☐
b. If No, consult the appropriate service information to repair or replace the faulty instrument panel components.	☐
5. Test clock spring operation by engaging the horn in different steering wheel positions.	☐
6. Check all wiring connections for damage or burnt conditions.	
a. Condition of wiring connections: Good: ☐ Bad: ☐	☐
b. Check all connectors to relays and control modules for looseness, cracking, and burn marks that may cause the system to malfunction.	☐
c. Condition of connectors: Good: ☐ Bad: ☐	☐
(Note: Any burn marks or discoloration of the connectors may indicate excessive amperage running through them.)	
7. If the connectors are found to be bad, make recommendations for repairing or replacing the connections:	☐
8. Test relay(s) and modules for proper operation.	☐

9. Check all wiring that is present to that circuit for bare spots, cracked insulation, and no connection to the connector or component. Perform voltage-drop tests to the circuit if necessary.	
a. Condition of wiring: Good: ☐ Bad: ☐	☐
10. If the wiring is found to be bad, make recommendations for repairing or replacing the wiring:	☐
11. Diagnose operation of wiper/washer.	
a. Utilizing a DVOM, measure the voltage at the wiper/washer circuit fuse according to manufacturer guidelines. Record your findings:	☐
12. Test the wiper motor switch by moving the switch through all of its positions to make sure it is operating as it should. Resistors determine the speeds of the wiper circuit.	
a. Operation of the switch: Pass: ☐ Fail: ☐	☐
13. Do the wipers park correctly when turned off? Yes: ☐ No: ☐	☐
14. If the switch fails to operate as designed, make recommendations for repair or replacement:	☐
15. Check all connectors to relays and control modules for looseness, cracking, and burn marks that may cause the system to malfunction.	
a. Condition of connectors: Good: ☐ Bad: ☐	☐
(**Note:** Any burn marks or discoloration of the connectors may indicate excessive amperage running through them.)	
16. Test relay(s) and modules for proper operation.	☐

© 2021 Jones & Bartlett Learning, LLC, an Ascend Learning Company

17. Check all wiring that is present to that circuit for bare spots, cracked insulation, and no connection to the connector or component. Perform voltage-drop tests to the circuit if necessary.	
a. Condition of wiring: Good: ☐ Bad: ☐	☐
18. If the wiring is bad, make recommendations for repairing or replacing the wiring:	☐
19. Inspect wiper motor transmission linkage.	
a. Check for linkage connections that have cracked or dry-rotted bushings.	☐
i. Condition of bushings: Pass: ☐ Fail: ☐	☐
b. Check for elongated linkage ends from loose or worn bushings.	☐
i. Are the linkage ends damaged? Yes: ☐ No: ☐	☐
c. Check for bent linkage arms.	☐
i. Are the linkage arms bent or damaged? Yes: ☐ No: ☐	☐
20. Test the windshield washer motor or pump/relay assembly switch through all of its positions to make sure it is operating as it should.	
a. Operation of the switch: Pass: ☐ Fail: ☐	☐
b. Check operation of pump for windshield fluid distribution. Pass: ☐ Fail: ☐	☐
21. Check all connectors to relays and control modules for looseness, cracking, and burn marks that may cause the system to malfunction.	
a. Condition of connectors: Good: ☐ Bad: ☐	☐
(**Note:** Any burn marks or discoloration of the connectors may indicate excessive amperage running through them.)	
22. Test relay(s) and modules for proper operation.	☐

23. Check all wiring that is present to that circuit for bare spots, cracked insulation, and no connection to a connector or component. Perform voltage-drop tests to the circuit if necessary.	
a. Condition of wiring: Good: ☐ Bad: ☐	☐
24. Check and test the operation and condition of seat belts and sleeper restraints.	
a. Seat belt operation: Good: ☐ Faulty: ☐	☐
b. If faulty, list the problems and your recommendation(s):	☐
25. Return the vehicle to its beginning condition, and return any tools you used to their proper locations.	☐
26. Discuss your findings with your supervisor/instructor.	☐

Non-Task-Specific Evaluations:	Step Completed
1. Tools and equipment were used as directed and returned in good working order.	☐
2. Complied with all general and task-specific safety standards, including proper use of any personal protection equipment.	☐
3. Completed the task in an appropriate time frame (recommendation: 1.5 or 2 times the flat rate).	☐
4. Left the workspace clean and orderly.	☐
5. Cared for customer property and returned it undamaged.	☐

Student signature _____ Date _____

Comments:

Have your supervisor/instructor verify satisfactory completion of this procedure, any observations made, and any necessary action(s) recommended.

Evaluation Instructions: The scoring box below is intended to act as a guide for both student and supervisor/instructor. Each criterion listed will help students understand what is expected of them and help supervisors/instructors articulate the level of success at a particular task. The scoring is set up to allow a second attempt at each task (see the Test and Retest columns). Scoring is also designed to award students points only for task criteria that were completed correctly. Points are lost for failure to complete the employability requirements (see Non-Task-Specific Evaluation criteria). When all criteria are evaluated, tally the points for a total at the bottom of each column.

Tasksheet Scoring

Evaluation Items	Test		Retest	
	Pass	**Fail**	**Pass**	**Fail**
Task-Specific Evaluation	**(1 pt)**	**(0 pts)**	**(1 pt)**	**(0 pts)**
Student detailed the 3 Cs on the submitted repair order and displayed use of manufacturer's repair information.				
Student properly performed diagnostic measurements.				
Student developed appropriate conclusions based on diagnostics.				
Student completed repairs as directed by the supervisor/instructor.				
Non-Task-Specific Evaluation	**(0 pts)**	**(−1 pt)**	**(0 pts)**	**(−1 pt)**
Student successfully completed at least three of the non-task-specific steps.				
Student successfully completed all five of the non-task-specific steps.				
Total Score: <total # of points/4 = %>				

Supervisor/Instructor:

Supervisor/instructor signature _____ Date _____

Comments:

Retest supervisor/instructor signature _____ Date _____

Comments:

CDX Tasksheet Number: MHT5G002

Student/Intern Information

Name _____ Date _____ Class _____

Vehicle, Customer, and Service Information

Vehicle used for this activity:

Year _____ Make _____ Model _____

Odometer _____ VIN _____

Materials Required

- Vehicle with possible electrical/electronic concern
- Engine manufacturer's workshop materials, including shematic wiring diagrams
- Manufacturer-specific tools depending on the concern/procedure(s)
- Vehicle/component lifting equipment, if applicable

Task-Specific Safety Considerations

- Activities may require test-driving the vehicle on the school grounds or on a hoist, both of which carry severe risks. Attempt this task only with full permission from your supervisor/instructor, and follow all the guidelines exactly.
- Lifting equipment and machines such as vehicle jacks and stands, vehicle hoists, and engine hoists are important tools that increase productivity and make the job easier. However, they can also cause severe injury or death if used improperly. Make sure you follow the manufacturer's operation procedures. Also make sure you have your supervisor's/instructor's permission to use any particular type of lifting equipment.
- Comply with personal and environmental safety practices associated with clothing; eye protection; hand tools; power equipment; proper ventilation; and the handling, storage, and disposal of chemicals/materials in accordance with federal, state, and local regulations.
- Always wear the correct protective eyewear and clothing and use the appropriate safety equipment, as well as wheel chocks, fender covers, seat protectors, and floor mat protectors.
- Make sure you understand and observe all legislative and personal safety procedures when carrying out practical assignments. If you are unsure of what these are, ask your supervisor/instructor.

▶ **TASK** Understand the operation of safety systems and related circuits, including speed control, collision avoidance, lane departure, and camera systems.

MTST
V.G.2; P3

Time off_____

Time on_____

Total time_____

Student Instructions: Read through the entire procedure prior to starting. Prepare your workspace and any tools or parts that may be needed to complete the task. When directed by your supervisor/instructor, begin the procedure to complete the task and check the box as each step is finished.

Note: This tasksheet may require the student to check the condition of miscellaneous vehicle fluids, some of which may be flammable and could damage the environment or cause health problems if not handled properly. Observe all safety precautions and follow local regulations for the proper disposal of fluids.

Procedure:	Step Completed
1. (**Note:** If the vehicle does not have any of the systems described below, research the Internet for required information.)	☐
2. While referencing the manufacturer's workshop materials, record the position of any supplemental restraint systems (SRSs):	☐
3. While referencing the manufacturer's workshop materials, record any special precautions/procedures when servicing/testing the SRS:	☐
4. While referencing the manufacturer's workshop materials, record the operation of any speed control systems:	☐
5. While referencing the manufacturer's workshop materials, record any special precautions/procedures when servicing/testing any speed control systems:	☐
6. While referencing the manufacturer's workshop materials, record the operation of any collision avoidance systems:	☐
7. While referencing the manufacturer's workshop materials, record any special precautions/procedures when servicing/testing any collision avoidance systems:	☐

8. While referencing the manufacturer's workshop materials, record the operation of any lane departure systems:	☐
9. While referencing the manufacturer's workshop materials, record any special precautions/procedures when servicing/testing any lane departure systems:	☐
10. While referencing the manufacturer's workshop materials, record the operation of any camera systems:	☐
11. While referencing the manufacturer's workshop materials, record any special precautions/procedures when servicing/testing any camera systems:	☐
12. While referencing the manufacturer's workshop materials and electronic service tool (EST), check for any fault codes related to the SRS, speed control, collision avoidance, lane departure, and camera systems.	
a. Within, manufacturer's specifications: Yes: ☐ No: ☐	☐
b. If No, list the recommended corrective action(s):	☐
13. Discuss your findings with your supervisor/instructor.	☐

Non-Task-Specific Evaluations:	Step Completed
1. Tools and equipment were used as directed and returned in good working order.	☐
2. Complied with all general and task-specific safety standards, including proper use of any personal protection equipment.	☐
3. Completed the task in an appropriate time frame (recommendation: 1.5 or 2 times the flat rate).	☐
4. Left the workspace clean and orderly.	☐
5. Cared for customer property and returned it undamaged.	☐

Student signature _____ Date _____

Comments:

```
_____
```

Have your supervisor/instructor verify satisfactory completion of this procedure, any observations made, and any necessary action(s) recommended.

Evaluation Instructions: The scoring box below is intended to act as a guide for both student and supervisor/instructor. Each criterion listed will help students understand what is expected of them and help supervisors/instructors articulate the level of success at a particular task. The scoring is set up to allow a second attempt at each task (see the Test and Retest columns). Scoring is also designed to award students points only for task criteria that were completed correctly. Points are lost for failure to complete the employability requirements (see Non-Task-Specific Evaluation criteria). When all criteria are evaluated, tally the points for a total at the bottom of each column.

Tasksheet Scoring

Evaluation Items	Test		Retest	
	Pass	**Fail**	**Pass**	**Fail**
Task-Specific Evaluation	**(1 pt)**	**(0 pts)**	**(1 pt)**	**(0 pts)**
Student properly identified service procedure/precautions of the SRS.				
Student properly identified service procedure/precautions of the speed control and collision avoidance systems.				
Student properly identified service procedure/precautions of the lane departure systems and camera systems.				
Student properly checked fault codes for the SRS, speed control, collision avoidance, lane departure, and camera systems.				
Non-Task-Specific Evaluation	**(0 pts)**	**(−1 pt)**	**(0 pts)**	**(−1 pt)**
Student successfully completed at least three of the non-task-specific steps.				
Student successfully completed all five of the non-task-specific steps.				
Total Score: <total # of points/4 = %>				

Supervisor/Instructor:

Supervisor/instructor signature _____ Date _____

Comments:

Retest supervisor/instructor signature _____ Date _____

Comments:

CDX Tasksheet Number: MHT5G003

Student/Intern Information

Name _____ Date _____ Class _____

Vehicle, Customer, and Service Information

Vehicle used for this activity:

Year _____ Make _____ Model _____

Odometer _____ VIN _____

Materials Required

- Vehicles or simulators with electrical faults such as electric windows, power seats, cruise control, electric door locks, and keyless remotes
- Vehicle manufacturer's workshop materials including schematic wiring diagrams
- Digital volt-ohmmeter (DVOM), PC-based software, and/or data scan tools
- Vehicle/component lifting equipment, if applicable

Task-Specific Safety Considerations

- Activities require you to measure electrical values. Always ensure that the instructor/ supervisor checks test instrument connections prior to connecting power or taking measurements. High current flows can be dangerous; avoid accidental short circuits or grounding the battery's positive connections.
- Air-conditioning systems have refrigerant gas within the system. When the system is running, high-pressure gas and liquid refrigerant will be circulating in the system. Use extreme caution when working around high-pressure hoses.
- This activity may require you to work with solenoid actuators. Actuators may create a crush injury hazard; keep fingers away from mechanisms.
- Electric motors may start up when you least expect it; keep fingers and clothing away from the mechanism.
- Activities may require test-driving the vehicle on the school grounds or on a hoist, both of which carry severe risks. Attempt this task only with full permission from your supervisor/ instructor, and follow all the guidelines exactly.
- Comply with personal and environmental safety practices associated with clothing; eye protection; hand tools; power equipment; proper ventilation; and the handling, storage, and disposal of chemicals/materials in accordance with federal, state, and local regulations.
- Always wear the correct protective eyewear and clothing, and use the appropriate safety equipment, as well as wheel chocks, fender covers, seat protectors, and floor mat protectors.
- Make sure you understand and observe all legislative and personal safety procedures when carrying out practical assignments. If you are unsure of what these are, ask your supervisor/ instructor.

▶ **TASK** Understand the operation of comfort and convenience systems and related circuits, including power windows, power seats, power locks, remote keyless entry, steering wheel controls, and cruise control.

MTST
V.G.3; P3

Time off_____

Time on_____

Total time_____

Student Instructions: Read through the entire procedure prior to starting. Prepare your workspace and any tools or parts that may be needed to complete the task. When directed by your supervisor/instructor, begin the procedure to complete the task and check the box as each step is finished.

Procedure:	Step Completed
1. Using appropriate service information for the vehicle you are working on, research how to inspect and test motors, switches, relays, connectors, terminals, wires, and control components/modules of power-side window circuits. List the results.	
a. Motors:	☐
b. Switches, relays, connectors, terminals, and wires:	☐
c. Control components/modules:	☐
2. Check your documented procedures with your supervisor/instructor. Supervisor's/instructor's initials:	☐
3. Using the appropriate service information, inspect and test motors, switches, relays, connectors, terminals, wires, and control components/ modules.	☐
4. List the results of conducting your tests:	☐
5. Determine and list any necessary action(s):	☐
6. Have your supervisor/instructor verify satisfactory completion of this section of the procedure. If instructed, carry out any rectification required. Supervisor's/instructor's initials:	☐

7. Using appropriate service information for the vehicle you are working on, research how to inspect and test motors, switches, relays, connectors, terminals, wires, and control components/modules of power seat circuits. List the results.	
a. Motors:	☐
b. Switches, relays, connectors, terminals, and wires:	☐
c. Control components/modules:	☐
8. Check your documented procedures with your supervisor/instructor. Supervisor's/instructor's initials:	☐
9. Using the appropriate service information, inspect and test motors, switches, relays, connectors, terminals, wires, and control components/ modules.	☐
10. List the results of conducting your tests:	☐
11. Determine and list any necessary action(s):	☐
12. Have your supervisor/instructor verify satisfactory completion of this section of the procedure. If instructed, carry out any rectification required. Supervisor's/instructor's initials:	☐
13. Using appropriate service information for the vehicle you are working on, research how to inspect and test switches, relays, connectors, terminals, wires, control components/modules, and actuator/solenoids of power-side window circuits. List the results.	
a. Controllers:	☐

b. Switches, relays, connectors, terminals, and wires:	☐
c. Actuators/solenoids:	☐
14. Check your documented procedures with your supervisor/instructor. Supervisor's/instructor's initials:	☐
15. Using the appropriate service information, inspect and test switches, relays, controllers, actuators/solenoids, connectors, terminals, and wires of electric door lock circuits.	☐
16. List the results of conducting your tests:	☐
17. Determine and list any necessary action(s):	☐
18. Have your supervisor/instructor verify satisfactory completion of this section of the procedure. If instructed, carry out any rectification required. Supervisor's/instructor's initials:	☐
19. Using appropriate service information for the vehicle you are working on, research how to check the operation of keyless and remote lock/unlock devices. List the results.	
a. Keyless and remote lock/unlock devices:	☐
20. Check your documented procedures with your supervisor/instructor. Supervisor's/instructor's initials:	☐
21. Using the appropriate service information, check the operation of keyless and remote lock/unlock devices.	☐
22. List the results of conducting your tests:	☐

23. Determine and list any necessary action(s):	☐
24. Have your supervisor/instructor verify satisfactory completion of this section of the procedure. If instructed, carry out any rectification required. Supervisor's/instructor's initials:	☐
25. Using appropriate service information for the vehicle you are working on, research how to inspect and test cruise control electrical components and steering wheel controls (if applicable). List the results:	☐
26. Check your documented procedures with your supervisor/instructor. Supervisor's/instructor's initials:	☐
27. Using the appropriate service information, inspect and test cruise control electrical components.	☐
28. List the results of conducting your tests:	☐
29. Determine and list any necessary action(s):	☐
30. Have your supervisor/instructor verify satisfactory completion of this section of the procedure. If instructed, carry out any rectification required. Supervisor's/instructor's initials:	☐
31. Return the vehicle to its beginning condition, and return any tools you used to their proper locations.	☐
32. Discuss your findings with your supervisor/instructor.	☐

Non-Task-Specific Evaluations:	Step Completed
1. Tools and equipment were used as directed and returned in good working order.	☐
2. Complied with all general and task-specific safety standards, including proper use of any personal protection equipment.	☐
3. Completed the task in an appropriate time frame (recommendation: 1.5 or 2 times the flat rate).	☐
4. Left the workspace clean and orderly.	☐
5. Cared for customer property and returned it undamaged.	☐

Student signature _____ Date _____

Comments:

Have your supervisor/instructor verify satisfactory completion of this procedure, any observations made, and any necessary action(s) recommended.

Evaluation Instructions: The scoring box below is intended to act as a guide for both student and supervisor/instructor. Each criterion listed will help students understand what is expected of them and help supervisors/instructors articulate the level of success at a particular task. The scoring is set up to allow a second attempt at each task (see the Test and Retest columns). Scoring is also designed to award students points only for task criteria that were completed correctly. Points are lost for failure to complete the employability requirements (see Non-Task-Specific Evaluation criteria). When all criteria are evaluated, tally the points for a total at the bottom of each column.

Tasksheet Scoring

Evaluation Items	Test		Retest	
	Pass	**Fail**	**Pass**	**Fail**
Task-Specific Evaluation	**(1 pt)**	**(0 pts)**	**(1 pt)**	**(0 pts)**
Student used the appropriate service information to research comfort and convenience systems and related circuits.				
Student accurately tested and inspected the comfort and convenience systems and related circuits.				
Student compared the results to the specifications, then correctly determined any necessary actions.				
Student reinstalled all removed components undamaged and in working order.				
Non-Task-Specific Evaluation	**(0 pts)**	**(−1 pt)**	**(0 pts)**	**(−1 pt)**
Student successfully completed at least three of the non-task-specific steps.				
Student successfully completed all five of the non-task-specific steps.				
Total Score: <total # of points/4 = %>				

Supervisor/Instructor:

Supervisor/instructor signature _____ Date _____

Comments:

Retest supervisor/instructor signature _____ Date _____

Comments:

CDX Tasksheet Number: MHT5G004

Student/Intern Information

Name _____ Date _____ Class _____

Vehicle, Customer, and Service Information

Vehicle used for this activity:

Year _____ Make _____ Model _____

Odometer _____ VIN _____

Materials Required

- Vehicle with possible engine concern
- Engine manufacturer's workshop materials, including schematic wiring diagrams
- Manufacturer-specific tools depending on the concern/procedure(s)
- Vehicle/component lifting equipment, if applicable

Task-Specific Safety Considerations

- Activities may require test-driving the vehicle on the school grounds or on a hoist, both of which carry severe risks. Attempt this task only with full permission from your supervisor/instructor, and follow all the guidelines exactly.
- Lifting equipment and machines such as vehicle jacks and stands, vehicle hoists, and engine hoists are important tools that increase productivity and make the job easier. However, they can also cause severe injury or death if used improperly. Make sure you follow the manufacturer's operation procedures. Also make sure you have your supervisor's/instructor's permission to use any particular type of lifting equipment.
- Comply with personal and environmental safety practices associated with clothing; eye protection; hand tools; power equipment; proper ventilation; and the handling, storage, and disposal of chemicals/materials in accordance with federal, state, and local regulations.
- Always wear the correct protective eyewear and clothing and use the appropriate safety equipment, as well as wheel chocks, fender covers, seat protectors, and floor mat protectors.
- Make sure you understand and observe all legislative and personal safety procedures when carrying out practical assignments. If you are unsure of what these are, ask your supervisor/instructor.

▶ **TASK** Understand the operation of entertainment systems and related circuits, including radio, DVD, navigation, speakers, antennas, and voice-activated accessories.

MTST
V.G.4; P3

Time off_____

Time on_____

Total time_____

Student Instructions: Read through the entire procedure prior to starting. Prepare your workspace and any tools or parts that may be needed to complete the task. When directed by your supervisor/instructor, begin the procedure to complete the task and check the box as each step is finished.

Note: This tasksheet may require the student to check the condition of miscellaneous vehicle fluids, some of which may be flammable and could damage the environment or cause health problems if not handled properly. Observe all safety precautions and follow local regulations for the proper disposal of fluids.

Procedure:	Step Completed
1. (**Note:** If the vehicle does not have any of the systems described below, research the Internet for required information.)	☐
2. While referencing the manufacturer's workshop materials, record the operation/position of any radio systems:	☐
3. While referencing the manufacturer's workshop materials, record any special precautions/procedures when servicing/testing the radio systems:	☐
4. While referencing the manufacturer's workshop materials, record the operation/position of any navigation systems:	☐
5. While referencing the manufacturer's workshop materials, record any special precautions/procedures when servicing/testing any navigation systems:	☐
6. While referencing the manufacturer's workshop materials, record the operation/position of any speaker systems:	☐
7. While referencing the manufacturer's workshop materials, record any special precautions/procedures when servicing/testing any speaker systems:	☐

8. While referencing the manufacturer's workshop materials, record the operation/position of any antennas:	☐
9. While referencing the manufacturer's workshop materials, record any special precautions/procedures when servicing/testing any antennas:	☐
10. While referencing the manufacturer's workshop materials, record the operation/position of any voice-activated accessories:	☐
11. While referencing the manufacturer's workshop materials, record any special precautions/procedures when servicing/testing any voice-activated accessories:	☐
12. While referencing the manufacturer's workshop materials and electronic service tool (EST), check for any fault codes related to the radio, DVD, navigation, speakers, antennas, or voice-activated accessories systems.	
a. Within, manufacturer's specifications: Yes: ☐ No: ☐	☐
b. If No, list the recommended corrective action(s):	☐
13. Discuss your findings with your supervisor/instructor.	☐

Non-Task-Specific Evaluations:	Step Completed
1. Tools and equipment were used as directed and returned in good working order.	☐
2. Complied with all general and task-specific safety standards, including proper use of any personal protection equipment.	☐
3. Completed the task in an appropriate time frame (recommendation: 1.5 or 2 times the flat rate).	☐
4. Left the workspace clean and orderly.	☐
5. Cared for customer property and returned it undamaged.	☐

Student signature _____ Date _____

Comments:

Have your supervisor/instructor verify satisfactory completion of this procedure, any observations made, and any necessary action(s) recommended.

Evaluation Instructions: The scoring box below is intended to act as a guide for both student and supervisor/instructor. Each criterion listed will help students understand what is expected of them and help supervisors/instructors articulate the level of success at a particular task. The scoring is set up to allow a second attempt at each task (see the Test and Retest columns). Scoring is also designed to award students points only for task criteria that were completed correctly. Points are lost for failure to complete the employability requirements (see Non-Task-Specific Evaluation criteria). When all criteria are evaluated, tally the points for a total at the bottom of each column.

Tasksheet Scoring

Evaluation Items	Test		Retest	
	Pass	**Fail**	**Pass**	**Fail**
Task-Specific Evaluation	**(1 pt)**	**(0 pts)**	**(1 pt)**	**(0 pts)**
Student properly identified radio systems, speaker systems, antennas, and voice-activated systems.				
Student properly identified service procedure/precautions of the radio systems, navigation systems, and navigation systems.				
Student properly identified service procedure/precautions of the speaker systems, antennas, and voice-activated systems.				
Student properly checked fault codes for the radio, DVD, navigation, speakers, antennas, and voice-activated accessories.				
Non-Task-Specific Evaluation	**(0 pts)**	**(−1 pt)**	**(0 pts)**	**(−1 pt)**
Student successfully completed at least three of the non-task-specific steps.				
Student successfully completed all five of the non-task-specific steps.				
Total Score: <total # of points/4 = %>				

© 2021 Jones & Bartlett Learning, LLC, an Ascend Learning Company

CDX Tasksheet Number: MHT5G005

Student/Intern Information

Name _____ Date _____ Class _____

Vehicle, Customer, and Service Information

Vehicle used for this activity:

Year _____ Make _____ Model _____

Odometer _____ VIN _____

Materials Required

- Vehicles or simulators with electrical faults within the auxiliary power systems
- Vehicle manufacturer's workshop materials, including schematic wiring diagrams
- Digital volt-ohmmeter (DVOM), PC-based software, and/or data scan tools
- Vehicle/component lifting equipment if applicable

Task-Specific Safety Considerations

- Activities require you to measure electrical values. Always ensure that the instructor/supervisor checks test instrument connections prior to connecting power or taking measurements. High current flows can be dangerous; avoid accidental short circuits or grounding the battery's positive connections.
- Air-conditioning systems have refrigerant gas within the system. When the system is running, high-pressure gas and liquid refrigerant will be circulating in the system. Use extreme caution when working around high-pressure hoses.
- This activity may require you to work with solenoid actuators. Actuators may create a crush injury hazard; keep fingers away from mechanisms.
- Electric motors may start up when you least expect it; keep fingers and clothing away from the mechanism.
- Activities may require test-driving the vehicle on the school grounds or on a hoist, both of which carry severe risks. Attempt this task only with full permission from your supervisor/instructor, and follow all the guidelines exactly.
- Comply with personal and environmental safety practices associated with clothing; eye protection; hand tools; power equipment; proper ventilation; and the handling, storage, and disposal of chemicals/materials in accordance with federal, state, and local regulations.
- Always wear the correct protective eyewear and clothing, and use the appropriate safety equipment, as well as wheel chocks, fender covers, seat protectors, and floor mat protectors.
- Make sure you understand and observe all legislative and personal safety procedures when carrying out practical assignments. If you are unsure of what these are, ask your supervisor/instructor.

Time off_____

Time on_____

▶ **TASK** Understand the operation of power inverters, protection devices, connectors, terminals, wiring, and control components/modules of auxiliary power systems.

MTST
V.G.5; P3

Total time_____

Student Instructions: Read through the entire procedure prior to starting. Prepare your workspace and any tools or parts that may be needed to complete the task. When directed by your supervisor/instructor, begin the procedure to complete the task and check the box as each step is finished.

Procedure:	Step Completed
1. Locate the wiring diagram for the auxiliary power outlet circuit that you are testing. Determine the purpose and operation of the components. Knowledge of how to read a wiring diagram is critical in diagnosing malfunctions in any given circuit. Understanding how components are designed to operate within a circuit will make problems easier to diagnose. (**Note:** The auxiliary power outlet or inverter can be used to power some convenient appliances, like TVs, microwaves, and toaster ovens, that operate on 110 volts.)	☐
2. Test the auxiliary power outlet with a DVOM to make sure it has the proper operating voltage required.	
a. Operation of the auxiliary power outlet: Pass: ☐ Fail: ☐	☐
b. Voltage applied to the outlet: _____ volts	☐
3. Check the mounting hardware for tightness.	☐
4. If the outlet fails to operate as designed, consult the manufacturer's service manual for proper procedures for testing. Make recommendations for repair or replacement:	☐
5. Check all connectors and terminals on control modules for looseness, cracking, and burn marks that may cause the system to malfunction.	
a. Condition of connectors: Good: ☐ Bad: ☐	☐
(**Note:** Any burn marks or discoloration of the connectors may indicate excessive amperage running through them.)	
6. If connectors and/or terminals are bad, make recommendations for repairing or replacing the connections:	☐

7. Test modules for proper operation.	
a. Consult the manufacturer's service manual, and record the proper procedures to test these components:	☐
8. Check all wiring that is present to that circuit for bare spots, cracked insulation, and no connection to the connector or component. Perform voltage-drop tests to the circuit if necessary.	
a. Condition of wiring: Good: ☐ Bad: ☐	☐
9. If the condition of the wiring is bad, make recommendations for repairing or replacing the wiring:	☐
10. Return the vehicle to its beginning condition, and return any tools to their proper locations.	☐
11. Consult with your supervisor/instructor and record any recommendations to bring the circuit back to manufacturer specifications:	☐

Non-Task-Specific Evaluations:	Step Completed
1. Tools and equipment were used as directed and returned in good working order.	☐
2. Complied with all general and task-specific safety standards, including proper use of any personal protection equipment.	☐
3. Completed the task in an appropriate time frame (recommendation: 1.5 or 2 times the flat rate).	☐
4. Left the workspace clean and orderly.	☐
5. Cared for customer property and returned it undamaged.	☐

Student signature _____ Date _____

Comments:

Have your supervisor/instructor verify satisfactory completion of this procedure, any observations made, and any necessary action(s) recommended.

© 2021 Jones & Bartlett Learning, LLC, an Ascend Learning Company

818 Cab and Chassis Electrical Systems

Evaluation Instructions: The scoring box below is intended to act as a guide for both student and supervisor/instructor. Each criterion listed will help students understand what is expected of them and help supervisors/instructors articulate the level of success at a particular task. The scoring is set up to allow a second attempt at each task (see the Test and Retest columns). Scoring is also designed to award students points only for task criteria that were completed correctly. Points are lost for failure to complete the employability requirements (see Non-Task-Specific Evaluation criteria). When all criteria are evaluated, tally the points for a total at the bottom of each column.

Tasksheet Scoring

Evaluation Items	Test		Retest	
	Pass	**Fail**	**Pass**	**Fail**
Task-Specific Evaluation	**(1 pt)**	**(0 pts)**	**(1 pt)**	**(0 pts)**
Student used the appropriate service information to research the auxiliary power systems.				
Student accurately tested and inspected the auxiliary power systems.				
Student compared the results to the specifications, then correctly determined any necessary actions.				
Student reinstalled all removed components undamaged and in working order.				
Non-Task-Specific Evaluation	**(0 pts)**	**(−1 pt)**	**(0 pts)**	**(−1 pt)**
Student successfully completed at least three of the non-task-specific steps.				
Student successfully completed all five of the non-task-specific steps.				
Total Score: <total # of points/4 = %>				

Supervisor/Instructor:

Supervisor/instructor signature _____ Date _____

Comments:

Retest supervisor/instructor signature _____ Date _____

Comments:

CDX Tasksheet Number: MHT5G006

Student/Intern Information

Name _____ Date _____ Class _____

Vehicle, Customer, and Service Information

Vehicle used for this activity:

Year _____ Make _____ Model _____

Odometer _____ VIN _____

Materials Required

- Vehicle with possible engine concern
- Engine manufacturer's workshop materials
- Manufacturer-specific tools depending on the concern/procedure(s)
- Vehicle/component lifting equipment, if applicable

Task-Specific Safety Considerations

- Activities may require test-driving the vehicle on the school grounds or on a hoist, both of which carry severe risks. Attempt this task only with full permission from your supervisor/instructor, and follow all the guidelines exactly.
- Lifting equipment and machines such as vehicle jacks and stands, vehicle hoists, and engine hoists are important tools that increase productivity and make the job easier. However, they can also cause severe injury or death if used improperly. Make sure you follow the manufacturer's operation procedures. Also make sure you have your supervisor's/instructor's permission to use any particular type of lifting equipment.
- Comply with personal and environmental safety practices associated with clothing; eye protection; hand tools; power equipment; proper ventilation; and the handling, storage, and disposal of chemicals/materials in accordance with federal, state, and local regulations.
- Always wear the correct protective eyewear and clothing and use the appropriate safety equipment, as well as wheel chocks, fender covers, seat protectors, and floor mat protectors.
- Make sure you understand and observe all legislative and personal safety procedures when carrying out practical assignments. If you are unsure of what these are, ask your supervisor/instructor.

▶ **TASK** Understand the operation of telematics systems. **MTST** *V.G.6; P3*

Time off_____

Time on_____

Student Instructions: Read through the entire procedure prior to starting. Prepare your workspace and any tools or parts that may be needed to complete the task. When directed by your supervisor/instructor, begin the procedure to complete the task and check the box as each step is finished.

Total time_____

Note: This tasksheet may require the student to check the condition of miscellaneous vehicle fluids, some of which may be flammable and could damage the environment or cause health problems if not handled properly. Observe all safety precautions and follow local regulations for the proper disposal of fluids.

Procedure:	Step Completed
1. (**Note:** If the vehicle does not have any of the systems described below, research the Internet for required information.)	☐
2. While referencing the manufacturer's workshop materials, record the operation/position of any factory telematics system:	☐
3. While referencing the manufacturer's workshop materials, record any special precautions/procedures when servicing/testing the factory telematics system:	☐
4. List the items that can be/are monitored by the factory telematics system:	☐
5. While referencing the manufacturer's workshop materials and electronic service tool (EST), check for any fault codes related to the factory telematics system.	
a. Within, manufacturer's specifications: Yes: ☐ No: ☐	☐
b. If No, list the recommended corrective action(s):	☐
6. While referencing the manufacturer's workshop materials, record the operation/position of any aftermarket telematics systems:	☐
7. While referencing the manufacturer's workshop materials, record any special precautions/procedures when servicing/testing any aftermarket telematics systems:	☐

	Step Completed
8. List the items that can be/are monitored by the aftermarket telematics system:	☐
9. While referencing the manufacturer's workshop materials and EST, check for any fault codes related to the factory telematics system:	
a. Within, manufacturer's specifications: Yes: ☐ No: ☐	☐
b. If No, list the recommended corrective action(s):	☐
10. Discuss your findings with your supervisor/instructor.	☐

Non-Task-Specific Evaluations:	Step Completed
1. Tools and equipment were used as directed and returned in good working order.	☐
2. Complied with all general and task-specific safety standards, including proper use of any personal protection equipment.	☐
3. Completed the task in an appropriate time frame (recommendation: 1.5 or 2 times the flat rate).	☐
4. Left the workspace clean and orderly.	☐
5. Cared for customer property and returned it undamaged.	☐

Student signature _____ Date _____

Comments:

Have your supervisor/instructor verify satisfactory completion of this procedure, any observations made,

and any necessary action(s) recommended.

Evaluation Instructions: The scoring box below is intended to act as a guide for both student and supervisor/instructor. Each criterion listed will help students understand what is expected of them and help supervisors/instructors articulate the level of success at a particular task. The scoring is set up to allow a second attempt at each task (see the Test and Retest columns). Scoring is also designed to award students points only for task criteria that were completed correctly. Points are lost for failure to complete the employability requirements (see Non-Task-Specific Evaluation criteria). When all criteria are evaluated, tally the points for a total at the bottom of each column.

Tasksheet Scoring

	Test		Retest	
Evaluation Items	**Pass**	**Fail**	**Pass**	**Fail**
Task-Specific Evaluation	**(1 pt)**	**(0 pts)**	**(1 pt)**	**(0 pts)**
Student properly recorded operation/position of the factory telematics system and service/testing of the factory telematics system.				
Student properly recorded operation/position of the aftermarket telematics system and service/testing of the aftermarket telematics system.				
Student properly checked fault codes associated with the factory telematics system.				
Student properly checked fault codes associated with the aftermarket telematics system.				
Non-Task-Specific Evaluation	**(0 pts)**	**(−1 pt)**	**(0 pts)**	**(−1 pt)**
Student successfully completed at least three of the non-task-specific steps.				
Student successfully completed all five of the non-task-specific steps.				
Total Score: <total # of points/4 = %>				

Supervisor/Instructor:

Supervisor/instructor signature _____ Date _____

Comments:

Retest supervisor/instructor signature _____ Date _____

Comments:

CDX Tasksheet Number: MHT5G007

Student/Intern Information

Name _____ Date _____ Class _____

Vehicle, Customer, and Service Information

Vehicle used for this activity:

Year _____ Make _____ Model _____

Odometer _____ VIN _____

Materials Required

- Vehicles or simulators with electrical faults within the auxiliary power systems
- Vehicle manufacturer's workshop materials, including schematic wiring diagrams
- Digital volt-ohmmeter (DVOM), PC-based software, and/or data scan tools
- Vehicle/component lifting equipment if applicable

Task-Specific Safety Considerations

- Activities require you to measure electrical values. Always ensure that the instructor/supervisor checks test instrument connections prior to connecting power or taking measurements. High current flows can be dangerous; avoid accidental short circuits or grounding the battery's positive connections.
- Air-conditioning systems have refrigerant gas within the system. When the system is running, high-pressure gas and liquid refrigerant will be circulating in the system. Use extreme caution working around high-pressure hoses.
- This activity may require you to work with solenoid actuators. Actuators may create a crush injury hazard; keep fingers away from mechanisms.
- Electric motors may start up when you least expect it; keep fingers and clothing away from the mechanism.
- Activities may require test-driving the vehicle on the school grounds or on a hoist, both of which carry severe risks. Attempt this task only with full permission from your supervisor/instructor, and follow all the guidelines exactly.
- Comply with personal and environmental safety practices associated with clothing; eye protection; hand tools; power equipment; proper ventilation; and the handling, storage, and disposal of chemicals/materials in accordance with federal, state, and local regulations.
- Always wear the correct protective eyewear and clothing, and use the appropriate safety equipment, as well as wheel chocks, fender covers, seat protectors, and floor mat protectors.
- Make sure you understand and observe all legislative and personal safety procedures when carrying out practical assignments. If you are unsure of what these are, ask your supervisor/instructor.

▶ TASK Diagnose faults in the engine block and engine oil heater(s); determine needed action. *MTST V.G.7; P2*

Time off_____
Time on_____
Total time_____

Student Instructions: Read through the entire procedure prior to starting. Prepare your workspace and any tools or parts that may be needed to complete the task. When directed

© 2021 Jones & Bartlett Learning, LLC, an Ascend Learning Company

Cab and Chassis Electrical Systems **825**

by your supervisor/instructor, begin the procedure to complete the task and check the box as each step is finished.

Procedure:	Step Completed
1. List the customer concern regarding the engine block and engine oil heater(s):	☐
2. Using appropriate service information for the vehicle you are working on, research how to inspect and test block heaters. List the results:	☐
3. Check your documented procedures with your supervisor/instructor. Supervisor's/instructor's initials:	☐
4. Using the appropriate service information, inspect and test block heaters.	☐
5. List the results of conducting your tests:	☐
6. Determine and list any necessary action(s):	☐
7. Return the vehicle to its beginning condition, and return any tools to their proper locations.	☐
8. Consult with your instructor, and record any recommendations to bring the circuit back to manufacturer specifications:	☐

Non-Task-Specific Evaluations:	Step Completed
1. Tools and equipment were used as directed and returned in good working order.	☐
2. Complied with all general and task-specific safety standards, including proper use of any personal protection equipment.	☐
3. Completed the task in an appropriate time frame (recommendation: 1.5 or 2 times the flat rate).	☐
4. Left the workspace clean and orderly.	☐
5. Cared for customer property and returned it undamaged.	☐

Student signature _____ Date _____

Comments:

Have your supervisor/instructor verify satisfactory completion of this procedure, any observations made,

and any necessary action(s) recommended.

Evaluation Instructions: The scoring box below is intended to act as a guide for both student and supervisor/instructor. Each criterion listed will help students understand what is expected of them and help supervisors/instructors articulate the level of success at a particular task. The scoring is set up to allow a second attempt at each task (see the Test and Retest columns). Scoring is also designed to award students points only for task criteria that were completed correctly. Points are lost for failure to complete the employability requirements (see Non-Task-Specific Evaluation criteria). When all criteria are evaluated, tally the points for a total at the bottom of each column.

Tasksheet Scoring

Evaluation Items	Test		Retest	
	Pass	**Fail**	**Pass**	**Fail**
Task-Specific Evaluation	**(1 pt)**	**(0 pts)**	**(1 pt)**	**(0 pts)**
Student used the appropriate service information to research engine block and engine oil heater(s).				
Student accurately tested and inspected the engine block and engine oil heater(s).				
Student compared the results to the specifications, then correctly determined any necessary actions.				
Student reinstalled all removed components undamaged and in working order.				
Non-Task-Specific Evaluation	**(0 pts)**	**(−1 pt)**	**(0 pts)**	**(−1 pt)**
Student successfully completed at least three of the non-task-specific steps.				
Student successfully completed all five of the non-task-specific steps.				
Total Score: <total # of points/4 = %>				

Supervisor/Instructor:

Supervisor/instructor signature _____ Date _____

Comments:

Retest supervisor/instructor signature _____ Date _____

Comments:

Appendix

2018 ASE Medium/Heavy Truck Master Service Technology (MTST) Task List Correlation Guide

ASE Task List	ASE Priority Number
Required Supplemental Tasks	
1. Identify general shop safety rules and procedures.	N/A
2. Utilize safe procedures for handling of tools and equipment.	N/A
3. Identify and use proper placement of floor jacks and jack stands.	N/A
4. Identify and use proper procedures for safe lift operation.	N/A
5. Utilize proper ventilation procedures for working within the lab/shop area.	N/A
6. Identify marked safety areas.	N/A
7. Identify the location and the types of fire extinguishers and other fire safety equipment; demonstrate knowledge of the procedures for using fire extinguishers and other fire safety equipment.	N/A
8. Identify the location and use of eye wash stations.	N/A
9. Identify the location of the posted evacuation routes.	N/A
10. Comply with the required use of safety glasses, ear protection, gloves, and shoes during lab/shop activities.	N/A
11. Identify and wear appropriate clothing for lab/shop activities.	N/A
12. Secure hair and jewelry for lab/shop activities.	N/A
13. Demonstrate awareness of the safety aspects of supplemental restraint systems (SRS), electronic brake control systems, and hybrid vehicle high-voltage circuits.	N/A
14. Demonstrate awareness of the safety aspects of high-voltage circuits (such as high-intensity discharge (HID) lamps, ignition systems, injection systems).	N/A
15. Locate and demonstrate knowledge of material safety data sheets (MSDS).	N/A
Tools and Equipment	
1. Identify tools and their usage in automotive applications.	N/A
2. Identify standard and metric designation.	N/A
3. Demonstrate safe handling and use of appropriate tools.	N/A
4. Demonstrate proper cleaning, storage, and maintenance of tools and equipment.	N/A
5. Demonstrate proper use of precision measuring tools (i.e., micrometer, dial-indicator, dial-caliper).	N/A
Preparing Vehicle for Service	
1. Identify information needed and the service requested on a repair order.	N/A
2. Identify purpose and demonstrate proper use of fender covers, mats.	N/A

3. Demonstrate use of the three Cs (concern, cause, and correction).	N/A
4. Review vehicle service history.	N/A
5. Complete work order to include customer information, vehicle identifying information, customer concern, related service history, cause, and correction.	N/A
Preparing Vehicle for Customer	
1. Ensure vehicle is prepared to return to customer per school/company policy (floor mats, steering wheel cover, etc.).	N/A
WORKPLACE EMPLOYABILITY SKILLS	
Personal Standards	
1. Reports to work daily on time; able to take directions and motivated to accomplish the task at hand.	N/A
2. Dresses appropriately and uses language and manners suitable for the workplace.	N/A
3. Maintains appropriate personal hygiene.	N/A
4. Meets and maintains employment eligibility criteria, such as drug/alcohol-free status, clean driving record.	N/A
5. Demonstrates honesty, integrity, and reliability.	N/A
Work Habits/Ethic	
1. Complies with workplace policies/laws.	N/A
2. Contributes to the success of the team, assists others, and requests help when needed.	N/A
3. Works well with all customers and coworkers.	N/A
4. Negotiates solutions to interpersonal and workplace conflicts.	N/A
5. Contributes ideas and initiative.	N/A
6. Follows directions.	N/A
7. Communicates (written and verbal) effectively with customers and coworkers.	N/A
8. Reads and interprets workplace documents; writes clearly and concisely.	N/A
9. Analyzes and resolves problems that arise in completing assigned tasks.	N/A
10. Organizes and implements a productive plan of work.	N/A
11. Uses scientific, technical, engineering, and mathematics principles and reasoning to accomplish assigned tasks.	N/A
12. Identifies and addresses the needs of all customers, providing helpful, courteous, and knowledgeable service and advice as needed.	N/A
I. DIESEL ENGINES	
A. General	
1. Inspect fuel, oil, Diesel Exhaust Fluid (DEF) and coolant levels, and condition; determine needed action.	P-1
2. Identify engine fuel, oil, coolant, air, and other leaks; determine needed action.	P-1
3. Listen for engine noises; determine needed action.	P-3

4. Observe engine exhaust smoke color and quantity; determine needed action.	P-2
5. Check engine no cranking, cranks but fails to start, hard starting, and starts but does not continue to run problems; determine needed action.	P-1
6. Identify engine surging, rough operation, misfiring, low power, slow deceleration, slow acceleration, and shutdown problems; determine needed action.	P-1
7. Identify engine vibration problems.	P-2
8. Check and record electronic diagnostic codes.	P-1
B. Cylinder Head and Valve Train	
1. Inspect cylinder head for cracks/damage; check mating surfaces for warpage; check condition of passages; inspect core/expansion and gallery plugs; determine needed action.	P-2
2. Disassemble head and inspect valves, guides, seats, springs, retainers, rotators, locks, and seals; determine needed action.	P-3
3. Measure valve head height relative to deck and valve face-to-seat contact; determine needed action.	P-3
4. Inspect injector sleeves and seals; measure injector tip or nozzle protrusion; determine needed action.	P-3
5. Inspect valve train components; determine needed action.	P-1
6. Reassemble cylinder head.	P-3
7. Inspect, measure, and replace/reinstall overhead camshaft; measure/adjust end play and backlash.	P-3
8. Inspect electronic wiring harness and brackets for wear, bending, cracks, and looseness; determine needed action.	P-1
9. Adjust valve bridges (crossheads); adjust valve clearances and injector settings.	P-2
C. Engine Block	
1. Perform crankcase pressure test; determine needed action.	P-1
2. Remove, inspect, service, and install pans, covers, gaskets, seals, wear rings, and crankcase ventilation components.	P-2
3. Disassemble, clean, and inspect engine block for cracks/damage; measure mating surfaces for warpage; check condition of passages, core/expansion and gallery plugs; inspect threaded holes, studs, dowel pins, and bolts for serviceability; determine needed action.	P-2
4. Inspect cylinder sleeve counter bore and lower bore; check bore distortion; determine needed action.	P-2
5. Clean, inspect, and measure cylinder walls or liners for wear and damage; determine needed action.	P-2
6. Replace/reinstall cylinder liners and seals; check and adjust liner height (protrusion).	P-2
7. Inspect in-block camshaft bearings for wear and damage; determine needed action.	P-3
8. Inspect, measure, and replace/reinstall in-block camshaft; measure/ adjust end play.	P-3

9. Clean and inspect crankshaft for surface cracks and journal damage; check condition of oil passages; check passage plugs; measure journal diameter; determine needed action.	P-2
10. Inspect main bearings for wear patterns and damage; replace as needed; check bearing clearances; check and correct crankshaft end play.	P-2
11. Inspect, install, and time gear train; measure gear backlash; determine needed action.	P-2
12. Inspect connecting rod and bearings for wear patterns; measure pistons, pins, retainers, and bushings; perform needed action.	P-3
13. Determine piston-to-cylinder wall clearance; check ring-to-groove fit and end gap; install rings on pistons.	P-3
14. Assemble pistons and connecting rods; install in block; install rod bearings and check clearances.	P-2
15. Check condition of piston cooling jets (nozzles); determine needed action.	P-2
16. Inspect crankshaft vibration damper; determine needed action.	P-3
17. Install and align flywheel housing; inspect flywheel housing(s) to transmission housing/engine mating surface(s) and measure flywheel housing face and bore runout; determine needed action.	P-3
18. Inspect flywheel/flexplate (including ring gear) and mounting surfaces for cracks and wear; measure runout; determine needed action.	P-2
D. Lubrication Systems	
1. Test engine oil pressure and check operation of pressure sensor, gauge, and/or sending unit; test engine oil temperature and check operation of temperature sensor; determine needed action.	P-1
2. Check engine oil level, condition, and consumption; determine needed action.	P-1
3. Inspect and measure oil pump, drives, inlet pipes, and pick-up screens; check drive gear clearances; determine needed action.	P-3
4. Inspect oil pressure regulator valve(s), by-pass and pressure relief valve(s), oil thermostat, and filters; determine needed action.	P-3
5. Inspect, clean, and test oil cooler and components; determine needed action.	P-3
6. Inspect turbocharger lubrication systems; determine needed action.	P-2
7. Determine proper lubricant and perform oil and filter change.	P-1
E. Cooling System	
1. Check engine coolant type, level, condition, and consumption; test coolant for freeze protection and additive package concentration; determine needed action.	P-1
2. Test coolant temperature and check operation of temperature and level sensors, gauge, and/or sending unit; determine needed action.	P-1
3. Inspect and reinstall/replace pulleys, tensioners and drive belts; adjust drive belts and check alignment.	P-1
4. Inspect thermostat(s), by-passes, housing(s), and seals; replace as needed.	P-2
5. Recover coolant, flush, and refill with recommended coolant/additive package; bleed cooling system.	P-1

6. Inspect coolant conditioner/filter assembly for leaks; inspect valves, lines, and fittings; replace as needed.	P-1
7. Inspect water pump and hoses; replace as needed.	P-1
8. Inspect, clean, and pressure test radiator. Pressure test cap, tank(s), and recovery systems; determine needed action.	P-1
9. Inspect thermostatic cooling fan system (hydraulic, pneumatic, and electronic) and fan shroud; replace as needed.	P-1
10. Inspect turbo charger cooling systems; determine needed action.	P-2
F. Air Induction and Exhaust Systems	
1. Perform air intake system restriction and leakage tests; determine needed action.	P-1
2. Perform intake manifold pressure (boost) test; determine needed action.	P-3
3. Check exhaust back pressure; determine needed action.	P-3
4. Inspect turbocharger(s), wastegate, and piping systems; determine needed action.	P-2
5. Inspect turbocharger(s) (variable ratio/geometry VGT), pneumatic, hydraulic, electronic controls, and actuators.	P-2
6. Check air induction system: piping, hoses, clamps, and mounting; service or replace air filter as needed.	P-1
7. Remove and reinstall turbocharger/wastegate assembly.	P-3
8. Inspect intake manifold, gaskets, and connections; replace as needed.	P-3
9. Inspect, clean, and test charge air cooler assemblies; replace as needed.	P-2
10. Inspect exhaust manifold, piping, mufflers, and mounting hardware; repair or replace as needed.	P-2
11. Inspect exhaust after treatment devices; determine necessary action.	P-2
12. Inspect and test preheater/inlet air heater, or glow plug system and controls; perform needed action.	P-2
13. Inspect exhaust gas recirculation (EGR) system including EGR valve, cooler, piping, filter, electronic sensors, controls, and wiring; determine needed action.	P-2
G. Fuel System	
1. Fuel Supply System	
1. Check fuel level, and condition; determine needed action.	P-1
2. Perform fuel supply and return system tests; determine needed action.	P-1
3. Inspect fuel tanks, vents, caps, mounts, valves, screens, crossover system, supply and return lines and fittings; determine needed action.	P-1
4. Inspect, clean, and test fuel transfer (lift) pump, pump drives, screens, fuel/water separators/indicators, filters, heaters, coolers, ECM cooling plates, and mounting hardware; determine needed action.	P-1
5. Inspect and test pressure regulator systems (check valves, pressure regulator valves, and restrictive fittings); determine needed action.	P-1
6. Check fuel system for air; determine needed action; prime and bleed fuel system; check primer pump.	P-1

2. Electronic Fuel Management System	
1. Inspect and test power and ground circuits and connections; measure and interpret voltage, voltage drop, amperage, and resistance readings using a digital multimeter (DMM); determine needed action.	P-1
2. Interface with vehicle's on-board computer; perform diagnostic procedures using electronic service tool(s) (to include PC based software and/or data scan tools); determine needed action.	P-1
3. Check and record electronic diagnostic codes and trip/operational data; monitor electronic data; clear codes; determine further diagnosis.	P-1
4. Locate and use relevant service information (to include diagnostic procedures, flow charts, and wiring diagrams).	P-1
5. Inspect and replace electrical connector terminals, seals, and locks.	P-1
6. Inspect and test switches, sensors, controls, actuator components, and circuits; adjust or replace as needed.	P-1
7. Using electronic service tool(s) access and interpret customer programmable parameters.	P-1
8. Perform on-engine inspections, tests and adjustments on electronic unit injectors (EUI); determine needed action.	P-2
9. Remove and install electronic unit injectors (EUI) and related components; recalibrate ECM (if applicable).	P-2
10. Perform cylinder contribution test utilizing electronic service tool(s).	P-1
11. Perform on-engine inspections and tests on hydraulic electronic unit injectors (HEUI) and system electronic controls; determine needed action.	P-2
12. Perform on-engine inspections and tests on hydraulic electronic unit injector (HEUI) high pressure oil supply and control systems; determine needed action.	P-2
13. Perform on-engine inspections and tests on high pressure common rail (HPCR) type injection systems; determine needed action.	P-2
14. Inspect high pressure injection lines, hold downs, fittings and seals; determine needed action.	P-2
H. Engine Brakes	
1. Inspect and adjust engine compression/exhaust brakes; determine needed action.	P-2
2. Inspect, test, and adjust engine compression/exhaust brake control circuits, switches, and solenoids; determine needed action.	P-3
3. Inspect engine compression/exhaust brake housing, valves, seals, lines, and fittings; determine necessary action.	P-3
II. DRIVETRAIN	
A. General	
1. Research vehicle service information, including fluid type, vehicle service history, service precautions, and technical service bulletins.	P-1
2. Identify drivetrain components, transmission type, and configuration.	P-1
3. Use appropriate electronic service tool(s) and procedures to diagnose problems; check, record, and clear diagnostic codes; interpret digital multimeter (DMM) readings.	P-1

B. Clutch	
1. Inspect and adjust clutch, clutch brake, linkage, cables, levers, brackets, bushings, pivots, springs, and clutch safety switch (includes push-type and pull-type); check pedal height and travel; determine needed action.	P-1
2. Inspect clutch master cylinder fluid level; check clutch master cylinder, slave cylinder, lines, and hoses for leaks and damage; determine needed action.	P-1
3. Inspect, adjust, repair, and/or replace hydraulic clutch slave and master cylinders, lines, and hoses; bleed system.	P-2
4. Inspect, adjust, lubricate, or replace release (throw-out) bearing, sleeve, bushings, springs, housing, levers, release fork, fork pads, rollers, shafts, and seals.	P-1
5. Inspect, adjust, and/or replace single-disc clutch pressure plate and clutch disc.	P-1
6. Inspect, adjust, and/or replace two-plate clutch pressure plate, clutch discs, intermediate plate, and drive pins/lugs.	P-1
7. Inspect and/or replace clutch brake assembly; inspect input shaft and bearing retainer; determine needed action.	P-1
8. Inspect, adjust, and/or replace self-adjusting/continuous-adjusting clutch mechanisms.	P-1
9. Inspect and/or replace pilot bearing.	P-1
10. Identify causes of clutch noise, binding, slippage, pulsation, vibration, grabbing, dragging, and chatter problems; determine needed action.	P-1
11. Remove and install flywheel; inspect mounting area on crankshaft; inspect rear main oil seal; measure crankshaft end play; determine needed action.	P-1
12. Inspect flywheel and starter ring gear; measure flywheel face; measure pilot bore runout; determine needed action.	P-1
13. Inspect flywheel housing-to-transmission housing/engine mating surface(s); measure flywheel housing face and bore runout; determine needed action.	P-2
C. Transmission	
1. Inspect transmission shifter and linkage; inspect and/or replace transmission mounts, insulators, and mounting bolts.	P-1
2. Inspect transmission for leakage; determine needed action.	P-1
3. Replace transmission cover plates, gaskets, seals, and cap bolts; inspect seal surfaces and vents; determine needed action.	P-1
4. Check transmission fluid level and condition; determine needed action.	P-1
5. Inspect transmission breather; inspect transmission oil filters, coolers, and related components; determine needed action.	P-2
6. Inspect speedometer components; determine needed action.	P-2
7. Inspect and test function of REVERSE light, NEUTRAL start, and warning device circuits; determine needed action.	P-1
8. Inspect, adjust, and replace transmission covers, rails, forks, levers, bushings, sleeves, detents, interlocks, springs, and lock bolts/safety wires.	P-2

9. Identify causes of transmission noise, shifting concerns, lockup, jumping out-of-gear, overheating, and vibration problems; determine needed repairs.	P-1
10. Inspect, test, repair, and/or replace air shift controls, lines, hoses, valves, regulators, filters, and cylinder assemblies.	P-2
11. Remove and reinstall transmission.	P-2
12. Inspect input shaft, gear, spacers, bearings, retainers, and slingers; determine needed action.	P-3
13. Inspect and adjust power take-off (PTO) assemblies, controls, and shafts; determine needed action.	P-3
14. Inspect and test transmission temperature gauge, wiring harnesses, and sensor/sending unit; determine needed action.	P-2
15. Inspect and test operation of automatic transmission, components, and controls; diagnose automatic transmission system problems; determine needed action.	P-2
16. Inspect and test operation of automated mechanical transmission, components, and controls; diagnose automated mechanical transmission system problems; determine needed action.	P-2
D. Driveshaft and Universal Joints	
1. Inspect, service, and/or replace driveshafts, slip joints, yokes, drive flanges, support bearings, universal joints, boots, seals, and retaining/mounting hardware; check phasing of all shafts.	P-1
2. Identify causes of driveshaft and universal joint noise and vibration problems; determine needed action.	P-1
3. Inspect driveshaft center support bearings and mounts; determine needed action.	P-1
4. Measure driveline angles; determine needed action.	P-2
E. Drive Axles	
1. Check and repair fluid leaks; inspect drive axle housing assembly, cover plates, gaskets, seals, vent/breather, and magnetic plugs.	P-1
2. Check drive axle fluid level and condition; check drive axle filter; determine needed action.	P-1
3. Inspect, adjust, repair, and/or replace air-operated power divider (inter-axle differential) assembly including: diaphragms, seals, springs, yokes, pins, lines, hoses, fittings, and controls.	P-2
4. Inspect drive axle shafts; determine needed action.	P-2
5. Remove and replace wheel assembly; check rear wheel seal and axle flange for leaks; determine needed action.	P-1
6. Inspect, repair, or replace drive axle lubrication system pump, troughs, collectors, slingers, tubes, and filters.	P-3
7. Identify causes of drive axle(s) drive unit noise and overheating problems; determine needed action.	P-2
8. Inspect and test drive axle temperature gauge, wiring harnesses, and sending unit/sensor; determine needed action.	P-2
9. Remove and replace differential carrier assembly.	P-2

10. Identify causes of drive axle wheel bearing noise and check for damage; determine needed action.	P-1
11. Inspect and/or replace components of differential case assembly including spider gears, cross shaft, side gears, thrust washers, case halves, and bearings.	P-3
12. Inspect and replace components of locking differential case assembly.	P-3
13. Inspect differential carrier housing and caps, side bearing bores, and pilot (spigot, pocket) bearing bore; determine needed action.	P-3
14. Inspect and replace ring and drive pinion gears, spacers, sleeves, bearing cages, and bearings.	P-3
15. Measure ring gear runout; determine needed action.	P-2
16. Measure and adjust drive pinion bearing preload.	P-3
17. Measure and adjust drive pinion depth.	P-3
18. Measure and adjust side bearing preload and ring gear backlash.	P-2
19. Check and interpret ring gear and pinion tooth contact pattern; determine needed action.	P-2
20. Inspect, adjust, or replace ring gear thrust block/screw.	P-3
III. BRAKES	
A. General	
1. Research vehicle service information, including fluid type, vehicle service history, service precautions, and technical service bulletins.	P-1
2. Identify brake system components and configurations (including air and hydraulic systems, parking brake, power assist, and vehicle dynamic brake systems).	P-1
3. Identify brake performance problems caused by the mechanical/foundation brake system (air and hydraulic).	P-1
4. Use appropriate electronic service tool(s) and procedures to diagnose problems; check, record, and clear diagnostic codes; interpret digital multimeter (DMM) readings.	P-1
B. Air Brakes: Air Supply and Service Systems	
1. Inspect, test, repair, and/or replace air supply system components such as compressor, governor, air drier, tanks, and lines; inspect service system components such as lines, fittings, mountings, and valves (hand brake/trailer control, brake relay, quick release, tractor protection, emergency/spring brake control/modulator, pressure relief/safety); determine needed action.	P-1
2. Test gauge operation and readings; test low pressure warning alarm operation; perform air supply system tests such as pressure build-up, governor settings, and leakage; drain air tanks and check for contamination; determine needed action.	P-1
3. Demonstrate knowledge and understanding of air supply and service system components and operations.	P-1
4. Inspect air compressor drive gear components (gears, belts, tensioners, and/or couplings); determine needed action.	P-3
5. Inspect air compressor inlet; inspect oil supply and coolant lines, fittings, and mounting brackets; repair or replace as needed.	P-1

6. Inspect and test air tank relief (safety) valves, one-way (single) check valves, two-way (double) check valves, manual and automatic drain valves; determine needed action.	P-1
7. Inspect and clean air drier systems, filters, valves, heaters, wiring, and connectors; determine needed action.	P-1
8. Inspect and test brake application (foot/treadle) valve, fittings, and mounts; check pedal operation; determine needed action.	P-1
C. Air Brakes: Mechanical/Foundation Brake System	
1. Inspect, test, repair, and/or replace service brake chambers, diaphragms, clamps, springs, pushrods, clevises, and mounting brackets; determine needed action.	P-1
2. Identify slack adjuster type; inspect slack adjusters; perform needed action.	P-1
3. Check camshafts (S-cam), tubes, rollers, bushings, seals, spacers, retainers, brake spiders, shields, anchor pins, and springs; perform needed action.	P-1
4. Inspect rotor and mounting surface; measure rotor thickness, thickness variation, and lateral runout; determine needed action.	P-1
5. Inspect, clean, and adjust air disc brake caliper assemblies; inspect and measure disc brake pads; inspect mounting hardware; perform needed action.	P-1
6. Remove brake drum; clean and inspect brake drum and mounting surface; measure brake drum diameter; measure brake lining thickness; inspect brake lining condition; determine needed action.	P-1
7. Diagnose concerns related to the mechanical/foundation brake system including poor stopping, brake noise, premature wear, pulling, grabbing, or dragging; determine needed action.	P-1
D. Air Brakes: Parking Brake System	
1. Inspect, test, and/or replace parking (spring) brake chamber.	P-1
2. Inspect, test, and/or replace parking (spring) brake check valves, lines, hoses, and fittings.	P-1
3. Inspect, test, and/or replace parking (spring) brake application and release valve.	P-1
4. Manually release (cage) and reset (uncage) parking (spring) brakes.	P-1
5. Identify and test anti-compounding brake function; determine needed action.	P-2
E. Hydraulic Brakes: Hydraulic System	
1. Check master cylinder fluid level and condition; determine proper fluid type for application.	P-1
2. Inspect hydraulic brake system for leaks and damage; test, repair, and/or replace hydraulic brake system components.	P-1
3. Check hydraulic brake system operation including pedal travel, pedal effort, and pedal feel; determine needed action.	P-1
4. Diagnose poor stopping, premature wear, pulling, dragging, imbalance, or poor pedal feel caused by problems in the hydraulic system; determine needed action.	P-2

5. Test master cylinder for internal/external leaks and damage; replace as needed.	P-2
6. Test metering (hold-off), load sensing/proportioning, proportioning, and combination valves; determine needed action.	P-3
7. Test brake pressure differential valve; test warning light circuit switch, bulbs/LEDs, wiring, and connectors; determine needed action.	P-2
8. Bleed and/or flush hydraulic brake system.	P-2
F. Hydraulic Brakes: Mechanical/Foundation Brake System	
1. Clean and inspect rotor and mounting surface; measure rotor thickness, thickness variation, and lateral runout; determine necessary action.	P-1
2. Inspect and clean disc brake caliper assemblies; inspect and measure disc brake pads; inspect mounting hardware; perform needed action.	P-1
3. Remove, clean, and inspect brake drums; measure brake drum diameter; measure brake lining thickness; inspect brake lining condition; inspect wheel cylinders; determine serviceability.	P-1
4. Check disc brake caliper assembly mountings and slides; replace as needed.	P-2
G. Hydraulic Brakes: Parking Brake System	
1. Check parking brake operation; inspect parking brake application and holding devices; adjust, repair, and/or replace as needed.	P-1
H. Power Assist Systems	
1. Check brake assist/booster system (vacuum or hydraulic) hoses and control valves; check fluid level and condition (if applicable).	P-1
2. Check operation of emergency (back-up/reserve) brake assist system.	P-1
3. Identify concerns related to the power assist system (vacuum or hydraulic), including stopping problems caused by the brake assist (booster) system; determine needed action.	P-2
4. Inspect, test, repair, and/or replace hydraulic brake assist/booster systems, hoses, and control valves.	P-1
I. Vehicle Dynamic Brake Systems (Air and Hydraulic): Antilock Brake System (ABS), Automatic Traction Control (ATC) System, and Electronic Stability Control (ESC) System	
1. Observe antilock brake system (ABS) warning light operation including trailer and dash-mounted trailer ABS warning light; determine needed action.	P-1
2. Observe automatic traction control (ATC) and electronic stability control (ETC) warning light operation; determine needed action.	P-2
3. Identify stopping concerns related to the vehicle dynamic brake systems: ABS, ATC, and ESC; determine needed action.	P-2
4. Diagnose problems in the vehicle dynamic brake control systems; determine needed action.	P-2
5. Check and test operation of vehicle dynamic brake system (air and hydraulic) mechanical and electrical components; determine needed action.	P-1
6. Test vehicle/wheel speed sensors and circuits; adjust, repair, and/or replace as needed.	P-1

7. Bleed ABS hydraulic circuits.	P-2
8. Verify power line carrier (PLC) operation.	P-3
J. Wheel Bearings	
1. Clean, inspect, lubricate, and/or replace wheel bearings and races/cups; replace seals and wear rings; inspect spindle/tube; inspect and replace retaining hardware; adjust wheel bearings; check hub assembly fluid level and condition; verify end play with dial indicator method.	P-1
2. Identify, inspect, and/or replace unitized/preset hub bearing assemblies.	P-2
IV. SUSPENSION AND STEERING SYSTEMS	
A. General	
1. Research vehicle service information, including fluid type, vehicle service history, service precautions, and technical service bulletins.	P-1
2. Disable and enable supplemental restraint system (SRS); verify indicator lamp operation.	P-1
3. Identify suspension and steering system components and configurations.	P-1
4. Use appropriate electronic service tool(s) and procedures to diagnose problems; check, record, and clear diagnostic codes; interpret digital multimeter (DMM) readings.	P-1
B. Steering Column	
1. Check steering wheel for free play, binding, and proper centering; inspect and service steering shaft U-joint(s), slip joint(s), bearings, bushings, and seals; phase steering shaft.	P-1
2. Diagnose causes of fixed and driver adjustable steering column and shaft noise, looseness, and binding problems.	P-1
3. Check cab mounting and adjust cab ride height.	P-2
4. Remove the steering wheel (includes steering wheels equipped with electrical/electronic controls and components); install and center the steering wheel.	P-1
5. Inspect, test, replace, and calibrate steering angle sensor.	P-2
C. Steering Pump and Gear Units	
1. Check power steering pump and gear operation, mountings, lines, and hoses; check fluid level and condition; service filter; inspect system for leaks.	P-1
2. Flush and refill power steering system; purge air from system.	P-1
3. Diagnose causes of power steering system noise, binding, darting/oversteer, reduced wheel cut, steering wheel kick, pulling, non-recovery, turning effort, looseness, hard steering, overheating, fluid leakage, and fluid aeration problems.	P-1
4. Inspect, service, and/or replace power steering reservoir, seals, and gaskets.	P-2
5. Inspect and/or replace power steering system cooler, lines, hoses, clamps, mountings, and fittings.	P-2
6. Inspect and/or replace power steering gear(s) (single and/or dual) and mountings.	P-2

D. Steering Linkage	
1. Inspect, service, repair, and/or replace tie rod ends, ball joints, king pins, pitman arms, idler arms, and other steering linkage components.	P-1
E. Suspension Systems	
1. Inspect, service, repair, and/or replace shock absorbers, bushings, brackets, and mounts.	P-1
2. Inspect, repair, and/or replace leaf springs, center bolts, clips, pins, bushings, shackles, U-bolts, insulators, brackets, and mounts.	P-1
3. Inspect, repair, and/or replace axle and axle aligning devices such as: radius rods, track bars, stabilizer bars, and torque arms; inspect related bushings, mounts, shims and attaching hardware; determine needed action.	P-1
4. Inspect, repair, and/or replace tandem suspension equalizer components; determine needed action.	P-3
5. Inspect, repair, and/or replace air springs, mounting plates, springs, suspension arms, and bushings.	P-1
6. Inspect, test, repair, and/or replace air suspension pressure regulator and height control valves, lines, hoses, dump valves, and fittings; check and record ride height.	P-1
7. Inspect and service king pins, steering knuckle bushings, locks, bearings, seals, and covers.	P-1
8. Measure, record, and adjust ride height; determine needed action.	P-1
9. Diagnose rough ride problems; determine needed action.	P-3
F. Wheel Alignment Diagnosis and Repair	
1. Demonstrate understanding of alignment angles.	P-1
2. Diagnose causes of vehicle wandering, pulling, shimmy, hard steering, and off-center steering wheel problems.	P-1
3. Check, record, and adjust camber.	P-2
4. Check, record, and adjust caster.	P-2
5. Check, record, and adjust toe settings.	P-1
6. Check rear axle(s) alignment (thrustline/centerline) and tracking.	P-2
7. Identify turning/Ackerman angle (toe-out-on-turns) problems.	P-3
8. Check front axle alignment (centerline).	P-2
G. Wheels and Tires	
1. Inspect tire condition; identify tire wear patterns; measure tread depth; verify tire matching (diameter and tread); inspect valve stem and cap; set tire pressure; determine needed action.	P-1
2. Diagnose wheel/tire vibration, shimmy, pounding, and hop (tramp) problems; determine needed action.	P-2
3. Check wheel mounting hardware; check wheel condition; remove and install wheel/tire assemblies (steering and drive axle); torque fasteners to manufacturer's specification using torque wrench.	P-1
4. Inspect tire and wheel for proper application (size, load range, position, and tread design); determine needed action.	P-2

H. Frame and Coupling Devices	
1. Inspect, service, and/or adjust fifth wheel, pivot pins, bushings, locking mechanisms, mounting hardware, air lines, and fittings.	P-1
2. Inspect frame and frame members for cracks, breaks, corrosion, distortion, elongated holes, looseness, and damage; determine needed action.	P-1
3. Inspect, install, and/or replace frame hangers, brackets, and cross members; determine needed action.	P-3
4. Inspect, repair, or replace pintle hooks and draw bars (if applicable).	P-2
5. Inspect, service, and/or adjust sliding fifth wheel, tracks, stops, locking systems, air cylinders, springs, lines, hoses, and controls.	P-2
V. ELECTRICAL/ELECTRONIC SYSTEMS	
A. General	
1. Research vehicle service information, including vehicle service history, service precautions, and technical service bulletins.	P-1
2. Demonstrate knowledge of electrical/electronic series, parallel, and series-parallel circuits using principles of electricity (Ohm's Law).	P-1
3. Demonstrate proper use of test equipment when measuring source voltage, voltage drop (including grounds), current flow, continuity, and resistance.	P-1
4. Demonstrate knowledge of the causes and effects of shorts, grounds, opens, and resistance problems in electrical/electronic circuits; identify and locate faults in electrical/electronic circuits.	P-1
5. Use wiring diagrams during the diagnosis (troubleshooting) of electrical/electronic circuit problems.	P-1
6. Measure parasitic (key-off) battery drain; determine needed action.	P-1
7. Demonstrate knowledge of the function, operation, and testing of fusible links, circuit breakers, relays, solenoids, diodes, and fuses; perform inspection and testing; determine needed action.	P-1
8. Inspect, test, repair (including solder repair), and/or replace components, connectors, seals, terminal ends, harnesses, and wiring; verify proper routing and securement; determine needed action.	P-1
9. Use appropriate electronic service tool(s) and procedures to diagnose problems; check, record, and clear diagnostic codes; interpret digital multimeter (DMM) readings.	P-1
10. Diagnose faults in the data bus communications network; determine needed action.	P-2
11. Identify electrical/electronic system components and configuration.	P-1
12. Check frequency, pulse width, and waveforms of electrical/electronic signals using appropriate test equipment; interpret readings; determine needed repairs.	P-2
13. Understand the process for software transfer, software updates, and/or reprogramming of electronic modules.	P-3
B. Battery System	
1. Identify battery type and system configuration.	P-1
2. Confirm proper battery capacity for application; perform battery state-of-charge test; perform battery capacity test, determine needed action.	P-1

3. Inspect battery, battery cables, connectors, battery boxes, mounts, and hold-downs; determine needed action.	P-1
4. Charge battery using appropriate method for battery type.	P-1
5. Jump-start vehicle using a booster battery and jumper cables or using an appropriate auxiliary power supply.	P-1
6. Check low voltage disconnect (LVD) systems; determine needed action.	P-1
7. Inspect, clean, and service battery; replace as needed.	P-1
8. Inspect and clean battery boxes, mounts, and hold-downs; repair or replace as needed.	P-1
9. Test, and clean battery cables and connectors; repair or replace as needed.	P-1
10. Identify electrical/electronic modules, radios, and other accessories that require reinitialization or code entry after reconnecting vehicle battery.	P-2
C. Starting System	
1. Demonstrate understanding of starter system operation.	P-1
2. Perform starter circuit cranking voltage and voltage drop tests; determine needed action.	P-1
3. Inspect and test starter control circuit switches (key switch, push button, and/or magnetic switch), relays, connectors, terminals, wires, and harnesses (including over-crank protection); determine needed action.	P-1
4. Diagnose causes of no-crank or slow crank condition; differentiate between electrical and engine mechanical problems; determine needed action.	P-1
5. Perform starter current draw tests; determine needed action.	P-2
6. Remove and replace starter; inspect flywheel ring gear or flex plate.	P-1
D. Charging System	
1. Identify and understand operation of the generator (alternator).	P-1
2. Test instrument panel mounted voltmeters and/or indicator lamps; determine needed action.	P-1
3. Inspect, adjust, and/or replace generator (alternator) drive belt; check pulleys and tensioners for wear; check fans and mounting brackets; verify proper belt alignment; determine needed action.	P-1
4. Inspect cables, wires, and connectors in the charging circuit.	P-1
5. Perform charging system voltage and amperage output tests; perform AC ripple test; determine needed action.	P-1
6. Perform charging circuit voltage drop tests; determine needed action.	P-1
7. Remove, inspect, and/or replace generator (alternator).	P-1
E. Lighting Systems	
1. Diagnose causes of brighter-than-normal, intermittent, dim, or no-light operation; determine needed action.	P-1
2. Test, replace, and aim headlights.	P-1
3. Inspect cables, wires, and connectors in the lighting systems.	P-1

4. Diagnose faults in tractor-to-trailer multi-wire connector(s), cables, and holders; determine needed action.	P-2
5. Diagnose faults in switches, relays, bulbs/LEDs, wires, terminals, connectors, sockets, and control components/modules of exterior lighting systems; determine needed action.	P-2
6. Diagnose faults in switches, relays, bulbs/LEDs, wires, terminals, connectors, sockets, and control components/modules of interior lighting systems; determine needed action.	P-2
7. Diagnose faults in switches, relays, bulbs/LEDs, wires, terminals, connectors, sockets, and control components/modules of auxiliary lighting circuits; determine needed action.	P-2
F. Instrument Cluster and Driver Information Systems	
1. Check gauge and warning indicator operation.	P-1
2. Diagnose faults in the sensor/sending units, gauges, switches, relays, bulbs/LEDs, wires, terminals, connectors, sockets, printed circuits, and control components/modules of the instrument cluster, driver information systems, and warning systems; determine needed action.	P-2
3. Inspect, test, replace, and calibrate (if applicable) electronic speedometer, odometer, and tachometer systems.	P-3
G. Cab and Chassis Electrical Systems	
1. Diagnose operation of horn(s), wiper/washer, and occupant restraint systems.	P-1
2. Understand operation of safety systems and related circuits (such as speed control, collision avoidance, lane departure, and camera systems).	P-3
3. Understand operation of comfort and convenience systems and related circuits (such as: power windows, power seats, power locks, remote keyless entry, steering wheel controls, and cruise control).	P-3
4. Understand operation of entertainment systems and related circuits (such as radio, DVD, navigation, speakers, antennas, and voice-activated accessories).	P-3
5. Understand the operation of power inverter, protection devices, connectors, terminals, wiring, and control components/modules of auxiliary power systems.	P-3
6. Understand operation of telematics systems.	P-3
VI. HEATING, VENTILATION, AND AIR CONDITIONING (HVAC)	
A. General	
1. Research vehicle service information, including refrigerant/oil type, vehicle service history, service precautions, and technical service bulletins.	P-1
2. Identify heating, ventilation, and air conditioning (HVAC) components and configuration.	P-1
3. Use appropriate electronic service tool(s) and procedures to diagnose problems; check, record, and clear diagnostic codes; interpret digital multimeter (DMM) readings.	P-1
4. Diagnose heating and air conditioning problems; determine needed action.	P-1

5. Identify refrigerant type; test for contamination; select and connect proper gauge set/test equipment; record temperature and pressure readings.	P-1
6. Perform A/C system performance test; determine needed action.	P-1
7. Perform A/C system leak test; determine needed action.	P-1
8. Inspect condition of refrigerant oil removed from A/C system; determine needed action.	P-1
9. Determine oil and oil capacity for system application and/or component replacement.	P-1
B. Refrigeration System Components	
1. Inspect, remove, and replace A/C compressor drive belts, pulleys, and tensioners; verify proper belt alignment.	P-1
2. Check A/C system operation including system pressures; visually inspect A/C components for signs of leaks; check A/C monitoring system (if applicable).	P-1
3. Inspect A/C condenser for airflow restrictions; determine needed action.	P-1
4. Inspect, test, service, and/or replace A/C compressor and clutch assembly; check compressor clutch air gap; determine needed action.	P-2
5. Inspect, service, and/or replace A/C system hoses, lines, fittings, O-rings, seals, and service valves.	P-2
6. Inspect, remove, and/or replace receiver/drier or accumulator/drier.	P-1
7. Inspect, remove, and/or replace expansion valve or orifice (expansion) tube.	P-2
8. Inspect evaporator housing water drain; perform needed action.	P-1
9. Diagnose A/C system conditions that cause the protection devices (pressure, thermal, and/or control module) to interrupt system operation; determine needed action.	P-2
10. Determine procedure to remove and reinstall evaporator.	P-3
11. Determine procedure to inspect and/or replace condenser.	P-2
C. Heating, Ventilation, and Engine Cooling Systems	
1. Inspect engine cooling system and heater system hoses and pipes; determine needed action.	P-1
2. Inspect HVAC system heater ducts, doors, hoses, cabin filters, and outlets; determine needed action.	P-1
3. Identify the source of A/C system odors; determine needed action.	P-1
4. Diagnose temperature control problems in the HVAC system; determine needed action.	P-2
5. Determine procedure to remove, inspect, reinstall, and/or replace engine coolant and heater system components.	P-2
D. Operating Systems and Related Controls	
1. Verify HVAC system blower motor operation; confirm proper air distribution; confirm proper temperature control; determine needed action.	P-1
2. Inspect and test HVAC system blower motors, resistors, switches, relays, wiring, and protection devices; determine needed action.	P-1

3. Diagnose A/C compressor clutch control systems; determine needed action.	P-2
4. Diagnose malfunctions in the vacuum, mechanical, and electrical components and controls of the HVAC system; determine needed action.	P-3
E. Refrigerant Recovery, Recycling, and Handling	
1. Understand correct use and maintenance of refrigerant handling equipment.	P-1
2. Understand how to identify A/C system refrigerant; test for sealants; recover, evacuate, and charge A/C system; add refrigerant oil as required.	P-1
3. Understand how to recycle, label, and store refrigerant.	P-1
VII. CAB	
A. General	
1. Research vehicle service information, including vehicle service history, service precautions, and technical service bulletins.	P-1
2. Use appropriate electronic service tool(s) and procedures to diagnose problems; check, record, and clear diagnostic codes; check and record trip/operational data; reset maintenance monitor (if applicable); interpret digital multimeter (DMM) readings.	P-1
B. Instruments and Controls	
1. Inspect mechanical key condition; check operation of ignition switch; check operation of indicator lights, warning lights and/or alarms; check instruments; record oil pressure and system voltage; check operation of electronic power take-off (PTO) and engine idle speed controls (if applicable).	P-1
2. Check operation of all accessories.	P-1
3. Understand operation of auxiliary power unit (APU)/electric power unit (EPU).	P-3
C. Safety Equipment	
1. Test operation of horns (electric and air); test warning device operation (reverse, air pressure, etc.); check condition of spare fuses, safety triangles, fire extinguisher, and all required decals; inspect seat belts and sleeper restraints; inspect condition of wiper blades, arms, and linkage; determine needed action.	P-1
D. Hardware	
1. Test operation of wipers and washer; inspect windshield glass for cracks or discoloration; check sun visor; check seat condition, operation, and mounting; check door glass and window operation; verify operation of door and cab locks; inspect steps and grab handles; inspect mirrors, mountings, brackets, and glass; determine needed action.	P-1
2. Record all physical damage.	P-2
3. Lubricate all cab grease fittings; inspect and lubricate door and hood hinges, latches, strikers, lock cylinders, safety latches, linkages, and cables.	P-2
4. Inspect cab mountings, hinges, latches, linkages, and ride height; determine needed action.	P-1
5. Inspect quarter fender, mud flaps, and brackets; determine needed action.	P-1

VIII. HYDRAULICS	
A. General	
1. Research vehicle service information, including vehicle service history, service precautions, fluid type, and technical service bulletins.	P-3
2. Verify placement of equipment/component safety labels and placards; determine needed action.	P-3
3. Identify hydraulic system components; locate filtration system components; service filters and breathers.	P-3
4. Check fluid level and condition; purge and/or bleed system; take a hydraulic fluid sample for analysis; determine needed action.	P-3
5. Inspect hoses and connections for leaks, proper routing, and proper protection; determine needed action.	P-3
6. Use appropriate electronic service tool(s) and procedures to diagnose problems; check, record, and clear diagnostic codes; interpret digital multimeter (DMM) readings.	P-3
7. Read and interpret system diagrams and schematics.	P-3
8. Perform system temperature, pressure, flow, and cycle time tests; determine needed action.	P-3
9. Perform system operational tests; determine needed action.	P-3
B. Pumps	
1. Identify causes of pump failure, unusual pump noises, temperature, flow and leakage problems; determine needed action.	P-3
2. Determine pump type, rotation, and drive system.	P-3
3. Remove and install pump; prime and/or bleed system.	P-3
4. Inspect pump inlet and outlet for restrictions and leaks; determine needed action.	P-3
C. Filtration/Reservoirs (Tanks)	
1. Identify type of filtration system; verify filter application and flow direction.	P-3
2. Service filters and breathers.	P-3
3. Identify causes of system contamination; determine needed action.	P-3
4. Inspect, repair, and/or replace reservoir, sight glass, vents, caps, mounts, valves, screens, supply, and return lines.	P-3
D. Hoses, Fittings, and Connections	
1. Diagnose causes of component leakage, damage, and restriction; determine needed action.	P-3
2. Inspect hoses and connections for leaks, proper routing, and proper protection; determine needed action.	P-3
3. Assemble hoses, tubes, connectors, and fittings.	P-3
E. Control Valves	
1. Pressure test system safety relief valve; determine needed action.	P-3
2. Perform control valve operation pressure and flow tests; determine needed action.	P-3

3. Inspect, test, and adjust valve controls (electrical/electronic, mechanical, and pneumatic).	P-3
4. Identify causes of control valve leakage problems (internal and external); determine needed action.	P-3
5. Inspect pilot control valve linkages, cables, and PTO controls; adjust, repair, or replace as needed.	P-3
F. Actuators	
1. Identify actuator type (single-acting, double-acting, multi-stage, telescopic, and motor).	P-3
2. Identify the cause of seal failure; determine needed action.	P-3
3. Identify the cause of incorrect actuator movement and/or leakage (internal and external); determine needed action.	P-3
4. Inspect actuator mounting, frame components, and hardware for looseness, cracks, and damage; determine needed action.	P-3
5. Remove, repair, and/or replace actuators.	P-3
6. Inspect actuators for dents, cracks, damage, and leakage; determine needed action.	P-3